W9-BLS-888
3 1611 00139 4961

THE CONSTITUTION IN CRISIS TIMES

The

New American Nation Series

EDITED BY

HENRY STEELE COMMAGER

AND

RICHARD B. MORRIS

THE CONSTITUTION IN CRISIS TIMES 1918 ★ 1969

By PAUL L. MURPHY

ILLUSTRATED

1817

HARPER & ROW, PUBLISHERS
New York, Evanston, San Francisco, London

 For information address Harper & Row, Publishers, Inc., 49 East 33rd Street, New York, N.Y. 10016. Published simultaneously in Canada by Fitzhenry & Whiteside Limited, Toronto.

FIRST EDITION

STANDARD BOOK NUMBER: 06-013118-7

LIBRARY OF CONGRESS CATALOG CARD NUMBER: 70-156570

For Helen

Contents

Illustrations

These photographs, grouped in a separate section, will be found following page 140

Editors' Introduction

THE recent ill-advised attempt on the part of the Department of Justice to enjoin the publication of the "Pentagon Papers" serves as one more reminder of that uniquely American habit of transforming complicated policy questions into legal issues. Americans invariably look to the Supreme Court of the United States to find in their venerable Constitution the definitive answer to moot problems. Most Americans still consider the Constitution to be a fixed point of reference for political discourse and behavior, and accept the High Court as its oracular interpreter. Most defer to the Court's decisions; the dissenters are wont to seek comfort in pillorying the *present composition* of the Court. So it has been since the days of John Marshall, and even before. Furthermore, by some mysterious process the gloss put upon the Constitution by the justices often takes on as much authority as the original text. Assuredly, future generations must continue to look for guidance both to the document itself and to the decisions of the Court.

In *The Constitution in Crisis Times 1918-1969* Paul L. Murphy traces the developments in constitutional history during a time of great challenge, beginning at the close of the First World War. He is aware that various groups in our body politic are constantly offering their own special interpretations of the Constitution to the high court for its consideration. He also understands that Congress and the President through their actions continually participate in the process of interpreting of vital provisions. So do the state and lower federal courts. But the most authoritative interpreter is the Supreme Court, and the effect of its rulings over a fifty year period make up a large part of Professor Murphy's analysis.

Our understanding of what is and what is not permissible under the Constitution has been much altered since 1918. The federal government now operates in many of the areas which had previously been considered solely the preserve of the states. Both state and federal governments now undertake without serious constitutional challenge a wide variety of social welfare responsibilities. Independent regulatory commissions and executive departments and agencies now operate under delegations of power from the Congress which were unheard of in 1918. The power of the executive in international affairs has vastly increased, not without strong dissent from Congress, however.

While the range of permissible activities in some areas, particularly those involving economic regulation, has burgeoned, in other areas government officials are now subject to constitutional checks where they were not in 1918. The actions of police officials, prosecutors, and trial judges in the administration of criminal justice are now subject to careful judicial scrutiny. The rights of Americans embodied in the first eight amendments are enforced against both the national and the state governments to a degree unimagined five decades ago. The parameters of the citizen's right to express himself and the press's right to inform have been largely drawn in the period described in this book. Unlike the situation in 1918 in which the right to vote was considered to be a state responsibility, the courts, Congress, and the executive now exercise control over state electoral practices. And, at least as a matter of constitutional doctrine, the United States may now no longer tolerate the practices of governmental segregation. Indeed, while the reverence for the Constitution may have remained a constant, the actual effective content of that document is remarkably different from what it was in 1918.

Yet, paradoxically, the existence of the Constitution and of the Supreme Court as its official interpreter has generally operated as a stabilizing influence, mediating the course of change, lessening its social costs, forcing political activists to look to one lodestone—the Constitution—and offering relatively powerless minorities the hope that their pleas will be heard.

Those who place blind faith in the Supreme Court will receive little comfort from Professor Murphy's book. Although the Court has experienced more than its share of glorious moments, and from 1954 to 1969 proved to be the most imaginative and creative of the three branches, it has too frequently crept ahead with timidity. The most vulnerable of government institutions, it has oftimes bent with the wind. Its record after World War I and during the first few years of the Great Depression, its rulings on the interned Japanese during the Second World War, and its decisions throughout the first decade of the Cold War, often displayed neither courage nor sensitivity towards individual liberties. And, if the Court took a decisive stride by its landmark desegregation decisions of 1954 and 1955, it was only erasing the stain of its own *Plessy* v. *Ferguson* while proving, in ensuing years, unable to deal effectively with those who would defy the letter and the spirit of its work. For all of its achievements, the Supreme Court reflects the gap in American society between the lessons of our heritage and our hesitations in its implementation.

The Constitution in Crisis Times 1918-1969 constitutes a volume in the New American Nation Series, a comprehensive and cooperative study of the history of the area now embraced in the United States from the days of discovery to our own time. Professor Loren P. Beth has already explored constitutional developments from 1877 to 1917. Three volumes to come, covering the period of the Confederation, the years between the birth of the Republic and the death of John Marshall, and the period from 1835 to 1877 will complete a constitutional history of the United States.

HENRY STEELE COMMAGER
RICHARD B. MORRIS

Preface

CONSTITUTIONAL government, American-style, has been under a constant state of challenge since Woodrow Wilson's wartime "dictatorship" of 1917–18. Such challenge has come from a widely disparate range of sources; has been the product of both in- and out-group discontent; and has been induced both by judicial intransigence and institutional rigidity and by excessive judicial activism and the shattering of restrictive legal and social institutions.

The average middle-class American of the "age of normalcy" undoubtedly felt he lived in a stable, constitutional world. When he thought of public law and its relation to social policy, his conceptualization was not unlike that of the English observer Sir Henry Maine, who, when describing the American system, had stated: "It all reposes on the sacredness of contract and the stability of private property, the first the implement, and the last the reward, of success in the universal competition." In this sense the courts in the 1920s were playing their proper role, sustaining legal structures that protected property, wealth, and economic power on the one hand, and striking down popularly enacted legislation that attempted to place too-rigid strictures on the free use of private property on the other. By the 1960s the same average American looked on the Constitution and the courts in a totally different way. Living in a society controlled by regulation from cradle to grave, he saw courts not as instruments for protecting property from desired social control, but rather as agencies concerned with the personal rights of the individual, and prepared to protect those rights both from the threat of private power on the one hand and governmental tyranny on the other. How this change came about is the subject of this work.

Here the almost unremitting crisis nature of the times is an important first element. Side by side with the constitutionally complacent American of the 1920s had stood his worried counterpart, the sensitive reformer and social critic, looking at the other side of the coin. He saw that the repressive behavior of entrenched wealth and power—its lack of social consciousness and responsibility, and its refusal to permit the constitutional structure to afford remedies to millions of depressed lower-class citizens—was producing a crisis of insensitivity that invited major social revolution. Such prescient individuals had clamored vainly for legal reform, emphasizing the necessity of a public concern for the individual who, being depressed, needed opportunity and freedom from those strictures that blocked his ability to do something for himself. Although this call was initially unheeded, despite its urgent quality, the depression crisis suddenly turned its Jeremiahs into honored prophets. The old legality was now seen by perceptive leaders, both off and on the bench, as an insensitive arrangement in need of a restructuring that would turn it from a conservative device for protecting the status quo into a constructive instrument for social change. Even so, strong judicial voices were unprepared to stride too far in the path of either rejecting traditional legal patterns or sanctioning and adapting experimental new constitutional programs. Until a Presidentially induced crisis in 1937 brought massive pressure to bear upon the judiciary, constitutional stalemate persisted at many levels.

Following the "switch" of 1937, a new Court was forced to rethink its proper role. The challenge of European dictatorship and the general collapse of constitutional government in western Europe contributed to a new focus on underwriting basic Bill of Rights guarantees. After the crisis of total war intervened, strong liberal forces urged expansion of this role. But the Cold War crisis produced counter concern for security, much as nervous Americans of the fifties and sixties later demanded a restructured balance between liberty and law and order, feeling that many of the newly emancipated were not sufficiently responsible to utilize freedom with a proper respect for the rights of others and of society generally.

Subthemes and more sophisticated questions are also raised by this constitutional revolution and its aftermath. Why did the Justices choose to cut themselves free from their role as broker for property and the economically powerful and make themselves a broker for have-nots of all stripes, seeking to gain meaningful protection for the rights guaranteed them by the Constitution? Did this reflect a change in the type of justice serving on the Court, or merely a changed attitude on the part of similar minds, confronting new circumstances and new challenges? To what extent was this change the result of the action of the other two branches of the government and the growth generally of big government with the threats it posed of destroying individuality and individual self-determination? Finally, what impact did such a change have on constitutional democracy? By abandoning its traditional role, did the Court become an instrument for making democracy work better, or did it revert once again to judicial paternalism and become merely a liberal quasi-legislative body using its traditional power to impose policies that a different group of citizens would not have chosen to support through their legislative and executive leaders?

Although such questions have concerned legal scholars and political scientists, their answers have frequently been sought devoid of the historical and social context in which vital developments took place. This work in attempting to relate closely shifting popular moods and public pressures regarding the desired utilization of law as an instrument for social control, seeks explanations as much within the value structure of the American people as in the formal record of legal adjudication and congressional action. As such it is a work of history, asking historical questions and seeking historical answers, answers in some ways only yieldable to the jack-of-all-trades historian with his unlikely bag of cluttered, and eclectic, methodological tools.

One builds up many obligations in the course of researching and writing a book, and is pleased to have the opportunity to acknowledge them if not to repay them fully. One does not venture along the path of recent constitutional history without quickly realizing his debt to earlier trailblazers. Particularly helpful to me was the work of Alpheus T. Mason, Walter F. Murphy, C. Herman Pritchett, Wallace Mendelson, and Milton Konvitz. I have also profited from the critical observations and suggestions of various colleagues. Here thanks go particularly to Lynn Castner, Harold Chase, Alfred Jones, Robert Lindsay, Robert Morris, Don Roper, and Frank Sorauf. I am also indebted to the editors, Richard B. Morris and Henry Steele Commager, for valuable suggestions and intelligent criticism. Various of my students over the years have had a role in this book either through direct research contributions or the stimulation of rigorous discussion in and out of seminars. Names that come to mind particularly are Robert Mollan, Margaret Horsnell, Carol Jenson, Kathryn Johnson, Robert Weinhagen, Charles Levenberg, Kenneth Smemo, Donald Belgum, Boyd Rist, and Jerold Simmons. I am indebted for compilation of the bibliography to two students, Fred G. Morgner and Robert Kaczorowski. Mr. Kaczorowski also carried out the difficult and exacting job of preparing the bibliographical essay, a task in which both his historical and legal expertise were of particular value.

Librarians are the indispensable handmaidens of successful research and in this regard I have been particularly fortunate. The staffs of Walter Library, Wilson Library, and the Law Library of the University of Minnesota have been generous with time and resources far beyond the call of normal duty. Again one must be selective in acknowledgment, but I benefited especially from the kindnesses of Robert Stumm, Arlette Soderberg, Siegfried Feller, James Kingsley, Douglas White, and Bill LaBissoniere.

The early stages of research for this project were generously supported by the Guggenheim Foundation; the latter, by the Graduate School of the University of Minnesota.

My wife, Helen Chase Murphy, improved the work greatly by comments and careful editing, all done in the process of typing the final draft. For patience and understanding at its frequently slow progress I am grateful both to her and to my two children, Pat Murphy and Karen Murphy, both of whom found their limited youthful patience tried repeatedly as promised vacations vanished, but who came up smiling, even if, at times, through their disappointment. One regrets that the study of constitutional crises must at times produce minor ones within his family.

PAUL L. MURPHY

THE CONSTITUTION IN CRISIS TIMES

CHAPTER 1

The Status of Law and the Constitution in Post–World War I America

WORLD WAR I produced constitutional developments unique in American history. Confronted with the immediate crisis of modern total war with very little in the way of precedents, Congress and the President were called upon to extend their powers to a vast new range of complex subjects that had hitherto been outside the orbit of national authority. The result had been multitudinous delegations of power to President Woodrow Wilson structured in such a way as to allow him and other members of the executive branch to evolve efficient programs to meet the changing requirements of a fluid war situation.

The breadth of such legislation was startling. Acts to achieve wartime economic mobilization and efficient use of national resources were augmented by a Selective Service Act, vesting the President with authority to raise an army by conscription. Espionage and sedition legislation afforded power to punish dissenting action or speech impeding the war effort. A Trading with the Enemy Act with power to license trade with the enemy and his allies was passed. Under it, all enemy properties in the United States were entrusted for the duration of the war to an alien property custodian. It also authorized censorship of all communications by mail, cable, radio, or otherwise, with foreign countries. Still other statutes clothed the President with authority to regulate the foreign-language press of the country, and the conduct of enemy aliens resident in the country and its possessions. The Chief Executive could take over and operate the rail and water transportation systems of the country, and the telegraph and telephone systems, and redistribute functions among the executive agencies of the national government.[1]

In operation this meant a modified executive dictatorship for the war period. Woodrow Wilson used this power fully when he felt emergency conditions demanded it. In March, 1917, he ordered an armed guard to be placed on all American merchant vessels, thus acting where Congress had refused.[2] On April 7, 1917, the day after the declaration of war on Germany, he issued an executive loyalty order authorizing any head of department or independent office to remove "forthwith any employee whose retention he had ground for believing would be inimical to the public welfare."[3] However, more characteristic was the wartime resort to administrative government with the President redelegating part or all of his powers to designated agents to act in his name. Such agents or the agencies which they manned were in turn authorized to issue in the name of the

1. See William F. Willoughby, *Government Organization in War Time* (New York, 1919); Clarence A. Berdahl, *War Powers of the Executive of the United States* (Urbana, Ill., 1921); Grosvenor B. Clarkson, *Industrial America in the World War* (Boston, 1923); Frank H. Dixon, *Railroads and Government: Their Relation in the United States, 1910–1921* (New York, 1922); Walker D. Hines, *War History of American Railroads* (New York, 1928); Harold A. Van Dorn, *Government-Owned Corporations* (New York, 1926); I. Leo Sharfman, *The American Railroad Problem* (New York, 1921); Homer Cummings and Carl McFarland, *Federal Justice* (New York, 1937), pp. 450 ff.; and for a general overview, Carl B. Swisher, *American Constitutional Development* (Boston, 1954), Chap. 27.

2. Swisher, *Amer. Constitutional Development*, pp. 599–600.

3. See Edward S. Corwin, *The President: Office and Powers, 1787–1957* (New York, 1957), pp. 384–385. See also Harry N. Scheiber, *The Wilson Administration and Civil Liberties, 1917–1921* (Ithaca, 1960). Revealing of Wilson's willingness to use Presidential power was an episode involving the refusal of strikers at the Remington Arms Company to heed a return-to-work order of the War Labor Board, a body the President had created by executive fiat. See Isaac Lippincott, *Problems of Reconstruction* (New York, 1919), pp. 103 ff. Wilson wrote the strikers, upholding the authority of the Board, pointed out that an appeal from it should be made through the regular channels and not by strike. He closed with the statement that if the strikers did not return to work they would be barred from any war work in Bridgeport for a year, that the United States Employment Service would not obtain positions for them elsewhere, and that the draft boards would be instructed to reject any claim for exemptions based upon their alleged usefulness in war production. This ended the strike. Edward S. Corwin, *Total War and the Constitution* (New York, 1947), p. 56.

President a vast mass of administrative regulations, which became the governing code for operating the rapidly created wartime bureaucracy.[4] Thus the earlier Progressive technique of commission government was copied and expanded to permit administrative control of aspects of American life ranging from information dispersal to liquor control. Such innovation in the area of emergency public administration was imitated by various states.[5]

With the armistice of November 11, 1918, immediate questions arose regarding such wartime constitutional developments. Would the whole structure be promptly and permanently dismantled, or would certain agencies be continued to handle demobilization problems? Would the Supreme Court, which had little opportunity to pass on any of this legislation during the war period, now validate its constitutionality? If so, would such validation be limited to the immediate actions taken during this war, or would it create broad precedents available for use in future wars and in situations of national emergency where quick and effective governmental action was called for? The answers to these questions obviously depended on the nature of Presidential leadership, the mood and philosophy of Congress, and above all the personnel and attitudes of the members of the high bench.

4. A good example was the Committee on Public Information, which was created by a presidential order, April 12, 1917. It quickly became the personal instrument of its executive director, George Creel, and ultimately became known as the Creel committee. Its *Official Bulletin* became the "Bible" of wartime regulations, containing executive proclamations and orders, rules and regulations promulgated by the departments, statutes, and judicial decisions bearing on the conduct of the war, and it directed the propagandist efforts of the government both at home and abroad. All this it did on the "sole authority of the President," even operating for a considerable time on the executive budget. Later it secured some appropriations from Congress. See Berdahl, *War Powers of the Executive,* pp. 197–199; James R. Mock and Cedric Larson, *Words that Won the War: The Story of the Committee on Public Information* (Princeton, 1939); and George Creel, *How We Advertised America* (New York, 1920).

5. A good example was the Minnesota Public Safety Commission, an appointive body of leading citizens who for all practical purposes mobilized and ran the state during the war years. See O. A. Hilton, "The Minnesota Commission of Public Safety in World War I, 1917–1919," *Bulletin of the Oklahoma Agricultural and Mechanical College,* Vol. LXVIII (May 15, 1951); and Charles S. Ward, "The Minnesota Commission of Public Safety in World War I: Its Formation and Activities" (unpublished M.A. thesis, University of Minnesota, 1965).

The suddenness of the armistice in 1918 took the American people, who were emotionally prepared for an invasion of Germany, almost as much by surprise as the country's rapid entry into war. Demobilization and reconstruction became immediate goals instead, with no clear plans having been evolved for either. The termination of the wartime emergency having immediately destroyed the basis for further centralized governmental control, a mad unplanned rush to demobilize resulted. The American Expeditionary Force was brought home and mustered out. Various war agencies rushed to wind up their affairs. For example, the War Industries Board, confident that the major problems of demobilization were ones that the business world could solve now, abandoned its control to industry almost immediately.[6] All such action was taken with general public approval, there being little feeling that governmental controls and planning were essential to a quick return to peacetime life.

Wilson, powerless to stay the momentum, and now confronted with a hostile Republican Congress selected only a few days before the armistice, watched domestic developments from Paris with increasing apprehension. Especially disturbing were runaway prices, growing unemployment, and the drawing of lines clearly presaging industrial conflict. Unable to obtain ameliorative legislation from Congress, the President called governors and mayors to the White House in March, 1919, to warn them of dangers ahead. He simultaneously established an Industrial Board to coordinate the efforts of various governmental purchasing agents in hopes of holding the line on prices. The board lacked statutory authority and the wartime emergency to make its need seem nationally vital. The result was that the business community ignored or defied the board; by May it was disbanded, after the Railroad Administration refused to permit it to fix prices for steel.[7]

Other Presidential action at the domestic level was equally abortive. Locked in a bitter struggle with Republican leadership over settlement of the war and obsessed by the need for gaining acceptance of his Fourteen Points, Wilson confined his domestic activities either to avoiding conflict with Congress or to attempting to turn domestic developments to his advantage in the foreign area. For

6. Bernard M. Baruch, *American Industry in War* (New York, 1941).

7. James R. Mock, and Evangeline Thurber, *Report on Demobilization* (Norman, 1944).

example, acknowledging the pressing need for modernizing governmental financial operations, he nonetheless cut off the movement toward a separate budgetary agency, insisting that until the Senate had acted on the treaty of peace, there could be no properly studied national budget. Then when Congress acted in defiance, Wilson vetoed, on narrow constitutional grounds, the statute creating a separate Bureau of the Budget.[8] When the California legislature moved toward the enactment of a stronger alien land law and vigorous anti-Japanese immigration proposals in April, 1919, the President intervened, through Secretary of State Lansing, to forestall their passage, fearing the effect on international negotiations.

This intransigence and the even greater powerlessness produced by the President's physical collapse from September, 1919, to late 1920,[9] created a vacuum of domestic Presidential guidelines which invited occupancy from at least two sources. Aggressive and ambitious administrators within the executive department like A. Mitchell Palmer and Albert Burleson moved cautiously but firmly to seize the reins of power, which Wilson had previously guarded so jealously, and to set up policies to advance their personal interests. Typical was Palmer's move, in light of the growing national apprehension of radicals and radicalism, to expand greatly the power and functions of the Justice Department and to develop within it a strong radical bureau to classify and maintain surveillance over politically radical, left-wing types.[10]

The desire by Republicans to reassert legislative authority was equally strong. Cognizant of Wilson's general domestic powerlessness, but alert to the problems that demobilization was producing

8. David F. Houston, *Eight Years with Wilson's Cabinet* (2 vols., New York, 1926), II, 8; *Congressional Record,* 66th Cong., 2d Sess., LIX (June 4, 1920), 8609. For a contemporary view see Thomas Reed Powell, "The President's Veto of the Budget Bill," *National Municipal Review, IX* (September, 1920), 538–545. Sufficient momentum had been generated that the measure was reintroduced and signed into law in June, 1921, as the Budget and Accounting Act (42 stat. 20), one of the few accomplishments of the Harding administration in successfully restructuring administrative procedures with the intent of serving broad public needs.

9. Richard H. Hansen, *The Year We Had No President* (Lincoln, Nebr., 1962); Gene Smith, *When The Cheering Stopped: The Last Years of Woodrow Wilson* (New York, 1964).

10. Stanley Coben, *A. Mitchell Palmer: Politician* (New York, 1963), pp. 155 ff.; Max Lowenthal, *The Federal Bureau of Investigation* (New York, 1950), pp. 72 ff. See also Don Whitehead, *The FBI Story* (New York, 1956), pp. 41 ff.; and Fred J. Cook, *The FBI Nobody Knows* (New York, 1964), pp. 90 ff.

and the responsibility this placed upon a Republican-controlled Congress, G.O.P. leaders moved to enact a number of significant pieces of legislation. The orientation of these statutes was important philosophically and in several cases constitutionally. Measures involving taxation policy, governmental control of railroads and the merchant marine, and congressional action in the area of natural resources were particularly revealing.

The War Revenue Bill of February, 1919, not sponsored, but signed happily, by the President, hardly represented a new departure in tax policy. The measure actually raised the prevailing tax burden and put almost four-fifths of a 250 per cent increase on large incomes, profits, and estates. It was thus in many ways an extension of the Democratic tax policy during wartime. Its need was justified in the necessity for providing funds to liquidate the war commitments at home, to care for returning service personnel, and to provide relief in Europe.[11]

Less Democratic, but in many ways progressive, was the Transportation Act of February, 1920.[12] The task of returning the railroads to private hands was a major concern of the nation at the time. Railroads were a key public service industry, still at this time the primary form of transportation for most Americans, and their proper operation was important to millions. Business leaders and especially railroad executives shrank from a policy of total laissez-faire. Clearly unwilling to return to the rate wars and cutthroat competition of prewar years, management favored continued rate regulation and governmental assistance in railroad consolidation and the elimination of unprofitable lines. Such a policy, they were convinced, would maximize service as well as profits. Congress responded accordingly.[13] Rejecting a plan suggested by Glenn E. Plumb, lawyer for the Railroad Brotherhoods, which would have continued nationalization of the railroads with workers given a share in their management and profit, the 1920 Act nonetheless stopped only short of nationalization. By terms of the Act the

11. Arthur S. Link and William B. Catton, *American Epoch* (New York, 1966), pp. 200–202.

12. 41 Stat. 456 (1920). See Rogers MacVeagh, *The Transportation Act of 1920* (New York, 1923).

13. Wilson took no part in the controversy. He simply announced on December 24, 1919, that he would return the railroads to their owners on March 1, 1920, unless Congress decided otherwise.

Interstate Commerce Commission had complete power to "initiate, modify, establish or adjust rates," even those set by state commissions. The I.C.C. was authorized to supervise the sale of railroad securities and the expenditure of proceeds. The Act contained a famous recapture clause, providing for the setting aside of a reserve fund from railroad earnings over a "fair return," with such recaptured funds to be distributed to keep less productive lines functioning. In addition the measure clearly reflected wide-scale public apprehensiveness toward labor troubles in public service industries in establishing a Railway Labor Board with authority to mediate labor disputes. As sanction, the framers planned to rally public opinion behind its rulings.[14]

Business and private capital was less regulation oriented when it came to the problem of disposing of the huge fleet of merchant vessels that had been developed by the government for the war period. Congress responded with the Merchant Marine Act of 1920 authorizing the sale of as many vessels as possible to American-owned firms. Highly favorable terms were offered with easy loans and tax inducements available. The measure did authorize a federally owned Merchant Fleet Corporation to open new shipping lines and operate surplus vessels, helping thereby to preserve American shipping and keep it out of foreign hands.[15]

Compromise was also reached in the natural resource area. The General Leasing Act of 1920 kept large naval oil reserves from private exploitation. In empowering the Secretary of the Interior to lease other public lands containing mineral and oil deposits to private firms, the Act insisted that the public interest be properly safeguarded. The Water Power Act of the same year, however, leaned toward accommodating private capital. The measure reflected a widely held business concern that in areas where uninhibited economic competition could be disastrous to participants there was need for the continued operation of rule-making agencies. However, it also reflected a strong desire for those agencies to be responsible to business pressures. The Federal Power Commission that the Water Power Act created was a body to be made up of the Secretries of War, Interior, and Agriculture, all serving ex officio. The

14. MacVeagh, *Transportation Act,* pp. 148 ff.; Sharfman, *American Railroad Problem,* pp. 428–439.

15. Carroll H. Wooddy, *The Growth of the Federal Government, 1915–1932* (New York, 1934), pp. 228 ff.

Power Commission was authorized to license water-power developments on public lands, on reservations, or on any navigable waters subject to national jurisdiction, and to police such licensees accordingly. In operation, the commission took little positive action and, lacking power and inefficient in operation, posed little threat to business. Power interests prepared to resist its authority. An ex officio commission composed of Cabinet officers with many other responsibilities worked inefficiently and understood poorly the specialized engineering and accounting work required by the Act. In 1930, after the commission was reorganized as an independent body of five full-time members, empowered to recruit its own staff, its operations began to resemble efficiency.[16]

The pre-Harding period saw the adoption of two previously introduced constitutional amendments; woman suffrage becoming official on June 4, 1919, and national prohibition ratified by the necessary number of states on January 29, 1919. Both measures were reflections of Progressivism. The right of women to vote constituted a further manifestation of Progressive faith in good government resulting from broader popular participation.[17] Prohibition, on the other hand, reflected Progressive faith in the law as an instrument for public morality. Many Progressive leaders, joining deeply conservative church groups, hailed its adoption as the greatest moral triumph since the abolition of slavery.[18]

The guidelines afforded the Supreme Court by such a conflicting set of executive and legislative action and inaction were in many ways distressingly vague. The body's task was significant and its range of constitutional options was wide. Clearly it had to deal with many pending challenges to wartime legislation ranging from government operation of service industries to restrictions on free speech and press. But the Court also had before it a number of cases raising

16. Merle Fainsod, Lincoln Gordon, and Joseph C. Palamountain, Jr., *Government and the American Economy* (New York, 1959), pp. 344–349. Ironically the body had become so associated in the minds of progressive congressmen with conservative pro-business policies, that in this new, more efficient form, it was challenged by depression-emboldened Senate liberals now prepared to oppose its conservative water-power policies.

17. Eleanor Flexner, *A Century of Struggle: The Woman's Rights Movement* (Cambridge, Mass., 1959); Alan Grimes, *The Puritan Ethic and Woman Suffrage* (New York, 1967); Aileen W. Kraditor, *Ideas of the Woman Suffrage Movement, 1890–1920* (New York, 1965).

18. James H. Timberlake, *Prohibition and the Progressive Movement 1900–1920* (Cambridge, Mass., 1965).

questions about traditional areas such as federal and state police power, and antitrust legislation as it applied both to business and labor. The question, traditional in judicial strategy, was one of taking action that the public would sanction and that would not run the body afoul of the other two branches of the government.

Public hostility to wartime coercion plus business antipathy to excessive governmental regulation afforded strong argument for total dismantling of the wartime administrative structure, softening of the antitrust structure, and the modification of police power regulations. Here the early wartime ruling in *Hammer* v. *Dagenhart,*[19] striking down the Federal Child Labor Law, afforded the kind of narrow constitutional precedents that provided the path.[20] Implicit in such an approach was the rejection of the law as an instrument for social change and the conversion of governmental legal institutions into instrumentalities exercising primarily negative police functions.

Congressional and public endorsement, on the other hand, of Progressive constitutional amendments, plus a clear reluctance even on the part of business to destroy effective regulatory bodies, seemed to point toward continuation of many prewar peacetime trends. Legally this meant extension of a line of cases that had sustained both federal and state police power enactments, endorsed commission control particularly of public service industries, and embraced a wide use of the federal taxing and commerce power for achieving governmental programs in the broad public interest.[21]

There was a segment of legal thought represented on the high bench by Louis Brandeis, John H. Clarke, and to a lesser degree

19. Hammer *v.* Dagenhart, 247 U.S. 251 (1918).

20. For an in-depth study of the constitutional aspects of the Child Labor movement see Stephen B. Wood, *Constitutional Politics in the Progressive Era: Child Labor and the Law* (Chicago, 1968).

21. These included Champion *v.* Ames, 188 U.S. 321 (1903); McCray *v.* U.S., 195 U.S. 27 (1904); Hipolite Egg Co. *v.* U.S., 220 U.S. 45 (1911); and Hoke *v.* U.S., 227 U.S. 308 (1913), in the federal area; and state cases such as Holden *v.* Hardy, 169 U.S. 366 (1898); Jacobson *v.* Massachusetts, 197 U.S. 11 (1905); Muller *v.* Oregon, 208 U.S. 412 (1908); Bunting *v.* Oregon, 243 U.S. 426 (1917); Stettler *v.* O'Hara, 243 U.S. 629 (1917); New York Central R.R. Co. *v.* White, 243 U.S. 188 (1917); Mountain Timber Co. *v.* Washington, 243 U.S. 219 (1917). See also U.S. *v.* Grimaud, 220 U.S. 205 (1911), on the discretionary power of federal administrative commissions and the cases sustaining broad federal authority over commerce: Swift *v.* U.S., 196 U.S. 375 (1905); Minnesota Rate Cases, 230 U.S. 352 (1913); Shreveport Rate Cases, 234 U.S. 342 (1914).

Oliver Wendell Holmes, Jr., and adhered to even more strongly in the broader liberal legal community, that saw the postwar period as an opportunity for significant social reconstruction with law as a positive instrument for social change. Such legal empiricists clearly called for law immediately adaptable to concrete postwar social and economic needs.[22] This meant the discarding of rigid legal structures such as the comparatively modern and in many ways novel concept of "freedom of contract" and strict "dual federalism," in favor of a jurisprudence clearly attuned to the social realities and social needs of a growingly urban, industrial, and national community.[23]

The Court that opened the October, 1918, term, and that served without the addition of new membership until taken over by William Howard Taft in October, 1921, was composed of three wings, representing sympathy to each of the three approaches. Its dominant figure and oldest member was Chief Justice Edward Douglas White.[24] White, a Louisiana Bourbon, a wealthy cane planter, president of a sugar refining company, and a former Confederate soldier, had been appointed initially an Associate Justice by Grover Cleveland in 1894. Upon the death of Chief Justice Fuller in 1910 he had been elevated to the Chief Justiceship by President William Howard Taft, becoming the first Associate Justice so honored, a move which had the warm endorsement of his judicial colleagues.[25] White's views were in some ways closer to Taft than to his fellow southern Democrat Woodrow Wilson.

22. For a general discussion of such a view see Henry S. Commager, *The American Mind* (New Haven, 1950), Chaps. 17, 18; Morton White, *Social Thought in America: The Revolt Against Formalism* (New York, 1949), Chaps. V-IX.

23. Chief Justice White was unimpressed with sociologically oriented Brandeis briefs frequently submitted to support such a view. When the attorney general of Washington submitted such a thick document to show that the practice of employment agencies imposing fees on workers was "non-useful, if not vicious" (Adams *v.* Tanner, 244 U.S. 590 [1917]), White retorted: "I could compile a brief twice as thick to prove that the legal profession ought to be abolished." Leo Pfeffer, *This Honorable Court* (Boston, 1965), p. 259.

24. White made clear at the outset of his term as Chief Justice that he was "going to stop this dissenting business," and he did manage to achieve a high degree of unanimity, there being few five-to-four decisions during his tenure. See Marie Carolyn Klinkhamer, *Edward Douglas White, Chief Justice of the United States* (Washington, 1943), pp. 61, 221.

25. Wood, *Constitutional Politics*, pp. 127–128.

Wilson, who conceived of the nation's courts not as "strait jackets" but as "instruments of the nation's growth," placed little hope for reform in the Court under White. (In his academic days he had likened the Supreme Court to "a constitutional convention in continuous session.") In fact, particularly in light of the Court's Taft-appointed majority, Wilson did not disagree with the expressed view of a confidant that when he took office there was not a single "progressive" on the bench. This was a circumstance he made clear that he hoped to correct.[26]

Yet, regarding White, such a view was harsh. As an Associate Justice he had shown a clear concern for the welfare of labor and labor unions. He had joined Harlan's strong dissent in the Lochner anti-maximum hour law ruling of 1905,[27] which while not as eloquent a denunciation of laissez-faire as Holmes', nonetheless emphasized the broad scope of the police power and the state's capacity to interfere with the right of free contract. Possibly demonstrating his Jesuit training, his earlier opinions had also invoked conceptions of fundamental principles of liberty and justice, especially in notions of "inherent" powers and "inherent" limitations and in the famous "rule of reason." The latter, which he had finally injected into antitrust adjudication in his majority opinion in the Standard Oil case of 1911,[28] he had set forth as early as 1897.[29] While to a constitutional literalist like Harlan, its adoption meant needlessly watering down the blanket application of such legislation, it was a logical application of the pragmatic position of Oliver Wendell Holmes, Jr., and a position to which Theodore Roosevelt had come in the latter part of his Presidency.

In the general area of property and particularly the relationship of property to the due process clause, White was more a Progressive than a nineteenth-century laissez-faire conservative. To him property's sacredness was clearly qualifiable when curtailment of its freedom was in the public interest. In fact, his biographer contends

26. Klinkhamer, *Edward Douglas White,* p. 61; Arthur Walworth, *Woodrow Wilson* (2 vols., New York, 1958), II, 57.

27. Lochner *v.* New York, 198 U.S. 45 (1905). On the details of the case see Sidney G. Tarrow, "Lochner Versus New York: A Political Analysis," *Labor History,* V (Fall, 1964), 277–312.

28. Standard Oil Co. *v.* U.S., 221 U.S. 1 (1911).

29. U.S. *v.* Trans-Missouri Freight Association, 166 U.S. 290, 344 (1897).

that his "theory of the supremacy of the legislature in determining the disposition of property within the constitutional framework . . . applied equally to state legislatures and to the national Congress, as plenary power over the property within its confines could not, to him, be denied to either."[30]

And the Louisianan who had fought for the losing cause of states' rights, had also come to a nationalistic view on war and war issues, manifesting in many ways the zeal of the convert. Typical was White's behavior in upholding the Wilson-sponsored Adamson Act of 1916 covering railroad labor, and his unqualified endorsement of conscription in the Selective Draft Law cases of 1917.

The Adamson Act had been passed in the hope of avoiding an impending massive railroad strike that the President was convinced threatened economic catastrophe. The measure established an eight-hour workday and imposed minimum floors on wages, an area into which government in this property-conscious era had not as yet intruded. White, in validating the law, sustained the principle of emergency legislation in a period of national crisis and emphasized the importance of public regulation of vital industries. While an emergency could not be made the source of new constitutional power, he maintained, it nonetheless could furnish a proper occasion for the exercise of living power already enjoyed. Further, Justice White denied that the measure violated due process, emphasizing that the wage-fixing provisions were temporary, and did not imply a general right in Congress to fix all rail wages.[31] Such a ruling rested upon a broad interpretation of the federal commerce power, an interpretation sharply challenged by four dissenting justices.

On conscription, White's nationalism was not only vigorous but emotional. The idea of conscription had not been an attractive one to Americans in their earlier history, although both the Union and the Confederacy resorted to it. Its clear association in 1917 with Prussian militarism did not enhance its palatability.[32] Thus the Selective Service Act of 1917 was passed over considerable congressional opposition and drew early fire, especially from critics who considered voluntarism not only the fairest and most effective but

30. Klinkhamer, *Edward Douglas White,* p. 238.

31. Wilson *v.* New, 243 U.S. 332 (1917). See Swisher, *Amer. Constitutional Development,* pp. 581–582.

32. Hoffman Nickerson, *The Armed Horde, 1793–1934: A Study of the Rise, Survival and Decline of the Mass Army* (New York, 1940), pp. 187–199.

the most democratic approach to public service.[33] The government moved quickly to bring challenges to the new Act up for rapid court test, and the Chief Justice's courtroom behavior in handling such cases was indicative of the result.[34] Rebuking an attorney who charged that the conscription act required men to take part in a war that had never received the approval of the people, he rejoined, "I don't think your statement has anything to do with the legal arguments and should not have been said to this court. It is a very unpatriotic statement to make."[35] He then went on to uphold the constitutionality of the law, finding full authorization to impose compulsory military service in the clause empowering Congress to declare war and "to raise and support armies." White denied that the statute unconstitutionally delegated power to state officials or vested legislative powers or judicial discretion improperly in administrative officers. Finally, he maintained that compulsory service in the army was not "involuntary servitude" within the meaning of the Thirteenth Amendment. He thus fully sustained federal war power and total federal sovereignty in a war situation.[36]

Justices Joseph McKenna and William R. Day, the former a McKinley appointee, the latter a McKinley confrere although a Theodore Roosevelt appointment, shared many of White's views, while lacking his charm and force of person. McKenna, also a Catholic, was a California lawyer and one of the few senators who had voted in 1887 against creation of the Interstate Commerce Commission. His legal career on the high bench was marked by a comparatively expansive attitude toward the rights of labor and a fairly permissive view toward the use of federal power.[37] His opinion sustaining the constitutionality of the Mann Act displayed a broad concept of the commerce clause as a basis for federal regulation.[38] In 1914 he had stoutly upheld state regulation of insurance rates,

33. J. S. Duggan, *Legislative and Statutory Development of the Federal Concept of Conscription for Military Service* (Washington, 1946), pp. 59–82.

34. Although the power to raise armies was given previously unheard-of extension by the rule that conceded the power to conscript men for service abroad, the Court entirely ignored prominent constitutional authority Hannis Taylor's striking amicus curiae brief opposing the government on this essential point.

35. *The New York Times* (December 14, 1917), p. 22.

36. Selective Draft Law Cases, Arver *v.* U.S., 245 U.S. 366 (1918).

37. Matthew McDevitt, *Joseph McKenna* (Washington, 1946).

38. Hoke *v.* U.S., 227 U.S. 308 (1913).

clearly designating the business as one affected with a public interest.[39] Day, whom Roosevelt had been convinced was "absolutely sane and sound" on the industrial question, pleased the President early by siding with the majority in the famed 1904 Northern Securities case, reviving the antitrust structure.[40] Day joined White in approving Harlan's dissent in Lochner, and had generally taken the position that the courts should utilize great restraint in negating state police power legislation, especially in the name of freedom of contract. By contrast, Day had written the opinion in *Hammer* v. *Dagenhart*. The ruling's narrowness had drawn broadsides from the liberal community. Of four dissents Holmes's was particularly incisive, in challenging its property-conscious social philosophy. McKenna also dissented, pointing out that the ruling contradicted earlier adherence to the broad use of federal police power in the famed McCray oleomargarine case of 1904.[41]

Oliver Wendell Holmes, Jr., had been the first Roosevelt appointee.[42] The indomitable Yankee had ascended the bench to the plaudits of national leaders, but the President was clearly apprehensive.[43] His early dissent in the Northern Securities case and his suggestion that the antitrust structure should be infused with a

39. German Alliance Insurance Co. *v.* Kansas, 233 U.S. 389 (1914).

40. Northern Securities Co. *v.* U.S., 193 U.S. 197 (1904). On Day's career see Joseph E. McLean, *William Rufus Day* (Baltimore, 1947); and Vernon William Roelofs, "William R. Day: A Study in Constitutional History" (unpublished Ph.D. dissertation, University of Michigan, 1942).

41. Hammer *v.* Dagenhart, 247 U.S. 251, 278 (1918).

42. The Holmes literature is voluminous. Max Lerner, *The Mind and Faith of Justice Holmes* (New York, 1943), pp. 452–460, indicates its nature to that time. Samuel J. Konefsky, *The Legacy of Holmes and Brandeis* (New York, 1956), *passim,* summarizes virtually everything written to its publication. Mark DeWolf Howe completed only two volumes of a projected five-volume biography: *Justice Oliver Wendell Holmes: The Shaping Years, 1841–1870* (Cambridge, Mass., 1957) and *The Proving Years, 1870–1882* (Cambridge, Mass., 1963). See also Howe (ed.), *The Holmes-Pollock Letters* (2 vols., Cambridge, Mass., 1941), and Howe (ed.), *The Holmes-Laski Letters* (2 vols., Cambridge, Mass., 1953). Valuable recent reassessments of Holmes include Yosal Rogat, "Mr. Justice Holmes: A Dissenting Opinion," *Stanford Law Review,* XV (1962, 1963), 3-44, 254–308; Samuel Krislov, "Oliver Wendell Holmes: The Ebb and Flow of Judicial Legendary," *Northwestern University Law Review,* LII (1957), 514–525; and a symposium, "Mr. Justice Holmes: Some Modern Views," *University of Chicago Law Review,* XXXI (1964), 213–278.

43. Felix Frankfurter, "Oliver Wendell Holmes, Jr.," in Harris E. Starr (ed.), *Dictionary of American Biography,* Supplement I, (New York, 1940), p. 422; Swisher, *American Constitutional Development,* pp. 518–519.

practical flexibility had induced Roosevelt to utter, "I could carve out of a banana a judge with more backbone than that."[44] Roosevelt, like most members of the prewar bench, did not comprehend or appreciate the thrust of Holmes's judicialism. In fact, Holmes had to wait until a later generation ascended the bench, one that agreed that the Fourteenth Amendment did not enact Herbert Spencer's *Social Statics,* to enjoy majority approval of his views. And little wonder. The son of the famous New England poet had shocked most traditional and entrenched legalists as early as the 1890s with the frank statement that "the life of the law has not been logic, it has been experience," and his further insistence that law should not be "dealt with as if it contained only the axioms and corollaries of a book of mathematics."[45] Holmes's repeated insistence that the law is power, and judges should not abuse such power, especially by converting doctrinal fictions into irrefragable facts, had come to be central to many irreverent assaults on the judiciary. Such a position had led Holmes to view with skeptical permissiveness federal and state experimentation in the area of social engineering. In fact, the Justice was prepared to uphold any reasonable social legislation enacted by a representative body.[46] The body, however, had to be clearly representative and responsible. Holmes was skeptical of commission government, distrusting the power wielded by bodies such as the I.C.C.[47] And while he was prepared to allow the federal government broad leniency in adopting programs of liberal nationalism based upon an expansive interpretation of the federal commerce and taxing powers, he nonetheless was prepared to draw the line on federal power when it threatened the personal freedoms and liberties of individuals. His ringing dissent in the Child Labor case of 1917 still reverberated in the postwar legal air. Whether such a call would be heeded by the high bench remained to be seen.

Two of the most conservative members of this late White Court were Taft appointees. Wills Van Devanter, appointed in 1910, had

44. Lerner, *Mind and Faith of Justice Holmes*, p. xxxiii.

45. Oliver Wendell Holmes, *The Common Law* (Boston, 1881), p. 5. For a comparable statement from the bench see Gompers *v.* U.S., 233 U.S. 604, 610 (1904).

46. For a judicial view on the value of state economic regulation see Noble State Bank *v.* Haskell, 219 U.S. 104, 110 (1911).

47. Howe (ed.), *Holmes-Pollock Letters,* I, 163.

geography going for him, and many people felt little more. Former Chief Justice of the Wyoming Supreme Court and after 1903 a federal circuit court judge, he had been a prominent railroad attorney, active in Republican politics,[48] and was known to be highly property-conscious and hostile to public regulation. Mahlon Pitney, who succeeded John Marshall Harlan in 1912, was a New Jersey state court judge whose conservative career had been particularly marked by anti–labor union sentiments. On the other hand, Pitney at times showed strong compassion for working-class people, upholding in 1917 a state workman's compensation law in Washington,[49] and later disagreeing with Taft himself over the validity of state anti-injunction legislation.[50]

The three Wilson appointees, McReynolds, Brandeis, and Clarke, bore out Wilson's intention of putting "progressives" on the Court in only two of the three cases. McReynolds, personally and legally traditional and illiberal, had impressed Wilson as a zealous trust-busting Attorney General. Upon mounting the bench, McReynolds' true colors emerged, and in many ways, no justice, not even Stephen Field, was ultimately more fanatically conservative than the petulant Tennesseean.[51]

Brandeis' appointment had been one of the most controversial in the Court's history. Opposed violently by conservatives like Taft and George Sutherland, and leaders of the American Bar Association, covertly because of his Judaism, openly because as an advocate of social causes and a crusader he lacked judicial temperament, his narrow confirmation was clearly a personal victory for President Wilson.[52] Brandeis' brief prewar and wartime judicial career had had less impact upon the Court than his pre-Court activities. A highly successful attorney, he had early devoted much time to the defense of unpopular causes, acting particularly as "the people's advocate

48. Maurice P. Holsinger, "Willis Van Devanter—the Early Years" (unpublished Ph.D. dissertation, University of Denver, 1964).

49. Mountain Timber Co. *v.* Washington, 243 U.S. 219 (1917).

50. Truax *v.* Corrigan, 257 U.S. 312, 353 (1921).

51. Stirling P. Gilbert, *James Clark McReynolds* (privately printed, 1946); John B. McCraw, "Justice McReynolds and the Supreme Court" (unpublished Ph.D. dissertation, University of Texas, 1949); Doris S. Blaisdell, "The Constitutional Law of Mr. Justice McReynolds" (unpublished Ph.D. dissertation, University of Wisconsin, 1953); Stephen T. Early Jr., "Mr. Justice McReynolds and the Judicial Process" (unpublished Ph.D. dissertation, University of Virginia, 1954).

52. Alden L. Todd, *Justice On Trial* (New York, 1964).

when public interests called for an effective champion."[53] As early as 1890 he had demonstrated his legal creativeness, coauthoring a famous article calling for the creation of a constitutional right of privacy.[54] In the constitutional area, he had engaged in far more incisive criticism of legal policy-making and the explicit and deleterious impact of a variety of public formulas and narrow high court rulings than Holmes. Further, where Holmes had eschewed concrete reforms and been little interested in carefully researched and detailed programs for social betterment, Brandeis' career had been built upon developing and advocating them. In evolving his famous sociological brief,[55] Brandeis had attempted to introduce into the law a highly detailed and explicit analysis of contemporary social evils and problems as a way of pointing up proper legal avenues to their relief and redress. As an intimate of Woodrow Wilson, Brandeis' name was clearly associated with the "New Freedom" and all of its various objectives from monetary reform and tariff revision to attacks on the "curse of business" as manifested in the trust structure.[56] In the latter regard he tended to place high reliance upon democratic solutions to social problems through state and local units of government. Brandeis was also identified with the positive encouragement of labor to achieve its goals, especially its rights to organize and use economic coercion. Thus, as an advocate of sociological jurisprudence, Brandeis' emphasis was different from both Pound's and Holmes's. Where Pound was concerned with what the law embraced, and Holmes in the way it worked, he was com-

53. The phrase was used by Woodrow Wilson in evaluating Brandeis. See 64th Cong., 1st Sess., *Senate Documents,* 17 (1916), 239–241. The standard biography is Alpheus T. Mason, *Brandeis: A Free Man's Life* (New York, 1946). Particularly valuable in its insights into both Brandeis and Holmes, and the inner working of the Court of the 1920s, is Alexander M. Bickel, *The Unpublished Opinions of Mr. Justice Brandeis* (Cambridge, Mass., 1957). On the Brandeis literature see Yale University Law School Library, *Louis Dembitz Brandeis, 1856–1941, a Bibliography* (New Haven, 1958).

54. Samuel D. Warren and Louis D. Brandeis, "The Right to Privacy," *Harvard Law Review,* IV (Dec. 15, 1890), 193–220.

55. Louis D. Brandeis, Brief for Defendant in Error, *Muller v. Oregon,* Transcripts of Records and File Copies of Briefs, 1907, Vol. XXIV (Cases 102–107, Library of the Supreme Court, Washington, D.C.).

56. Brandeis' obsession with the dangers and moral dilemmas posed by the rise of giantism and his compulsion to assail it has led one writer to maintain that he had "one of the finest minds of the nineteenth century." Paul A. Freund, "Mr. Justice Brandeis," in Philip B. Kurland and Allison Dunham (eds.), *Mr. Justice* (Chicago, 1964), p. 177.

mitted to seeing that it served a constructively useful and equitable social function. Social justice democratically achieved was to Brandeis the prime objective of jurisprudence.

The junior member of the bench, John H. Clarke, like Day, an Ohioan, was a democrat and friend of the former Progressive mayor of Cleveland, Tom Johnson, and of Attorney General Thomas W. Gregory. Clarke had been a highly successful railroad attorney who chose to act as a conscience for the business community he served. Wilson's Secretary of War, Newton D. Baker, had urged that Clarke be placed on a lower federal bench as one of several men whom he felt worthy of grooming for subsequent elevation to the Supreme Court. When Charles Evans Hughes resigned to run for the Presidency, Baker convinced Wilson that Clarke could be relied upon for a "liberal and enlightened view of the law."[57] Closer to Brandeis than any other judge, Clarke believed in broad governmental intervention in the economy to protect the underprivileged. He confronted the postwar period equally hopeful that concepts of sociological jurisprudence could in time come to pervade the American legal system.[58]

The Court's 1918–19 term had opened before the armistice, and had seen a renewed dispute over the issue of federal police power —whether, in the absence of a constitutional grant of the police power to Congress more general delegated powers such as commerce, taxing, and postal could be used for coercive purposes to secure the general welfare. Justice Day, for a unanimous Court, now moved away from the sharply restrictive doctrines of the Child Labor case, thus seeming to indicate that no permanent precedent had there been created. In upholding a challenge to the federal Meat Inspection Act, the Court made clear that enactment of the law was "within the power of Congress in order to prevent interstate and foreign shipment of impure or adulterated meat products."[59] Three months later, without alluding to *Hammer* v. *Dagen-*

57. Ray Stannard Baker, *Woodrow Wilson, Life and Letters* (8 vols., Garden City, N.Y., 1927–1938), VI, 116. On Clarke see Hoyt Landon Warner, *The Life of Mr. Justice Clarke* (Cleveland, 1959).

58. Wood, *Constitutional Politics,* p. 133.

59. Pittsburgh Melting Co. *v.* Totten, 248 U.S. 1 (1918). The commerce clause was widened even further the following June when White wrote an eight-to-one opinion maintaining that federal commerce power could extend to subjects that were not commerce, but that obstructed or interfered with its free flow. U.S. *v.* Ferger, 250 U.S. 199 (1919).

hart, five of the justices also supported broad congressional use of the taxing power. In a case challenging the Federal Narcotics Act, Day sustained the measure, making clear that it could not "be declared unconstitutional because its effect may be to accomplish another purpose as well as the raising of revenue."[60] Why Congress's purpose in enacting the legislation was irrelevant here, and not in the Child Labor case, he did not explain. Four justices including White dissented, however, indicating that a slight change in Court membership might well revitalize the Hammer positions.

Probably the most extreme example of the use of the federal government acting to regulate the "health, morals, and welfare" of the American people was prohibition. Here the postwar White Court was called upon in several ways. The earlier Webb-Kenyon Act of 1913 had been upheld during the war period,[61] and the Court turned away further challenges in cases immediately following the war. The measure had made use of the commerce power to assist the states in enforcement of their various prohibition laws. The White Court did not depart appreciably from such a policy of cooperative federalism in other areas.[62]

Prohibition had also been imposed nationally as an aspect of the war effort, a move that had brought joy to the hearts of dry crusaders. This gave them added momentum for the constitutional amendment that they had long sought. Prior to ratification of that January, 1919, enacted measure and ten days after the armistice,

60. U.S. *v.* Doremus, 249 U.S. 86 (1919).

61. Clark Distilling Company *v.* Western Maryland Railway Co., 242 U.S. 311 (1917).

62. The Court was generally tolerant toward the use of state police power in these years. See Payne *v.* Kansas, 248 U.S. 112 (1918); Hebe Co. *v.* Shaw, 248 U.S. 297 (1919); Merchants Exchange *v.* Missouri, 248 U.S. 365 (1919); LaTourette *v.* McMaster, 248 U.S. 465 (1919); Middleton *v.* Texas Power and Light, 249 U.S. 152 (1919); Corn Products *v.* Eddy, 249 U.S. 427 (1919); Arizona Employer Liability Cases, 250 U.S. 400 (1919); McCloskey *v.* Tobin, 252 U.S. 107 (1920); Whipple *v.* Martinson, 256 U.S. 41 (1921). Holmes in a 1919 case reflected a general attitude running through such decisions, maintaining that "the Fourteenth Amendment is not a pedagogical requirement of the impossible." "A state may do what it can to prevent what is deemed an evil . . . stopping short of those cases in which the harm to the few concerned is thought less important than the harm to the public that would ensue if the rule laid down were mathematically exact." He admitted that this required judicial line-drawing since such distinctions were distinctions of degree but, he contended, "the constant business of the law is to draw such lines." Dominion Hotel *v.* Arizona, 249 U.S. 265, 268 (1919).

Congress passed a Wartime Prohibition Act, relying on its war powers to extend federal restriction on through until the completion of demobilization. Challenge to the legislation came early and raised not only questions of due process, but of the length of time Congress could rely upon its war powers to deal with postwar problems. Taking a realistic instead of a legalistic view, the Court sustained the measure, noting that "the treaty of peace has not yet been concluded, that the railways are still under national control by virtue of the war powers, that other war activities have not been brought to a close, and that it cannot even be said that the man power of the nation has been restored to a peacetime footing. . . ."[63] But Brandeis took the opportunity, for a unanimous Court, to suggest that the Court should not pass upon the necessity of the exercise of a power possessed by Congress, and to argue that an emergency situation called for a leniency toward congressional solutions.

Later in the same term, two other prohibition programs received judicial sanction. The Volstead Act, enacted to carry out the purpose of the Eighteenth Amendment, had also sought to cover the period before the amendment became effective by utilizing the Wartime Prohibition Act for prior enforcement. Woodrow Wilson had vetoed the measure because it merged enforcement based on war powers with that based on the constitutional amendment. Congress then passed it over his veto. The Supreme Court validated Congress, sustaining the measure as a proper exercise of merged war and police power.[64] It also, in an unprecedented ruling in early 1920, turned away strong and unique challenges to the constitutionality of the Eighteenth Amendment. Prominent critics, including Elihu Root, had questioned particularly whether the substance of the amendment was not illegal and incapable of becoming a part of the Constitution, the area being one limited to the states by the Tenth Amendment. This the Court denied, making clear by its ruling that the federal police power could clearly be used for the accomplishment of desirable social purposes.[65]

63. Hamilton *v.* Kentucky Distilleries, 251 U.S. 146 (1919).

64. Ruppert *v.* Caffey, 251 U.S. 264 (1920).

65. Rhode Island *v.* Palmer, 253 U.S. 350 (1920). A useful discussion of the case is in Alfred H. Kelly and Winfred A. Harbison, *The American Constitution: Its Origins and Development* (New York, 1970), pp. 681–683.

Challenges to other wartime legislation met a similar fate. Cases reached the Court in early 1919 questioning the government take-over of the railroads,[66] and of the telephone and telegraph lines,[67] challenging a conviction under the Trading with the Enemy Act,[68] and questioning the wartime use of cable property by the federal government.[69] All were turned away. White set the tone in the first, arguing, in defending Presidential seizure and operation of the railroads, that "the complete and undivided character of the war power of the United States is not disputable."[70] The fact that the program was an encroachment upon state authority, he found in no way abnormal for a wartime period. Sustaining of the other measures followed logically from such a position. Particularly indicative of the balance the court was willing to reach regarding emergency curtailment of the free use of private property were rulings in the Emergency Rent cases.[71] There the "just compensation" clause of the Fifth Amendment was held to be less restrictive of governmental power "in a public exigency" than in normal times. "Housing is a necessary of life," wrote Holmes for a Court split five to four. "All the elements of a public interest justifying some degree of public control are present." "The only matter that seems to us open to debate is whether the statute goes too far."[72] Overly restrictive and unreasonable regulation, the Justice was quick to admit, clearly was unwarranted, but such a decision should be made based upon careful examination of the application of the legislation.

Of much more interest to many Americans, particularly to a growing group of citizens concerned over wartime abrogation of personal rights and civil liberties, were challenges to the wartime espionage and sedition legislation. These laws had been, in many

66. Northern Pacific *v.* North Dakota, 250 U.S. 135 (1919).

67. Dakota Central Telephone *v.* South Dakota, 250 U.S. 163 (1919).

68. Rumely *v.* McCarthy, 250 U.S. 283 (1919); Central Union Trust Co. *v.* Carvin, 254 U.S. 554 (1921); Stoehr *v.* Wallace, 255 U.S. 239 (1921).

69. Commercial Cable *v.* Burleson, 250 U.S. 360 (1919).

70. Northern Pacific *v.* North Dakota, 250 U.S. 135, 149 (1919).

71. Bloch *v.* Hirsh, 256 U.S. 135 (1921); Marcus Brown Holding Co. *v.* Feldman, 256 U.S. 170 (1921). The latter, a New York state case, had produced an eloquent amicus curiae brief by Louis Marshall of the American Jewish Committee sharply condemning public control of private rental property when facilities serving the public such as inns, hotels, bridges, etc., had not been subjected to wartime price-fixing.

72. Block *v.* Hirsh, 256 U.S. 135, 156 (1919).

ways, as revolutionary a legal departure as wartime administrative measures.[73] Not since the infamous Alien and Sedition Acts of 1798 had the federal government launched so vigorous a campaign to curtail dissent and attack critics of wartime government. However, to many the legislation had even more ominous overtones. Not unlike its eighteenth-century predecessors it was aimed as much against unpopular critics of the government as against true enemy agents and sympathizers. The Espionage Act[74] provided punishment for making or conveying false reports for the benefit of the enemy and seeking to cause disobedience in the armed forces. Most important, it found its real teeth in a provision aimed at willfully obstructing the recruiting or enlistment service. This section was used widely to curtail activities of persons not in sympathy with the conduct of the war. Its 1918 amendment, the Sedition Act,[75] was an even less subtle device. Passed by the pressure of western senators and modeled after a Montana Industrial Workers of the World statute, its purpose was to undercut both the performance and advocacy of undesirable, i.e., general antiwar, activity.

Arrests under the legislation made clear its target. Alien radicals, members of the anarcho-syndicalist Industrial Workers of the World, leaders of the Socialist party, including Eugene V. Debs, and the agrarian Nonpartisan League, verbal and visible anarchists and militant pacifists all found themselves indicted under its terms,[76] or under comparable state laws enacted to accomplish similar pur-

73. On the background of the legislation see Zechariah Chafee, Jr., *Freedom of Speech* (New York, 1920), pp. 38–42; Harry N. Scheiber, *The Wilson Administration and Civil Liberties—1917–1921* (Ithaca, 1960), pp. 17–20; 22–26; Thomas F. Carroll, "Freedom of Speech and of the Press in Wartime: The Espionage Act," *Michigan Law Review,* XVII (June, 1919), 622 ff.

74. 40 Stat. 217 (1917).

75. 40 Stat. 553 (1918). For background see Paul L. Murphy, "Sources and Nature of Intolerance in the 1920's," *Journal of American History,* LI (June, 1964), 62–66.

76. Scheiber, *Wilson Admin. and Civil Liberties,* pp. 61–63 contains a numerical summary of Espionage Act prosecutions. See also National Civil Liberties Bureau, *War-Time Prosecutions and Mob Violence* (New York, 1919); and Philip Taft, "The Federal Trials of the IWW," *Labor History,* III (Winter, 1962), 57–91. On Debs see Ray Ginger, *The Bending Cross* (New Brunswick, 1949), pp. 358 ff.; and Forrest R. Black, "Debs *v.* the United States—A Judicial Milepost on the Road to Absolutism," *University of Pennsylvania Law Review,* LXXXI (1932), 160–175.

poses.[77] Challenge particularly on First Amendment grounds had come early, but unlike the Selective Draft Cases the government had not been anxious to push immediate Court test while the war was on.[78]

Six major cases involving the convictions under the legislation reached the Supreme Court in the immediate postwar period, three in the spring of 1919 and three more in the winter of 1919–20. The first, *Schenck* v. *U.S.*,[79] again set the tone for sustaining such convictions, but its implications and overtones were far more complex.

Schenck, a prominent Socialist leader, had been indicted for inciting young men to resist the draft. He had mailed circulars to men who had passed exemption boards, that not only declared conscription to be unconstitutional despotism, but urged the recipients in impassioned language to assert their rights. Such utterances could fairly be considered a direct and dangerous interference with the power of Congress to raise armies. Clearly, in accordance with Judge Learned Hand's earlier interpretations of the statute,[80] such action could be construed as counseling unlawful action.

Justice Holmes, to whom the majority opinion was assigned, saw the occasion as a vital one in which to clarify broadly the law of free speech. Federal cases on the subject were virtually nonexistent. The only real precedents that existed were from English common law and a few state rulings, primarily from the nineteenth century.

77. For a summary of such state laws see Eldridge F. Dowell, "A History of the Enactment of Criminal Syndicalism Legislation in the United States" (2 vols., doctoral dissertation, Johns Hopkins University, 1936). Thomas Reed Powell, teacher of two generations of Harvard constitutional law students, showed an early and constant concern for such legislation. See his "Precautionary Regulation" (unpublished MS.), Powell Papers, Treasure Room, Harvard Law School Library. See also John M. Smith and Cornelius P. Cotter, "Freedom and Authority in the Amphibial State," *Midwest Journal of Political Science,* I (1957), 40–59.

78. The number of indictments under the legislation ran into the thousands, with many of the resulting cases unreported. The Attorney General in his *Annual Report for 1919–1920* alluded to 877 convictions out of 1,956 cases commenced.

79. Schenck *v.* U.S. 249 U.S. 47 (1919).

80. Hand, in linking speech with action, had emphasized the nature of the words used. The normal test for the suppression of speech in a democratic government, he argued, was neither the justice of its substance nor the decency and propriety of its temper, but the strong danger that it would cause injurious acts. He did place outside the limits of free speech, however, one who counseled or advised others to violate existing laws. Masses Publishing Co. *v.* Patten, 244 Fed 535 (S.D. N.Y., 1917).

Turning to the common-law rule of proximate causation, which maintained that to prove improper intent it was necessary to show a direct and immediate relationship between the spoken word and some illicit act, Holmes set out to make more precise the proper lines of application of the legislation, something that was highly vague from its congressional wording. Exempting nonpolitical speech from First Amendment protection at the outset (the most stringent protection of free speech would not protect a man in falsely shouting fire in a theater and causing a panic), he defined the true scope of the First Amendment, as it related to political expression, as follows:

> The question in every case is whether the words used are used in such circumstances and are of such a nature as to create a clear and present danger that they will bring about the substantive evils that Congress has a right to prevent. It is a question of proximity and degree. When a nation is at war, many things that might be said in time of peace are such a hindrance to its effort that their utterance will not be endured so long as men fight and no Court could regard them as protected by any constitutional right.[81]

Two cases similar to Schenck were decided one week later. In one, the Court sustained conviction, under the Schenck rule, of a newspaper editor whose German-language paper had contained articles challenging the constitutionality and merits of the draft and the purposes of the war.[82] In the other, which involved conviction of Eugene V. Debs for a militant antiwar speech, Holmes was willing to accept the jury's verdict of proof that actual interference with the war was intended and was the proximate effect of the words used.[83]

These three decisions came, in the words of Zechariah Chafee, Jr., as a "great shock to forward-looking men and women who had consoled themselves through the war-time trials with the hope that

81. 249 U.S. 47, 52 (1919). On the background of the concept see Phillip L. Sirokin, "The Evolution of the Clear and Present Danger Doctrine" (unpublished M.A. thesis, University of Chicago, 1947). See also Wallace Mendelson, "Clear and Present Danger: From Schenck to Dennis," *Columbia Law Review,* LII (1952), 313–317; Chester J. Antieau, "The Rule of Clear and Present Danger—Its Origin and Application," *University of Detroit Law Journal,* XIII (1950), 198–213.

82. Frowerk *v.* U.S., 249 U.S. 204 (1919).

83. Debs *v.* U.S., 249 U.S. 211 (1919).

the Espionage Act would be invalidated when it reached the Supreme Court."[84] "They were especially grieved," Chafee went on, in his classic and influential work on *Freedom of Speech,* "that the opinions which dashed this hope were written by the Justice who for their eyes had long taken on heroic dimensions."

Holmes was early disturbed by the broad use to which the government now set out to put what he had hopefully set forth as a narrow and limited test for punishment of free expression. In the three cases of the following term, he dissented strongly, and was joined by Brandeis as well.

The Abrams case,[85] which came eight months after Debs had been sent to prison, struck Holmes as a good example of the kind of expression the government has no business suppressing. Abrams, an obscure Lower East Side Russian Jewish immigrant, had been indicted, along with four other Bolshevik sympathizers, for the publication and distribution of Yiddish and English leaflets attacking the government's policy in dispatching American troops to Vladivostok and Murmansk in the summer of 1918. Tried before a repressive-oriented district court judge, the government was confronted with demonstrating that the action in some way interfered with the war with Germany. The charge was only provable through the claim that the leaflets had a tendency to cause armed revolts and strikes and thus diminish the supply of troops and munitions available against Germany on the regular battlefield. The government presented what it claimed was clear proof of its charge, and the Supreme Court, with Justice Clarke speaking for a seven-man majority, upheld its contention on appeal.

Holmes's dissent has been called the "most eloquent and moving defense of free speech since Milton's *Areopagitica.*"[86] Maintaining that the government had not shown successfully that the leaflets had had any effect upon its war efforts, or that it had been the appellants' purpose to have such an effect, Holmes reiterated his earlier contention that it was only present danger of immediate evil or the intent to bring it about that warranted Congress to set limits on freedom of expression. This, he argued, was not the

84. Zechariah Chafee, Jr., *Free Speech in the United States* (Cambridge, Mass., 1941), p. 86.
85. Abrams *v.* U.S., 250 U.S. 616 (1919).
86. Kelly and Harbison, *American Constitution,* p. 678.

situation here. "Nobody can suppose," he stated, "that the surreptitious publishing of a silly leaflet by an unknown man, without more, would present any immediate danger that its opinions would hinder the success of the government arms or have any appreciable tendency to do so." "We should be eternally vigilant against attempts to check the expression of opinions that we loathe and believe to be fraught with death, unless they so imminently threaten immediate interference with the lawful and pressing purposes of the law that an immediate check is required to save the country."[87]

In the Schaefer case[88] decided four months later in March, 1920, Brandeis entered the dialogue, speaking in dissent for Holmes and Clarke as well. The case involved a Philadelphia German-language newspaper accused of publishing articles unpatriotic in tone, critical of the Allies, and generally favorable to the German cause. The Brandeis dissent was an eloquent, probing exploration of the utility of freedom of speech and the social consequences of its use and abuse. The Justice weighed carefully the desirability of public knowledge of the truth about the war against the importance of the suppression of information which might lead to national defeat. Brandeis called not only for a rule of reason in giving the benefit of the doubt to the critic, but a careful and responsible examination of all the facts by an impartial jury. The jury would be responsible in its obligation to apply hard-and-fast tests of criminality to allegedly dangerous action. Above all Brandeis condemned the injection of prejudice or emotional antipathy to the actions and words of critics of American policy.

The last of the major Espionage cases was *Pierce* v. *U.S.*[89] This case involved prosecution of three Socialists for being local distributors of a strongly antiwar pamphlet by St. John Tucker, a

87. 250 U.S. 616, 630 (1919). Dean John H. Wigmore assailed Holmes's Abrams dissent since it betrayed Holmes's naïveté in failing to realize that "hundreds of well-meaning citizens—'parlor bolsheviks' and 'pink radicals' are showing . . . complaisance or good-natured tolerance to the licensing of the violence-propaganda." John H. Wigmore, "Freedom of Speech and Freedom of Thuggery in War-Time and Peace-Time," *Illinois Law Review,* XIV (1920), 539. Holmes's response was philosophic. Writing to Pollock, he stated: "I was sorry to see Wigmore carried away by the panic mongers. His reasons amounted to saying that it is wrong to criticize an indictment for murder because homicide is a very dangerous offense and many murderers are very wicked men." Howe (ed.), *Holmes-Pollock Letters,* II, 48.

88. Schaefer *v.* U.S., 251 U.S. 468 (1920).

89. Pierce *v.* U.S., 252 U.S. 239 (1920).

prominent Episcopalian clergyman. Speaking for the majority, Justice Pitney took it upon himself to deny the truth of certain contentions within the pamphlet, particularly the allegation that the war had had economic causes.[90] Such a false view, Pitney was convinced, would not help but have deleterious even if indirect impact upon successful war efforts. Again Brandeis and Holmes dissented, questioning whether matters of opinion and judgment could be ruled false, and if they could whether any future existed for free speech and free discussion as a democratic instrument, particularly in periods of national crisis. The Schaefer case and the others before it thus left a restrictive legal residue available for governmental use more immediate and ominous than in any of the other war power areas.[91]

Concern for permissible expression, radical views, and the general rights of critics of the American system existed elsewhere within American society at this time. National developments in the latter months of 1919 and early 1920 were responsible. These included growing national discontent in the form of inflation, unemployment, and particularly the outbreak of hundreds of strikes throughout the country, which had aroused conservatives to demand repression. The result was ominous, particularly to civil libertarians. State legislatures rushed sedition, criminal syndicalism, and red flag laws onto their statute books to take the place of the federal wartime Espionage and Sedition laws. In New York, Illinois, California, and New Jersey such legislation quickly became the

90. Chafee observed caustically: "According to the Pierce case, it was a criminal falsehood to say that we entered the war to save the Morgan loans. During the hearings of the Nye Committee of the Senate in 1934, it was almost a crime to say that we did not enter the war to save the Morgan loans." Chafee, *Free Speech,* p. 95. Woodrow Wilson, following the war, had made a similar statement. Speaking on September 5, 1919, six months before the Pierce ruling, he had stated: "Is there any man here, or woman . . . who does not know that the seed of war in the modern world is industrial and commercial rivalry. This was a commercial and industrial war." Albert Fried (ed.), *A Day of Dedication: The Essential Writing & Speeches of Woodrow Wilson* (New York, 1965), pp. 431–433.

91. The Court also sustained the section of the Espionage Act closing the mails to publications violating its provisions. The case involved Victor Berger's *Milwaukee Leader,* a Socialist organ, which had been highly critical of the war. U.S. *ex rel* Milwaukee Social Democratic Publishing Co. *v.* Burleson, 255 U.S. 407 (1921). Holmes and Brandeis again dissented, contending the question was one of statutory construction and that the statute did not confer upon the Postmaster General the privilege of denying second-class privileges to all issues of a newspaper of which some issues contained "non-mailable" materials.

basis for the arrest of such figures as Benjamin Gitlow, Charles Ruthenberg, "Big Jim" Larkin, Rose Pastor Stokes, "Big Bill" Haywood, William Bross Lloyd, and Charlotte Anita Whitney, all alleged radicals whose continued activities were feared to be subversive of the American way.[92] Many states created antisubversive bodies. Typical was the Lusk Committee in New York, which quickly assumed the responsibility for staging raids on radical headquarters and the seizing of the files and publications of various bodies felt to be subversive.[93]

Not to be outdone, Congress set out to enact federal peacetime sedition legislation. Attorney General A. Mitchell Palmer, taking such action as a cue for Justice Department activism, began a series of harassments against critics of the government that ended in midnight raids upon alleged radical groups and radical headquarters throughout the country. The raid on January 2, 1920,[94] ended with the roundup of over four thousand victims, some of whom were held long periods in crowded jails. The raids were conducted without warrant and with almost total disregard for the elementary procedural rights of the victims. Although eliciting immediate endorsement from conservative sources, they also drew vigorous condemnation from many liberal church leaders, labor leaders, professional men, and alert members of the media. The simultaneous high-handed refusal of the New York Assembly to seat five duly elected Socialist members further disturbed citizens sensitive to the importance of preserving democratic processes.[95] By February and March of 1920, the national reaction

92. Paul L. Murphy, *The Meaning of Freedom of Speech, 1918–1933* (Westport, Conn., 1971), Chaps. 4, 5.

93. On the activities of the committee see Lawrence H. Chamberlain, *Loyalty and Legislative Action* (Ithaca, 1951), Chap. I.; Robert K. Murray, *Red Scare: A Study in National Hysteria* (Minneapolis, 1955), pp. 94–102, 197, 235–238; Murphy, *Meaning of Freedom of Speech,* Chap. 4. The committee's massive report, *Revolutionary Radicalism* (4 vols., New York, 1920), composed largely of material from radical bodies commandeered in its raids, became a standard right-wing source of exposé material throughout the 1920s for "proving" that organizations ranging from liberal labor unions to peace organizations and the American Civil Liberties Union were Communist fronts.

94. Coben, *A. Mitchell Palmer,* pp. 217–245; Murray, *Red Scare,* pp. 112 ff.

95. Merlo J. Pusey, *Charles Evans Hughes* (2 vols., New York, 1951), pp. 390 ff.; Louis Waldman, *Labor Lawyer* (New York, 1944) pp. 97–104; Charles Reznikoff (ed.), *Louis Marshall: Champion of Liberty* (2 vols., Philadelphia, 1957), II, 977–985; Chafee, *Free Speech,* pp. 269 ff. For contemporary reaction see "Albany's Ousted Socialists," *Literary Digest,* LXIV (January 24, 1920), 20.

was so hostile that even Palmer, who earlier had been calling for vigorous peacetime antisubversive legislation, now felt compelled to reassert his basic commitment to freedom of speech and press. The movement for a federal peacetime sedition law collapsed in ignominy and public hostility.[96]

The Supreme Court and a number of members of the lower federal bench were affected by this development.[97] Members of the high bench had opened their October, 1919, term sustaining wartime Espionage Act convictions, but by later January were of a mood to deplore illegal search and seizure techniques. The case, *Silverthorne Lumber Company* v. *United States*,[98] involved an action in which two suspects had been indicted by a federal grand jury and taken into custody. While so detained, Justice Department officials "without a shadow of authority" raided their offices and "made a clean sweep of all the books, papers, and documents found there." Holmes, who at the height of the "Red Scare" activities had publicly deplored such a national development,[99] spoke for the Court in branding the government's action an "outrage." Further, he not only condemned the seizure tactics,

96. Murphy, *Meaning of Freedom of Speech,* Chap. 5.

97. Judge Charles F. Amidon of the Federal District Court at Fargo, North Dakota, was outspoken in his criticism of national leadership. As he wrote in 1920: "The Federal Government under the dull and massive administration of Mr. Harding seems to be sliding down on the American people like a glacier and wiping out whatever the little sanhedrin of senators who are to be in control may be pleased to call 'radicalism.' Economically they threaten to destroy all that labor has gained for a century through labor unions. There seems to be no temper for education and kindness. The wave of greed and hatred that is to cover the earth will be as much worse in experience as the great war has been greater than previous wars." Charles F. Amidon to Zechariah Chafee, Jr., Nov. 22, 1920. Amidon Papers, University of North Dakota Library, Grand Forks, N.D. On Amidon see I. Kenneth Smemo, "Progressive Judge: The Public Career of Charles Fremont Amidon" (unpublished Ph.D. dissertation, University of Minnesota, 1967). Other eloquently liberal judges in the decade included George W. Anderson of Massachusetts, George M. Bourquin of Montana, Orrin N. Carter in Illinois, Learned Hand and Cuthbert Pound in New York, and Kimbrough Stone in Missouri. On Bourquin see Arnon Gutfeld, "The Ves Hall Case, Judge Bourquin and the Sedition Act of 1918," *Pacific Historical Review,* XXXVII (May, 1968), 163–178.

98. Silverthorne Lumber Co. *v.* U.S., 251 U.S. 385 (1920).

99. "Prating Patriots Worse Than Reds," New York *World,* January 13, 1920. Holmes's oft-quoted statement avowed that "with effervescing opinion as with the not yet forgotten champagne, the quickest way to let them get flat is to let them be exposed to the air." "The Red Hysteria," *New Republic,* XXI (January 28, 1920), 250.

but insisted that material so obtained not only could not be used before a court but "shall not be used at all." The ruling was an important cornerstone in the creation of the "exclusionary rule" developed by a later generation of judges.[100] Shortly thereafter, Federal District Court Judge George M. Bourquin applied the Silverthorne dictum to forestall, through a writ of habeas corpus, the deportation of an alleged radical because evidence used against him had been illegally obtained.[101]

In *Colyer* v. *Skeffington,* in June,[102] District Judge George W. Anderson sternly rebuked the Justice Department for its unwarranted raids and seizures and its "hang-first-and-try-afterwards" techniques. "A mob is a mob," wrote the judge, who had joined Holmes in contemporaneous condemnation of national resort to vigilantism, "whether made up of government officials acting under instructions from the Department of Justice, or of criminals, loafers, and the vicious classes." The ruling had a pronounced effect upon the Labor Department, which had joined in the national suppression by launching a vigorous policy of deporting "dangerous radicals." It now greatly curtailed these activities, confining its future action to a handful of "incorrigible" aliens.[103]

Contradictory legal trends and precedents precluded the Court from moving to any set of new liberal positions defending personal rights and civil liberties at this time. The general commitment to the primacy of business and the sacredness of private property still prevailed strongly, as several key cases demonstrated.

100. Jacob W. Landynski, *Search and Seizure and the Supreme Court* (Baltimore, 1966), p. 69. See also Gouled *v.* U.S., 255 U.S. 289 (1921), in this regard.

101. National Popular Government League, *To The American People: Report upon the Illegal Practices of the United States Department of Justice* (Washington, 1920), p. 11.

102. Colyer *v.* Skeffington, 265 Fed. 17 (D. Mass., 1920).

103. Murray, *Red Scare,* pp. 250–251. The same sentiments prevailed at the Supreme Court level, in a case in June involving highly arbitrary action by the Secretary of Labor in refusing to permit an American-born Chinese from re-entering the country after a sojourn abroad. After decrying the "manifestly unfair" aspects of the proceedings involved, Justice Clarke maintained that governmental power, such as that possessed by the Secretary of Labor, "is power to be administered, not arbitrarily and secretly, but fairly and openly, under the restraints of the tradition and principles of free government applicable where the fundamental rights of men are involved, regardless of their origin or race." Kwock Jan Fat *v.* White, 253 U.S. 454, 464 (1920).

In the search and seizure area, June, 1921, brought a ruling denounced by liberals, which a majority of the high bench had no difficulty seeing as consistent within the Silverthorne rule. McDowell, an officer in a business enterprise, had been dismissed for fraud. Another officer of the business was dispatched to Pittsburgh where McDowell was located. He took possession of his office, as well as two safes, and although the latter were McDowell's personal property, he nonetheless had them blasted open by a private detective with much of the material so obtained shipped to the head offices of the business in New York. Some of the material so obtained was turned over to the government, which used it to prosecute McDowell for fraudulent use of the mails. Although he fought back, charging that the government was making illegal use of stolen papers, the Supreme Court rejected his appeal. Speaking through Justice Day, the Court contended the Fourth Amendment was a restraint on government and not on private persons. The wrong done McDowell was the act of one individual taking the property of another, an act in which the government did not share. "No constitutional principle," wrote Justice Day, with exact legal literalness, "requires exclusion of the evidence in this case."[104]

A similar adherence to *stare decisis* led the Court to turn aside challenge to one of the more appalling examples of wartime vigilantism. The case concerned centered on the infamous Bisbee deportations in which over a thousand striking copper miners and their sympathizers had been forcibly transported by action of their employers into New Mexico and released in the desert, and then threatened with death or bodily harm should they ever return to the state of Arizona.[105] Rejecting a strong plea by the appellants' counsel, Charles Evans Hughes, the Court again made clear that the factual evidence presented showed that the action was perpetrated by private parties, not by the state. Hence it was beyond federal protection.[106] Edward S. Corwin expressed widely held liberal reaction at the outcome: "Although the decision unquestionably follows conventional lines," he wrote,

104. Burdeau *v.* McDowell, 256 U.S. 465 (1921).

105. H. C. Peterson and Gilbert C. Fite, *Opponents of War, 1917–1918: The Story of the Persecution of Antiwar Groups* (Madison, Wis., 1957), pp. 54, 314, 358.

106. U.S. *v.* Wheeler, 254 U.S. 281 (1920).

it leaves one not entirely satisfied. Perhaps the time will come when with the spread of the Ku Klux Klan or some equally egregious form of *imperium in imperio*, it will become necessary to discard the outworn artificiality of the decisions in the Slaughter House and the Civil Rights Cases. Certainly, it is rather dismaying to be told in one breath that national citizenship is "paramount and dominant" and in the next that all our most fundamental rights come from the states and are dependent on them for protection.[107]

But the Court was, in certain areas, equally reluctant to challenge state action, carried out, allegedly, in the public interest. In a landmark ruling in December, 1920, involving indictment of a prominent Nonpartisan League leader under a state sedition statute,[108] the body sustained the measure as a legitimate exercise of state police power. By implication this ruling gave a green light to other state loyalty programs enacted during and immediately following the war.[109] Only White and Brandeis challenged the action. White contended in typical nationalist form that federal laws in this area had preempted the field and were within the exclusive war power of Congress. Brandeis, by contrast, called for federal action in behalf of the individual and frank rejection of the majority view that "the liberty guaranteed by the Fourteenth Amendment includes only liberty to acquire and to enjoy property."[110]

107. Edward S. Corwin, "Constitutional Law in 1919–1920," *American Political Science Review*, XVI (1920), 37–38. The only case in the period involving the Jim Crow system, in an era when race riots had burst forth in a number of cities, was an April, 1920, ruling sustaining a Kentucky segregation ordinance demanding separate cars by interurban railroad companies for white and colored passengers. South Covington & Cincinnati Street Railway Co. *v.* Kentucky, 252 U.S. 388 (1920).

108. Gilbert *v.* Minnesota, 254 U.S. 325 (1920). On the background of the case see Dwight W. Jessup, "Joseph Gilbert and the Minnesota Sedition Law" (unpublished M. A. thesis, University of Minnesota, 1965).

109. A more highly publicized assault on the League involved the trial for conspiracy of its founder and guiding light, A. C. Townley, in a lower Minnesota court in mid-1919. Townley was convicted and jailed, a ruling the Minnesota Supreme Court upheld in April, 1921 (State *v.* Townley, 149 Minn. 5); and on which the Supreme Court denied certiorari, 257 U.S. 643 (1921). See Robert L. Morlan, *Political Prairie Fire: The Nonpartisan League, 1915–1922* (Minneapolis, 1955), pp. 336–338; and Carol Jenson, "Agrarian Pioneer in Civil Liberties: The Non-Partisan League in Minnesota" (unpublished Ph.D. dissertation, University of Minnesota, 1968).

110. Gilbert *v.* Minnesota, 254 U.S. 325, 343 (1920). The Court also failed to see

The White Court took a middle-of-the-road position regarding areas less security-charged and less oriented to personal freedom. Here distinctions were drawn that reflected the majority's concept of the "national interest." Governmental action geared to stimulate industrial consolidation and uninhibited business growth was encouraged on the one hand, and the curtailment of forces that might impede that growth was endorsed on the other. This trend was particularly noticeable in the antitrust area.

The original Sherman Act of 1890 had been strengthened in 1914 through the enactment of the Clayton Antitrust Act. This new measure had made explicit what had been implicit in Sherman Act interpretation. This was the prohibition of certain practices previously illegal only as part of proven conspiracies or with proven illicit intent. It had also placed new emphasis on prevention rather than punishment, especially with the addition of an administrative tribunal, the Federal Trade Commission. The body was empowered to expand the definition of unfair trade practices and apply them to new situations rather than leaving this task to the ordinary process of civil litigation. The measure also had sought to clarify the government's relationship to labor through the antitrust structure. A deliberate attempt was made to return to the original intent of the framers of the earlier measure, by explicitly exempting the actions of labor unions from its application and also exempting labor from having its legitimate activities enjoined.[111] Thus, while the measure had strengthened the government's hand in supervising business, its sponsors had sought to shield labor from constant governmental intervention to hinder achievement of labor's concrete objectives.

Judicial interpretation of the new antitrust structure had to await the termination of wartime conditions, but the postwar White Court gave early indication of its sentiments. In cases in December,

---

civil liberties denial in the May, 1921, case of Newberry *v.* U.S. 256 U.S. 323. (For background see Spencer Ervin, *Henry Ford vs. Truman H. Newberry* [New York, 1935]). Justice McReynolds, in a Court split five to four, ruled that despite clear evidence of violation by a candidate for the U.S. Senate of the Federal Corrupt Practices Act of 1910, the power of Congress to regulate elections did not extend back to the regulation of the nominating process.

111. 42 Stat. 20 (1921).

1918,[112] and June, 1919,[113] it unanimously rejected governmental attempts to curtail business activities alleged to be destructive of open competition. Then, in early 1920, it nullified antitrust action against the United States Steel Corporation, the nation's largest industrial complex. United States Steel had just displayed its massive power by decisively crushing its employees' demands for better working conditions, hours, and wages, and especially for unionization.

United States Steel had been charged, as leader of the industry, with using its power to force its competitors to standardize prices, wages, and costs, thereby eliminating competition within the industry. The company's success lay in the fear it was able to throw into the minds of independents of a price war against a rival with the size and financial connections of the corporation. Justice McKenna rejected the government's suit to dissolve U.S. Steel into component parts.[114] He conceded that the corporation's promoters had at one point intended to monopolize the industry, but contended that they had not succeeded. He further insisted that the competition had not been illegally restrained since the company had made no efforts to suppress the independents by unfair means. To stretch the antitrust structure to cover informal cooperation and brand it restraint of trade, was clearly unreasonable, contended Justice McKenna. In fact, the majority opinion spoke so sanguinely of the benefits to be gained from such a stabilization that the net result of the ruling was to encourage renewal of the old system of business agreements. Once again industry-wide operations came to be formalized through price and policy arrangements made by various trade associations.

Similar judicial curtailment of government regulatory power took place three months later. Speaking through Justice McReynolds, the Court sharply undermined the authority of the Federal Trade Commission.[115] Questioning critically the body's

112. Buckeye Powder Co. *v.* Dupont, 248 U.S. 55 (1918).

113. U.S. *v.* Colgate, 250 U.S. 300 (1919).

114. U.S. *v.* U.S. Steel Corp., 251 U.S. 417 (1920).

115. F.T.C. *v.* Gratz, 253 U.S. 421 (1920). The Court's further F.T.C. rulings in the decade merely followed and extended Gratz. See F.T.C. *v.* Beech-Nut Packing Co., 257 U.S. 441 (1922); F.T.C. *v.* Curtis Publishing Co., 260 U.S. 568 (1923); F.T.C. *v.* American Tobacco Co., 264 U.S. 298 (1924). Carl McFarland, *Judicial Control of the Federal Trade Commission and the Interstate Commerce Commis-*

presumed authority to investigate "unfair methods of competition," McReynolds argued that such methods were not defined in the statute. It was for the courts, not the commission, ultimately to determine as a matter of law what unfair competition included. The decision had the effect of destroying the commission's capacity to demarcate new areas of unfair trade practice. With the Court making clear it would review any other rulings by the body, the effect was to undermine the finality of the commission's actions, tarnishing its competence in the public eye.[116] Thus the Federal Trade Commission, already hampered by conservative membership and generally unpopular in the business world, found its effective power to police industry, the purpose for which it was originally created, minimal in virtually every regard.[117]

The White Court also saw the hindrance of business objectives by labor union harassment as a proper subject for judicial curtailment. Section 20 of the Clayton Act had provided that "no

---

sion, 1920–1930 (Cambridge, Mass., 1933); Gerard C. Henderson, *The Federal Trade Commission* (New Haven, 1924); Thomas C. Blaisdell, *The Federal Trade Commission* (New York, 1932); Myron W. Watkins, "An Appraisal of the Work of the Federal Trade Commission," *Columbia Law Review,* XXXII (February, 1932), 272–289; and Robert E. Cushman, *Independent Regulatory Commissions* (New York, 1941). Public acquiescence in such judicial emasculation was in sharp contrast to its demands for a strong agency to control commercial radio. The abuse of an instrument reaching hourly into millions of homes, plus the general confusion that had been created by the pell-mell rush of broadcasters to get their word first to susceptible consumers, eventually forced Congress to enact the Radio Act of 1927, creating a five-man Federal Radio Commission charged with classifying radio stations, prescribing service, assigning frequency bands, regulating chain broadcasting, and generally inspecting and controlling the activities of radio operators and apparatus. See Carl J. Friedrich and Evelyn Sternberg, "Congress and the Control of Radio Broadcasting," *American Political Science Review,* XXXVII (1940), 797–818, 1014–1026. See also Thomas P. Robinson, *Radio Networks and the Federal Government* (New York, 1943); and Walter B. Emery, *Broadcasting and Government* (East Lansing, Mich., 1961).

116. The Court had reached a similar position regarding state-created commissions. When a Pennsylvania Public Service Commission law failed to provide opportunity, by way of appeal to the courts or by injunctive proceedings, to test whether rates fixed by the commission were confiscatory, it ruled that further orders of the commission establishing maximum future rates were illegal as a violation of due process of law. Ohio Valley Co. *v.* Ben Avon Borough, 253 U.S. 389 (1920).

117. On the fate of the commission in the twenties see G. Cullom Davis, "The Transformation of the Federal Trade Commission, 1914–1929," *Mississippi Valley Historical Review,* XLIX (December, 1962), 437–455.

restraining order or injunction shall be granted by any court of the United States in any case between employer and employees . . . unless necessary to prevent irreparable injury to property, or to a property right." The section also prohibited the issuing of injunctions against peaceful persuasion of others to strike, and insured that no injunctions could be issued against primary boycotts. In the January, 1921, case of *Duplex Printing Press Co.* v. *Deering,* [118] a case with origins in prewar days, Justice Pitney held that the Clayton Act did not legalize the secondary boycott and immunize workers responsible for it from the operations of the principles of equity. Pitney made clear that Section 6 of the Clayton Act was not a blanket exemption of labor from the antitrust laws. It merely protected unions in "lawfully carrying out their legitimate objectives." Secondary boycotts being unlawful, unions who encouraged them were subject to having their actions stopped by injunction. As to Section 20, Pitney ruled that the restrictions upon injunctions must be construed very narrowly to apply only to the immediate parties concerned in the dispute. Only actual strikers were thus apparently exempt from injunctions. A union conducting them was not. The ruling, coming after business's smashing victory at the polls with the election of Harding, seemed to indicate that the injunction was open once again for use against unions almost without restraint. The fact was clearly validated by the issuance of nearly three hundred injunctions to applying railroad companies during the course of the Railroad Shopman's Strike in 1922 alone.[119]

Yet the justices were able to compartmentalize their thought on governmental action in such a way as to draw lines between the use of governmental power to enhance business interests and to conduct other public policy actions. Two rulings handed down in

118. Duplex Printing Press Co. *v.* Deering, 254 U.S. 443 (1921). Pitney's attitude toward labor seemed to have changed little since 1902 when he wrote, in a case involving the right to picket (Frank & Dugan *v.* Herold, 52 Atl. 152), that a picket who wished to remain within the law might accost a worker or a prospective employer and politely ask, "May I have a moment of your time, sir?" and speak to him if he consented to listen.

119. George W. Pepper, *Men and Issues* (New York, 1924), p. 159. See also Zechariah Chafee, Jr., *The Inquiring Mind* (New York, 1928), pp. 198 ff.; Edward Berman, *Labor and the Sherman Act* (New York, 1930), pp. 140–149; and Felix Frankfurter and Nathan Greene, *The Labor Injunction* (New York, 1930).

the spring of 1920 were revealing. *Missouri* v. *Holland*,[120] a landmark case in the development of the federal treaty power, grew out of controversy over the flight patterns of migratory wildfowl, treaty provisions governing them, and state game laws declaring open season on the wildfowl. Counsel for Missouri contended that the subject matter of both a treaty with Great Britain and a statute enacted in pursuance of this agreement went beyond the enumerated powers of the federal government, invaded the powers of the state, and violated the Tenth Amendment. A treaty, he contended, could not convey powers to the national government that it did not already possess by virtue of the powers of the Congress.

Justice Holmes, speaking for six of his brethren, rejected this argument, upholding federal predominance through an interpretation of the treaty power so broad that by the 1950s senators viewing the ruling in light of the nation's new international commitments sought to undo it by constitutional amendment. The crux of the Holmes opinion was that since treaties were made under the authority of the United States, while acts of Congress were enacted under the authority of the Constitution, the powers of the central government were almost limitless if written into a treaty. Theoretical, noneconomic centralized federal power was thus apparently permissible even to a conservative of the stripe of McReynolds. Only Van Devanter and Pitney failed to go along with the majority viewpoint.

Similarly, the power of the states to utilize tax revenues with broad discretion was sustained without opposition. The case of *Green* v. *Frazier*[121] involved the legislation program of the Nonpartisan League of North Dakota, which had used tax monies to establish what critics charged was a socialistic state bank, a state warehouse, elevator and flour mill system, and a state home building project. Court action on it was being watched eagerly, especially by liberals.[122] Rejecting the contention that the legislation authorized taxation for purposes not public, and therefore constituted deprivation of property without due process of law, Justice Day pointed to the fact that the authority of the constitu-

120. Missouri *v.* Holland, 252 U.S. 416 (1920).

121. Green *v.* Frazier, 253 U.S. 233 (1920).

122. Edward T. Devine, "North Dakota—The Laboratory of the Non-Partisan League," *The Survey*, XLIII (March 6, 1920), 685–689.

tion and laws prevailing in North Dakota, the people, the legislature, and the highest court of the state had all declared the purpose for which these several acts were passed to be of a public nature and within the taxing authority of the state. "With this united action of people, legislature and court," he contended, "we are not at liberty to interfere, unless it is clear beyond reasonable controversy that rights secured by the federal Constitution have been violated." Such judicial restraint was a marked contrast to judicial monitoring of antitrust and Federal Trade Commission activities.

The White Court completed its final term in a general mood of caution and restraint, a factor contributed to by the declining health and death on May 19, 1921, of its Chief Justice. Although it had handed down rulings in a number of vital areas of law, public response to its actions was sparse and generally unemotional. Such a reaction was possibly a reflection of broader attitudes toward law and its limited role generally, which a majority of Americans by 1921 had come to hold.

Government actions during the "Red Scare" particularly had played a prominent part in shaping that broader attitude. The widely distributed "Report Upon the Illegal Practices of the United States Department of Justice," issued in early 1920 by twelve prominent lawyers including Zechariah Chafee, Jr., Felix Frankfurter, Ernst Freund, Roscoe Pound, and Frank P. Walsh, had been an eloquent and courageous exposé of wrongdoing by government officials. "For more than six months we, the undersigned lawyers, whose sworn duty it is to uphold the Constitution and Laws of the United States, have seen with growing apprehension the continued violation of that Constitution and breaking of those Laws by the Department of Justice of the United States government," the Report had begun,[123] said it had appealed for the reestablishment of proper procedure with respect to the law, calling upon bench and bar alike to return to the code of ethics of the legal profession.

As other prominent, respected, and conservative citizens had openly espoused similar views, and as "Red Scare" excesses had been otherwise exposed, significant segments of the public had found

123. National Pop. Govt. League, *To the American People*, p. 3.

their earlier Progressive views toward law as an instrument for morality and positive social good sharply shaken. Law, especially when it afforded broad authorization for the indiscriminate use of governmental power, could, it was now seen, become in cynical hands an immoral instrument, destructive of fundamental, historical American rights. Significantly this view was shared by liberals, civil libertarians, and conservative business leaders alike.[124]

Since it was the business leaders who were in decision-making positions at the time, it fell to them to make quick readjustments. Realizing that the conservatives had overplayed their hand in endorsing and encouraging the use of legal restrictions to curtail severely those who espoused broad-scale postwar social reorganization, they now saw the clear advantage for coupling their own desire for less government in business with a posture of less overt legal restraints in society. The best avenue for restoring respect for the law, they were convinced, was to push law into the background as a conscious control factor, shifting its enforcement and administration to more benign and subtle hands who could accomplish much the same ends with it, but could do so easily and quietly without fear of arousing further public hostility and distrust. John Hays Hammond, influential business leader and public figure, nicely encapsulated such a view in an article in *Collier's* in early 1921 when he pointed out: "What the average American wants out of the government is civility." He went on to make an eloquent plea for the restoration of an atmosphere of general laissez-faire within society, urging Americans to "forget the notion that we are going to find perfection in government or that an excessive faith in the efficacy of laws is going to substitute for a reasoned intelligence on the part of the individual."[125]

What this meant to business leadership was return of effective social control to private hands, or "government," as Norman

124. Such a reassessment of the potential sources of morality greatly jolted many liberal theologians and refocused their attitude toward government and law. For a contemporary analysis of this development see "Freedom of Opinion and the Clergy," *New Republic*, XXI (February 11, 1920), 304. See also Paul A. Carter, *The Decline and Revival of the Social Gospel* (Ithaca, 1954), pp. 26–27; and William F. McKee, "The Social Gospel and the New Social Order, 1919–1929" (unpublished Ph.D. dissertation, University of Wisconsin, 1961).

125. John Hays Hammond, "Can We Make Happiness by Law?," *Collier's*, LXVII (January 8, 1921), 7.

Hapgood wrote in October, 1920, "by the stronger elements of society."[126] This, on the contrary, did not necessarily mean a return to mechanical jurisprudence or even to nineteenth-century laissez-faire law. It meant, for such citizens, a clear rejection of law as an instrument or catalyst for social change, with judges and courts acting primarily as impartial umpires to see to it that parties respected the status quo, and played by the basic rules of a business civilization.

The White Court had been influenced by these pressures in only a minor way. It would remain to be seen whether the justices under new leadership would be fully swayed by them.

126. Norman Hapgood, "Liberal or Reactionary," *Yale Review,* X (October, 1920), 26.

CHAPTER 2

Majority Legal Assumptions and Their Impact in the Twenties

WILLIAM HOWARD TAFT had coveted the Chief Justiceship of the United States since well before his days in the White House. The office was to him the ideal public assignment, offering "power without worry" and affording the most effective vantage point for stemming the advancing tide of social democracy.[1] Taft was convinced that the way to undermine social reformers' crusades was through a firmly administered and equitable judicial system. He had long hoped to be in a position to upgrade and make more efficient the operations of the entire federal judiciary, which by 1920 was in dire need of modernization. Yet such a Marshallian view was clearly related to the explicit national needs of the early twenties. Such needs Taft saw primarily as erecting new safeguards for private property, and undermining its most dangerous enemies—Socialists, Communists, Progressives and militant champions of labor and labor unions.

Taft's appointment to the Court followed logically from the events of 1920 and 1921. During the Presidential campaign of

1. Alpheus T. Mason, *William Howard Taft: Chief Justice* (New York, 1964), pp. 17 ff. See also Henry F. Pringle, *The Life and Times of William Howard Taft* (2 vols., New York, 1939), II, 960 ff.; and Walter F. Murphy, "In His Own Image: Mr. Chief Justice Taft and Supreme Court Appointments," *1961 Supreme Court Review* (Chicago, 1961), p. 161.

1920 he had openly supported Harding, making clear that his reasons for doing so were strongly tied to his concern for the proper rule of law. Wilson's appointments to the Court, particularly Brandeis and Clarke, represented to the former President an unfortunate "new school of constitutional construction which if allowed to prevail will greatly impair our fundamental law."[2] With four justices presumably near retirement, he was not hesitant to state that "there is no greater domestic issue in the election than the maintenance of the Supreme Court as the bulwark to enforce the guaranty that no man shall be deprived of his property without due process of law."[3] The death of Chief Justice White finally afforded Taft the opportunity to claim the prize that he clearly felt due him. Harding, after procrastinating in a way painful to the former President, announced the appointment on June 30, 1921.[4]

The appointment drew wide comment, some of it sharply critical. Labor and liberal publications were particularly quick to view Taft's antilabor, lower-court record with alarm and to express concern over his proclivity for placing property above personal rights.[5] Both the *Nation* and the *New Republic* raised the question of why a President whom the voters had rejected as too conservative in 1912 should now be given unchecked power to shape national policies.[6] Such comments, and those of congressional insurgents, Taft dismissed as insignificant, preferring rather

2. William Howard Taft, "Mr. Wilson and the Campaign," *Yale Review* (October, 1920), pp. 19–20.

3. *Ibid.*, p. 20.

4. Mason, *Taft*, Chap. 3; Pringle, *Taft*, II, Chap. 50.

5. Taft's record as a lower federal judge had been particularly featured by the readiness with which he was prepared to issue injunctions against labor activities. In 1908 he stated that "the writ of injunction is one of the most beneficial remedies known to the law." William Howard Taft, *Present Day Problems: A Collection of Addresses Delivered on Various Occasions* (New York, 1908), p. 266. The labor press was particularly bitter on this point. A typical editorial ran: "As Chief Justice . . . we should not expect too much from Taft. . . . We know his sentiments and qualities as a judge upon the Ohio federal bench, where he invented the process of interfering with labor by injunctions. His ideas were accepted by other courts. He achieved fame and promotion through the success of such legal ideas. Is he now expected to recede from the position that brought him fame and honor?" "The New Chief Justice," *Labor Clarion* (San Francisco), XX (July 8, 1921), 3–4.

6. "Chief Justice: A Mistaken Appointment," *Nation*, CXIII (July 13, 1921), 32; "Mr. Chief Justice Taft," *New Republic*, XXII (July 27, 1921), 230–231.

to revel in the general approbation of the business community. This group, he was convinced, represented majority American opinion, and their interests, he felt, could be most beneficially served.[7]

The question was one of tactics, particularly in light of the national mood of 1920 and 1921. Taft was much more alert to public wishes than had been the ailing White. Taft read the election returns of 1920 and the public reaction against the too-ambitious use of governmental power in the "Red Scare" as a call for returning the control of the nation to the hands of private leadership. This in turn meant rejecting law as an instrument for social change. It reflected a logical although modified application of his earlier progressivism. The unlikelihood of upper-class men of talent and wealth continuing to assert their leadership through formal government positions was apparent. Taft clearly felt the proper road lay in throwing the weight of the law to them in their private capacity. "The cornerstone of our civilization is the proper maintenance of the guarantees of the 14th and 5th amendments,"[8] he wrote Elihu Root in 1922. Translated into nonlegal terms this meant for Taft freeing men of property and talent from ill-guided restrictions on the creative use of that property. Specifically, this entailed legal undermining of dubious attempts at public regulation and other forms of social control passed into law by the whim of capricious, socially irresponsible majorities.

Judicial activism was thus to be the instrument for the recreation of laissez-faire policies, especially in light of executive and legislative inactivism. For not only did Taft view these branches as dangerously susceptible to the pressures of "democratic idiocy,"[9] their effectiveness in 1921 was clearly in doubt. The election of Harding had been ample reassurance to opponents of Wilsonian activism that the Presidency would remain where Wilson's illness had landed it—in virtual impotence. And those who urged legislative activism were a handful of progressive legislators who continued to advocate public programs attacking specific social evils or benefiting certain deprived groups within society. But even their record was poor. A few pieces of minor legislation, such as

7. "Chief Justice Taft," *Literary Digest,* LXX (July 16, 1921), 13.

8. William Howard Taft to Elihu Root, Dec. 21, 1922, Taft Papers, Library of Congress.

9. Mason, *Taft,* pp. 14, 264–265.

the Packers and Stockyards Act of 1921;[10] the Fess-Kenyon Act,[11] appropriating money for disabled veteran rehabilitation; and the Sheppard-Towner Act,[12] subsidizing state infant and maternity welfare activities, were passed. But generally, *The New York Times* summed up a broadly held public attitude toward legislative effectiveness when it stated editorially in December, 1921:

> Congress had a good deal of public confidence last April. Now it has almost wholly lost it. The people expected definite policies and vigorous leaders at the head of a united party. But they got neither. It is evident, and it is freely admitted in Washington, that the public is not counting any longer upon sound and constructive legislation from Congress.[13]

In order for the Court to play the role that Taft envisioned for it, it had to be unified and its power enhanced. Taft effectively accomplished both. As Chief Justice he early made clear to Harding and other leaders of the administration that he planned to exert his authority to get men with the proper ideological orientation onto the bench.[14] In this he succeeded surprisingly well. George Sutherland, whom Harding appointed to replace retiring Justice Clarke in 1922,[15] shared Taft's ideological views almost without

10. 42 Stat. 159 (1921). The investigations that prompted the Act can be found in Federal Trade Commission, *Report of the Meat Packing Industry* (6 vols., Washington, 1918–20).

11. 41 Stat. 735 (1920).

12. 42 Stat. 224 (1921). On the Act generally, see J. Stanley Lemons, "The Sheppard-Towner Act: Progressivism in the 1920's," *Journal of American History,* LV (March, 1969), 776–786. On constitutional aspects of grants-in-aid see V. O. Key, Jr., *Administration of Federal Grants to States (*Chicago, 1937); Austin F. MacDonald, *Federal Aid: A Study of the American Subsidy System* (New York, 1928); and Edward S. Corwin, "The Spending Power of Congress Apropos the Maternity Act," *Harvard Law Review,* XXXVI (March, 1923), 548–582.

13. "The Regular Session," *The New York Times,* (Dec. 6, 1921), p. 18, col. 1.

14. Murphy, "In His Own Image," p. 163; Mason, *Taft,* pp. 160–161; Walter F. Murphy, Elements of Judicial Strategy (Chicago, 1964), pp. 73 ff. A revealing case study is that involving the appointment of Pierce Butler to the Supreme Court: David J. Danelski, *A Supreme Court Justice Is Appointed* (New York, 1964). Taft hoped at the outset to ease Holmes off the Court. "The Bench would be well rid of him," he wrote his brother Horace, "for his influence is not good on the Bench. He is always or generally with Brandeis." William Howard Taft to Horace D. Taft, June 7, 1921, Taft Papers, Library of Congress.

15. Clarke's resignation greatly disturbed Woodrow Wilson, who wrote him at the time: "Like thousands of other liberals throughout the country, I have been counting on the influence of you and Justice Brandeis to restrain the Court in some measure from the extreme reactionary course which it seems inclined to follow." Woodrow Wilson to John H. Clarke, Sept. 5, 1922, Wilson Papers, Library of Congress.

exception. As a Republician senator and as president of the American Bar Association, and as an opponent of the appointment of Brandeis to the Court, Sutherland had demonstrated not only his opposition to change but his capacity for fluent, philosophical justification for conservatism. Sutherland ultimately enjoyed the dubious reputation of writing more decisions that were subsequently overruled than any justice who ever served on the high bench. Pierce Butler, a Catholic and a Democrat, who replaced Day the same year, was clearly Taft's candidate for the position. The Chief Justice told his close friend Van Devanter, "Butler is our man."[16] And although opposition arose to the appointment, particularly in light of Butler's high-handed interference with academic freedom at the University of Minnesota, confirmation posed no problem.[17] A look at his Supreme Court record attests to Butler's conservatism. In the entire history of that body only three justices showed stronger resistance to overruling precedents than the former railroad attorney.[18]

Taft was pushed into greater conservatism than he instinctively espoused by the inevitable majority that resulted when Sutherland and Butler joined Van Devanter and McReynolds. These "Four Horsemen" were fully committed to the protection of a social order uniquely explained and justified by the tenets of John Locke, Adam Smith, the Manchester economists, Blackstone, Cooley, and Spencer. They themselves had matured and prospered during an earlier period of America's economic growth. They fully espoused a social ethic that stressed self-reliance, individual initiative and responsibility, and the survival of the fittest. Such views emphasized unquestionably the virtual uninhibited privilege of private property and rationalized the growth of corporate collectivism in terms of individual liberty and private enterprise.[19]

16. Murphy, "In His Own Image," p. 172.

17. Danelski, *A Supreme Court Justice Is Appointed,* pp. 134–139.

18. John R. Schmidhauser, "Stare Decisis, Dissent, and the Background of the Justices of the Supreme Court of the United States," *University of Toronto Law Journal,* XIV (May, 1962), 196–212.

19. Ronald F. Howell, "Conservative Influence on Constitutional Development —1923–1937: The Judicial Theory of Justices Van Devanter, McReynolds, Sutherland, and Butler" (unpublished Ph.D. dissertation, Johns Hopkins University, 1952), is a useful composite analysis. Studies of the individual justices include: Maurice P. Holsinger, "Willis Van Devanter—The Early Years" (unpublished Ph.D. dissertation, Denver University, 1964); John B. McGraw, "Justice Mc-

The task of enhancing the power of the federal judicial branch posed different problems for Taft, but ones that he nonetheless surmounted admirably. The mounting work load confronting the entire judiciary was reaching a point by the mid-1920s where it took almost two years to bring on a case to be heard. Appointing a committee of his own Court to prepare a bill, known publicly as the Judges' Bill, Taft rallied sufficient support to see it into law as the Judiciary Act of 1925.[20] Under this Act the Supreme Court was granted almost unlimited discretion to decide for itself what cases it would hear. This meant that the Court could take no more cases than it could handle expediently and could restrict adjudication to matters of more general interest. The result was an upgrading of the importance of the cases that the body did agree to hear and a commensurate enhancement of the Court's own prestige and power.[21]

The legal path to the social objectives of the Taft Court was clearly marked out. Just as the country was being restored to normalcy, it was time to restore it to its traditional constitutional bases. This meant the re-creation of a predictable and symmetrical legal system, resting primarily on judicial interpretation of a static Constitution and an immutable natural law. Such a legal system could best be achieved by the application of fixed concepts such as "liberty of contract" and "substantive due process," and what E. S. Corwin was to label "dual federalism." This meant the creation of a twi-

---

Reynolds and the Supreme Court" (unpublished Ph.D. dissertation, University of Texas, 1949); Doris S. Blaisdel, "The Constitutional Law of Mr. Justice McReynolds" (unpublished Ph.D. dissertation, University of Wisconsin, 1953); Stephen T. Early Jr., "Mr. Justice McReynolds and the Judicial Process," (unpublished Ph.D. dissertation, University of Virginia, 1954); Sterling P. Gilbert, *James Clark McReynolds* (privately printed, 1946); Joel F. Paschal, *Mr. Justice Sutherland, A Man Against the State* (Princeton, 1951); Francis J. Brown, *The Social and Economic Philosophy of Pierce Butler* (Washington, 1945.).

20. 43 Stat. 936 (1925). Taft's hand in the measure was acknowledged contemporaneously, Felix Frankfurter and James M. Landis writing in 1927: "Congress gave the Supreme Court what it wanted . . . deferring to the prestige of the Supreme Court and its Chief Justice, whose energetic espousal largely helped to realize the Court's proposal." Felix Frankfurter and James M. Landis, *The Business of the Supreme Court* (New York, 1927), p. 280.

21. The measure drew sharp opposition, however, not only from certain liberal senators such as Thomas J. Walsh, but from Charles Evans Hughes, who questioned especially the wisdom of the Court exercising more discretionary authority. Mason, *Taft,* p. 111.

light zone between federal and state power where neither sovereignty had legal authority to act.[22] The majority of the Court was thoroughly committed to liberty in this sense, and took a narrow view of liberty to criticize or challenge the system. The limits of such liberty were to be drawn far before liberty reached the status of license. When the state imposed legal restrictions upon radicals, labor leaders, and overly aggressive reformers, who were clearly seeking to abuse their liberty by assailing the status quo, the majority's eagerness to sustain such restrictions was clear.[23]

Such a trend was clear from Taft's first majority opinion in the American Steel Foundry case handed down on December 5, 1921. The case had been argued even before the Duplex decision, but it had fallen to Taft to render the opinion.[24] It involved the peaceful picketing of an industrial plant, which the company's management had sought to stop by injunction. This the picketers claimed was illegal under the Clayton Act's Section 20, forbidding injunctions to restrain employees from peaceful picketing in promotion of their side of a labor controversy. Taft had from the outset viewed the labor provisions of the Clayton Act with a jaundiced eye. He rejected the picketers' appeal for suspension of the injunction on the grounds that group picketing was not peaceful, but by its very nature intimidating. Although he felt Section 20 did give labor some claim for freedom from injunctive processes, he indicated that the Court would have to decide on a case-to-case basis when such relief

22. Corwin's writings in this area and on constitutional law generally are voluminous. See the bibliography in Alpheus T. Mason and Gerald Garvey (eds.), *American Constitutional History: Essays by Edward S. Corwin* (New York, 1964), pp. 216–229. See also Gerald J. Garvey, "Corwin on the Constitution: The Content and Context of Modern American Constitutional Theory" (unpublished Ph.D. dissertation, Princeton University, 1962).

23. Taft was highly hostile to dissent within his own Court, especially toward the end of his term when he began to feel that his essentially "sound" positions were being undermined by the "unpatriotic" and the "disloyal." Alpheus T. Mason, *The Supreme Court from Taft to Warren* (Baton Rouge, 1958), p. 66.

24. American Steel Foundries *v.* Tri-City Central Trades Council, 257 U.S. 184 (1921). The background of the case is traced in Elias Lieberman, *Unions Before the Bar* (New York, 1950), pp. 108–117. See also Stanley I. Kutler, "Labor, the Clayton Act, and the Supreme Court," *Labor History,* III (Winter, 1962), 19–38; and Thomas Reed Powell, "The Supreme Court's Control over the Issue of Injunctions in Labor Disputes," *Proceedings of the Academy of Political Science,* XIII (1928), 37–77. Picketing and its relation to freedom of expression is examined in detail in Joseph Tannenhaus, "Organized Labor and Freedom of Speech" (unpublished Ph.D. dissertation, Cornell University, 1953).

was valid. In a general way, with regard to picketing he made clear that in a normal labor dispute, strikers and their sympathizers should be limited to one representative for each point of ingress and egress from the plant. All others could clearly be enjoined from congregating or loitering in the vicinity.

Two weeks later, in *Truax* v. *Corrigan,*[25] Taft revealed even more clearly his labor attitudes. The case involved an Arizona restaurant owner who had gone unsuccessfully to a state court for an injunction claiming that picketing had drastically diminished his business, thus adversely affecting his property. The court's refusal, on the grounds of a state law restricting the use of injunctions in labor disputes, deprived him, he charged, of his property rights without due process of law. Taft promptly gave him the relief he wanted by ruling the law unconstitutional. "The legislative power of the state," he made clear, was limited and "could be exerted only in subordination to the fundamental principles of right and justice which the guaranty of due process in the Fourteenth Amendment was intended to preserve." The Arizona law was clearly an arbitrary and capricious exercise of that power, whereby a wrongful and highly injurious invasion of property rights was practically sanctioned and the owners stripped of all real remedy. The ruling left no doubt that to Taft business was property and any infringement upon the way it was conducted was a potential infringement of property rights.[26]

A case the same day indicated that in 1921 Taft had not fully "massed the Court" behind an unqualified support of business practices. The impact of the United States Steel case of 1920 had been to encourage the development of trade associations within American industry. These groups exchanged information regarding prices, wages, and production quotas so as effectively to "stabilize" industries through elimination of competition within

25. Truax *v.* Corrigan, 257 U.S. 312 (1921).

26. Even Mahlon Pitney, whose lower-court record was strongly antilabor and who had written the majority opinion in the Duplex case, dissented. "I can find no ground," he wrote, "for declaring that the State's action is so arbitrary and devoid of reasonable basis that it can be called a deprivation of liberty or property without due process of law, in the constitutional sense. In truth, the States have a considerable degree of latitude in determining, each for itself, their respective condition of law and order, and what kind of civilization they shall have as a result." Truax *v.* Corrigan, at 349.

them. In the American Column and Lumber decision,[27] Justice John Clarke, after examining the impact of such practices within the hardwood lumber industry, ruled them in violation of the antitrust structure. In this critical ruling Clarke pointed to the fact that association meetings and market reports were studded with repeated warnings against "overproduction," and a number of suggestions for price maintenance or increase. There could be little question, he contended for a six-man majority, that such actions constituted a preventable conspiracy prohibited by the Sherman Act. Curiously both Holmes and Brandeis dissented. Holmes pragmatically suggested that if business wished to experiment with new ways of operation that might in the long run benefit the public as well as itself, it should be permitted to do so.[28] Brandeis, on the other hand, argued that if such informal exchange of information were prevented, the alternative would be the redevelopment of formal trusts. Such an eventuality he considered threatening, since the Court had already seemed to sanction it in the U.S. Steel case.[29]

As the decade progressed, administrative action was sufficiently influential to alter judicial views in this area. Secretary of Commerce Herbert Hoover early had deplored liberal assault upon the "open competition" associations. He felt that as long as their activities lead to public dispersal of information, they performed a useful purpose. It should be the purpose of government to aid as well as control business,[30] he contended after the American Column and Lumber case. Deeply committed to efficiency in all phases of public life and using the Commerce Department as a clearinghouse, Hoover stepped in. Through the Commerce Department Hoover collected extensive information and made it available to all competitors within various industries. In this new climate, the Court altered its focus on the trade associations. In 1925, in an opinion rendered by newly appointed Justice Harlan Fiske Stone, six of the justices agreed that such activities tended "to stabilize

27. American Column and Lumber Co. *v.* U.S., 257 U.S. 377 (1921).

28. *Ibid.*, p. 413.

29. *Ibid.*, p. 419. Justice Clarke was highly disturbed by Brandeis' action, writing Woodrow Wilson that he had felt it essential to defeat "the 'open competition' plan which was devised with all the cunning astute lawyers and conservative business men could command to defeat or circumvent the law." John H. Clarke to Woodrow Wilson, Sept. 9, 1922, Wilson Papers, Library of Congress.

30. "Open Competition," *The New York Times* (Dec. 21, 1921), p. 18.

trade and industry and to avoid the waste which inevitably attends the unintelligent conduct of economic enterprise."[31] The effect of the decision was to stimulate the mushrooming of even more trade associations, which now grew up in almost two hundred industries. A number of these associations wrote codes of competition that standardized profits, wages, and provided penalties for price cutting. This was often done with the help and advice of Department of Commerce officials.[32]

Probably the best summary of the operations of the antitrust structure as it applied to business in the 1920's was given a few years later by a New York industrial engineer, Charles A. Stevenson. In a nostalgic speech in June, 1934, he pointed out:

> Practically, under the Harding, Coolidge and Hoover administrations, industry enjoyed to all intents and purposes a moratorium from the Sherman Act, and through the more or less effective trade associations which were developed in most of our industries, competition was, to a very considerable extent, controlled. The Department of Justice acted with great restraint and intelligence and only enforced the Sherman Act against those industries who violated the law in a flagrant and unreasonable manner.[33]

Later cases in Taft's first two terms indicated that there were to be juridical contradictions during the Taft years other than the restriction of labor's prerogatives on the one hand and the expansion of business's on the other. In December, 1921, the Court, speaking through Justice Van Devanter, gave a new extension to the commerce clause. "Where goods are purchased in one state for transportation to another, the purchase is interstate commerce quite as much as the transportation,"[34] Van Devanter insisted. The impact was to restrict state power in the commerce area by insisting that in any potential conflict such power was transcended by federal authority. The implication of this development was seen when the

31. Maple Flooring Manufacturers's Assn. *v.* U.S., 268 U.S. 563, 582 (1925).

32. Robert F. Himmelberg, "Relaxation of Federal Anti-Trust Policy as a Goal of the Business Community During the Period 1918–1933" (unpublished Ph.D. dissertation, Pennsylvania State University, 1963).

33. Quoted in Marshall E Dimock, *Business and Government: Issues of Public Policy,* 4th ed. (New York, 1961), p. 110. A useful survey of judicial interpretation of the antitrust structure is Edward P. Hodges, *The Antitrust Act and the Supreme Court* (St. Paul, 1941).

34. Dahnke-Walker Milling Co. *v.* Bondurant, 257 U.S. 282, 290 (1921).

rule was applied shortly thereafter to set aside a vital part of North Dakota's plan for controlling the marketing of grain in the interests of the growers.[35]

A similar constitutional thrust emerged from a case challenging the Transportation Act of 1920.[36] Under that measure the business-dominated Interstate Commerce Commission had issued an order increasing interstate passenger and freight rates. In Wisconsin, for example, the minimum passenger rate was set at 3.6¢ per mile, while a state statute set the maximum passenger fare in that state at 2¢ per mile.

The validity of this order was assailed by Wisconsin and twenty other states, but the Court unanimously upheld the federal intrastate regulation. It was the commission's duty under the Transportation Act, Taft felt, to secure the roads a fair income. If intrastate rates were too low, the road would be obliged to charge excessive interstate rates to secure fair total income. When necessary, intrastate rates could be revised even when not in direct competition with interstate rates. The practical effect of the decision was to place all rail rates within the commission's direct control, and virtually to obliterate the distinction between interstate rates and intrastate commerce as far as commission control was concerned.[37]

Stafford v. *Wallace* in May, 1922,[38] moved the same principle into a different area. The Packers and Stockyards Act of 1921[39] had struck hard at unfair, discriminatory, and deceptive practices in the meat-packing industry. It authorized the Secretary of Agriculture to supervise rates for handling livestock in the yards and to issue cease and desist orders, with the force of law, to halt what he considered unwarranted behavior not in the public interest. "The

35. Lemke *v.* Farmers' Grain Co., 258 U.S. 50 (1922).

36. Railroad Commission of Wisconsin *v.* C.B. and Q., 257 U.S. 563 (1922).

37. Later in the decade the Court upheld the recapture provisions of the Act, Taft making clear that a "public service" industry had no constitutional right to more than a fair operating income upon the value of its properties. Dayton-Goose Creek Railway Co. *v.* U.S., 263 U.S. 456 (1924). The recapture technique did not work well, however, and after the I.C.C. recommended repeal in each of its annual reports for 1930, 1931, and 1932, Congress finally in 1933 repealed the provision as part of a program "to relieve the existing national emergency in relation to interstate railroad transportation." 48 Stat. 211, 220 (1933).

38. Stafford *v.* Wallace, 258 U.S. 495 (1922).

39. 42 Stat. 159 (1921).

stockyards are not a place of rest or final destination," wrote Taft in upholding the measure, "but are a throat through which the current [of commerce] flows and the transactions which occur therein are only incident to this current from the West to the East and from one state to another."[40] The ruling seemed to indicate that the special obligation of those in public service activities carried over to the behavior of certain private manufacturers and productive concerns clearly reachable by federal commerce power if they were not performing in the public interest.

But if federal authority under the commerce clause was to be looked upon as broad, federal taxing power was suddenly subjected to new Taftian inhibitions. Clearly the most interesting and revealing decision of Taft's first term to students of constitutional theory and government was the famous ruling in *Bailey* v. *Drexel Furniture Co.* It was popularly known as the Second Child Labor case.[41] In it the court voided a special tax levied by act of Congress of February 24, 1919, on the incomes of concerns employing child labor. Taft ruled the tax was not intended to raise revenue, but to regulate the employment of children, and was a matter reserved to the states by the Tenth Amendment. The ruling seemed to contradict the White Court's ruling three years earlier upholding the federal narcotics act, which had been based upon the taxing power. Taft distinguished between a tax and a penalty, the proper intent of the former being the collection of revenue, and of the latter, some ulterior design. He thus made legislative motive the test of legislative action. Any attempt by Congress to bring within its

40. Stafford *v.* Wallace, at 516.

41. Bailey *v.* Drexel Furniture, 259 U.S. 20 (1922). On the child labor movement in the 1920s see Clarke A. Chambers, *Seedtime of Reform* (Minneapolis, 1963), pp. 29–58; Richard B. Sherman, "The Rejection of the Child Labor Amendment," *Mid-America,* XLV (January, 1963), 3–17; and for a special study, Jeremy Felt, *Hostages of Fortune: Child Labor Reform in New York State* (Syracuse, 1965). The majority apparently agreed with Representative Clark of Florida, who summarized much of the opposition position, insisting that federal restrictions on child labor "deny to the poor boy, perhaps alone in the world, the chance to carve out his own fortune by honest labor and write his name high on the scroll of fame, as so many before him have done. Give him a chance in the race of life, and do not hamper him with misfit legislation born of a sickening sentimentality which has no place in a government like ours." Quoted in James E. Anderson, *The Emergence of the Modern Regulatory State* (Washington, 1962), p. 84.

control matters normally falling to the states alone raised questions of valid motive.

Such a narrow view of the taxing power was extended to other areas. On the same day as *Bailey* v. *Drexel Furniture* the Chief Justice struck down certain sections of the Future Trading Act of 1921. In this case Congress had attempted broad regulation of boards of trade.[42] Taft ruled local dealings of this sort could not be brought constitutionally under federal control by means of the taxing power. Whether such legislation might be valid as a legitimate exercise of the commerce power, the Chief Justice left unanswered. The logical follow-up to the ruling came the next year. After *Hill* v. *Wallace,* Congress had taken the Court's hint. It immediately passed another measure, which, according to the preamble, was for the prevention of obstructions and burdens upon interstate commerce in grain. This legislation regulated transactions on grain futures exchange. The Court upheld the new statute as a legitimate regulation of interstate commerce. Taft likened the regulation of the sale of grain futures to the regulation of business conducted in the stockyards.[43]

The landmark case of *Massachusetts* v. *Mellon* in June, 1923, raised a different type of taxing-power question.[44] Here taxpayers had challenged the Sheppard-Towner Act of 1921, a typical federal grant-in-aid program, on the grounds that the states in accepting such funds accepted also federal supervision of their dispensation. The measure provided that financial aid for reducing maternal and infant mortality be extended only to such states as would accept and comply with the provisions of the act. Justice Sutherland, for a unanimous Court, denied there was any undue compulsion involved in such an arrangement. The state, he ruled, could avoid involvement simply by refusing to accept the provisions of the act. As for the effect of the Act upon citizens of the state, they were also citizens of the United States, and a state had no power to institute judicial proceedings to protect them from the operation of federal statutes. The ruling inferred that the high bench would not interfere when revenue raised by national taxation was used

42. Hill *v.* Wallace, 259 U.S. 44 (1922). A further section of the same measure was struck down four years later. Trusler *v.* Crooks, 269 U.S. 475 (1926).

43. Board of Trade *v.* Olsen, 262 U.S. 1 (1923).

44. Massachusetts *v.* Mellon, 262 U.S. 447 (1923).

for economic and social purposes usually within the domain of the states.

When it came to dealing with state activity and regulation in conflict only with the federal Constitution and its provisions, the Court struck a slightly different pose. Particularly revealing was its ruling of June, 1922, rejecting challenge, on civil liberties grounds, to Missouri's Service Letter Law.[45] The measure required every corporation doing business in the state to furnish, upon request to any employee, when discharging or leaving its service, a letter signed by the superintendent or manager setting forth the nature and duration of his service to the corporation and stating the true cause of his leaving. The measure was challenged on the ground that letters having been demanded and used by other employers to deny employment to their bearers, served as an arbitrary interference with freedom of contract amounting to a deprivation of liberty without due process of law. Attorneys further attempted to protect clients from the necessity for revealing such information on freedom of speech grounds, deducing from that concept a parallel "liberty of silence" guaranteed to citizens against state encroachment. Pitney, for the Court, did not feel this was a legitimate liberty-of-contract situation. The relation between a corporation and its employees and former employees are matters of wholly private concern. The Fourteenth Amendment nor any other provision of the Constitution "imposes upon the States any restrictions about 'freedom of speech' or the 'liberty of silence'; nor we may add, does it confer any right of privacy upon either persons or corporations." In a conflict between civil rights and property rights the higher priority of the latter was essential.

The same reluctance to challenge state prerogatives was evident in *Moore* v. *Dempsey*[46] early the following year. Holmes spoke for the Court in declaring the conviction of blacks, sentenced to death on trumped-up charges by an all-white jury, unconstitutional as a denial of life and liberty without due process of law. A mob-dominated trial is not a fair trial, he maintained, adding that the state's

45. Prudential Insurance Co. *v.* Cheek, 259 U.S. 530 (1922).

46. Moore *v.* Dempsey, 261 U.S. 86 (1923). For details on the case see Loren Miller, *The Petitioners* (Cleveland, 1966), pp. 232–41. See also Elvin Overton and J. S. Waterman, "Federal Habeas Corpus Statutes and Moore v. Dempsey," in *Selected Essays in Constitutional Law* (4 vols., Chicago, 1938), II, 1477–1491.

whole proceeding was a mask. Nonetheless, he was careful to state that appeal to federal courts should be a last resort for any citizen. He went on to contend courts should in ascertaining the validity of facts, leave, as far as possible, state proceedings undisturbed.

By contrast, when Nebraska passed a law prohibiting the teaching of any subject in any public school in any other language except English, McReynolds found the statute a violation of the "liberty" protected by the Fourteenth Amendment. He inferred that this term could, in this instance, embrace a teacher's right to teach and the right of the parents to hire him so to teach.[47] The justice augmented this rule two years later. Oregon, prodded by the Ku Klux Klan, had enacted a law aimed at eliminating parochial and private schools by requiring children between the ages of eight and sixteen to attend public schools. Defenders of the measure argued that the alarming increase in juvenile crime could be attributed to the lack of public school education by many children; that religious prejudices might result from religious segregation; that subversive economic doctrines might be taught in non-public schools; and that a system of compulsory public education was necessary to encourage the patriotism and insure the loyalty of future citizens. McReynolds held the Oregon statute unconstitutional. Such coercion he saw as destroying property rights in private schools as well as violating the freedom of the parents to utilize educational facilities of their own choice.[48]

But if liberty under the Fourteenth Amendment seemed to vary in application in noneconomic situation, its meaning in the area of state

47. Meyer *v.* Nebraska, 262 U.S. 390 (1923). Holmes and Sutherland filed a separate dissent, appending it to the companion case of Bartels *v.* Iowa, 262 U.S. 404, 412 (1923). Adopting a position of judicial self-restraint, they contended that the state program was a legitimate experiment and the statute creating it a lawful and proper one. Holmes had misgivings about the lawfulness of the means adopted toward the end desired, but ultimately did not feel it unreasonable. His position has been called his "most illiberal view and vote." Fred Rodell, *Nine Men* (New York, 1955), p. 205. Strong defenders exist, however. See especially Samuel J. Konefsky, *The Legacy of Holmes and Brandeis* (New York, 1956), pp. 258–260. For a broader view of the legislation here under fire, and its reflection of the values of the 1920s see Kenneth B. O'Brien, Jr., "Education, Americanization and the Supreme Court," *American Quarterly*, XIII (Summer, 1961), 161–171. See also Orville H. Zabel, *God and Caesar in Nebraska* (Lincoln, 1955).

48. Pierce *v.* Society of Sisters, 268 U.S. 510 (1925).

regulation of business activities was perfectly clear. *Adkins* v. *Children's Hospital*,[49] a case which became the bête noir for liberals in the twenties, showed the resiliency of latent "Spencerianism." In striking down a statute calling for a minimum wage for women in the District of Columbia, Justice Sutherland reaffirmed vigorously the vitality of the principles of freedom of contract in the economic realm—"such freedom . . . is the general rule and restraint the exception; and the exercise of legislative authority to abridge it can be justified only by the existence of exceptional circumstances." Sutherland based his decision on the solemn ground that the ruling protected the freedom of women who were emancipated to work for as little as they found necessary without majority interference. But Sutherland went further, offering an insightful vignette into the social values of the business society of the time. Maintaining that this particular type of interference prescribing the fixing of a wage affected "the heart of the contract," he denied that it could be permitted under any circumstance. Human necessities, he made clear, in spite of an elaborate Brandeis-type brief by Felix Frankfurter to the contrary,[50] simply could not be regarded as superior to economic rights. The Court's move to sustain the individual freedom of action contemplated by the Constitution was not to strike down the common good, but to exalt it. Justice Sutherland wrote: ". . . surely the good of society as a whole can not be better served than by the preservation of the liberties of its constituent members."

Even Taft was taken aback by the ruling and registered one of his twenty dissents of the decade. "I agree," he wrote, "that it is a disputable question in the field of political economy how far a statutory requirement of maximum hours or minimum wages may be a useful remedy [for social evils] . . . but it is not the function of this Court to hold congressional acts invalid simply because they are passed to

49. Adkins *v.* Children's Hospital, 261 U.S. 525 (1923).

50. Felix Frankfurter *et al.*, *Brief for Appellant: District of Columbia Minimum Wage Case* (New York, 1923). See also Harlan B. Phillips (ed.), *Felix Frankfurter Reminisces* (New York, 1960), pp. 103–104. Frankfurter was apparently bitter because he had not been able to reach Butler with his arguments and stated somewhat angrily, shortly after the decision: "He [Pierce Butler] does not generalize. He is a farmer, and spent twenty to thirty years of his life in working up a practice. This is very confining and limiting." Transcript of special conference of the National Consumers League, N.C.L. collection, Library of Congress.

carry out economic views which the Court believes to be unwise or unsound." Holmes was more pithy. Deploring the fact that liberty of contract, which had started as an "innocuous generality," had now become a "dogma," he responded to Sutherland's claim that, especially in light of woman suffrage, women did not need special legislation, by observing: "It will need more than the Nineteenth Amendment to convince me that there is no difference between women and men."

More revealing of the sort of fine distinctions the Taft Court was prepared to draw in the general area of state regulation was the Chief Justice's opinion in the Wolff Packing Co. case of June, 1923.[51] The decision addressed itself to a unique situation at the time. State legislatures following World War I had generally confined their law-making to procedural aspects of daily living. Occasionally, however, attempts had been made to readapt the legal structure to current and local needs through the creation of wholly new institutions. As an example, Kansas had startled the nation in 1920 with the enactment of an Industrial Relations Act providing for the compulsory arbitration of all disputes in key industries—food, clothing, and fuel—through a specially appointed Industrial Court. The authorizing statute further contained legally enforcible restrictions against workers striking and employers locking out workers or stopping production in these industries. Such provisions were to be enforced by the Industrial Court, which also had power to fix wages and oversee working conditions. Other states had experimented with various types of administrative bodies, from warehouse commissions to public safety agencies, in an attempt to establish more effective social control through law.[52]

In the Wolff case, the Chief Justice ruled the Kansas Industrial Relations Act unconstitutional, destroying the Industrial Court and in the process writing an important essay on the proper application of the "public interest" doctrine. A mere declaration by a state legislature that a business was affected with a public interest did not

51. Wolff Packing Co. *v.* Industrial Court, 262 U.S. 522 (1923).

52. Domenico Gagliardo, *The Kansas Industrial Court: An Experiment in Compulsory Arbitration* (Lawrence, Kans., 1941), discusses the experiment. Its demise was hailed not only by business but by labor as well, Samuel Gompers having assailed it from the outset. See *Debate Between Samuel Gompers and Henry J. Allen At Carnegie Hall* (New York, 1920).

justify public regulation, he made clear. There were only limited types of business affected with a public interest and these were confined principally to public utilities or similar endeavors serving the public virtually all the time—businesses whose revealing characteristic was the fact that controls of natural economic law did not operate within them. Regulation of businesses other than these was a violation of freedom of contract and due process of law, and state laws attempting such regulation were clearly vulnerable. If there was question as to proper category or if business took on a new and more public form, "the circumstances of its alleged change from the status of a private business and its freedom from regulation into one in which the public was to have come to have an interest are always a subject of judicial inquiry."[53]

Looking back at the Court's performance during its initial terms under Taft, it was easy to agree with the contemporaneous evaluation of Edward S. Corwin, that the new Chief Justice was "manifestly determined that the Court shall remain a real factor of the national life."[54] It is equally easy to agree with a later scholar when he contended that the new Chief Justice was clearly determined to utilize the power of his new judicial "super-legislature" "almost solely in behalf of property interests."[55] This was especially clear when one evaluated the Taftian approach to normal constitutional sources of federal power. Afforded broad and narrow precedents for interpretation of both the commerce and taxing powers, he found ways of utilizing both to accomplish his economic goals. When it was advantageous for the federal government to regulate activities detrimental to or of no consequence to legitimate business, the Chief Justice had no difficulty dipping into the broad line. He even expanded federal power under the commerce clause in areas of railroad regulation and in the control of threatening labor activity. Combined with actions keeping alive the progressive tradition of nationalism in predominantly noneconomic areas, this enabled him to keep federal power available through the commerce clause for future exigencies. Broad federal commerce power could well serve the purpose of undermining too-ambitious state regulatory programs of

53. Wolff Packing Co. *v.* Indust. Ct., at 536.

54. Edward S. Corwin, "Constitutional Law in 1921–1922," *American Political Science Review,* XVI (November, 1922), 638–639.

55. Mason, *Taft to Warren,* p. 67.

business activity. By ruling that state action was entering a field clearly preempted by federal authority, it was possible to create a twilight zone between the two where the states could not regulate and the federal government had no intention of doing so. On the other hand, when a narrow interpretation of the clause would serve the interests of conservative property rights, the Taft majority did not hesitate either to turn to narrow precedents restricting federal authority or to play the "dual federalism" game in reverse. Taft maintained that federal exercise of the commerce power was limited to specific areas; and where it got into a field clearly reserved to the states by the Tenth Amendment, it was no longer a proper device for bringing local activities constitutionally under federal control.

With regard to the taxing power, the pattern, although somewhat similar, was modified. Clearly the power was a far more limited device for federal regulatory purposes. The line of precedents that had earlier made it available as a device for correcting objectionable features of industrial and generally detrimental human behavior was largely turned aside. On the other hand, the Taft court did not reject the device as a potential basis for limited federal programs of a social welfare nature, even when such programs had within them features coercing the states into their acceptance. Thus advocates of child labor, following the Bailey decision, were forced to turn to the amendment process for striking at that evil[56] while the possibilities for further federal grants-in-aid programs grounded on a permissible taxing power base still existed.

With regard to the constitutionality of state actions, Taft played the same game of floating options. In general, if the subject was noneconomic, or if the states were striking at enemies of property interests, the conservative majority was prepared to defend their local prerogatives fully. But when state legislatures experimented with a variety of social welfare laws, geared to imposing popular restrictions upon property rights and business activities, they were quickly reminded of the legal presence of the Fourteenth Amendment and its vital due process clause. Particularly, when such programs interfered

56. The child labor amendment (43 Stat. 670 [1924]) was attacked bitterly as an unwarranted federal invasion of a field of regulation traditionally belonging to the states and was never ratified. See Carl B. Swisher, *American Constitutional Development,* 2nd ed. (Boston, 1954), pp. 729–732.

with "liberty of contract" or deprived property of its guaranteed liberty, such programs had to go. This necessitated a steady exercise in legal line-drawing by the justices, and injection of concepts of judicial reasonableness. But Taft found this welcome and traditional—welcome because it enchanced the power of the Court, and traditional because it seemingly tied his Court's actions to those of its progressive predecessors. The problem was that wielding such a "rule of reason" was a totally subjective process, and related clearly to the public values of the period. And while Taft might feel he was acting progressively, an important shift was present. In the new business atmosphere of the 1920s with a changed membership on the bench, what was reasonable in 1923 and 1924 differed appreciably from what had been considered reasonable in 1918, or even, as his critics were quick to point out, in 1908.[57]

Subsequent terms of the decade produced few surprises, the decisions emerging from the body on major points of law being largely extensions of the constitutional tack which the Taft majority had early charted. Nonetheless, numerous refinements on these patterns produced significant constitutional points. Taft's complete willingness to keep alive the progressive tradition of nationalism in noneconomic areas resulted in several key rulings of considerable significance. The question through American history of the limits of the President's power to remove federal executive officers of all ranks had created problems for leaders as divergent as Andrew Jackson, Andrew Johnson, and Woodrow Wilson. Seeking once and for all to clarify the point and speaking with the inner knowledge of once having held the Presidential office, Taft wrote a lengthy seventy-one-page opinion making clear that the President's removal power was an inherent part of executive prerogative, apart from any authority specifically delegated to him by the Constitution. As such it could not be controlled or restricted by Con-

57. Felix Frankfurter, in observing the trend, wrote in 1930: ". . . the Court has invalidated more legislation than in fifty years preceding. Views that were antiquated twenty-five years ago have been resurrected. . . . Merely as a matter of arithmetic this is an impressive mortality rate. But a numerical tally of the cases does not tell the tale. . . . The discouragement of legislative efforts through a particular adverse decision and the general weakening of the sense of legislative responsibility are destructive influences not measurable by statistics." Felix Frankfurter, "The United States Supreme Court Molding the Constitution," *Current History* (May, 1930), p. 239.

gress except where the Constitution specifically so provided.[58] Given the benign Presidential officeholders of the twenties the ruling was immediately academic, but theoretically serious. Such expansion of Presidential prerogative technically threatened the status of minor federal officials frequently guaranteed by civil service legislation. It even raised the further possibility that the President could now at will remove the members of independent federal commissions, in spite of the fact that in most instances the condition for the removal of such officers was stipulated by Congress.

In somewhat similar spirit, the Court gave strong legal support to the investigatory privileges of congressional committees. It read broadly the limits of committee powers, particularly those of a quasi-judicial nature. After the fall of the corrupt Harding administration, and particularly the shattering exposés emerging from Attorney General Daugherty's malfeasance in the Justice Department, a Senate committee investigated the Department and the activities of its officials. When subpoenaed evidence, supposedly in the possession of Daugherty's brother, Mally, was not produced on the grounds the committee was preempting essentially judicial powers and thus violating the principle of separation of powers, Justice Van Devanter not only rejected the contention, but ruled that the power of inquiry, with the process to enforce it, was essential to the legislative function.[59] A legislative body could not legislate wisely or effectively in the absence of information respecting the conditions which the legislation was expected to affect or change, argued the Court. Therefore the power to subpoena both witnesses and information was a valid part of the legislative process. Two years later, the Court went a step further, sustaining the power of a committee to punish a witness for contempt, as a valid component of law making.[60]

Later commerce clause interpretation followed the constitutional inconsistency previously established. The Court could find few business activities either in commerce or which sufficiently threat-

58. Myers *v.* U.S., 272 U.S. 52 (1926). The three dissents, by Holmes, McReynolds, and particularly Brandeis, greatly annoyed and angered the Chief Justice, as he was not reluctant to point out. See Mason, *Taft,* pp. 225–226. See also Edward S. Corwin, "Tenure of Office and the Removal Power Under the Constitution," *Columbia Law Review,* XXVII (April, 1927), pp. 353–399.

59. McGrain *v.* Daugherty, 273 U.S. 135 (1927).

60. Barry *v.* U.S. *ex rel.* Cunningham, 279 U.S. 597 (1929).

ened to interfere with commerce to warrant federal control. However, it had no trouble stretching the clause to the limit in other areas. In 1925 the Court was called on to sustain the constitutionality of the National Motor Vehicle Theft Act of 1919, forbidding the movement of stolen automobiles in interstate commerce. It did so, ignoring the obvious similarity between the measure and the first Child Labor Law, which had been ruled unconstitutional for laying an absolute provision upon the movement of things not in themselves harmful.[61]

Further critics at the time wondered openly whether the movement of stolen property by a thief was commerce in any traditional sense of that term.[62] This argument Taft met largely by insisting that the moral purpose of the act was valid and certainly federal authority could be extended without the concern for legal fine points to achieve a socially desirable end.

Even less neutral were decisions in 1926 and 1927 sanctioning further the use of injunctions to curb violations of antitrust legislation.[63] Both rulings emphasized how little the Clayton Act had helped labor. The latter, the Bedford Cut Stone case, particularly aroused labor's hackles. It involved a handful of exploited and dissatisfied, but peaceful, local stonecutters who, in conformity to their union's constitution, which stated that no union workers should work on any limestone cut by nonunion workers, refused to handle stone cut by the unorganized Bedford Cut Stone Company. The company went to court for an injunction, but in order to enjoin the strikers it was necessary for the Sherman Act's strictures on all secondary boycotts to be reaffirmed. This the Court did by turning to a highly expansive commerce clause interpretation. Thus, unlike business, the most minute form of local activity became interstate commerce when circumstances made it necessary to protect a manufacturer against "unreasonable" interference by a labor union.[64]

61. Brooks *v.* U.S., 267 U.S. 432 (1925).

62. Thomas Reed Powell, "Commerce, Congress and the Supreme Court, 1922–1925, II," *Columbia Law Review,* XXVI (November, 1926), 524.

63. U.S. *v.* Brims, 272 U.S. 549 (1926); Bedford Cut Stone Co. *v.* Journeymen Stone Cutters' Assn., 274 U.S. 37 (1927).

64. The Bedford ruling, as the high point in the trend toward utilizing the antitrust structure to curb labor activity, aroused vigorous labor and liberal protest and great unrest and dissension within the Supreme Court. See Mason, *Taft,* pp. 228–230; and Irving Bernstein, *The Lean Years: A History of the American Worker, 1920–1933* (Cambridge, Mass., 1960), pp. 213–215.

The second of the Coronado Coal cases also hinged upon unions, commerce, and the antitrust structure.[65] The ruling grew out of efforts of the United Mine Workers to unionize the southern coal mines, and thereby prevent the competitive undermining of northern labor standards. Holding that coal mining itself was not interstate commerce and therefore not subject to the federal antitrust laws, Chief Justice Taft maintained that violence on the part of union members aimed at stopping the interstate shipment of non-union coal, did fall within the prohibitions of the Sherman Act. A strike was primarily a collective withholding of labor, which the Clayton Act declared not to be an article of commerce subject to the antitrust laws. Thus any union action which had the intent and not merely the incidental result of interfering with interstate commerce, became an illegal restraint of trade.

The Court in dealing with state legislation, particularly in the area of economic regulatory and police power measures, reached an all-time high in judicial activism. The Adkins case, which involved a District of Columbia law, but was a precedent for state legislation, gave a green light to business not only to challenge postwar statutes, but to call boldly for reassessment of earlier measures in light of the Court's obvious new intention of strengthening "liberty of contract" as a device for curtailing frivolous social experiments. The new result is measurable statistically. Between 1920 and 1930, before Hughes took over the Chief Justiceship, the Court ruled nearly 140 state laws unconstitutional, a large percentage on the grounds that they were in violation of the protections of liberty of property and of contract as guaranteed by the due process clause of the Fourteenth Amendment.[66] The pattern of the rulings is revealing.

Many state police power measures when they interfered with

65. Coronado Coal Co. *v.* U.M.W., 268 U.S. 295 (1925). In the first Coronado case, Coronado Coal Co. *v.* U.M.W., 259 U.S. 295 (1925), the Court had ruled that triple damages under the Sherman Act could be recovered from a union, even an unincorporated union, in its quasi-corporate capacity, provided that official responsibility could be shown for members' action protested against. See Stanley I. Kutler, "Chief Justice Taft, Judicial Unanimity and Labor," *Historian*, XXIV (November, 1961), 68–83.

66. Benjamin F. Wright, *The Growth of American Constitutional Law* (New York, 1942), p. 113, alludes to 141 decisions against state laws during Taft's Chief Justiceship. Norman J. Small (ed.), *The Constitution of the United States of America* (Washington, 1964), pp. 1453–1473, lists 118 state acts held unconstitutional during the same period.

business activities were now ruled unreasonable interferences with the nation's vital productive forces.[67] A Pennsylvania statute forbade mining in such a way as to cause damage to any human habitation, public street or building. It thereby made commercially impractical the removing of some valuable coal deposits. The Court voided it as arbitrary and a deprivation of property without due process.[68] A Nebraska statute designed to prevent the palming off of smaller loaves of bread than the label on the package proclaimed was ruled unconstitutional as an "intolerable burden" by Justice Butler.[69] An Arkansas statute imposed special assessments on lands acquired by private owners from the United States, because such benefits resulted from road improvements completed before the United States parted with the title. These assessments were held to effect a taking of the new owner's property without due process of law.[70] Iowa contractors, in turn, had their due process violated by a law which imposed penalties when workers on state projects were paid less than the current rate of per diem wages in the locality where the work was performed.[71] A Pennsylvania health measure that prohibited the use of shoddy in the manufacture of bedding materials was held so arbitrary and unreasonable as to be violative of due process.[72] Thus if one takes a sardonic view, liberty in this area in the 1920s meant judicially enforced freedom for private homes to fall in coal mines, for bakers to sell underweight bread, for private parties to gain nontaxable federal land improvements, for contractors to chisel on their workers' wages, and for manufacturers to stuff mattresses with floor sweepings.[73]

67. The concept of state police power stems from at least at early as Roger B. Taney's enunciation of it, as attorney for the state, in Brown *v.* Maryland, 12 Wheaton 419 (1827).

68. Pennsylvania Coal Co. *v.* Mahon, 260 U.S. 393 (1922). Holmes wrote the majority opinion, over a bitter dissent by Brandeis and with hostile reactions from a number of liberal sources. See Max Lerner, *The Mind and Faith of Justice Holmes* (New York, 1943), pp. 185–186.

69. Jay Burns Baking Co. *v.* Bryan, 264 U.S. 504 (1924).

70. Lee *v.* Osceola Imp. Dist., 268 U.S. 643 (1925).

71. Connally *v.* General Const. Co., 269 U.S. 385 (1926).

72. Weaver *v.* Palmer Bros. Co., 270 U.S. 402 (1926).

73. The Court had no trouble sustaining a Virginia statute permitting sterilization of inmates in institutions for the feebleminded. In this noneconomic area, the Court was willing to tolerate social experimentation, agreeing with Holmes that "three generations of imbeciles are enough." Buck *v.* Bell, 274 U.S. 200 (1927).

The course charted in the Wolff Packing case afforded the legal rationale for even more vigorous assaults upon statutes directly regulating business's behavior. Narrowing the public interest doctrine to such a degree that it covered only public utilities and a few parallel industries had had the effect of converting this legal principle into a negative device by which to exclude previously covered areas and thereby remove them from public control. New York sought to protect theatergoers against the excessive charges demanded by licensed brokers who trafficked in ticket resale. The Court maintained, in a widely renowned and criticized opinion, *Tyson* v. *Banton,*[74] that theaters were not public utilities or affected with a public interest. Theaters served only a small percentage of the public and they could enjoy no special governmental protection or privilege. Neither could the limited public they served. In the following year, the Court struck down a New Jersey law empowering the Secretary of Labor to fix the fees charged by employment agencies. Holding in *Ribnik* v. *McBride*[75] that even though such a measure was clearly designed to protect the welfare of the large numbers of people who found it necessary to thus seek employment, the business, not being affected with a public interest, was thus not subject to governmental regulation. The law, it maintained, must be voided as a violation of the liberty of the owners of the agencies.

The Ribnik case afforded Sutherland, who gave the majority opinion, the opportunity to speak generally about the whole question of state interference in the area of price and wage control. "It is no longer fairly open to question," he wrote, "that the fixing of prices for food, clothing, house rental, wages to be paid, whether minimum or maximum, is beyond the legislative power."[76] Ironically, in a period when the U.S. Department of Commerce was aiding business in every way to take similar action privately, the Court lost little time in applying the formula. In 1921, it cut

74. Tyson *v.* Banton, 273 U.S. 418 (1927). On the legal background and historical development of the "public interest" doctrine see Walton H. Hamilton, "Affectation with a Public Interest," *Yale Law Review*, XXXIX (June, 1930), 1089–1112; and Breck P. McAllister, "Lord Hale and Business Affected with a Public Interest," *Harvard Law Review*, XLIII (March, 1930), 759–791.

75. Ribnik *v.* McBride, 277 U.S. 350 (1928).

76. *Ibid.*, p. 357.

down a Tennessee statute attempting to stabilize gasoline prices, again on the categorical grounds that unless the business was vested with a public interest, as was not the case here, there was no power in the state to assume such a task—even if large portions of the general public might otherwise be adversely affected thereby.[77] Thus in the area of state police power, as with the antitrust laws, the Court had little trouble in reviving or evolving legal devices by which to underwrite the right of the propertied individual to liberty of person and freedom of contract, although a minority steadily protested that such formulas were sterile legalisms.

Informed legal criticism of the Court's obsession with property rights acknowledged that its legal hairsplitting was traditional and contrasted it with the more socially conscious decisions of an earlier day. Maurice Finkelstein wrote at the time in the *Columbia Law Review:*

> That official decisions have in the past been replete with principles, distinctions and differences which neither guide, distinguish nor indicate helpful differentiations is now a commonplace in juristic thought. The standards reiterated in the Tyson case are without doubt such principles and distinctions.[78]

But Finkelstein, along with other vigorous critics, was quick to emphasize the sharp departure such preemptive judicial arbitrament represented from Holmes's principle of weighing state laws on the basis of the importance of their ends and the reasonableness of the means adapted to reach those ends. "Time was," Finkelstein wrote, "when the majority of the Court . . . paid tribute to this principle; but today after the series of decisions of which Tyson v. Banton is the culmination and latest expression, it is difficult to avoid the conclusion that the principle, to all intents and purposes, has been abandoned."[79]

To legal outsiders, this aggravated judicial preemption of determining what was proper public policy betrayed both a double standard and a gratuitous overloading of the scale on the side of those with adequate sources of private power who hardly needed

77. Williams *v.* Standard Oil Co., 278 U.S. 237 (1929).

78. Maurice Finkelstein, "From Munn v. Illinois to Tyson v. Banton: A Study in the Judicial Process," *Columbia Law Review,* XXVII (November, 1927), 770.

79. *Ibid.,* p. 783.

more special favor. In virtually every case in which labor was involved, the liberty guaranteed was of the nature to make labor's demands and hopes ineffectual, especially those seeking concessions in the form of better hours, wages, and working conditions, while in virtually every case in which business prerogatives threatened the public welfare, the liberty on whose side the Court came up was liberty of business to continue its practices and the liberty of the public to accept and adjust to them on business's terms. Such a posture seemed even more questionable to many in light of the Court's callous unwillingness to protect the freedoms and liberties of the dissenters and have-nots within American society against whom the Court had little difficulty in upholding and enforcing state-authorized proscriptions and inhibitions. Little wonder that such citizens and their defenders and champions came early to agree on the futility of judicial relief and the necessity for seeking solutions in other ways, while a minority of the high bench itself warned with increasing urgency of the potential danger of its course.

The judicial majority in the 1920s, while it may have found internal legal consistencies in its own mind, and proper service of the central needs of American society in its principles and formulas, at no time convinced even the entirety of its own membership of its rightness. Rather it exalted in its ability to utilize virtually uninhibited judicial power, basking in the praise of the business establishment for so doing.[80] It was confident that, if there were shortcomings in its positions, the fact that they were designed to insure the even greater success of the business civilization with its assurance of prosperity for all, would eventually engulf and reorient even the bitterest of its critics.

80. Business was fully appreciative of the favor Taft showed it, the National Association of Manufacturers as early as 1923 passing resolutions commending the Court for its intelligent rulings and hailing it as the "indispensable interpreter of our written Constitution," particularly given the fact that it was insulated from the "babel voices of the mob" and hence, as the most important check upon the power of agencies more responsive to the demands of the crowd, "the safest repository of power." John E. Edgerton, "Annual Address of the President," *Proceedings,* National Association of Manufacturers (New York, 1924), pp. 114–115. Herbert Hoover shared this view, and was further convinced that unless the enterprise system operated free from popular controls, all constitutional freedoms would die. Herbert Hoover, *The New Day: Campaign Speeches of Herbert Hoover, 1928* (Stanford, 1928), pp. 16, 162–163.

CHAPTER 3

Normalcy and Freedom: The Awakening Concern for National Standards

ALTHOUGH conservative legal thought dominated the bench and bar during the Republican ascendency of the 1920s, it did not go unchallenged. On the contrary, the cry for a more humane, socially responsible and realistic jurisprudence was heard from a wide range of voices throughout the decade, from leaders in legal education and legal practice to figures in public life at the national, state, and local levels. The sources and motivations for this protest varied as greatly as the range of Americans who voiced it. Yet all agreed on the common purpose of returning the Constitution to the people and curtailing it as an instrument for special privilege. Such a view remained that of a decided minority but the minor breakthroughs scored in the decade came in time to be significant far beyond their limited initial impact.

While liberals, reformers, champions of labor and of the welfare state had suffered severely at the hands of the executive department and from the narrow partisanship of the judiciary, their zeal was unabated. But by 1921, the challenge had changed. The ascendency of Taft, and Harding normalcy, and the downgrading of the government as an overtly repressive agency forced liberals to reassess the methods of constitutional modernization. Court rulings such as the Duplex case,[1] *Truax* v. *Corrigan*,[2] *Bailey* v. *Drexel*

1. Duplex Printing Press Co. *v.* Deering, 254 U.S. 441 (1921).
2. Truax *v.* Corrigan, 257 U.S. 312 (1921).

Furniture,[3] *and Adkins* v. *Children's Hospital*[4] all but precluded the possibility of judicial avenues to the attainment of their ends. Legislative ones looked equally blocked. As Justice Sutherland's biographer wrote later of the Adkins opinion, "taken at its face value, it could only be interpreted as asserting that under the constitution it was impossible to attempt the solution of certain modern social problems by legislation."[5] Other decisions created the same impression. Under Harding and Coolidge, the White House offered few rays of hope, while administrative agencies and commissions were dominated by conservative appointees. State governors like Alfred E. Smith in New York[6] and Gifford Pinchot in Pennsylvania[7] developed reform programs, but they were the exception and even their power to push through new liberal approaches was limited by the *laissez-nous faire* business climate of the times.

Constitutional reform clearly had to come from challenging the system. And as frustrating as such a prospect seemed in a period of ostensible national prosperity, many conscience-ridden Americans were prepared to develop tactics for doing so. With the urging and support of national organs like the *Nation,* the *New Republic,* and the *Survey* and large segments of the labor, Socialist, and reform press, a number of social workers, certain liberal clergymen, pacifists, militant labor leaders, and intellectuals sought alternatives to the business culture and its legal values. One organization that crystallized and fulfilled their desires was the American Civil Liberties Union.[8] Organized initially during World War I

3. Bailey *v.* Drexel Furniture Co., 259 U.S. 20 (1922).

4. Adkins *v.* Children's Hospital, 261 U.S. 525 (1923).

5. Joel F. Paschal, *Mr. Justice Sutherland: A Man Against the State* (Princeton, 1951), pp. 123–124.

6. Smith had publicly denounced the highly restrictive Lusk legislation. Lawrence H. Chamberlain, *Loyalty and Legislative Action* (Ithaca, 1951), pp. 42–44; *Progressive Democracy: Addresses and State Papers of Alfred E. Smith* (New York, 1928), pp. 272–282; Henry E. Pringle, *Alfred E. Smith: A Critical Study* (New York, 1927), pp. 236 ff. Smith had crusaded for a variety of reform measures. Oscar Handlin, *Al Smith and His America* (Boston, 1958).

7. Pinchot was a particularly active campaigner for industrial peace in the state's strife-torn mining regions and made major strides toward undercutting owner tyranny by removing the state police as coercive instruments of the operators, a trend that his successor made every effort to reverse. M. Nelson McGeary, *Gifford Pinchot: Forester–Politician* (Princeton, 1960).

8. Donald Johnson, *The Challenge to American Freedoms: World War I and the Rise of the American Civil Liberties Union* (Lexington, Ky., 1963); Charles

to defend critics and opponents of the war, it was reorganized in 1920 and its base broadened to include a wide spectrum of opponents of social and economic injustice. Roger N. Baldwin, its founder and most active leader, tended to focus its activities on the protection of labor and workingmen now weakened and generally stigmatized by their participation in postwar strikes and protests. To this former social worker, civil liberties flowed from economic power, and artificial impediments to the achievement of that power had to be removed.[9]

Concretely this meant that the A.C.L.U. was prepared to attack the system, its premises and values, and even its foundations, in a number of ways. It launched an active campaign to release the "political prisoners" still incarcerated as punishment for wartime espionage or sedition, with the added hope of dramatizing the deleterious effects of government curtailment of freedom of speech.[10] It mounted vocal and well-reasoned opposition to the further abuse of state sedition and criminal syndicalism laws, and launched campaigns for their repeal.[11] It aimed similar protest at the use of the labor injunction to intimidate workers and undermine their causes.[12] Attorneys like Albert DeSilver, Walter Nelles, Walter Pollak, Arthur Garfield Hays, and Morris Ernst denounced the concept that only property had liberty, and sought new legal formulas to enlist the federal government into active protection of personal rights threatened by state action.

L. Markmann, *The Noblest Cry: A History of the American Civil Liberties Union* (New York, 1965); Barton Bean, "Pressure for Freedom: The American Civil Liberties Union" (unpublished Ph.D. dissertation, Cornell University, 1955). For the more intimate experiences of a leading member of the body see Arthur Garfield Hays, *Let Freedom Ring* (New York, 1929) and *Trial by Prejudice* (New York, 1933).

9. In assessing the activities of the organization in the late 1920s, Roger Baldwin, its founder and guiding light, estimated that 90 per cent of the work of the body involved protecting rights "which labor asserts in its contest with employers or with civil authorities." *Social Work Year Book, 1929* (New York, 1929), I, 85. See also Roger N. Baldwin and Clarence B. Randall, *Civil Liberties and Industrial Conflict* (Cambridge, Mass., 1938), p. 17.

10. Johnson, *Challenge to American Freedoms,* pp. 176 ff.

11. Eldridge F. Dowell, "A History of the Enactment of Criminal Syndicalism Legislation in the United States" (2 vols., Ph.D. dissertation, Johns Hopkins University, 1936), *passim,* contains discussion of numerous such attempts through the 1920s.

12. Irving Bernstein, *The Lean Years: A History of the American Worker, 1920–1933* (Boston, 1960), pp. 391–415.

The body also mounted steady and vigorous protest against the high-handedness of law-enforcement officials. A particular target was William Burns, Jr.,[13] Attorney General Harry M. Daugherty's choice for chief of the Bureau of Investigation, who used that agency as an instrument to root out enemies of the government, particularly left-wing political critics. Its leaders publicly deplored and assailed local police tyranny, especially in instances where it was clear that the police were working closely with economic power to deny the legitimate rights of workingmen and minority groups.[14] When such general techniques failed, A.C.L.U. leaders and supporters openly risked arrest and even physical assault to challenge a wide battery of local statutes and regulations used by "creative" law-enforcement agents as the basis for curtailing any kind of action that seemed a threat to the local power structure.[15] Such A.C.L.U. activity was designed to restore true meaning to the Bill of Rights, and particularly to the due process and equal protection clauses of the Fourteenth Amendment.

Many men in public life were equally concerned that constitutional government had become a hollow facade and was not working equitably. A number of senators and congressmen, like William E. Borah of Idaho, Robert La Follette of Wisconsin, George Norris of Nebraska, Henrik Shipstead of Minnesota, and Thomas J. Walsh and Burton K. Wheeler of Montana, deplored various aspects of governmental malfunctioning. Borah deplored

13. On Burns's career see Don Whitehead, *The F.B.I. Story* (New York, 1956), pp. 55–59; Max Lowenthal, *The Federal Bureau of Investigation* (New York, 1950), pp. 269 ff., 309 ff.; Alpheus T. Mason, *Harlan Fiske Stone: Pillar of the Law* (New York, 1956), pp. 149–150; Methodist Federation for Social Service, *The Social Service Bulletin* (February, 1920), pp. 1–4; *ibid.*, (September, 1924), pp. 1–4; New York *World*, February 9, 1923, p. 31. Later in the decade Burns was convicted of jury tampering. *The New York Times*, February 22, 1928, p. 1.

14. The A.C.L.U. issued two informal reports on the police and civil liberties in the decade. American Civil Liberties Union, *The Police and Radicals: What 88 Police Chiefs Think and Do About Radical Meetings* (New York, 1921); *Blue Coats and Reds* (New York, 1929). See also the popular summarization of the findings of the Wickersham Commission: Ernest J. Hopkins, *Our Lawless Police: A Study of the Unlawful Enforcement of the Law* (New York, 1931).

15. Looking back some years later, Arthur Garfield Hays observed: "In the old days, we used to go into the coal fields or over to New Jersey, and hold test meetings and get ourselves locked up. We were right in the front lines then. Now we file a brief. Governors speak at our dinners. I think we were a more effective organization before we became respectable. Hell, there was a time when we were all jailbirds together." Dwight McDonald, "Profiles: The Defense of Everybody," II, *The New Yorker*, XXIX (July 18, 1953), 57.

the travesty of the guarantee of freedom of speech by the government's continued refusal to release wartime critics from federal prisons, particularly the redoubtable Socialist leader Eugene V. Debs.[16] Norris and Shipstead were outspoken critics of the revival of the labor injunction to curtail legitimate union activities.[17] Walsh read the adverse findings of the *Illegal Practices of the Justice Department* into the *Congressional Record* and called for the resignation of the lawless William J. Burns.[18] La Follette geared much of his campaign for the Presidency in 1924 to the irresponsibility of the federal judiciary which, he charged, had "usurped . . . the power to nullify laws duly enacted by the legislative branch of the government in plain violation of the Constitution. . . ."[19] He called for a constitutional amendment to permit direct election of judges on fixed terms and to enable Congress to override a judicial veto. This, he argued in his campaign, was essential to the re-creation of responsible public control of private economic power.

Ultimately, the most significant legal activity of the decade took place within the normally conservative legal community. "Legal realism," which sought to go beyond the sociological jurisprudence of the prewar period and focus legal adjudication into primary consideration of societal reality, gained vigorous adherents in the 1920s. In fact, Benjamin Cardozo was to observe in 1932 that "the most distinctive product of the last decade in the field of jurisprudence is the rise of a group of scholars styling themselves real-

16. Claudius O. Johnson, *Borah of Idaho* (Seattle, 1967), pp. 217–218; Johnson, *Challenge to American Freedoms,* pp. 192–193.

17. On Norris see George W. Norris, *Fighting Liberal: The Autobiography of George W. Norris* (New York, 1945); Alfred Lief, *Democracy's Norris* (New York, 1939). On Shipstead, see Mary R. Lorentz, "Henrik Shipstead—Minnesota Independent" (unpublished Ph.D. dissertation, Catholic University, 1965).

18. *Congressional Record,* 67th Cong., 4th Sess., LXIV (February 5, 1923), 3005 ff.

19. The platform of La Follette's Progressive party of 1924 began with a general assault upon the callous usurpation of power by the federal courts and its use to destroy the liberties of the people. Kirk H. Porter and Donald B. Johnson, *National Party Platforms* (Urbana, Ill., 1956), p. 252. Hughes's appointment as Chief Justice afforded another occasion for senatorial assault upon excessive judicial power, Borah, for example, declaring that the Supreme Court had become the "economic dictator in the United States"—*Congressional Record,* 71st Cong., 2d Sess., LXXII (February 11, 1930), 3449–3450—and urging the justices to stop treating the Fourteenth Amendment as a sole protection for property and elevate it as a guarantee of individual liberty.

ists."[20] Prominent among the group were Karl Llewellyn of the University of Chicago, Jerome Frank, a corporation lawyer in that city, Morris and Felix Cohen of C.C.N.Y., Thurmond Arnold of Yale, and Justice Cardozo himself, as well as a group of research scholars, all anxious to convert Poundian idealism into new forms of social control.[21] Influenced by pragmatism, behaviorist psychology, psychoanalysis, and statistical sociology, these legalists deplored the decade's emphasis on rigid formulas and the application of formal rules of law, rather placing emphasis upon the role of the judge and his own psychological composition as a prime factor in judicial decision making.[22] Judges actually decide cases according to their own political or moral tastes, and then choose an appropriate legal rule as a rationalization, they argued. What was needed was a "scientific" approach that would fix on what judges do, rather than what they say, and the actual impact their decisions have on the larger community.

Such a posture led them to criticize sharply the retrogressive economic and social sources of the predilections that led the Taft majority to rule as it did. A typical criticism was that of Harvard's Thomas Reed Powell, who, in evaluating the Adkins ruling, observed:

20. "Jurisprudence," *Selected Writings of Benjamin Nathan Cardozo,* ed. Margaret E. Hall (New York, 1947), pp. 7–8. Ten years earlier, Cardozo had viewed with great hope a trend that he hoped would "touch all departments of the law," the change in emphasis urged by Roscoe Pound from "the content of the precept and the existence of the remedy to the effect of the precept and the availability and efficiency of the remedy to attain the ends for which the precept was devised." Benjamin N. Cardozo, *The Nature of the Judicial Process* (New Haven, 1921), p. 73.

21. This was particularly the ambition of Herman Oliphant, who saw the scientific training of lawyers lagging behind the education of doctors. See Herman Oliphant, "Parallels in the Development of Legal and Medical Education," *Annals,* CLXVII (1933), 162.

22. Llewellyn quite correctly saw the advocates of legal realism not as an integrated "school," but as an unintegrated "movement" whose overall effect was primarily to call attention to social needs and policy implications, and prepare the ground for the introduction of new kinds of materials on social relationships into the process of making legal decisions. Karl N. Llewellyn, "Some Realism About Realism," *Harvard Law Review,* XLIV (1931), 1234. See also Wilfrid E. Rumble, Jr., *American Legal Realism* (Ithaca, 1968); Julius Paul, *The Legal Realism of Jerome N. Frank* (The Hague, 1959); and Eugene V. Rostow, "The Realist Tradition in American Law," in Arthur M. Schlesinger, Jr., and Morton White (eds.), *Paths of American Thought* (Boston, 1963), pp. 203–218.

This vote was determined by the capacity of economic analysis and the views of public policy of five individuals. It is their preference which has rendered minimum-wage legislation invalid. It is not wholly true that the elucidation of the question of its validity cannot be aided by counting heads. Only because in the final vote some heads rather than others are the ones to be counted is minimum-wage legislation invalid.[23]

Thus, despite a decade and a half of introducing sociological material to the Court through detailed briefs, the realists had to admit that the validity of such data was not yet accepted. The majority still relied on their personal economic and social philosophy and then justified their actions by traditional legal rationalizations.

The realists thus came to see that a new emphasis upon the practicality of empirical research and data was essential. This led the Institute of Law of the Johns Hopkins University to launch significant social research on the operation and functioning of law.[24] It induced most major law schools to adopt a new type of casebook featuring the inclusion of a substantial body of factual or "extra-legal" material. At Columbia, under such scholars as Herman Oliphant and Underhill Moore, and at Yale under Dean Robert Hutchins and a group of young legal iconoclasts who turned the law school of Taft's alma mater into a "hotbed of legal realism," it saw a revision of law school curriculum to include economic and social theory, psychological and sociological data.[25] Finally it resulted in the appointment to law school faculties of a number of distinguished social scientists such as political economist Walton

23. Thomas Reed Powell, "The Judiciality of Minimum Wage Legislation," *Harvard Law Review,* XXXVII (1924), 572.

24. The Institute, established in 1928, lasted only until 1933, but, with its brilliant staff of social science–oriented lawyers, launched a number of useful empirical studies on the function of law, its impact on society, and more specifically on the use for lawyers of psychology, psychiatry, sociology, criminology, etc. See Walter Wheeler Cook, "Scientific Method and the Law," *American Bar Association Journal,* XIII (1927), 303–309; and Rumble, *American Legal Realism,* pp. 15–19.

25. Rumble, *American Legal Realism,* p. 24. Legal liberalism moved from Columbia to Yale in the mid-twenties, according to John W. Hopkirk, "The Influence of Legal Realism on William O. Douglas," in Gottfried Dietze (ed.), *Essays on the American Constitution* (Englewood Cliffs, N.J., 1964), pp. 63–64. See also the comments of Thurman Arnold, *Fair Fights and Foul* (New York, 1965), pp. 35, 57 ff.

H. Hamilton and political behaviorist Harold Lasswell at Yale, economist and regulatory specialist Robert L. Hale at Columbia, and criminologist Sheldon Glueck at Harvard.

A particular emphasis of the legal realists, in a decade of rapid and dramatic technological change, was upon the need for a dynamic law. They stressed the inability of old rules to provide clear guidance for the unprecedented situation characteristic of a world in flux and the need for judges to confront present reality. "New instruments of production, new modes of travel and of dwelling, new credit and ownership devices, new concentrations of capital, new social customs, habits, aims and ideals—all these factors of innovation," wrote Jerome Frank, "make vain the hope that definitive legal rules can be drafted that will forever after solve all legal problems."[26]

The challenge to the realists was selling the "new law" to judges in a position to implement it. They had, however, a number of judicial sympathizers. A handful of courageous lower-court judges during the decade were not loath to use the realists' yardstick to measure the validity of social legislation, and from the Supreme Court Holmes and Brandeis provided not only hope but inspiration. Brandeis especially had been an active crusader throughout and even before his judicial career. Like many frustrated liberals, he and Holmes were prepared to face realistically the challenges of the new climate of normalcy and tailor their activities to meet it effectively.

The question was one of tactics. Here the two men differed appreciably. Holmes was highly disturbed by the judicial activism of the Taft Court because its actions represented hostility toward the democratic process. Dissenting sharply from Taft's Truax opinion, he rejected the notion that any activity conducted by a legitimate business was merely the extension of a sacred property right, to be protected categorically against state interference. To Holmes, there was clear danger in such "delusive exactness" in applying the Fourteenth Amendment to void state laws. To call business "property" made it seem like land and thereby invited the conclusion that "a statute cannot substantially cut down the

26. Jerome N. Frank, *Law and the Modern Mind* (New York, 1930), p. 6.

advantages of ownership existing before the statute was passed."[27] Legislation, such as the state anti-injunction law, Holmes felt, could clearly begin where an evil began. He denounced sharply Taft's assertion that the Constitution was intended as a perpetual bar to legislative experimentation. The proper function of the Court was, he thought, to encourage experimentation carried out by the elective branches, the validity of such experimentation to be determined largely by a general societal evaluation of the desirability of the social results thereby achieved.[28] This posture of judicial self-restraint meant that the Court, while serving a liberalizing function, should no more play a positive role in achieving specific liberal social policies than a negative one in invalidating experimental regulatory legislation. Rather it should interpret the law in such a way as to make it possible for the people's representatives to move in the direction they felt desirable.

Similarly, when it came to the ongoing question of the permissible limits of dissent, Holmes, now sobered by the turning of his "clear and present danger rule" into a rationalization for suppression by the decisions of 1919 and 1920, once again struck a pose for reason. He insisted that the rule only be enforced restrictively when empirical information indicated that the threat to society was real. In light of the calm of post-Red scare days, and the dominance of conservative business power, he could see even less clear and present danger of social evil from social critics in the halcyon days of normalcy.[29]

Brandeis, by contrast, tended to step up his use of the high bench as a didactic podium for urging explicit social responsibility. He too saw judicial self-restraint as essential and participatory democracy at the local level to be encouraged rather than quashed, but he still felt that judges should clearly set forth alternative social

27. Truax *v.* Corrigan, 257 U.S. 312, 342 (1921).

28. This attitude, which is more formally called "rule-skepticism," assumes both that extralegal factors are essential as considerations in litigation, and that the predictive values of legal rules for unprecedented exigencies is limited and must be supplemented by consideration of factors "in good measure outside these . . . traditional rules." Karl N. Llewellyn, *"Jurisprudence: Realism in Theory and Practice"* (Chicago, 1962), p. 61.

29. See especially his dissent in Gitlow *v.* New York, 268 U.S. 652, 672–673 (1925). See also Samuel J. Konefsky, *The Legacy of Holmes and Brandeis* (New York, 1956), pp. 226–228.

values and alternative approaches to constitutional reality.[30] His Truax dissent, involving objection to Taft, and the conservative majority's invalidation of a state anti-injunction law, differed from Holmes's, stressing far more the social needs produced by changing conditions and circumstances. Arguing that the rights of property and the liberty of the individual must be remolded from time to time to meet the changed needs of society, he extended the arguments of his earlier *Gilbert* v. *Minnesota* dissent, arguing that the "law of property was not appropriate for dealing with the forces beneath social unrest."[31] But he also took the occasion to decry what he considered the unwarranted revival of the use of the labor injunction to thwart labor's legitimate demands. By limiting the injunction, he had contended in his Duplex dissent, Congress had in the Clayton Act confronted a social need realistically and established legitimate national standards fair to both parties in the industrial struggle.[32] Here as there, it was not the prerogative of judges to undo such action on the ground that it did not square with their own particular economic and social views.

Parallel circumstances produced a similar Brandeisian response later in the decade. The 1927 Bedford Cut Stone ruling was a classic example of the worst aspects of the old jurisprudence. Having developed a general rule and general approach early in the decade through which reasonable restraints of trade by such business structures as the United States Steel Corporation and the trade associations could be sustained within the antitrust structure, the conservatives rejected their own rule when asked to sustain the reasonable activities of a labor union, even when it was clearly

30. Brandeis' relationship with Taft, who had fought his initial appointment bitterly, fluctuated sharply. Upon Taft's taking over the Chief Justiceship, Brandeis sought carefully to create a working relationship, but by the late twenties, Taft's initial suspicions had returned to the point that his antagonism "bordered on the irrational." Alpheus T. Mason, *William Howard Taft: Chief Justice* (New York, 1965), pp. 225–226. During the congenial period Brandeis was capable of maneuvering Taft skillfully in certain instances. An outstanding example was the First Coronado Coal case, U.M.W. *v.* Coronado Coal Co., 259 U.S. 344 (1922), in which an unpublished Brandeis dissent induced the Chief Justice to revise his views and use Brandeis' arguments to write a unanimous majority opinion. Alexander Bickel, *The Unpublished Opinions of Mr. Justice Brandeis* (Cambridge, Mass., 1957), pp. 97–99.

31. Truax *v.* Corrigan, 257 U.S. 312, 368 (1921).

32. Duplex Printing Press Co. *v.* Deering, 254 U.S. 443, 484–485 (1920).

demonstrable that such activities were being carried out to prevent a combination of powerful corporations from destroying its very existence.[33] The obvious shuffling of constitutional principles that the majority found necessary in order to arrive at this legal conclusion was so clearly an implementation of judicially desired social and economic results that the dissenting critique, even though couched in legalisms, served to rally considerable public opinion against the majority's position. So also did Brandeis' objection to the majority's frivolous application of the clear and present danger rule in the free speech area, particularly when he posed more practical alternatives for the handling of dissent.

Brandeis and Holmes gained some cautious, but at times effective, judicial support for their posture as the decade advanced. When Joseph McKenna retired in 1925, Calvin Coolidge chose as his successor Harlan Fiske Stone. Stone, an old friend from Amherst College days, had been rigidly pro-business in his views and during his tenure as dean of the Columbia University Law School from 1910 to 1923 he had clearly put himself in the bailiwick of legal conservatism, his associations being predominantly with those of that view.[34] However, liberal signs had crept forth. Stone had strongly disapproved the violence to due process inherent in the "Red Scare" tactics of the government, endorsing the famous lawyers' broadside against the illegal practices of the Justice Department in 1920. He was particularly offended by the fact that under Attorney General Daugherty certain personnel in the Justice Department, particularly William J. Burns, head of the Bureau of Investigation, and Gaston B. Means, one of the most heavy-handed of its special investigators, had made serious attempts to keep alive the atmosphere of Red hysteria and witch-hunting that had prevailed in the early and now clearly repudiated period. When Coolidge appointed Stone Attorney General to replace the publicly discredited Daugherty, one of his first acts was not only to call for Burns' resignation, but to make clear that the bureau was being taken out of politics with its radical-chasing activities terminated. In a public pronouncement in May, 1924, Stone stated forcibly his belief that

33. Bedford Cut Stone *v.* Journeymen Stone Cutters' Assn., 274 U.S. 37, 65 (1927). On the general significance of the ruling and the dissent see Charles O. Gregory, *Labor and the Law* (New York, 1961), pp. 219–220.

34. Mason, *Harlan Fiske Stone,* Chaps. 6–9.

there is always the possibility that a secret police may become a menace to free government and free institutions because it carries with it the possibility of abuses of power which are not always quickly apprehended or understood. It is important that the Bureau's activities be strictly limited to those functions for which it was created and that its agents themselves be not above the law or beyond its reach. The Bureau . . . is not concerned with political or other opinions of individuals. It is concerned with their conduct and then only with such conduct as is forbidden by the laws of the United States.[35]

The action drew a wide range of favorable liberal comment. Particularly enthusiastic were Civil Liberties Union leaders and general opponents of big government who could see no justification for a secret police, particularly in an era in which freedom from governmental tyranny of all kinds—economic, social, and political—was so much the order of the day. And while its implications greatly distressed ultraconservative patriots—the D.A.R., the American Legion, professional military leaders, and various groups dubbed by Brandeis' close friend Norman Hapgood "professional patriots"[36]—it was sufficiently incisive and resounding to keep the government out of an active concern for hunting down left-wingers and political "subversives" until Martin Dies successfully launched the House Un-American Activities Committee in 1938.

Much less prominent, but by no means insignificant, was Justice Edward T. Sanford, appointed to replace Pitney in late January of 1923. Sanford, while aligning himself frequently with the conservative majority on questions of economic policy, nonetheless showed occasional liberal tendencies in the civil liberties area, writing in the Gitlow, Whitney, and Fiske cases[37] three of the more

35. American Civil Liberties Union, *The Nation-Wide Spy System Centering in the Department of Justice* (New York, 1924), p. 3. See also Lowenthal, *Federal Bureau of Investigation,* p. 298.

36. Norman Hapgood, *Professional Patriots* (New York, 1927). Hapgood concentrated on groups such as the National Security League, the American Defense Society, the Better America Federation, and the National Civic Federation, whose work, unlike the D.A.R. and the veterans' groups, was geared to little but superpatrioteering. On the D.A.R. see Martha Strayer, *The D.A.R.* (Washington, 1958). On the work of veterans' groups, Marcus Duffield, *King Legion* (New York, 1930); and Rodney G. Minott, *Peerless Patriots* (Washington, 1962), are suggestive in this regard.

37. Gitlow *v.* New York, 268 U.S. 562 (1925); Whitney *v.* California, 274 U.S. 357 (1927); Fiske *v.* Kansas, 274 U.S. 380 (1927). Sanford, while voting with the majority in the Bedford Cut Stone case, had also disagreed strongly with its reasoning. 274 U.S. 37 (1927).

centrally important opinions in the decade. He also endorsed fully Holmes's eloquent dissent in the Rosika Schwimmer case in which the famed female pacifist was denied citizenship because of her concrete refusal to bear arms in a war period.[38]

Upon mounting the bench, Stone was quickly influenced by Holmes's logic regarding the permissible limits of state police power, sharing his antagonism toward the use of rigid legal formulas to frustrate it. Holmes had made that antagonism implicit in his Adkins dissent. Responding to Sutherland's ruling that minimum wage legislation was an abrogation of "freedom of contract," he seriously challenged whether that concept was any more than an "innocuous generality expanded into a dogma."[39] Contract, Holmes maintained, was not specifically mentioned in the Constitution and the original concept was merely an unpretentious assertion of the liberty to follow ordinary callings. Thus, he contended, since pretty much all law consists of forbidding men to do some things they want to do, and contract is not more exempt from law than other acts, the use of the concept to prevent legal action for the public good was highly unwarranted.

Holmes raised similar objections to the use of the "public interest" doctrine for curtailing legitimate social control. In *Tyson* v. *Banton,* in which the majority voided the New York anti–ticket scalping law since it was not technically "in the public interest," he questioned whether such a technical criterion was necessary to justify legislative action. The Legislature, he argued, when it had sufficient force of public opinion behind it, should have the power to forbid or restrict any business without legal apology.[40]

Stone, in his dissent in *Ribnik* v. *McBride,* picked up the ball from Holmes and ran further. Deploring the voiding of New Jersey's employment agency regulation by the use of the same nar-

38. U.S. *v.* Schwimmer, 279 U.S. 644, 655 (1929). Actually the majority merely ruled that two sections of the oath clauses of the Naturalization Act of 1906 did require such a display of willingness, thus validating that act, but super-patriots promptly interpreted it as meaning that pacifists generally were not qualified to enjoy the rights of full American citizenship. On the background of the case see Milton R. Konvitz, *The Alien and the Asiatic in American Law* (Ithaca, 1946), pp. 97–100; and Rocco J. Tresolini, *Justice and the Supreme Court* (Philadelphia, 1963), pp. 68–76, 169–170.

39. Duplex Printing Press Co. *v.* Deering, 254 U.S. 443, 484–485 (1920).

40. Tyson *v.* Banton, 273 U.S. 413, 446 (1927).

row "public interest" formula, he charged the majority with employing not only a negative, but a vague and illusionary standard that precluded it from coping realistically with basic social issues. If the Court did not wish to continue begging the question to be decided, Stone maintained, it must stop using artificial tests and examine the circumstances that called forth the regulation initially.[41] Taft's response was one of disgust. "Stone has become subservient to Holmes and Brandeis," he wrote his brother Horace. "I am very much disappointed in him; he hungers for the applause of the law-school professors and the admirers of Holmes."[42]

And by 1928, the majority's excessive legal literalness was not even free from criticism by an occasional conservative. Taft's ruling upholding the use of wiretap evidence in the Olmstead case of that year, produced a sharp if homely protest from Justice Butler. The Minnesotan rejected the majority's narrow interpretation of the breadth of coverage afforded by the Fourth Amendment, and took Taft to task both for ignoring the principles upon which the amendment was founded and for waving aside the implied "safeguards against all evils that are like and equivalent to those embraced within the ordinary meaning of its words."[43] And although the case dealt basically with civil liberties and personal freedom, and only indirectly with the rights and liberties of private property, Butler's insistence that such rights should also have high constitutional and hence judicial priority constituted yet another assault upon the deleterious social effects produced by the majority's blind and insensitive focus upon disembodied legal logic.

The social values and objectives that emerged from the composite protest launched by liberal jurists and legalists against the majority's economic rulings, while affording no concrete avenues toward relief and solution, at least acknowledged pressing necessity for creation of higher and more responsible national social and economic standards. The road to their attainment obviously lay in the future, as the failure of liberals to achieve even such a minimal objective as a national child labor law clearly indicated. But at least roadblocks, in the form of legal literalness and intransigence, could be removed.

41. *Ibid.,* p. 454.
42. Mason, *William Howard Taft,* p. 228.
43. Olmstead *v.* U.S., 277 U.S. 438, 487 (1928).

And although there was little to do during the decade but bemoan the fact that a majority of Justices, by striking down, in one test case, one piece of state social welfare legislation, could successfully undermine such efforts to cope with national problems, here a shift in legal emphasis was not impossible to work for. By hammering away at the way in which such judicial tyranny blocked the considered wishes of the people's representative, liberals hoped to appeal to popular frustration, particularly in areas where responsible social legislation was clearly needed to undermine the abuses of private capital and irresponsible economic power.

Liberals were also crusading for minimal national standards in the area of civil liberties and civil rights. Here they hoped that the broadly held antipathy toward excessive governmental power might work in their behalf, particularly as they set out to strike down a large number of state and local restrictions and regulations clearly curtailing personal liberty. Such was not the case, however. Again conservative opposition had to be surmounted. For while the influential business community had, on one hand, turned to judges to develop legal formulas through which to strike down social and economic regulation, it had been equally as energetic and successful in encouraging state legislatures to pass measures restricting the personal freedom of its critics and opponents, and in persuading the courts to develop rigid legal formulas by which to uphold them. Popular opinion generally agreed and supported their enforcement. Labor unrest and discontent, strikes, and protest picketing were most easily explained as the work of irresponsible agitators spurred on by "parlor bolsheviks and pink radicals."[44] And it was but one

44. Charles L. Markmann, *The Noblest Cry: A History of the American Civil Liberties Union* (New York, 1965), pp. 149–151; Irving Bernstein, *The Lean Years: A History of the American Worker, 1920–1933* (Boston, 1960). Dean John H. Wigmore had assailed Holmes's Abrams dissent since it betrayed Holmes's naïveté in failing to realize that "hundreds of well-meaning citizens—'parlor bolsheviks' and 'pink radicals,' are showing . . . complaisance or good-natured tolerance to the licensing of the violence-propaganda." John H. Wigmore, "Freedom of Speech and Freedom of Thuggery in War-Time and Peace-Time," Illinois Law Review, XIV (1920), 539. Holmes's response was philosophic. Writing to Pollock, he stated: "I was sorry to see Wigmore carried away by the panic mongers. His reasons amounted to saying that it is wrong to criticize an indictment for murder because homicide is a very dangerous offense and many murderers are very wicked men." Mark D. Howe (ed.), *The Holmes-Pollock Letters* (2 vols., Cambridge, Mass., 1941) II, 48.

step further to insist that while personal liberty and due process were guaranteed by the Constitution, such guarantees did not cover "license" and the abuse of freedom. Here local law enforcement had to be trusted to deal with irresponsible personal action as it saw fit even if this meant uses of local power frequently with utter disregard for any element of fair procedure or for any uniform national standards of minimal human rights.[45]

But nationalization of the Bill of Rights against the states, a goal of certain of the more advanced post–Civil War reconstructionists, had not been forgotten over the years. The majority opinion in the 1923 case of *Prudential Insurance Co.* v. *Cheek*[46] had seemed to set the tone for the decade by insisting that abrogation of civil rights and civil liberties were matters beyond federal control. Yet despite Pitney's insistence that the Fourteenth Amendment was not a legal vehicle for introduction of that control, certain legal liberals became more and more convinced that this was the only viable legal path to the development of national standards. The case of *Gitlow* v. *New York*,[47] which eventually reached the Supreme Court in 1925, after a series of appeals and a number of elaborate lower-court opinions, afforded the occasion for their first assault. The case involved conviction under New York's 1902 Criminal Anarchy Act for the publication of a left-wing newspaper, a "Left-Wing Manifesto," and other allegedly subversive documents. Preparing the brief for Benjamin Gitlow, a prominent figure in the Communist party of the time, were Civil Liberties Union attorneys Walter Nelles, Albert DeSilver, and most significantly Walter H. Pollak, the logic and eloquence of whose argument before the bench was such, as Zechariah Chafee, Jr., was later to write, that he successfully "convinced the Court that 'liberty' in the Fourteenth Amendment includes liberty of speech and of the press."[48]

Following the earlier lead suggested by Brandeis in his *Gilbert* v. *Minnesota* dissent, Pollak's brief challenged Pitney's Prudential Insurance position head-on. Here he already had support from an unexpected source. Justice McReynolds in the 1923 case ruling un-

45. Paul L. Murphy, *The Meaning of Freedom of Speech, 1918–1933*, Chap. 8.
46. Prudential Insurance Co. *v.* Cheek, 259 U.S. 530 (1922).
47. 268 U.S. 562 (1925).
48. Zechariah Chafee, Jr., "Walter Heilprin Pollak," *Nation*, CLI (October 12, 1940), 319.

constitutional a Nebraska statute, which forbade teaching any subject in any school in the state in any language other than English, had stressed the breadth of the "liberty" protected by the due process clause of the Fourteenth Amendment. That liberty, the Tennessee conservative had insisted, included

> not merely freedom from bodily restraint, but also the right of the individual to contract, to engage in any of the common occupations of life, to acquire useful knowledge, to marry, establish a home and bring up children, to worship God according to the dictates of his own conscience, and generally to enjoy those privileges long recognized at common law as essential to the orderly pursuit of happiness by free men.[49]

If the Fourteenth Amendment's liberty was that inclusive, it could surely, Pollak argued, protect freedom of speech and of the press as well.[50] He thus sought to give open discussion the same protection against the states that the essentially negative First Amendment presumably gave it against the nation. And the Court, speaking through Justice Sanford, accepted the argument, thus legitimizing a legal tool with the potential to create broad national standards in the civil liberties area by striking down local restrictions when they clearly abrogated the personal rights guaranteed as an aspect of United States citizenship.

However, although Pollak made his point abstractly, he failed to do so concretely. The majority did not accept his argument that the New York statute was an unwarranted restriction on liberty. Indeed, Sanford carefully refuted his contention that only in circumstances where the exercise of that liberty bore a causal relation with some substantive evil, consummated, attempted, or likely was restraint war-

49. Meyer *v.* Nebraska, 262 U.S. 390, 399 (1923). One authority has noted: "McReynolds wrote the opinion in this case and also in the one invalidating the Oregon statute abolishing private schools for children between the ages of eight and sixteen (Pierce v. Society of Sisters, 268 U.S. 510 [1925]), as if only property rights were involved." Benjamin F. Wright, *The Growth of American Constitutional Law* (New York, 1942), p. 152. Cf. Konefsky, *Legacy of Holmes and Brandeis,* pp. 259–260.

50. Walter H. Pollak and Walter Nelles, *Brief for Plaintiff-in-Error,* Gitlow *v.* New York, p. 11. Sanford merely stated categorically: "For the present purposes we may and do assume that freedom of speech and of the press—which are protected by the First Amendment from abridgment by Congress—are among the fundamental personal rights and 'liberties' protected by the due process clause of the Fourteenth Amendment from impairment by the states. . . ." Gitlow *v.* New York, 268 U.S. 652, 666 (1925).

ranted. Rather, Sanford stayed within the restrictive tradition of the "clear and present danger rule" while refining it further. The rule, he made clear, was intended to apply only to cases where the statute "merely prohibits certain acts involving the danger of substantive evil without any reference to language itself."[51] He rejected it altogether as a test of the constitutionality of a statute expressly directed against words of incitement. Words could be punished for their bad nature, he insisted, regardless of the Court's opinion that there is no danger of bad acts, if legislative findings had resulted in statutes aimed clearly at curtailing the dissemination of sentiments destructive to the ends of society. Thus although Governor Alfred E. Smith of New York promptly pardoned Gitlow by executive edict, the attempt to secure reversal of his earlier conviction through a Holmesian application of "clear and present danger" still demonstrated its basic legal nonacceptance.

Those of a liberal legal view were not through, however. In 1927, the same year that the execution of anarchists Sacco and Vanzetti terminated one of the greatest and most widely supported liberal causes célèbres of the period,[52] they got a new opportunity to press their case. Charlotte Anita Whitney, like Gitlow, had been a victim of "Red Scare" hysteria, having been arrested under a state criminal syndicalism law for alleged involvement in the organization of the Communist Labor party in California, a group that advocated governmental change by revolution. A niece of former ultraconservative Justice Stephen J. Field, and a member of a distinguished California family, she turned to respectable, conservative California legal talent, retaining John Francis Neylan, Hearst lawyer and prominent counsel for a number of large local corporations, and

51. Gitlow *v.* New York, 671 (1925).

52. The Sacco-Vanzetti case has never ceased to arouse controversy in the years since its supposed termination. The standard work was long Louis C. Joughin and Edmund M. Morgan, *The Legacy of Sacco and Vanzetti* (New York, 1948), now partially superseded by Herbert B. Ehrmann, *The Case That Will Not Die: Commonwealth vs. Sacco and Vanzetti* (Boston, 1969). Recent studies include Francis Russell, *Tragedy in Dedham: The Story of the Sacco-Vanzetti Case* (New York, 1962); and David Felix, *Sacco-Vanzetti and the Intellectuals* (Bloomington, Ind., 1965). Felix argues that the furor was largely the product of the need for liberal intellectuals to have martyrs to dramatize the social injustice of the age. The sharp response by mid-1960 old left types would seem to indicate that the same is even true in retrospect.

Thomas L. Lennon of San Francisco as her attorneys. However, given their partial success in the Gitlow case, Nelles and Pollak were also quickly involved.[53] Again, however, conservatism triumphed and conviction was sustained.

But the eloquence of judicial liberals made telling points. Holmes had protested vigorously against the Gitlow ruling, again arguing for the value of the free trade in ideas, and stating that "if what I think the correct test is applied, it is manifest that there was no danger of attempt to overthrow the government by force on the part of the admittedly small minority who shared the defendant's view."[54] In the Whitney case, he merely concurred in Brandeis' opinion. The latter, apparently discouraged by the lack of success attained through head-on opposition to majority rigidity, picked up Holmes's torch, but did so by carefully concurring in the majority's position. This enabled him to challenge majority legal assumptions while suggesting potential new avenues to liberal success.

What emerged from the Brandeis opinion was a further reaffirmation of his basic faith in local participatory democracy. The Supreme Court, in applying the whole body of restrictive legal strictures to First Amendment freedoms, he argued, was operating on a highly unfortunate set of assumptions. Basically what the Court had done was to gauge the limits of free speech by evaluating the potential danger it might have to property interest. This, he felt was to use a negative, biased, and unwarranted scale. Like Holmes, he felt that the criteria to be used should be the extent to which the speech was serving the general welfare of the whole community. Hence the test for permissible restraint should be evolved against the backdrop of broad social needs. Unless free speech posed a clear and present danger to society at large, there was much more to be lost in its suppression than in its expression. This enabled him to suggest that since the Court's majority had failed to develop reasonable and explicit standards, it was the duty of the legislatures to do so. Specifically he urged them to repeal overly suppressive legislation already on their statute books, and if they felt the real necessity, to replace it with legislation of a more realistic and sensitive nature.

53. John Francis Neylan, Thomas L. Lennon, Walter Nelles, and Walter H. Pollak, *Brief for Plaintiff-in-Error,* Whitney *v.* California.

54. Gitlow *v.* New York, 268 U.S. 652, 673 (1925).

In terms of a standard, he suggested what came to be called his "time to answer theory." "No danger flowing from speech can be deemed clear and present," he argued, "unless the incidence of the evil apprehended is so imminent that it may befall before there is an opportunity for full discussion." "If there be time to expose through discussion the falsehood and fallacies, to avert the evil by processes of education, the remedy to be applied is more speech, not enforced silence."[55]

Later in the same year the first budding fruit of such legal liberalism quietly emerged. In reversing a conviction under the Kansas criminal syndicalism law, Justice Sanford, although careful not to challenge the constitutionality of the measures, nonetheless ruled that its application in punishing an organizer for the Industrial Workers of the World, for attempting by speech and pamphlet to solicit membership for his organization, unwarrantedly infringed his liberty in violation of the due process clause of the Fourteenth Amendment.[56] While hardly a smashing victory for civil liberties it was significant that up until this time it had been either tacitly assumed or openly stated that virtually every activity of the I.W.W. was automatically punishable under the criminal syndicalism laws, normally with no hearing necessary. The Court's surprising willingness to examine the way the laws were functioning and the actual impact they had upon individual rights represented an important new sensitivity not earlier present. On the other hand, such action could now be taken with some degree of judicial equanimity since, with the exceptions of a few scattered pockets, the effective power of the I.W.W. had been largely shattered and the organization itself largely decimated.[57]

The failure of the Court to rule the Kansas criminal syndicalism law unconstitutional was another example of the indifference of the

55. Whitney *v.* California, 274 U.S. 357, 377 (1927). The reason for Brandeis' concurrence is conjectural. In the opinion he reiterated an oft-stated liberal contention that there was no legal need or justification for legislation such as the criminal syndicalism laws, the criminal codes of the states adequately covering such actions as conspiracy, libel, etc., Apparently, playing the realist, and seeing no judicial relief, he sought to encourage popular action in this area as in others, urging legislatures to adopt more realistic free speech standards.

56. Fiske *v.* Kansas, 274 U.S. 380 (1927).

57. On the waning of the body, particularly its legal difficulties, see John S. Gambs, *The Decline of the I.W.W.* (New York, 1932).

majority of that body toward Bill of Rights guarantees as they applied to state statutes. Generally all challenges to such statutes on civil liberties grounds were turned aside in the decade. The only exception involved an Ohio law providing that the mayor of rural villages might try offenses against the state prohibition law without jury, in turn retaining the amount of cost in case of conviction. Here lack of due process was sufficient to negate the law because of the pecuniary interest of the judge in the outcome of the trial.[58]

In interpreting the procedural rights of Amendments Four through Eight, the majority justices took few decisive steps that created permanent precedents. Called upon to guarantee such rights in a number of disparate situations running from alleged illegal search seizures to the rights of aliens and the clearly second-class treatment of southern Negroes, the Court found it possible to leave standards strictly to the states where this seemed to fit the pressures of the times, inject a modest degree of federal authority where it did not, and to stand sharply behind the full meaning of such protections only when flagrant flouting brought national demands for minimal decency.

The Fourth Amendment's search and seizure guarantee presented peculiar and often uniquely new challenges. Fluctuating demands for the enforcement of prohibition coupled with the clear intent of large numbers of citizens to defy it, at times created perplexing judicial dilemmas. As Zechariah Chafee remarked in 1922:

> Interpretation of the search and seizure provision received new life from the fact that infractions of the Fourth Amendment frequently interfered with the consumption of liquor in violation of the Eighteenth.[59]

Holmes's Silverthorne opinion had set one tone in this regard. Outraged when two suspects were taken into custody and, while they were detained, representatives of the Department of Justice and the United States marshal had, "without a shadow of authority," seized books and papers from their office, his opinion insisted that "the knowledge gained by the government's own wrong cannot be used by it in the way proposed."[60] Six of the justices had joined him

58. Tumey *v.* Ohio, 273 U.S. 510 (1927).

59. Zechariah Chafee, Jr., "The Progress of the Law, 1919–1922," *Harvard Law Review,* XXXV (April, 1922), 673, 694.

60. Silverthorne Lumber Co. *v.* U.S., 251 U.S. 385, 392 (1920).

in sounding a note against official flouting of the amendment's basic standards for securing evidence on which to prosecute. The ruling was naturally analyzed with an eye to its relevance to the prohibition situation as a variety of cases reached the docket. One such was *Carroll* v. *U.S.* in 1925 in which judicial realism emerged sharply. Since illegal bootleg liquor was clearly not going to be left easily accessible for seizure by prohibition agents, the Court relaxed the constitutional barrier and permitted search and seizure, without warrant, of automobiles used for its illegal transport. The only qualification was Taft's assertion that "where the securing of a warrant is reasonably practicable it must be used,"[61] but circumstances themselves of searching an automobile on the road made such a situation unlikely.

The technological fascination of the decade became clear in later search and seizure situations. The gradual shift from its 1920 concern with violation of the rights of individuals to emphasis upon gadgetry, efficiency, and the need of the government to utilize the latest mechanical methods in its relentless crusade against lawlessness and organized crime led to its logical close on the note that securing evidence by wiretapping did not violate the Fourth Amendment. "A standard which would forbid the reception of evidence if obtained by other than nice ethical conduct by government officials," wrote Taft for a badly split Court, "would make society suffer and give criminals greater immunity than has been known heretofore."[62] "For my part I think it a less evil that some criminals should escape than that the government should play an ignoble part," retorted Brandeis bitterly. "If government becomes a lawbreaker it breeds contempt for law."[63] And Holmes, in a remark

61. Carroll *v.* U.S., 267 U.S. 132, 156 (1925). Bitter protest to the ruling came from both inside and outside the Court. McReynolds in dissent deplored the green light this seemed to give to officials to search cars on the slightest provocation, at 163–174. Professor Forrest R. Black wrote a devastating critique in the same vein. Forrest R. Black, "A Critique of the Carroll Case," *Columbia Law Review,* XXIX (November, 1929), 1068–1098. See also Jacob W. Landynski, *Search and Seizure and the Supreme Court* (Baltimore, 1966), pp. 87–91.

62. Olmstead *v.* U.S., 277 U.S. 438, 468 (1928). See Walter F. Murphy, *Wiretapping on Trial* (New York, 1965), p. 125. On details of the case see Norman H. Clark, *The Dry Years: Prohibition and Social Change in Washington* (Seattle, 1965).

63. Olmstead *v.* U.S., 485.

quoted frequently by wiretap opponents over the subsequent years, referred to the practice as "dirty business."[64]

Somewhat similar patterns emerged in regard to the rights of aliens, rights which had been abused above all others in the "Red Scare" days. Here, although liberal attorneys such as Louis Marshall and Walter Nelles made pleas for the Constitution to apply equally to all those under its protection, whether temporary or permanent, the liberal minority on the bench acquiesced fully in a series of careful legal line-drawings clearly designed to keep the alien more clearly in his proper place.[65] The Court thus reflected with clarity and accuracy the majority sentiments of a decade that had seen growing demand for immigration curtailment result in the highly restrictive Immigration Act of 1924,[66] with its rigid quota structure clearly biased against southern and eastern European and Asiatic peoples. One clear reason for antagonism to the former was their association, in the public mind, with political and economic radicalism. In the case of Chinese, Japanese, Filipinos, and Hindus such antagonism was more clearly based on economic hostility with racial bias never far beneath the surface.

Prior to the 1920s members of the Malayan and Mongolian races had generally been conceded the rights of naturalization by lower

64. Olmstead *v.* U.S., 470. Congress moved to counteract the Court's ruling, denying wiretap use to agents enforcing the National Prohibition Act in a 1933 statute (47 Stat. 1371, 1381) and, more significantly, introducing into the Federal Communications Act of 1934 a section forbidding the divulging of information received by wire or radio by any person not entitled thereto (48 Stat. 1064, 1103). The Court subsequently interpreted the act to prohibit the use in federal courts of information acquired by federal agents through wiretapping. Nardone *v.* U.S., 302 U.S. 338 (1939).

65. In 1915, the Court had upheld the right of an alien resident to earn a living by following an ordinary occupation, Truax *v.* Raich, 239 U.S. 33 (1915), although it had sustained a lower court ruling by Justice Cardozo, sustaining a New York law prohibiting their employment on public works projects, Heim *v.* McCall, 239 U.S. 175 (1915). The value orientation of the 1920s added an interesting note. In Ohio *ex rel.* Clarke *v.* Deckenbach, 274 U.S. 392 (1927), the Court upheld a Cincinnati ordinance disqualifying aliens from operating poolrooms, on the grounds that pool halls were by nature centers of iniquity and this was a way to restrain them.

66. U.S. Bureau of Immigration, *Annual Report of the Commissioner-General of Immigration* (Washington, 1924). The measure was, in a sense, a replacement for early laws enacted in 1917 and 1921 which had proved unsatisfactory to a majority of congressmen since they admitted too large a number of immigrants and did not discriminate sufficiently in favor of immigration from northern and western Europe.

courts.[67] Yet such action was based, constitutionally, on the fact that the first naturalization statute of 1790, in assuring naturalization for "all free white aliens," did not explicitly exclude them. Congress did explicitly make Negroes eligible for naturalization through an act of 1870,[68] and excluded Chinese by formal legislation. But it was not until the 1922 Ozawa case[69] that the question of Asiatic eligibility reached the high bench. Speaking through Justice Sutherland, that body had little trouble ruling unanimously that the Act could be interpreted to exclude Japanese from American citizenship. White persons within the meaning of the statute, the Court ruled, were members of the Caucasian race. Clearly, others, unless specifically exempted by Congress, were ineligible to claim naturalization rights. The grounds for this ruling merely followed the thrust of the statute, the Court admitted, which "imputed a racial and not an individual test."[70] The ruling was thus the inevitable concomitant of a social order based on race. Having taken this step, the Court had little difficulty excluding on similar grounds Filipinos[71] and Hindus.[72] In the latter case, the majority opinion went into the question of whether racial intermingling in India involved a "destroying to a greater or less degree of the purity of the 'Aryan' blood," in a man-

67. Konvitz, *Alien and Asiatic*, p. 81; Maurice R. Davie, *World Immigration: With Special Reference to the United States* (New York 1936), p. 328.

68. 16 *Stat.* 256 (1870).

69. Ozawa *v.* U.S., 260 U.S. 178 (1922). On the Japanese experience see Roger Daniels, *The Politics of Prejudice: The Anti-Japanese Movement in California and the Struggle for Japanese Exclusion* (Berkeley, 1962).

70. Ozawa *v.* U.S., 197.

71. Toyota *v.* U.S., 268 U.S. 402 (1924). The exclusion of Filipinos came as an obiter dictum, the Court ruling that since they owed allegiance to the U.S. as nationals, they were not "aliens," but they were not citizens, and since the 1790 Act provided for the naturalization of "aliens," the Filipinos were therefore ineligible. The case had raised the point of whether a Japanese member of the armed forces during World War I had properly been awarded a naturalization certificate by a lower court. The Court ruled he had not, basing its reasoning on the fact that while Congress in 1918 and 1919 had passed acts providing that "any alien" serving in the armed forces during the War could file for naturalization, those acts had not given any indication of eliminating from the definition of eligibility, in the 1790 Act, the distinction based on race or color. This was somewhat unusual given the fact that in the same year Congress extended the full rights of citizenship to American Indians, an action which some critics saw as strangely gratuitous given the fact that the Constitution already granted citizenship to all persons born in the country.

72. U.S. *v.* Bhagat Singh Thind, 261 U.S. 204 (1923).

ner now seen as chillingly similar to the racist analysis of Nazi Germany.[73]

Such rulings induced the Court also to consider more precisely the rights of those aliens now ineligible for citizenship. Again the results were restrictive. No dissent was forthcoming when the Court upheld various state laws denying aliens who had not declared their intention of becoming citizens the ability to own or acquire any interest in land within the state.[74] There was no deprivation of due process or equal protection of the laws in such a state measure, wrote Justice Butler in 1923 in a Washington case where Orientals were clearly the target even though under recent interpretation of federal statutes Japanese and Chinese were not entitled to become citizens and could not file legal declarations of intention to become citizens. And again reflecting the subjectivism of the majority, the justice, whose antagonism to state economic legislation was notable, now argued that while Congress had exclusive jurisdiction over immigration, naturalization, and the disposal of the public domain, each state in the absence of any treaty provision to the contrary had full legislative power to deny aliens the economic right to own land within its border or even to own stock in a corporation holding land for agricultural purposes.[75]

Taft, although an avowed partisan of the "little brown brother" during his earlier tenure as civil governor of the Philippines, held an equally adamant view about the limited rights of alien "brothers," brown, yellow, olive, or white, when their stateside behavior was someway not sufficiently orthodox by his standards. Interpreting a 1920 statute passed to expedite the deportation of undesirable aliens, many of whom had been charged with violation of wartime statutes, the Chief Justice rejected the contention that such a measure was invalid as an ex post facto law. The sovereign power to deport is limited only by treaty obligations, Taft argued, and an alien may therefore be deported for doing an act that was entirely legal when done but that has subsequently been declared illegal or criminal. Deportation, while burdensome and severe, was

73. *Ibid.*, p. 213. See Bernard Schwartz, *A Commentary on the Constitution of the United States: Rights of the Person* (2 vols., New York, 1968), II, 719.

74. Terrace *v.* Thompson, 263 U.S. 197 (1923); Porterfield *v.* Webb, 263 U.S. 313 (1923); Frick *v.* Webb, 263 U.S. 326 (1923).

75. Terrace *v.* Thompson, 217.

not punishment, he maintained, and the rights of such individuals were always subservient to the broader right to guarantee the safety and welfare of society.[76] Further, few procedural rights were to be afforded such an individual. If he claimed to be a citizen, he was entitled to a judicial trial, on the question of citizenship, but only on that question.[77] And the government was generally free from having to afford such a party the constitutional protection accorded to persons accused of crime—counsel, right to confront witnesses, right against self-incrimination. Indeed, the government was free from the restrictions guaranteed against unreasonable search and seizure in gathering information on potential deportable aliens.[78]

Finally the 1920s saw acknowledgment that there were constitutional aspects of the "Negro problem" that could not escape ultimate consideration. The presence of black Americans within the society was brought home clearly by events of the immediate postwar years. The intolerance of the "Red Scare" era spilled over into an ugly outburst of racism as well. Wartime labor shortages had drawn Negroes north. Most had stayed to compete with postwar white labor. Negro troops abroad had been accorded an equality they had never known in America. White Southerners were terrified at the thought of so many Negro men learning the use of firearms and the ways of equality, and were thus prepared to use violent means to remind returning Negro veterans that the war to make the world safe for democracy had been no war for racial democracy in America. Just such black frustrations led to new interest and support for unified action. The N.A.A.C.P., at the end of the war in militant hands, was determined to undertake an active crusade for expanded Negro rights, particularly in the courts. The by-products of such tension were ominous. Lynchings more than doubled between 1917 and 1919, with southern white terrorism also finding expression in a revival of the Ku Klux Klan that early made clear it had no intention of extending to its victims any semblance of due process of law. Race riots erupted in a dozen cities with the one in Chicago in July, 1919, leading ultimately to thirty-eight deaths, over five hundred injuries, more than one thousand families left homeless, and a riot

76. Mahler *v.* Eby, 264 U.S. 32, 39 (1924).
77. Ng Fung Ho *v.* White, 259 U.S. 276 (1921).
78. Bilokumsky *v.* Tod., 263 U.S. 149 (1923).

commission report whose findings were repeated with depressing similarity by a similar national body in the 1960s. Cooler heads in both the black and white communities sought some middle ground, eventually inducing the House of Representatives to pass an anti-lynching bill in 1921, making lynching a federal crime.[79] But the measure was defeated by a southern filibuster in the Senate leaving the courts the one possible agency of government in a position to afford any meaningful relief.

Judicial conservatives offered little encouragement to rising black expectations. Indeed, in certain areas the Taft majority even retreated from postures struck by the body under former southern Chief Justice White. In 1917 it had held a Louisville, Kentucky, ordinance providing that Negroes might not move into residential blocks where the occupants were primarily whites, to be undue interference with property rights and hence a denial of due process.[80] In 1926, Justice Sanford for a unanimous Court upheld a challenged restrictive covenant that provided that property should never be leased or sold to a Negro, maintaining that since no state action was involved, no violation of due process was present.[81] In *Nixon* v. *Herndon,* by contrast, Holmes, speaking for a unanimous Court, made clear that Texas could not by statute exclude Negroes from the Democratic primary without thereby violating the clause of the Fourteenth Amendment guaranteeing equal protection of the laws.[82] The ruling had little impact, however, since party leaders promptly found ways to make the essential primary decisions prior to the election, and by moving to deny Negroes membership in the party, in effect accomplished the same disfranchisement privately without having to resort to statutes. Thus, as in many other areas, it was

79. The figures on lynching in the decade are not self-revealing. The rise from thirty-eight in 1917 to eighty-three in 1919 clearly reflects immediate postwar tension, yet steady decline through the decade, with the exception of the year 1926, fits no easily ascertainable set of causative factors as does the sudden rise in 1933, 1934, and 1935. For data see Harry A. Ploski and Roscoe C. Brown, Jr. (eds.), *The Negro Almanac* (New York, 1967), pp. 212–215. The most revealing study is Robert L. Zangrando, "The Efforts of the National Association for the Advancement of Colored People to Secure Passage of a Federal Anti-Lynching Law, 1920–1940" (unpublished Ph.D. dissertation, University of Pennsylvania, 1963).

80. Buchanan *v.* Warley, 245 U.S. 60 (1917).

81. Corrigan *v.* Buckley, 271 U.S. 323 (1926). On the background of this and the Buchanan *v.* Warley case see Loren Miller, *The Petitioners: The Story of the Supreme Court of the United States and the Negro* (Cleveland, 1966), pp. 246–255.

82. Nixon *v.* Herndon, 273 U.S. 536 (1927).

possible to withdraw quickly to the sanctity of private or quasi-legal forms of discrimination, an area that even the most advanced judicial liberal was unwilling to enter, at least as long as the illusion of some degree of due process of law was maintained.

The Taft Court was reluctant to challenge the deeply ingrained legal code of the South and to take appeals involving issues such as miscegenation, segregated schools and juries, subtle disfranchisement, discrimination in public accommodations, and further restrictive covenant situations.[83] But it could not in good conscience submit to mob rule and lynch law with equanimity, when clearly such rule not only violated the entire spirit of the Bill of Rights, but offended millions of law-abiding and decent Americans. In the case of *Moore* v. *Dempsey,* which reached the Supreme Court in 1923, not only was a locally sanctioned judicial lynching ruled a denial of due process of law, but the majority approved Holmes's frank insistence that when legal proceedings were smoke screens for deeper injustices, the Court had a clear duty to "secure to the petitioners their constitutional rights."[84] And the situation could not have been more overt. As Max Lerner wrote in summary:

> one gets rapid glimpses of the entire pattern of power and opinion in the sharecropping South; the attempts to organize in the face of landowners terrorism, the meeting in the Negro church, the armed attack, the manhunt by vigilantes, the lynching mob, the Committee of Seven, the torturing of witnesses, the intimidation of counsel, the skeleton trial, the resolutions by the American Legion and the Rotary and Lions Clubs, the attempts to appease the mob spirit by hastening execution.[85]

83. The Court fully sustained the "separate but equal" concept in transportation in 1920, South Covington and Cincinnati R.R. *v.* Kentucky, 252 U.S. 399 (1920). However, a variety of lower court rulings clearly demonstrating anti-Negro bias did not reach it. See Wilson *v.* State, 101 So. 417, 20 Ala. App. 137 (1924); Weaver *v.* State, 116 So. 893, 22 Ala. App. 469 (1928); Jackson *v.* State, 129 So. 306, 23 Ala. App. 555 (1930); Chandler *v.* Neff, 298 Fed. 515 (1924); Ware *v.* State, 225 S.W. 626, 146 Ark. 321 (1920); Washington *v.* State, 116 So. 470, 95 Fla. 289 (1928); Bruster *v.* State, 266 P. 486, 40 Okl. Cr. 25 (1928); State *v.* Albritton, 224 P. 511, 98 Okl. 158 (1924); Bryant *v.* Barnes, 106 So. 113, 144 Miss. 732 (925); Berry *v.* City of Durham, 119 S.E. 748, 186 N.C. 420 (1923); Los Angeles Inv. Co. *v.* Gary, 186 P. 596, 181 Cal. 680 (1920); Tyler *v.* Harmon, 104 So. 200, 158 La. 439 (1925); Wyatt *v.* Adair, 110 So. 801, 215 Ala. 363 (1926); Goff *v.* Savage, 210 P. 374, 122 Wash. 194 (1922); and State *v.* Brown, 212 P. 663, 112 Kan. 814 (1923).

84. Moore *v.* Dempsey, 261 U.S. 86, 91 (1923).

85. Max Lerner, *The Mind and Faith of Justice Holmes* (New York, 1943), p. 347.

Little wonder that the President of the N.A.A.C.P., Moorfield Storey, worked to bring the case to the Supreme Court and appeared himself as one of the counsel for the Negroes.[86]

Similarly, despite bitter protest, the Justices did not find it difficult to reflect legally the broad-scale national hostility to the Ku Klux Klan. In a case in 1928, decided comfortably after the organization's broad-scale effectiveness had been decimated by internal scandal as well as effective countercampaigns against its irresponsible use of power, the Court upheld as no violation of equal protection a 1923 New York civil rights law that required organizations like the Klan to file sworn copies of constitutions, by-laws, rules, regulations, oaths of membership, rosters of membership, and lists of officers, even though other private and in some cases secret bodies like the Masons, Odd Fellows, and Knights of Columbus were exempted. One member charged that such revelation impaired his personal liberty. To this Justice Van Devanter replied, in an opinion in which his contempt for the body was implicit if not explicit, "his liberty in this regard, like most other personal rights, must yield to the rightful exertion of the police power."[87]

The achievements of legal liberalism in the 1920s are hard to evaluate. Immediate triumphs were few. But conceiving and enunciating the need for new national economic and social standards, while comprehending the difficulty of easy achievement, led to the exploration of the question of legal means, a process thereby possible with few inhibitions. The residue was a body of liberal legal alternatives important, given the precedent nature of American law, when later Courts sought to move to more emancipated and socially responsible positions.[88] Particularly important in this regard were the

86. Mark D. Howe, *Portrait of an Independent: Moorfield Storey* (Boston, 1932), pp. 250–257. Storey had also taken part in two earlier important Negro cases—Guinn *v.* U.S. (the Grandfather Clause case), 238 U.S. 347 (1915); and Buchanan *v.* Warley (the Louisville Residential Segregation case), 245 U.S. 60 (1917). See William B. Hixson, Jr., "Moorfield Storey and the Struggle for Equality," *Journal of American History,* LV (December, 1968), 545 ff.

87. New York *ex rel.* Bryant *v.* Zimmerman, 278 U.S. 63, 72 (1928). In a few cases where overt discrimination actually could not be conducted without running afoul of state legislation, the lower courts were willing to uphold the punishment of violations of it. See e.g., Hutson *v.* Owl Drug Co., 249 P. 525, 79 Cal. App. 390 (1926); Pickett *v.* Kuchan, 153 N.E. 667, 323 Ill. 138 (1926); Bolden *v.* Grand Rapids Operating Corp., 239 N.W. 241, 239 Mich. 318 (1927).

88. In comment on judicial behavior, Paul A. Freund has pointed to the accepted pattern of "throwing up bridges before and the burning of them behind, characteristic of juridical advance." Paul A. Freund, "The Supreme Court and

dissenting arguments of Holmes and Brandeis, and the carefully reasoned, but generally rejected, briefs presented to the Court by liberal attorneys from Felix Frankfurter and Louis Marshall to Walter Pollak and Moorfield Storey.

The fact that there were eloquent liberal dissenting voices on the high bench, and before it, was undoubtedly a blessing in disguise to its conservative majority. Much of the liberal left, and even a preponderance of national labor leaders, held increasingly skeptical views of the possibility of equal justice from the judicial establishment of the time. By posing the prospect of potential future liberalization and relief, the dissenting justices headed off what might well have become an open rejection or even unqualified assault upon that body had total reaction been its sole earmark.

Outside the courtroom it was hard to miss the ferment which was taking place in the scholarly world of law. While the realists by no means prevailed, their voices were widely heard and their critique of both legal methods and materials drew wide comment. Their students, in turn, not only carried the message, but moved quickly into important positions in government and education. It was significant, for example, that by the later years of the decade law review articles were beginning to be used as a legitimate adjunct to legal decision making, joining precedent, earlier treatises, and a priori social and economic predilections.[89]

Conditions in years following 1929 proved the stimulus for serious nationwide attention to the dissenters of the normalcy decade. The great crash of 1929 and the subsequent depression made governmental concern for the human needs of its citizens the nation's primary task. It was then that the ten-year crusade of legal liberals began to realize its deeply felt objectives. For with acknowledgment of the bankruptcy of conservative approaches, the legal course that liberalism had charted was now turned to eagerly. It suddenly seemed to present one option well worth exploring as a plausible way out of the nation's massive and bewildering crisis.

Civil Liberties," *Vanderbilt Law Review,* IV (April, 1951), 533. Undoubtedly, in retrospect, liberal opinions did serve as the bridges eventually crossed to new civil liberties positions.

89. See Max Radin, "Sources of Law—New and Old," *Southern California Law Review,* I (July, 1928), 411–421; and Chester A. Newland, "Legal Periodicals and the United States Supreme Court" (unpublished Ph.D. dissertation, University of Kansas, 1958).

CHAPTER 4

The Depression and the Emergence of Legal Realism

THE impact of the crash of 1929 upon the American psyche was profound. Initial shock and disbelief was quickly succeeded by bewilderment and despair. There was scapegoating too, with special bitterness directed at the pre-1929 pitchmen who had been glibly predicting that the "Era of Perpetual Prosperity" was near at hand. Surely the leadership of U.S. business had based its forecast on untenable assumptions or misinformation, or both, the critics said. Whatever the reasons for the miscalculation, the result was a widespread rejection of big business and its value system. And concomitant with this wholesale disenchantment was a sharp intensification of the pre-crash discontent with the American judicial system and what was perceived as its increasingly antisocial interpreters.

Judicial leadership had partially brought such stigma upon itself. By allying itself with the business community, the bench had made of itself an equally vulnerable target when the survivors of the economic disaster arose to search for the perpetrators. Clearly the crusade for insuring national prosperity and broad-scale social and economic opportunity through the uninhibited functioning of private capitalism, had flown false colors. Yet such admission, given the nature of the functioning of courts, had to come in the form of subtle legal recantations buried in the logic of formal opinions. It was thus bound to provide distressingly slow relief. Moreover, between 1929 and 1937 at least four Associate Justices of the Supreme Court were steadfast in their unwillingness to admit error in their previous judgments.

Americans in general, fighting panic and a sense of hopelessness, sought positive pathways out of the crisis. There seemed to be a national realization that out of the agonizing experience of the moment meaningful gain for the Republic could be achieved, that "much that was destroyed would never be recovered; much that was salvaged would be transformed and show only slight resemblance to the old."[1] If nothing else the years of the Great Depression enabled fresh study of the American institutional system. In the legal area this invited challenge of the continued application of general principles and their defense with flatulent rationalizations. Continued legal adherence to unworkable processes invited sharp criticism and calls for the finding of new paths to social, political, and economic stability. In this context formerly disregarded critics of the system in the twenties were now accorded serious attention.

And as the depression sloughed onward, demands for a restructuring of the entire political framework became stronger. Certainly it was by now evident that a legal system founded on the assumption that the law's central responsibility was to make the nation safe for unfettered use of private property was no longer viable. Why, indeed, turn to the Supreme Court as the wellspring of legal wisdom—a Court whose majority held consistently that under the Constitution it was impossible to attempt the solution of certain modern social problems by legislation. The times called, in the law, as in all other areas, for hardheaded realism derived from sharp and relentless analysis of the facts, with the solutions evolved to be ones geared to serve the needs of all the citizens of the nation through the establishment of uniform national standards. These would have to be based on what Karl Llewellyn claimed, in 1931, was the consensus of liberal demands, "an insistence on evaluation of any part of the law in terms of its effect, and an insistence on the worthwhileness of trying to find these effects. . . ."[2] The Constitution and the law it created would have to be enlisted in the redirected crusade

1. Albert U. Romasco, *The Poverty of Abundance: Hoover, the Nation, the Depression* (New York, 1965), p. viii.

2. Karl N. Llewellyn, "Some Realism About Realism," *Harvard Law Review*, XLIV (1931), 1237.

with due regard for the warning that "laws were a means to social ends, not ends in themselves."[3]

The political leadership to whom Americans looked for practical programs and workable institutions responded quickly. The Hoover administration had even taken a few timid steps in this direction in the months before the great crash. Alarmed by popular nose-thumbing at prohibition, Hoover had set up a National Commission on Law Observance and Enforcement, known as the Wickersham Commission, to study the whole problem of law enforcement.[4] The commission, although headed by Taft's former Attorney General, George W. Wickersham, drew upon the assistance of a number of liberals. Among these were Zechariah Chafee, Jr., of the Harvard Law School, who for the past decade had called for a reoriented law focused on the pursuit of social justice; and Walter H. Pollak, who in his briefs in Gitlow, Whitney, and Burns had devised a powerful federal deterrent for the abuse of power by local authorities.[5]

Hoover had also shown a serious concern for the farmer, urging legislation to treat agriculture as a national problem demanding national solutions.[6] And despite some straining of his political and

3. *Ibid.,* p. 1243. Much of the legal realists' most influential writing came during the depression period. See Llewellyn's *The Bramble Bush* (New York, 1930) and "The Constitution as an Institution," *Columbia Law Review,* XXXIV (1934), 1–40; Jerome Frank, *Law and the Modern Mind* (New York, 1930); and Thurman Arnold, *The Symbols of Government* (New Haven, 1935). Felix S. Cohen, *Ethical Systems and Legal Ideals: An Essay on the Foundations of Legal Criticism* (Ithaca, 1933), differed from other realist writing in seeking to set forth an ethical standard of legal criticism, while Fred Rodell's *Woe unto You, Lawyers!* (New York, 1939) was an iconoclastic assault upon legal pomposity written largely for the layman.

4. The body, known as the National Commission on Law Observance and Enforcement, produced in mid–1931 a fourteen-volume *Report* dealing with virtually every aspect of the functioning of the law from the operations of the federal courts and penal institutions, to criminal procedure and the cause and cost of crime (Washington, 1931).

5. Chafee and Pollak, along with Carl S. Stern, as members of a subcommittee of the National Commission charged with the particular study of "lawlessness in law enforcement," used the occasion to probe deeply into California's decade-long cause célèbre, the Tom Mooney affair. Their special report, however, was suppressed by the Commission and only published separately, and privately, after much liberal pressure; *The Mooney-Billings Report* (New York, 1932). See Curt Gentry, *Frame-Up: The Incredible Case of Tom Mooney and Warren Billings* (New York, 1957); and Richard H. Frost, *The Mooney Case.* (Stanford, 1968).

6. Hoover's Agricultural Marketing Act of 1929 (46 *Stat.* 11 [1929]) with its Federal Farm Board, contained a number of approaches to the agriculture program that had a strong influence on later New Deal legislation. Its constitutional

constitutional scruples, he in time also came to concede the need for relief of unemployment even though his proposed techniques to this end were inhibited by his narrow view of the law's role and scope.[7]

The depression also had sharp impact upon congressional leadership. Liberal reformers of the pre-crash years gained new stature and power, especially as the relevancy of their earlier criticism became more widely acknowledged. Typical was Senator George Norris, Nebraska Republican. After years of fighting the sale of the government's multimillion-dollar Muscle Shoals facilities to private industry for a few cents on the dollar, Norris saw his dream of a Tennessee Valley Authority unfold to complement a triumph of a few years earlier—enactment of the Twentieth or "Lame Duck" Amendment, aimed at enhancing congressional efficiency and responsibility.[8]

The times also effected a new look at the nation's benches. In 1930, Hoover appointed as Taft's successor one of the most highly respected legalists and statesmen of the day, Charles Evans Hughes. This caused congressional liberals to unleash an unexpected salvo of criticism against the former Justice, Presidential candidate, and Secretary of State. Although this failed to prevent Hughes's nomination, it left no doubt in his mind that his tenure on the Court would be subjected to constant liberal surveillance and criticism.[9]

---

base differed sharply, however. See Alexander Legg, *The Agricultural Marketing Act* (Washington, 1930).

7. Romasco, *Poverty of Abundance,* pp. 129 ff.

8. John W. Bystrom, "Senator George W. Norris and the Muscle Shoals Struggle" (unpublished Ph.D. dissertation, University of Minnesota, 1960). For Norris' views see *Fighting Liberal: The Autobiography of George W. Norris* (New York, 1945). The definitive study of Norris, by Richard Lowitt, is being written, Volume one, *George W. Norris: The Making of a Progressive, 1861–1912* (Syracuse, 1963), having appeared. An interpretive study is Norman L. Zucker, *George W. Norris* (Urbana, Ill., 1966).

9. Hughes's semiofficial biographer, Merlo J. Pusey, is undoubtedly correct in contending that "the Insurgents were striking more at the Taft court and the Hoover Administration than at Hughes as an individual. For the moment Hughes was made an unwitting symbol of the philosophy which they believed to be responsible for the country's economic convulsions." Merlo J. Pusey, *Charles Evans Hughes* (2 vols. New York, 1951), pp. ii, 659. As Senator Clarence Dill of Washington said at the time, "the insurgents merely wished to place in the Record . . . a warning" and arouse the public to the fact that if they "would free themselves and have justice at the hands of their Government they must reach the Supreme Court . . . by putting men on that bench who hold economic theories which are fair and just to all, and not in the interest of the privileged few." *Congressional Record,* 71st Cong., 2d Sess., LXXII (Feb. 12, 1930), 3500.

Other Hoover appointees met similar response. Later in the same year when Associate Justice Sanford retired, Hoover named as his replacement a faithful southern Republican, Judge John J. Parker of North Carolina. But when Parker's antilabor record and anti-Negro attitudes were revealed in the press, the Senate rejected the nomination and Hoover had no choice but to withdraw it.[10]

The President then nominated Owen J. Roberts, a noncontroversial Philadelphia lawyer, in time to become one of the most controversial justices in Supreme Court history. Roberts, scion of a prosperous and conservative Philadelphia family, had served publicly as assistant district attorney of Philadelphia and special prosecutor in espionage cases in that region during World War I. On the recommendation of Harlan Fiske Stone, President Coolidge had appointed him to prosecute the Teapot Dome oil case, and his careful but relentless legal work had sent Secretary of Interior Albert B. Fall to prison. Generally, however, his pre-Court career had been spent in private law—as a member of a staid law firm; as professor at the University of Pennsylvania Law School; and as attorney for the Pennsylvania Railroad and member of the board of a half-dozen other large companies. Roberts privately, at the time, expressed serious doubts about his capacity for high court service. Writing to Felix Frankfurter, he indicated that he accepted the nomination with "a good deal of trepidation."[11] But he went on to indicate he considered legal adjudication to be essentially a process of finding the right principle and applying it properly, a view that seemed to

10. Richard L. Watson, "The Defeat of Judge Parker: A Study in Pressure Groups and Politics," *Mississippi Valley Historical Review,* L (September, 1963), 213–234; William C. Burris, *The Senate Rejects a Judge: A Study of the John J. Parker Case* (Chapel Hill, N.C., 1962). Actually Parker's later record as a federal circuit court judge was marked by strong support both of Negro voting rights (Rice *v.* Elmore, 165 F. 2d 387 [1947], Baskin *v.* Brown, 174 F. 2d 391 [1949]) and racial integration (Mayor and City Council of Baltimore *v.* Dawson, 220 F. 2d 386 [1955]; Fleming *v.* South Carolina Electric and Gas Co., 224 F. 2d 752 [1956]).

11. Owen J. Roberts to Felix Frankfurter, May 20, 1930, Frankfurter Papers, Library of Congress. The harassed Hoover was slow to read the public pulse correctly. In early 1932, shortly after Holmes's resignation, he named Judge James H. Wilkerson of Chicago to the 7th Circuit Court of Appeals. Wilkerson was known for having sentenced Al Capone to prison, but any advantage thus accrued was overshadowed by his name being synonymous with the hated injunction of the Shopmen's Strike of the early 1920s. Public furor exceeded that against Parker, and Wilkerson eventually requested the President to withdraw his name. See Irving Bernstein, *The Lean Years* (Boston, 1960), pp. 411, 550–551.

recognize neither the dynamic quality of the law nor the impossibility of a judge freeing himself from his basic predispositions.

Roberts' appointment did not assuage public demand for more progressive members of the bench. When Holmes retired in 1932, the clamor for a liberal successor who would epitomize as nearly as possible his humanism, common sense, and socially enlightened skepticism, virtually forced Hoover, against his better judgment and natural instincts,[12] to replace him with Benjamin N. Cardozo. Cardozo's widely respected Yale lectures, *The Nature of the Judicial Process,* had identified him with legal pragmatism, and a view that formal legal rules should be measured by their social value and the extent to which they contributed to the welfare of society.[13] A member of New York's highest court, the Court of Appeals, it was generally acknowledged that he had been the primary force in elevating it into the second most distinguished tribunal in the United States largely by translating common-law principles into workable legal rules for an industrial society.

Taft closed out his nine years in the Chief Justiceship on a note of apprehensive defiance, fearing that his carefully erected legal structure would have to be protected, virtually by fair means or foul.[14] Hughes entered the same position far more sensitive to the

12. William E. Borah is generally held to be responsible for convincing a reluctant Hoover, disturbed both by Cardozo's "geography" (Hughes and Stone were both New Yorkers) and his religion (there was one Jew on the bench, Brandeis) that neither objection was valid and that "just as John Adams is best remembered for his appointment of John Marshall to the Supreme Court, so you, Mr. President, have the opportunity of being best remembered for putting Cardozo there." Felix Frankfurter, "Benjamin Nathan Cardozo," in the *Dictionary of American Biography* (New York, 1958), Supp. I, pp. 94–95. See also Claudius O. Johnson, *Borah of Idaho* (Seattle, 1967), pp. 452–453.

13. Benjamin N. Cardozo, *The Nature of the Judicial Process* (New Haven, 1921), pp. 66, 102, 150. Cardozo was more circumspect than the legal realists with regard to departure from precedent, however. Convinced that there was justice in legal consistency, he argued that litigants had to have faith in the even-handed administration of justice in the courts. Wilfrid E. Rumble, Jr., *American Legal Realism* (Ithaca, 1968), pp. 193–194. There is no adequate biography of Cardozo. Existing works include Joseph P. Pollard, *Mr. Justice Cardozo* (New York, 1938); George S. Hellman, *Benjamin Nathan Cardozo* (New York, 1940); and Beryl H. Levy, *Cardozo and the Frontiers of Legal Thinking* (New York, 1938). See also "Mr. Justice Cardozo," *Harvard Law Review,* LII (1939), 353–498; and Walter Gouch, "The Legal Theory of Justice Benjamin Cardozo" (unpublished Ph.D. dissertation, Johns Hopkins University, 1954).

14. Alpheus T. Mason, *William Howard Taft: Chief Justice* (New York, 1964), pp. 294–297.

risks the Supreme Court would run should it persist in its antisocial intransigence. A legal system geared only to guaranteeing the privileges of private property was a growing target of articulate social critics. The premise that the law was essentially a compilation of legal "thou shalt nots" was rapidly losing support. Even the popular press was insisting that positive legal ways had to be devised to underscore the obligations of property in a democratic society. Hughes realized that the Supreme Court would have to take the lead in evolving new legal guarantees that would insure that attempts at the positive solution of social and economic problems through the elected branches of the government would not fall victim to the judicial ax before extended operation afforded an opportunity to test their practicality.

The question was one of legal means. But there was no dearth of options. The dissents of Holmes, Brandeis, and Stone, while speaking negatively to antisocial rulings of the 1920s, contained in a general way constructive alternatives. The legal realists, although their concern was more with the method and content of jurisprudence than concrete programs, had stimulated a body of analysis of explicit legal problems that made their dimensions more realistic. By 1930, it was becoming a more broadly accepted judicial practice, particularly in weighing the legality of a statute, to "recognize that almost any official source contemporary with [its] passage might be used in its interpretation."[15] The effect of such background evidence was to be gauged by its credibility, and not by its compliance with formal rules of competence. Similarly, there was strong pressure to square legal practices with their historic evolution and purpose and to bring some degree of functioning harmony between such easily mouthed legal clichés as due process of law, equal protection of the laws, freedom of speech and press, and especially federalism, with actual observance and practice. But whether the road was to be through judicial activism or judicial self-restraint, statutory construction or strong judicial review was not clear.

Disagreement clearly existed on the bench. Brandeis, whose influence was now strong and increasing, pressed for solutions grounded

15. James Willard Hurst, *The Growth of American Law* (Boston, 1950), p. 187.

heavily in his early Wilsonian Progressivism and in the utility of rejuvenating federalism. His strong conviction persisted that man could be reformed through reforming society, and that man, being rational, could solve his own problems if given the opportunity to exert some mastery over his own destiny without constant legal harassment and restriction. He called now, more insistently, for the reinvigoration of state responsibility and state functions. Such a posture was not new. Brandeis, in fact, had felt so strongly that "the new Progressivism requires local development—quality not quantity," that he had earlier endorsed Taft's voiding of the second Child Labor Act, clearly on these grounds. Such a posture, he hoped, would stimulate the beginning of an epoch, "the epoch of State Duties."[16]

Yet Brandeis himself was not uninfluenced by Holmes's healthy skepticism in this regard. He had no starry-eyed conviction that the people by democratic processes through their elected state assemblies would attain perfect, or even the most practicable, solutions for all problems. He was willing to admit, with Holmes and Stone, that local democracy's greatest asset lay in the potential it had for enabling the group conflicts inevitable in all society to find a relatively harmless outlet in the give and take of legislative compromise.[17] But the alternative made him highly apprehensive. His chronic fear of the insensitivity of bigness gave him a stake in the greater desirability of local solutions, which he saw as viable instruments for dealing with national economic and social problems. The same view helps to explain the jaundiced eye he cast on massive, untried national programs and panaceas early evolved by New Deal planners.

Hughes and Roberts, representing a modern strand of judicial thought, were challenged to reassess their responsibilities in the light of the developing depression. In his public career, Hughes had responded with sensitivity to what he conceived to be the realities of power and national leadership. As a Taft-appointed

16. Alpheus T. Mason, *Brandeis: A Free Man's Life* (New York, 1946) p. 558. Holmes, despite his earlier dissent in Hammer *v.* Dagenhart, 247 U.S. 251 (1917), had joined Taft also in voiding the second child labor measure. Speculation still exists as to his unarticulated reasons. See Mason, *Taft,* pp. 248–249.

17. Irving Dilliard (ed.), *The Spirit of Liberty: Papers and Addresses of Learned Hand* (New York, 1953), pp. 203–204.

Associate Justice in the years 1910 to 1916, his opinions, particularly on the interpretation of the commerce clause, had reflected Progressive faith in the salutary impact of positive public regulation of the economy.[18] His 1916 campaign for the Presidency against Woodrow Wilson had stressed his general concern with the public interest. Although he returned to private law practice following his narrow defeat, he remained alert to public developments, deploring particularly the "Red" hysteria that swept the nation in late 1919 and early 1920. Ever aware of the public responsibilities of men of his class and position, he leaped into the fray when five duly elected Socialist members of the New York Assembly were arbitrarily denied their seats due solely to their political commitments. Joining with a number of other prominent conservatives both in the New York City and State bar associations, he publicly decried such a prostitution of the democratic process, leading a delegation of lawyers to Albany to protest to the Assembly directly.[19] The reaction, particularly against irresponsible power-hungry public officials, stemming from the "Red Scare," impelled Hughes to manifest concern for the restoration of the proper rule of law. But despite his acceptance of the Secretaryship of State under Harding, he did not acquiesce in the return of power to the hands of self-aggrandizing business leaders. Rather, he saw the decade as requiring the return of the control of society to the hands of responsible private individuals, who, in a new spirit of private paternalism and stewardship, would accept the responsibility of continuing to advance the morality of American society. This did not mean that self-appointed natural leadership should personally take power away from irresponsible government officials, even if this were possible. It did mean that a restoration of informal social controls, through which it would be possible to maintain a type of peaceful, orderly society, had to be reestablished. Such leadership could function smoothly without resort to overt legal coercion

18. On the early phase of Hughes's judical career see Samuel Hendel, *Charles Evans Hughes and the Supreme Court* (New York, 1951).

19. Merlo J. Pusey, *Charles Evans Hughes* (2 vols., New York, 1951), I, 391 ff.; Zechariah Chafee, Jr., *Free Speech in the United States* (Cambridge, Mass., 1941), pp. 269 ff.; Louis Waldman, *Labor Lawyer* (New York, 1944), pp. 97–104; Charles Reznikoff (ed.), *Louis Marshall: Champion of Liberty* (2 vols., Philadelphia, 1957), II, pp. 977–985.

or open governmental flaunting of its authority, and could find private ways to minimize social tensions and prevent open outbreaks without resort to harsh curtailment. Such an attitude led Hughes to encourage the further development of legal aid clinics and to work personally in the Legal Aid Society; to support the work of various private welfare organizations; and to join with his later successor as Chief Justice, Harlan Fiske Stone, in founding the American Arbitration Association in 1926. This nonprofit body quickly became the principal agency for commercial arbitration in the nation, affording an efficient and speedy way for the resolving of commercial disputes.[20]

Hughes saw the depression underscoring a clear necessity for the relocation of power and leadership. With the prestige and socially responsible image of private leaders badly tarnished and the magnitude of the social and economic problems facing the nation unprecedented, it was unrealistic for the law to continue to benefit solely private property owners and private leaders on the assumption that they in turn could bring stability and successful operation to society. Clearly new people had to be found to accept such leadership. And with virtually all people in the nation now actively seeking national solutions to the chaos that affected all, it was now much more plausible to extend power more broadly to wider numbers and once more trust the democratic process. In fact, courts might well play a significant role in stimulating such a development as well as act as a solicitous monitor, encouraging experimentation, while standing ready to draw the line when democracy resorted to clearly extreme and irresponsible approaches. The immediate challenge was to recreate public respect for the judiciary in order that it might stand some chance of success in playing this role.

In the years between 1930 and early 1937, the Justices took the initiative in significant decisions in which they followed their particular predilections toward restoring national stability. Such actions paralleled, but were independent of (and frequently in contradiction to) the dramatic new national programs of the New Deal. Almost without exception, such judicial policy-reshaping involved sharp modification of the legal principles and presump-

20. Frances Kellor, *American Arbitration: Its History, Functions and Achievements* (New York, 1948).

tions of the previous decade. Only to the extent that Taft had increased the formal and institutional power of the Supreme Court, did the body build on his contributions.

In the area of state police power, action early in Hughes's regime presaged significant legal liberalization. On January 5, 1931, the Court handed down a ruling in a complex insurance case cited as *O'Gorman and Young* v. *Hartford Fire Insurance Company.* Over the vigorous protest of Van Devanter, McReynolds, Sutherland, and Butler, who held resolutely to formulas and procedures such as freedom of contract, the restrictive alteration of the public interest doctrine, and the pressing judicial obligation to check any legislative interference with property, Brandeis upheld a New Jersey price-fixing statute regulating commissions paid fire insurance agents. Hughes and Roberts voted with the majority. In contrast with the dissenters' strong allegation that the Court "must determine whether thus construed, and in the absence of any emergency, the statute necessarily conflicts with the Fourteenth Amendment,"[21] Brandeis contended that the facts surrounding the statute's origins and its operation should be determinative—"the presumption of constitutionality must prevail, in the absence of some factual foundation of record for overthrowing the statute." The business of insurance, he argued, "is so far affected with a public interest that the state may regulate the rates.[22] As to the insurance company's argument that "liberty of contract cannot be arbitrarily and unnecessarily interfered with under the guise of protecting the public," he merely made clear that, in his opinion, "the statute here questioned deals with a subject clearly within the scope of the police power."[23]

A complete judicial switch was far from automatic, however. Hughes, who came to sustain the powers of the states in virtually all police power situations, joined the conservatives in 1932 to strike down an Oklahoma law regulating the ice business.[24] An alarmed Brandeis wrote an eloquent and hopefully didactic dissent renewing his pleas for judicial toleration of state legislative activity. In an opinion that necessitated rather sharp confinement of his instinctive antimonopoly principles (the state was clearly fostering

21. O'Gorman and Young *v.* Hartford Fire Ins. Co., 282 U.S. 251, 266 (1931).
22. *Ibid.,* p. 257.
23. *Ibid.,* pp. 256–257.
24. New State Ice Co. *v.* Liebmann, 285 U.S. 262 (1932).

monopoly by forbidding anyone from entering the ice business without first obtaining from the State Corporation Commission a certificate of convenience and necessity), Brandeis resorted to legal pragmatism. He rejected any implication that monopoly could not be stimulated by the state when the public welfare demanded, or that the scope of governmental regulation depends upon the character of the business involved. "The notion of a distinct category of business 'affected with a public interest' employing property 'devoted to public use' rested upon historical error," he argued. "The true principle is that the state's power extends to every regulation of any business reasonably required and appropriate for the public protection." And he went on to contend that only by inquiring into "conditions existing in the community" could it be determined whether the regulation of a particular business or service was permissible.[25]

But Brandeis also criticized the majority for not taking adequate account of depression conditions throughout the nation, conditions producing "an emergency more serious than war." Sutherland's majority opinion had argued that no matter how pressing the conditions out of which such legislation emerged, there were "certain essentials of liberty" that must not be interfered with "in the interest of experiments."[26] Brandeis rejoined that in circumstances of national emergency, government must be even more free to experiment with various attacks on the grave economic problems facing the country. "I cannot believe," the justice observed, "that the framers of the Fourteenth Amendment, or the States which ratified it, intended to deprive us of the power to correct the evils of technological unemployment and excess productive capacity which have attended progress in the useful arts." "It is one of the happy incidents of the federal system," he concluded, "that a single courageous State may, if its citizens choose, serve as a laboratory; and try novel social and economic experiments without risk to the rest of the country." And he again expressed his deep belief that for the justices to set themselves up as an agency to check such experimentation created the serious danger that "we erect our prejudices into legal principles."[27]

25. *Ibid.*, p. 303.
26. *Ibid.*, p. 280.
27. *Ibid.*, pp. 307–308.

As the depression intensified, the Court came quickly to recognize the dangers inherent in rejecting depression-spawned emergency legislation and became equally as sensitive to the need for enlightened judicial experimentation with emergency theories that might serve to uphold it. In 1933, the Minnesota legislature, in the face of mounting pressure from angry farmers, threatened through wholesale foreclosures with the loss of their means of production and livelihood, enacted a Mortgage Moratorium Law.[28] The statute, clearly an emergency measure, was designed to postpone executive sales after mortgages had been foreclosed, thus allowing the extension by court order of the redemption period, and thereby offering property owners time to save their homes and farms. The law was promptly attacked by equally distressed creditors as an unconstitutional impairment of the obligation of contracts, even though a specific provision had been included in the statute for the interim payment of rent or fees from income derived during the moratorium period.

Hughes's opinion sustaining the measure was a masterpiece both of legal realism and pragmatic readaption of the law to the era. Citing a chain of precedents for the exercise of police power in regard to the health, welfare, and morals of the people, he spoke of the "growing appreciation of public needs and of the necessity of finding ground for a rational compromise between individual rights and public welfare." "The settlement and consequent contraction of the public domain, the pressure of a constantly increasing density of population, the interrelation of the activities of our people and the complexity of our economic interests, have inevitably led to an increased use of the organization of society in order to protect the very bases of individual opportunity," argued the Chief Justice. "Where, in earlier days, it was thought that only

28. The enactment capped widespread farmer lawlessness in the state, plus a caravan of several thousand farmers descending upon the legislature, making demands and threats and uttering dire predictions. The governor threatened to invoke martial law in aid of the farmers and actually issued an executive order directing all sheriffs to refrain from conducting foreclosure sales until after the legislative session. William L. Prosser, "The Minnesota Mortgage Moratorium," *Southern California Law Review,* VII (1934), 353–355; Edward S. Corwin, "Moratorium over Minnesota," *University of Pennsylvania Law Review,* LXXXII (1934), 311–316; Jane P. Clark, "Emergencies and the Law," *Political Science Quarterly,* XXXIX (1934), 268–283.

the concerns of individuals or of classes were involved, and that those of the state itself were touched only remotely, it has later been found that the fundamental interests of the state are directly affected; and that the question is no longer merely that of one party to a contract as against another, but of the use of reasonable means to safeguard the economic structure upon which the good of all depends."[29] Quoting with approval John Marshall's memorable warning: "We must never forget that it is a Constitution we are expounding . . . a Constitution intended to endure for ages to come and consequently to be adapted to the various *crises* of human affairs,"[30] the Chief Justice found legal justification for modifying the rigid constitutional stricture against states impairing the obligation of contracts. This, he argued, derived from the higher need for readapting that clause so as to insure the capacity of the states to protect their fundamental interest through the recognition of public needs. This in turn reflected the clear relationship of individual right to public security.

Sutherland's predictable and traditional dissent, joined in by his three conservative soulmates, brought into focus even more sharply the boldness of Hughes's new path. He objected strongly to Hughes's contention that "although an emergency does not create power, it may furnish occasion for the exercise of power," and that "the constitutional question presented in the light of an emergency is whether the power possessed embraces the particular exercise of it in response to particular conditions."[31] Such a course, he warned, was the road to potential catastrophe. "He simply closes his eyes to the necessary implications of the decision who fails to see in it the potentiality of future gradual but ever-advancing encroachments upon the sanctity of private and public contracts," wrote Sutherland. "The effect of the Minnesota legislation, though serious enough in itself, is of trivial significance compared with the far more serious and dangerous inroads upon the limitations of the Constitution which are almost certain to ensue as a consequence naturally following any step beyond the boundaries fixed by that instrument."

29. Home Building and Loan Assn. *v.* Blaisdell, 290 U.S. 398, 442 (1934).

30. McCulloch *v.* Maryland, 4 Wheaton 316, 407, 415 (1819). For perceptive observations on Hughes's use of history in the decision see Charles A. Miller, *The Supreme Court and the Uses of History* (Cambridge, Mass., 1969), Chap. 3.

31. Home Building and Loan Assn. *v.* Blaisdell, 426.

The Constitution, he argued, was not merely a collection of political maxims to be adhered to or disregarded according to the prevailing sentiment, but a law enacted by the people in their sovereign capacity that could not be changed by events, nor was it "competent for any department in the government to change . . . or declare it changed, simply because it appears to be ill adapted to a new state of things."[32]

Sutherland also made clear the growing distinction between judicial liberals and judicial conservatives over the nature of the judicial function. Hughes had asserted that the generality of the contract clause required a "process of construction . . . to fill in the details."[33] The anguished dissenter retorted that it was not a judge's business to interpret; he had only to apply the Constitution. That instrument carried its own interpretation since it spoke "in such plain English words that it would seem that the ingenuity of man could not evade them." Therefore, wrote Sutherland (that prime architect in readapting the law in the twenties to fit the needs of business and in reembodying the principles of laissez-faire, and who was shortly to join with enthusiasm in the negation of a battery of nationally enacted statutes), "a judge must declare the law as written, leaving it to the people themselves to make such changes as new circumstances may require."[34] Not only could it not be changed by events; it could not be changed by judges so long as they acted judicially.

Despite the pronouncement of such a plague upon the liberals' new course, they continued to follow it. Less than two months later a five-man majority upheld the price-fixing provisions of a 1933 New York statute creating a state Milk Control Board with broad regu-

32. *Ibid.*, p. 448. In Ashton *v.* Cameron County Water District, 298 U.S. 513 (1936), the Court made clear that the question of state finances was a matter of sovereignty, voiding a Municipal Bankruptcy Act permitting municipalities and other political subdivisions of states to file petitions in voluntary bankruptcy. If emergency power was to be wielded by local units, the conservatives, at least, felt they should not be too local, and certainly it was not the role of the federal government to bypass the state governments and encourage their lesser units to operate independently, even though the states were encouraged to take this kind of action vis-à-vis the national government.

33. *Ibid.*, p. 435.

34. *Ibid.*, p. 452.

latory powers.[35] The statute, whose enactment paralleled national attempts at stabilizing industry through the public elimination of cutthroat competition, was promptly challenged. After the board fixed nine cents as the minimum retail store price for a quart of milk, Leo Nebbia, a Rochester grocer, was caught selling two quarts of milk and a five-cent loaf of bread for eighteen cents. Convicted of violating the board's order, he appealed on the ground that the statute violated his rights under the due process and equal protection clauses of the Fourteenth Amendment by imposing unwarranted restrictions upon the use of property and the making of contracts. The milk industry, it was also contended, was not a business affected with a public interest, and as such public control of rates or prices within it was per se unreasonable and unconstitutional.

Justice Roberts' opinion was a resounding assertion of the necessary predominance of the general public interest over all private rights of property and contract. Specifically, Roberts sustained the power of a state to adopt whatever economic policy it might deem reasonable to best promote the public welfare, including price control if such seemed warranted.[36] "Under our form of government," he wrote, "the use of property and the making of contracts are normally matters of private and not public concern. The general rule is that both shall be free of governmental interference. But neither property rights nor contract rights are absolute; for government cannot exist if the citizen may at will use his property to the detriment of his fellows, or exercise his freedom of contract to work them harm. Equally fundamental with the private right

35. The New York State Milk Control Act (New York Code, Chapter 158, Laws of 1933) had created a control board with power "to regulate the entire milk industry of New York State, including the production, transportation, manufacture, storage, distribution, delivery and sale." After considering "all conditions affecting the milk industry including the amount necessary to yield a reasonable return to the producer and to the milk dealer," the board was required to order the minimum wholesale and retail prices to be charged for milk handled within the state, See Victor G. Rosenblum, *Law as a Political Instrument* (New York, 1955), pp. 12–37.

36. Nebbia *v.* New York, 291 U.S. 502 (1934). Roberts thus, in effect, elevated to majority status the earlier dissents of Stone in Ribnik *v.* McBride, 277 U.S. 350, 360–361 (1927), and Brandeis in New State Ice *v.* Liebmann, 285 U.S. 262, 304 (1932), in which each had argued that there was no difference between price control and other forms of regulation, each being clearly within the state's legislative power.

is that of the public to regulate it in the common interest. . . ."[37]

The decision was a landmark, also, in the permanent retirement of one of the principal legal tools of the conservatives. In responding to the charge that the milk industry was not affected with a public interest, Roberts admitted this to be true, in the traditional context of that concept. He then went on to declare the concept irrelevant to modern conditions, stating categorically that "there is no closed class or category of business affected with a public interest." A realistic approach to public regulation demanded that the only judicial basis for modifying it would be that its functioning demonstrated that a specific measure was unreasonable, arbitrary, or discriminatory. "With the wisdom of the policy adopted," Roberts stated, "with the adequacy or practicability of the law enacted to forward it, the courts are both incompetent and unauthorized to deal."[38]

Despite the seeming finality of the position, substantive due process as a device for limiting state power did not die with the Nebbia ruling. Other portions of the New York Milk Control Act were subsequently ruled unconstitutional,[39] and to the great distress and alarm of not only judicial liberals, but high-level New Deal administrators, and even prominent liberal Republicans, the Court took a disturbing step backward in June, 1936, in throwing out New York's 1933 minimum wage law.[40] Roberts in this instance

37. Nebbia *v.* New York, 291 U.S. 502, 523 (1934).

38. *Ibid.,* p. 536. The position brought a predictable rejoinder from McReynolds, speaking for the minority. "I think," he wrote, "this Court must have regard to the wisdom of the enactment." *Ibid.,* p. 556. Or, as Alpheus T. Mason has written: "That is, the Supreme Court under the Fourteenth Amendment, must act as a super-legislature." Alpheus T. Mason, *The Supreme Court from Taft to Warren* (Baton Rouge, 1958), p. 83.

39. Baldwin *v.* Seelig, 294 U.S. 511 (1935); Borden's *v.* Ten Eyck, 297 U.S. 251 (1936); Mayflower Farms *v.* Ten Eyck, 297 U.S. 266 (1936). The cases differed in that a complicating question of interstate commerce was introduced in each. Prior to this the Court had extended the Nebbia doctrine, Hegeman Farms *v.* Baldwin, 293 U.S. 163 (1934), by adding to the public health considerations of the statute the importance of sustaining the power of the state to legislate for the economic welfare of an industry vital to the state. See also Panhandle Co. *v.* Highway Comm'n., 294 U.S. 613 (1935).

40. Morehead *v.* New York *ex rel.* Tipaldo, 298 U.S. 587 (1936). Stone in his dissent was adamant that "we should follow our decision in the Nebbia case and leave the selection and the method of the solution of the problems to which the statute is addressed where it seems to me the Constitution has left them, to the legislative branch of the government" (at 636). Hughes expressed similar distress, finding nothing in the federal Constitution "which denies to the State the power to protect women from being exploited . . ." (at 619).

joined with the conservatives in a puzzling rejection of his earlier position.[41] Thus it took the pressure of Roosevelt's threat to "pack" the Court in early 1937 to solidify the liberal position of broad permissibility for state economic regulation. And only with Hughes's famous ruling in the case of *West Coast Hotel* v. *Parish* was the formerly devastating weapon of the conservatives, "liberty of contract," retired once and for all as a device for those seeking legal refuge from regulation by state authority.[42]

In other areas of legal adjudication, the new Hughes bench made strong efforts to overcome the social insensitivity of its predeçessor. Among the most bitter critics of the Taft Court had been the spokesmen for organized labor. What irked them the most was the overt abuse of the injunction to stymie labor's efforts to improve its plight. But the labor injunction was a double-edged sword. A few months after Hughes's return to the bench he handed down an utterly unpredicted decision sustaining the Railway Labor Act of 1926 and the issuance under it of an injunction to members of a labor organization seeking to enjoy its benefits. The Texas and New Orleans Railroad Company had, through pressure and coercion, forced its employees to reject the Brotherhood of Railway and Steamship Clerks as a collective bargaining agent and confine their membership solely to the company's union. In sustaining

41. Pusey, *Charles Evans Hughes,* II, 701, contends that Roberts voted with the conservatives because he felt the counsel for New York's reasoning was disingenuous, but later felt the reactionary tone of Butler's majority opinion was very distasteful. On Roberts' vote here and his later controversial reversal see John W. Chambers, "The Big Switch: Justice Roberts and the Minimum-Wage Cases," *Labor History,* X (Winter, 1969), 44–73.

42. West Coast Hotel *v.* Parish, 300 U.S. 379 (1937). In his majority opinion, Hughes queried: "What is this freedom? The Constitution does not speak of freedom of contract. It speaks of liberty and prohibits the deprivation of liberty without due process of law. In prohibiting that deprivation the Constitution does not recognize an absolute and uncontrollable liberty. Liberty in each of its phases has its history and connotation. But the liberty safeguarded is liberty in a social organization which requires the protection of law against the evils which menace the health, safety, morals and welfare of the people. Liberty under the Constitution is thus necessarily subject to the restraints of due process, and regulation which is reasonable in relation to its subject and is adopted in the interests of the community is due process" (at 391). See Robert L. Stern, "The Problems of Yesteryear—Commerce and Due Process," *Vanderbilt Law Review,* IV (1951), 446–468; Robert E. Rodes, "Due Process and Social Legislation in the Supreme Court—a Post Mortem," *Notre Dame Lawyer,* XXXIII (1957), 5–33; John A. C. Hetherington, "State Economic Regulation and Substantive Due Process of Law," *Northwestern University Law Review,* LIII (1958), 13–32, 222–251; Virginia Wood, *Due Process of Law, 1932–1949* (Baton Rouge, 1951).

the workers' move to enjoin such action, Hughes made it clear that freedom of choice in the selection of representatives, as provided by the Act, was basic and not a deprivation of due process of the company. He also suggested that the statutory requirements were susceptible of enforcement by appropriate proceedings. Citing John Marshall that "the right is created and the remedy exists,"[43] he made clear that the carriers subject to the act had no right to interfere with the freedom of the employees to make such selection as seemed most beneficial for securing their interests and demands. Further he found no grounds for complaint against the statute on constitutional grounds. Yet Hughes was clearly acting to implement a specific congressional action in a specific area.[44] While labor was heartened by Hughes's apparent desire to make the injunction available equally to employers and employees, any broad-scale application of this principle or of the wider one of undercutting the use of the injunction as a general legal restraint on strikes, picketing, and other forms of nonviolent labor pressure had to await further congressional legislation. The demand for action in this area had clearly preceded the depression crisis. Labor's fulminations against the revival of the injunction in the Duplex case, and particularly its cries of "foul" following the massive use of governmental-promoted injunctions to break the Railway Shopmen's strike in 1922 had reached a good many sensitive ears beyond those of rank and file membership. Not only did such legal action seem unfair in weighing the law so heavily on the side of one class, but its concrete results were distressing. Instead of producing industrial harmony through a coerced acknowledgment of property's transcendent rights, such denial of relief through orderly legal channels invited resort to extralegal ones. The result was inevitable violence. As Irving Bernstein has pointed out, "no other advanced nation in the world conducted its industrial relations with such defiance of the criminal law as the United States in the 1920s."[45]

The campaign for congressional relief, when mounted in 1927,

43. Texas and New Orleans Railroad *v.* Brotherhood of Railway & Steamship Clerks, 281 U.S. 548, 569–570 (1930).

44. Further, Hughes saw the situation as one fundamentally affecting interstate commerce, which the federal government could protect and advance through appropriate legislation. *Ibid.*, p. 570.

45. Bernstein, *The Lean Years,* p. 204.

drew the support of numerous aroused individuals. Warnings from men like Newton D. Baker, William E. Borah, and George Wharton Pepper, that judges invited disrespect for the law and courts if justice became obviously one-sided,[46] were expanded upon by legal liberals, notably Zechariah Chafee, Jr., Felix Frankfurter,[47] and the American Civil Liberties Union. That body, by the latter years of the decade, had made legislation curtailing the injunction one of its prime objectives. Its annual report of 1928–29 stated: "The most extensive restrictions on free speech and assemblage are caused by injunctions in industrial conflicts. It is the weapon of repression most difficult to combat."[48] And when, in late 1927, Senator Henrik Shipstead of Minnesota introduced an anti-injunction bill into the Senate, and the measure was referred to a subcommittee of the Senate Judiciary Committee, chaired by George Norris, a national sounding board quickly developed for widespread public assault upon the evils of what labor was more and more calling government by injunction.[49]

It took hard depression realism and growing apprehensions over the danger of internal revolution to produce the added momentum necessary for enacting a major congressional statute. By 1931, such disparate groups as the Federal Council of Churches; the Commission on Industrial Inquiry of the business-oriented, ultraconservative National Civic Federation; and the conservative leadership of the A.F. of L. joined hands with the earlier liberal advocates. The result was the enactment of the Norris–La Guardia Act in March, 1932. The affirmative vote in both houses of Congress was overwhelming.[50] Further, the action stimulated a number of lib-

46. *Ibid.*, p. 394.

47. Zechariah Chafee, Jr., *The Inquiring Mind* (New York, 1928) pp. 183–216; Felix Frankfurter and Nathan Greene, "The Use of the Injunction in American Legal Controversies." *Law Quarterly Review,* XLIV, XLV (1928), 164–197, 353–380, 19–59; and Felix Frankfurter, *Law and Politics* (New York, 1962), pp. 218–228. See also Albert DeSilver, "The Injunction—A Weapon of Industrial Power," *Nation,* CXIV (January 25, 1922), 89–90.

48. American Civil Liberties Union, *The Fight for Civil Liberty* (New York, 1929), pp. 18–19.

49. U.S. Congress. Senate. Subcommittee of the Committee on the Judiciary. Hearings. *Limiting Scope of Injunctions in Labor Disputes,* 70th Cong., 1st Sess. (1928).

50. The measure, 47 Stat. 70 (1932), passed the Senate 75 to 5, and the House 362 to 14.

erally dominated state legislatures to reject the Court's earlier ruling in *Truax* v. *Corrigan* and pass new state anti-injunction measures to complement the national measure.[51]

The implications of such action were significant. The Act made yellow-dog contracts unenforceable in federal courts, forbade the issuance of injunctions against a number of hitherto outlawed union practices, and guaranteed jury trials in cases involving violations of criminal injunctions. It thereby afforded the machinery for undercutting a variety of informal antilabor devices. The federal government was now projected between the citizen and overt local pressures in such a way as to give him access to concrete and uniform relief when he felt his rights of national citizenship were being abridged.

Judicial reaction to such legislative legal change was cautious. At the time he signed the measure, President Hoover, through his unenthusiastic Attorney General William D. Mitchell, threw the gauntlet to the courts by urging early judicial clarification of the measure's "controversial provisions."[52] But the Supreme Court, at least, was not anxious to challenge Congress in this area, denying certiorari in appeals from lower federal court rulings that had upheld the constitutionality of the law.[53] Finally a new and more liberal Court of the late 1930s took cases on the measure, finding it not only constitutional, but approving fully what Justice Roberts maintained was the evident purpose of Congress in passing the law, "to obviate the results of the judicial construction" of the Clayton Act.[54]

The actions of the Hughes Court in the civil liberties area complemented predictably the general social and legal assumptions supporting the use of the states' police power. If the law was to be interpreted pragmatically so as to encourage state experi-

51. Edwin E. Witte, *The Government in Labor Disputes* (New York, 1932), pp. 270–273; Felix Frankfurter and Nathan Greene, *The Labor Injunction* (New York, 1930), pp. 187 ff.

52. William S. Myers (ed.), *The State Papers and Other Public Writings of Herbert Hoover* (2 vols., New York, 1934), II, 145–146.

53. Cinderella Theatre Co. *v.* Sign Writers' Local Union, 6 F. Supp. 164 (1934); Levering and Garrigues Co. *v.* Morris, 7 F. (2d) 284 (1934); United Electric Coal Companies *v.* Rice, 80 F. (2d) 1 (1935).

54. New Negro Alliance Co. *v.* Sanitary Grocery Co., 303 U.S. 552, 562 (1938); see also Lauf *v.* Shinner & Co., 303 U.S. 323 (1938).

mentation in seeking solutions to economic and social problems, a certain general consistency demanded that similar lenience be extended individuals desirous of suggesting and purveying unique ideas and panaceas also geared toward producing social and economic change. Similarly, if one accepted the premise that it was no longer possible within a highly complex industrial society for every man to take care of himself on an individual basis, realism now demanded that legal acknowledgment be made of the fact that just as government had an obligation to improve social and economic conditions, it also had an obligation to eliminate legal strictures that prevented the constructive use of personal liberty.

The difficulty was that the obtainment of such an objective involved sharply different if not contradictory legal paths. The former demanded the enactment of a variety of new pieces of state legislation with the object in mind of striking at social and economic forces inhibiting individual self-determination. The latter entailed the disentanglement of individuals from existing legislation, the enforcement of which had chronically denied their civil rights and civil liberties. More explicitly, the former necessitated curtailing the use of the Fourteenth Amendment's due process clause as a legal device for ruling such legislation unconstitutional. The latter required extending and expanding it as a device for guaranteeing personal liberty by striking down laws infringing upon that liberty.

The Hughes Court's determination to take such action emerged early and resoundingly. Almost simultaneously with Brandeis' opinion in the O'Gorman case, Hughes handed down two eloquent rulings involving freedom of speech and press[55] that decisively enthroned Walter H. Pollak's nationalization principle, acceded to but not implemented in the Gitlow ruling. "It is no longer open to doubt," wrote the new Chief Justice, "that the liberty of the press and of speech is within the liberties safeguarded by the due process clause of the Fourteenth Amendment from invasion by state action."[56] And significantly, both cases had involved what a majority of the justices agreed was both a needless abuse of state power to restrict personal freedom and the unwarranted utilization of in-

55. Stromberg *v.* California, 283 U.S. 359 (1931); Near *v.* Minnesota, 283 U.S. 697 (1931).

56. Near *v.* Minnesota, 707.

formal local power to which such legislation inevitably gave a clear green light.

In *Stromberg* v. *California,* the Court ruled unconstitutional the key portion of a state red flag law, which had been exhumed to justify vigilante action on the part of local American Legionnaires against a Communist-sponsored summer camp for children in the southern California hills.[57] "The maintenance of the opportunity for free political discussion," wrote Hughes, "to the end that government may be responsive to the will of the people, and that changes may be obtained by lawful means, an opportunity essential to the security of the republic, is the fundamental principle in our constitutional system. A statute which upon its face and as authoritatively construed is so vague and indefinite as to permit the punishment of the fair use of this opportunity, is repugnant to the guarantee of liberty contained in the Fourteenth Amendment."[58]

And if Stromberg proscribed one kind of local action unwarranted by its clear abrogation of national standards, Hughes's equally direct and incisive opinion in the Near case undercut another. Here the Chief Justice, utilizing Blackstone's historic condemnation of "prior restraint," struck down a Minnesota censorship statute under which public officials had closed down a local "scandal-sheet."[59] The majority was particularly disturbed by the fact that under the statute a single violation invoked the thrust of permanent suppression of a periodical, whatever its contents. In his opinion, Hughes went even further in demanding harmony between commitments to liberty, freedom, and equal protection of the law on the part of the nation and local states. As Hughes saw it, "the question is whether a statute authorizing such proceedings in restraint of publication, is consistent with the conception of the liberty of the press as historically conceived and guaranteed."[60] His answer was resoundingly negative.

57. Transcript of Record, Yetta Stromberg, Appellant *v.* People of the State of California, Filed December 9, 1930, 22 ff.; American Civil Liberties Union, *The California Red Flag Case* (New York, 1930).

58. Stromberg *v.* California, 369.

59. For the facts behind the case see Transcript of Record, J. M. Near, Appellant *v.* State of Minnesota *ex rel.* Floyd B. Olson, filed, April 25, 1930, 8 ff.; and John E. Hartmann, "The Minnesota Gag Law and the Fourteenth Amendment," *Minnesota History,* XXVII (December, 1960), 161–173. On the broader implications of the ruling see Edward Gerald, *The Press and the Constitution, 1931–1947* (Minneapolis, 1948), pp. 127 ff.

60. Near *v.* Minnesota, 713.

National response to the rulings was not only generally favorable but showed an understanding of the Court's objectives. Alluding to the Court's recent rulings in O'Gorman, and Near, the *Literary Digest* proclaimed them "just about the biggest Washington news of the decade." The editors then went on to quote Mark Sullivan:

> The cleavage between liberal and conservative and the dominance of the former appear particularly in two areas of decisions. One, speaking broadly, emphasizes human rights and constitutional guarantees to the individual, such as freedom of speech. These human rights the liberals of the Court tend to protect or enlarge. The other group of decisions . . . tends to restrain private property rights and to enlarge the powers of State governments in dealing with private property.[61]

The Near and Stromberg rulings proved merely the initial steps in a new judicial campaign that sought to undermine irresponsible state or state-sanctioned action, action which numerous members of the new majority felt was undermining confidence in the very state governments that they hoped might provide enlightened relief for their citizens in the social and economic areas. When Louisiana's "Kingfish" Huey Long launched a subtle assault upon the hostile urban press of his state, the one medium of enlightened protest against his dictatorial tendencies, by imposing a two per cent gross receipts tax on newspapers having a circulation of more than twenty thousand per week, Justice Sutherland struck down the law. Relying upon the Near and Stromberg rulings against which he had earlier dissented, he voiced the classical liberal objection to state coercion. The vital interest at stake, he argued, was the "natural right" of a people to be informed about the

61. "The Supreme Court's Shift to Liberalism," *Literary Digest,* CIX (June, 13, 1931), 8. Similar sentiments were expressed in D. E. Wolfe, "Supreme Court in a New Phase," *Current History,* XXXIV (July, 1931), 592–593. For legal comment see Harry Shulman, "The Supreme Court's Attitude Toward Liberty of Contract and Freedom of Speech," *Yale Law Journal,* LXI (1931), 262–271; George Foster, Jr., "The 1931 Personal Liberty Cases," *New York University Law Quarterly Review,* IX (1931), 64–81; Malcolm P. Sharp, "Movement in Supreme Court Adjudication: A Study of Modified and Overruled Decisions," *Harvard Law Review,* XLVI (1933), 360–403; Pendleton Howard, "The Supreme Court and State Action Challenged Under the Fourteenth Amendment, 1930–1931," *University of Pennsylvania Law Review,* LXXX (1932), 483–521; and Walton H. Hamilton, "The Jurist's Act," in Felix Frankfurter (ed.), *Mr. Justice Brandeis* (New Haven, 1932), pp. 171–192.

"doings or misdoings" of their rulers.[62] To the Utah conservative, whatever other good might be achieved from a free press, its great utility was the protection it offered to the individual in his never-ending struggle with organized society, and the immediate issue at hand brought this home in a way in which informal restraints clearly had not.

The Court, on the other hand, clearly had no intention of upholding every vague challenge to local authority simply because local citizens felt that their rights were in one way or another being abrogated. It rejected, in 1935, the plea of a Negro Communist organizer in Georgia that an ancient insurrection statute under which he had been arrested deprived him of his constitutional rights. Its denial was based on the fact that he failed to specify which rights were being violated.[63] Only when, in subsequent appeal, specific charges of free speech violation were leveled did the justices consider the issue. Then, speaking through Justice Roberts, they held that the statute as construed and applied was repugnant to the Fourteenth Amendment in that it furnished no sufficiently ascertainable standard of guilt and that it interfered unduly with speech and assembly not demonstrably creating a clear and present danger of the use of force against the state. Thus Holmes's earlier rule gained new life in being used for the first time to strike down a state statute.[64]

Although cautious, the justices did not hesitate to nationalize other portions of the First Amendment against local violation of citizens' nationally guaranteed rights. In a case decided the month before Roosevelt tossed his court-packing bomb, the right to freedom of assembly was guaranteed against state interference, again in a situation in which high-handed local police tactics, clearly a projec-

62. Grosjean *v.* American Press Co., 297 U.S. 233, 249 (1936). For background see Allan P. Sindler, *Huey Long's Louisiana* (Baltimore, 1956), pp. 89–90. The same principle was used to throw out a comparable Arizona law two years later. See Arizona Publishing Co. *v.* O'Neil, 304 U.S. 543 (1938).

63. Herndon *v.* Georgia, 295 U.S. 441 (1935). On the background of the case see Angelo Herndon, *Let Me Live* (New York, 1937).

64. Herndon *v.* Lowry, 301 U.S. 242 (1937). The case marked the only occasion during the decade in which the majority utilized the concept, although Cardozo, in dissenting in Herndon *v.* Georgia, *supra,* had called for its utilization. See Wallace Mendelson, "Clear and Present Danger: From Schenck to Dennis," *Columbia Law Review,* LII (1952), 317.

tion of conservative local hostility to "radicals," had been the instrument for assailing and breaking up a peaceful meeting.[65]

The justices even took some faltering steps toward elevating the guarantees of Amendments Four through Eight into areas of national concern. This trend had a particular impact on the Negro. Like labor, depression attitudes tended to create a greater tolerance and understanding for the black American. The Court, however, in squaring national ideals with concrete practice in the fields of civil rights and liberties, took the first steps of a legal revolution in which black leadership would eventually mount a national campaign for full first-class citizenship.

The rifle shots that touched off an avalanche were the famous Scottsboro cases, which emerged from litigation running from 1931 to 1935. The arrest in March, 1931, of nine Negro boys charged with the rape of two white girls, and the unseemly haste in which the accused seemed doomed to the Alabama electric chair, with only a modicum of regard for justice, quickly aroused the nation. Liberals insisted not only on the accused being given a proper defense but also demanded a thoroughgoing examination of the functioning of the Bill of Rights in the South.[66] The new attitude of the Court was revealed in its treatment of the legal questions involved—the right to counsel and to a fair trial by a fair and impartial jury. In earlier cases, the Court had been generally willing, if the record showed that proper procedural forms had been followed, to inquire no further as to whether federal rights had been denied. Now, confronted with an eloquent and devastatingly documented brief by Attorney Walter H. Pollak, detailing not only the facts but the

65. De Jonge *v.* Oregon, 299 U.S. 353 (1937). On the case see Zechariah Chafee, Jr., *Free Speech in the United States* (Cambridge, Mass., 1941) 384–388; Glenn Abernathy, *The Right of Assembly and Association* (Columbia, S.C., 1961), pp. 16, 161; and Charles E. Rice, *Freedom of Association* (New York, 1962), pp. 132–134. The Court was still highly cautious about blanket nationalization of even all the First Amendment guarantees at this time. See Hamilton *v.* Board of Regents, 293 U.S. 245 (1934).

66. The literature on Scottsboro is extensive. See Allan K. Chalmers, *They Shall Be Free* (New York, 1951); Arthur Garfield Hays, *Trial By Prejudice* (New York, 1933), pp. 25–150; Haywood P. Patterson, *Scottsboro Boy* (Garden City, N.Y., 1950); Quentin Reynolds, *Courtroom: The Story of Samuel S. Leibowitz* (New York, 1950); and Dan T. Carter, *Scottsboro: A Tragedy of the American South* (Baton Rouge, 1969).

entire atmosphere surrounding the proceedings,[67] it determined to explore whether such rights had been denied in operational reality. Having set itself such a task, its conclusions were foregone.

Justice Sutherland spoke for the Court in the first of two cases to reach it examining the issue of whether the right to counsel had truly been afforded. He took note of the fact that the lower court judge had, in a grandstanding fashion, designated "all members of the Bar" as counsel, but found this too indefinite. He also found that that guarantee had not been met by the designation on the morning of the trial of one attorney to be definitely responsible for the defense. Such action, wrote the justice, amounted to "a denial of effective and substantial aid in that regard." "Without counsel," he went on, "though a defendant be not guilty, he faces the danger of conviction because he does not know how to establish his interest. If that be true of men of intelligence, how much more true, it is of the ignorant and illiterate, or those of feeble intellect." Hence the lower court's actions regarding token counsel had been strictly sham, and "violative of the due process clause of the Fourteenth Amendment."[68]

Hughes wrote the 1935 opinion concerning the jury question in the second of the Scottsboro cases to reach the Supreme Court. Responding again to Pollak's prodding brief,[69] he explored thoroughly the actual functioning of the all-white jury system in the two counties involved, not only in the immediate case, but over a period of time. Such hard viewing of the record led him promptly to rule that the Negroes had been denied a fair trial since the equal protection of the laws, as guaranteed by the Fourteenth Amendment, had been denied. He found that Negroes were systematically excluded from jury duty on the basis of their race, a denial particularly indefensible considering the fact that many were not only willing but fully competent to serve.[70]

67. Walter H. Pollak, Brief for Petitioner, Powell *v.* Alabama, Filed September 19, 1931, p. 2.

68. Powell *v.* Alabama, 287 U.S. 45, 46 (1932). On the legal context of the case see William M. Beaney, *The Right to Counsel in American Courts* (Ann Arbor, 1955), pp. 151–157.

69. Walter H. Pollak and Osmond K. Fraenkel, Petition and Brief for Support of Application for Certiorari, Norris *v.* Alabama, Filed Nov. 17, 1934.

70. Norris *v.* Alabama, 294 U.S. 587 (1935). The Alabama law, which deliberately did not discriminate on the basis of race, was nonetheless sufficiently ambiguous so that it could easily be applied to exclude Negroes. However, the fact that no Negro could ever be found to meet its qualifications was partially

A case in 1936, although not a part of the Scottsboro situation, found the Court functioning in the same spirit, upsetting as a denial of due process a conviction that rested solely upon confessions of three Negroes, shown to have been extorted by third-degree methods, virtually bestial in their nature. In writing the majority opinion, Hughes made clear for a unanimous Court that because a state may exercise discretion in regulating the forms of trial, it did not follow that "it may substitute trial by ordeal." "The rack and torture chamber may not be substituted for the witness stand." "It would be difficult to conceive of methods more revolting to the sense of justice than those taken to procure the confessions of these petitioners," wrote the Chief Justice, "and the use of the confessions thus obtained as the basis for conviction and sentence was a clear denial of due process."[71]

Yet there were still high legal barriers inhibiting the Negro that the Court was not willing to lower. The establishment of voting qualifications in America and the administration of elections had been traditionally a matter of state control. Despite clear evidence that such control was abused to disfranchise eligible Negroes, the Court was willing only to question such proceedings when their legal validity seemed clearly in doubt as an integral part of discriminatory state action. This it had ruled to be the case in its 1927 assault upon the Texas white primary.[72] The Texas legislature had then passed a new statute authorizing the state executive committee of any political party to determine who may vote in its primary. The Democratic state committee promptly passed a rule excluding Negroes from the Democratic primary in 1928. The Court now held that Negroes were denied the equal protection of the laws since the state law authorized the discrimination.[73] Texans now

---

undermined by the fact that a number of Negroes had served on federal courts in the area, which had fully as demanding qualifications. See Hughes's response for the majority at 596–599. The majority had earlier expressed its views on the relevancy of racial bias to a fair trial. See Aldridge *v.* U.S., 283 U.S. 308 (1931).

71. Brown *v.* Mississippi, 297 U.S. 278, 285–286 (1936). The Court did insist that litigants exhaust all rightful state remedies first, however, denying in the famed Mooney case the right of appeal even though evidence was overwhelming that Mooney's conviction had been secured on the basis of state-secured perjured testimony. Mooney *v.* Holohan, 294 U.S. 103 (1935).

72. Nixon *v.* Herndon, 273 U.S. 536 (1927).

73. Nixon *v.* Condon, 286 U.S. 73 (1932).

got the cue and turned the disfranchisement process over to the Democratic party as a private body. This the Court was unwilling to question. Even though only white citizens were allowed to participate in the party's councils and deliberations (and by clear implication its primary), it found no constitutional right denied. It did not deny resultant exclusion of Negroes from the voting process, but found that this was not the result, direct or indirect, of any state law or the act of any state official. The Democratic party, wrote Justice Roberts for a unanimous Court, is a private and not a governmental body, and private persons or groups cannot violate the Fourteenth Amendment.[74]

Similarly, aliens and pacifists, particularly with war clouds brewing in Manchuria and belligerent Fascists and Nazis marching in Italy and Germany, found there were clear limits to the extent of the Court's solicitude for rights that might in any way be taken to challenge the sovereignty of the state. Hopeful that Holmes's vigorous dissent in the earlier Schwimmer case might gain new status under a more liberal bench, two pacifists again challenged the denial of their rights to obtain citizenship on the grounds of their beliefs. One was a Canadian-born professor of divinity at Yale University, the other a Canadian-born nurse who had spent nine months in the service of the United States government in France, nursing soldiers and aiding in psychiatric work. Each indicated a willingness to take the oath of allegiance but each sought to qualify the categorical requirement of bearing arms for the nation—Macintosh, the theologian, by insistence upon weighing into the situation the greater needs of humanity, Miss Bland by adding to the phrase "defend the United States against all enemies" the phrase "as far as my conscience as a Christian will allow." The Court found the positions of both enough to deny citizenship, turning both rulings on the nation's essential right of survival.[75] Hughes dissented eloquently, in what has been called "perhaps his most memorable opinion."[76] He was joined by Holmes, Brandeis, and Stone.

74. Grovey *v.* Townsend, 295 U.S. 45 (1935). The Court was cautious in cases involving other racial minorities, insisting only upon procedural regularities in ruling on a case involving California's clearly discriminatory Alien Land Law. Morrison *v.* California, 291 U.S. 82 (1934).

75. U.S. *v.* Macintosh, 283 U.S. 605 (1931); U.S. *v.* Bland, 283 U.S. 636 (1931).

76. Rocco Tresolini, *Justice and the Supreme Court* (Philadelphia, 1963), p. 89.

Possibly the most penetrating comment on the rulings came a decade later, and only a few years before a new majority, under Chief Justice Stone, reversed both rulings.[77] In a 1940 revision of his distinguished work on free speech Zechariah Chafee, Jr., wrote:

> There is something humorous in the denial of American citizenship to persons of high intelligence, public spirit, and humanitarian sympathies . . . on the single ground of their unwillingness to bear arms, while during the same decade of Prohibition a considerable number of naturalized citizens were disturbing the country by their excessive willingness to bear arms, especially sawed-off shotguns and machine guns. A wise naturalization policy should not make everything turn on a single opinion of the petitioner, especially when age or sex makes that opinion of little practical importance.[78]

The cases were among the few in the period in which questions of deprivation of rights by the federal government were raised. Normally it was with the activity of the states in this area with which the Hughes Court was concerned. And this concern was central to an understanding of much of its philosophy. That Court, in the years prior to early 1937, when acting on its own and not concerned with national legislation fostered by Roosevelt and New Deal leaders, continually kept the states, their rights, prerogatives and privileges, and their favorable image in mind. Such a faith in local democracy and the power of the people through their state government to shape and control their destiny, through the intelligent and responsible control of their social, economic, and political institutions, seemed vital to majority membership. The insinuation of national leadership and massive national control into these areas produced different and frequently negative responses and at times seemed to place the justices in the somewhat peculiar position of endorsing federalism when its component parts operated successfully, but not when its powerful monolithic center sought to impose upon the nation its programs for the solution of many of the same problems.

77. Girouard *v.* U.S., 328 U.S. 61 (1946).
78. Chafee, *Free Speech in the U.S.*, p. 374.

CHAPTER 5

Constitutional Crisis over Controlling a National Economy

IF Franklin D. Roosevelt had a legal philosophy, it was, at its clearest, a vague synthesis of the views of Holmes and Brandeis, especially their endorsement of the value of social experimentation, and their focus upon the vital relationship of the law to the social and economic forces that control society. Confronted with a prostrate nation in March, 1933, in which *laissez-nous faire,* despite conservative protests, was no longer viable, the new President early made clear his intention to turn to the positive use of governmental power to arrest and reverse the economic trends. This, he realized, would demand public acceptance of constitutional tolerance and expansiveness. "Our Constitution," he argued in his first inaugural address, "is so simple and practical that it is possible always to meet extraordinary needs by changes in emphasis and arrangement without loss of essential form." "That is why," he went on, "our constitutional system has proved itself the most superbly enduring political mechanism the modern world has produced."[1]

Yet even here, the President sounded a warning. Anticipating traditional intransigence, he suggested that, should stalemate arise in the securing of essential national programs, he was prepared to

1. Samuel I. Rosenman (ed.), *The Public Papers and Addresses of Franklin D. Roosevelt* (13 vols., New York, 1938–50), II, 14–15.

ask Congress for "broad executive power to wage a war against the emergency, as great as the power that would be given me if we were, in fact, invaded by a foreign foe." That sentiment, which produced the biggest demonstration during the address, and even made his own wife apprehensive,[2] constituted a commitment of massive activism that Roosevelt quickly made clear he fully intended to honor.

The overwhelming amount of national legislation enacted during F.D.R.'s now legendary "First Hundred Days" in office was as frankly experimental as might have been expected in an area where few constitutional guidelines existed. Unfortunately it was put together by architects whose hastily contrived blueprints were all too often structurally and functionally questionable. Framed by a battery of intellectuals and young lawyers who left depression-wracked practices to descend upon Washington and join the great New Deal experiment,[3] such legislation rested upon vague constitutional theories and imprecise legal foundations. Such framers turned to the alternate set of broad commerce clause and taxing power precedents, many rooted in the Progressive period and even the 1920s. When specific actions by administrative agencies seemed warranted, bland and broad-scale delegation of legislative authority was proposed and sought from Congress, with the result that agency discretion increased with few guidelines or restrictions. If no other constitutional base could be contrived, the World War I–spawned "doctrine of emergency powers" was thrown in as an excuse for constitutional experimentation. Such a hodgepodge constitutional justification, however, was fraught with danger. Claims of authority under it were soon so broad, plenary, and unqualified as to betray little concern either for traditional constitutional limitations, or for the parallel authority of the states, still a factor in an inherently federal governmental system.

The character of the early New Deal helps to explain its constitutional outlook. Many of the initial influential "brain trusters"

2. Arthur M. Schlesinger, Jr., *The Coming of the New Deal* (Boston, 1958), pp. 1–2. On the crisis atmosphere of the thirties see Clinton Rossiter, *Constitutional Dictatorship: Crisis Government in the Modern Democracies* (New York, 1963), Chap. 17.

3. William E. Leuchtenburg, *Franklin D. Roosevelt and the New Deal, 1932–1940* (New York, 1963), p. 64.

were heavily oriented toward central planning and generalized solutions to the recovery of business and agriculture, currency reform, and general relief. Such an orientation, in practice more an abstract than a concrete reality, explains the early carelessness that marred the blueprints for functioning and implementation. Typical of such "First New Deal" legislation were the National Industrial Recovery Act of 1933[4] and the Agricultural Adjustment Act of the same year.[5]

The NIRA with its "blue eagle" and "codes of competition" within various industries, quickly came to be synonymous in a large part of the public mind with Roosevelt and the New Deal. The measure was framed by a divergent and often disparate group of primarily noncongressional drafters, principally Raymond Moley, Hugh Johnson, Donald Richberg, Lewis Douglas, Rexford Tugwell, A. A. Berle, and a leading devotee of national economic planning, Under Secretary of Commerce John Dickinson.[6] It sought to bring about national recovery through general elimination of damaging competition in business and industry. Specifically, as Roosevelt stated in his message urging congressional approval, the measure sought such ends by regulations to "shorten the working week to pay a decent wage for the shorter week and to prevent unfair competition and disastrous overproduction."[7] And the President demonstrated his prescience, later adding, "History probably will record the National Industrial Recovery Act as the most important and far-reaching legislation ever enacted by the American Congress,"[8] even though at the time he hardly anticipated the degree to which that importance would have negative as well as positive implications.

However grandiloquent the goals, the constitutional foundation for such a measure was shaky. Frankly cast as an "emergency" measure, "doubtless in part," as Carl B. Swisher once wrote, "to

4. 48 *U.S. Statutes at Large* 195 (1933). On its passage see Murray R. Benedict, *Farm Policies of the United States* (New York, 1953), pp. 276 ff.; and Leuchtenburg, *Franklin D. Roosevelt,* pp. 48–50.

5. 48 *U.S. Statutes at Large* 31 (1933). On its constitutional aspects see Oliver P. Field, "The Constitutional Theory of the National Industrial Recovery Act," *Minnesota Law Review,* XVIII (1934) 269–318.

6. Ellis W. Hawley, *The New Deal and the Problem of Monopoly* (Princeton, 1966), pp. 21–25.

7. Rosenman, *Public Papers of FDR,* II, 202.

8. Rosenman, *Public Papers of FDR,* II, 246.

show its necessity, and in part also to gather up any accretions to constitutionality, if such there were, that derived from the existence of a national emergency,"[9] its only clearly indicated basis for constitutionality was the commerce clause. Further, the interpretation its framers gave to that grant of congressional power was so expansive as to be all but unlimited. Granted, constitutional terminology such as "public welfare" and "general welfare" was also thrown in to show the necessity of the statute and to promote good will for it, neither phrase was calculated to sustain the measure if subjected to the scrutiny and assault of hostile constitutional lawyers. Further, by turning over power to private industrial groups to write codes for their own control, which in turn became certified and enforced as national law, Congress prescribed no standards, laid down no rules, and gave no indication of what such codes of "fair competition" should include. Republican Senator William E. Borah spoke for a number of hostile old Progressives such as George Norris and Burton K. Wheeler, as well as apprehensive reformers such as Hugo Black. Such codes, Borah charged apprehensively, apparently could include anything "which industry agrees upon and can get approved."[10] Equally troublesome to such critics was the temporary suspension of the antitrust laws that the act provided. They also saw the measure as potentially encouraging company unions, if not giving a green light to renewed use of the yellow-dog contract and the labor injunction.

The Agricultural Adjustment Act was equally as sweeping, and as constitutionally vulnerable. Drawn up, as with NIRA, with acquiescence of the interested groups to be regulated, the measure was, if anything, even more socially and legally inventive in setting forth new and untrod paths than was its companion piece for business and labor. Its broad objective of creating "parity" for the farmer was to be achieved through reducing agricultural production, direct government purchase of storable commodities, governmental subsidization of crop storage, and the licensing and taxing of processors of farm goods. The revenue so obtained would be returned to the farmer to bolster his position. Three potential constitutional

9. Carl B. Swisher, *American Constitutional Development* (Boston, 1954), p. 892.

10. Hawley, *New Deal and Problem of Monopoly,* p. 20; Schlesinger, *Coming of the New Deal,* pp. 100–102.

bases were considered by its framers. The measure's preamble stressed the theory of emergency powers, spoke confidently of the general welfare, and stressed the importance of Congress keeping the "normal currents of commerce" in farm commodities open, unburdened, and unobstructed. The central focus, however, devolved upon federal taxing power and the right to appropriate for the general welfare.[11] But such a foundation was highly vulnerable constitutionally. The Supreme Court in previous years, especially in its unanimous ruling in the second child labor case,[12] had taken a dim view of the use of the taxing power as a device primarily for regulation. Further, the fact that the statute authorized the raising of revenue from one group within society to pay to another, raised questions as to whether processors were not being deprived of property without due process of law as protected by the Fifth Amendment. Finally, the nature of the general welfare power itself was highly vague. General taxation, such as Sutherland had upheld in sustaining the Massachusetts Maternity Act ten years earlier,[13] might not be held coercive, but certainly a system in which individual farmers who did not cooperate in acreage reduction would not receive tax payments had a strong odor of unjustified coercion.

Constitutional questions also arose early as these new structures went into operation. This was especially true as those to whom responsibility fell for the actual administration of the program frequently took a highly cavalier attitude toward the fine points of legal responsibility when pushing them into action. The National Recovery Administration under the leadership of expansive, power-hungry Hugh Johnson, moved carelessly but relentlessly to project its authority through vague provisions into an ever growing number of new areas hardly contemplated by its framers.[14] It especially moved to bring dozens of new industries under the codes and sanction new breadth of code restrictiveness, especially in the wage-price area. The Agricultural Adjustment Administration derived similar stimulation from Assistant Secretary of Agriculture Rexford G.

11. Paul L. Murphy, "The New Deal Agricultural Program and the Constitution," *Agricultural History,* XXIX (1955), 160–169.

12. Bailey *v.* Drexel Furniture, 259 U.S. 20 (1922).

13. Massachusetts *v.* Mellon, 262 U.S. 447 (1923).

14. Hawley, *New Deal and Problem of Monopoly,* pp. 53 ff. For Johnson's version of the experiment see Hugh Johnson, *The Blue Eagle from Egg to Earth* (Garden City, N.Y., 1935).

Tugwell, its volatile general counsel, legal realist and innovator Jerome Frank, and a galaxy of largely intellectual-type, city-bred modernists.[15] Such leadership pushed ahead to secure its broad objectives, leaving in its wake the slaughter of little pigs and plowing under of crops, confusion as to its purpose, and growing antagonism both toward its methods and objectives. Thus while lesser pieces of New Deal reform and relief legislation were often framed upon far more careful, precise, and sound constitutional grounds, a task made easier by their less ambitious scope and objectives, the heart of the program was vulnerable at the outset. This proved particularly true in the case of the majority membership of the federal judiciary, which shared few, if any, of the careless constitutional assumptions of its framers and had slight sympathy for the "creative" tactics of its implementers.

The instinctive response of the Court to Roosevelt and the New Deal was predictable but vitally important. The conservative "Four Horsemen," Van Devanter, McReynolds, Sutherland, and Butler, shocked already by the green light that their liberal colleagues were giving state economic regulation, were appalled by unprecedented moves to bring the nation's economy under centralized national control, and were especially disturbed that the new President, who inevitably recalled "that earlier Democratic autocrat, Woodrow Wilson,"[16] was rushing it through a pliant Congress in record time, with little debate and less dissent. Hughes, by contrast, could not help resent the New Dealers' bland ignoring of what the Court was doing on its own, constructively, to create a new spirit of national tolerance and experimentation through its rulings at the state level. Having made a serious effort to wipe off the stigma that attached to the body because of its previous social insensitivity, and clearly seeking to restore both its prestige and its power through new demonstration of public responsibility, Roosevelt's seeming indifference to these contributions could not have been other than frustrating, even given his cordiality and professed wish to work

15. A frequently quoted story, supposedly illustrative of such a view, has Lee Pressman, attending a meeting to work out a macaroni code, asking aggressively what the code would do for the macaroni growers. Schlesinger, *Coming of New Deal,* pp. 50–51. On one of the leading critics, see Gilbert Fite, *George N. Peek and the Fight for Farm Parity* (Norman, Okla., 1954).

16. For a summary of such legislation see James M. Burns, *Roosevelt: The Lion and the Fox* (New York, 1956), pp. 165–171.

harmoniously with the justices.[17] Similarly a judge who had castigated state leadership for irresponsibility in both law framing and law enforcement in cases like Near and Stromberg, would hardly be enamored of somewhat parallel tactics at the national level in connection with business, labor, and agriculture programs that affected a majority of the people of the nation.

The liberals, by contrast, had other misgivings. Brandeis and to a lesser degree Stone and Cardozo could not help but be apprehensive about national programs that did not seem pointed toward a healthily diversified economy and a decentralized society. Devoted to local experiment, but highly realistic in acknowledging that only the national government could exorcise the cure of bigness, Brandeis nonetheless preferred that federal authority, when its use was necessary, be aimed at halting the march of bigness by reforming the financial arrangements of modern capitalism. This clearly would call for Congress to use its wide national powers to regulate commerce, tax, and spending, but regulation should be aimed at unwarranted financial speculation combating the unhappy trend toward combination and merger, guaranteeing resale price maintenance and other fair-trade measures to protect the small merchant, and establishing progressive taxation that could reduce the advantage and profits of bigness.[18] Little wonder that the old Wilsonian empathized slightly, if at all, with the NIRA and the AAA or that his colleague Cardozo, so imbued with the necessity for a public servant's sense of discipline and obligation,[19] viewed with alarm the casual way Congress was delegating its power to the very agents whose careful regulation was essential. Little wonder that Roberts, who was to become the "swing man" between the four conservatives and four liberals, and who initially looked for direction to liberal leadership, felt he had received reassurance to move to the right and

17. Roosevelt attempted especially to draw upon common ties with Hughes as fellow New Yorkers and former governors of the state in his hope to "have the same type of delightful relations with the Supreme Court which I had with the Court of Appeals in Albany." Merlo J. Pusey, *Charles Evans Hughes* (2 vols., New York, 1951), II, 733.

18. Alpheus T. Mason, *Brandeis: A Free Man's Life* (New York, 1946), pp. 614–619; Arthur M. Schlesinger, Jr., *The Politics of Upheaval* (Boston, 1960), pp. 220–222, 678.

19. See Walton H. Hamilton, "Cardozo the Craftsman," *University of Chicago Law Review,* VI (1938), 1–22; Dean G. Acheson, "Mr. Justice Cardozo and Problems of Government," *Michigan Law Review,* XXXVII (1939), 513–539.

join with those questioning broad national economic regulatory power almost from the outset.[20]

The final constitutional liability of Roosevelt's first New Deal became clear as legal challenge to new governmental programs necessitated their defense. Attorney General Homer Cummings had not recruited top talent in staffing the Justice Department. Himself interested in the reform of federal crime legislation and unification of practice and procedure in the federal courts, he had chosen as Solicitor General J. Crawford Biggs, who promptly lost ten of seventeen cases in his first months in that role.[21] Assistant Attorney General Harold Stephens, politically conservative and more conscientious and incisive than the ineffectual old gentleman from North Carolina, frequently found himself with little enthusiasm for attempting to defend slipshod framing and practices, and betrayed his distaste in court.

The initial confrontation of the New Deal and the high bench endeared neither to the other. High administration officials had sought nervously to delay such a showdown as long as possible, particularly since search for test cases in order best to demonstrate the constitutionality of New Deal measures had disclosed the effect of haste in drafting legislation, executive orders, and codes, and in working out procedures.[22] One of the serious errors discovered was in the code of fair competition for the petroleum industry. After the President, as authorized by the original Act, had modified the code, that modification was printed with the penalty provision of the code, which gave it legal sanction, inadvertently omitted. The Petroleum Administration had proceeded to enforce the code only

20. Erwin N. Griswold, "Owen J. Roberts as a Judge," *University of Pennsylvania Law Review,* CIV (1955), 332–349.

21. Schlesinger, *Politics of Upheaval,* p. 261. Roosevelt's initial lack of concern over top-flight personnel in the Justice Department paralleled similar attitudes toward other agencies which in the 1920s had come to be stigmatized for many liberals because of their reactionary, or with justice, repressive policies. This was especially true of the Department of Commerce, which had symbolized normalcy, and with the depression, the instability of the business world of the twenties.

22. Alpheus T. Mason, *The Supreme Court: Vehicle of Revealed Truth or Power Group, 1930–1937* (Boston, 1953), pp. 21–22. Robert L. Stern, "The Commerce Clause and the National Economy, 1933–1946," *Harvard Law Review,* LIX (1946), 656 ff.; Robert F. Carr, *The Supreme Court and Judicial Review* (New York, 1942). Carr insists New Deal leadership would have been wise to have pushed for immediate constitutional tests of its legislation, thus avoiding the apprehension and politics of the waiting period.

to find that a party arrested and jailed for violating it had violated a law that did not exist. Whereupon the government promptly and with considerable embarrassment dropped the case.[23]

In December of 1934, the justices heard argument on a suit challenging broader provisions of the National Industrial Recovery Act as it applied to the petroleum industry.[24] Quickly, they were regaled by private counsel with accounts of both the missing provision of the code and the careless way in which codes were enacted, amended, and enforced in general. It was further disclosed that orders having the force of law were being issued without any systematic publication. Queried by Justice Brandeis, "Is there any way by which to find out what is in these executive orders when they are issued?" Harold Stephens was forced to admit, "I think it would be rather difficult, but it is possible to get certified copies of the executive orders and codes from the N.R.A." Such a reply, the Washington *Post* reported, induced Justice Van Devanter to query, "Is that advantage open to the staff of the Justice Department?" Mr. Stephens' affirmative was lost in the titter of laughter that swept the courtroom.[25]

But the blow to the New Deal was as much to its functioning as to its composure. The Court, in holding that the conferring upon the President of power to prohibit by executive order the interstate and foreign shipment of oil left him without the prescription of a policy or standard to guide his decision and was thus an unconstitutional delegation of legislative power, immediately returned the oil industry to a state of uncontrolled competition.[26] This in turn, threw an ominous shadow over the broader aspects of NIRA and AAA due soon for Court test themselves.[27] Roosevelt's response to

23. Stern, "Commerce Clause and National Economy," pp. 655–657.

24. Panama Refining Co. *v.* Ryan, 293 U.S. 388 (1935).

25. Quoted in Edward S. Corwin, *Constitutional Revolution, Ltd.* (Claremont, Calif., 1941), pp. 40–41.

26. On the delegation issue generally see Louis L. Jaffe, "An Essay on Delegation of Legislative Power," *Columbia Law Review,* XLVII (1947), 359–376, 561–593.

27. Department of Agriculture officials reacted speedily with proposed amendments to the AAA, which Congress quickly passed, revising the statute to meet the test of delegation of power, and to limit the control over agriculture to products that clearly entered interstate commerce. Edwin G. Nourse, *Marketing Agreements Under the A.A.A.* (Washington, 1935), pp. 423 ff.

the ruling, while typical, hardly enhanced the New Deal image. Professing annoyance at judicial nit-picking, he seemed to condone earlier legal carelessness by casually suggesting that "there may be half a dozen more court decisions before they get the correct language and before they get things straightened out according to correct constitutional methods."[28]

Disturbed, Attorney General Cummings decided to argue the next case himself, calling upon Stanley Reed of the RFC for advice and assistance. Involved was the administration's controversial monetary policy, particularly the voiding of clauses in public and private bonds pledging redemption in gold, now being challenged by bondholders as a violation of the sanctity of contracts. Cummings pulled out all the stops. He relied heavily upon the doctrine of emergency powers, stressed the essentiality of solving the nation's economic crisis, and called upon the "power of self-preservation," which required transcending the "supposed sanctity and inviolability of contractual obligations" that the government had entered into.[29] The government thus shakily won its case by a narrow five-to-four decision, retaining essential control over national monetary policy and seeing the New Deal's current program for its manipulation validated.[30] The victory was narrow, however, and was due in large part to a majority opinion by Chief Justice Hughes, which Arthur M. Schlesinger, Jr., has characterized as "a masterpiece of judicial legerdemain, hardly matched in the annals of the Court since Marshall's opinion in Marbury v. Madison."[31] This was only accomplished over the vitriolic dissent of Justice McReynolds, whose opinion was in places too bitter for the formal record and was read

28. F.D.R. Press Conference #173, January 9, 1935, quoted in Schlesinger, *Politics of Upheaval,* p. 255.

29. Carl B. Swisher (ed.), *Selected Papers of Homer Cummings* (New York, 1939), pp. 112–120.

30. Norman *v.* B. and O. RR. Co., 294 U.S. 240 (1935); Nortz *v.* U.S., 294 U.S. 317 (1935); Perry *v.* U.S., 294 U.S. 330 (1935).

31. Schlesinger, *Politics of Upheaval,* p. 259. Detailed commentary on the cases includes: John P. Dawson, "The Gold-Clause Decisions," *Michigan Law Review,* XXXIII (1935), 647–684; John Dickinson, "The Gold Decisions," *University of Pennsylvania Law Review,* LXXXII (1935), 715–725; and Henry M. Hart, Jr., "The Gold Clause in United States Bonds," *Harvard Law Review,* XLVIII (1935) 1057–1099.

with muttered asides that "the Constitution is gone," and that "this is Nero at his worst."[32]

And Nero was frankly disturbed by the handwriting on the wall. The advanced sheets on the gold clause rulings were scarcely out when Roberts, speaking for the "Four Horsemen," not only ruled a 1934 Railroad Retirement Act unconstitutional, but made clear that any compulsory pension act for railroad employees was beyond the scope of congressional power.[33] His basis was a highly restrictive interpretation of the commerce clause in one industry, the railroads, which even the Taft Court had held was clearly interstate in its nature and fully subject to federal control. Chief Justice Hughes, who twenty-one years earlier had written a landmark decision extending federal power even to intrastate roads,[34] dissented sharply. "I think the conclusion is a departure from sound principles," Hughes wrote, "and places an unwarranted limitation upon the commerce clause of the Constitution."[35]

But the worst was yet to come. The Pension Act ruling was handed down only a few days after a case challenging the constitutionality of NIRA was argued and three weeks before it was decided, and its implications for the latter, based so heavily upon a highly expansive interpretation of the commerce clause, were clear. The Schechter brothers, whose case somewhat inadvertently became the test case on the entire NIRA,[36] were Kosher poultry dealers operat-

32. Alpheus T. Mason, *Harlan Fiske Stone: Pillar of the Law* (New York, 1956), p. 391 n.; Corwin, *Constitutional Revolution Ltd.*, pp. 45–46. A later commentator observed: "He completely departed from his written opinion and went to the country with an extemporaneous denunciation of repudiation of contracts and devaluation of the currency which electrified his auditors, sympathetic and unsympathetic alike. . . . He has often been quoted as saying, 'The Constitution is gone.' It is believed that the expression he used was, "The Constitution as we know it is gone." 334 U.S. ix–x (1948). A copy of the dissent is in the McReynolds MSS., University of Virginia Library.

33. Retirement Board *v.* Alton RR. Co., 295 U.S. 330 (1935).

34. Shreveport Rate Cases, 234 U.S. 324 (1914).

35. Retirement Board *v.* Alton RR. Co., 374. Thomas Reed Powell treats this ruling and the subsequent Schechter decision in "Commerce, Pensions and Codes," *Harvard Law Review*, XLIX (1935), 1–43, 193–238, maintaining that both were based on unnecessarily restrictive interpretations of the commerce clause, and could as easily have been disposed of on other grounds.

36. The government had initially sought to make its case in defense of the Lumber Code, which had clear interstate overtones. However, the code had peculiarities making it atypical of many of the codes, so the case it initially

ing in New York City, charged by the government with violating trade practice provisions of the live poultry code as well as its wage and hour provisions. Government attorneys had prepared a lengthy transcript on the case that they felt would show clearly the interstate implications of the operations of the poultry industry. But as a Justice Department official of the time pointed out,

> the apparent superiority of the record vanished when it was searched for material showing how the practices and wages and hours of poultry slaughterers in New York affected commerce. . . . The labor and trade practices occurred in the slaughter houses, and no amount of economic research to unearth judicially noticeable matter could fortify the meagre record on the crucial point so as to show in a convincing manner that these practices in New York substantially affected the interstate poultry market.[37]

On May 27, 1935, the Court unanimously, speaking through Chief Justice Hughes, struck down the recovery act, insisting that only intrastate practices "directly" affecting interstate commerce were subject to federal authority.[38] Now in contrast with his Minnesota moratorium ruling,[39] the Chief Justice rejected any theory of emergency power ("extraordinary conditions do not create or enlarge constitutional power"[40]) and suggested that all other areas not so

---

proposed to take to the high court was dismissed. U.S. *v.* Belcher, 294 U.S. 736 (1935). The Schechter case at first blush looked promising, since the Supreme Court had sustained an antitrust suit against the live poultry industry in New York two years before. Local 167 *v.* U.S., 291 U.S. 293 (1934).

37. Stern, "Commerce Clause and the National Economy," p. 660.

38. Schechter *v.* U.S., 295 U.S. 495 (1935). Earlier the same day the Court had struck directly at Roosevelt by limiting sharply the President's power to remove officers, not essentially executive and whose removal had been restricted by Congress. Humphrey's Executor *v.* U.S., 295 U.S. 602 (1935). Roosevelt early in his administration had forced the resignation of a conservative, aggressive, and outspokenly pro-big-business member of the Federal Trade Commission, William Humphrey. The Court now held Humphrey's removal to have been unwarranted since it had been the intent of Congress to confer upon the Commission independence from the President, and the Commission was the agent of Congress and the judiciary, not the executive. The ruling, which did not allude to Taft's earlier broad grant of removal authority in Myers *v.* U.S. (272 U.S. 52 [1926]), was another clear act of judicial disapproval of Roosevelt's conception of executive power. See William E. Leuchtenburg, "The Case of the Contentious Commissioner: Humphrey's Executor v. U.S.," in Harold M. Hyman and Leonard W. Levy (eds.), *Freedom and Reform* (New York, 1967), pp. 276–312.

39. Home Bldg. and Loan Assn. *v.* Blaisdel, 290 U.S. 398 (1934).

40. Schechter *v.* U.S., 295 U.S. 495, 528.

"directly" affected were reserved for state control by the Tenth Amendment. And pushing further the newly created weapon of unconstitutional delegation of power from the Panama Oil ruling, he thoroughly condemned Congress's blanket authorization of code making with "no standards for any trade, industry, or activity."[41] Justice Cardozo, who had registered the only dissent in Panama Oil, added a widely quoted concurring phrase. "This," he maintained, "is delegation running riot."[42]

Roosevelt could do little but protest publicly, lick his wounds, and call for new approaches to solving the depression. Yet the ruling loomed as an obstacle in this regard. As the President pointed out, the delegation of power point did not present an insurmountable obstacle. Future statutes could be written giving definite direction to administrators or quasi-legislative bodies that would be acceptable. But the Court's "horse-and-buggy" interpretation of interstate commerce could not be so easily surmounted.[43] As the Court also had made clear in the pension case, it was closing doors to any but the most essential and obvious national economic regulation[44] and suggesting that, to as large a degree as possible, this was an area of state authority. And even this option was limited. Before the year was out, the conservative majority had created a new legal tool for striking down state action. In a case striking sharply at state monitoring of interstate business activity, Justice Sutherland elevated the long dormant privileges and immunities clause of the Fourteenth Amendment as a new weapon for the defense of property

41. *Ibid.*, p. 541.

42. *Ibid.*, p. 553. For comment on the case see Robert H. Jackson, *The Struggle for Judicial Supremacy* (New York, 1949), pp. 109–114; Edward S. Corwin, "The Schechter Case—Landmark or What?," *New York University Law Quarterly Review,* XIII (1936), 151–190; J. A. C. Grant, "Commerce, Production, and the Fiscal Power of Congress," *Yale Law Journal,* XLXV (1936), 751–778, 991–1021, and Powell, "Commerce, Pensions and Codes." See also Schlesinger, *Politics of Upheaval,* pp. 487–488.

43. Rosenman, *Public Papers of FDR,* IV, 207, 221.

44. David W. Minar points out (*Ideas and Politics: The American Experience* [Homewood, Ill., 1964], pp. 309–310) that it was the tendency of the pre-1937 Court to decide questions concerning the national economic regulatory power on grounds other than those concerning the proper scope of political authority as such. Thereby, all one learned from its rulings was the precise nature of the commerce and taxing power and virtually nothing of the extent to which the electorate could use its supposed democratic power to control and shape society.

1. Oliver Wendell Holmes, Jr.

(Harris & Ewing)

2. Supreme Court members (left to right) Brandeis, Van Devanter, Chief Justice Taft, Holmes, Butler, Sanford and Stone, inspect a model of the proposed new Supreme Court building in 1929.

(Underwood and Underwood)

3. "The Nine Old Men" in 1932. (Front) Brandeis, Van Devanter, Chief Justice Hughes, McReynolds, Sutherland; (back row) Roberts, Butler, Stone, Cardozo.

(Underwood and Underwood)

4. Louis D. Brandeis
(Harris & Ewing)

5. Benjamin N. Cardozo
(Harris & Ewing)

SHOPS

VIL
BERTIES
AWYERS

Walter H. Pollak, noted civil liberties rney, whose briefs and arguments in Gitlow, Whitney, and Scottsboro cases, to landmark rulings.

urtesy of Mrs. Walter H. Pollak)

8. Morris Ernst, moving force behind the National Lawyers Guild, after a confrontation with Jersey City Mayor Frank Hague over C.I.O. organization activities in that city.

(Underwood and Underwood)

Roger S. Baldwin, founder, and head the American Civil Liberties Union during its first thirty years.

Underwood and Underwood)

10. Attorney General A. Mitchell Palmer, whose 1920 "Red Raids" climaxed the anti-radical hysteria of post–World War I America.

(Underwood and Underwood)

11. Citizen's response to the "law and order" issue during the 1919 Boston Police Strike. Here a department store owner, flanked by two assistants prepares for looters and strikers.

(U.P.I.)

12. Assistant Attorney General, Robert H. Jackson (left) welcomed by chairman Henry F. Ashurst to the Senate Judiciary Committee hearings on F.D.R.'s "court packing" bill. Ashurst's desultory tactics belied his public support of the measure and aided its defeat.

(Underwood and Underwood)

13. Willis Van Devanter, Charles Evans Hughes, and Louis Brandeis in a rare appearance before the Senate Judiciary Committee. All three opposed F.D.R.'s "court packing" measure.

(Underwood and Underwood)

14. The Scottsboro boys with their attorney Samuel S. Leibowitz.

(Brown Brothers)

15. Farmer protest, such as this Minnesota march, led to mortgage moratorium. The Hughes court upheld such emergency laws to the joy of debtors and the concern of conservatives.

(Minnesota Historical Society)

16. The World War II Court. (Back row) James Byrnes, William Douglas, Frank Murphy, Robert Jackson; (front) Stanley Reed, Owen Roberts, Chief Justice Harlan Stone, Hugo Black, Felix Frankfurter.

(Harris & Ewing)

17. Los Angeles Nisei ready to be moved to relocation centers during World War II. (Los Angeles Times)

18. Efficient Army action helped expedite movement of Japanese-Americans. (National Archives)

19. The House Un-American Activities Committee in its late 1940's heyday. L. to R., Reps. John McDowell, Richard M. Nixon, J. Parnell Thomas (chairman), Robert E. Stripling (chief investigator) and Rep. John E. Rankin.

(U.P.I.)

20. G. W. McLaurin, although admitted to the University of Oklahoma, was forced to sit in an anteroom in class.

(U.P.I.)

21. Martin Luther King's first arrest in Montgomery, Alabama, 1958.

(Charles Moore—Black Star)

22. Birmingham police turning dogs on black militants brought new civil rights support.

(Charles Moore—Black Star)

23. White hostility to court ordered integration of Little Rock's Central High School, such as shown here, eventually forced armed military protection of black students, and a famous court ruling.

(U.P.I.)

24. Gov. George Wallace, symbolically, and unsuccessfully, blocks the door of the University of Alabama to black students, defying Deputy U.S. Attorney General Nicholas Katzenbach, and a federal court order.

(U.P.I.)

25. The Warren Court of 1965. Back row, Byron White, William Brennen, Potter Stewart, Abe Fortas; front, Tom Clark, Hugh Black, Earl Warren, William Douglas, John Harlan.

(Harris & Ewing)

26. "Separate but equal" in West Memphis in the early 1950's.

(Ed Clark, *Life* Magazine © Time Inc.)

27. Thurgood Marshall, special counsel for the N.A.A.C.P., flanked by attorneys George E. C. Hayes and James Nabrit, Jr., following the Supreme Court's ruling in their favor in *Brown* v. *Board of Education.*

(U.P.I.)

28. An early (1960) "Impeach Earl Warren" sign showing the results of some typical responses.

(Paul Conklin-Pix)

against legislative control, thus reaffirming a legal twilight zone in which neither sovereignty could function.[45]

The range of response to this sharply restrictive turn was vast and varied. The lower federal courts, still at the time dominated by Republican judges, now intensified their already snowballing tendency to issue injunctions against the further enforcement of national legislation. By late 1933, as Assistant Attorney General Robert H. Jackson later pointed out, some sixteen hundred injunctions restraining officers of the federal government from carrying out acts of Congress were granted by federal judges, a more voluminous outpouring of judicial rulings in restraint of acts of Congress than at any time in American history. Clearly, unless broad change of public climate could someway be effected and mustered against the process, it would continue and intensify.[46]

Business leaders, and conservatives generally, at first highly sanguine about the NIRA and general New Deal approaches to recovery, now seemed to delight in its failure, to which they frequently contributed by a variety of forms of noncompliance. The American Liberty League was organized in 1934 and 1935 by a militant group of critical voices now thoroughly aroused to the threats of central planning and national economic regulatory programs. The well-financed body promptly made one of its early orders of business the creation of a special committee to study and challenge, as to constitutionality, the remaining national statutes.[47] An early target was the National Labor Relations Act of 1935. The measure constituted a new attempt to inject federal authority into the area of

45. Colgate *v.* Harvey, 296 U.S. 404 (1935); Jackson, *Struggle for Judicial Supremacy*, pp. 168–170. On the general question of "dual federalism" see the writings of Edward S. Corwin, who coined the term, especially his *Twilight of the Supreme Court* (New Haven, 1934), *Commerce Power versus States Rights* (Princeton, 1936), and *Court over Constitution* (Princeton, 1938).

46. Jackson, *Struggle*, pp. 115–123. See also Felix Frankfurter and Adrian S. Fisher, "The Business of the Supreme Court at the October Terms, 1935 and 1936," *Harvard Law Review*, LI (1938), 611 ff. Company attorneys evolved a clever method of challenging the constitutionality of laws, and preventing their enforcement by injunction and still keeping the government from entering the court and defending the threatened enactment. The technique was a stockholders' suit in which the company would be sued to prevent it from obeying the law on the grounds that if it did, damage to the stockholders' interests would result.

47. George Wolfskill, *The Revolt of the Conservatives: A History of the American Liberty League* (Boston, 1962), pp. 71–78.

management labor relations, creating a special board, the NLRB, with authority to determine appropriate collective bargaining units subject to elections it supervised at the request of the workers, and to issue cease and desist orders against employers' unfair labor practices. Its framers drafted the measure with legal fastidiousness, carefully prohibiting only unfair labor practices that threatened to obstruct interstate commerce. The League's fifty-eight-member Lawyers' National Committee promptly proclaimed the whole measure unconstitutional and urged business to adopt policies of noncompliance by reassuring them of the measure's inability to stand up against Court test.[48] "When a lawyer tells a client that a law is unconstitutional," explained Earl F. Reed, chief counsel for Weirton Steel Company, and chairman of the subcommittee that drafted the report, "it is a nullity and he need no longer obey that law."[49]

The failure of the American Bar Association to condemn outright such action encouraged the League Committee to take similar steps with regard to other pieces of New Deal legislation. These included the 1935 Bituminous Coal Conservation Act, the Potato Control Act, the TVA Act, and the Public Utility Holding Company Act. Thus, despite broad-scale public hostility to such acts of defiance on the part of the conservative legal profession and despite the editorial opinion of the conservative *United States Law Review* that such tactics had nothing to recommend them,[50] the League persisted in setting itself above the "misguided" administration as a self-appointed supercourt and seemed to be willing, in the acerbic words of Secretary of the Interior Harold Ickes, "to take on the work of the executive and legislative branches of the government as well."[51]

New Deal tactics had already begun to change prior to such

48. National Lawyers Committee of the American Liberty League, *Report on the Constitutionality of the National Labor Relations Act* (Pittsburgh, 1935). One of the fullest statements of Liberty League constitutionalism was Raoul E. Desvernine, *Democratic Despotism* (New York, 1936); he was chairman of the Lawyer's Committee.

49. Wolfskill, *Revolt of Conservatives,* p. 72.

50. "The Fifty Eight Lawyers," *United States Law Review,* LXIX (1935), 505–507; Sveinbjorn Johnson, "The Fifty Eight Lawyers," *United States Law Review,* LXX (1936), 22–30. See also "A Conspiracy of Lawyers," *Nation,* CXLI (Oct. 2, 1935), 369; and "Liberty League Lawyers," *New Republic,* LXXXIV (Oct. 2, 1935), 203.

51. Wolfskill, *Revolt of Conservatives,* p. 73.

assault. By 1935, high administration leaders were prepared to admit that the NIRA approach of economic management, direct planning, and national coordination and control had not only failed in the courts but in practice as well. That recovery which had taken place had largely been in spite of such programs, not because of them. Further, many of the elements now so vitriolic in their criticism of New Deal policy had been its greatest benefactors. The focus of programs such as the NIRA and AAA upon the elimination of competition and the general standardization of production and costs had primarily benefited powerful manufacturers and large farmers, in some instances at the expense of the general public. Thus a refocus of general ends was both tactically and politically essential.

Now the views of Louis Brandeis suddenly took on new relevance. The justice had been as pleased by the implications of the Schechter ruling as had conservative New Deal critics. Privately he had hailed it at the time as "most beneficent . . . compelling a return to human limitations."[52] Roosevelt's thinking now seemed to be moving toward the ideas of the old advocate of the New Freedom. The administration tack now called for redesigning the structure of competition through induced diversification and decentralization. In a message to Congress in March, 1935, the President called specifically for new regulation to break up giant holding companies, whose evils had been thoroughly revealed by lengthy Federal Trade Commission investigations. The message had broader implications, however. Its tone was clearly unsympathetic to government-business cooperation along earlier lines, stressing the dangers of financial complexity in general and calling for reversal of processes leading to "the private socialism of concentrated private power."[53] And the new lieutenants who quickly emerged as the draftsmen of a second New Deal tended inevitably to reflect this new orientation.

This "Harvard crowd," a number of youthful products of the Harvard Law School, careful students of Thomas Reed Powell, and generally protégés of Felix Frankfurter, had good reason to hew to the Brandeisian philosophy. James M. Landis, Dean Acheson, William Sutherland, and Paul Freund had been Brandeis' former

52. Mason, *Brandeis*, p. 620. See also Schlesinger, *Politics of Upheaval*, p. 280.
53. Rosenman, *Public Papers of F.D.R.*, IV, 98–103.

law clerks, while Thomas Corcoran, Lloyd Landau, the Hiss brothers, and James Rowe had served similar apprenticeships with his cohort Holmes. Joining with Frankfurterites Benjamin Cohen, David Lilienthal, and Charles Wyzanski, they set out to implement the Vienna-born legalist's Brandeisian doctrine that "competitive enterprise had to be at the base of the American system." This meant creating a more favorable climate for the "multitudinous activities, experiments and strivings of all those whom Lincoln called the common people."[54]

Through the efforts of Corcoran and Cohen particularly, a proposed Public Utility Holding Company Act was framed. The measure vested in the Federal Power Commission authority to regulate interstate transmission of electric power; in the Federal Trade Commission authority over gas; and in the Securities and Exchange Commission authority over financial practices of such companies. It contained, in addition, a "death sentence" clause that set a term of five years, at the end of which any holding company that could not demonstrate its localized, useful, and efficient character would be dissolved. As a constitutional base, the framers relied heavily upon a broad interpretation of the commerce clause. Similarly, an accompanying measure creating a national social security program relied constitutionally on a broad taxing power base. Constitutional misgivings were present, however. Critics questioned the power of the federal government to grant money to a state for expenditures on projects such as aid to the blind, aid to dependent and crippled children, maternal and child welfare, and public health projects upon which the federal government itself could not spend directly. Others questioned the fact that unemployment compensation features virtually coerced states to set up plans in this area, raising the question of whether the taxing power was being used legitimately, or as a penalty. And clearly the Court's ruling a few days after the Senate Finance Committee began executive sessions on the measure

54. Schlesinger, *Politics of Upheaval*, p. 223. Schlesinger tends to draw indefensibly tight lines between first and second New Deal, with the first non-Brandeisian, the second, both in spirit and personnel, a projection of the justice's views and philosophy. Leuchtenburg, *Franklin D. Roosevelt and New Deal*, pp. 163–164, warns, wisely, against so sharp a delineation. See also Burns, *Roosevelt*, pp. 266–268; and Bernard Sternsher, *Rexford Tugwell and the New Deal* (New Brunswick, N.J., 1964), pp. 151, 308, 325 ff.

holding unconstitutional the Railroad Retirement Act had to be distinguished.[55]

But if Frankfurter's "Happy Hot Dogs" were as ambitious and energetic as the Donald Richberg–A. A. Berle–Rex Tugwell group of central planners whom they replaced, they differed sharply in technical approach. Assiduously careful legal draftsmen, painfully aware of the legal structures that would have to be surmounted and the philosophy of the judges who would view their handiwork, they thought through every point with technical punctiliousness and always showed a meticulous regard for legal continuities. Thus, while, ironically the National Industrial Recovery Act was, on the whole, a less complicated piece of legislation than the Public Utility Holding Company Act, the latter did survive, due not in small part to its legal fastidiousness and superiority. The same was true of the social security measure.[56]

Brandeis was delighted to have emerged as the senior statesman of this new turning toward decentralization. He and his devotees were sufficiently realistic to acknowledge, however, that this could not mean restoring full control over the national economy to the states. The federal government still had a duty to control and regulate the adverse tendencies of private power and property when it threatened to destroy man's liberty and economic self-determination, and constitutional ways had to be found to do so. Further, while Brandeis himself clung to a certain optimism about the ability to reform man, his realistic devotees, reflecting the general cynicism of the decade, had no such illusions. Feeling that what could realistically be done was to update and revise the institutions with which humans interacted, they set out to make them function equitably, efficiently, and realistically, and above all honestly rather than hypocritically. Clearly in a decade engulfed in the tangles of eco-

55. On the Holding Company Act (48 *Stat.* 881 [1935]) see Herman H. Trachsel, *Public Utility Regulation* (Chicago, 1950), pp. 220–222, 398–406. On the Social Security Act (49 *Stat.* 620 [1935]) see Eveline M. Burns, *Toward Social Security* (New York, 1936), pp. 218–230; and Edwin E. Witte, *The Development of the Social Security Act* (Madison, Wis., 1962), pp. 33, 100, 116. The counsel of the drafting committee, Thomas Eliot, was specifically responsible for the precise constitutional arrangements of the latter measure.

56. The same careful draftsmanship went into the National Labor Relations Act. See Irving Bernstein, *The New Deal Collective Bargaining Policy* (Berkeley, 1950), pp. 63, 88, 104–105.

nomic depression, the central institutions that would have to be so reformed were economic institutions. The type of power that would have to be checked and channeled into constructive paths was economic power—and this, in light of the early New Deal experience, would have to be done not by telling business what it must do, but by telling business what it must not do.[57]

That this was a federal task they had no doubt, nor did most realistic state and local leaders. For if the fact that the states were incompetent to cope with national economic problems was not clear in 1932, it was resoundingly obvious by 1935. Of thirty-seven governors polled in that year, only one indicated he was willing to have the states resume responsibility for relief.[58] And when suggestion was made that functions now carried on by the federal government might have to be shunted back to local authorities, a kind of panic seemed inevitably to result, with mayors going to Washington to protest that essential activities, such as relief, recovery, and major reform, were quite beyond the power and ability of local government to carry on. The need for national protection for the citizen and his rights in competition with corporate power also was widely felt in the populace. The revelations by the La Follette Committee of the ruthless use of business power to protect the self-interest of private property,[59] came as no surprise to working people in the mid-decade, victimized themselves by business's aggressive crusade to crush the growing labor movement, especially the C.I.O. drive toward industrial unionism.[60]

Five of the justices in Washington, however, seemed totally oblivious to such strong currents of public opinion. The Agricultural Adjustment Act of 1933 eventually reached the high bench in early January of 1936. A majority insisted dogmatically, through Roberts' majority opinion, that not only was agriculture a local problem, reserved clearly for state control, but that the fact that

57. Leuchtenburg, *Roosevelt*, pp. 338–341.

58. *Today*, III (Jan. 12, 1935), 4.

59. Senate, Subcommittee of the Committee on Education and Labor, *Hearings*, Violations of Free Speech and Rights of Labor, 74th Cong., 2nd Sess.—76th Cong., 3rd Sess. (75 pts., 1936–40). For an analysis of the work of the committee see Jerold S. Auerbach, *Labor and Liberty: The La Follette Committee & the New Deal* (Indianapolis, 1966).

60. Joseph G. Rayback, *A History of American Labor* (New York, 1964), pp. 346 ff. See also Foster Rhea Dulles, *Labor in America* (New York, 1949), pp. 288 ff.

local conditions throughout the nation had created national problems and a situation for national concern, still in no way afforded Congress the authority to "ignore constitutional limitations on its own powers and usurp those reserved to the states." Relying once more on the dubious contention that the Tenth Amendment in someway prevented the federal government from extending its authority into new areas, a direction that it had consistently taken since the 1890s,[61] Roberts wrapped the government's power to tax and spend for the general welfare in as severe strictures as those already limiting its power to regulate interstate commerce. For justification he turned to the argument that such a position was the only one which a virtually mechanical judging process could sustain.[62]

Such a total lack of realism carried with it the implication that national economic problems could not even be attacked with national programs. This brought forth loudly critical challenge to the Court's peculiarly unrealistic assumptions. Critics also deplored the impertinence of the conservative majority in proceeding as if it had a mandate to set straight the ill-guided judgments of the peoples' representatives in the legislative and executive branches. Justice Stone had chafed for some time at the majority's societal myopia. Now, as an expert on taxation, he let fire not only at the majority's drastic restriction on the scope of the national taxing power, but upon judicial usurpation in general. Roberts' peculiarly apprehensive view that such federal power unless judicially limited would be put to disastrous and constitutionally prohibited ends,

61. U.S. *v.* Butler, 297 U.S. 1, 77 (1936). Disturbed by Roberts' reiteration of Hughes's contention in Schechter that the Tenth Amendment intended the reserve powers of the states to constitute a limitation on the power of Congress, Justice Stone wrote the historian Charles A. Beard inquiring if this was the proper historical interpretation of the amendment as indicated by the intent of its framers. Beard replied that it was not. Rather it was their intent "to put all 'general interests' under the federal government and to restrict the states to matters of local interest." Mason, *The Supreme Court,* p. 32.

62. U.S. *v.* Butler, 291 U.S. 1, 62. For comments on the ruling see Russel L. Post, "Constitutionality of Government Spending for General Welfare," *Virginia Law Review,* XXII (1935), 1–38; Charles S. Collier, "Judicial Bootstraps and the General Welfare Clause: The A.A.A. Opinion," *George Washington Law Review,* IV (1936), 211–242; John W. Holmes, "Federal Spending Power and States Rights," *Michigan Law Review,* XXXIV (1936), 637–649; and G. Merle Bergman, "Federal Power to Tax and Spend," *Minnesota Law Review,* XXXI (1947), 328–354.

Stone contended, "hardly rises to the dignity of an argument." Maintaining that "courts are not the only agency of government that must be assumed to have capacity to govern," he sounded an ominous warning against further abuse of judicial power, and called for a restoration of legal realism based on responsible judicial self-restraint.[63] And Stone's distress found resounding echoes off the bench. "What we face now," wrote Dean Lloyd K. Garrison of the Wisconsin Law School, "is not how government functions shall be shared, but whether in substance we shall govern at all."[64] Senator Hugo Black protested that "this means that 120,000,000 are ruled by five men," while George W. Norris castigated the body as a "continuous constitutional convention," and in Iowa, irate farmers hung in effigy the six justices who had destroyed AAA.[65]

Unperturbed, the five conservatives, buoyed by the praise of the Liberty League, next took a passing swipe at the investigatory authority and the administrative methods of the Securities and Exchange Commission.[66] They then extended the same ruling on the unconstitutionality of national economic solutions to the problems of labor, holding the Bituminous Coal Conservation Act of 1935 unconstitutional. The ruling revealed a growing division within the Court, particularly over the limits of that body's control of the people's elected representatives.

Coal had been one industry that had benefited from the NRA codes. With administration urging, Congress, in the 1935 Guffy-Snyder Coal Conservation Act, had salvaged the bituminous coal code and reestablished the NRA coal code authority. This new post-Schechter measure established a National Bituminous Coal Commission, composed of management, labor, and public repre-

63. U.S. *v.* Butler, 297 U.S. 1. 87. For comment on Stone's frame of mind see Mason, *Harlan Fiske Stone,* pp. 405–418; and Schlesinger, *Upheaval,* pp. 472–474.

64. Lloyd K. Garrison, "The Constitution and the Future," *New Republic,* LXXXV (Jan. 29, 1936), 328–330.

65. Schlesinger, *Upheaval,* pp. 488–489.

66. Jones *v.* S.E.C., 298 U.S. 1 (1936). Stone's response to the ruling was even more frankly critical than it had been to U.S. *v.* Butler; see Mason, *The Supreme Court,* p. 41. Hughes had been with the conservative majority in increasing judicial reexamination of agency and commission fact-finding, thereby taking a step backward in the movement to lighten the burden of the courts and relieve them of tasks others were better equipped to perform. See Crowell *v.* Benson, 285 U.S. 22 (1932); and St. Joseph Stockyards Co. *v.* U.S. 298 U.S. 38 (1936). See also Brandeis' devastating dissent in the former, at 65.

sentatives empowered to control production and prices through district boards in various coal-producing areas. Moreover, the Act guaranteed collective bargaining, stipulating that when wages and hours agreements were signed by the miners' union and producers of two-thirds of the national tonnage, such agreements should go into effect in the entire industry. It also levied a tax of 15 per cent on all coal sold at the mine head, nine-tenths of which was to be remitted to producers who accepted the code provisions. Framed with the Schechter rulings clearly in mind, its preamble stressed that coal was an industry "affected with a national public interest," and that the production and distribution of coal directly affected interstate commerce and so made federal regulation necessary.[67] Generally approved by much of the industry, including management and labor alike, a legal overturn of the Act appeared tactically difficult. The conservative justices, however, in a ruling that actually upheld the power of the Tennessee Valley Authority to dispose of power generated at Wilson Dam,[68] suggested a path. In that case, they validated the right of company stockholders to sue company officials obeying federal laws on the ground that such laws were unconstitutional. Such a suit brought the Guffy Act into Court in early 1936.

Sutherland delivered the majority opinion in a case cited as *Carter* v. *Carter Coal Co.* Rejecting, for all practical purposes, over twenty years of congressional study of an essential national resource and ignoring the protest of a number of the states themselves (seven had filed a brief supporting the act, maintaining that federal regulation was the only salvation for the industry), Sutherland voided the entire Coal Act. Despite the framer's intention that its sections be considered separately, he ruled the labor provisions unconstitutional, even though they had not been put into operation

67. 49 *Stat.* 991 (1935). On the conditions surrounding passage of the Act see Ralph H. Baker, *The National Bituminous Coal Commission* (Baltimore, 1941); and Jackson, *Struggle*, 153–159. The framers carefully separated its price-fixing and fair-tradition provisions from its labor clauses, making clear through a special clause that the provisions should be treated separately. On the technique, then in common use, see Robert L. Stern, "Separability and Separability Clauses in the Supreme Court," *Harvard Law Review*, LI (1937), 76–128.

68. Ashwander *v.* T.V.A., 297 U.S. 288 (1936). See Helen Martell, "Legal Aspects of the Tennessee Valley Authority," *George Washington University Law Review*, VII (June, 1939), 983–1012.

at the time of the case and there was no record involving their functioning, and concluded that the other provisions of the act, as inseparably linked with the labor provisions, were unconstitutional as well. He thus not only put the industry beyond federal aid, but outlawed federal monitoring of its internal operations, thereby suggesting that matters of fair price, decent wages, and collective bargaining were at the least state concerns, and preferably private considerations. The ruling, which again turned on a highly restrictive interpretation of interstate commerce, not only heightened Stone's disaffection, but prompted sharply critical comments from both Hughes and Cardozo. The Chief Justice objected particularly to Sutherland's flouting of the Act's separability provisions, arguing that the fact that the labor provisions were invalid did not by simple implication void the price provisions.[69] Cardozo was frankly disturbed by the Court's ignoring of social reality. If an industry in as anarchic a state as coal and as central to life was immune to federal regulation, he saw little hope for solution of the nation's general economic problems.[70]

Again public protest swelled as the implications of the ruling were understood. It grew more intense when two weeks later the four conservative members plus Roberts ruled unconstitutional New York's model state minimum wage law as a violation of freedom of contract, thereby by implication invalidating similar statutes in seventeen other states.[71] The ruling seemed a contradiction of the conservatives' own broader logic. One week earlier, in invalidating a federal Municipal Bankruptcy Act,[72] they had stressed that eco-

69. Carter *v.* Carter Coal Co., 298 U.S. 238, 321 (1936). Samuel Hendel, *Charles Evans Hughes and the Supreme Court* (New York, 1951), pp. 243–244; Pusey, *Hughes*, II, 746.

70. Carter *v.* Carter Coal, 329–332. For pithy contemporary comment see Irving Brant, *Storm over the Constitution* (New York, 1936), p. 144.

71. Morehead *v.* New York *ex rel* Tipaldo, 298 U.S. 587 (1936). One conservative journal reported that 79 per cent of commenting newspapers (in a period when the press was overwhelmingly Republican) called the ruling "regrettable," while 21 per cent found some reason for abstaining from condemnation. "Wage Law Decision as Viewed by Press," *United States News*, IV (June 8, 1936), 12. See also William E. Leuchtenburg, "The Origins of Franklin D. Roosevelt's 'Court-Packing' Plan," *Supreme Court Review* (1966), pp. 376–377; and John W. Chambers, "The Big Switch: Justice Roberts and the Minimum-Wage Cases," *Labor History*, X (Winter, 1969), 54–55.

72. Ashton *v.* Cameron County Water Improvement Dist., 298 U.S. 512 (1936).

nomic matters were state concerns. The action against New York now made it impossible for regulation to be carried on by state governments, the one public authority that they argued did have power to act. Such a posture was so blatantly irresponsible that even Herbert Hoover publicly protested, insisting that action would have to be taken "to give back to the states the powers they thought they already had,"[73] and leaders from both parties suggested constitutional amendment as a way of revalidating state authority.

The clearest manifestation of public hostility toward returning management of the nation's economic life to private hands, and the concomitant endorsement of the second New Deal's clearly avowed intention of pushing for national solutions to the depression and the nation's general economic problems, came at the polls in November, 1936.[74] All the frequently voiced conservative contentions that Roosevelt's election in 1932 was not a mandate for the type of massive national actions he had pushed through were belied as voters in forty-six of the forty-eight states gave the administration as resounding a vote of confidence and endorsement as any before or since in modern American history. To convince the conservative judicial majority of the wisdom of surrendering to the popular will meant modifying its absolutist position on the inviolability of property rights and curtailing its use of judicial review. And Roosevelt decided that an inevitable showdown should come sooner rather than later, especially since the Court was about to rule on the validity of the Social Security Act, the Wagner Labor Relations Act, the Railway Labor Act, the Commodity Exchange Act, state minimum-wage and unemployment compensation laws, and the powers of the PWA, SEC, and the Federal Communications Commission. Even the gold clause resolution faced another contest. Rigid adherence to narrow commerce and taxing precedents, to say nothing of narrow state regulatory prerogatives, spelled the doom of the whole New Deal program.

73. *Newsweek*, VII (June 13, 1936), 12.

74. The Republican candidate, Alfred M. Landon, was careful not to embrace the position of the Court's conservative majority, but stood clearly behind a platform that generally called for national solutions to economic problems, and specifically supported state regulation of hours and wages for women and children. Republican National Committee, *Text Book of the Republican Party* (Washington, 1936), pp. 33, 121.

The question was one of tactics. The President had come to feel that large elements of public opinion were now aware, especially in light of growingly more hostile dissent by liberal minority justices, that the obstacle to New Deal success lay not in the Constitution itself but in the composition of this particular Court. Here he clearly underestimated the degree of blind public adherence to both as stable symbols in unstable times. Nonetheless, after lengthy discussion with Attorney General Homer Cummings over some months, he decided that the Court could be curbed by act of Congress. The question was the form of action to be requested from that body. A variety of suggestions occurred. A constitutional amendment might be sought to end judicial review, but this tack was quickly discarded as cumbersome and time-consuming. The Court might be required to produce a two-thirds majority in order to establish the unconstitutionality of an act of Congress, but this might either produce noncompliance or might coerce justices anxious to preserve the prestige of the Court to join unwillingly with the majority so as to make a decision of the Court effective. The Court might be deprived of jurisdiction over certain subjects or of appellate jurisdiction generally. But this would still leave it with original jurisdiction, especially in cases involving conflicts among the states, and would also not get at the power of lower courts.[75] Finally Cummings, seeking to implement various suggestions by Princeton political scientist Edward S. Corwin, came upon a seemingly viable if ironic plan.

Justice McReynolds, while Attorney General under Woodrow Wilson, had set forth a proposal for retirement at seventy at full pay of judges on U.S. courts with the added suggestion that when one did not avail himself of the privilege, "the President be required, with the advice and consent of the Senate, to appoint another judge, who would preside over the affairs of the Court and have precedence over the older one."[76] With careful study, but little alteration the proposal was now applied to the Supreme Court as well. With six members of the high bench now in this category, congressional approval would insure Roosevelt the ability to name

75. Swisher, (ed.), *Papers of Homer Cummings*, pp. 146–154; Leuchtenburg, "Roosevelt's 'Court-Packing' Plan," pp. 384 ff.

76. *Report of the Attorney General for the Fiscal Year Ending June 30, 1913* (Washington, 1914), p. 5.

six new justices. It was this proposal that Roosevelt suddenly submitted to Congress on February 5, 1937, as part of a broader plan of judicial reorganization. In an accompanying message the President explained the necessity for the proposal, hanging it largely on problems such as crowded dockets and delay in judicial business caused by insufficient and infirm personnel. Only in a subsequent "fireside chat" did he reveal the policy implications of his move, stating them candidly: "Our difficulty with the Court today rises not from the Court as an institution but from human beings within it . . . we cannot yield our constitutional destiny to the personal judgment of a few men who, fearful of the future, would deny us the necessary means of dealing with the present."[77]

The resultant political battle over the measure constituted the bitterest domestic controversy of Roosevelt's long Presidency. Attacked as executive usurpation and as an attempt to destroy judicial independence, the measure became a political rallying point for Republicans and dissident Democrats who until that time had been hesitant to launch a head-on attack on the popular Chief Executive. Following heated hearings,[78] the Senate Judiciary Committee in June rejected the proposal in a report that insinuated that the President was trying to subvert American institutions and overturn the Constitution by questionable methods. The report deplored any attempt to make the federal judiciary "subservient to the pressures of public opinion of the hour."[79] Long before the proposed measure

77. *Senate Reports*, 75th Cong., 1st Sess. (Mar. 9, 1937), Report No. 711, I, 42. The statement was a part of a "fireside chat" which Roosevelt made to the American people on radio. Felix Frankfurter's role in the controversy was peculiar. Sworn by the President to silence and public neutrality, the future justice only near the end of his life revealed that he had been a confidant and adviser in the latter stages of the controversy. See Max Freedman (ed.), *Roosevelt and Frankfurter: Their Correspondence, 1928–1945* (Boston, 1967), 372 ff.

78. Senate, Committee on the Judiciary, *Hearings: Reorganization of the Federal Judiciary*, 75th Cong., 1st Sess. (1937). See also Leonard Baker, *Back to Back: The Duel between FDR and the Supreme Court* (New York, 1967), pp. 149 ff.

79. *Senate Reports*, 75th Cong., 1st Sess., Report No. 711, I, 21. The detailed literature on the episode is enormous. See Florence S. Hellman (comp.), *List of Speeches on the United States Supreme Court Issue*, U.S. Library of Congress, Division of Bibliography (Washington, 1937); and *The Supreme Court Issue: A Selected List of References*, U.S. Library of Congress, Division of Bibliography (Washington, 1938); Burns, *Roosevelt*, pp. 521–523; Schlesinger, *Upheaval*, pp. 699–701; Joseph Alsop and Turner Catledge, *The 168 Days* (New York, 1938); Pusey, *Hughes*, Vol. II, Chap. 70; Mason, *Stone*, Chap. 28; Jackson, *Struggle*, pp. 187–196, 328–353.

reached action stage, however, the justices responded themselves to such pressures and in a dramatic reversal promptly altered their attitude toward New Deal legislation and their concept both of national economic needs and their own role within the political system.

This immediate, and as it turned out, extended switch which saw the high bench and gradually the lower federal courts turned into instruments of popular government rather than makeweights against democratic sovereignty and governmental power, proved to be the crucial turning point in modern constitutional history. And although induced by an immediately contrived crisis on the part of the President, it had been in the making for some years.

The Supreme Court historically had gained its power as an agency trusted to establish and enforce constitutional limitations on the excessive use of government authority. In the 1930s it had made this power the basis of a virtually unlimited mandate to thwart the democratic process in the name of establishing proper limits on executive and legislative authority. Its four conservative members not only felt such a role would be vindicated, but saw no danger to the body in thus setting itself against the popular will in the name of preserving traditional constitutional limitations.[80] At least three of its members, along with its tactically shrewd Chief Justice, perceived the folly of such a course.

Negative government was not relevant to the needs of the times. A nation as deep in the throes of an economic crisis as the United States, forced to cope with nationwide economic problems that defied either private or local solutions, had to be able to utilize the one instrument capable of reaching such problems, the national government, which was, after all, the creature and implement of the general public will. Further, denial of the ability of that will to make itself felt by decisions almost solely negative and devoid of reasonable constitutional alternatives, seemed an admission of judicial irresponsibility calculated to destroy faith in those opinions

80. Felix S. Cohen was undoubtedly correct in 1935 when he wrote that the majority of the American people had come to expect the Supreme Court to act "more like a brake than a motor in the social mechanism." "Transcendental Nonsense and the Functional Approach," *Columbia Law Review*, XXXV (1935), 809.

creating positive precedents.[81] Seldom in the Court's history had the justices exercised such a degree of power.[82] But seldom had informed public opinion been so critical of its social obtuseness. Even elements of the conservative community could no longer view such an exercise in judicial supremacy as impartial action. The Philadelphia *Record* summed up a growing national sentiment. "By their own admission," observed the newspaper editorially, "they read their personal bias, their individual economic predilections into our fundamental law. Instead of utilizing their unequaled independence to serve the Constitution, they twist the Constitution to serve their notions. And today the document dedicated to the general welfare is employed to destroy the general welfare. . . . The Supreme Court's usurpation of power is the issue of the hour."[83]

It was Charles Evans Hughes's task to shepherd the body in publicly acceptable ways. Before 1937, he had still felt that this was possible through careful maneuvering to mitigate the sting of overly reactionary rulings.[84] But the Court-packing crisis made this seem no longer a viable course. Initially rebutting the President's charges through a widely quoted letter, written with the approval of Justices Van Devanter and Brandeis, he also looked for ways to change tactics. The problem was to visualize continued judicial authority through constitutional approval rather than constitu-

81. Stone was particularly outspoken in this regard, complaining bitterly in 1936: "I can hardly see the use of writing judicial opinions unless they are to embody methods of analysis and of exposition which will serve the profession as a guide to the decision of future cases. If they are not better than an excursion good for this day and trip only, they do not serve even as protective coloration for the writer of the opinion, and would much better be left unsaid." Harlan F. Stone to Felix Frankfurter, Feb. 17, 1936, quoted in Mason, *Supreme Court*, p. 41.

82. The Court between 1934 and 1936, e.g., had thrown out more pieces of federal legislation than in any comparable period in American history. See Norman J. Small (ed.), *The Constitution of the United States* (Washington, 1964), pp. 1398–1399.

83. Philadelphia *Record*, June 3, 1936, p. 8.

84. Hughes's voting pattern in the pre-1937 years is revealing. Apparently anxious to project a liberal image, but happy with conservative rulings, he willingly wrote opinions when he was on a liberal majority, but assigned them to one of the "Four Horsemen" when he was not. As one contemporary comentator pointed out: "When Charles Evans Hughes is a liberal, he proclaims it to the world. When he is a reactionary, he votes silently and allows somebody else to be torn to pieces by the liberal dissenters." Irving Brant, "How Liberal Is Justice Hughes?," *New Republic*, XCI (1937), 295–298; 329–330.

tional limitation, without turning the Court into an obedient rubber stamp, and the Chief Justice now moved to join those who had no trouble with such a challenge. Stone, Brandeis, Cardozo, and even, belatedly, Roberts could see clear ways whereby judicial acquiescence in the use of executive and legislative power would not have to mean the destruction of judicial authority. Judicial self-restraint had strong historic roots as a legitimate judicial role. Courts clearly had the right and duty to adapt, apply, and structure public laws so their impact could produce salutary public economic and social policies. In fact, certain of the conservatives even came in time to see that there was as much power to be gained from determining the way a law should be enforced and the areas to which it would be applied as there was in negating it.[85] The practice of adhering to stare decisis was not readily overcome, and it must be borne in mind that judicial approval of New Deal legislation clearly necessitated the reversal of a whole string of very recent precedents. Here the logic of legal liberals and realists provided possible rationalizations. Since the Near and Stromberg cases of 1931, the Court had been upholding the right of citizens to turn to national authority to protect their personal rights against encroachment by local authority and private power. A certain logical consistency could underwrite a similar utilization of federal power to protect those same citizens from economic exploitation by private interests supported by local pressures. It could also provide grounds for vindicating congressional programs designed to undermine dehumanizing factors such as unemployment, poverty, old-age, ignorance, hunger, and the privately uncontrollable business cycle.

The Court took its first strike down this path in late March, 1937. In a case virtually indistinguishable from the New York

85. A modern political scientist argues that the heart of this shift lay in the judges' acknowledgement of the greater importance of their being "goal-oriented" than "role-oriented," i.e., "having a stronger concern for achieving the right result in the controversies that come before them than in the process by which the Court arrives at that result." C. Herman Pritchett, "The Judicial Revolution and American Democracy," in Thomas R. Ford (ed.), *The Revolutionary Theme in Contemporary America* (Lexington, Ky., 1965), pp. 67–68. As to the extent to which Hughes himself shifted or changed his views see Alpheus T. Mason, "Charles Evans Hughes: An Appeal to the Bar of History," *Vanderbilt Law Review*, VI (December, 1952), 1–19.

minimum-wage case of the previous spring, Hughes, speaking for a five-man majority, upheld a challenged state of Washington law, and in the process not only eliminated freedom of contract as a legal stricture on state social legislation, but made clear that such a legal contrivance had no place in limiting general programs for human social betterment.[86] The ruling pulled the Court sharply back into the path it had begun in 1931 and 1932 in sustaining state police power. On the same day, the Court dealt squarely with three federal statutes, all similar to ones recently annulled in the 1934–36 period, upholding laws providing for farm debtors' relief,[87] collective bargaining on the nation's railroads,[88] and a penalizing tax on firearms, designed to enhance law enforcement.[89] The latter was particularly significant since it sustained a use of the taxing power for regulation parallel to that which the Court had voided in the Butler, AAA decision.

Two weeks later the constitutional revolution entered its second stage. Sustaining the constitutionality of the National Labor Relations Act, the Chief Justice gave Congress a green light to utilize the commerce clause as a device for tackling the nation's economic problems, and also launched the Court on its new affirmative course of applying, implementing, and extending positive federal economic power. "When industries organize themselves on a national scale, making their relation to interstate commerce the dominant factor in their activities," Hughes wrote, "how can it be maintained that their industrial labor relations constitute a forbidden field into which Congress may not enter when it is necessary to protect interstate commerce from the paralyzing consequences of industrial war." "We have often said that interstate commerce itself is a prac-

86. West Coast Hotel *v.* Parrish, 300 U.S. 379 (1937). On the implications of the ruling see Rolbert L. Stern, "The Problems of Yesteryear—Commerce and Due Process," *Vanderbilt Law Review*, IV (1951), 446–468; Robert E. Rodes, "Due Process and Social Legislation in the Supreme Court—A Post Mortem," *Notre Dame Lawyer,* CCCIII (1957), 5–33; John A. C. Hetherington, "State Economic Regulation and Substantive Due Process of Law," *Northwestern University Law Review*, LIII (1958), 13–32, 226–251; Robert G. McCloskey, "Economic Due Process and the Supreme Court: An Exhumation and Reburial," *Supreme Court Review* (1962), pp. 34–62; and Virginia Wood, *Due Process of Law* (Baton Rouge, 1951), pp. 151 ff.

87. Wright *v.* Vinton Branch, 300 U.S. 441 (1937).

88. Virginia Ry. *v.* Federation, 300 U.S. 313 (1937).

89. Sonzinsky *v.* U.S., 300 U.S. 506 (1937).

tical conception," wrote the Chief Justice in a Holmesian vein. "It is equally true that interferences with that commerce must be appraised by a judgment that does not ignore actual experience." "The power to regulate commerce is the power to enact all appropriate legislation for its protection and advancement . . . that power is plenary and may be exerted to protect interstate commerce no matter what the sources of the dangers which threaten it. . . ."[90] The same day the Court in four other cases[91] extended that principle into more specific and narrower areas and left no doubt that it intended to continue doing so, to the extent practical to accomplish national economic goals.[92]

In some respects the nonconstitutional implications of the ruling were more important than the legal ones. Prior to 1937, the Wagner Act had been a highly maligned, frequently challenged, widely defied piece of "experimental" federal legislation, a situation that Congress and the executive branch could do little to change. The Court had now given it constitutional status, functional breadth, legal teeth, formal sanction, and popular legitimization, and as a result, turned it into an effective instrument for a whole new epoch in management-labor relations. No longer would Liberty League challenge to its constitutionality produce the type of noncompliance that had characterized its life prior to 1937. Congress's policy now had been made operational. The National Labor Relations Board, which had previously been seriously apprehensive about its own permanence, now was so overwhelmed with complaints that had been held in abeyance until the constitutionality of the Act had been determined, that its business rose by nearly 1000 per cent, quickly becoming more than the board's staff could handle.[93]

90. N.L.R.B. *v.* Jones & Laughlin Steel Co., 301 U.S. 1, 41, 37 (1937).

91. N.L.R.B. *v.* Freuhauf Trailer Co., 301 U.S. 49 (1937); N.L.R.B. *v.* Friedman-Harry Marks Clothing Co., 301 U.S. 58 (1937); Associated Press *v.* N.L.R.B., 301 U.S. 103 (1937); Washington, Virginia & Maryland Coach Co. *v.* N.L.R.B., 301 U.S. 142 (1937).

92. Subsequent cases turned largely upon coverage. Operating upon the principle enunciated in Jones & Laughlin that "it is the effect upon commerce, not the sources of the injury which is the criterion," the Court went on to extend the Act into more and more local situations, leaving, in the end, no doubt that any type of labor-management controversy could be brought under its aegis. See Herbert O. Eby, *The Labor Relations Act in the Courts* (New York, 1943).

93. National Labor Relations Board, *Second Annual Report* (1937), p. 31. On the background and rulings see Richard C. Cortner, *The Jones & Laughlin Case* (New York, 1970).

The Court's action, and its broad impact, encouraged Congress to take another long step in the creation of national standards. In what turned out to be the last major piece of domestic legislation enacted prior to World War II, Congress, disturbed by the great variations in patterns nationally in maximum hours, minimum wages, and restrictions upon child labor, sought through the Fair Labor Standards Acts of 1938 to establish minimum national requirements.[94] With the Court having now accepted the principle of Congress's ability to enact such legislation as a legitimate exercise of its commerce power, the constitutional questions that arose regarding it almost exclusively concerned the Act's coverage. Here as with the NLRA, the Court assumed the positive responsibility for extending and legitimizing that coverage, at times into areas so remote from interstate commercial activities as to raise questions of whether it or the commerce power had any definable limits.[95]

This concern for labor's condition also saw the Court extending its power through its new activism in virtually rewriting its prior restrictive labor rulings and the federal statutes that permitted such restrictions. By 1941, it had not only removed, for all practical purposes, labor's activities from proscription under the antitrust laws,[96] but had interpreted the provisions of the Norris–La Guardia Act so as to make clear that under its definition of a permissible labor dispute a union might strike, picket, engage in all the other acts specifically enumerated in Section 20 of the Clayton Act, without fear of injunction, damage suit, or prosecution as far as the antitrust laws were concerned.[97] In addition, exemption from the

94. 52 U.S. Statutes at Large 1060 (1938).

95. See E. Merrick Dodd, "The Supreme Court, and Organized Labor, 1941–1945," *Harvard Law Review*, LVIII (1945), 1018–1071; and E. Merrick Dodd, "The Supreme Court and Fair Labor Standards, 1941–1945," *Harvard Law Review*, LIX (1946), 321–375; Paul H. Douglas and Joseph Hackman, "The Fair Labor Standards Act of 1938," *Political Science Quarterly*, LIII, LIV (1939), 491–515, 29–55; and Herman A. Wecht, *Wage-Hour Law Coverage* (Philadelphia, 1951).

96. Apex Hosiery Co., *v.* Leader, 310 U.S. 469 (1940). The case, a dramatic one involving sit-down strikers in a Philadelphia hosiery plant, is discussed in Elias Lieberman, *Unions Before the Bar* (New York, 1950), pp. 225–240. See also Charles O. Gregory, *Labor and the Law* (New York, 1961), pp. 255–269.

97. U.S. *v.* Hutcheson, 312 U.S. 219 (1941). Lieberman, *Unions*, pp. 241–251; Gregory, *Labor*, pp. 269–288. Justice Frankfurter's opinion constituted an extensive reorientation and harmonizing of existing statutes applying to labor unions and brought sharp criticism of the professed advocate of judicial self-restraint

coercive old practice of yellow-dog contracts was expanded to new limits.[98]

The breadth with which the Court was now prepared to interpret the commerce clause afforded similar authorization and extension of a variety of other pieces of federal legislation that later New Deal statute framers had so carefully tied to a commerce base. The second attempt of the federal government to enter the area of agriculture and agricultural production had been effected through a composite body of legislation enacted between 1935 and 1938.[99] As various segments of the structure met legal challenge and underwent judicial surveillance, the Court systematically erected a constitutional framework on which to sustain the whole program. Starting with a 1935 Tobacco Inspection Act, Hughes made clear that under its power to regulate interstate commerce, Congress could validly prescribe the conditions under which interstate sales of agricultural goods could be made.[100] Moving ahead, the Agricultural Marketing Agreement Act of 1937 was validated and with it regulation of sales both in intrastate and interstate transactions.[101] "The Commerce power," wrote Chief Justice Stone in 1942, in what turned out to be the last major challenge to that measure, "extends to those intrastate activities which in a substantial way interfere with or obstruct the exercise of the granted power."[102]

Significantly, it was Justice Roberts who validated the most ambitious of these laws, the second Agriculture Adjustment Act of 1938. Pointing out that the Act's various production restrictions,

---

not only from the bench (see Roberts' comments in dissent, 312 U.S. 219, 236) but from legal analysts. See especially Walton H. Hamilton and George D. Braden, "The Special Competence of the Supreme Court," *Yale Law Journal*, L (1941), 1363; and Charles O. Gregory, "The New Sherman-Clayton-Norris-La-Guardia Act," *University of Chicago Law Review*, VIII (1941), 503–516.

98. Phelps Dodge *v.* N.L.R.B., 313 U.S. 177 (1941).

99. Such legislation included a 1935 Tobacco Inspection Act, Potato Control Act, and Soil Conservation Act; a 1936 Soil Conservation and Domestic Allotment Act; a 1937 Agricultural Marketing Agreement Act; and a second Agricultural Adjustment Act in 1938. See Murphy, "New Deal Agriculture Program."

100. Currin *v.* Wallace, 306 U.S. 1 (1939).

101. U.S. *v.* Rock Royal Cooperative, 307 U.S. 533 (1939); H. P. Hood & Sons *v.* U.S., 307 U.S. 588 (1939).

102. U.S. *v.* Wrightwood Dairy, 315 U.S. 110, 119 (1942). For a general discussion of this line of cases see Ashley Sellers and Jesse E. Baskette, Jr., "Agricultural Marketing Agreement and Order Programs, 1933–1943," *Georgetown Law Journal*, XXXIII (1945), 123–152.

controls, and quotas were valid, since "any rule . . . intended to foster, protect and conserve . . . commerce, or to prevent the flow of commerce from working harm to the people of the nations, is within the competence of Congress,"[103] he established the power of the federal government to regulate the quantity of a commodity that could be sold, a type of regulation that in practical effect controlled the amount produced in an interstate industry. Thus Roberts in effect sanctioned, under the commerce power, the type of agricultural regulation he had struck down when it had been attempted under the taxing power.[104] Finally, in 1942, the Court, in defining the coverage of the Act, removed the categorical distinction between commerce and production, so much a part of the earlier interpretation of the clause in areas from antitrust regulation to child labor. "Whether the subject of the regulation in question was production, consumption, or marketing, is . . . not material for purposes of deciding the question of federal power before us," Jackson wrote in *Wickard* v. *Filburn.*[105] The test of the power to regulate any local activity was now a practical economic one and turned on the extent of the economic effect the activity in question had upon interstate commerce.

Similar patterns of validation emerged from judicial interpretation of the Public Utilities Holding Company Act of 1935[106] and the later Bituminous Coal Act of 1937.[107] Further, without benefit

103. Mulford *v.* Smith, 307 U.S. 38, 48 (1939).

104. Roberts was much maligned for so reversing himself, but actually quite unfairly. As Justice Jackson pointed out: "The two opinions by Mr. Justice Roberts are not legally inconsistent, since they are not concerned with the same power of Congress. . . . I would agree, however, that the latter opinion indicates a broader and more tolerant approach to the constitutional problem than did his first opinion." Jackson, *Struggle,* p. 238. Roberts' own 1951 comment here is revealing. Speaking at Harvard, he stated: "Looking back, it is difficult to see how the Court could have resisted the popular urge for uniform standards throughout the country—for what in effect was a unified economy." Owen J. Roberts, *The Court and the Constitution* (Cambridge, Mass., 1951), p. 61. See also Felix Frankfurter, "Mr. Justice Roberts," *University of Pennsylvania Law Review, CIV* (December, 1955), 311–316; and Chambers, "The Big Switch," pp. 64–65.

105. Wickard *v.* Filburn, 317 U.S. 111, 124 (1941).

106. Electric Bond and Share Co. *v.* S.E.C., 303 U.S. 419 (1938); North American Co. *v.* S.E.C., 327 U.S. 686 (1946).

107. Sunshine Anthracite Coal Co. *v.* Adkins, 310 U.S. 331 (1940). The measure constituted a reenactment of most of the provisions of the 1935 act with the exception of the granting of certain powers to the Coal Commission and the tax levied on noncooperating producers.

of the opportunity to validate specific legislation, the justices moved to extend federal regulation to the insurance business[108] and to the control of non-navigable inland streams,[109] thus placing federal authority over waterways upon a far broader constitutional basis than had previously been felt possible.

The commerce clause was not the only constitutional provision which the justices reinterpreted in their zeal for finding legitimate bases for new types of federal control. In two eloquent decisions, Justice Cardozo, sustaining both the unemployment insurance[110] and old-age pension[111] provisions of the Social Security Act, set forth a highly expansive interpretation of the federal taxing and spending power, underwriting with Court sanction Congress's premises about the national need to serve the general welfare implicit in the assumptions underlying the measure. "The purge of nation-wide calamity that began in 1929 has taught us many lessons," wrote the justice. "Not the least is the solidarity of interests that may once have seemed to be divided." "Unemployment is an ill not particularly, but generally, which may be checked, if Congress so determines, by the resources of the Nation . . . the problem is plainly national in area and dimensions. . . . Moreover, laws of the separate states cannot deal with it effectively. Only a power that is national can serve the interests of all."[112]

Such general underwriting of federal activism, even including final vindication of the power of Congress to create new power centers through proper delegation of its powers to various agen-

108. Polish National Alliance *v.* N.L.R.B., 322 U.S. 643 (1944); U.S. *v.* Southeastern Underwriters Assn., 322 U.S. 533 (1944). Congress promptly moved to undo the decisions by enacting federal legislation returning full control of the insurance business to the states. See Thomas Reed Powell, "Insurance As Commerce," *Harvard Law Review*, LVII (1944), 937–1008; see also Paul L. Murphy, "The New Deal and the Commerce Clause" (unpublished Ph.D. dissertation, University of California, 1953), pp. 243–251.

109. U.S. *v.* Appalachian Electric Power Co., 311 U.S. 377 (1940); Oklahoma *ex rel.* Phillips *v.* Atkinson, 313 U.S. 508 (1941).

110. Stewart Machine Co. *v.* Davis, 301 U.S. 548 (1937). Justice McReynolds, in dissent, turned to the annals of history, citing as relevant an 1854 message of President Franklin Pierce vetoing a grant of public lands to the several states for the benefit of indigent insane persons, as proof that this kind of concern was not legitimately one of the federal government, at 600 ff.

111. Helvering *v.* Davis, 301 U.S. 619 (1937).

112. 301 U.S. 619, 641, 644.

cies,[113] could not help but force a thorough reevaluation and readjustment of the relationship between such power and that of the states. Such readjustment necessitated the consideration of a large number of factors both constitutional and practical. The two particular areas of concern involved state police power and the raising of revenue to finance expanded state activities through new and varied approaches to taxation.

The Court's strides toward authorizing broad state regulatory power, which had momentarily wavered in 1935–36 after the course had seemingly been well plotted in the first five years of the decade, were resumed resoundingly with *West Coast Hotel* v. *Parrish.* [114] By the latter years of the decade such impact was resoundingly clear, as the state governments collected and spent more money, employed more people, and engaged in more activities than ever before in their history. Not the least of their activities was the broadened regulation of many aspects of the local economy. Yet coming at a time when federal power was expanding, the danger of the two sovereignties conflicting was ever present, especially as the federal government continued to expand its power into intrastate activities and the states more and more found themselves attempting to cope with interstate activities having a deleterious effect upon the local community.[115] This was particularly troublesome given the scope the Court was now conceding to the commerce power.

113. Opp Cotton Mills *v.* Administrator, 312 U.S. 126, 145 (1941). Stone, in setting straight the delegation issue, stated: "The essentials of the legislative function are the determination of the legislative policy and its formulation as a rule of conduct. Those essentials are preserved when Congress specifies the basic conclusions of fact upon ascertainment of which, from relevant data by a designated administrative agency, it ordains that its statutory command is to be effective" (at 145). This policy was defended at the time as traditional. See Jackson, *Struggle,* pp. 92–93.

114. Hughes later told his official biographer that the decision to switch in the Parrish case was not influenced by the President's court-packing proposal but had been reached in the confines of the Court well before publication of the President's plan. Pusey, *Hughes,* II, 757, 771, inferring that the Court had seen the light on reaffirming the legitimacy of state police power before any Presidential pressure was put upon it.

115. The reversal of the old Hammer *v.* Dagenhart precedent in 1941 in U.S. *v.* Darby (312 U.S. 100) eased the situation somewhat by removing the barrier created in 1918 to the proper exercise by Congress of its power over the actual movement of goods in interstate commerce. See Charles Fahy, "Notes on Developments in Constitutional Law, 1936–1949," *Georgetown Law Journal,* XXXVIII (1949), 14.

Clearly, in the absence of congressional action there was a permissible area of state control.[116] But where the Court in the 1920s had defined it largely in terms of the encroachment its use might have upon private property, the justices of the thirties developed more practical measures, curtailing such power only when its use seemed to pose a threat to the broad public interest. In the majority of cases in which the Court was required to make such a delineation, the justices tended to come up on the side of state police power. Only if the state law questioned was discriminatory or tended to retard, burden, or obstruct the flow of such commerce so as to serve the state's narrow economic advantage did the justices balk. And again, despite some sharp opposition from minority members of the Roosevelt-appointed post-1938 bench, the high bench seemed to relish the drawing of such lines, thereby constituting itself a powerful umpire in monitoring local economic as well as national policy.[117]

To a large extent the Court also willingly accepted a central role in judging the worth and validity of state taxing programs. Prior to the depression the states had relied principally upon real and personal property taxes as their chief source of revenue. But following 1929, many property holders were unable to pay even the normal levies and widespread sale of property for delinquent taxes was both politically and economically disastrous. The states were thus faced with the problem of finding new sources of revenue since the expenses of municipal and state government had increased sharply, especially in light of the great rise in unemployment and relief expenditures. New forms of taxation were thus evolved out of necessity and ranged from state and local sales taxes to taxes on the use of goods that had been bought in interstate commerce and upon which no sales tax had been paid, license taxes, taxes on chain stores,

116. In 1940, the Court expanded that area, eliminating a barrier to its exercise by reversing its 1936 Colgate *v.* Harvey ruling (296 U.S. 404 [1935]) and once again negating the privileges and immunities clause as a device for blocking state economic and social legislation. Madden *v.* Kentucky, 309 U.S. 83 (1940).

117. See William Anderson, *The Nation and the States: Rivals or Partners* (Minneapolis, 1956); Joseph E. Kallenbach, *Federal Cooperation with the States under the Commerce Clause* (Ann Arbor, 1942); Samuel J. Konefsky, *Chief Justice Stone and the Supreme Court* (New York, 1945); Ruth L. Roettinger, *The Supreme Court and State Police Power* (Washington, 1957), pp. 1–137; John R. Schmidhauser, *The Supreme Court as Final Arbiter in Federal-State Relations* (Chapel Hill, N.C., 1958), pp. 162–183; and Stern, "Problems of Yesteryear," pp. 451–460.

privilege, occupation, net income, and gross receipt taxes. The problems created here were potentially more serious than those involving local regulation for the health, safety, and welfare of local citizens. Great fear was aroused that state taxation might be used to discriminate against interstate competition, or against out-of-state business in favor of local business activity, and talk of "Balkanization of the United States" not infrequently arose. Further, the threat of multiple taxation continually posed a challenge, as more states sought new ways to raise the much-needed revenue.[118]

Again the justices attempted to devise workable judicial rules. Clearly discriminatory taxing schemes were viewed with a jaundiced eye. The delineation between direct and indirect burdens upon interstate commerce that such taxation might produce became a widely used although frequently challenged touchstone. But generally, in the late thirties and early forties, the Court underwrote its enthusiasm for a new cooperative federalism and federal-state partnership.[119] It encouraged both sovereignties to expand their activities in the economic and social areas by customarily sustaining their taxing proposals.[120] It was only in the late forties, when the nation's economic status had sharply changed, that a later Court tended to

118. For discussion of the problem see Konefsky, *Chief Justice Stone,* pp. 46–97; Paul J. Hartman, *State Taxation of Interstate Commerce* (Buffalo, 1953); Edward L. Barrett, Jr., "State Taxation of Interstate Commerce—'Direct Burdens,' 'Multiple Burdens,' or What Have You?," *Vanderbilt Law Review,* IV (1951), 496–532; and "Governmental Market Barriers: A Symposium," in *Law and Contemporary Problems,* VIII (April 1941).

119. One manifestation of this new tolerance came in reversal of the longstanding practice of intergovernmental tax immunity, with the Court upholding a state income tax levied on a federal employee. Graves *v.* New York *ex rel.* O'Keefe, 306 U.S. 466 (1939). On the details of this development see Thomas Reed Powell, "The Waning of Intergovernmental Tax Immunities," *Harvard Law Review,* LVIII (1945), 633–674; and Powell, "The Remnant of Intergovernmental Tax Immunities," *Harvard Law Review,* LVIII (1945), 757–805.

120. The final legal barrier to such expansion was eliminated in 1941 when Chief Justice Stone in U.S. *v.* Darby, 312 U.S. 100, ruled that the Tenth Amendment "states but a truism that all is retained which has not been surrendered. There is nothing in the history of its adoption to suggest," wrote Stone, in a deliberate effort to use history to validate his conclusions (Mason, *Stone,* p. 553), "that it was more than declaratory of the relationship between the national and state governments as it had been established by the Constitution before the amendments, or that its purpose was other than to allay fears that the new national government might seek to exercise powers not granted, and that the states might not be able to exercise fully their reserved powers" (at 123–124). On the implications of the move see Edward S. Corwin, "The Passing of Duel Federalism," *Virginia Law Review,* XXXVI (1950), 1–34.

jam the brakes on new forms of taxation, thereby strengthening the appeal to state revenue officials of sales taxes—in many respects the most problem-free form of taxation from an administrative standpoint.[121] Thus, much as with positive federal programs, the Court found that there were ways to be followed that would insure a type of judicial supremacy other than through applying constitutional limitations to state sovereignty.

The new Roosevelt Court of the late 1930s and early 1940s, having settled into its role as validator of positive governmental regulation of the economy, came quickly to realize that there were many unexpected dimensions to this new role. Always heretofore the servant of a conservative, property-conscious constituency, it now found itself praised and complimented by the liberal elements within society, particularly those who since well before the turn of the century had called for governmental and legal enforcement of social responsibility upon private property. In the same vein, a liberal executive and New Deal leadership in Congress acquiesced happily in such a role. The Court, in shelving its power of judicial review[122] and making their policies more effective, uniform, and universal in application, eased their task immeasurably.

But in winning new friends the Court also lost old ones, and found frequently to its distress that its new seeming indifference to property alienated large segments of its former supporters, particularly within the business world and the oligarchy of the American bar. And since such a shift had also involved a strong turnaway from traditional concepts of "mechanical" jurisprudence to a more highly pragmatic view toward the law and constitution, its former status as a vehicle of revealed truth evaporated, at least for this class. As Robert J. Harris wrote in 1948, "no longer could it be said by the late forties, as it could in the period when the Court was guaranteeing the right of a corporate oligarchy to be free of governmental regulation, that taking the judicial oath was comparable to the religious rites of anointment, ordination, or the laying on of

121, John P. Frank, "Court and Constitution: The Passive Period," *Vanderbilt Law Review*, IV (1951), 413.

122. The Court was not hesitant to review its own earlier rulings and reverse them, however. For a list of such actions see C. Herman Pritchett, *The Roosevelt Court* (New York, 1948), pp. 300–301.

hands."[123] Performing cooperatively, within a now recognized governmental framework, deciding issues of policy within that framework, the justices, even had they desired, were in a poor position to pose as remote oracles transmitting eternal verities into the control of human affairs. They were now another power group, working in cooperation with the other two branches of the government, determined to maintain and expand their general powers. Such a position hardly enabled them to set themselves apart from the normal human frailties of members of the legislative and executive branches.

But such a tacit admission of fallibility and pattern of general acquiescence and cooperation required that as the most vulnerable branch of the government, highly dependent upon popular respect and adherence for the implementation of its rulings, the justices surround themselves with a different mystique of authorization. And here, as New Deal leaders had found in other contexts, there was a usable past on which to draw. As the one branch of the government in many ways best situated for construing established statutes and legal language in the context of both initial meaning and intent and the later recasting that occurs when precedents are inadequate to cope with the needs produced by changing situations, the Court was in good position to project itself as logical guardian and vital protector of the nation's heritage.[124]

John Marshall proved particularly relevant in this regard. The early Chief Justice's conceptualization of the broad areas of federal power permissible through Congress's grants of authority, particu-

123. Robert J. Harris, "The Decline of Judicial Review," *Journal of Politics*, X (1948), 18. One authority has characterized the Court's action as the rejection of "legal fundamentalism." See Theodore L. Becker, *Political Behavioralism and Modern Jurisprudence* (Chicago, 1964), pp. 42–43.

124. Paul L. Murphy, "Time to Reclaim: The Current Challenge of American Constitutional History," *American Historical Review*, LXIX (1963), 74. Justice Black even wanted to reverse the process. In a startling dissent in Connecticut General Life Insurance Co. *v.* Johnson, 303 U.S. 77, 83 (1938), he argued that the Court should return to the original historic meaning of the due process clause of the Fourteenth Amendment, and wipe off half a century of unwarranted gloss during which the term "person" had incorrectly been interpreted to include corporations and grant them unjustified legal protection from valid public regulation. On the validity of Black's history see Andrew C. McLaughlin, "The Court, the Constitution and Conkling," *American Historical Review*, XLVI (1940), 45–63.

larly the power to regulate interstate and foreign commerce, was especially attractive.[125] A bit of rationalization was necessary, however. Marshall had given great breadth to the commerce clause for totally different reasons than had New Dealers. Seeking to undercut local interference with property rights, he had blocked out large areas of potential authority from state entry by claims of primary federal control with full knowledge that in an era of negative government, Congress would make little attempt to utilize such control through broad federal programs of economic regulation. As the Court moved to embrace broad commerce precedents, New Deal leaders both off and on the bench were quick to insist that this constituted returning the nation to the bedrock principles of the Founding Fathers.[126] When in 1946 Justice Frank Murphy wrote that the national government's economic regulatory power under the commerce clause "was as broad as the economic needs of the nation,"[127] his ruling was hailed as being particularly Marshallian.

125. Edward S. Corwin was particularly impressed with the nationalistic doctrines of Marshall as a basis for developing a proper body of national economic power, as well as his strong conviction that the Constitution, in order to endure, had to be adapted to the various crises of human affairs. See Gerald J. Garvey, "Corwin on the Constitution" (unpublished Ph.D. dissertation, Princeton University, 1962). Another deliberate attempt to tie a broad interpretation of the commerce clause to the initial intent of the framers of the Constitution was Walton H. Hamilton and Douglass Adair, *The Power to Govern* (New York, 1937).

126. Notable in this regard was Stone's majority opinion in U.S. *v.* Darby, 312 U.S. 100 (1941), and Jackson's opinion in Wickard *v.* Filburn, 317 U.S. 111 (1942), and the government's constitutional argument supporting passage of the Public Utilities Holding Company Act, *Memorandum on the Constitutionality of Title II of the Wheeler-Rayburn Public Utility Bill,* in Senate: Committee on Interstate Commerce, Hearings on S. 1725, 74th Cong. 1st Sess. (1935), pp. 797 ff. See also Carr, *Supreme Court and Judicial Review,* pp. 135 ff.; James Hart, "Limits of Legislative Delegation," *Annals of the American Academy,* CCXXI (1942), pp. 87–88; Robert H. Jackson, "Back to the Constitution," *American Bar Association Journal,* XXV (1939), 745; Raymond Gram Swing, "F.D.R.—Counter-Revolutionist," *Ken,* II (July 28, 1938), 12; Max Lerner, "John Marshall and the Campaign of History," *Columbia Law Review* (1939), pp. 396–431; Hugh E. Willis, "Growth in the Constitution and Constitutional Law Since the Decision in the Case of West Coast Hotel *v.* Parrish," *Tulane Law Review,* XX (October, 1945), 22–55; and especially Bernard Schwartz, *The Supreme Court: Constitutional Revolution in Retrospect* (New York, 1957), pp. 28–38. Schwartz has been historically obtuse in missing the implications of the maneuver to wrap New Deal actions in Marshallian justifications, failing completely to come to terms with the motives underlying Marshall's actions.

127. American Power & Light Co. *v.* S.E.C., 328 U.S. 90, 141 (1946). For a comparable earlier statement see 327 U.S. 686, 705–706 (1946).

The immediate solution of the Court to its power and status problem was clearly temporary, however. Approving and extending programs of economic reform, while important at a time when further expansion of domestic programs by Congress had virtually been terminated, could go on just so long. Discovering the areas in which proper adjudication would remove logjams and create easier ways by which future social problems could be solved before they got to the point of adjudication, while a path to greater societal stability, lessened the essentiality of a judicial umpire. Decisions such as the one in *Wickard* v. *Filburn,* giving virtual carte blanche authority to federal economic regulation, removed the body from the field of socioeconomic policy making and line drawing. Comparable elimination of legal limitations in other like economic areas produced similar results and served further to confine the Court's role to such tasks as monitoring the limited economic relationship between the states and the federal government, or handling technical questions of the permissible coverage of federal statutes.[128]

Yet the times produced challenges that demanded legal adjudication. Even before its economic role had come in for such sharp assault and reassessment, the body had begun to concern itself with problems of individual rights and personal freedom, and the creation of conditions in which such historic guarantees could be more completely utilized. Now, with the constitutional crisis over the government's positive ability to control the national economy resolved, it could devote more attention to such issues and in the process transfer its centrality and prestige as an umpire into new and pressing areas.

128. Wallace Mendelson has pointed out that "the view that economic policy is a matter for legislatures and voters again prevails. Since Mr. Justice McReynold's departure from the bench in 1941, there has not even been a laissez faire dissent." Wallace Mendelson, *The Supreme Court: Law and Discretion* (Indianapolis, 1967), p. 136. See also his observations on the "new economic activism" at pp. 33 ff.

CHAPTER 6

Big Government and the Rights of the Individual

THE American Civil Liberties Union, like a number of other liberal bodies, viewed the early New Deal's adventures with massive application of federal authority, particularly its aid to business and private power, with a highly jaundiced eye. Habituated to thinking of positive government as an instrument of repression, either through its use to curtail radical activities or to underwrite the application of various forms of private power, its leaders found it virtually incomprehensible that such power could be used to protect citizens' civil liberties and civil rights from abuse. They particularly viewed with skepticism the possibility that government could be counted on to intervene positively, on a continuing basis, to check business leaders and establishment organizations who traditionally exercised firm social control. Such a radical assault upon generally accepted private power agencies, they felt, would necessitate a role for government foreign to its traditional behavior, and one for which it had little enthusiasm, and even fewer instrumentalities.[1]

1. In its first annual report under the New Deal, the A.C.L.U. expressed concern at the new administration's action in throwing the weight of government on the side of employers, while doing little to prevent such employers from encouraging company unions and engaging in a great variety of traditional repressive tactics against working people. "Alarms are widely expressed over alleged dictatorship by the President, the abrogation of States' rights and the vast

As the decade progressed, civil libertarians rubbed their eyes with delighted astonishment. The American Civil Liberties Union, which in its annual report for 1934 was still viewing with alarm the danger of encroachment of federal authority, especially following Roosevelt's gains in the off-year elections,[2] filled its 1936 report with paeans of praise for the healthy new civil liberties climate that the government had created. For the A.C.L.U., the administration particularly was no longer the seat of repression. "The greatest single attack upon American liberties is the resort to force and violence by employers, vigilantes, mobs, troops, private gunmen and compliant sheriffs and police. These bulk far larger and more serious than restrictions by law."[3] Further, its leaders welcomed the creation of the La Follette Committee in early 1936, with its specific charge to investigate violations of free speech and assembly, and interference with the rights of labor. The 1936 A.C.L.U. Annual Report hailed the action as "a sweeping country-wide investigation of violations of civil liberties and collective bargaining, the first such Congressional investigation in American history, which for the first time will put the reactionaries on the defensive."[4] Although in the long run the union was disappointed with the lack of concrete results flowing from that committee's[5] lengthy and revealing investigation of company espionage, strikebreaking, and use of private arms and armies, it was gratified that the government was so oriented as to be willing to question such practices and cast them as civil liberties violations.

Civil libertarians for years had argued that it was economic discrimination that created a depressed body of second-class citizens unable and unwilling to demand their full civil rights and civil liberties. Leaders of the A.C.L.U. viewed the passage of the Wagner Act, the subsequent action of its National Labor Relations Board in enforcing collective bargaining, and the Supreme Court's actions

---

economic powers of the federal government," it stated. American Civil Liberties Union, *Liberty Under the New Deal: The Record for 1933–34* (New York, 1934), pp. 3, 9–10.

2. American Civil Liberties Union, *Land of the Free* (New York, 1935), pp. 3–4, 8–9.

3. American Civil Liberties Union, *How Goes the Bill of Rights?* (New York, 1936), p. 7.

4. *Ibid.*, pp. 5–6.

5. On the history of the committee see Jerold S. Auerbach, *Labor and Liberty: The La Follette Committee and the New Deal* (Indianapolis, 1966), pp. 197 ff.

in consistently upholding the legality of the measure and vindicating the actions of the board, as a triumph for civil liberties. Its 1937–38 report, for example, referred to such action as "the most important single step toward the attainment of meaningful freedom of speech which has taken place in modern times."[6]

Yet to certain advanced libertarian thinkers, even actions of this kind left much to be desired. It was gratifying to be able to read such implications into the actions of Congress, and to praise the President for moderation in the use of national power and for creating a healthy new climate for civil liberties. But there was still a disturbing feeling that neither the executive nor legislative branch had an active, consistent, and ongoing program for their full realization. New Dealers generally were not, as a group, individualistically oriented. Nor did they place high values upon the free individual operating with maximum self-determination within society. Rather, as William Leuchtenburg has pointed out, individualism in the thirties "gave ground to a new emphasis on social security and collective action."[7] Roosevelt may very well have expressed public sentiments of concern for the depressed within American society. Yet he saw them in the conglomerate, as "one-third of a nation" rather than individually. New Deal programs dealt with people in the plural, assuming that if enough governmental largesse were distributed, it would have the effect of restoring human dignity, out of which the individual could make as much of his own individuality as possible. Nevertheless, the Democratic party at its 1936 convention adopted a platform plank pledging support of First Amendment freedoms, as, in fact, did the Republican party.[8] By 1940 the Democrats were stressing the added urgency of protecting such freedoms "in the keen realization that the vivid contrast between the freedom we enjoy and the dark repression which prevails in the lands where

6. American Civil Liberties Union, *Let Freedom Ring* (New York, 1937), pp. 4–5; American Civil Liberties Union, *Eternal Vigilance* (New York, 1938), pp. 3–4, 7. The process was extended at the state level with strong civil libertarian approval as well. See "State Labor Relations Boards," *International Juridical Assn. Monthly Bulletin*, VIII (August, 1938), 13; "Little Wagner Acts—Amended Style," *International Juridical Association Monthly Bull.*, VII (June, 1939), 137.

7. William E. Leuchtenburg, *Franklin D. Roosevelt and the New Deal, 1932–1940* (New York, 1963), p. 340.

8. Kirk H. Porter and Donald B. Johnson, *National Party Platforms, 1840–1964* (Urbana, Ill., 1966), pp. 358, 369.

liberty is dead, affords warning and example to our people to confirm their faith in democracy."[9] Yet neither Democrats nor Republicans afforded any concrete ways by which civil liberties might gain the special protection that each party seemed to feel they needed. The same remained true through the 1940s.

Similarly, the ultraconservative, business-oriented Liberty League, although it never missed an opportunity to point out how big government was crushing the individual within American society and depriving him of his freedom and his rights, tended to think of those rights almost solely in economic terms. There may have been room for dissent against Roosevelt at Liberty League banquets, but certainly the Liberty League had no intention of utilizing its massive resources to support radical dissenters or other depressed individuals anxious to exert their individuality. Neither did it intend to lend its auspices to guaranteeing more fully meaningful practice of the Bill of Rights for all citizens.[10]

Others' concern was for positive action, however. John Dewey in 1936 called for rethinking the state's role in relation to civil liberties, indicating that the state had a positive responsibility for utilizing social control for their advancement.[11] Other advanced liberal thinkers referred to the necessity for reassessing American liberty with the idea of shifting its focus from being that of negative liberty—freedom from government and arbitrary restraints—to positive liberty—freedom to participate more fully in the democratic process.

9. *Ibid.*, p. 383. Americans had already come, in practice, however, to expect that practical protection of their civil liberties would come from courts—so much so, that as early as 1938 Grenville Clark, chairman of the American Bar Association's Special Committee on the Bill of Rights, warned of "excessive reliance on the Court to vindicate such basic rights as freedom of speech and assembly," arguing it was still primarily a private responsibility. Grenville Clark, "Civil Liberties; Court Help or Self Help," *Annals of the American Academy*, CIXXXXV (January, 1938), Supp. 1. For a similar but more pungent statement, see Thomas Reed Powell, "A Constitution for an Indefinite and Expanding Future," *Washington Law Review,* XIV (1939), 99, 108.

10. On the body and especially its civil liberties posture see George Wolfskill, *The Revolt of the Conservatives: A History of the American Liberty League, 1934–1940* (Boston, 1962), p. 30. In this regard, Herbert Hoover, who consistently refused to join the body, wrote a friend: "I have no more confidence in the Wall Street model of human liberty which this group so well represents, than I have in the Pennsylvania Avenue model." *The Memoirs of Herbert Hoover: The Great Depression, 1929–1941* (New York, 1952), III, 455.

11. John Dewey, "Liberalism and Civil Liberties," *Social Frontier,* II (February, 1936), 138.

Only thereby would all the advantages of life within a democracy be made available equally to all citizens.[12]

By the late 1930s, the times were ripe for actions along these lines. The growing threat of Nazi and Fascist tyranny, to say nothing of the infamous Moscow purge trials, brought home clearly and dramatically to the American people the dangers of legally uninhibited statism, creating new apprehensiveness regarding their own liberties and the clear necessity for positive action to protect them. Such a sentiment ran through a broad spectrum of American thought from far left-wing Communists and radicals, anxious to preserve their right to dissent and disseminate their doctrines, to ultraconservative opponents of the New Deal, as deeply concerned lest "that man in the White House" develop further dictatorial tendencies of his own, and they be insulated from governmental powers that they feared might be used to curtail their operations and diminish their property.

It is revealing to consider some disparate manifestations of conservative sentiment. In 1936, a New York division of the American Legion surprised both liberals and conservatives alike by authorizing and distributing a pamphlet on Americanism that placed strong emphasis upon the need for advancing civil liberties and stressing the attainment of more equitable human relations. So extensive were the requests for the pamphlet that they both startled its sponsors and outraged national leadership, which promptly denounced it as an "illegitimate Legion offspring," placing much too much emphasis upon freedom of speech and not enough on the fundamentals of religion. This liberal upthrust was quickly quelled, but not before the issue had been taken to the national convention where surprising strength for the liberal position was evident.[13] The Disabled Veterans of America (D.A.V.) in 1940 had much the same experience. After a special commission had come up with a new definition of Americanism that emphasized adherence to the Constitution and practice of the Bill of Rights, top officials promptly insisted upon

12. Frederic Heimberger, "Our Outworn Civil Liberties," *Christian Century*, LIII (Apr. 22, 1936), 599–600; T. Richard Witner, "Civil Liberties and the Trade Union," *Yale Law Journal*, L (February, 1941), 622. Such a view had been expressed in the 1920s by such figures as Dewey, Zechariah Chafee, Jr., and Horace M. Kallen. See Kallen (ed.), *Freedom in the Modern World* (New York, 1928), pp. 1–2, 22, 113, 150.

13. See Rodney G. Minott, *Peerless Patriots: Organized Veterans and the Spirit of Americanism* (Washington, 1962), p. 65.

qualifying both by expressing their unalterable view that there was no place in America for anyone not in direct and complete accordance with the principles of the American government.[14]

Much more significant was the action of the American Bar Association. That body, through its conservative leadership, had become highly political in the 1930s, fighting much of the New Deal legislation, and bitterly opposing Franklin Roosevelt's Court-packing plan. Its "tory" and "economic royalist" stances, however, did not go unchallenged. In late 1936 and early 1937, legal liberals such as Morris Ernst, Frank P. Walsh, and the former Chief Justice of Minnesota, John P. Devaney, set up a rival organization, the National Lawyers Guild, "on behalf of thousands of lawyers who believe in liberal and democratic action in government. . . ."[15] This move, plus growing internal pressure for liberalizing the A.B.A.'s image, produced a quiet campaign for regaining public support for the body, particularly as a firm bastion against the excesses of governmental centralization. Its conservative, but politically astute incoming 1938 president, Frank Hogan, supplied an attractive avenue in his acceptance speech. Hogan, who still viewed big government as an error and an evil, whether it curtailed property rights or the civil liberties of the First and Fifth Amendments, suggested the formation of an association committee on civil liberties to study violations and to work out a program to protect the rights of citizens.[16] A resultant Committee on the Bill of Rights was created with Grenville Clark of New York as its chairman and with members from both the conservative and liberal-moderate wing of the association participating. These ranged from Hearst counsel John Francis

14. *Ibid.*, p. 69.

15. "The Quarterly," *National Lawyers Guild Quarterly* I (1937), 1. The guild in its stormy history tended to attract a liberal, and ultimately radical, membership. When the A.B.A. returned to its traditional position of nonalignment on political issues during the Second World War, its liberal members largely defected. By the 1950s the Justice Department attempted to designate the body as a Communist organization, which it claimed had been the case since 1946, a move announced to the American Bar Association in a speech by Herbert Brownell in August, 1953. Although the action was unsuccessful, largely due to procedural complications, it stigmatized the body sufficiently to destroy its further respectability. The group's changing posture can be followed in its organ, the *National Lawyers Guild Quarterly*, which changed its name in 1940 to the *Lawyers Guild Review*.

16. Frank J. Hogan, "Lawyers and the Rights of Citizens," *American Bar Association Journal*, XXIV (1938), 617. On the forming of the committee see *Report of the American Bar Association*, LXIII (1938), 174–175.

Neylan and Charles Taft to Lloyd Garrison and Zechariah Chafee, Jr. Clark felt it essential for the association that the public be convinced that its conservative members shared an equal concern for civil liberties. "Leaders of conservative opinion have been unfortunately quiescent in the face of violations where the rights of minority groups advocating unpopular opinions have been involved,"[17] he warned. And he went on to make clear to the conservative members of the association that if they did not come to the defense of the rights of liberal groups, the time would come when they would not be able to state their case to the public. Significantly, the first legal action of the committee was the filing of a brief, prepared by Chafee, supporting the right of speech and assembly for the C.I.O. and the Socialist party in Jersey City, rights flouted by Mayor Frank ("I am the Law") Hague.[18]

This case, and others which the committee entered, were strictly chosen to demonstrate the evils inherent in the abuse of governmental power. Its membership developed little in the way of a positive program to gain freedom for individuals, within the context of big government, along lines that Dewey and other liberal thinkers were urging. In fact the limited scope of the committee's activities and purposes made even more clear that if meaningful action were going to be taken toward positive advancement of civil liberties, it would have to be by individuals in government acting primarily on their own, to evolve subtle techniques, outside the normal range of executive orders or congressional legislation.

Fortunately a number of such individuals existed. Such a quiet but effective figure was Frank Murphy. Murphy, former governor of Michigan and governor general of the Philippines, had been appointed on January 1, 1939, to the office of Attorney General to succeed Homer Cummings.[19] He promptly cleaned house at the

17. Grenville Clark, "Conservatism and Civil Liberties," *American Bar Associational Journal,* XXIV (1938), 640.

18. The brief is included in the U.S. Reports. See Hague *v.* C.I.O., 307 U.S. 496, 678–682 (1939). For a discussion of the case and the committee's role see Glenn Abernathy, *The Right of Assembly and Association* (Columbia, S.C., 1961), pp. 115–124; and Zechariah Chafee, Jr., *Free Speech in the United States* (Cambridge, Mass., 1941) pp. 409–431.

19. The literature on Murphy is extensive. See Rocco J. Tresolini, *Justice and the Supreme Court* (Philadelphia, 1963), pp. 176–178. See also J. Woodford Howard, Jr., *Mr. Justice Murphy: A Political Biography* (Princeton, 1968); and on Murphy's pre-Court activities, Richard D. Lunt, *The High Ministry of Government: The Political Career of Frank Murphy* (Detroit, 1965).

Justice Department, replacing a number of political appointees with skillful civil liberties–oriented attorneys, and within a month after his appointment had established a Civil Liberties Unit in the Criminal Division to prosecute violators of federal civil rights statutes.[20] In making public his order creating the unit, Murphy indicated that "in a democracy, an important function of the law enforcement branch of government is the aggressive protection of fundamental rights inherent in a free people." And he went on to indicate that through the unit, a central purpose of the Department of Justice would be "to pursue a program of vigilant action in the prosecution of infringement of these rights."[21]

Subsequent implementation made clear the direction in which Murphy had in mind moving. The department would now concern itself with being both a shield to protect citizens against arbitrary deprivation of their rights, and a sword to cut away at legal structures capable of being used to deprive people of their liberties at a future time. As a sword it might also move positively to discourage destructive private action through the revitalization of a number of forms of federal protection that had withered and become ineffective due either to misuse or restrictive court interpretations. In the latter regard, the unit set out to revitalize the Thirteenth, Fourteenth, and Fifteenth Amendments and statutes passed under their aegis, as a way of finding a new basis for a positive federal program of safeguarding civil rights within the express terms of the Constitution. Significantly the section won its first important case, *U.S.* v. *Classic,* in 1941 when the Court upheld the conviction of a crooked New Orleans politician, guilty of the crudest kind of election frauds, on the grounds that his actions had violated two sections of the old

20. Robert K. Carr, *Federal Protection of Civil Rights: Quest for a Sword* (Ithaca, 1947), pp. 1–32. See also Henry A. Schweinhaut, "The Civil Liberties Section of the Department of Justice," *Bill of Rights Review,* I (Spring, 1941), 206–216. Murphy tended to use the terms "civil liberties" and "civil rights" somewhat interchangeably. At the suggestion of its 1941 chief, Victor Rotnem, the unit's name was changed to the Civil Rights Section, with its activities in later years shifting largely to the civil rights area. See Auerbach, *Labor and Liberty,* pp. 208–209.

21. Carr, *Fed. Protection of Civil Rights,* p. 1. On the same day Murphy wrote to Roger Baldwin of the American Civil Liberties Union, "I am anxious that the weight and influence of the Department of Justice should be a force for the protection of the people's liberties." See Jerold S. Auerbach, "The La-Follette Committee: Labor and Civil Liberties in the New Deal," *Journal of American History,* LI (December, 1964), 455.

Ku Klux Klan Enforcement Act of 1870, which forbade obstruction or interference with the rights guaranteed to citizens by the Constitution or statutes of the United States. Stone in his majority opinion made clear that the Court was no longer prepared to tolerate official local misaction under the color of law, and thus not only struck a clear blow at the abuse of governmental power, but sustained the Justice Department's positive program of seeking to ferret out and discipline such abuses of civil liberties.[22]

The case reached the Court after Murphy had been appointed an Associate Justice to replace the deceased Pierce Butler, and leadership of the department had passed to his successor Robert H. Jackson. While not participating therein, Murphy, in other cases as a justice, pursued the line of affording special and positive protection to the rights of the individual.[23] Yet, though this was a logical extension of his behavior as Attorney General, his actions along these lines actually postdated similar decisions of the Court that had been handed down several years earlier by individual justices, particularly two of the "nine old men," Benjamin Cardozo and Harlan Fiske Stone.

Cardozo, an admirer of Holmes, with a long and distinguished liberal career of his own, had made clear early in his career on the high bench his commitment to permissible legislative experimentation in the area of state economic regulation.[24] And, reflecting the Brandeisian position, he had, while not writing majority opinions, joined the Hughes Court in throwing out state restrictions on freedom of speech, press, and assembly as well as abrogation of procedural rights and suffrage guarantees.[25] But as the clamor for

22. U.S. *v.* Classic, 313 U.S. 299 (1941).

23. See Harold Norris, *Mr. Justice Murphy and the Bill of Rights* (Dobbs Ferry, N.Y., 1965); Vincent M. Barnett, Jr., "Mr. Justice Murphy, Civil Liberties and the Holmes Tradition," *Cornell Law Quarterly*, XXXIII (November, 1946), 177–211; and Howard, *Mr. Justice Murphy*, pp. 238 ff., 265–299.

24. Williams *v.* Mayor, 289 U.S. 36, 42 (1933). See Dean G. Acheson, "Mr. Justice Cardozo and Problems of Government," *Michigan Law Review*, XXXVII (February, 1939), 522; and Andrew L. Kaufman, "Mr. Justice Cardozo," in Allison Dunham and Philip B. Kurland (eds.), Mr. Justice (Chicago, 1964), pp. 268, 271.

25. Cardozo had been with the majority in both Scottsboro cases, Powell *v.* Alabama, 287 U.S. 45 (1932); Norris *v.* Alabama, 294 U.S. 587; and in Morrison *v.* California, 291 U.S. 82 (1934); Grosjean *v.* American Press Co., 297 U.S. 233 (1936); Brown *v.* Mississippi, 297 U.S. 78 (1936); De Jonge *v.* Oregon, 299 U.S. 353 (1937); Herndon *v.* Lowry, 301 U.S. 242 (1937). Only in the Negro voting rights area did Cardozo rule against a complainant, Grovey *v.* Townsend, 295 U.S. 45 (1935), being unwilling to strain the Constitution to reach nongovernmental discrimination.

expansion of civil liberties intensified, he, as a careful student of the judicial process, felt the need to draw a sharp legal line marking off the boundaries of nationalization to guarantee the Bill of Rights against infringement by the states and their officials. While in no way deploring the process, he saw danger in blanket nationalization of all provisions of Amendments Two through Eight. On the other hand, he did not feel that experimentation along lines of nationalizing certain of the latter, and to him less basic, of the guarantees of the procedural amendments should be discouraged.

Cardozo's majority opinion in the December, 1937, case of *Palko v. Connecticut*[26] combined both a summing up of the past performance of one Court regarding the process, and a strong hint as to the proper path ahead. The case involved the limited question of whether the Fourteenth Amendment embraced the guarantee against double jeopardy in the Fifth Amendment. Cardozo ruled that it did not. This enabled him to make clear that the Fourteenth did not automatically protect all the rights extended by the first eight amendments. The question then was: which ones did it encompass? Here Cardozo's own values emerged clearly. To him only those rights "implicit in the concept of ordered liberty," and those principles of justice "so rooted in the traditions and conscience of our people as to be ranked as fundamental" should be nationalized by the Court. There was no doubt that these would include the First Amendment guarantees, particularly those of thought and speech. These were sufficiently basic, and of such "social and moral value" that they constituted the "matrix, the indispensable condition, of nearly every other form of freedom."[27] As to the others, the Court would clearly have to decide which were sufficiently "implicit." This process would leave in its hands both the task of evaluating, virtually on a case-to-case basis, whether the legislative estimate of contemporary needs properly respected individual rights, and the technical constitutional means for the "modernization" of the Bill of Rights.

26. 302 U.S. 319 (1937).

27. Cardozo was on record in this regard, writing in a 1931 article that "only in one field is compromise to be excluded, or kept within the narrowest limits. There shall be no compromise of the freedom to think one's thoughts and speak them, except at those extreme borders where thought merges into action. There is to be no compromise here, for thought freely communicated . . . is the indispensable condition of intelligent experimentation, the one test of its validity." Benjamin N. Cardozo, "Mr. Justice Holmes," *Harvard Law Review,* XLIV (1931), 688.

The latter encouraged the justices to formulate new liberties if they felt modern economic and social conditions necessitated their creation. Read by attorneys and civil liberties advocates, it seemed an invitation to obtain for citizens more meaningful use of their liberties by casting them as problems that were clearly part of "ordered liberty."

Almost simultaneously, Harlan Fiske Stone was rethinking the position in which the Court now found itself with the collapse both of economic due process and of restrictive constitutional formulas on the commerce and taxing powers. Stone too was concerned that the greatest and freest popular participation be protected and expanded. And particularly with new emphasis upon democratic problem-solving through political processes, the Court had a special responsibility to have regard for their purity. Only a month after Cardozo's Palko ruling Stone had written a majority opinion indicating his sensitivity to the subtleties involved in the problem. The case involved state regulation of interstate trucking firms and clearly constituted the type of economic regulation that the Court now was generally upholding. Stone, in validating the law, nonetheless placed emphasis upon the fact that if out-of-state truckers found such legislation unfair and overly punitive they should clearly have a popular remedy for taking action. To him, freedom to influence political action was the most basic freedom. And, as a matter of practicality, he pointed out that when regulation "is of such a character that its burdens fall principally upon those without the state, legislative action is not likely to be subjected to those political restraints which are normally exerted on legislation where it affects adversely some interests within the state."[28]

Stone was impressed by the Palko ruling in other ways as well. Through it, as he wrote Raymond L. Wise, he now saw it possible to apply special constitutional safeguards necessary for protecting individual freedoms without the necessity for constitutional amendment.[29] And in his immediately obscure, but later to become famous, Carolene footnote of April, 1938, he reaffirmed the thrust of Car-

28. South Carolina Highway Dept. *v.* Barnwell Bros., 303 U.S. 177, 185 (1938). See Allison Dunham, "Mr. Chief Justice Stone," in Dunham and Kurland, *Mr. Justice,* pp. 240–242.

29. Alpheus T. Mason, *Harlan Fiske Stone: Pillar of the Law* (New York, 1956), p. 516.

dozo's position. The Court in the future, he suggested, would be perfectly in order to give a much higher presumption to the validity of state regulation of economic matters, than to attempts by the state to curtail individual freedom and justice through the legislative process.[30] Once again his thrust was that civil liberties and civil rights had a preferred position above economic liberties and property rights. But as Stone's later opinions implementing the position made clear, he too subscribed to the Cardozo philosophy which placed First Amendment freedoms at the top of the scale of values as most basic. Deprive society of them, and freedom would be over. Deprive society of the lesser freedoms and through the First Amendment guarantees, society would have means for resuscitating and rejuvenating them.

This preferred-freedoms or preferred-position doctrine had roots as far back as Holmes's eloquent opinion in the Abrams case,[31] and Brandeis' sharp dissent in *Pierce* v. *U.S.* in 1920.[32] It was, in a sense, not unrelated to the Court's clear resuscitation and positive use of the clear and present danger doctrine, a process that had been begun cautiously, but clearly, in Roberts' *Herndon* v. *Lowry* ruling in April, 1937, a case in which the Court for the first time applied the test to uphold the civil liberties claims of the defendant against

30. The precise wording was: "There may be narrower scope for operation of the presumption of constitutionality when legislation appears on its face to be within a specific prohibition of the constitution, such as those of the first ten amendments, which are deemed equally specific when held to be embraced within the Fourteenth. . . . It is unnecessary to consider now whether legislation which restricts those political processes which can ordinarily be expected to bring about repeal of undesirable legislation, is to be subjected to more exacting judicial scrutiny under the general prohibitions of the Fourteenth Amendment than are most other types of legislation. . . . Nor need we enquire whether similar considerations enter into the review of statutes directed at particular religious, . . . or national, . . . or racial minorities, . . . whether prejudice against discrete and insular minorities may be a special condition, which tends seriously to curtail the operation of those political processes ordinarily to be relied upon to protect minorities, and which may call for a correspondingly more searching judicial inquiry." U.S. *v.* Carolene Products Co., 304 U.S. 144, 152–153 (1938). Stone's law clerk, Louis Lusky, had a major hand in formulating both the idea and the statement in the footnote. See Mason, *Harlan Fiske Stone,* p. 513.

31. Abrams *v.* U.S., 250 U.S. 616 (1919).

32. Pierce *v.* U.S., 252 U.S. 239, 270–273 (1920)

restrictive state action.[33] Stone's concept of its proper thrust emerged more clearly in his opinion in the famous case involving Mayor Frank Hague (the Carolene case had, curiously, not involved civil liberties in any way). Here, as his biographer points out, he again stressed the primacy of the First Amendment, in agreeing to take judicial action against restrictions on free speech and assembly, but also "claimed for the Court a special responsibility for safeguarding the political process." For unless it stepped in, interference with this primary mechanism for obliging government to control itself might render free government a sham.[34]

Opponents of the position and its implications clearly existed from the start. McReynolds consistently deplored what to him was the danger of the shift in emphasis away from the essential protection of property rights, as did others of the conservative senior justices.[35] A number of conservative moralists condemned the position for its departure from traditional natural law principles, with law as a device for restricting man's immoral impulses. A legal approach that struck all types of inhibitions from individuals and encouraged them to act freely and without restraint in their rela-

33. Herndon *v.* Lowry, 301 U.S. 242 (1937). The conviction in the case was upset principally on the grounds that the vagueness of the statute involved offended due process of law. Justice Roberts, however, clearly used preferred freedoms language in his opinion: "The power of a state to abridge freedom of speech and of assembly is the exception rather than the rule and the penalizing even of utterances of a defined character must find its justification in a reasonable apprehension of danger to organized government" (at 258).

34. Mason, *Stone,* p. 517.

35. McReynolds and Butler both dissented in the Hague case, 307 U.S. 496, 532 (1939), as did McReynolds in Schneider *v.* Irvington, 308 U.S. 147 (1939), a case in which the rest of the bench, including Frankfurter, raised Stone's Carolene suggestion to majority doctrine. Frankfurter, later to become the principal critic of preferred freedom, took a step toward the doctrine in Milk Wagon Drivers Union *v.* Meadowmoor Dairies, 312 U.S. 287, 299. "Freedom of speech and of the press," he wrote, "cannot be too often invoked as basic to our scheme of society." He then quickly went on to make clear that the state could place reasonable restrictions on such freedoms when the public interest warranted. Butler, curiously, dissented in the Palko case without opinion, even though the decision went against the plaintiff. It was thus not clear whether he opposed Cardozo's plan for selective nationalization, too heavy emphasis on the First Amendment, or the ruling itself. Black had explicitly refused to concur in that portion of the Carolene ruling which contained Stone's footnote. He also joined the majority in Palko. Clearly, at the time, Black was far more concerned with sustaining the democratic process than with the proper configurations of judicial review. See, e.g., his dissent in Polk *v.* Glover, 305 U.S. 5, 18 (1938).

tions with their fellow man, these critics maintained, was inherently immoral. Nor did they accept the relativism, realism, and pragmatism of the champions of such a posture who maintained that open and free participation in the democratic process could and would result in man balancing his evil temptations against those of his neighbors, with the public interest eventually served as a result of such interaction.[36] And in time, as the membership of the Court changed radically, such concerns became intrajudicial, with the dispute about the Court's proper role becoming increasingly more acrimonious, and splitting the Roosevelt-appointed liberals almost as sharply as economic issues had divided the pre-1937 bench.

Interestingly, the first Roosevelt appointee was, at the time of his appointment, clearly unaware of the subtleties of the question. He was, in time, to become the most vocal champion of carrying preferred freedoms to its fullest extreme. Hugo L. Black was an Alabaman with a long career in public life, a career with strong liberal and even populist overtones.[37] Committed from an early age to the position that the people had the right through their government to improve the condition of their daily lives, Black, starting as a police court judge in Birmingham, had empathized with the frustrations and ambitions of lower-class people. Elected county prosecuting attorney in 1914, he had enforced the law just as vigorously against

36. Holmes, in time, became a major target of the moral law critics, as he was singled out as the father of the new legal liberalism, or as one writer charged: "Holmes was the agnostic prophet for an agnostic age." Harold R. McKinnon, "The Secret of Mr. Justice Holmes: An Analysis," *American Bar Association Journal,* XXVI (April, 1950), 345. Earlier writers linked him with Hobbes and Hitler and charged him with being an amoral majoritarian. See John C. Ford, S.J., "The Fundamentals of Holmes' Juristic Philosophy," *Proceedings of the Jesuit Philosophical Association* (1941), pp. 49–77; and "The Totalitarian Justice Holmes," *Catholic World,* CLIX (May, 1944), 114; Francis E. Lucey, S.J. "Natural Law and American Legal Realism: Their Respective Contributions to a Theory of Law in a Democratic Society," *Georgetown Law Journal,* XXX (April, 1942), 493–533; and Ben W. Palmer, "Hobbes, Holmes and Hitler," *American Bar Association Journal,* XXXI (November, 1945), 569–573. For refutation of such views see Mark D. Howe, "The Positivism of Mr. Justice Holmes," *Harvard Law Review,* LXIV (February, 1951), 514–525; and Francis Biddle, *Justice Holmes, Natural Law and the Supreme Court* (Cambridge, Mass., 1961).

37. The literature on Black is large and growing. For a preliminary bibliography see Irving Dilliard (ed.), *One Man's Stand for Freedom: Mr. Justice Black and the Bill of Rights* (New York, 1963), pp. 487–491. See also Tresolini, *Justice and the Supreme Court,* pp. 173–175; and Stephen Strickland (ed.), *Hugo Black and the Supreme Court* (Indianapolis, 1967).

entrenched local interests such as coal and insurance companies as against bootlegging and gambling rings. Further he had launched an unpopular but successful investigation of police brutality against Negroes in the town of Bessemer, a suburb of Birmingham. Highly ambitious and knowledgeable regarding the avenues to power for a southern politician, Black in the earlier years of the 1920s joined a number of organizations: the Masons, Odd Fellows, Moose—and the Ku Klux Klan. Elected to the U.S. Senate in 1927, he promptly identified himself with the liberal wing of the Democratic party, and although he opposed the NIRA in the early New Deal days because it gave too much price-fixing power to business, he generally became one of the most loyal of Roosevelt's congressional lieutenants. In this capacity, he lead the fight for a national wage and hour law, and launched effective investigations of subjects ranging from corruption in the United States Shipping Board to the highly dubious lobbying activities of the utility holding company systems. These powerful bodies were, at the time, using every device possible, including huge sums of money, to defeat a proposed Wheeler-Rayburn "death sentence" provision in a public utility holding company bill, designed to break up their pyramided financial structures.[38]

Having campaigned vigorously for the reelection of President Roosevelt in 1936, and having supported fully the Court-packing bill, Black was rewarded with an appointment to replace the retiring Justice Willis Van Devanter in the late summer of 1937. Ironically, however, while the strongest misgivings about Black stemmed from his social and economic liberalism,[39] opponents of his nomination rallied around the sudden revelation in the early fall of 1937 of his former Klan membership.[40] In Europe at the time, Black hurried

38. So determined was committee chairman Black that he attempted to use the power of his Senate committee to subpoena supposedly bogus telegrams which the utility lobby had poured into Congress, sent over the names of unknowing citizens gathered from city and telephone directories. This invasion of privacy led to his censure by a Congress apparently highly sensitive to charges of violating individual freedom. See Dilliard, *One Man's Stand for Freedom,* pp. 16–17; and for details *The New York Times,* Mar. 6, 1936, pp. 1, 20; Mar. 12, 1936, p. 1; Mar. 24, 1936, pp. 15, 22.

39. Dilliard, *One Man's Stand,* pp. 18–21. See also Charlotte Williams, *Hugo L. Black: A Study in the Judicial Process* (Baltimore, 1950), pp. 14–18.

40. The story broke through a series of articles in the strongly anti–New Deal Pittsburgh *Post-Gazette,* beginning Sept. 13, 1937. See Strickland, *Hugo Black and the Supreme Court,* pp. 80–83.

home to deliver a nationwide radio address in which he both admitted his earlier Klan tie and rejected fully the charge that this in any way affected his personal attitude or his ability to deal fairly with all citizens. "I believe that my record as a Senator refutes every implication of racial and religious intolerance," he stated. "It shows that I was of that group of liberal Senators who have consistently fought for the civil, economic, and religious rights of all Americans without regard to race or creed."[41] With this admission, the storm of protest and controversy abated. Three days later Black sat as a member of the Court for the first time.

Nonetheless, Black was destined for continued controversy through his long judicial career.[42] Initially more knowledgeable regarding public social and economic needs and general justice than the fine points of legal adjudication, and having as yet developed no well-conceived judicial theories, he joined the majority and acceded to Cardozo's position regarding selective incorporation of the Bill of Rights in the Palko case, a position that ten years later he rejected for blanket nationalization.[43] More dramatically, he shocked his brethren with an early 1938 dissent by not only insisting that history be set straight by rejecting categorically the idea that the word "person" in the Fourteenth Amendment includes corporations, but by contending that "the doctrine of *stare decisis,* however appropriate and even necessary at times, has only a limited application in the field of constitutional law."[44] Two years later he joined with

41. John P. Frank, *Mr. Justice Black: The Man and His Opinions* (New York, 1949), p. 105; and Dilliard, *One Man's Stand,* p. 20.

42. Another flap that filled the public press was his acrimonious controversy on the bench with Justice Robert H. Jackson. While ostensibly involving Black's role in a portal-to-portal pay case, Jewell Ridge Coal Co. *v.* Local No. 6167, 325 U.S. 161 (1945), in which a former law partner took part, the underlying and root issue was Jackson's ambition for the Chief Justiceship and his fear that in his absence at Nuremberg, as chief American prosecutor at the war crimes trials, Black was gaining support for the position and for his particular legal views. On the incident see Wesley McCune, *The Nine Young Men* (New York, 1947), pp. 164–187; C. Herman Pritchett, *The Roosevelt Court* (New York, 1948), pp. 23–44; Eugene C. Gerhart, *America's Advocate: Robert H. Jackson* (Indianapolis, 1958), pp. 234–277; Frank, *Mr. Justice Black,* pp. 123–131; Williams, *Hugo Black,* pp. 172–187.

43. Adamson *v.* California, 332 U.S. 46, 68–125 (1948).

44. Connecticut General Life Ins. Co. *v.* Johnson, 303 U.S. 77 (1938). The quotation was from a concurring opinion of Stone and Cardozo in St. Joseph Stock Yards Co. *v.* U.S., 298 U.S. 38, 94 (1936), but taken with the call for admitting that sixty years of litigation was on an improper constitutional base,

Roberts in his opinion in the Hague case, in urging that the privileges and immunities clause of the Fourteenth Amendment be resuscitated as a special protection for personal freedom, a position that Stone at the time, carefully seeking ways to expand such freedom, categorically rejected as unwise and impractical.[45]

On the other hand, Black's basic instincts for justice and fair procedure were more easily translated into manageable constitutional principles. In a 1938 case, he spoke out strongly regarding the importance of extending the right of counsel and habeas corpus to all citizens.[46] The following year he sharply condemned the conviction of a Louisiana Negro by a clearly prejudiced all-white jury.[47] And on Lincoln's birthday, 1940, he deplored the practice of coerced confessions, in a case involving Negroes clearly subjected to third-degree tactics, pointing out that

> under our constitutional system, courts stand against any winds that blow as havens of refuge for those who might otherwise suffer because they are helpless, weak, outnumbered or because they are non-conforming vic-

---

it shocked even Stone. As one lawyer has written: "Stone was no more bothered by precedents than was Black; but there were accepted ways of getting around them, and Black did not use those ways. As a revolutionary, he wasted no time in carefully wrapping the idols in cotton and placing them away out of use and also out of harm; he would simply sweep them all out of the door." Leo Pfeffer, *This Honorable Court* (Boston, 1965), p. 329. Walton Hamilton, "Mr. Justice Black's First Year," *New Republic,* LXXXXV (June 8, 1938), 121, wrote at the time: "Justice Black has had legal training enough. What he needs is a course in hallowed platitudes."

45. Hague *v.* C.I.O., 307 U.S. 496 (1939). His heavy commitment to the democratic process led him also to call for sharp curtailment of state power over interstate commerce with the courts drawing lines between proper federal and state authority. "Spasmodic and unrelated instances of litigation," he wrote, in a 1940 dissent joined by Douglas and Frankfurter, "cannot afford an adequate basis for the creation of integrated national rules which alone can afford that full protection for interstate commerce intended by the Constitution. . . . Congress alone can, in the exercise of its plenary constitutional control over interstate commerce, not only consider whether such a tax as now under scrutiny is consistent with the best interests of our national economy, but can also on the basis of full exploration of the many aspects of a complicated problem devise a national policy fair alike to the States and our Union." McCarroll *v.* Dixie Greyhound Lines, 309 U.S. 176, 189 (1940). Liberal critics who, following 1937, had hoped the Court could be turned into a more enlightened and liberal third branch of the legislature, now wondered aloud whether Black was not the harbinger of the virtual abolition of the third branch.

46. Johnson *v.* Zerbst, 304 U.S. 458 (1938).

47. Pierre *v.* Louisiana, 306 U.S. 354 (1939).

tims of prejudice and public excitement. Due process of law, preserved for all by our Constitution, commands that no such practice as that disclosed by this record shall send any accused to his death. No higher duty, nor more solemn responsibility, rests upon this Court, than that of translating into living law and maintaining this constitutional shield deliberately planned and inscribed for the benefit of every human being subject to our Constitution—of whatever race, creed or persuasion.[48]

Yet, in the pre–World War II years, Black had clearly not evolved the consistent theory with regard to preferred freedoms which he would later favor. And his own views with regard to the proper relationship between the substantive rights of the First Amendment and the procedural rights of the later ones, although clear in cases in which such rights conflicted directly, still lacked definitive enunciation.

If Black had a counterpart, it was William O. Douglas, appointed to the Court by Roosevelt in April, 1937, to replace Louis Brandeis.[49] Douglas too was from small-town America, having grown up in the Pacific Northwest and climbed the ladder to prominence largely through his own efforts and ingenuity. The youngest of the Roosevelt choices at the time of his appointment and the youngest justice appointed to the Court in 125 years, Douglas had served as a member of the faculty of the Yale Law School in the freewheeling days when Robert M. Hutchins was its dean, doing pioneer work in recasting the law of business along functional lines. He also became a specialist in bankruptcy and during the depression years directed government-sponsored clinical studies of the causes of business failure. Under the early New Deal his knowledge in the latter area was sought, and as a part-time consultant he produced

48. Chambers *v.* Florida, 309 U.S. 227 (1940). On the background of the case see Tresolini, *Justice and the Supreme Court,* pp. 107–114, 175–176. One publication that had bitterly attacked Black's appointment characterized his Chambers opinion as "far and away the most direct, sweeping, and brilliantly written application of the Fourteenth Amendment to human rights that has come from our highest court." John A. Ryan, "Due Process and Mr. Justice Black," *Catholic World,* CLI (April, 1940), 38.

49. Representative of the Douglas literature is Vern Countryman (ed.), *Douglas of the Supreme Court* (Garden City, N.Y., 1959); Gilbert L. Oddo, "Mr. Justice Douglas and the Roosevelt Court" (unpublished Ph.D. dissertation, Georgetown University, 1952); Leon D. Epstein, "Justice Douglas: A Case Study in Judicial Review" (unpublished Ph.D. dissertation, University of Chicago, 1949). For a critical assessment see Yosal Rogat, "Mr. Justice Pangloss," *New York Review of Books* (Oct. 22, 1964), pp. 5–7.

an extended study of the manner in which equity receiverships were operated for the profit of the bankers at the expense of investors.[50] This work laid the basis for new laws including a key section of the Bankruptcy Act of 1938 that brought corporate reorganization under the administration of the bankruptcy courts and the Securities and Exchange Commission, and left the S.E.C. responsible for monitoring future actions by investment agencies.

Douglas then seemed especially qualified to serve on the S.E.C. In September, 1937, he became its chairman, promptly turning the agency into an aggressive instrument for bringing about self-reform and greater public responsibility by investment banking houses and the New York Stock Exchange, prodding the latter to set its house in order by launching revealing investigations of its past malfeasance, utilizing the strictures of the new Public Utility Holding Company Act as an added weapon.[51]

Douglas' image as a civil libertarian then was nebulous at the time of his Court appointment, but his instinctive championing of the underdog and the broad public interest were implicit in his career. Further, he never had concealed his devotion to the principles and judicialism of his idol, Louis D. Brandeis. Still, his early years on the Court produced little in the way of majority opinions that identified him clearly as a strong advocate of the new civil liberties line. Indeed, he registered one of the three dissents in the 1941 case of *U.S.* v. *Classic,* denying that a seventy-year-old congressional statute intended the constitutional power of Congress to authorize federal monitoring of congressional primaries.[52] Nonetheless, on the basis of his voting record in civil liberties cases in the period 1939 to 1946, the analyst of the Roosevelt Court, C. Herman Pritchett, placed him "with the left-wing grouping of Murphy, Rutledge and Black."[53]

50. Countryman, *Douglas of the Supreme Court,* p. 12.

51. See Marver H. Bernstein, *Regulating Business by Independent Commission* (Princeton, 1965), pp. 251 ff. For Douglas' own account of his experience as commission chairman see William O. Douglas, *Democracy and Finance* (New Haven, 1940).

52. U.S. *v.* Classic, 313 U.S. 299, 329 (1941).

53. Pritchett, *Roosevelt Court,* p. 130. Douglas was a good example of one of the new generation of law students trained in legal realism. See John W. Hopkirk, "The Influence of Legal Realism on William O. Douglas," in Gottfried Dietze (ed.), *Essays on the American Constitution* (Englewood Cliffs, N.J., 1964), pp. 59–76.

Others of the earlier Roosevelt appointees varied sharply with regard to their degree of commitment to the new civil liberties emphasis of the period. Stanley Reed, who replaced Sutherland in January, 1938, was strictly a moderate in the area, inclined more often to support legislative than personal freedom.[54] Reed, an affable and uncontroversial Kentuckian, who had been general counsel for Herbert Hoover's ill-fated Federal Farm Board and later for the Reconstruction Finance Corporation, had been a New Deal faithful in carrying out the difficult job of Solicitor General in the climactic days of 1936 and 1937. Further he had agreed with Stone in the Hague case that the path to effective protection of personal liberties was not, as the majority had suggested, through the privileges and immunities clause.[55] On the other hand, the argument that the times warranted special protections against government infringement upon the individual had little appeal to Reed, and although he did emerge as spokesman for the majority in the landmark 1944 case of *Smith* v. *Allwright,* in which the Court veered sharply to guarantee Negro voting rights,[56] such positions in his long career were normally the exception and not the rule.

Robert H. Jackson, who followed Murphy to the Attorney General's office, followed him to the Court as well. The resignation of Chief Justice Charles Evans Hughes at the end of the 1940–41 term, left Roosevelt with the task of naming a new Chief Justice; and after considerable deliberation, he elevated Stone to that position.[57] The maneuver opened Stone's Associate Justice seat, which promptly went to Jackson, whose public career to that point had followed the

54. Mark J. Fitzgerald, "Justice Reed: A Study of a Center Judge" (unpublished Ph.D. dissertation, University of Chicago, 1950); William O'Brien, "Mr. Justice Reed and Democratic Pluralism," *Georgetown Law Journal,* XLV (Spring, 1957), 364–387.

55. Hague *v.* C.I.O., 307 U.S. 496 (1939).

56. Smith *v.* Allwright, 321 U.S. 649 (1944). Reed's assignment to the case was a tactical maneuver. Originally it had been assigned to Frankfurter, but on the persuasion of Jackson, Chief Justice Stone was convinced that the white South would accept with less bitterness a ruling written by a native son than by a northeastern Jew not in his career particularly sympathetic with the Democratic party. Mason, *Harlan Fiske Stone,* p. 615.

57. Hughes strongly recommended Stone for the position, and although Roosevelt also considered Robert H. Jackson, Frankfurter leaned toward Stone, particularly since he was a Republican and the nation needed unity on the eve of potential hostilities abroad. Merlo J. Pusey, *Charles Evans Hughes* (2 vols, New York, 1951), II, 787–788. Mason, *Stone,* pp. 563 ff.

familiar pattern of New Deal service and political loyalty, combined with a commitment to support the new judicial self-restraint–oriented jurisprudence in the area of economic regulation that had marked the post-1937 rulings. Jackson's widely circulated 1940 book, *The Struggle for Judicial Supremacy,* had been a rationalization for Roosevelt's actions in checking the irresponsible power-wielding of the old Court, par excellence,[58] and once on the bench, he extended its thrust, taking the Court further out of the sphere of economic monitoring of government policies.[59] A successful lawyer in upstate New York, where he was known locally as a champion of the underdog, Jackson had come to Washington as counsel for the Bureau of Internal Revenue, moved to the Justice Department where he headed up the antitrust division, and revitalized the government's role in antitrust prosecutions with a vengeance. With Reed's elevation to the high bench, he moved into the position of Solicitor General compiling a notable record as a successful government advocate before the Court.

With Murphy's Court appointment, Jackson took over the Justice Department. He promptly found himself confronted, on the one hand, with the responsibility for continuing the civil liberties patterns Murphy had launched,[60] and on the other, with sharp new pressures for guaranteeing national security. These new pressures were intensified by the Nazi-Soviet rapprochement, suggesting an increasing necessity for the government to protect its defense plants in the face of domestic sabotage, real or imagined. In the same period, he raised the eyebrows of many members of the legal profession by affording President Roosevelt the legal rationalizations he needed to carry off his constitutionally shaky destroyers-for-bases deal with Great Britain. Similarly, many liberals were disturbed when Jackson innovated new and more efficient techniques for the regis-

58. Robert H. Jackson, *The Struggle for Judicial Supremacy* (New York, 1940).

59. Jackson's opinion in Wickard *v.* Filburn, 317 U.S. 111 (1942), gave the government virtually carte blanche constitutional authority in the agriculture area. See Paul L. Murphy, "The New Deal Agriculture Program and the Constitution," *Agricultural History,* XXIX (1955), 160–169.

60. Jackson's biographer contends that he was apprehensive that he might have to either carry out or extricate himself from policies Murphy had launched in the sedition area, in possible prosecution of the Teamsters Union under the antitrust laws, and in dismissing J. Edgar Hoover. Gerhart, *America's Advocate,* pp. 183–189.

tration and monitoring of the the activities of aliens.[61] Frequently mentioned for the Presidency in 1940, if Roosevelt did not choose to run, his appointment to the high bench occasioned little opposition, but also no great wave of enthusiasm from advanced civil libertarians.

But if Jackson and Reed displayed little concern or enthusiasm for aggressive and overt championing of civil liberties and preferred freedoms, Felix Frankfurter began, fairly early in his tenure, to challenge the concepts as ill-guided and to evolve a counter theory regarding the proper role of the Court in the civil liberties area.[62] Frankfurter, always hyperconscious of the fact that he was sitting in the seat formerly held by both Cardozo and the great Holmes, felt that the Court should not only follow a Holmesian pattern of self-restraint with regard to economic matters but that it should adhere largely to the same pattern in the civil liberties area.[63] Popular

61. Gerhart, *America's Advocate,* pp. 197–200. Jackson's defense of his destroyer-base opinion appeared some years later, Robert H. Jackson, "A Presidential Legal Opinion," *Harvard Law Review,* LXVI (June, 1953), 1353–1361. For contemporary views see Herbert Briggs. "Neglected Aspects of the Destroyer Deal," *American Journal of International Law,* XXXIV (1940), 569–587; Quincy Wright, "Transfer of Destroyers to Great Britain," *Ibid.,* 680–689; and Edwin Borchard, "The Attorney General's Opinion of the Exchanging of Destroyers for Naval Bases," *Ibid.,* 690–697.

62. On Frankfurter see Helen S. Thomas, *Felix Frankfurter: Scholar on the Bench* (Baltimore, 1960); Samuel J. Konefsky, *The Constitutional World of Mr. Justice Frankfurter* (New York, 1939); Wallace Mendelson, *Felix Frankfurter: The Judge* (New York, 1964), *Felix Frankfurter: A Tribute* (New York, 1964), and *Justices Black and Frankfurter* (Chicago, 1961). The law review literature on Frankfurter is voluminous. See especially "A Symposium on Justice Felix Frankfurter, *Yale Law Journal,* LXVII (December, 1957), 179–323; and "Mr. Justice Frankfurter," *Harvard Law Review,* LXII (June, 1950), 353–412.

63. Frankfurter's critics early questioned both the degree to which he was committed to self-restraint and whether his seizing upon that aspect of Holmes's philosophy to the exclusion of others was not needlessly doctrinaire. On the former point two Yale law professors could not help but note his virtual rewriting of the antitrust structure in the 1941 case of U.S. *v.* Hutcheson, 312 U.S. 219, pointing out that when he felt the end proper he could "discover the true intent of Congress; write a marginal note into the Norris-LaGuardia Act; use this to resolve the ambiguities of the Clayton Act; and eventually bring the moving gloss to rest within the Sherman Act itself." Walton H. Hamilton and George D. Braden, "The Special Competence of the Supreme Court," *Yale Law Journal,* L (June, 1941), 1363. Even Roberts, at the time, replied in dissent that the Court's interpretation seems "a usurpation by the courts of the function of Congress not only novel but fraught as well with the most serious danger to our constitutional system of division of powers" (312 U.S. 219, 472). On his excessive obsession with self-restraint see Harry Kalven, Jr., "Justices Black and Frankfurter," *Indiana Law Journal,* XXXVII (1962), 572–573.

government proceeded from the elected representatives of the people and their will should prevail as fully as possible. If policies were arbitrary, legislative solutions should be sought and the Court should encourage such action, thereby giving weight and support to the democratic process. In the civil liberties area, this meant that legislative assessment of current needs should be respected, unless the judges, following a Holmesian "reasonable-man" approach, clearly felt that such action was flagrantly in defiance of the community's sense of values and general wishes, and that access to legislative relief was clearly stymied.[64]

Frankfurter took a slightly different view of the procedural rights, however. As he wrote in the famous McNabb "moonshiner" case in 1943, "the history of liberty has largely been the history of observance of procedural safeguards,"[65] and since, in this area of law, the Court normally was not being asked to evaluate legislative enactments, but to determine whether the action of law enforcement officials and lower court judges squared with traditional legal procedures and precepts, the process did not involve challenging legislative policy but protecting and enforcing historic legal guarantees. Nonetheless, even in this area, he was prepared to emphasize the limited nature of the Court's role. Clearly there was a task of judicial supervision of the administration of criminal justice in the federal courts, which implied the duty of establishing and maintaining civilized standards of procedure and evidence. But in Frankfurter's jurisprudence the Supreme Court could only require of state courts that they enforce fundamental principles of liberty and justice, and at best, the intervention by the Supreme Court in the criminal process of states was delicate business. Such intervention should not be encouraged unless no reasonable doubt was left that a state had

64. Clyde E. Jacobs, *Justice Frankfurter and Civil Liberties* (Berkeley, 1961).

65. McNabb *v.* U.S., 318 U.S. 332, 347 (1943). The case involved illiterate Tennessee moonshiners suspected of shooting a revenue officer, taken into custody by federal officials and questioned over a period of two days, without the presence of friends or counsel, until a confession was secured. The Court voided the conviction, not on the grounds of unconstitutional self-incrimination, but because the prisoners had not been taken before the nearest judicial officer, "without unnecessary delay" for hearing, commitment, or release on bail, as required by statute.

denied or refused to exercise means of correcting a claimed infraction of the United States Constitution.[66]

Hence, where Black, Douglas, Murphy, and later Rutledge were prepared to make the Court the ever sensitive and vigilant protector of personal liberties, both substantive and procedural, Frankfurter was the strongest spokesman for the opposite wing of the Court, viewing such a position as unrealistic, both as manifesting an insensitivity to the wishes of legislatures, and as unwarranted policy making based on the private preferences of a few independent judges. "After all," as he wrote in 1948, "this is the Nation's ultimate judicial tribunal, not a super-legal-aid bureau."[67]

Frankfurter felt that such a position was in no way inconsistent with his long previous career in public life. Civil libertarians felt differently. To them, he was associated with such things as opposition to A. Mitchell Palmer's "Red" raids, the founding of the American Civil Liberties Union, condemnation of the Sacco-Vanzetti miscarriage of justice, and the fight against child labor and the labor injunction.[68] They thus found his performance on the bench disappointing from the outset. Frankfurter's appointment had produced somewhat ironically sharp challenges, particularly before the Senate Judiciary Committee, that he was a foreign-born radical and hence unfit to serve on the nation's high bench. He felt publicly compelled to deny before the committee that he was or ever had been a Communist.[69]

One other aspect of Frankfurter contributed to the mixed feelings about him. As a long-time professor of law at the Harvard Law

66. A typical statement of this view occurred in Hysler *v.* Florida, 315 U.S. 411 (1942), in which Frankfurter reasserted his view that "each state is free to devise its own way of securing essential justice."

67. Uveges *v.* Pennsylvania, 335 U.S. 437, 449–450 (1948). The case involved reversal of the indictment of a seventeen-year-old Pennsylvania youth charged with four burglaries with a maximum aggregate sentence of eighty years, since the plaintiff had not been advised of his right of counsel or been offered counsel at any time between arrest and conviction.

68. Frankfurter's earlier career comes through best in his own writings and memoirs. See Harlan B. Phillips (ed.), *Felix Frankfurter Reminisces* (New York, 1956); Archibald MacLeish (ed.), *Law and Politics* (New York, 1939); Philip Elman, *Of Law and Men* (New York, 1956); and Philip B. Kurland (ed.), *Of Law and Life and Other Things That Matter* (New York, 1965).

69. Pritchett, *Roosevelt Court,* p. 10; U.S. Congress, Senate, Committee on the Judiciary, "Hearings on the Nomination of Felix Frankfurter," 76th Cong., 1st Sess., Jan. 11, 12, 1939.

School, with numerous young former law student protégés in government (the "happy hot dogs"), Frankfurter frequently tended to behave like a professor on the bench, writing numerous long, discursive, sometimes cloyingly didactic concurring and dissenting opinions, in which he lectured his brethren on legal points which he indirectly or overtly seemed to infer they had not grasped.[70] One of his most consistent detractors and denigrators, Professor Fred Rodell of the Yale Law School, liked to allude contemptuously to his "judicial needle work."[71] This plus his often overly pretentious vocabulary and his proclivity for constant qualification of qualifications made his postures difficult ones around which to rally. A good summary of liberal annoyance with him came from Wesley McCune, who wrote in 1947:

> After years and years of fighting for changes in the interpretation of the Constitution, Frankfurter came to the Court after the basic changes had been made. Moreover, he hadn't been there long before a liberal bloc consisting of Black, Douglas and Murphy appeared at one side of the Court—and without benefit of a blessing from the great expert on constitutional law, Felix Frankfurter. This bloc, with votes occasionally from others, began to jell into a group which would seldom let red tape stand in its way of arriving at an end it felt to be desirable. In trying to stave off departure from procedural barriers, which Felix thinks make freedom rather than destroy freedom, he was driven into fancy dialectics and picayunish distinctions. He withdrew into a strict construction of his favorite document and laws passed by legislatures. Hence his many separate concurrences and dissents.[72]

However valid such criticism, Frankfurter was conceded to be the most knowledgeable lawyer on the bench and overall the preeminent

70. Frankfurter had long been close to Roosevelt, and had periodically acted as advisor on constitutional issues, a fact that did not diminish his sense of being close to New Deal orthodoxy. See Max Freedman, *Roosevelt and Frankfurter: Their Correspondence, 1928–1945* (Boston, 1967).

71. Fred Rodell, "The Supreme Court Is Standing Pat," *New Republic,* CXXI (Dec. 19, 1949), 12. Rodell had begun his assault early, a 1941 article having caused wide comment and some bitter rejoinders by Frankfurter's champions. Fred Rodell, "Felix Frankfurter, Conservative," *Harper's,* CLXXXIII (October, 1941), 449–459.

72. McCune, *Nine Young Men,* p. 83. For a similar latter-day evaluation see J. A. C. Grant, "Felix Frankfurter: A Dissenting Opinion," *U.C.L.A. Law Review,* XII (1965), 1042.

justice of his day.[73] Ironically, though, his role served to expose the Court's acrimonious divisions on the subject of civil liberties.

The implicit invitation on the part of Cardozo in his Palko opinion for individuals to cast their public grievances in the form of civil liberties issues evoked response initially by a religious group, the Jehovah's Witnesses. The Witnesses' unorthodox religious practices of door-to-door solicitation and street-corner sale of their publication, plus their desire to hold parades and public meetings in parks and on other public property, combined with their frank refusal to acknowledge the legitimacy of temporal authority, which frequently acted to curtail such actions, led their attorneys to raise First Amendment questions regarding their rights.[74] Specifically the question was raised as to whether governmental enforcement of local ordinances against their activities was not a violation of freedom of speech and press and the provision assuring that "Congress shall make no law . . . prohibiting the free exercise [of religion]." Prior judicial interpretation of the latter section had come largely as a result of Mormon polygamy, which the nineteenth-century Court had refused to authenticate as a "religious" practice.[75] The Witnesses now sought to "nationalize" it against state and local government action through the Fourteenth Amendment.

In March, 1938, the first of what was to become a series of Witness cases reached the Court. The results, an eight-to-nothing favorable ruling, encouraged the sect, despite their rejection of most temporal authority, to continue appealing to judges at least in an attempt to gain the carte blanche freedom from governmental authority that they desired. This first case, *Lovell* v. *Griffin*,[76] both produced a supporting brief from the American Civil Liberties Union and a vigorous defense by Chief Justice Hughes of the group's right to distribute their literature. Hughes held that a city ordinance being invoked against such distribution "was invalid on its face and estab-

73. Mendelson, *Felix Frankfurter: A Tribute,* p. 6.

74. Herbert H. Stroup, *The Jehovah's Witnesses* (New York, 1945), discusses the sect and its method of operations. The body had a legal department, with cooperating Witness attorneys in various parts of the country. Generally, however, Witness defendants were expected to conduct their own defenses at the trial level following a set of instructions issued by the Society. David R. Manwaring, *Render unto Caesar: The Flag-Salute Controversy* (Chicago, 1962), p. 27.

75. Reynolds *v.* U.S., 98 U.S. 145 (1879); Davis *v.* Beason, 133 U.S. 333 (1890).

76. Lovell *v.* Griffin, 303 U.S. 444 (1938).

lished a censorship of the press." By the time the second of the Witness cases reached the bench in late November, 1939, Douglas and Frankfurter had replaced Brandeis and Cardozo. In the case, *Schneider* v. *Irvington*,[77] the Court extended the principle of the previous year's decision one step further, invalidating an ordinance which forbade canvassing or distribution of literature from house to house without permission of the police.

Yet the ruling was more important in some ways to the liberal justices than to the Witnesses, for in it Roberts, speaking for a seven-to-one Court, with only McReynolds dissenting, transferred the principle suggested in Stone's Carolene footnote into a rule of law, giving the preferred freedoms initial majority enunciation.[78] Interestingly, Frankfurter made no protest. The Court, again, turned the case on freedom of the press. It was not until six months later, in May of 1940, when it threw out a local restriction working adversely on the Witnesses' desires to operate in defiance of local authority, that the Court invoked the "free exercise" principle.[79] In doing so, Roberts again, for a unanimous majority, drew a line that was to be important in later cases, clearly indicating that in embracing the two concepts regarding religion—freedom to believe and freedom to act—the First Amendment was dealing with an absolute in the first instance, but not in the second. Clearly freedom to act had to be balanced against the social impact of that action, with society's needs balanced against the individual's rights. Two weeks later, Frankfurter demonstrated how truly relative those latter rights could be.

For some years controversy had surrounded the Witnesses' views regarding saluting the flag, an act that they considered worshiping a graven image and proscribed by the Ten Commandments, but which a number of annoyed citizens considered their patriotic duty. The Court had earlier refused to take a Witness appeal on the

77. Schneider *v.* Irvington, 308 U.S. 147 (1939).

78. Roberts' statement was: "In every case . . . where legislative abridgement of the rights [to freedom of speech and press] is asserted, the courts should be astute to examine the effect of the challenged legislation. Mere legislative preferences or beliefs respecting matters of public convenience may well support regulation directed at other personal activities, but be insufficient to justify such as diminishes the exercise of rights so vital to the maintenance of democratic institutions. And so, as cases arise, the delicate and difficult task falls upon the courts to weigh the circumstances and to appraise the substantiality of the reasons advanced in support of the regulation of the free enjoyment of the rights." Schneider *v.* Irvington, 308 U.S. 147, 161 (1939).

79. Cantwell *v.* Connecticut, 310 U.S. 296 (1940).

issue.[80] But the facts of the 1940 situation, plus the fact that both the A.B.A. Committee on the Bill of Rights and the A.C.L.U. had made the flag-salute situation a major target area, now brought adjudication. Two Witness children, Lilian and William Gobitis, who had refused to salute the flag in the school classroom had been evicted from the school by order of the local board of education. Their parents had then promptly run afoul of another law, the state compulsory school attendance measure. Unable financially to send the children to private schools, the parents sought relief in the form of readmission to the schoolroom with attendance not contingent upon their being forced to take actions in contradiction to their religious beliefs. The situation clearly demanded a balancing of interests—the community's needs, weighed against the individuals' prerogative.

Frankfurter wrote the majority opinion of the Court, placing heavy emphasis upon the former. The times gave his position added support. With national headlines telling of Nazi armies overrunning France and the Low Countries, with Americans feeling their security challenged as it had not been for over a century, and with patriotic fervor mounting on all sides, Frankfurter lost no chance to stress that "national unity is the basis of national security," and that such unity is "fostered by the symbols we live by." These included first and foremost the flag, which he contended "transcended all internal differences, no matter however large, within the framework of the Constitution."[81] Such a posture enabled the justice to take his next desired step toward judicial self-restraint, and to stress the Court's proper role of refraining from challenging legislative judgments, even though their impact might be to curtail certain types of freedom.[82]

80. See Hollis W. Barber, "Religious Liberty v. the Police Power: Jehovah's Witnesses," *American Political Science Review,* XLI (1947), pp. 226–247.

81. Minersville School District *v.* Gobitis, 310 U.S. 586 (1940). Frankfurter drew his reverence for symbols from Holmes, yet Holmes had been circumspect here. "We live by symbols," Holmes had once stated, and then had added: "what shall be symbolized by any image of the sight depends upon the mind of him who sees it." Oliver Wendell Holmes, Jr., *Speeches* (Boston, 1913), p. 87.

82. The justice here equated a school board order with legislative policy, making it possible to argue judicial self-restraint, even though a school board order was hardly the order of a state agency. See Royal C. Gilkey, "Mr. Justice Frankfurter and Civil Liberties As Manifested in, and Suggested by, the Compulsory Flag-Salute Controversy" (unpublished Ph.D. dissertation, University of Minnesota, 1957).

Such a position was a direct repudiation of Stone's preferred freedoms posture and drew a sharp dissent from him, although to Frankfurter it incorporated the same principle of respect for legislative judgment as Stone had urged in his Butler dissent.[83] In Stone's opinion, the flag salute requirement suppressed freedom of speech and free exercise of religion, coercing children "to express a sentiment violative of their deepest religious convictions."[84] He also felt compelled to use the immediate situation as a clear illustration of why he felt the Court did have a special obligation to protect the freedom of helpless minorities, even if it supplanted the legislative judgment in doing so. Examining Frankfurter's contention that "so long as the remedial channels of the democratic process remain open and unobstructed, personal liberty is most secure," he made clear the inability of a minority group like the Witnesses, in a situation like the one at hand, to gain any meaningful relief through such channels, a circumstance that the hysteria of the time clearly intensified.[85] Nonetheless, Stone's dissent was the only one, and the case ushered in an unhappy period for the Witnesses, who now found the Court more than ready to place society's needs above their demands for individual noncompliance.

As the wartime situation progressed, however, and Nazi and Fascist tyranny grew, governmental coercion of individuals and general thought-control became increasingly unpalatable to Americans. In this climate, three of the liberal justices who had had some misgivings in the initial case, found their doubts regarding the flag salute situation strengthened. In a case in early June, 1942, which again

83. Frankfurter at the time wrote to Stone to this effect, stressing that his opinion would "be a vehicle for preaching the true democratic faith of not relying on the Court for the impossible task of assuring a vigorous, mature, self-protecting and tolerant democracy." This task, he contended, was the responsibility of "the people and their representatives." For the text of the letter see Alpheus T. Mason, *Security Through Freedom: American Political Thought and Practice* (Ithaca, 1955), pp. 217–220.

84. Minersville School District *v.* Gobitis, 310 U.S. 586, 601 (1940). Stone's biographer describes his agitated state at the time and the emotion with which he read his dissent. Mason, *Stone,* pp. 528–531.

85. Stone had replied to Frankfurter's letter in the same vein, distinguishing between a "vulgar intrusion of law" in the domain of conscience and in legislation dealing with the control of property. The Court's responsibility is the larger, he wrote, in the domain of conscience. See Mason, *Security Through Freedom,* p. 132.

found the Court, speaking through Justice Reed, ruling against the Witnesses, Black, Douglas, and Murphy took the unprecedented step of confessing repentance for their part in the earlier flag salute decision, while joining Stone, now Chief Justice, in a renewed demand for shifting the balance back to individual freedom.[86] The cases, in this instance, involved local peddling ordinances being used to prevent Witness activities.

Yet full reassertion of the preferred freedoms concept had to await change in the Court's membership. This came, however, only shortly thereafter. James Byrnes, who had replaced McReynolds at the beginning of the 1941 term,[87] was "drafted" from the bench for wartime administrative work by President Roosevelt in late 1942, and his seat was promptly filled with a member of the United States Court of Appeals for the District of Columbia, Wiley Rutledge, the only Roosevelt appointment with lower court judicial service. Rutledge, former dean of the Washington University and University of Iowa law schools, came to the Court, unlike Byrnes, as a frank champion of individual freedom, with clear sympathy for the preferred freedoms position.[88] In fact, in a subsequent case, *Thomas*

86. Jones *v*. Opelika, 316 U.S. 584, 623 (1942). Five of the justices here supported the validity of municipal license fees on transient merchants or book agents as applied in three different cities to Witnesses engaged in door-to-door peddling of religious tracts, on the ground that the taxes imposed were not unduly burdensome and were nondiscriminatory. "The First Amendment does not require a subsidy in the form of fiscal exemption," Justice Reed stated for the majority.

87. Byrnes's brief career on the Court was uneventful. His one major ruling, Edwards *v*. California, 314 U.S. 160 (1941), many felt was placed on the wrong constitutional base. The case involved California's anti-Okie law, which made it a misdemeanor for anyone to bring an "indigent person" into the state. Byrnes voided it as an unconstitutional barrier to commerce. Four members of the Court preferred to rest it on the "privileges and immunities" clause of the Fourteenth Amendment. In other opinions Byrnes voided a Georgia peonage law, Taylor *v*. Georgia, 315 U.S. 25 (1942), and upheld New York teamsters against prosecution under the federal anti-kickback law, Local 897 *v*. U.S., 315 U.S. 521 (1942). See William Pettit, "Justice Byrnes and the United States Supreme Court," *South Carolina Law Quarterly*, VI (June, 1954), 423–428.

88. Fowler V. Harper, *Justice Rutledge and the Bright Constellation* (Indianapolis, 1965); Tresolini, *Justice and the Supreme Court*, pp. 180–181; Alfred O. Canon, "The Constitutional Thought of Wiley Rutledge" (unpublished Ph.D. dissertation, Duke University, 1953); Robert H. Birkby, "Justice Wiley B. Rutledge and Individual Liberties" (unpublished Ph.D. dissertation, Princeton University, 1963); and "Symposium to the Memory of Wiley B. Rutledge," *Iowa Law Review*, XXXV (Summer, 1950), 541–699.

v. *Collins,* in 1945, he set forth what has been characterized as the "strongest assertation of this position,"[89] insisting that it was the Court's task "to say where the individual's freedom ends and the State's power begins," and contending that "any attempt to restrict those liberties must be justified by clear public interest, threatened not doubtfully or remotely, but by clear and present danger."[90] He now joined the majority in a May, 1943, case to produce a direct reversal of the peddling ruling of the previous fall, subscribing willingly to a decision by Douglas which stated categorically: "Freedom of press, freedom of speech, freedom of religion, are in a preferred position."[91] One month later, he joined five of the justices in reversing the flag-salute decision of 1940.

The case, *West Virginia State Board of Education* v. *Barnette,*[92] had the advantage for the Witnesses of coming after two years under the previous ruling had produced numerous and in some cases shocking examples of persecution of their children for refusal to accede to the patriotic orthodoxy that it demanded.[93] It again produced strong briefs supporting the Witness position from both the A.B.A. and the A.C.L.U. Justice Jackson, who normally sided with the public interest, now wrote an eloquent statement for the majority, condemning governmental actions geared to produce uniformity of sentiments by coercion. Alluding to the practices of the very enemies America was fighting and the posture America sought as leader of the free world, he contended that "compulsory unification of opinion achieves only the unanimity of the graveyard." He also went on to infuriate Justice Frankfurter by insisting that the frank purpose of the Bill of Rights was to withdraw freedom of speech, press, religion, and other basic rights from the reach of legislatures and popular majorities, using Holmes's "clear and present danger" test as support for his conclusions.[94]

89. Norman J. Small (ed.), *The Constitution of the United States: Analysis and Interpretation* (Washington, 1964), pp. 883–884.

90. Thomas *v.* Collins, 323 U.S. 516, 529 (1945).

91. Murdock *v.* Pennsylvania, 319 U.S. 105 (1943).

92. 319 U.S. 624 (1943).

93. Manwaring, *Render Unto Caesar,* pp. 163–186.

94. West Virginia State Board of Education *v.* Barnette, p. 639. Frankfurter was particularly outraged at the use of Holmes's clear and present danger doctrine to void the state's policy, charging that it was quite inappropriate as applied to this type of legislation.

Frankfurter's irate dissent was both an attack upon the ruling and upon judicial activism generally. "It can never be emphasized too much," he wrote, "that one's opinion about the wisdom or evil of a law should be excluded altogether when one is doing one's duty on the bench." He contended that "the only opinion of our own even looking in that direction that is material is our opinion whether legislators could in reason have enacted a law."[95] But temporarily, at least, Frankfurter was in the minority, and subsequent cases generally now saw the pendulum swinging back to the Witnesses' side. Such rulings were not without protest, however, particularly by Reed, who in few instances was willing to support the group's contentions.[96] Also somewhat ironically, Jackson found himself in frequent dissent, viewing virtually all the sect's activities, except their claim to freedom of conscience on the flag salute, with a sharp and jaundiced eye. His most acid comments regarding their proclivity for "riding roughshod over others simply because their consciences tell them to do so," he reserved for a series of three cases handed down on the same day in May, 1943.[97] Here his opinion chronicled and documented both the intolerant doctrines and practices that the group followed, leading such a respected constitutional scholar as Edward S. Corwin of Princeton to concur and to question seriously whether

> the right of people to resort to their own places of worship and listen to their chosen teachers stands on a constitutional level with the right of religious enthusiasts to solicit funds and peddle their doctrinal wares in the street, to ring doorbells and disturb householders, and to accost passersby and insult them in their religious beliefs.[98]

Nonetheless, despite the cogency of this argument, the Court tended to stay on the individual freedom side of the free exercise equation

95. Barnette, p. 645.

96. William O'Brien, *Justice Reed and the First Amendment: The Religion Clauses* (Washington, 1958).

97. Murdock *v.* Pennsylvania, 319 U.S. 105 (1943); Martin *v.* Struthers, 319 U.S. 141 (1943); Douglas *v.* Jeannette, 319 U.S. 157 (1943). Jackson's opinion occurs in the latter case at 166.

98. Edward S. Corwin, *The Constitution and What It Means Today,* 8th ed. (Princeton, 1946), pp. 180–181.

through Witness cases that continued to appear until early 1946.[99]

Cardozo's Palko rule, particularly his encouragement of modernization of the Bill of Rights, also led to a significant move on the part of champions of organized labor to advance labor's cause through such a mechanism. Subsequent development along this line was also clearly related to the preferred freedoms policy, both in its conceptualization and in its implementation. When the majority of the Supreme Court determined in its 1937 self-reorientation that the judiciary had no special obligation to protect property rights through the application of special legal mechanisms, labor was quick to challenge a number of the traditional strictures which had been so regularly applied against its activities. Further prosecution under the antitrust structure for illegal restraint of trade, use of the labor injunction, and the continued use of the yellow-dog contract quickly came under challenge. And in cases in 1940 and 1941,[100] the Court took the dramatic, if not unexpected, step of abdicating its former role of guaranteeing business power through the utilization of these devices, making clear that it no longer felt that its task was to afford business artificial legal advantages in dealing with its employees and their representatives.

But despite labor's gratification, its leaders were clearly aware that this was negative freedom in the sense of being a freedom from former restrictions. Seeking positive guarantees that these rights were basic and always available, they set out to use the preferred freedoms sword, hoping to induce the courts to acknowledge that such rights were indeed aspects of Bill of Rights guarantees, and as such, worthy of special judicial protection, particularly from legislative encroachment.

Brandeis, in a case in 1937, had already suggested somewhat tentatively that picketing might well contain elements of free speech.[101] The case involved a Wisconsin legislative enactment authorizing the

99. Two 1946 rulings raised unique questions of the right of the Witnesses to solicit in an Alabama company town, Marsh *v.* Alabama, 326 U.S. 501, and to distribute literature on a federal housing authority project, Tucker *v.* Texas, 326 U.S. 517. The Court upheld the sect in both instances, with Frankfurter joining the majority, but with Stone, somewhat unpredictably, joining Reed and Burton in dissent.

100. Apex Hosiery Co. *v.* Leader, 310 U.S. 469 (1940); U.S. *v.* Hutcheson, 312 U.S. 219 (1941); Phelps Dodge Co. *v.* N.L.R.B., 313 U.S. 177 (1941).

101. Senn *v.* Tile-Layers' Protective Union, 301 U.S. 468 (1937).

giving of publicity to labor disputes, and making peaceful picketing lawful and nonenjoinable. And although the decision was somewhat ambiguous and drew dissent from four members of the bench, it encouraged labor to think of this right as a civil liberty. This tendency gained added momentum as government and the public came to accept a strong labor movement as a desirable element in American life. The lower courts moved to follow the precedent, especially as the Court further underwrote the C.I.O.'s organizational rights by wrapping them with the protection of freedom of speech and assembly in the Hague case of 1939.

But the question still remained whether the Court would exempt labor from the proscriptions of an anti-picketing statute, thereby substituting its new commitment to the basic nature of the Bill of Rights for a legislative judgment. The answer was afforded resoundingly in 1940 in the famous Thornhill case.[102] There an eight-to-one Court, speaking through Justice Murphy, struck down such an Alabama law, insisting that the measure was invalid on its face. "If freedom of discussion is to fulfill its historic function," Murphy wrote, "it must embrace all issues about which information is needed or appropriate to enable the members of society to cope with the exigencies of their period." "In the circumstances of our times," he went on, "the dissemination of information concerning the facts of a labor dispute must be regarded as within the area of free discussion that is guaranteed by the Constitution." The position, which later analysts came to see in retrospect as the "high-water mark in the Constitutional rights of labor,"[103] drew dissent only from Justice McReynolds. But Stone had been apprehensive about throwing out the statute categorically, and had suggested that a more practical approach might have been to rule it void only as applied to the particular petitioner. This would have made clear, he felt, that picketing was not an absolute right, and that clearly situations would arise in which its curtailment might well be neces-

102. Thornhill *v.* Alabama, 310 U.S. 88 (1940).

103. Sidney Fine, "Frank Murphy, the Thornhill Decision, and Picketing as Free Speech," *Labor History*, VI (Spring, 1965), 99–120. Strong criticism of the ruling came at the time, however, with a number of legal commentators feeling it was "unguarded" and that Murphy was more concerned with speaking out against intolerance and oppression than with legal craftsmanship. See Fine at pp. 108–109.

sary to prevent imminent and aggravated dangers to lawful interest.[104]

Frankfurter, who went along with Murphy in the Thornhill case, certainly did not interpret the Murphy rule in this light. Clearly, to him, there was constant need for evaluating social needs and the public interest on a case-to-case basis against the type of freedom that labor was attempting to claim. In two cases in 1941, the justice, who had played a prominent role in the framing of the Norris–La Guardia anti-injunction law, and who a few weeks earlier had engaged in an exercise of judicial activism par excellence in judicially rewriting that law to make it applicable to conditions in 1941, spoke for the Court.[105] He sustained in one case, and rejected in another, the right of state courts to enjoin picketing. In sustaining picketing by parties not immediately involved in a labor dispute, he sharply challenged an Illinois law making such activity illegal.[106] In the second case, however, although making clear that "freedom of speech and of the press cannot be too often invoked as basic to our scheme of society," he nonetheless maintained that utterance in a context of violence "can lose its significance as an appeal to reason and become part of an instrument of force."[107] Such utterance, he contended, was not meant to be sheltered by the Constitution. Black, Reed, and Douglas dissented sharply.

The following year saw the pendulum swing back even more sharply. In a five-to-four decision, Frankfurter qualified picketing, this time peaceful, by weighing it against the public interest. Admitting that "by peaceful picketing workingmen communicate their grievances," and that "as a means for communicating the facts of a labor dispute peaceful picketing may be a phase of the constitutional right of free utterance," he nonetheless contended that "recognition of peaceful picketing as an exercise of free speech does not imply that the states must be without power to confine the sphere of communication to that directly related to the dispute."[108]

104. Fine, "Frank Murphy," pp. 109–110. See also Archibald Cox, "The Influence of Mr. Justice Murphy on Labor Law," *Michigan Law Review,* XLVIII (April, 1950), 767–810.

105. U.S. *v.* Hutcheson, 312 U.S. 219 (1941). See the comments in fn. 63, *supra.*

106. American Federation of Labor *v.* Swing, 312 U.S. 321 (1941).

107. Milk Wagon Drivers' Union *v.* Meadowmoor Dairies, 312 U.S. 287 (1941).

108. Carpenters and Joiners Union *v.* Ritter's Cafe, 315 U.S. 722 (1942). On the general subject of picketing as free speech see Joseph Tanenhaus, "Picketing as a Tort: The Development of the Law of Picketing from 1880–1940," *University of Pittsburgh Law Review,* XIV (Winter, 1953), 170–198.

Thus, two years after the Thornhill ruling, the Court had moved sharply back to the position that picketing might be free speech, but that even if it was, it was entitled to protection only at certain times and under certain conditions. On this point, therefore, advocates of the preferred freedoms position did not prevail even though, somewhat ironically, the position espoused by Frankfurter left the justices the responsibility of utilizing their own judgment on a virtual case-to-case basis to determine the legitimacy of this type of labor activity and legislative actions relating to it.

Curiously, on the peripherally related subject of labor's rights to assemble for purposes of organization, the Court, speaking through Justice Rutledge, went sharply in the other direction. In the 1945 case of *Thomas* v. *Collins,* the Court reversed the conviction of a union organizer arrested under a Texas statute requiring all labor union officials operating in the state to secure organizer's cards from the secretary of state before soliciting members. Maintaining that the statute was an invalid interference with freedom of speech and assembly, Rutledge ruled that it constituted a "restriction so destructive of the right of public discussion that it could not be upheld."[109]

In two other areas, revealing divisions emerged on civil liberties issues in the post-1937 Roosevelt Court. The importance of guaranteeing fair procedure on the part of law enforcement officials and judges was brought into sharp focus for a large number of Americans by the drumhead trials and police-state tactics of the governments of the totalitarian states rising so rapidly at the time. Yet while this undoubtedly intensified the Court's sense of general responsibility for sensitive evaluation of the administration of justice at the federal level, it in no way propelled the justices toward assuming the role of constant monitor and censor of state criminal procedures. It did produce a new concern on the part of some for seeing that "fairness" be guaranteed in state trial and pretrial procedures. Here Black's 1940 Chambers ruling stood out.

In maintaining that coerced confessions could not be used in a criminal trial without violating rights guaranteed the accused by the Federal Constitution, Black argued resolutely that the due process provision of the Fourteenth Amendment has led few to doubt "that it was intended to guarantee procedural standards

109. 323 U.S. 516 (1945).

adequate and appropriate, then and thereafter, to protect, at all times, people charged with or suspected of crime by those holding positions of power and authority."[110] The thrust of the argument was clear. The federal government did have a duty to guarantee due process in state as well as federal courts and that included a "fair trial." The difficulty lay in specifying the essential ingredients for a "fair trial." Clearly the admission of coerced evidence would destroy such fairness. But which of the other procedural guarantees of Amendments Four through Eight were equally essential, Black and the Court at large were unprepared to say. Rather, the justices chose to take cases on a wide range of subjects from the right to counsel and fair and impartial jury,[111] to search and seizure,[112] and

110. Chambers *v.* Florida, 309 U.S. 227, 236 (1940). In evolving a more clear criterion, the Court had little to go on, only in 1923, in Moore *v.* Dempsey, 261 U.S. 86, having begun to interfere with state criminal convictions. Subjectivity was clearly a strong consideration, the facts of each case, as well as the feelings of the justices, determining whether or not a particular state proceeding violated the due process clause of the Fourteenth Amendment. Holmes had once expressed this earthily, contending state administration of criminal law offends due process "if it makes you vomit." William O. Douglas, *We the Judges* (Garden City, N.Y., 1956), p. 272. But other factors prevailed. A tradition of federalism had established that due process was not solely a federal standard or that of any particular state. Rather it was legitimately divergent, provided only that local juridical standards, expressive of different combinations of historical and practical considerations, did not conflict with fundamental principles of liberty and justice, or more explicitly, that they represented the civilized standards of the Anglo-American world. Thus, turning to Bill of Rights absolutes was a temptation, but also a deceptively easy out.

111. In the jury area, the Court moved to, and then back away from, the concept that the commandment of the Sixth Amendment, which requires a jury trial in criminal cases in the federal courts, is picked up by the due process clause of the Fourteenth Amendment so as to become a limitation on the states. See Hill *v.* Texas, 316 U.S. 400 (1942); Akins *v.* Texas, 325 U.S. 398 (1945); Thiel *v.* Southern Pacific, 328 U.S. 217 (1946); Ballard *v.* U.S., 329 U.S. 187 (1946); Fay *v.* New York, 332 U.S. 261 (1947); and Moore *v.* New York, 333 U.S. 565 (1948).

112. In the search and seizure area the Court, although badly split in almost every case, consistently upheld governmental action in seizing incriminating evidence, either directly or by subterfuge or electronic means. See Goldstein *v.* U.S., 316 U.S. 114 (1942); Goldman *v.* U.S., 316 U.S. 129 (1942); Davis *v.* U.S., 328 U.S. 582 (1946); Zap *v.* U.S., 328 U.S. 624 (1946); Harris *v.* U.S., 331 U.S. 1945 (1947). The Court here could hardly have been uninfluenced by the government's generally lenient position on the use of wiretapping by the F.B.I. in situations involving national defense, and on Attorney General Jackson's careful line between interception and divulgence. "Any person," Jackson argued, "with no risk of penalty, may tap telephone wires and eavesdrop on his com-

to evaluate each based upon the circumstances of the case at hand. Thus even Black advocated no absolutist pattern at this time. And if he had, he would have mustered little support for such a position.

Typical of the Court's dilemmas and internal divisions in this area was its approach to the question of the right to counsel. The Scottsboro case of *Powell* v. *Alabama* in 1932,[113] had seemed to establish fairly firmly the point that in capital cases, where the defendant was unable to employ counsel, it was the duty of the Court to assign counsel to him as a necessary requisite of due process of law. And in one of his earliest decisions, Black had reiterated the principle in a case involving two nearly illiterate South Carolinians.[114] But in 1942, the Court, speaking through Justice Roberts, questioned seriously whether the right was under all circumstances a fundamental one, arguing that a number of state constitutions did not recognize it, and that it was not required by the common law.[115] This Betts rule drew sharp dissent from Black, Douglas, and Murphy, however, who contended that the right was a fundamental one whose denial "is shocking to the universal sense of justice."[116] And with Rutledge joining them, they temporarily swung the pendulum back, in the 1944 term, toward guarantee of the right,[117] only to see the Frankfurter-Roberts-Jackson wing moving it the other way in

---

petitor, employer, workman, or others, and act upon what he hears or make any use of it that does not involve divulging or publication." William S. Fairfield and Charles Clift, "The Wiretappers," in Max Ascoli (ed.), *Our Times: The Best from the Reporter* (New York, 1960), p. 59. See also Jacob W. Landynski, *Search and Seizure and the Supreme Court* (Baltimore, 1966), pp. 227–278; Alan F. Westin, *Privacy and Freedom* (New York, 1967), pp. 176–177. President Roosevelt was sanguine about the use of wiretapping in the national security area. See David W. Helfeld, "Justice Department Policies on Wiretapping," *Lawyers Guild Review,* IX (1949), 60; "Congressional Wiretapping Policy Overdue," *Stanford Law Review,* II (1949), 750; and J. Edgar Hoover, "Rejoinder," *Yale Law Journal,* LVIII (1949), 423.

113. 287 U.S. 45 (1932).

114. Johnson *v.* Zerbst, 304 U.S. 458 (1938).

115. Betts *v.* Brady, 316 U.S. 455 (1942).

116. *Ibid.,* at p. 476. For contemporary comment see the letter of Benjamin V. Cohen and Erwin N. Griswold to *The New York Times* in James M. Smith and Paul L. Murphy, *Liberty and Justice: A Historical Record of American Constitutional Development* (2 vols., New York, 1968), II, 466. See also William M. Beaney, *The Right to Counsel in American Courts* (Ann Arbor, 1955), pp. 160–164.

117. Williams *v.* Kaiser, 323 U.S. 471 (1945); Tomkins *v.* Missouri, 323 U.S. 485 (1945); Mouse *v.* Mayo, 323 U.S. 24 (1945); Rice *v.* Olson, 324 U.S. 786 (1945).

subsequent rulings.[118] Thus the right remained relative and was not to be fully guaranteed for another decade and a half.

Two unrelated but celebrated cases further illustrated the Court's concerns in the procedural area. In cases in 1941, one involving the conservative Los Angeles *Times*,[119] the other, the left-wing and radical head of the West Coast longshoremen, Harry Bridges,[120] the Court was called to balance the First Amendment guarantee of freedom of the press against the procedural rights implicit in due process and a fair trial. In each case the issue was whether inflammatory publicity produced during the course of judicial proceedings was sufficiently threatening as to prevent a fair trial. In both cases, the Court came up on the side of the First Amendment guarantee, with Black making clear, in his preferred freedoms–oriented joint opinion, that only if press comment created a clear and present danger to the actual rendering of impartial justice, could its curtailment be considered.

The other case, *Screws* v. *U.S.*,[121] involved police brutality, specifically the beating to death of a Negro suspect by a Georgia sheriff. When Georgia authorities refused to act, the Murphy-created Civil Rights Section of the Justice Department moved to make the situation a federal case, once again seeking to use sections of the old post–Civil War Reconstruction statutes as a basis for such action. The Court was split not only sharply but acrimoniously. Clearly the statute under which the government was seeking conviction was broad and vague and failed to provide ascertainable standards of guilt, thus leaving state law enforcement officers uncertain as to what rights they must respect in order to avoid criminal prosecution under it. Douglas wrote the majority opinion, in which Black and Reed joined. While clearly shocked by the circumstances, and personally convinced of the need for legal action, he was highly troubled by the vagueness of the statute and at most was willing to read it with a gratuitous tightness and order a new trial. Murphy, on the other hand, felt such legal hair-splitting was needless. The sheriff

118. Carter *v.* Illinois, 329 U.S. 173 (1946); Gayes *v.* New York, 332 U.S. 145 (1947); Foster *v.* Illinois, 332 U.S. 134 (1947).

119. Times-Mirror Co. *v.* Superior Court of California, 314 U.S. 252 (1941).

120. Bridges *v.* California, 314 U.S. 252 (1941).

121. Screws *v.* U.S., 325 U.S. 91 (1945). On the case see Robert K. Carr, "Screws vs. United States: The Georgia Police Brutality Case," *Cornell Law Quarterly*, XXXI (1945), 48–67.

had brutally killed a prisoner in his custody. The statute made it a federal crime for a public official to deprive a person of a constitutional right. Therefore clearly the sheriff was guilty. Roberts, Frankfurter, and Jackson, by contrast, were all of the opinion that the statute was frankly unconstitutional since it was so vague as not to afford clear standards. And since its vagueness was so clear, they were alarmed at the thought that, if validated and used further, it would serve as a device for authorizing massive and insensitive federal interference into state criminal procedure at all levels. To Frankfurter particularly, the solution of the problem of the breakdown of state criminal justice lay not in the Supreme Court but in the people, who should be encouraged through their state legislatures to raise standards generally by statute.

The Negro fared better in other regards in the period, however. Frankfurter spoke for a seven-man majority in 1939 in putting finally to rest the highly discriminatory grandfather clause, used for nearly half a century to restrict Negro suffrage.[122] And Reed, in 1944, in *Smith* v. *Allwright*,[123] pronounced the same benediction for the Southern white primary, in the process cautiously, but clearly, reversing a decision of only nine years earlier that had permitted political parties to organize as "private clubs" and thus bar Negroes from their counsels, thereby avoiding the charge that such discrimination was "state action."[124]

On the more central question of segregation, however, different patterns evolved. By the late 1930s, Negro leadership had zeroed in on two target areas. One was school segregation practices; the other, the chronic pattern in southern states of paying Negro public school teachers lower salaries than were paid to white teachers of the same classification level and experience. Launching a campaign for equal educational opportunities for Negroes, both were charged as violating the constitutional guarantee of equal protection of the law.

In each area, the courts moved with considerable caution. In the former they were asked to consider especially the almost total lack in the South of provisions for collegiate, graduate, and professional educational opportunities for Negroes. As late as 1937, graduate

122. Lane *v.* Wilson, 307 U.S. 268 (1939).

123. Smith *v.* Allwright, 321 U.S. 649 (1944). On the case see Robert E. Cushman, "The Texas 'White Primary' Case—Smith v. Allwright," *Cornell Law Quarterly,* XXX (1944), 66–85.

124. Grovey *v.* Townsend, 295 U.S. 45 (1935).

instruction was available to Negro students in only three publicly supported Negro institutions in the region. Professional training was available in none. Further, nine southern states made no provision whatsoever for graduate or professional training for Negroes despite the fact that such was provided at public expense for white students.

These practices were challenged first in Maryland and later in Missouri. Subsequent cases were instituted on the salary issue in Virginia, Maryland, and North Carolina. In the initial Maryland case, a state court ordered the admission of a Negro to the state university law school, turning aside the state's contention that "out-state" scholarships, affording Negroes training in the institutions of other states, maintained equality of educational opportunity.[125] The Missouri case went all the way to the Supreme Court. It involved denial to a Missouri Negro of admission to the state's segregated law school clearly on the ground of his race. Operating on the basis of the "separate but equal" rule of the 1896 case of *Plessy* v. *Ferguson,* Hughes for the Court startled Southerners and lawyers alike by insisting on reading the provision literally. Only if separate facilities were truly equal, he maintained, could they meet the gloss on the equal protection clause that the rule involved. Clearly in the immediate case, the absence of such equality was patent and the Negro would have to be admitted.[126] Rulings by the lower federal courts struck similarly at salary discrimination, carrying with them the added implication that the state as an employer may not discriminate against any employee on the basis of race and color.[127]

125. University of Maryland *v.* Murray, 169 Md. 478 (1936). On the case and its importance see Bernard H. Nelson, *The Fourteenth Amendment and the Negro Since 1920* (Washington, 1946), pp. 115–118.

126. Missouri *ex rel* Gaines *v.* Canada, 305 U.S. 339 (1938). Missouri's compliance with the ruling left much to be desired, and elicited a second case. Here, however, a lower federal court ruled against a Negro applicant to Missouri's Graduate School of Journalism. Bluford *v.* Canada, 32 F. Supp. 707 (D.C.W.D. Mo., 1940).

127. Mills *v.* Board of Education of Anne Arundel County, 30 Fed. Supp. 245 (1939); Alston *et al. v.* School Board of City of Norfolk, 112 Fed. (2d) 995 (1940). "Discrimination in Rate of Compensation Between Colored and White Teachers Held Unconstitutional," *Harvard Law Review,* LIII, (1940), 669–670; "Discrimination in Rate of Compensation Between White and Colored Teachers," *Bill of Rights Review,* I (1940), 142–144. After the Norfolk case the movement to equalize salaries gained momentum. Within two years fifty-three city and county school boards in Virginia had made or agreed to make the adjustments necessary to equalize salaries. Court action for similar compliance was instituted in Florida, Louisiana, Kentucky, North and South Carolina, and Missouri.

Yet few of these decisions were unaminous. McReynolds, speaking for himself and Butler, dissented in the Missouri case, setting forth a view that was strangely similar to that of Frankfurter, particularly in his Screws opinion. Since the state of Missouri had acted on the view that the best interests of her people demanded separation of whites and Negroes in the schools, it was hardly the Court's responsibility to challenge such a generally agreed-upon community value. Implementation of the ruling, the Tennessee justice maintained, could result in only two alternatives, both unfortunate—forcing the state to abandon its law school and thereby disadvantaging its white citizens, or breaking down the subtle practice concerning separate schools, and thereby, as indicated by experience, "damnifying both races."[128]

Certainly such a view represented an extreme enunciation of the right of the local community to maintain its own standards, even if the rights of American citizens were being violated thereby, and evidenced little concern for the broad question of general human rights. But the fact that even the liberal justices were unwilling to reject the "separate but equal" concept indicated an equally insensitive, if unarticulated, reluctance to challenge more than the surface manifestations of the broad-scale segregation practiced in both the South and the North at the time. Clearly no judicial absolutism in the name of the achievement of full civil rights appeared here. At best Negroes could bring case-to-case challenges to traditional discriminatory practices and hope to find the justices in a sanguine mood as situations were elaborated.

Thus despite the Roosevelt Court's clear commitment to the task of upgrading the rights of the individual and making America a showcase of democracy in the face of rising foreign tyranny, very few clear rules emerged from its rulings. Certainly it did not succeed in building a coherent constitutional theory on the question of Bill of Rights freedoms. And the increasingly sharp splits which the adjudication surrounding them produced, particularly regarding the proper role of the Court, precluded immediate and fixed solutions in the near future.[129]

128. Missouri *ex rel* Gaines *v.* Canada, p. 354.

129. For contemporary comment see "Ten Years of the Supreme Court, 1937–1947," *American Political Science Review,* XLI (December, 1947), 1142–1181, XLII (February, 1948), 32–67, especially the pieces by Robert E. Cushman on "Civil Liberties," Robert J. Harris on "Due Process of Law," and C. Herman Pritchett on "The Roosevelt Court: Votes and Values."

Yet all these developments took place in an era when the nation was moving quietly but irresistibly toward war. Despite a mounting focus upon national security and the unity, loyalty, patriotism, and sublimation of individuality to group needs that such a climate elicited, the Court maintained its general resoluteness in not being stampeded into abandoning its civil liberties commitments. Granted, it was being asked to concern itself with essentially nonsecurity questions—the religious practices of Jehovah's Witnesses, labor's right to picket and organize, procedural rights, and the Negro franchise—these were still not areas from which security considerations were absent. With the exception of Frankfurter's opinion in the first flag-salute case, however, the Court carefully and assiduously refused to inject into its considerations the qualifying strictures of security considerations and maintained its commitment to act for the citizen against the excess power of governmental authority.

But if the focus upon security did not obviously emerge from Court rulings, it was a major consideration of the other two branches of the government. In the years in which the Court was concerning itself with the proper thrust of preferred freedoms and the degree to which personal rights should be protected, both the executive branch and Congress were envolving a set of national policies and programs geared to putting the nation on a wartime basis.

CHAPTER 7

Total-War Crisis and Its Impact on the Constitution

ON August 24, 1936, Franklin Roosevelt quietly summoned to the White House the director of the Federal Bureau of Investigation, J. Edgar Hoover. The President was frankly worried about Communist and Fascist activities in the United States, particularly in relation to the economic and political life of the country. Upon being told by Hoover that there was no governmental agency compiling such general intelligence, and that the F.B.I. had no specific authority to make such investigations, Roosevelt, chagrined to find that the President himself could not grant such authorization, arranged that it be undertaken through the Department of State. The immediate result was that the F.B.I. set out to obtain, from all possible sources, information concerning subversive activities being conducted in the United States. The move at the time was kept highly confidential and the F.B.I. was careful to keep its own activities classified and instruct its agents not to overstep the bounds which its limited authorization afforded.[1]

Roosevelt's concern with national security was natural in light of the privileged information that he as President had regarding the intensifying European situation. Yet such security concern was not

1. Donald F. Whitehead, *The FBI Story* (New York, 1956), pp. 157 ff.

limited to the executive branch. Many members of Congress had for years been apprehensive both about the danger of domestic subversion and the absence of any positive governmental policy to curb it. That lack could be put down to the reaction toward earlier governmental "Red" hunters and their excesses in the "Red Scare" of the early 1920s. When, in the depths of the depression, it was proposed that the government mount a large-scale campaign against Communists and other left-wing individuals and groups, the public reaction was hardly favorable.[2] Intensifying concern over security now afforded Congress justification for instigating action in its own behalf. Under the aggressive leadership of Representative Martin Dies of Texas, Congress plunged into the security area with the creation of a special House committee to investigate un-American activities, in May, 1938.[3] This Dies Committee from the outset was nowhere near as discreet or as restrained in its antisubversive activities as was the F.B.I. under Presidential surveillance. The committee was highly partisan and strongly anti-administration.[4] It made clear that it saw its primary function as ridding the government of Communists, radicals, Fascists, "crackpots" and "internationalists," and while Dies stated publicly that the committee's purpose was

2. Conspicuous in this regard were the highly publicized Fish Committee investigations in 1930, which produced nineteen volumes of testimony, largely from far-right-wing groups. See Earl Latham, *The Communist Controversy in Washington: From the New Deal to McCarthy* (Cambridge, Mass., 1966), pp. 28–34; August R. Ogden, *The Dies Committee: A Study of the Special House Committee for the Investigation of Un-American Activities* (Washington, 1945), pp. 23–30. A good cross section of national newspaper opinion on the committee (which was primarily hostile) is in the American Civil Liberties Union Collection, Microfilm Reel 464, New York Public Library.

3. Ogden, *The Dies Committee,* is the standard treatment. See also William Gellermann, *Martin Dies* (New York, 1944), and for Dies's own account of his anti-Communist activities see Martin Dies, *The Trojan Horse in America* (New York, 1940) and *Martin Dies Story* (New York, 1963).

4. Harold Ickes wrote at the time: "Dies is in a fair way to build up the same kind of reputation that A. Mitchell Palmer built up during the last war. As I have felt all along would happen, he has become an actual menace. Fundamentally, he is after the New Deal. He keeps saying that soon he is going to give out names of prominent New Dealers in the Administration connecting them with communistic activities. I know perfectly well that he will try to smear me if he can, but I do not propose to let him get away with it without knowing that he has been in a fight." *The Secret Diary of Harold L. Ickes* (3 vols., New York, 1954), III, 33. See also Telford Taylor, *Grand Inquest: The Story of Congressional Investigations* (New York, 1955), pp. 73–74.

not to seek publicity or arouse hatred or distrust, its subsequent behavior raised serious doubts on this score. In addition, its methods and techniques disturbed civil libertarians. Dies had stated upon assuming the chairmanship that "we must keep in mind that in any legislative attempt to prevent un-American activities, we might jeopardize fundamental rights far more important than the objective we seek."[5] The committee's frequent disregard for procedural rights guaranteed in any court verified the statement, sometimes in appalling degree.

Although the committee showed little interest in investigating anyone except left-wing groups, largely ignoring the growing internal Nazi movement of the times,[6] it did not hesitate to attack the administration's failure in that regard. In November, 1938, the committee demanded an investigation by the State Department to determine whether the German-American Bund, among other organizations, was not actually composed of unregistered agents of foreign governments operating in violation of federal law. Roosevelt, already at war with the committee, and convinced of the baseness of its motives, nonetheless moved to take the sting out of its charges, by authorizing the F.B.I. to start investigations under the Foreign Agents Registration Act.[7] But the President also moved to fight fire with fire. Tired of the Dies Committee's irresponsible charges and allegations, he designated the F.B.I., by executive order, as the official and exclusive agency to take charge of the investigation of all espionage and cognate matters, working in cooperation with the War Department's Military Intelligence Division, and the Office of Naval Intelligence. The F.B.I. then went ahead, publicly, to expand its operations, investigating individuals and groups charged with subversive activity detrimental to internal security, and compiling

5. *Congressional Record,* 75th Cong., 3d Sess., p. 7570.

6. The Committee's grant of authority was virtually verbatim the same as the March, 1934, House-adopted Dickstein resolution, which had authorized investigation of "the extent, character, and objects of Nazi propaganda activities in the United States." The only difference was the substitution of the word "un-American" for Nazi, and a provision covering propaganda "of a domestic origin." Latham, *The Communist Controversy,* pp. 34–35; Taylor, *Grand Inquest,* pp. 72–73.

7. Ogden, *The Dies Committee,* p. 115; Whitehead, *FBI Story,* pp. 164–166; William Leuchtenburg, *Franklin D. Roosevelt and the New Deal* (New York, 1963), pp. 280–281.

a general index on individuals whose activities it felt should be kept under surveillance.[8]

Congress, in the meantime, was joining the security campaign in other ways. In early August, 1939, it passed the Hatch Act[9]—to prevent pernicious political activities—and the measure, while geared largely to protect government employees from being pressured into active politics against their will, nonetheless contained a section embodying the first anti-Communist prohibition in federal employment. Significantly, Roosevelt, in his message accompanying the approval of the measure, designated the Civil Liberties Section of the Justice Department as the suitable agency for its administration and enforcement.[10]

International events affected all such action. The Russo-German nonaggression pact of August 23, 1939, temporarily aligning the Communists with the Nazis, had a marked effect both upon the behavior of domestic Communists and those law-enforcement agencies entrusted with their surveillance. The Annual Report of Attorney General Frank Murphy for 1940 stated categorically, "The effect of the needs of national defense is reflected in practically every division and bureau of the Department."[11] In March of 1940, Congress reenacted the Espionage Act of 1917, with increased penalties for peacetime violation.[12] And with Communist sabotage of American defense industries clearly a threat, Congress had little trouble

8. *Annual Report of the Attorney General, 1939* (Washington, 1940), p. 8. Liberal apprehension about this move was fanned by a series of F.B.I. raids in early February, 1940, against leaders of the left-wing Abraham Lincoln Brigade, an organization of American volunteers who had fought on the side of the Loyalists in the Spanish civil war. Cries arose that this was an example of the kind of FBI activities that would come from its new authority. One article, "American Ogpu," *New Republic,* CII (February, 1940), 230–231, so aroused Republican Senator George Norris that he read it into the *Congressional Record* and called for investigation of the episode. Ultimately Attorney General Jackson acted to quash the resultant indictments and calm the storm of criticism they had produced. See Whitehead, *FBI Story,* pp. 170–176; Fred J. Cook, *The FBI Nobody Knows* (New York, 1964), pp. 244 ff.

9. 53 Stat. 1147 (1939). On the background of the measure see Dorothy G. Fowler, "Precursors of the Hatch Act," *Mississippi Valley Historical Review,* XLVII (September, 1960), 247–262. See also Thomas I. Emerson and David M. Helfeld, "Loyalty Among Governmental Employees," *Yale Law Journal,* LVIII (December, 1948), 1–143.

10. *Annual Report of the Attorney General, 1940* (Washington, 1941), pp. 1–2.

11. *Loc. cit.*

12. 40 Stat. 217 (1917) reenacted as 54 Stat. 79 (1940).

enacting an Alien Registration Act in June, 1940, aimed primarily at Communists, but broadly phrased so as to punish not only those conspiring to overthrow the government, but those advocating or conspiring to advocate its overthrow.[13] Under the measure nearly five million aliens were registered and fingerprinted within a short period, with Attorney General Jackson and Solicitor General and later Attorney General Francis Biddle exercising great caution and tact in insisting that such actions be taken sympathetically and with solicitude for the rights and feelings of those so handled.[14]

At the same time questions arose of the permissible extent of the use by the F.B.I. of wiretap devices in conducting its investigations. Jackson, in taking over as Attorney General, had ordered an investigation into the F.B.I. to explore critical charges that the body was using "third degree" methods in investigating cases. He subsequently ordered the F.B.I. to stop using wiretap methods, at the same time asking Congress for authority to authorize limited use of wiretapping for law-enforcement officials with the appropriate legal safeguards.[15] In this area the President was less concerned about civil liberties than the Attorney General, and insisted that the latter have power to order wiretaps for investigatory bodies, with authorization to be particularly available to the F.B.I.[16] The Supreme Court, apparently picking up the President's cue, sanctioned such techniques,[17] even going so far in one case as to uphold F.B.I. action in a case involving a forgery suspect, which a later authority referred to as the "most extensive search without warrant ever to receive the Court's sanction."[18]

13. 54 Stat. 670 (1940).

14. *Annual Report of the Attorney General, 1941* (Washington, 1942), p. 8. See also Francis Biddle, *In Brief Authority* (New York, 1962), pp. 112 ff.; and Robert E. Cushman, "Civil Liberties," *American Political Science Review*, XXXVII (February, 1943), 52–53.

15. Eugene C. Gerhart, *America's Advocate: Robert H. Jackson* (Indianapolis, 1958), p. 198.

16. Jacob W. Landynski, *Search and Seizure and the Supreme Court* (Baltimore, 1966), p. 221; Alan F. Westin, Privacy and Freedom (New York, 1967), pp. 176–177; and Whitehead, *FBI Story*, pp. 179, 342.

17. Goldman *v.* U.S., 316 U.S. 129 (1942); Goldstein *v.* U.S., 316 U.S. 114 (1942). See also Walter F. Murphy, *Wiretapping on Trial: A Case Study in the Judicial Process* (New York, 1965), pp. 141 ff.

18. Landynski, *Search and Seizure and the Supreme Court*, p. 103. The case was Harris *v.* U.S., 331 U.S. 145 (1947).

Such actions seemed to diminish very little the enthusiasm of the Dies Committee for further disclosure of the laxity and the "Red" tinge of the administration. It now launched demands that "Reds" be removed from the federal payroll. In early 1943, Dies scored heavily, as Congress attached to a vital appropriation bill a rider severing three "Red"-designated government officials from the federal payroll. The action was denounced by critics as divergent as *The New York Times,* the American Political Science Association, and the President.[19] Roosevelt especially charged the action was not only technically illegal as a bill of attainder but was an unwarranted encroachment upon the authority of both the executive and judicial branches. In 1964, after Dies had departed from the Committee and from politics in the face of mounting criticism, the Supreme Court unanimously validated the bill of attainder charge, holding an act of Congress unconstitutional for the first time since the Court-packing fight of 1937.[20] The episode was another reflection of the security drama of the years from 1938 to 1947 with, as one critic saw it, "Congress on one side in the active, and even offensive posture, and the administration on the other, in an attitude of guardedness and wary assurance, convinced in its impassivity that the motives of Congressional critics were largely impure in that they contained elements of personal ambition, partisan antagonism, and historic hostility, fixed in the constitutional separation of power and fed by rivalry to control the courses of statecraft."[21]

Such security problems were minor when compared with the massive challenges of the international situation of the times. Here constitutional government was being put to the test not only of surviving but acting as the instrument for the protection and preservation of representative government throughout the world. In this challenge the President's position as national leader was vital.

19. Robert E. Cushman, "Civil Liberty After the War," *American Political Science Review,* XXXVIII (February, 1944), 10; *The New York Times,* May 20, 1943, p. 20; May 28, 1943, p. 20. For a legislative history of the case and the constitutional issues involved; see Frederick L. Schuman, " 'Bill of Attainder' in the Seventy-Eighth Congress," *American Political Science Review,* XXXVII (1943), 819–829.

20. U.S. *v.* Lovett, 328 U.S. 303 (1946). See also Robert E. Cushman, "The Purge of Federal Employees Accused of Disloyalty," *Public Administration Review,* III (1943), 297–316.

21. Latham, *The Communist Controversy,* p. 273.

Here the changing constitutional nature of the office was equally basic. The crisis of the depression and its worldwide impact had raised to new heights the need for dynamic executive leadership. Roosevelt had been quick to accept the challenge and to utilize power fully and expansively, playing particularly upon the emergency and crisis aspects of the situation. Congress and the courts had, to a large degree, gone along. The President's prerogative in the area of international trade policy, particularly tariff adjustment, was expanded to new limits.[22] The Supreme Court, speaking through Justice Sutherland in 1936, had given constitutional approval to the "plenary and exclusive power of the President as the sole organ of the federal government in foreign relations." This was a power, said the conservative justice, "which does not require as a basis for its exercise an act of Congress."[23]

Starting in the mid-1930s Roosevelt had used his foreign policy prerogative in a great many areas, particularly as constitutional support for a number of extraordinary agreements with foreign governments that he considered basic to the nation's general security. In September, 1939, he had taken a further step. In keeping with what Clinton Rossiter once labeled "the love of crisis which Mr. Roosevelt was never bashful in exhibiting,"[24] he declared a "limited" national emergency, a step which enabled him to use various

22. The Trade Agreements Act of 1934, 48 Stat. 943 (1934), had authorized the President to enter into trade agreements with foreign nations. To that end Congress authorized him to modify duties and other import restrictions up to 50 per cent of existing rates. It also authorized him to deny the benefits of such lower rates to the products of countries that discriminated against the commerce of the United States.

23. U.S. *v.* Curtiss-Wright Export Corporation, 299 U.S. 304 (1936). For the background of the case see Robert A. Divine, "The Case of the Smuggled Bombers," in John A. Garraty (ed.), *Quarrels That Have Shaped the Constitution* (New York, 1962), pp. 210–221. The following year the Court went a step farther, holding in U.S. *v.* Belmont, 301 U.S. 324 (1937), that the recognition of Soviet Russia in 1933 and the accompanying executive agreements constituted an international compact that the President was authorized to enter into without consulting the Senate. Moreover, such agreements had the same effect as treaties in superseding conflicting state laws. This latter point it reenforced in U.S. *v.* Pink, 315 U.S. 203 (1942). Stone was greatly disturbed by the latter ruling, contending that it aided and abetted what he considered to be the President's autocratic pretensions. Alpheus T. Mason, *Harlan Fiske Stone: Pillar of the Law* (New York, 1956), p. 649.

24. Clinton Rossiter, *Constitutional Dictatorship: Crisis Government in the* Modern Democracies (New York, 1948), p. 267.

emergency statutes, particularly regarding expansion of the peacetime army and navy, without having to go through other channels, and without rousing the excitement and concern of a still predominantly isolationist-minded public.

The real emergency of Pearl Harbor underwrote the validity of the President's preliminary preparedness actions, and if anything, encouraged further broader exercise of executive prerogative. Less than two weeks following the surprise attack, Congress enacted the First War Powers Act, reinstating the provisions of the Overman Act of World War I, authorizing the President to reorganize the federal government virtually as he saw fit.[25] Roosevelt chose to act largely through the Office of Emergency Management, which had been set up by an administrative order of the President in May of 1940. The OEM speedily became a coordinating body for much of the wartime executive structure. It included the War Production Board, the Office of Defense Transportation, the War Shipping Administration, the War Manpower Commission, the Office of War Information, the Office of Civilian Defense, and a score of other agencies, twenty-nine of which were still alive and functioning at the end of the war period. Few in their creation or operations raised any serious constitutional problems. Most were sensitively managed. The OWI, as an example, under the leadership of liberal newsman Elmer Davis, deliberately sought to avoid the excesses of the World War I Creel Committee. Its censorship authority was similarly utilized with utmost restraint.[26]

The power that Roosevelt did not assume without reference to statutory provision, Congress afforded him through the enactment of a series of critical statutes authorizing vast federal powers for

25. The measure had a certain irony, given the vigorous opposition that had crushed Roosevelt's proposed reorganization measure of the late 1930s. See Richard Polenberg, *Reorganizing Roosevelt's Government: The Controversy over Executive Reorganization, 1936–1939* (Cambridge, Mass., 1966). For Roosevelt's actions and the Court's consideration of them, see Clinton Rossiter, *The Supreme Court and the Commander-in-Chief* (New York, 1951).

26. See Elmer Davis and Byron Price: *War Information and Censorship* (Washington, 1943); Byron Price, "Governmental Censorship in War-Time," *American Political Science Review,* XXXVI (1942), 837–849; H. C. Shriver and Cedric Larson, "Office of Censorship," *Bill of Rights Review,* II (Spring, 1942), 189–200. For a discussion of the extent to which the courts accepted the constitutionality of wartime executive actions, see Nathan Grundstein, "Presidential Subdelegation of Administrative Authority in Wartime," *George Washington Law Review,* XVI (April, 1948), 301–341, 478–507.

prosecution of the war. A peacetime draft was authorized in September, 1940, through the Selective Service Act.[27] The Lend-Lease Act of March, 1941, gave the President virtually carte blanche executive authority over the distribution of some fifty billion dollars of war supplies to the country's allies. It represented, in the words of one authority, "the broadest delegation of spending power in American history."[28] The two war powers acts of December, 1941, and March, 1942, were catchall measures, giving governmental authorization for actions as diverse as censorship of overseas communications, dealing with alien property, negotiating defense contracts, and providing penalties for trading with the enemy.

And if such authority were not enough, Roosevelt made very clear that he was prepared to exercise any other powers essential to the success of the war effort. In demanding that Congress repeal a provision of the Price Control Act of January 31, 1942, the President indicated that should Congress not accede, "it will leave me with an inescapable responsibility to the people of this country to see to it that the war effort is no longer imperiled by threat of economic chaos." "In the event that the Congress should fail to act, and act adequately, I shall accept the responsibility, and I will act." "The President has the power, under the Constitution and under Congressional acts," he made clear, "to take measures necessary to avert a disaster which would interfere with the winning of the war. . . ." But he was quick to concede that "the American people can be sure that I will use my powers with a full sense of my responsibility to the Constitution and to my country. When the war is won, the

27. 54 Stat. 885 (1940). The measure delegated to local draft boards the responsibility for making classifications for service, the policy-making power for the enforcement of the overall measure to reside in a director of Selective Service. Congressional opposition to the measure on constitutional grounds emerged in both the Senate and the House as well as in the testimony of representatives of a number of organizations in the committee hearings. See *Congressional Record,* 75th Cong., 3d Sess., pp. 9606, 9607, 10113, 10296, 11361; and U.S. Congress, Senate, Military Affairs Committee, *Selective Compulsory Military Training and Service,* 76th Cong., 3d Sess. (Washington, 1940); U.S. Congress, House, Military Affairs Committee, *Selective Compulsory Military Training and Service,* 76th Cong., 3d Sess. (Washington, 1940). See also Harry Emerson Fosdick, "Conscripts for Conquest," *Christian Century,* LVII (Aug. 21, 1940), 1030–1031; "Conscription and the Churches," *Christian Century,* LVII (Sept. 25, 1940), 1168–1170. See also Clyde E. Jacobs and John F. Gallagher, *The Selective Service Act* (New York, 1967).

28. Rossiter, *Constitutional Dictatorship,* pp. 269–270.

powers under which I act automatically revert to the people—to whom they belong."[29]

A number of American citizens, in Congress and elsewhere, were prepared to challenge such a massive use of governmental authority.[30] Particularly anathema to property-conscious Americans were the actions of the Office of Price Administration, the agency set up by executive order to administer the Emergency Price Control Act. That measure had provided broad delegation of power to the OPA to fix prices, and had even set up an Emergency Court of Appeals with the exclusive jurisdiction to determine the validity of any regulation or order of the price administrator. The measure's price-fixing provisions, as well as other restrictions on economic liberty such as rationing, government control of industry, and government ceilings on salaries, rankled those who felt that the law of supply and demand should still operate freely in a wartime period. The measure was thus the one part of the war program openly challenged in Court. Such action was unsuccessful. After initially validating the special Emergency Court, the Supreme Court, following the peacetime ruling it had formulated in a Fair Labor Standards Act case in 1941,[31] strongly defended broad delegation of discretionary authority. Even dissenting Justice Rutledge, although questioning whether Congress had set proper limits on the use of the power it had delegated, and decrying the fact that the measure unduly limited the jurisdiction of regular courts, admitted that "war calls into play the full power of government in extreme emergency." "Citizens," he stated, "must surrender or forego exercising rights which in other times could not be impaired."[32]

In subsequent cases, an OPA order penalizing an oil distributor

29. Quoted in Merlo J. Pusey, *The Way We Go to War* (Boston, 1969), p. 77. For contemporary comment see Edward S. Corwin, "The War and the Constitution: President and Congress," *American Political Science Review*, XXXVII (February, 1943), 18–24. See also Arthur T. Vanderbilt, "War Powers and Their Administration," *Annual Survey of American Law, 1942* (New York, 1942), pp. 106–231.

30. A. Russell Buchanan, *The United States and World War II* (2 vols., New York, 1964), II, 321; Roland Young, *Congressional Politics in the Second World War* (New York, 1956), pp. 90–108. For the work of one congressional committee exploring dubious wartime administrative practices see Donald H. Riddle, *The Truman Committee* (New Brunswick, 1966).

31. Opp Cotton Mills *v.* Administrator, 312 U.S. 126 (1941).

32. Yakus *v.* U.S., 321 U.S. 414, 461 (1944).

for violating the rationing system was upheld as a necessary implication of the Second War Powers Act of 1942, even though the OPA order was alleged to be punishment without proper judicial process.[33] The Court, also in 1944, passed favorably upon a rent-fixing directive, insisting: "A nation which can demand the lives of its men and women in the waging of a war is under no constitutional necessity of providing a system of price control on the domestic front which will assure each landlord a 'fair return' on his property."[34]

Similarly, when it came to the question of the prices the federal government should pay for wartime services and products, the Court sustained Congress and federal policy. The Renegotiation Act of 1942 had attempted to protect the public from profiteering on government contracts by authorizing the reopening of contracts when evidence indicated that the government was being "gouged."[35] Again, many citizens anxious to "cash in" on the economic opportunities of wartime complained. The Court refused to hear challenge to the policy during the war period. With the war safely over, however, it took a case challenging the measure as unconstitutional on the ground of violation of contract rights by means of unconstitutional delegation of renegotiation authority to administrative officials. Justice Burton, speaking for a unanimous Court, turned back the charge, arguing that it permitted America to win World War II "without abandoning our traditional faith in and reliance upon private enterprise, and individual initiative devoted to the public welfare."[36]

Complaints were also raised with regard to the activities of the National War Labor Board. The board, acting as an arbitration

33. Steuart and Co. *v.* Bowles, 322 U.S. 398 (1944). On the OPA see Julius Hirsch, *Price Control in the War Economy* (New York, 1943); D. D. Holdoegel, "The War Powers and the Emergency Price Control Act of 1942," *Iowa Law Review,* XXIX (1944), 454–462; J. W. Willis, "The Literature of OPA. Administrative Techniques in Wartime," *Michigan Law Review,* XLII (1942), 235–256; George P. Adams, *Wartime Price Control* (Washington, 1942); and Paul M. O'Leary, "Wartime Rationing and Governmental Organization," *American Political Science Review,* XXXIX (1945), 1089–1106.

34. Bowles *v.* Willingham, 321 U.S. 503, 518 (1944). See generally Robert A. Sprecher, "Price Control in the Courts," *Columbia Law Review,* XLIV (1944), 34–64.

35. 56 Stat. 226 (1942).

36. Lichter *v.* U.S., 334 U.S. 742 (1948).

or mediation agency, had wage-approving power, and was in a position of using the "indirect sanctions" of publicity and governmental seizure against recalcitrant labor or management. The latter was used sparingly, but vigorously when necessary. Its defiance, especially by John L. Lewis and his mine workers in refusing to terminate a national strike, brought so strong a Labor Disputes Settlement Act from Congress that Roosevelt vetoed it as too drastic. Nonetheless its provisions, imposing penalties on labor leaders who provoked strikes in plants working on government contracts, went into effect over his veto.[37] No Court challenge was taken in this area.

The furor of the public, and particularly of business, over restrictions on the liberty of property and freedom of contract, brought little judicial relief or consideration. The Court's late 1930 abandonment of such protection in its peacetime rulings hardly signaled new wartime concern and special protection. Public protest against governmental restrictions on the rights and freedoms of the individual, however, occurred in a different climate and forced the courts to square their tendency to go along with virtually any federal program in the area of economic regulation with their advanced civil libertarian concerns, so vigorously proclaimed in the immediate prewar era.

Dilemmas promptly occurred. Prewar civil liberties rulings had almost without exception challenged the abuse of governmental power at the local level by local officials. Precedent for challenging broad-scale congressional enactments, or Presidential orders on civil liberties grounds, were few and weak. Painfully cognizant that the Bill of Rights was an explicit restriction on federal authority, most judicial leaders hoped at all costs to avoid finding themselves in situations of judicial defiance of measures and actions clearly geared to the war effort and national security. Hope existed in the careful posture of Roosevelt, and particularly his Attorney General Francis Biddle, an advanced civil libertarian and member of the

37. Biddle, *In Brief Authority,* pp. 311–312; Buchanan, *United States and World War II,* pp. 139, 319; Leonard B. Boudin, "The Authority of the National War Labor Board over Labor Disputes," *Michigan Law Review,* XLIII (1944), 329–382; Wayne L. Morse, "The National War Labor Board Puts Labor Law Theory into Action," *Iowa Law Review,* XXIX (1944), 175–201; Wayne L. Morse, "The National War Labor Board: Its Power and Duties," *Oregon Law Review,* XXII (December, 1942), 1–45.

American Civil Liberties Union. Roosevelt had made clear prior to Pearl Harbor that "free speech and a free press are still in the possession of the people of the United States and it is important that it should remain there." "Suppression of opinion and censorship of news are among the mortal weapons that dictatorships direct against their own peoples and direct against the world," he went on, insisting that "it would be shameful use of patriotism to suggest that opinion should be stifled in its service."[38]

Biddle, in turn, was on record as being intent upon avoiding the inexcusable excesses of World War I in the civil liberties area. Ten days following Pearl Harbor he informed United States Attorneys throughout the country that "prosecution of persons arrested for alleged seditious utterances must not be undertaken unless consent is first obtained from the Department of Justice." Four days later he dismissed complaints lodged against three men for alleged seditious utterances, stating categorically that "free speech as such ought not to be restricted."[39]

The Supreme Court revealed early that it shared such concerns. Both the President and Biddle had expressed their views at the time of the passage of the Alien Registration Act that this area should be a federal concern. They feared that attempts by the states or municipalities to deal with aliens and alleged subversives would result both in undesirable confusion and in a heavy-handed and nonuniform set of local "war" activities sure to jeopardize personal rights. In January, 1941, the Supreme Court made such a policy official, revoking a Pennsylvania statute requiring aliens to register and carry identification on the grounds that federal action had super-

38. *The New York Times* (Apr. 18, 1941), p. 8. Roosevelt was, however, somewhat of a "fair weather" civil libertarian at numerous points. See James M. Burns, *Roosevelt: The Soldier of Freedom* (New York, 1970), pp. 216–217.

39. *The New York Times* (Dec. 21, 1941), p. 21. The Department did prosecute under the Smith Act a group of Trotskyites. In 1941, eighteen members of the Socialist Workers party, active in Minneapolis in the militant labor movement, were convicted for advocating and conspiring to effect insubordination in the armed forces and violent overthrow of the government. Their convictions were sustained by the Court of Appeals for the Eighth Circuit, and the Supreme Court denied certiorari. Dunn *v.* U.S., 138 F. 2d 137, 320 U.S. 790 (1941). For Biddle's discussion of this and other wartime free speech problems, see Biddle, *In Brief Authority*, pp. 151–152, 233–251. For the political factors behind the action see Ralph C. and Estelle James, "The Purge of the Trotskyites from the Teamsters," *Western Political Quarterly*, XIX (March, 1966), 5–15.

seded such state legislation.[40] As a follow-up, a series of federal-state meetings were arranged to insure state and federal cooperation in enforcing wartime legislation, with a meeting of state attorneys general in August, 1941, recommending that in view of the national character of sedition, no state sedition laws be adopted.[41]

As the war progressed, mounting pressure grew from many patriotic citizens and even from the President for the restriction of criticism of the war effort, particularly of right-wing pro-Nazi critics. Biddle was forced to walk a tightrope in his proceedings against such critics, notably against so stormy and controversial a figure as Father Charles Coughlin, against a number of ultra-right-wing, generally anti-Semitic self-proclaimed patriots, patently fascist in their views, and against the anti-administration Chicago *Tribune,* which had shockingly violated security matters by its sensational reporting.[42] Again the Supreme Court offered wartime guidelines. In June, 1941, the Court considered an indictment under the revitalized sedition act of 1917 of an American citizen, charged through speaking and writing with willfully attempting to cause insubordination and disloyalty, and attempting to obstruct recruitment and enlistment in the armed forces.[43] In a five-to-four ruling, Murphy, speaking for the majority, threw out the conviction. "The mere fact that such ideas are enunciated by a citizen is not enough by itself to warrant finding of criminal intent to violate the Espionage Act," he ruled. "Unless there is sufficient evidence from which a jury could infer beyond a reasonable doubt that he intended to bring about the specific consequences prohibited by the Act," the Justice maintained, "an American citizen has a right to discuss these matters by temperate reasoning, or by immoderate and vicious invective without running afoul of the Espionage Act."[44] The ruling, a literal application of

40. Hines *v.* Davidowitz, 312 U.S. 52 (1941).

41. Biddle, *In Brief Authority,* pp. 111–112.

42. Cushman, "Civil Liberties," *American Political Science Review,* XXXVII (1943), 51; Rossiter, *Constitutional Dictatorship,* p. 277; Biddle, *In Brief Authority,* pp. 233 ff.

43. Hartzel *v.* U.S., 322 U.S. 680 (1944).

44. *Ibid.,* p. 689. In two other wartime cases, the Court reversed, over Black and Douglas' dissent, the conviction of George Sylvester Viereck for violating the Foreign Agents Registration Act. Here the majority held that Viereck was required under the statute merely to report to the Secretary of State propaganda activities undertaken as the agent of a foreign principal, and was under no

Holmes's "clear and present danger" test, went a long way toward discouraging further prosecutions for unpopular oral or written expression during the war period.

The same concern for the rights of citizens was evident in rulings regarding treason. In one of the most melodramatic episodes of the early war period, eight Nazis, who had been brought to the American shore in submarines, were put ashore on Long Island and in Florida, with instructions to attempt to sabotage and otherwise to cripple U.S. industrial plants. All eight were quickly apprehended and picked up by the F.B.I. and the Coast Guard, but not before two had made contact with American citizens whom they hoped to use to facilitate their plans. The Americans, in one case a friend, in another the father of one of the Nazis, were also promptly arrested and charged with treason for giving aid and comfort to the enemy. In April, 1945, the Court reversed the conviction of the former. Jackson, speaking for a sharply divided Court, maintained that the "overt acts" with which the man was charged—meeting and talking with the saboteur, and offering to handle his money—were not sufficiently dangerous to warrant punishment. An overt act must manifest on its face an obvious intent to commit treason, the justice argued. It is not enough that some action might indirectly be connected with treason.[45]

Only with the war over, did a later Court sustain the treason conviction. Then, in a case involving the implicated father, it upheld a treason conviction for the first time in American history. On the evidence, the prisoner had sheltered his son, obtained a car for him, and secured him a job in a factory manufacturing the Norden bombsight for the Air Corps. In an eight-to-one decision, Justice Jackson termed these actions more than casually useful, and denounced them as "steps essential to his design for treason."

---

obligation to report similar activities undertaken on his own initiative. Viereck *v.* U.S., 318 U.S. 236 (1943). Stone was highly aroused by the government's action. Mason, *Stone,* pp. 683–685. In the second, it reversed the conviction of twenty-four leaders of the German-American Bund on the ground that the evidence offered was not sufficient to convict them of conspiring to counsel evasion of or resistance to the draft. Keegan *v.* U.S., 325 U.S. 478 (1945).

45. Cramer *v.* U.S., 325 U.S. 1 (1945). On treason law from Burr to Cramer see J. Willard Hurst, "Treason in the United States," *Harvard Law Review,* LVIII (December, 1944), 226–272, 395–444, 806–846.

Only Murphy felt the evidence showed sufficiently indirect "overt acts" to warrant a contrary finding.[46]

In such cases, the Court, while challenging the application of certain of the wartime security statutes and actions, did not set itself up to challenge their general validity and constitutionality. The same was not true with regard to the constitutional rights of naturalized citizens. Here civil liberties–minded judges, particularly Murphy, Douglas, and Rutledge, drew sharper lines. Early in the war, the Justice Department, acting under provisions of the Naturalization Act of 1906 and the Nationality Act of 1940, set out to curtail the activities of dissentious naturalized citizens, particularly Italians and Germans, by showing that their disloyal conduct proved that they had initially received their citizenship illegally and under false pretenses. This would then make it possible to cancel their citizenship and deport them as undesirable aliens. By the end of 1942, forty-two such actions had been successfully completed, three hundred suits were pending in the courts, and well over two thousand cases were being actively investigated.[47] In the first important test case on the policy the Court struck hard at the program. The case involved a Communist, whose party membership at the time of naturalization the government contended precluded "true faith and allegiance to the United States."[48] The case had come to the attention of the 1940 Republican Presidential candidate, Wendell Willkie, who appeared before the Court as opposing attorney and made such an eloquent case against the injustice of condemning a person for alleged adherence to abstract principles, that the Court ruled against the government. It would be necessary, wrote Murphy for the majority, to produce clear, unequivocal, and convincing evidence that the petitioner fraudulently and illegally procured his certificate initially. Subsequent views of the person's qualifications or fitness for citizenship, particularly due to controversial actions and beliefs, were not pertinent to such an evaluation.[49]

46. Haupt *v.* U.S., 330 U.S. 631 (1947).

47. Cushman, "Civil Liberties," *American Political Science Review,* XXXVII (1943), 54.

48. Schneiderman *v.* U.S., 320 U.S. 119 (1943).

49. Willkie's comment on the decision was: "I have always felt confident as to how the Supreme Court would decide a case involving such fundamental American rights. My bafflement has been as to why the Administration started and prosecuted a case in which, if they had prevailed, a thoroughly illiberal precedent would have been established." Ellsworth Barnard, *Wendell Willkie: Fighter for Freedom* (Marquette, Mich., 1966), p. 404.

The Justice Department reacted with disappointment. The decision, it maintained, now forced the government to carry "an onerous burden of proof in establishing lack of attachment to principles of the American Constitution."[50] Yet the Department still felt that such a burden of proof could be sustained in other cases. Its optimism was only partly justified. In June, 1944, the Court was confronted with a denaturalization order of a naturalized German, who following his naturalization in 1932, became an enthusiast of Hitler and his doctrines of Aryan superiority. Frankfurter reversed the order for a unanimous Court. The most eloquent statement emerging from the bench in this instance came from Justice Murphy, in a concurring opinion. "American citizenship is not a right granted on a condition subsequent that the naturalized citizen refrain in the future from uttering any remark or adopting an attitude favorable to his original homeland or those there in power, no matter how distasteful such conduct may be to most of us," Murphy wrote. "He does not lose the precious right of citizenship because he subsequently dares to criticize his adopted government in vituperative or defamatory terms. The naturalized citizen has as much right as the natural-born citizen to exercise the cherished freedoms of speech, press, and religion. . . ."[51] Murphy's view was in sharp contrast to that maintained earlier in American history by opponents of immigration who had questioned seriously the ability of the foreign-born citizen to understand and utilize American freedoms properly.[52] It was particularly significant coming against the backdrop of wartime emergency, and was clear indication that wartime pressures had not diminished the commitment of certain of the more liberal justices to the extension of the preferred freedoms concept.

Only in 1946 did the Court sustain a denaturalization proceeding. In this case, however, evidence was clear that the naturalized citizen in question was following at the time of his naturalization "a clear course of conduct . . . designed to promote the Nazi cause in this country."[53] Even here Rutledge and Murphy disagreed, arguing once more that the policy applied a double standard, preventing

50. *Annual Report of the Attorney General, 1943* (Washington, 1944), pp. 10–11.

51. Baumgartner *v.* U.S., 322 U.S. 665 (1944).

52. See, for example, Henry Pratt Fairchild, *The Melting-Pot Mistake* (Boston, 1926), pp. 255–256; and the attitudes of Chief Justice Taft, Chap. III, *supra*, which the Taft Court translated into the law.

53. Knauer *v.* U.S., 328 U.S. 654, 656 (1946).

naturalized citizens from engaging in the same type of activities as native-born, and thus placing them in a separate and inferior class.

Conscientious objection during World War II was made possible through the terms of the Selective Service Act of 1940 which exempted from combatant training and service anyone who "by reason of religious training or belief, is consciously opposed to participation in war in any form." Administration was left largely to local draft boards, some of which took an unduly narrow view of the words "religious training and belief," but the majority of which handled the law equitably.[54] By contrast, the Nationality Act of 1940 had, by in no way indicating otherwise, included the principle that an alien holding similar pacifist views was ineligible for naturalization, thus acquiescing in earlier Supreme Court rulings to that effect. On April 22, 1946, the Court took a contrary view, ruling that a pacifist who refused to bear arms but was willing to serve in the army as a noncombatant, could be admitted to citizenship under the Act. Noting that the man's religious scruples would not disqualify him from becoming a member of Congress or holding other public office, Douglas, for the Court, questioned whether Congress should set a stricter standard for aliens seeking admission to citizenship than it did for officials who made and enforced the laws of the nation.[55] In taking this position, the Court overruled three earlier cases barring naturalization on the grounds of pacifism. It thereby posthumously vindicated Oliver Wendell Holmes, Jr., who had dissented vigorously in the first, wondering out loud whether people were undesirable citizens "who believe more than some of us do in the teachings of the Sermon on the Mount."[56]

The decision, rendered a day before his death, presented Chief Justice Stone with a sharp dilemma that in many respects proved a microcosm of his entire career. Ever the careful craftsman, highly cognizant of the Court's obligation toward judicial self-restraint

54. On the constitutional status and experience of World War I conscientious objectors see Mulford Q. Sibley and Philip E. Jacob, *Conscription of Conscience: The American State and the Conscientious Objector, 1940–41* (Ithaca, 1952). The Court was cautious on the question, sustaining, for example, the refusal of Illinois to admit a CO to the bar of that state even though he was willing to take an oath to support the state constitution. Since such oath included potential service in the state militia, it was contended he could not do so in good faith. *In re* Summers, 321 U.S. 561 (1945).

55. Girouard *v.* U.S., 328 U.S. 61, 65 (1946).

56. U.S. *v.* Schwimmer, 279 U.S. 644, 655 (1929).

with regard to congressional legislation, but on the other hand, sensitive and socially conscious and no great adherent of stare decisis for its own sake, Stone found himself confronting the overruling of earlier precedents against which he had himself dissented. Since he clearly felt that Congress had "adopted and confirmed the construction of the naturalization laws given by the Court in the earlier cases," he now contended it was the Court's responsibility to sustain congressional intent. Thus the Chief Justice, who in his judicial career had seen more of his dissenting opinions and positions become the law of the Court than any other justice in history, ended his career opposing the elevation of one more of them into ruling law.[57] Such a note was typical of the selflessness and devotion to principle of the man, who had fought the Court's own sacrifice of principle when it had selfishly fought the New Deal on dubious constitutional grounds, and who had gone on to shepherd the body through one of its most difficult periods—the crisis of war and the threat to basic human freedoms that wartime crisis produced.

Harry Bridges was the head of the International Longshoremen's Union on the Pacific Coast. Because of the aggressive and successful tactics of his union, he had been the subject of bitter assault by conservative West Coast employers for a number of years, particularly since he led the maritime workers' strike on the Pacific Coast in 1934. Bridges had come to the United States from Australia in 1920 but had never become naturalized. The government had attempted unsuccessfully to deport him in 1938 on the ground that he was a member of the Communist party. Dean James M. Landis of the Harvard Law School, acting as a special government examiner, had concluded that the evidence did not sustain the charges. The Secretary of Labor had then dismissed the proceedings.[58] The

57. Allison Dunham, "Mr. Chief Justice Stone" in Allison Dunham and Philip B. Kurland, *Mr. Justice* (Chicago, 1964), p. 229.

58. Biddle, *In Brief Authority*, pp. 120, 296. The House of Representatives then proceeded to pass a resolution directing the Attorney General "notwithstanding any other provision of law," immediately to deport Harry Bridges, "whose presence in this country the Congress deems hurtful." 76th Cong., 3d Sess. (1940), House Resolution, 9766. See the debate for constitutional objections, *Congressional Record*, 76th Cong., 3d Sess., pp. 8181–8214. The measure died in Senate committee, although that body urged deportation as a result of Bridges' political views and affiliations, calling for amending the deportation laws to facilitate such action.

Alien Registration Act of 1940 contained a provision for deportation of any alien who was "at the time of entering the United States, or has been at any time thereafter" a member of or affiliated with an organization of the character attributed to the Communist party. A second deportation proceeding was promptly instituted under the new measure and again lengthy hearings were held. The basis of the charges rested largely upon Bridges' public utterances and his publications. Douglas, for a six-to-three Court, refused to sanction such action. Focusing upon Bridges' actions, Douglas found that his associations with various Communists groups "seemed to indicate no more than cooperative measures to attain objectives which were wholly legitimate." Stressing that "freedom of speech and of press is accorded aliens residing in this country," Douglas further maintained that while Bridges' literature and utterances revealed a militant advocacy of the causes of trade unionism, they did not teach or advocate or advise the subversive conduct condemned by the statute. Three of the justices, speaking through Chief Justice Stone, disagreed sharply, arguing that the fact that Bridges was a demonstrable Communist was enough to bring him under the proscriptions of the Act.[59]

Failing to secure alien deportation through this measure, the Attorney General reached for a page of history, and moved to expel aliens clearly identified with enemy nations under the Alien Enemy Act of 1798. The measure provided that such aliens had no legal rights to a hearing before deportation, and no right to judicial review. Again, a postwar court finally took a case testing the action, and splitting five to four, sustained the provisions. Bitter protest arose, especially from Justice Black, that such a waving of basic procedural guarantees made "individual liberty less secure tomorrow than it was yesterday."[60]

The Court's reluctance to challenge national policy clearly tied to alleged military necessity was most clear with regard to the

59. Bridges *v.* Wixon, 326 U.S. 135, 157 (1945). Bridges subsequently became a naturalized U.S. citizen, only to have evidence introduced that he had perjured himself in the deportation hearings. Tried and convicted, the action became grounds for cancellation of his naturalization. Back then in alien status, but now guilty of having broken laws, he was again subject to deportation. Once again, however, the Supreme Court set aside his conviction on the grounds that the statute of limitations prevented the government from prosecuting him at such a late date. Bridges *v.* U.S., 346 U.S. 209 (1953).

60. Ludecke *v.* Watkins, 335 U.S. 160, 183 (1948).

government's highly controversial policy toward a special group of American citizens—the Japanese on the West Coast. Prejudice against the 112,000 persons of Japanese descent resident on the West Coast had existed for many years. Roughly two-thirds were citizens, and more would clearly have been, if they had not been barred by the federal naturalization laws. Yet for those who disliked the Japanese, this fact was minor compared with hostility toward their religious views and social patterns, and particularly toward their economic success as skilled agricultural workers and truck gardeners and their entrepreneurial acumen in other commercial ventures. Such prejudice clearly played a role in the fate of the Japanese.[61] The idea of evacuating the Japanese from the West Coast did not take shape and gain momentum until some weeks after Pearl Harbor. Initially even West Coast military leaders had not contemplated such action. General J. L. DeWitt, head of the West Defense Command, told a Justice Department official fully a month after Pearl Harbor that "any proposal for mass evacuation was 'damned nonsense!' "[62] Restrictive areas around military installations from which all aliens should be excluded were fully adequate, he added. Civilian West Coast leaders, however, hostile to the Japanese, mounted a vigorous campaign for immediate evacuation. Some of the more violent and vigorous, such as the Native Sons of the Golden West, encouraged rapid and permanent deportation, even suggesting that long-standing legal precedents giving native-born children of noncitizens the full rights of citizenship be either ignored or overruled so that that process could extend to all Orientals.[63]

61. The literature is voluminous. For background see Roger Daniels, *The Politics of Prejudice: The Anti-Japanese Movement in California and the Struggle for Japanese Exclusion* (Berkeley, 1962). The most extensive study is the three-volume work: Dorothy S. Thomas and Richard S. Nishmoto, *The Spoilage* (Berkeley, 1946), Dorothy S. Thomas, *The Salvage* (Berkeley, 1952), and Jacobus Ten Broek, Edward N. Barnhart, and Floyd W. Matson, *Prejudice, War and the Constitution* (Berkeley, 1954). See also Morton Grodzins, *Americans Betrayed: Politics and the Japanese Evacuation* (Chicago, 1949); Allan R. Bosworth, *America's Concentration* (New York, 1967); Maurice Alexandre, "Wartime Control of Japanese-Americans," *Cornell Law Quarterly,* XXVIII (June, 1943), 385–413; and Harrop A. Freeman, "Genesis, Exodus and Leviticus—Genealogy, Evacuation and Law," *Cornell Law Quarterly,* XXVII (June, 1943), 414–458.

62. Biddle, *In Brief Authority,* p. 215.

63. Edward S. Corwin, *Total War and the Constitution* (New York, 1947), pp. 93–95.

By late January, in spite of the release of the report of the Commission on Pearl Harbor, headed by Justice Owen J. Roberts, indicating no evidence of espionage activities on the coast, General DeWitt had apparently been reached. He now took the position that the fact that there had been no sporadic attempts at sabotage showed an "exercised control" on the part of the Japanese. This meant that when sabotage came, he contended, it would be on a mass basis. As Francis Biddle, then Attorney General, wrote some years later, "he was feeling the impact of aroused public opinion, particularly among the 'best people in California.' "[64] The Justice Department then assigned Texan Tom Clark as agent to coordinate the work of enemy alien control with the army. Clark promptly acceded almost completely to the wishes of the military. California Attorney General Earl Warren had by this time also come around to endorsing evacuation and was also prepared to cooperate with Clark and the military in all ways possible.[65]

Such views did not reflect the general position of the Attorney General and his staff, however. Yet Mr. Biddle, who later indicated that the information afforded him did not indicate any necessity for evacuation, at the same time was not fully informed of the actual military situation. Recognizing mounting hysteria, and the general prestige of the military, he was clearly cognizant of the fact that it could not be stopped on an issue it defined as a military one. For the Justice Department to set itself against a program claimed to be a military necessity without adequate information would be a grave risk to its status and authority. Thus both he and his staff wound up, in final analysis, aiding in the drawing up of the evacuation proclamation that was presented to the President as a joint document of the War and Justice Departments. The President was thus presented with an order to sign. And without discussion, even with his cabinet, he made it official on February 19, 1942.[66] Thus the first acquiescence

64. Biddle, *In Brief Authority,* p. 216; Grodzins, *Americans Betrayed,* p. 281.

65. Richard Polenberg (ed.), *America at War: The Home Front, 1941–1945* (Englewood Cliffs, N.J., 1968), pp. 98–103; Biddle, *In Brief Authority,* p. 216.

66. Grodzins takes the position that Roosevelt took no part in conceiving or developing the evacuation program, and was thus not responsible for it. Grodzins, *Americans Betrayed,* p. 272. Ten Broek disagrees, maintaining Roosevelt bears a large share of the responsibility "not only in the inert and formal sense that he was the chief executive . . . and hence accountable for the acts of his subordinates, but . . . also in the immediate and active sense that he deliberately

to what was later to be called "the most drastic invasion of the rights of citizens of the United States by their own government that had thus far occurred in the history of our nation"[67] was made by the officers of a Department acutely aware of their responsibilities as guardians of civil liberties and protectors of civil rights. But if the army was to be solely responsible for the program and its consequences, its lawyers wanted more authority than the executive order. Consequently a month later Congress also acquiesced, passing a statute that sustained the order and prescribed sharp penalties for citizens who did not submit to evacuation.[68] Subsequently a War Relocation Authority was established in the Department of the Interior, again by executive order, to assist in carrying out evacuation and conducting confinement camps in which evacuees were to be placed.[69]

The resultant temporary confinement of the Japanese in coastal assembly centers and their subsequent relocation in confinement areas in the interior, resulted not only in great personal trauma and hardship, but frequently heavy financial loss as the result of being forced overnight to dispose of land, stores, homes, and personal property. Most adapted to the situation with amazing docility and cooperation, given the immense disruption it brought to their lives. Many of the young men volunteered to serve in the army and a number made up one of the most highly decorated units in the European theater in the later years of the war.

Many American citizens were highly disturbed by the program from the outset. It clearly proceeded on questionable racist assumptions, and was a direct abrogation of the civil liberties and civil rights of American citizens. Its challenge in the Courts was thus inevitable

---

and knowingly authorized the program through the issuance of Executive Order 9066, thereafter supplemented it by other executive orders and personally directed that its termination be delayed until after the presidential election of 1944." Ten Broek, *Prejudice War and the Constitution,* p. 331.

67. Corwin, *Total War and the Constitution,* p. 91.

68. 56 Stat. 173 (1942).

69. Its authority came from Executive Order 9102, 7 *Federal Register* 2165 (1942). The authority published extensive reports, including a bibliography on Japanese and Japanese Americans in the United States. For an analysis of its constitutional position see U.S. Department of the Interior, War Relocation Authority, *Legal and Constitutional Phases of the War Relocation Authority* (Washington, 1946).

and drew support from a number of concerned civil libertarians. The first case to reach the Supreme Court involved a University of Washington senior, Gordon Hirabayashi, a citizen, arrested for failing to report to a control station to undergo exclusion, and for violating a military commander's curfew order requiring him to remain at home after 8 P.M. daily. The Supreme Court, in taking the case, carefully limited its considerations to the second point, upholding the curfew and indicating that there was no need to consider the conviction of the first count.

Subsequently the Court took two further cases involving other phases of the program. Fred Korematsu, also an American citizen, had been rejected for army service because of ulcers. Hoping to enlist otherwise in the war effort he used his $150 savings to learn welding. With Pearl Harbor and General DeWitt's subsequent confinement and exclusion orders he found himself in the contradictory position of being forbidden by military order to be found within that zone, unless he were in an Assembly Center. As Justice Jackson stated in his dissenting opinion, Korematsu

> . . . was convicted of an act not commonly a crime . . . being present in the state whereof he is a citizen, near the place where he was born, and where he lived all his life. Even more unusual is the series of military orders which make this conduct a crime. They forbid such a one to remain, and they also forbid him to leave. They were so drawn that the only way Korematsu could avoid violation was to give himself up to the military authority. This meant submission to custody, examination, and transportation out of the territory, to be followed by indeterminate confinement in detention camps.[70]

The court, in taking the case, was again confronted with two issues, the legitimacy of the exclusion order, and forced detention in a relocation center. Again it chose the narrow path, sustaining the former and ignoring the latter.

Mitsuye Endo, also a citizen, whose loyalty had clearly been established, applied for a writ of habeas corpus to gain her freedom from the detention camp in which she was being held. She hoped, as did the American Civil Liberties Union,[71] to challenge the detention

70. Korematsu *v.* U.S., 323 U.S. 214, 243 (1944).

71. The A.C.L.U. filed amicus curiae briefs in all three cases. The American Bar Association's Bill of Rights Committee, significantly, did not enter any of the three.

of loyal citizens on one hand, and the entire detention program on the other. Douglas for a unanimous Court authorized the writ. He carefully avoided ruling upon the constitutionality of the confinement program in its entirety, thus completing the Court's general dodging of the larger question at a time when such action might have brought some meaningful relief.

The constitutional issues raised by this set of wartime cases, and the various judicial postures and attitudes that emerged from them, had immediate and long-range implications. Stone, who wrote the first of the decisions, found himself in the difficult position of having to decide whether the Court would sacrifice its usual standards of review in civil liberties cases by accepting an army General's evaluation of the necessity for curbing fundamental rights. The initial case also raised, in an unavoidable way, the question of the ultimate limits of the war power. These, Stone quickly made clear, "we need not now attempt to define." Unhappily, having once taken such a posture, the Court continued to remain aloof from such a definition through the series of cases that followed. It went on to acquiesce in Stone's further contention that if the confinement or evacuation was "reasonably related" to the war effort, it was justifiable. Caught between sharply divergent elements on his own bench, Stone attempted to make clear that DeWitt's actions in proclaiming the Japanese dangerous as a group were unfortunate ("by their very nature odious to a free people whose institutions are founded upon the doctrine of equality") and that only because of the danger of espionage and sabotage was the Court accepting them. Clearly it was not approving them.[72] But Stone, trapped in his own deep belief in separation of powers and the necessity for the judiciary confining its activities to its own proper functions clearly by deferring to the military's actions, gave them a form of judicial sanction. This factor was even more clear when one considers the thrust of his ultimate position, which virtually was that military acts, justified by military leaders as proper exercise of the war power, were not subject to the same review as courts give other acts of government. This was ironic contrast to the thrust of his Carolene footnote that statutes directed at "national . . . or racial minorities were to be subjected to more exacting judicial scrutiny . . . than . . . most other types of legisla-

72. Hirabayashi *v.* U.S., 320 U.S. 81, 100 (1943).

tion," and his inference that "prejudice against discrete and insular minorities" should call for "more searching judicial inquiry" than normally required.[73]

Frankfurter, the most advanced war hawk on the Court, was prepared to go even further than Stone. Taking the general position that civil liberties could be suspended any time such action was necessary to win the war, he argued that such suspension would not result in their attrition. Rather, they could be resuscitated easily once the national emergency had been successfully surmounted. Otherwise, Frankfurter felt clearly, the danger was created of having the entire system and structure of government destroyed by an enemy, an action that would make such liberties not only meaningless but would destroy them permanently. Jackson in the Korematsu case had dissented, contending that the Court's action distorted the Constitution to approve all that the military may deem expedient. He deplored the precedent that such action seemed to be setting. Further, he viewed this as a dangerous general precedent for the unrestricted use of other kinds of official power—lying "like a loaded weapon ready for the hand of any authority that can bring forward a plausible claim of an urgent need."[74] Frankfurter saw no such implications. "If a military order . . . does not transcend the means appropriate for conducting war," he contended in reply, "such action by the military is as constitutional as would be any authorized action by the I.C.C. within the limits of the constitutional power to regulate commerce."[75]

Jackson's view, however, had strong public sympathy, coming not long after his eloquent statement in the second flag-salute case condemning the excesses created in the name of official orthodoxy on the part of authoritarian government officials. It also heartened civil libertarians, who clearly endorsed his added contention that "a commander in temporarily focusing the life of a community on defense is carrying out a military program; he is not making law in the sense that the Courts know the term. He issues orders, and they may have a certain authority as military commands, although they may be very bad as constitutional law. . . . If we cannot confine

73. Sidney Fine, "Mr. Justice Murphy and the Hirabayashi Case," *Pacific Historical Review,* XXXIII (May, 1964), 199–200.

74. Korematsu *v.* U.S., 323 U.S. 214, 246 (1944).

75. *Ibid.,* at 224–225.

military expedients by the Constitution, neither would I distort the Constitution to approve all that the military may deem expedient." "I cannot say, from any evidence before me," he went on, "that the orders of General DeWitt were not reasonably expedient military precautions, nor could I say that they were. But even if they were permissible military procedures, I deny that it follows that they are constitutional. If, as the Court holds, it does follow, then we may as well say that any military order will be constitutional and have done with it."[76]

Black and Douglas found themselves in many ways compromised in the situation, partly by their advanced New Dealism and general loyalty to the President, partly by their devotion to the necessity for winning the war, and considerably by their civil liberties consciences. Black was able to reconcile these views more easily than Douglas. Going along very largely with the Stone position, and basing his majority Korematsu opinion heavily upon Stone's logic, he again stressed the difficulty for the Court in setting itself up as an agency to weigh and measure national defense needs. Although maintaining that all legal restrictions that curtail civil rights of a single racial group are immediately suspect, he was still reluctant to utilize such suspicion to question the program. "We cannot say," he wrote, "that the war making branches of the Government did not have ground for believing that in a critical hour such persons could not readily be isolated and separately dealt with. . . ."[77] Waving aside the charge of Korematsu's attorney that "the government had borrowed the device of 'protective custody' " from the Nazis by simply failing to consider the detention program, he sought some personal vindication in the fact that in a 1942 case he had himself condemned the inherent racism of an action to deprive an alien Japanese of rightful wages on the grounds that a state of war existed between Japan and the United States.[78]

Douglas, who had grown up on the West Coast and had great personal sympathy for the Japanese, was highly cognizant of the types of arguments that had traditionally been made against them

76. *Ibid.*, at 245.

77. *Ibid.*, at 218.

78. *Ibid.*, at 219. The case was *ex parte* Kawato, 317 U.S. 69 (1942). See Irving Dilliard (ed.), *One Man's Stand for Freedom: Mr. Justice Black and the Bill of Rights* (New York, 1963), p. 114.

by professional anti-Orientals. "Racial solidarity and lack of assimilation do not show lack of loyalty as I see it," he wrote Stone, urging the Chief Justice to narrow and qualify his Hirabayashi opinion more sharply.[79] Yet Douglas also admitted that the speed that the army maintained was essential in acting to prevent internal damage, and clearly precluded immediate determination between the loyal and the disloyal Japanese. He also agreed that "we must credit the military with as much good faith . . . as we would any other public official acting pursuant to his duties."[80] Still he continued to press for actions that would expedite the process of reaching such determinations, in the meantime encouraging internees to bring habeas corpus suits in the district courts as a device for individually breaking out from under the program and the mass stigma that it carried. In this regard, his majority opinion, sustaining Miss Endo's writ, was, in his own mind, a minor triumph.

If any judicial civil libertarian kept the faith in the situation it was Murphy. An instinctive champion of the underdog, a vigorous opponent of conservative power and the type of faulty rationalization it used to sustain and justify its desired positions, Murphy rose to the height of eloquence in denouncing the entire program. Pressured hard by the Chief Justice not to dissent in the Hirabayashi case and thereby put the majority in the light of "wanting to destroy the liberties of the United States,"[81] he nonetheless left no doubt in his concurring opinion that he felt the racial implications of the program were "at variance with the principles for which we are now waging war." The program, he stated, "bears a melancholy resemblance to the treatment accorded to members of the Jewish race in Germany. To sanction discrimination between groups of

79. Mason, *Stone,* p. 673.

80. Hirabayashi *v.* U.S., 320 U.S. 81, 106 (1943). The concession made generally by the majority justices is difficult to reconcile with the fact that such speed did not take place. The evacuation was not completed until five months after its authorization by the President, and eight months after Pearl Harbor. Further, the Court had ample evidence that the army was making no attempt to screen for loyalty in spite of the fact that accepted procedures had clearly been developed for it, and were available. See Nanette Dembitz, "Racial Discrimination and the Military Judgment," *Columbia Law Review,* XLV (March, 1945), 175–239.

81. Fine, "Mr. Justice Murphy and the Hirabayashi Case," p. 206.

United States citizens on the basis of ancestry . . . goes to the very brink of constitutional power."[82] By the Korematsu case, he was no longer willing to give deference either to the Chief Justice or the military. He now condemned the latter's actions, bringing out the clear racism involved in the army's position, particularly in DeWitt's public statements.[83] Keeping the faith also with the modern trend toward sociological jurisprudence, he pointed out incisively and directly that justification for the exclusion was sought "mainly upon questionable racial and sociological grounds, not ordinarily within the realm of expert military judgment, supplemented by certain semi-military conclusions drawn from an unwarranted use of circumstantial evidence." I dissent, he stated boldly, "from this legalization of racism. Racial discrimination in any form and in any degree has no justifiable part whatever in our democratic way of life."[84] He also reminded the bench that there were adequate precedents for its own intervention in such a situation. It is essential, he pointed out, that there be definite limits to military discretion. "Individuals must not be left impoverished of their constitutional rights on a plea of military necessity that has neither substance nor support." And he quoted cases from 1851 to 1932, in which prior Courts had made clear that "what are the allowable limits of military discretion, and whether or not they have been overstepped in a particular case, are judicial questions."[85]

The Court's overall posture in the Japanese cases was in some

82. Hirabayashi *v.* U.S., 320 U.S. 81, 110 (1943).

83. Korematsu *v.* U.S., 323 U.S. 214, (1944). DeWitt had stated: "I don't want any of them [persons of Japanese ancestry] here. They are a dangerous element. This is no way to determine their loyalty. . . . It makes no difference whether he is an American citizen, he is still a Japanese. American citizenship does not necessarily determine loyalty. . . . You needn't worry about the Italians at all except in certain cases. Also, the same for the Germans except in individual cases. But we must worry about the Japanese all the time until he is wiped off the map. Sabotage and espionage will make problems as long as he is allowed in this area. . . ." U.S. Congress, House Naval Affairs Subcommittee to Investigate Congested Areas, Part 3, 78th Cong., 1st Sess., pp. 739–40. See Grodzins, *Americans Betrayed,* pp. 282–283.

84. 323 U.S. 214, 242 (1943).

85. *Ibid.,* at 234. The cases included Mitchell *v.* Harmon, 13 Howard 115, 134 (1851); U.S. *v.* Russell, 13 Wallace 623, 627–628 (1871); Raymond *v.* Thomas, 91 U.S. 712, 716 (1875). Murphy was quoting Sterling *v.* Constantine, 287 U.S. 378, 401 (1932).

ways understandable, given the state of total war, national emphasis upon full cooperation in the war effort, the high status the military held at the time, and the reluctance of the Commander in Chief to do anything but acquiesce fully in military decision. It was nonetheless out of step with the justices' professed prewar and wartime commitment to the preferred position of individual rights. Nonetheless, the Court's actions in hiding behind fine legal distinctions as a way of avoiding conflict, public hostility, and thereby potential criticism, to say nothing of loss of power and status, was ironically unsuccessful. Even the contemporary public was not convinced by the Court's general insistence that positive action would plunge it into the unwarranted area of policy making. By acquiescing to a military posture that was anathema to much of the public and unjustifiable in many ways, it positively acquiesced in the very policy from which it claimed it wished to disassociate itself. As Morton Grodzins wrote in 1949, "The Court by the very process of adopting weak review standards made a social judgment in favor of the evacuation."[86] Little wonder that the then dean of American constitutional lawyers, Edward S. Corwin, characterized the cases as bringing "the principle of constitutional relativity to the highest pitch yet,"[87] and that a contemporary commentator entitled his critique "The Japanese American Cases—a Disaster."[88]

Acquiescence to military domination on other fronts was not as full. Immediately following Pearl Harbor, Hawaii was placed under martial law by its governor, an action President Roosevelt approved two days later. Civil and criminal courts were forbidden to try cases, and military tribunals were set up to replace them. As time went on, this resulted in the trial of civilians, without jury, and without the normal procedural safeguards of the Bill of Rights, a practice that became increasingly unpopular as the continued need for martial law in the islands became less obvious.[89] Military control was gradually relaxed and the courts authorized

86. Grodzins, *Americans Betrayed,* p. 357.

87. Corwin, *Total War and the Constitution,* p. 100.

88. Eugene V. Rostow, "The Japanese American Cases—A Disaster," *Yale Law Journal,* CIV (June, 1945) 489–533. Rostow also wrote a popular contemporary piece denouncing the program, "America's Greatest Wartime Mistake," *Harper's Magazine,* CXCI (September, 1945), 193–201.

89. C. Herman Pritchett, *The Roosevelt Court: A Study in Judicial Politics 1937–1947* (New York, 1948), pp. 156–157.

to conduct criminal trials. However, prosecution for violation of military orders, many of which applied to civilian activities, were still required to be conducted before military tribunals. In 1946, the Court finally took a case on the question, splitting seven to two. The justices drew fairly sharp boundaries around the limits of military authority even under martial law. Speaking through Justice Black, the Court maintained clearly that the term in the Hawaii Organic Act was intended to authorize the military to act vigorously for the maintenance of an orderly civil government and for the defense of the island against actual or threatened rebellion or invasion. It was not intended, however, to authorize the supplanting of courts by military tribunals. Clearly this inferred further that martial law could not become the basis for suspending the constitutional guarantees of fair trial that applied elsewhere in the United States.[90]

The war tested the extent to which constitutional guarantees must prevail in the activities of military bodies in two other divergent, but vital, areas. Partly as a result of sensitivity to the need for America to display her commitment to civil liberties in the fact of European tyranny, public sentiment even developed favoring giving the Nazi saboteurs a judicial hearing. The Court thus met in special session in the summer of 1942 to consider the saboteurs' claim that their trial by military procedures before a military tribunal, instead of by a civil court, denied them proper constitutional safeguards. After serious consideration the Court nonetheless ruled that the Presidentially created commission had followed lawful procedures in conducting the trial. The result was thus inconclusive for the appellants, but did stand as a warning to the military that the Court did not consider the actions of its judicial bodies beyond its surveillance.[91]

90. Duncan *v.* Kohonomoku, 327 U.S. 304 (1946). On the episode see J. Garner Anthony, *Hawaii under Army Rule* (Stanford, 1955); Charles Fairman, "The Supreme Court on Military Jurisdiction: Martial Rule in Hawaii and the Yamashita Case," *Harvard Law Review,* LIX (July, 1946), 833–882; and John P. Frank, "Ex Parte Milligan v. The Five Companies: Martial Law in Hawaii," *Columbia Law Review,* XLIV (1944) 639–668. Frank points out that martial law was clearly a device to keep Hawaii's labor movement under military control.

91. *Ex parte* Quirin, 317 U.S. 1 (1942). On the case see Robert E. Cushman, "The Case of the Nazi Saboteurs," *American Political Science Review,* XXXVI (1942), 1082–1091; Cyrus Bernstein, "The Saboteur Trial," *George Washington Law Review,* XI (1943), 131–190.

The end of the war produced different kinds of problems. With victory in sight and the extent of Nazi and Japanese atrocities and violations of the laws of war and international conventions gradually revealed, strong world sentiment arose for the trial as war criminals of national leaders who had urged or condoned such actions. The result was the setting up of an International Military Tribunal to meet in Nuremberg, Germany. Justice Robert H. Jackson of the Supreme Court was named representative of the United States to sit with representatives from France, the United Kingdom, and the U.S.S.R. on that body. The subsequent trial, which resulted in the death sentence for twelve and imprisonment for seven other Nazi leaders, was to be hectic for all parties. It also set disturbing precedents for the future. Jackson was clearly sensitive to strong charges that the tribunal was branding as offenses crimes that were not clearly outlawed by any rule of international law, and hence was engaging not only in adjudication but in legislation of the nature of ex post facto law.[92] He was also disturbed by rumors that his longed-for chances of being elevated to Chief Justice were being undercut by his absence. It was in this climate that he launched his unfortunate attack from Nuremberg on his feared rival Justice Black. The net result was to be injurious to both parties, to embarrass the Court generally, and to lead Harry Truman, President at the time of the death of Chief Justice Stone, to look outside the bench and name to the position a former member of the Court of Appeals for the District of Columbia, wartime Director of Economic Stabilization, and his current Secretary of the Treasury, Kentuckian Fred M. Vinson.[93] As to Nuremberg itself, the Supreme Court stayed totally aloof from the proceedings and expressed itself in no way regarding the trial and its legitimacy.

92. The original Nuremberg prisoners made no effort to obtain review either from the Supreme Court or from British, French, or Russian courts. See Charles Fairman, "Some New Problems of the Constitution Following the Flag," *Stanford Law Review,* I (1949), 590–603.

93. The literature on Vinson is varied. See Francis A. Allen, "Chief Justice Vinson and the Theory of Constitutional Government: a Tentative Appraisal," *Northwestern University Law Review,* XLIX (March-April, 1954), 3–35; John P. Frank, "Fred Vinson and the Chief Justiceship," *University of Chicago Law Review,* XXI (Winter, 1954), 212–246; John J. Parker, "Chief Justice Fred M. Vinson: Meeting the Challenge to Law and Order," *American Bar Association Journal,* XLI (April, 1955), 324–326, 363; James J. Bolner, "Mr. Chief Justice Vinson: His Politics and His Constitutional Law" (unpublished Ph.D. dissertation, University of Virginia, 1962).

When a later trial of war criminals was held at Tokyo, however, certain defendants sought review by the Court of the right of trial by such a military tribunal. The Court, walking on egg-shells, denied leave to file petitions for habeas corpus, maintaining that such leave could be granted only if the tribunal holding the prisoners was a tribunal of the United States. Certainly a military tribunal set up as an international instrument of the Allied powers was a body not subject to review by the judiciary of any one of them.[94]

Murphy dissented in this case, however, extending, once again, his hostility to the surrender of the principle of due process under any circumstances in which personal rights were involved. The ruling was a logical projection of his dissent three years earlier in the celebrated case of Japanese General Tomoyuki Yamashita, the notorious "Tiger of Malaya," who had been tried and sentenced to death by an American military tribunal in the Philippines. Murphy, and with him Rutledge, were particularly disturbed by the drumhead nature of the trial. Murphy especially objected to the fact that "the petitioner was rushed to trial under an improper charge, given insufficient time to prepare an adequate defense, deprived of the benefits of some of the most elementary rules of evidence, and summarily sentenced to be hanged."[95] Rutledge possibly summarized the more general misgivings of civil libertarians. He could not, he maintained, accept the view that "anywhere in our system resides or lurks a power so unrestrained to deal with any human being through any process of trial." "No human being," he argued, "has heretofore been held to be wholly beyond elementary procedural protection. I cannot consent to even implied departure from that great absolute." Quoting Thomas Paine, he stated: "He that would make his own liberty secure must guard even his enemy from oppression; for if he violates this duty he establishes a precedent that will reach himself."[96]

Stone's majority opinion prevailed, however, and the proper

94. Hiroto *v.* McArthur, 338 U.S. 197 (1948). On the case see Fowler *v.* Harper, *Justice Rutledge and the Bright Constellation* (Indianapolis, 1965), pp. 196–198.

95. *In re* Yamashita, 327 U.S. 1, 27 (1946). On the case see Frank A. Reel, *The Case of General Yamashita* (Chicago, 1949); and J. Gordon Feldhaus, "The Trial of Yamashita," *South Dakota Bar Journal,* XV (October, 1946), 181–193, for the recollections of one of the defense lawyers.

96. 327 U.S. 1, 81 (1946). See Rocco Tresolini, *Justice and the Supreme Court* (Philadelphia, 1963), pp. 131–149; and Harper, *Justice Rutledge,* pp. 180 ff. A parallel case was Homma *v.* Patterson, 327 U.S. 759 (1946).

limits of military authority and its obligation to adhere to Bill of Rights guarantees in overseas areas had to await the postwar period for more explicit and precise definition. With armies of occupation and service personnel surrounding the globe, this was inevitable.[97]

The overall impact of the World War II crisis on the American Constitution is difficult to assess precisely. Clearly the power of the President in the area of foreign relations was expanded to new limits. Such limits were generally acceded to by Congress at the time, however, as easy ratification of even the controversial Yalta agreement testifies. The President's use of war power, drawn to a large degree from actions of previous Presidents, primarily Lincoln and Wilson, went beyond that of any of his predecessors and at times seemed virtually unlimited. The wartime prerogatives of the military were also swollen. These were still tied closely to Presidential power and prestige, however, and the reluctance of the Court to challenge them undoubtedly stemmed in considerable part from the personal respect and attachment of the majority of the justices to Franklin Roosevelt and not from any sudden doctrinal shift to judicial self-restraint. The willingness of Congress to acquiesce in Presidential war management, and give the President a green light in most areas where he felt certain kinds of action necessary, was also a war-related development. But as far as changing traditional relationships, or any permanent surrender of congressional prerogative, even the most acquiescent congressman saw no such implications in such emergency action.

The extent of the permanent constitutional changes resultant from the wartime years, focusing as they did upon Presidential power, would be best seen when that office passed to a different individual. Much of the power that acceded to the office was a function of the fact that it was occupied by Franklin D. Roosevelt. Roosevelt clearly was a constitutional opportunist and pragmatist. Throughout his Presidency he showed far more interest in the content of policy than in governmental traditions or machinery.

97. In Johnson *v.* Estranger, 339 U.S. 763 (1950), the Court refused access to American courts of Germans captured in China and tried for aiding the Japanese in the war. There were three dissents, however, Black particularly stressing that the power of judicial inquiry should follow in the footsteps of American tribunals no matter where set up.

The end to be reached was the important consideration. If constitutional means were not at hand, they would have to be evolved. A President with a different conception of the office, and of the Constitution, could clearly terminate such informal and loose procedural constitutional precedents. A reinvigorated Congress or an unsympathetic Court could also find more formal devices for blocking and undercutting them. The Court's favorable civil liberties record was in some ways one of the most remarkable aspects of the war period, particularly when one compares it with the black picture of World War I.[98] Again, however, the future would determine the fate of the civil liberties that remained in 1946. It would also test the degree to which Frankfurter's wartime relativism was valid, and whether the various examples of suspension that did occur were temporary expedients or the blueprint for a more sharply limited concept of civil liberties and civil rights that would operate in the postwar period.

98. Rossiter, *Constitutional Dictatorship,* p. 276. The fact that the war was without question the most popular ever fought eliminated the kinds of civil liberties challenges present so familiarly in the Civil War, World War I, and Vietnam.

CHAPTER 8

The Fair Deal and Judicial Pragmatism, 1946–50

IN his annual message to Congress of January 11, 1944, Franklin D. Roosevelt provided a rough blueprint of his ambitions for postwar America. The President placed particular emphasis upon the necessity for complementing continued adherence to traditional rights of free speech, press, and worship, with governmental guarantees of man's economic rights. "We have accepted," Roosevelt contended, "a second Bill of Rights under which a new basis of security and prosperity can be established for all, regardless of station, race or creed." And he went on to set forth what he considered the elements of minimal economic security, "without which realization of true individual freedom cannot exist."[1] It fell to his successor, Harry S. Truman, who took office on April 12, 1945, to generate concrete programs toward the realization of such ends.

Truman's task was momentous. Lacking the capacity of his predecessor for stirring enthusiasm for social reforms, he entered the White House to be confronted by a Congress impatient to reassert its own authority in the area of public policy-making and national leadership, and a Republican party thirsting for power

1. Samuel Rosenman (ed.), *The Public Papers and Addresses of Franklin D. Roosevelt* (13 vols, New York, 1938–50), XIII, 32.

after twelve dry years. Thus, although he called for a postwar "Fair Deal" to extend previous New Deal objectives into broader areas, it quickly became clear that successes would be few and limited. This was particularly true in light of his enormous task in confronting the massive complications of postwar reconversion and attendant problems. As a result he quickly found himself in the uncomfortable position of being forced to devote his energies in the reform area to preserving New Deal programs from conservative assault.

Even conservatives, however, were not prepared to return the nation's economy to the unregulated control of private business leaders. Depression lessons had been painful and had left a permanent scar on the memories of a generation of Americans. The Full Employment Act of 1946, warmly endorsed by the President, was passed by Congress on February 20 of that year.[2] The measure wrote into American public law the concept that it was the government's task to take all steps necessary to maximize employment, production, and purchasing power. Through a newly created three-man Presidential Council of Economic Advisors, the nation's economic patterns were to be constantly studied and analyzed, with the government responsible for evolving new controls when these seemed essential to the nation's economic security. These included tax rates, designed to produce a predetermined deficit or surplus (based on whether it was wished to stimulate or cool off the economy); controlling the ease or tightness of credit; raising and lowering of public spending levels and wage and price guidelines. The measure was a constitutional landmark. It terminated officially the precept that the main responsibility of the government in the economic sphere was the maintenance of a free enterprise system, to be achieved negatively by preserving, through laws and court decisions, a hands-off policy toward American economic activities.

Even this measure did not go through Congress in the form Truman wished, and was sharply watered down by conservative congressmen who, while subscribing to the goal of economic stability, were disturbed by the economic management that it ob-

2. 60 Stat. 23 (1946). On the background and passage of the measure see Stephen K. Bailey, *Congress Makes a Law: The Story Behind the Employment Act of 1946* (New York, 1950).

viously necessitated. That such a view was a minority one, however, was indicated by the enactment by Congress in 1947 of the Housing and Rent Act,[3] extending into peacetime the provisions of the wartime Price Control Act. The measure in this instance was challenged legally. But the Supreme Court, in a case in 1948,[4] made clear that the war power could legitimately continue, even after the shooting had ceased, in certain areas of economically essential public policy.

One target of conservative wrath was labor's power. Republican take-over of Congress in 1946, plus a wave of disruptive national strikes in various key industries, presaged the development of new legal restrictions on labor's rights. When contract negotiations between management and the miners broke down in the spring of 1946, a government agency declared that the shortage of coal was creating a national disaster. Harry Truman, responding to the crisis, seized the mines on May 21, justifying the step on the ground that coal production was essential both to the war effort and for the continued operation of the national economy during the transition from war to peace.[5] The miners, with John L. Lewis' clever but silent assent, promptly refused to work in government-held pits pending contract negotiations, despite a court order prohibiting a work stoppage.[6] The result was the levying of a $3.5 million fine against the United Mine Workers, and $10,000 against Lewis for contempt of the court order, an action which the Supreme Court upheld in March, 1947, despite the supposed inhibitions afforded by federal antilabor injunction legislation. "We hold," wrote Chief Justice Vinson, "that in a case such as this, the Norris-LaGuardia Act does not apply."[7]

General public approbation encouraged Republican leaders in Congress to push for new legislation to water down and curtail the 1935 Wagner Act, then the nation's principal labor law. The enactment of the Taft-Hartley Act in 1947 opened a new chapter

3. 61 Stat. 193 (1947).
4. Woods *v.* Miller, 333 U.S. 138 (1948).
5. *The New York Times,* May 22, 1946, p. 24.
6. John L. Blackman, Jr., *Presidential Seizure in Labor Disputes* (Cambridge, Mass., 1967), p. 34. See also Arthur F. McClure, *The Truman Administration and the Problems of Postwar Labor, 1945–1948* (Cranbury, N.J., 1969).
7. U.S. *v.* United Mine Workers and John L. Lewis, 330 U.S. 258 (1947).

in the history of U.S. labor-management relations.[8] The measure clearly sought to eliminate an alleged prolabor bias in the law by arming management with new rights and imposing limitations on long-established trade-union practices such as the closed shop. It included a specific provision requiring labor union officials, in order to use the facilities of the National Labor Relations Board, to sign affidavits denying not only membership in the Communist party but also Communist beliefs. It also sought to curtail union influence by prohibiting unions, but not the management with which they dealt, from making contributions to political campaigns. President Truman vetoed the measure, calling it "completely contrary to the national policy of economic freedom" and "a threat to the successful working of our democratic society."[9] But Congress easily passed it over his veto and it became law in late June of 1947. Arthur Link has called it "the most important conservative triumph of the postwar era."[10]

Emboldened by congressional actions, thirty states also enacted a variety of antilabor laws, particularly "right to work" statutes and antipicketing measures. In January, 1949, a unanimous Court, speaking through Justice Black, over the protest of the C.I.O. and a brief by its counsel, Arthur Goldberg, upheld a Nebraska constitutional amendment and a North Carolina statute forbidding closed shop contracts, maintaining that they were not, as labor contended, a violation of its freedom of contract, speech, and assembly.[11] Three months later, Black took another step toward unwrapping labor from the protection of Bill of Rights guarantees, acknowledging, as the Court was coming to do generally, that picketing was

8. 61 Stat. 136 (1947). See Harry Milles and Emily Brown, *From the Wagner Act to Taft-Hartley* (Chicago, 1950).

9. Barton J. Bernstein and Allen J. Matusow (eds.), *The Truman Administration: A Documentary History* (New York, 1966), pp. 124–128. See Senator Taft's reply to the veto, *ibid.*, pp. 128–131.

10. Arthur S. Link, *American Epoch: A History of the United States Since the 1890's* (New York, 1967), p. 676. Strong contemporary objections were raised to the measure's constitutionality. See Arthur E. Sutherland, Jr., "The Constitutionality of the Taft-Hartley Law," *Industrial and Law Relations Review*, I (1948), 177–205; and James D. Barnett, "Constitutionality of the Expurgatory Oath Requirement of the Labor Management Relations Act of 1947," *Oregon Law Review*, XXVII (1948), 85–96.

11. Lincoln Federal Labor Union *v.* Northwestern Iron & Metal Co., 335 U.S. 525 (1949).

bound up with elements of coercion, restraint of trade, labor relations, and other social and economic problems of intimate concern to society at large. He sustained a Missouri injunction prohibiting picketing that had been carried on in an attempt to force an employer to an agreement in violation of the state's antitrust laws. Taking the position that the right to picket had to be balanced against other social needs, Black pointed out that "it is clear that appellants were doing more than exercising a right of free speech or press. They were exercising their economic power to compel the [employer] to abide by union rather than state regulation of trade."[12]

Black drew the line, however, at any further retreat. In a 1950 case in which the Court, speaking through Frankfurter, took the position that a state might prohibit picketing even when directed to an end in itself lawful, he reasserted his commitment to his position in the 1942 Ritter's Cafe case,[13] where he had contended that orderly regulated picketing was within the protection of the Fourteenth Amendment against state encroachment. Joining in dissent, Justice Minton added, "it seems to me, too late now to deny that [earlier picketing cases] were rooted in the free speech doctrine. I think we should not decide the instant cases in a manner so alien to the basis of prior decisions."[14]

The Court heard one further challenge to the new labor legislation in the pre–Korean war period. On the same day that it virtually cut away the free speech protection from picketing, it sustained the non-Communist affidavit provision of the Taft-Hartley Act. Chief Justice Vinson maintained in his ruling that although Congress had undeniably discouraged the lawful exercise of political

12. Giboney *v.* Empire Storage and Ice Co., 336 U.S. 490 (1949). The Court had taken the same position earlier in a case involving "Caesar" Petrillo, head of the Musicians Union, U.S. *v.* Petrillo, 332 U.S. I (1947), and followed the rule in Building Service Employees Union *v.* Gazzam, 339 U.S. 532 (1950); and Local Union No. 10 *v.* Graham, 345 U.S. 192 (1953). Both cases involved picketing for a purpose declared unlawful by statute. In Hughes *v.* Superior Court of California, 339 U.S. 460 (1950), it went a step further, striking at picketing proscribed by judicial judgment as to proper public policy. See Joseph Tanenhaus, "Picketing as Free Speech: The Growth of the New Law of Picketing from 1940 to 1952," *Cornell Law Quarterly*, XXXVIII (Fall, 1952), 1–50.

13. Carpenters and Joiners Union *v.* Ritter's Cafe, 315 U.S. 722 (1942).

14. International Brotherhood of Teamsters *v.* Hanke, 339 U.S. 470, 483 (1950).

freedom by demanding oaths relating to personal beliefs, this abridgment of free speech had to be weighed against the government's power to regulate commerce. He thus upheld the oath as a valid commercial regulation rather than a speech restriction. He also felt compelled to allude to Holmes's "clear and present danger" test, weighing it against the power of constitutional government to survive. Coming up clearly on the security side of the ledger, the Chief Justice warned that "The Court's interpretations of the Constitution [should not] be reduced to the status of mathematical formulas."[15] Black's dissent was strong and sharp, protesting against what he considered a clear violation of freedom of conscience and the ability of American citizens to participate freely in the political process. He particularly denied that the "Commerce Clause restricts the right to think."[16] His opinion also was laden with overtones of annoyance over the Court's alleged departure from its own proper function of actively safeguarding the personal freedoms of American citizens against their abrogation by other branches of the government. "Fears of alien ideologies have frequently agitated the nation and inspired legislation aimed at suppressing advocacy of those ideologies," he wrote. "At such times the fog of public excitement obscures the ancient landmarks set up in our Bill of Rights. Yet then, of all times, should this Court adhere most closely to the course they mark."[17]

Other actions of the postwar period also indicated a strong intention on the part of congressional leaders to reassert congressional dominance of the government and cut down sharply on Presidential power and prerogative. Many Republicans had never forgiven Franklin Roosevelt for running for a third, to say nothing of a fourth, term for the Presidency. Many also still nursed the wounds

15. American Communications Association *v.* Douds, 339 U.S. 382, 394 (1950).

16. *Ibid.*, p. 446. For support of Black's position see Francis D. Wormuth, "Legislative Disqualifications as Bills of Attainder," *Vanderbilt Law Review*, IV (1951), 603–619.

17. American Communications Association *v.* Douds, 453. Three of the justices held that the "belief" provisions of the Act were unconstitutional, a fact Vinson carefully ignored in his opinion. In a subsequent case, Osman *v.* Douds, 339 U.S. 846 (1950), four of the justices so held, although Douglas wavered, contending that the provisions of the oath were not separable, and consequently his holding that the "belief" provisions were unconstitutional made it unnecessary for him to consider the constitutionality of the other part of the oath.

of frustration, carried as a result of being forced to accede to Roosevelt's near wartime dictatorship. The move for the Twenty-second Amendment to the Constitution, to limit future Presidents to two terms in office, was thus a highly partisan measure, as the resultant furor in and out of Congress demonstrated. Both proponents and opponents referred repeatedly to Roosevelt's record as President, and even Dwight Eisenhower later stated, when President, that he "feared the Amendment was in large degree an act of retroactive vindictiveness against the late Franklin D. Roosevelt rather than the result of judicious thinking about the institutions of the Republic."[18] Nonetheless the measure passed Congress and was ratified by the necessary number of states, and marked another example of the growing postwar constitutional trend in which Congress implemented constitutional restraints, legalistically, with an eye to enhancing its own power. Certainly, as Harry Truman later stated, "the measure was a potential instrument for making a 'lame duck' out of every second-term President for all time in the future,"[19] thereby enhancing congressional authority and prestige.

But if there was a real showdown between President and Congress in the struggle for public power, status, prestige, and favor, it lay more in the area of civil liberties and civil rights, brought into special focus in this period by the growing popular concern for the problems of national security. The Dies Committee had lost much of its initial force as the United States entered World War II. The reasons were varied. Administration hostility to it was open. Much of the public found its flamboyant headline-hunting activities distasteful. Its partisanship raised wide doubts that it was seeking impartial justice, one of its dissident members even proclaiming publicly that it was too consciously "a political instrument of definite conservative bias."[20] Its records and staff became increasingly the personal appurtenances of Mr. Dies. When that right-wing Texan, realizing he could not be renominated for Congress, withdrew from the race in 1944, the Committee expired

18. *The New York Times,* Oct. 6, 1956, p. 10.

19. *Ibid.,* p. 1. See the discussion of Congress's action in Donald G. Morgan, *Congress and the Constitution* (Cambridge, Mass., 1966), pp. 226–245.

20. Quoted in Telford Taylor, *Grand Inquest: The Story of Congressional Investigations* (New York, 1955), p. 74. See also August R. Ogden, *The Dies Committee* (Washington, 1945), p. 296.

and Dies himself vanished temporarily into political oblivion.[21]

When the Seventy-ninth Congress assembled on January 3, 1945, conservative racist, anti-Roosevelt, Democratic Representative John Rankin of Mississippi skillfully resuscitated the committee, and induced a somewhat reluctant House membership to turn it into a permanent instrument of that body.[22] Its activities over the next two years were minimal, however. But with Republican victory in the 1946 congressional elections, and the rise to the chairmanship of Congressman J. Parnell Thomas, the committee was prepared to launch a vigorous and broad-gauge assault upon internal subversion, designating as its first objective its intention "to expose and ferret out the Communists and communist sympathizers in the Federal Government."[23]

Support for the committee grew rapidly. The F.B.I.'s activities

21. Dies and two other members of the committee had been the particular targets of the Political Action Committee of the C.I.O. Dies's oblivion lasted eight years. In 1952, in the height of the McCarthy era, he was again elected to Congress as representative-at-large from Texas. In 1945, a new committee sought advice from the Brookings Institution concerning proper procedural and substantive standards for loyalty testing. The institution's report emphasized the need for restraint on the part of legislators and for cooperation between Congress and President if internal security was to be obtained without infringing upon civil liberties. Brookings Institution, *Suggested Standards for Determining Un-American Activities* (Washington, 1945).

22. Robert K. Carr, *The House Committee on Un-American Activities, 1945–1950* (Ithaca, 1952), pp. 19–23; Walter Goodman, *The Committee: The Extraordinary Career of the House Committee on Un-American Activities* (New York, 1968), pp. 167 ff.

23. Taylor, *Grand Inquest,* p. 76. Other objectives ranged from exposing Communist leadership in labor unions, education, and science, especially those who would "dissipate our atomic bomb knowledge for the benefit of a foreign power," to investigating Communist influence in Hollywood; and under the leadership of Chairman J. Parnell Thomas, it was quickly clear that earlier concern for proper procedure and substantive standards had declined sharply. The committee's probe of substantive indoctrination through the movies led to convictions for contempt of Congress of the famed "Hollywood Ten" following hearings that departed sharply from basic principles of due process. See Gordon Kahn, *Hollywood on Trial* (New York, 1948); John Cogley, *Report on Blacklisting* (2 vols., New York, 1956), Vol. I; and Goodman, *The Committee,* pp. 207–225. The body also issued damaging reports allegedly demonstrating Communist domination of organizations such as American Youth for Democracy, the Civil Rights Congress, and the Southern Conference for Human Welfare. The latter, put together rapidly in hopes of discrediting Henry Wallace's Progressive party, is analyzed carefully and devastatingly in Walter Gellhorn, "Report on a Report by the House Committee on Un-American Activities," *Harvard Law Review,* LX (1948), 1193–1234. See also Thomas A. Krueger, *And Promises to Keep: The Southern Conference for Human Welfare, 1938–1948* (Nashville, 1967).

in the security area in the immediate postwar period, although it was now undertaking its first comprehensive investigation of Communist organizations, hardly served to allay public anxiety. Neither did action by various departments in Washington to undertake their own disjointed and often ineffective investigations in 1945 and 1946. Public apprehensions, particularly over the famous *Amerasia* case, and the break-up of a Soviet spy ring in Canada, led to vigorous demands for more aggressive action.[24]

Truman moved cautiously. In November, 1946, he established a Temporary Commission on Employee Loyalty and was promptly given a taste of the type of criticism he would expect when he moved into the loyalty area. Conservatives interpreted his action as a confession of guilt, and an effort to cover up previous malfeasance. Liberals decried the action as unwarranted governmental interference with private rights. Increasing security pressures dictated expansions of the program, however, and by early 1947, with the F.B.I. and security officers in Washington calling for a massive drive against the Communists, the President set up a full-scale Federal Loyalty and Security Program. Executive Order 9835[25] inaugurated a comprehensive investigation of all federal employees, with any negative information from any sources a potential basis for a security dismissal. A list of subversive organizations was to be prepared by the Attorney General with membership in any to be grounds for "reasonable doubt" as to an employee's loyalty. The only guideline the Act provided was that to be so designated an organization must be "totalitarian, Fascist, Communist, or subversive," or one adopting a policy of "approving the commission of acts of force or violence to deny to others their constitutional rights."[26]

24. Fred J. Cook, *The F.B.I. Nobody Knows* (New York, 1964), pp. 277–283; Eleanor Bontecou, *The Federal Loyalty-Security Program* (Ithaca, 1953), pp. 21–22.

25. *Federal Register,* XII (Mar. 25, 1947), 1935–1938. See Harold D. Lasswell, *National Security and Individual Freedom* (New York, 1950); John Lord O'Brian, *National Security and Individual Freedom* (Cambridge, Mass., 1955); Ralph S. Brown, *Loyalty and Security: Employment Tests in the United States* (New Haven, 1958); and for a defense of the Truman program by the former chairman of the Loyalty Review Board, Seth W. Richardson, "The Federal Employee Loyalty Program," *Columbia Law Review,* LI (May, 1951), 546–563.

26. Bontecou, *Federal Loyalty-Security Program,* pp. 29, 157 ff. Eighty-two organizations were eventually named, and the list distributed with the admonition that the United States government did not accept the principle of "guilt by

Liberals attacked the new program on constitutional lines. They charged that the new program presumed an employee to be subversive and hence eligible for dismissal unless he could prove himself innocent. They were equally disturbed by the program's explicit lack of procedural protections, a charge they also raised chronically against H.U.A.C. Former Attorney General Francis Biddle wrote: "Where a man is accused of a crime . . . our Constitution and laws protect him so far as possible with the strength of objective and impartial procedure; a court independent of the State, a jury trial, definite charges, no hearsay evidence, an open public proceeding, the presumption of innocence. He is treated thus because so much is at stake—his livelihood, his freedom, his good name. All these considerations are present in the loyalty cases."[27] And Biddle went on to insist that the government had a special obligation to adhere to such procedures in its screening process.

On the whole, the administration moved with regard for justice and civil rights during its loyalty probe. By early 1951, the Civil Service Commission had cleared more than 3 million federal employees. The F.B.I. had made some fourteen thousand full-scale investigations of doubtful cases. Over two thousand employees had resigned, although in very few cases because of the investigation, and 212 persons had been dismissed on the grounds that there was a reasonable doubt as to their loyalty. The executive branch also acted in a way that it felt demonstrated its responsibility in the security area, winning indictments of the twelve national leaders of the Communist party, on July 20, 1948, under the Smith Act, from a special federal grand jury. A lengthy and bombastic trial followed, with all twelve subsequently convicted of conspiring to advocate

---

association." Those using it, however, tended to operate on the contrary principle that once a person's membership in such a body was revealed, it was up to him to prove that he was not disloyal. The House Committee on Un-American Activities prepared its own list independently, eventually citing 624 organizations as Communist, or otherwise determined to overthrow the government by unconstitutional means.

27. Francis Biddle, *The Fear of Freedom* (New York, 1951), p. 210. See Bernstein and Matusow, *The Truman Administration,* pp. 363–366, for a typical conservative critique. See also Bontecou, *Federal Loyalty-Security Program,* pp. 30–34.

the overthrow of the government by force and violence, but not before a variety of legal points and constitutional challenges had been raised.[28]

The House Committee on Un-American Activities, however, chose to interpret such actions as support for its enlarged role. The feeling of several of its leading members, particularly Representatives Carl Mundt of South Dakota and Richard M. Nixon of California, was that a true housecleaning of the executive department and full exposure of its past dereliction with regard to Communists would only come from a body in no way corrupted by ties to that department. The sensational Hiss-Chambers hearings and the resultant conviction of Hiss, a former New Deal official, for perjury in connection with the turning over of security information, added to the prestige of the committee.[29] By 1948, it was prepared to sponsor legislation to require the Communist party and front organizations to register with the Department of Justice and supply the names of all officers and members, and of all publications. In essentials, the bill reflected the approach of Morris Ernst, prominent civil liberties lawyer, who argued that the constitutional way to

28. The trial, which lasted nine months, raised questions as to the objectivity of the jury (the issue had been raised in a different connection earlier when one of the same defendants had refused to obey a subpoena served on him by the Un-American Activities Committee, before a District of Columbia jury on which sat seven government employees). Dennis had contended unsuccessfully that a Communist could not get a fair trial from government employees, because the "aura of surveillance and intimidation" resulting from the federal loyalty check would make them fearful of rendering anything but a guilty verdict. Dennis *v.* U.S., 339 U.S. 162 (1950)). Also, the behavior of the Communists' lawyers was ruled "wilfully obstructive" of the conduct of the trial by Judge Harold Medina, U.S. *v.* Sacher, 182 F. 2d at 423, leading eventually to a Supreme Court ruling on the issue, Sacher *v.* U.S., 343 U.S. 1 (1952), and one of the lawyers was eventually disbarred both by the state of New Jersey and from practice before the Supreme Court. *In re* Isserman, 345 U.S. 286 (1953). For two opposite versions of the trial see Hawthorne Daniel, *Judge Medina: A Biography* (New York, 1952), pp. 217 ff.; and George Marion, *The Communist Trial: An American Crossroads* (New York, 1950). See also Nathaniel L. Nathanson, "The Communist Trial and the Clear-and-Present Danger Test," *Harvard Law Review,* LXIII (1950), 1167–1175.

29. The Hiss case raised few constitutional issues, but many political ones, and produced a voluminous literature. See especially Whittaker Chambers, *Witness* (New York, 1956); Fred J. Cook, *The Unfinished Story of Alger Hiss* (New York, 1958); Alistair Cooke, *A Generation on Trial: U.S.A. vs. Alger Hiss* (New York, 1950); Alger Hiss, *In the Court of Public Opinion* (New York, 1957); Earl Jowitt, *The Strange Case of Alger Hiss* (New York, 1953); and Richard B. Morris, *Fair Trial* (New York, 1953), Chap. XIV.

fight Communism was to force Communists out into the open.[30] Nonetheless, although the measure passed the House by a comfortable margin, it ironically got caught in the Republican political crossfire of an election year. Nixon had, at the time, tied his political hopes to the rising star of Harold Stassen. But Thomas E. Dewey resented the Stassen challenge, and when Stassen sought to pin his preconvention hopes to the Mundt-Nixon bill, Dewey destroyed both them and the bill with a vigorous assault upon its anti–civil libertarian implications. "Stripped to its naked essential," he contended in a Portland, Oregon, debate with Stassen, "this is nothing but the method of Hitler and Stalin. It is thought control borrowed from the Japanese. It is an attempt to beat down ideas with a club. It is surrender of everything we believe in."[31]

Leading newspapers in all parts of the country joined in Dewey's protest. *The New York Times* predicted that the bill "could be used to impose restraints on freedom such as the American people have not known for one hundred and fifty years." While the *Christian Science Monitor* contended that it could easily set up "the precedents and the machinery for a kind of political proscription which could be turned by any party in power against any minority."[32] Thus successful congressional action in the way of legislation in the security area had to await the crisis conditions produced by Korea, and H.U.A.C. and other congressional committees were thrown back on their own investigatory powers as the principal way of making congressional contributions to the security crusade.

Harry Truman's own position on civil liberties and civil rights, although not clearly defined at the time of his accession to the Presidency, were tied to an instinctive sense of fair play, and deep concern for the importance and rights of the individual. As a young politician in Missouri he had suffered political defeat as a result of his opposition to the Ku Klux Klan, and his election to the Senate in 1940 had come as a large part due to the vote of workers,

30. Milton R. Konvitz, *Expanding Liberties: Freedom's Gains in Postwar America* (New York, 1966), p. 115. See the constitutional objections raised to the measure in Murray Cohen and Robert F. Fuchs, "Communism's Challenge and the Constitution," *Cornell Law Quarterly*, XXXIV (1948), 182–219, 352–375.

31. William Costello, *The Facts About Nixon: An Unauthorized Biography* (New York, 1960), p. 189.

32. *Ibid.*, p. 189. See also *Time*, LI (May 31, 1948), p. 13.

farmers, and Negroes.[33] Truman clearly found the antics of H.U.A.C. distasteful, at one point maintaining that "the capitol hill spy scare is a 'red herring' to divert public attention from inflation."[34] In his veto of the Taft-Hartley Act he had particularly objected to the non-Communist affidavit. He was quite convinced that the problem of Communists, both in and out of government, could be handled quietly and effectively by agencies of the executive branch. His Attorney General, Tom Clark, was not reluctant to state publicly that congressional investigations seriously impaired the work of the Justice Department.[35] Others in the administration shared with the President the clear feeling that Congress's overzealous desire to muddy the waters in the security area was a form of highly partisan politics.

Truman, however, felt that his political opponents sinned more greatly in their refusal to take positive actions in the area of civil rights. Here, in contrast to the area of civil liberties, he came to have the last word.

The Negro during World War II had begun to press more strongly than at any time since Reconstruction for the equal protection of the laws that the Fourteenth Amendment, on its face, seemed to afford him. Roosevelt's slowness to take action against employers who stubbornly refused to hire black workers produced the threat of a Negro protest march on Washington. The President was thus pressured to issue an executive order on June 25, 1941, directing that Negroes be admitted to job-training programs, forbidding discrimination in work on defense contracts, and establishing a Fair Employment Practices Committee to investigate charges of discrimination on account of race.[36]

33. On Truman and civil liberties see Alan D. Harper, *The Politics of Loyalty: The White House and the Communist Issue, 1946–1952* (Westport, Conn., 1969); Athan Theoharis, *Harry S. Truman and the Origins of McCarthyism* (Chicago, 1971). See also Harry S. Truman, *Memoirs by Harry S. Truman* (2 vols., New York, 1955–56).

34. *The New York Times,* Aug. 6, 1948, p. 1.

35. *The New York Times,* Aug. 16, 1948, p. 1.

36. On the experience under the measure see Louis Ruchames, *Race, Jobs, and Politics* (New York, 1953); Louis C. Kesselman, *The Social Politics of FEPC: A Study in Reform Pressure Movements* (Chapel Hill, N.C., 1948), pp. 1–24; Samuel Krislov, *The Negro in Federal Employment: The Quest for Equal Opportunity* (Minneapolis, 1967), pp. 28–35; and Herbert Garfinkel, *When Negroes March: The March on Washington Movement in the Organizational Politics for FEPC* (Glencoe, Ill., 1959).

Initially, Mr. Truman also trod gingerly in this area. Shortly after becoming President he permitted Congress to strangle the special wartime commission. He did ask Congress to create a permanent F.E.P.C. and on December 5, 1946, the President's Committee on Civil Rights was established, made up of distinguished Southerners, Negroes, and leaders in religion and education throughout the country. Its charge was to determine in what respects current law-enforcement measures might be strengthened, and improved to safeguard civil rights, and to recommend "more adequate and effective means and procedures for the protection of the civil rights of the people of the United States."[37] The committee's famous report, "To Secure These Rights," which was released in October, 1947, explored the entire range of Bill of Rights guarantees, recommending their full protection and extension in a variety of ways. Its major concern was racial discrimination, however, and here it placed special emphasis on the opportunity of each individual to obtain useful employment, and to have access to services in the fields of education, housing, health, recreation, and transportation. "These," it urged, "must be provided with complete disregard for race, color, creed, and national origin." "Without this equality of opportunity," the report went on, "the individual is deprived of the chance to develop his potentialities and to share the fruits of society." "The group also suffers," it maintained, "through the loss of the contributions which might have been made by persons excluded from the main channels of social and economic activity."[38] For implementation, the report called for strengthening the Civil Rights Section of the Justice Department, using the F.B.I. in cases involving violations of civil rights, enacting antilynching and anti–poll tax laws, and establishing a permanent F.E.P.C.

Southern opposition to the report was almost instantaneous.[39] And when Truman sent a special message to Congress on Civil Rights on February 2, 1948, calling for its prompt implementation,[40] the Southerners threatened a filibuster. Truman's posture

37. Bernstein and Matusow, *The Truman Administration,* p. 95.

38. *To Secure These Rights;* The Report of the President's Committee on Civil Rights (Washington, 1947), p. 6.

39. Kesselman, *Social Politics of FEPC,* pp. 166–177; Bernstein and Matusow, *Truman Administration,* pp. 108–110.

40. 80th Congress, 2d Sess., House Document No. 516.

was also largely responsible for the secession of the Dixiecrats in the Presidential election of that year, when they ran their own candidate, J. Strom Thurmond, on a "states rights" platform calling for "segregation of the races," and denouncing proposals for national action in behalf of civil rights as a "totalitarian concept . . . which threatens the integrity of the states and the basic rights of their citizens."[41] But even though Truman overcame this challenge at the polls, no implementation of his recommendations was forthcoming from Congress during his Presidency.

Truman still had power to act in his executive capacity, however, and he used it fully. He strengthened the Civil Rights Section by executive action and began the practice of having the Justice Department assist private parties in civil rights cases. Subsequently the Department submitted amicus curiae briefs before the Supreme Court arguing the unconstitutionality of restrictive covenants and segregation in the public schools. He appointed Negroes to high federal position, and named the first Negro federal judge. More importantly he issued two executive orders in 1948, abolishing segregation in federal employment, and calling for full integration of the armed services.[42]

Congressional rejection of F.E.P.C. also brought important compensating action at the state level. The New York legislature in 1945 had enacted the first state Fair Employment Practices Act, creating a State Commission Against Discrimination with power to prevent and to stop discrimination in employment. A number of Northern states followed suit, and within a decade and a half nearly two-thirds of the population was covered by such legislation.[43]

The postwar Supreme Court was confronted with a series of difficult challenges. Its membership could not help being cognizant of the executive-legislative struggle for power then taking place, and the new "cold war" emphasis on security. This, plus its own changing personnel, and intensifying internal divisions, made its own perception of its proper role ambiguous and clouded. The

41. Kirk H. Porter and Donald B. Johnson, *National Party Platforms, 1840–1964* (Urbana, Ill., 1966), pp. 467–468.

42. *Federal Register,* XVIII (July 26, 1948), p. 722.

43. See Monroe Berger, *Equality by Statute: The Revolution in Civil Rights* (Garden City, N.Y., 1968), pp. 169 ff.; and Milton R. Konvitz and Theodore Leskes, *A Century of Civil Rights* (New York, 1961) pp. 197–224.

man who succeeded Harlan Fiske Stone as Chief Justice differed from his predecessor in judicial training and temperament as well as social and political orientation. Essentially a mediator, Fred M. Vinson had been appointed partly because of his lack of strong commitments and partly because it was felt that he could reconcile the factional differences that were tearing the Roosevelt Court apart. He now sought in every way possible to accommodate the Court to the tensions of the times, to avoid public controversy, and to minimize the Court's role as a policy-making and power body. Second of the Truman appointees (the conservative Ohio Republican Harold Burton having replaced the retiring Roberts in 1946),[44] Vinson was a pragmatist par excellence. Uninterested in brooding over principles of law, he was convinced the law could be adapted to the felt necessity of almost any human situation if the facts of that situation were carefully studied and understood. "Nothing is more certain in modern society," he wrote in perhaps the most famous of his opinions, "than the principle that there are no absolutes, that a name, a phrase, a standard has meaning only associated with the considerations which gave birth to the nomenclature. . . . To those who would paralyze our government by encasing it in a semantic strait-jacket, we must reply that all concepts are relative."[45]

Truman's third and fourth appointees shared similar views. Tom Clark and Sherman Minton both ascended the high bench in October, 1949. Both were close personal friends of the President, the former as his Attorney General, the latter as a former Senate colleague and party regular who had stood firmly behind Franklin Roosevelt's Court-packing proposal in 1937.[46] Neither had a distinguished legal mind and each tended to view his function as a justice in much the same light as Vinson, particularly with regard to the expendability of various civil liberties guarantees in the

44. Daniel S. McHargue, "One of Nine—Mr. Justice Burton's Appointment to the Supreme Court," *Western Reserve Law Review*, IV (1953), 128–131; Ray Forrester, "Mr. Justice Burton and the Supreme Court," *Tulane Law Review*, XX (1945), 1–21.

45. Dennis *v.* U.S., 341 U.S. 494, 508 (1951).

46. C. B. Dutton, "Mr. Justice Clark," *Indiana Law Journal*, XXVI (1951), 169–184; George D. Braden, "Mr. Justice Minton and the Truman Bloc," *Indiana Law Journal*, XXVI (1951), 153–168; Harry S. Wallace, "Mr. Justice Minton: Hoosier Justice on the Supreme Court," *Indiana Law Journal*, XXXIV (1959), 377–422.

face of the pressure of national security and, so some critics maintained, of political assault. The two men they replaced, Justices Murphy and Rutledge, had continued to adhere to their advanced preferred freedoms positions, even in the face of mounting stress upon national security. Memorializing both, Vinson had stated: "Saddened by our losses, but inspired by their examples of devotion to duty . . . we turn to the work before us."[47] Of this, Black's former law clerk, John P. Frank, later ironically observed: "within six weeks the country knew that the 'work before us' consisted in large part of rejecting the civil-rights views of the late Justices."[48] And, in fact, with civil libertarian ranks now depleted, Black and Douglas were forced, even more than previously, to assume responsibility for their judicial protection.

This the two justices were fully prepared to do. Douglas, keeping the liberal faith, wrote a majority opinion in a 1948 case ruling that a city ordinance prohibiting the use of sound trucks was a violation of the First Amendment. Although acknowledging that a balancing process had to take place between community interests and individual rights, he still stressed that in that process Courts "should be mindful to keep the freedoms of the First Amendment in a preferred position."[49] Black, in turn, had emerged from the war period more resolute in his commitment to the concept that the Court had a special obligation to upgrade the civil liberties, particularly of citizens suffering from their impairment as a result of state and local actions. In a famous opinion in the 1948 case of *Adamson* v. *California,* he called for blanket nationalization of the entire Bill of Rights against the states, insisting, in a vigorous dissent, that "this Court is endowed by the Constitution with boundless power under 'natural law' periodically to expand and contract constitutional standards to conform to the Court's conception of what, at a particular time, constitutes 'civilized decency' and 'fundamental liberty and justice.' " "I would follow what I believe was the original

47. 388 U.S. viii (1949).

48. John P. Frank, *Marble Palace: The Supreme Court in American Life* (New York, 1961), p. 190.

49. Saia *v.* New York, 334 U.S. 558, 562 (1948). On the case and the broader issue see "Free Speech and the Hostile Audience," *New York University Law Review,* XXVI (1951), 489–505; and Charles L. Black, "He Cannot Choose But Hear: The Plight of the Captive Auditor," *Columbia Law Review,* LIII (1953), 960–972.

purpose of the Fourteenth Amendment," he added, "to extend to all the people of the nation the complete protection of the Bill of Rights."[50]

Black and Douglas also responded negatively to the implications of the political power shift in the country, especially the growing aggressiveness of conservative congressmen and senators and the new orientation of so many powerful leaders away from the previous concept of the proper governmental role as vigilant defender of the rights of all Americans. Viewing its performance in retrospect, C. Herman Pritchett, historian of the Vinson Court, wrote in 1954:

> The strong legislature-weak judiciary formula, said Justices Black and Douglas, was only appropriate when legislatures were doing things *for* people. When the legislature was doing things *to* people, then the judiciary's role was to act vigorously to guarantee to individuals their constitutionally protected rights against governmental coercion. When the government was engaged in criminal prosecutions; when it was deporting aliens; when legislative investigating committees were grilling witnesses; when Negroes were subjected to discrimination; when people were being taxed or coerced to support religious doctrines; when qualified citizens were being denied the right to vote—in these situations the liberal judicial activists saw intervention by the courts as the essential guarantee of the Constitution's libertarian text.[51]

50. Adamson *v.* California, 332 U.S. 46, 69, 89 (1948). Black's position, especially his "historical" argument, drew great fire and strong rebuttal. See Charles Fairman, "Does the Fourteenth Amendment Incorporate the Bill of Rights? The Original Understanding," *Stanford Law Review,* II (1949), 5–140; Stanley Morrison, "Does the Fourteenth Amendment Incorporate the Bill of Rights? The Judicial Interpretation," *Stanford Law Review,* II (1949), 140–173. For a later similar view see Wallace Mendelson, "Mr. Justice Black's Fourteenth Amendment," *Minnesota Law Review,* LIII (1969), 711–727. In rebuttal, Professor William Crosskey argued that it was the precise intention of the framers of the Fourteenth Amendment to make the Bill of Rights applicable to the states. This was accomplished, he believed, through the insertion of the privileges and immunities clause. William W. Crosskey, *Politics and the Constitution in the History of the United States* (2 vols., Chicago, 1953), II, 1083–1118, 1381. See also Crosskey, "Charles Fairman, 'Legislative History' and the Constitutional Limitations on State Authority," *University of Chicago Law Review,* XXII (1954), 1–143; and Charles Fairman, "A Reply to Professor Crosskey," *University of Chicago Law Review,* XXII (1954), 144–156. Howard J. Graham, one of the leading authorities on the Fourteenth Amendment, has wondered whether any of the lengthy disputes has broken any new ground in truly getting at its origins. See Howard J. Graham, *Everyman's Constitution* (Madison, Wis., 1968), p. 240.

51. C. Herman Pritchett, *Civil Liberties and the Vinson Court* (Chicago, 1954), p. viii.

Their antagonist, Felix Frankfurter, had also become more resolute in adhering to his contrary conviction that the Court's role was essentially passive, and that it could not and should not accept any real responsibility for the formulation of public policy. This meant, even more than previously, that the body should not stand in the way of the political branches that did have that responsibility. Frankfurter was particularly determined to shoot down the preferred freedoms concept. In a second prior restraint case in January, 1949, again involving sound trucks and similar amplifying devices emitting loud and raucous noises, he condemned "the preferred position of freedom of speech" as a mischievous phrase because it "radiates a constitutional doctrine without avowing it."[52] He then traced the evolution of the concept from *Herndon* v. *Lowry* through the *Thomas* v. *Collins* case of 1946, seeking to demonstrate that the phrase expressed a complicated process of constitutional adjudication by a deceptive formula, and thus in its absolutism was an impractical device for dealing with case-to-case situations. Clearly to Frankfurter, in the free speech area, as in others, rigid doctrines, such as "incorporation" (of all the Bill of Rights against the states) and "preferred position," had to give way to flexible ones such as "judicial self-restraint" and "neutralism." To him this was the only proper judicial function as well as the logical projection of Holmesian jurisprudence in a latter-day context.[53]

Ironically, the members of the bench least concerned, in many ways, with judicial philosophy—the Truman appointees and Justice Reed—were in a position to throw their weight decisively to resolve this conflict. The result proved a victory for the Frankfurter philosophy, with, of course, varied ramifications and implications.

Such a shift was reflected in the difficult area of prior restraints on freedom of expression by the Court's second sound truck ruling in early 1949, and its decisions sustaining antipicketing laws and injunctions. It had even been observable in a 1947 decision sustaining restrictive Civil Service Commission actions. Here a congressional

52. Kovacs *v.* Cooper, 336 U.S. 77, 90 (1949).

53. See Walter P. Kremm, "Justice Holmes on Constitutionality and Evidence of His Influence on the Vinson Court, 1946–1949" (unpublished Ph.D. dissertation, University of North Carolina, 1961); Walter Berns, *Freedom, Virtue and the First Amendment* (Chicago, 1965); and Wallace Mendelson (ed.), *The Supreme Court: Law and Discretion* (Indianapolis, 1967), pp. 489–502.

statute had been under fire. Certain employees of the executive branch of the federal government had sued for an injunction against the members of the commission to prohibit them from enforcing the section of the Hatch Act that forbade such employees from "taking any active part in political management or in political campaigns." They had also asked for a declaratory judgment on the unconstitutionality of the section. The Court, speaking through Justice Reed, rejected the claim, denying particularly that it was an unconstitutional invasion of the employees' rights of freedom of speech. "It is accepted constitutional doctrine," Reed wrote, in an opinion joined by Frankfurter, Vinson, and Burton, "that fundamental human rights are not absolute." "This Court must balance the extent of the guarantee of freedom against Congressional enactment to protect the democratic society against the supposed evil of political partisanship by employees of the government."[54] Justices Black, Douglas, and Rutledge would have held the statute unconstitutional. Black's argument was particularly cogent. He interpreted the statute as empowering the Commission "with the awesome power to censor the thoughts, expressions, and activities of law-abiding citizens in the field of free expression from which no person should be barred by a government which boasts that it is a government of, for and by the people—all the people."[55] One month later the Court refused to review the case of a federal officer dismissed on a finding, by the commission, of "reasonable doubt as to his loyalty to the government of the United States."[56] The Court's refusal to review seemed a tacit judicial approval of loyalty proceedings by the executive branch, and coming only four days before the issuance of President Truman's Executive Order No. 9835, seemed to assure a judicial hands-off policy in the implementation of the executive's new loyalty program.

When it came to questions of subsequent punishment for the use of First Amendment freedoms, the Court took a slightly different tack. The reason, some critics argued, was that the individual whose speech had been curtailed was not a loyalty problem but an unfrocked Fascist-type Catholic priest and follower of the rabble-rousing

54. United Public Workers *v.* Mitchell, 330 U.S. 75, 95–96 (1947).
55. *Ibid.*, p. 115.
56. Friedman *v.* Schwellenbach, 330 U.S. 838 (1947).

racist Gerald L. K. Smith. Father Terminiello had made a speech in a Chicago auditorium in 1946 that not only aroused the eight hundred people in the hall, but stimulated a larger crowd outside to picket the building in protest, throw rocks and stink bombs through the windows, and attempt to break down the doors. The Court promptly narrowed the issue to a consideration of the constitutionality of the city ordinance under which Terminiello had been arrested. This enabled Douglas, speaking for a strange coalition of Reed, Black, Murphy, and Rutledge, to avoid confronting squarely the broader question of whether speech composed of derisive, fighting words, and calculated to cause violent reaction, was entitled to constitutional protection.[57] Rather, Douglas' opinion, which was widely quoted in the press as an indication of the high level of tolerance prevalent in the America of the time, was primarily "an academic lecture about the importance of 'unrest' or even 'anger' in preventing the 'standardization of ideas.' "[58]

With regard to procedures, the Court took federal cases dealing with coerced confessions, the right to counsel, and jury trial, but issued no startling changes of rules in any.[59] Its primary concern proved to be the determination of the extent of the protections afforded by the Fourth Amendment's proscription of unreasonable search and seizure. Here the Court swung from one extreme to the other with no workable rule emerging. Thus, in the 1947 term, it viewed with lenience the action of federal officers in a broad, but only partially warranted search of a person's premises.[60] In 1948, it swung back sharply to the position that a search without a warrant, even though made in the course of a lawful arrest, was unreasonable when there was time to obtain a warrant in advance.[61] By 1950, it had gone back to the 1947 position of lenience, inducing Justice Black to comment that "in no other field has the law's uncertainty been more clearly manifested."[62]

57. Terminiello *v.* Chicago, 337 U.S. 1 (1949).

58. Pritchett, *Civil Liberties and the Vinson Court,* p. 61.

59. See Von Moltke *v.* Gillies, 332 U.S. 708 (1948); Upshaw *v.* U.S., 335 U.S. 410 (1948); Frasier *v.* U.S., 335 U.S. 497 (1948); and L. B. Schwartz, "Federal Criminal Jurisdiction and Prosecutors' Discretion," *Law and Contemporary Problems,* XIII (1948), 64–85.

60. Harris *v.* U.S., 331 U.S. 145 (1947). See Benjamin H. Kizer, "The Fourth Amendment to the Federal Constitution—The Harris Case," *Lawyers Guild Review,* VII (1947), 122–128.

61. Trupiano *v.* U.S., 334 U.S. 699 (1948).

62. U.S. *v.* Rabinowitz, 339 U.S. 56, 67 (1950).

At the state level, the Court continued the application of its "fairness" doctrine, measuring state criminal procedures against its own evaluation of what ingredients were necessary for a "fair trial." This resulted in a series of fairly consistent rulings against coerced confessions, even though a number of its members were prepared to exclude situations that they considered only "inherently coercive."[63] In the right-to-counsel area, the justices followed Frankfurter's position that "when a crime subject to capital punishment is not involved each case depends on its own facts."[64] Thus where clearly lack of counsel had led to denial of justice, the Court reversed convictions.[65] In other instances it normally supported the state.[66] When attempts were made to nationalize further of the procedural guarantees, the Court consistently balked. These included the protection of the Sixth and Seventh Amendments relative to jury trial,[67] including the use of "blue ribbon" juries,[68] the Fifth Amendment's guarantee against double jeopardy, and the Eighth's against cruel and unusual punishment.[69]

The 1949 case of *Wolf* v. *Colorado* was in many ways a typical example of the justices' approach to procedural problems. Speaking through Frankfurter, the Court held unanimously that "the security of one's privacy against arbitrary intrusion by the police . . . is basic to a free society,"[70] thus suggesting that the prohibition against unreasonable searches and seizures in the Fourth Amendment was applicable against state officials as an integral ingredient in its concept of "ordered liberty." The Court then proceeded to rob the statement of much of its apparent meaning, refusing to require state courts to exclude evidence secured by admittedly unreasonable search and seizure techniques. The ruling thus left it up to the

63. Ashcraft *v.* Tennessee, 322 U.S. 143 (1944); Haley *v.* Ohio, 332 U.S. 596 (1948); Watts *v.* Indiana, 338 U.S. 49 (1949); Turner *v.* Pennsylvania, 338 U.S. 62 (1949); Harris *v.* South Carolina, 338 U.S. 68 (1949).

64. Quicksall *v.* Michigan, 338 U.S. 660 (1950).

65. De Meeler *v.* Michigan, 329 U.S. 663 (1947); Townsend *v.* Burke, 334 U.S. 736 (1948); Wade *v.* Mayo, 334 U.S. 672 (1948); Gibbs *v.* Burke, 337 U.S. 773 (1949).

66. Carter *v.* Illinois, 329 U.S. 173 (1947); Foster *v.* Illinois, 332 U.S. 134 (1947), Quicksall *v.* Michigan 338 U.S. 660 (1950).

67. Gayes *v.* New York, 332 U.S. 145 (1947).

68. Fay *v.* New York, 332 U.S. 261 (1947).

69. Louisiana *ex rel* Francis *v.* Resweber, 329 U.S. 459 (1947). See Arthur E. Sutherland, "Due Process and Cruel Punishment," *Harvard Law Review*, LXIV (1958), 271–279.

70. Wolf *v.* Colorado, 338 U.S. 25, 27 (1949).

states to decide whether they would follow the example of the federal government and exclude from their courts any incriminating evidence the police might pick up in the course of an arbitrary intrusion. It thus became a classic example of a basic right for which no judicial remedy was provided.[71]

The hottest time given the Vinson Court in the pre-Korean period, resulted from its rulings in the area of religion. The establishment-of-religion provision in the First Amendment had been virtually untested in American history. But in 1947, the Court accepted a case involving the important and highly sensitive question of public aid to private schools, particularly Catholic parochial schools, and promptly found itself in the midst of a storm center. The deceptive easiness of pinpointing precisely what, in the area of religious and quasi-religious practices, the traditional wall of separation between church and state separated, quickly became apparent. The case involved the use of public tax money to reimburse New Jersey parents for bus fare spent in transporting their children to religious schools. Justice Black, speaking for a sharply divided, five-to-four bench, wrote eloquently of the historical importance of the principle of separation, indicating that its logical thrust precluded taxes in any amount, large or small, being levied to support any religious activities or institutions. He endorsed as the proper meaning of the First Amendment the principle that the state was required to be neutral in its relation with groups of religious believers and nonbelievers. "The wall of separation must be kept high and impregnable," he contended. "We could not approve the slightest breach." And then, in what seemed an anticlimatic and contradictory concluding sentence, he stated, "New Jersey has not breached it here."[72] Justice Jackson's evaluation of the opinion was shared by much of the informed public. "The case which irresistibly comes to mind as the most fitting precedent," remarked the dissenting justice, "is that of Julia who, according to Byron's reports, 'whispering "I will ne'er consent,"—consented.' "[73]

71. Francis A. Allen, "The Wolf Case: Search and Seizure, Federalism, and Civil Liberties," *Illinois Law Review,* XLV (1950), 11–13; and "Federalism and the Fourth Amendment: A Requiem for Wolf," in Philip B. Kurland (ed.), *1961 Supreme Court Review* (Chicago, 1961), pp. 1–48. See also Frankfurter's dissent in Irvine *v.* California, 347 U.S. 128, 142 (1954).

72. Everson *v.* Board of Education, 330 U.S. 1, 18 (1947).

73. *Ibid.,* p. 19.

The decision stirred up a mixed reaction ranging from sharply critical to cordially approving. It split religious groups acutely. One response was the setting up of a national organization, Protestants and Other Americans United for Separation of Church and State, as a watchdog to protect the public treasury against further raids by the Catholic Church. Catholic circles, as could be expected, hailed the decision as a victory for religious freedom and a recognition of the equal status of public schools and Catholic parochial schools. The ruling thus fanned long-smoldering religious controversy.[74] The Court's ruling, striking down an Illinois program authorizing the use of public schools for religious instruction, expanded the controversy, but drew its fire from conservatives.[75] Particularly upset that the decision expunged religious instruction of all kinds, by all denominations, from the schools, they argued vehemently that the Court's assumed posture of neutrality regarding religion was a misinterpretation of history and violated the intent of the framers of the Constitution and the Bill of Rights. The Founding Fathers did not intend by the First Amendment to forbid completely all government aid to religion, its critics argued, but only such aid as favored one religion over another. The Court, they maintained, was adopting policies of religious absolutism and inflexibility inappropriate to a Christian nation. It was at the same time, in the words of Professor E. S. Corwin, setting itself up as a "national school board."[76]

74. For a detailed discussion of this reaction see Theodore Power, *The School Bus Law: A Case Study in Education, Religion, and Politics* (Middletown, Conn., 1960).

75. McCollum *v.* Board of Education, 333 U.S. 203 (1948). See Vashti McCollum, *One Woman's Fight* (New York 1951)

76. Edward S. Corwin, "The Supreme Court as National School Board," *Thought,* XXIII (1948), 665–683. See also Paul G. Kauper, *Religion and the Constitution* (Baton Rouge, 1964); Robert F. Drinan, *Religion, the Courts, and Public Policy* (New York, 1963); Conrad H. Moehlman, *The Wall of Separation Between Church and State* (Boston, 1951); Dallin H. Oaks (ed.), *The Wall Between Church and State* (Chicago, 1963); and Wilbur Katz, *Religion and American Constitutions* (Evanston, Ill., 1964). The law review literature on the subject is voluminous. See especially "Religion and the State," *Law and Contemporary Problems,* XIV (Winter, 1949), 1–159; Leo Pfeffer, "Church and State: Something Less than Separation," *University of Chicago Law Review,* XIX (1951), 1–29; Arthur E. Sutherland, "Due Process and Disestablishment," *Harvard Law Review,* LXII (1949), 1306–1344; and Paul M. Butler and Alfred Scanlan, "The Wall of Separation—Judicial Gloss on the First Amendment," *Notre Dame Lawyer,* XXXVII (1962), 288–308.

The Vinson Court's behavior in the area of civil rights again suggested its self-restraint. Here also it was reluctant to launch massive onslaughts on legislatively authorized policies and programs, even when they tended, on their face or in their operation, to deny equal protection of the laws. Voting rights were a conspicuous case in point. Here historical patterns, reinforced by Frankfurter's deep conviction that the judiciary should not project its authority into the area of electoral matters, clearly came to prevail. Indeed, the concept that certain matters were non-justiciable, as so-called "political questions" to be decided by the two policy-making departments of the government, was as old as John Marshall. It had been applied to the voting arrangement of states as early as the famous 1849 case of *Luther* v. *Borden*.[77] The rule complemented nicely Frankfurter's general belief in judicial self-restraint, and the Vinson majority's desire to avoid needless public controversy and critical assault. Nonetheless, the growing underrepresentation of urban and suburban areas in rural-dominated legislatures undermined further the possibility of citizens whose voting rights were thereby watered down gaining any meaningful relief through legislative or executive branches. It was thus inevitable that cases would be brought charging that such practices were a denial of due process, equal protection, and the privileges and immunities of citizenship.

Such was the situation in the 1946 case of *Colegrove* v. *Green*. The case involved malapportionment in Illinois and refusal by the Illinois legislature, in spite of population shifts, to revise its legislative districts since the apportionment of 1901. Frankfurter, for the Court, was quick to reject the idea that the federal courts had any authority to reconstruct the electoral process of Illinois. The issue was, he maintained "of a peculiarly political nature, and therefore not meet for judicial determination."[78] If there was any authority in the federal government to compel such reconstruction, Frankfurter made clear, it belonged to Congress and not the Courts. The decision, however, was four to three, and strong dissents by Black, Douglas, and Murphy encouraged other citizens who felt their franchise invalidated, to consider the possibility of judicial relief.

77. Luther *v.* Borden, 7 Howard 1 (1849). For background see Charles G. Post, "The Supreme Court and Political Questions," in *Johns Hopkins Studies in History and Political Science,* Vol. LIV (Baltimore, 1936).

78. Colegrove *v.* Green, 328 U.S. 549, 552 (1946).

The same three justices dissented in a 1948 case involving the refusal of Illinois election officials to honor Progressive party petitions to get the name of Henry Wallace on the Illinois ballot.[79] The denial was clearly the result of an Illinois law that required the signatures of twenty-five thousand voters on a petition, but demanded that this include two hundred voters in each of at least fifty counties within the state, thereby giving a few rural counties a virtual veto over the process. The majority still found no justiciable issue. By 1950, with the death of Murphy, the dissenters had been reduced to two. Nonetheless, speaking through Douglas, protest was raised against a per curiam ruling in which the Court again held that a state's geographical distribution of electoral strength among its political subdivisions is a political question. To Douglas, the Georgia "County Unit System" being considered, a scheme that assigned to each county electoral votes that went to the candidate receiving the highest popular vote, was clearly designed to disfranchise the urban Negro. It was a device, wrote the justice, "as deeply rooted in discrimination as the practice which keeps a man from the voting booth because of his race, creed, or color. The creation by law of favored groups of citizens and the grant to them of preferred political rights is the worst of all discriminations under a democratic system of government. . . ."[80]

Like caution existed in other areas of racial discrimination. In 1948, two highly supercharged racial covenant situations reached the Court. In each, Negroes had protested against private agreements denying access to real estate for which they were prepared to pay. Solicitor General Philip B. Perlman argued the case for the United States, as amicus curiae, supporting the petitioners. Even so, the Court limited its ruling to the narrowest extent. There was no doubt that the equal protection clause of the Fourteenth Amendment, under which the first of these actions was brought, was clearly directed against the actions of states rather than individuals. The leading precedent on the subject involved refusal to take jurisdiction in a case in 1926 challenging a private covenant. Such covenants entered into by property owners binding themselves not to sell or lease their property to Negroes, or other racial, national, or religious groups, were a type of private action, the Taft Court had ruled.

79. MacDougall *v.* Green, 335 U.S. 281 (1948).
80. South *v.* Peters, 339 U.S. 276, 281 (1948).

Hence they were not contrary to the Constitution or to public policy. The 1948 Court did not depart from this view. It focused upon the legitimacy of state action in the form of formal judicial enforcement of such covenants by state courts, maintaining only that such enforcement violated the equal protection clause. The result was not to proscribe such covenants per se, but merely to make them legally unenforceable. In practice, this forced a Negro, determined in the future to break one, into the expensive and psychologically difficult position of taking the initiative to force a court test.[81] Three of the justices, Reed, Jackson, and Rutledge, did not participate in the case, or the companion one, raising similar questions about covenants in the District of Columbia, reportedly because each of them owned property that was covered by a restrictive covenant.[82]

Other forms of segregation, while generally producing unanimous judicial proscription, were carefully confined to narrow rules and the immediate circumstances that brought them to adjudication. In the area of segregated education, the Court took a series of cases involving aspects of professional education beyond the college level. In 1948, it insisted that a qualified Negro had to be admitted to the state law school in Oklahoma or be furnished an equivalent education by the state.[83] Once again, separate facilities, it was maintained, had to be fully equal. Nothing less would be tolerated. When a Negro graduate student was admitted to the University of Okla-

81. Shelley *v.* Kraemer, 334 U.S. 1 (1948). In the companion case of Hurd *v.* Hodge, 334 U.S. 24 (1948), the Court applied the same principle to the District of Columbia, turning the case, however, on the Civil Rights Act of 1866, again following arguments in the Justice Department brief. See Charles Abrams, *Race Bias in Housing* (New York, 1947); Clement E. Vose, *Caucasians Only: The Supreme Court, the NAACP, and the Restrictive Covenant Cases* (Berkeley, 1959); and Donald M. Cahen, "The Impact of Shelley *v.* Kraemer on the State Action Concept," *California Law Review,* XLIV (1956), 718–736.

82. Pritchett, *Vinson Court,* p. 142. The cases left open the issue of whether the signer of a covenant who breached its provisions could be sued for damages by other participants in the covenant. Numerous conflicting rulings were handed down by the lower court until the Supreme Court in Barrows *v.* Jackson, 346 U.S. 249 (1953), held such action invalid. California, Justice Minton argued, could not coerce a property owner to pay damages for failure to observe a covenant that the state had no right to incorporate in a statute or enforce in equity, and that federal courts could not enforce because of its being contrary to public policy.

83. Sipuel *v.* Board of Regents of the Univ. of Oklahoma, 332 U.S. 631 (1948).

homa he was segregated, sitting in a separate row for Negroes in classrooms, reading at a separate table in the library, and eating at a separate table in the cafeteria. Justice Vinson for the Court held that the equal protection clause assured the Negro student the same treatment by the state as other students.[84]

In two other cases, decided the same day, the Court made it evident that the days of the "separate-but-equal" doctrine were numbered. In a case involving a Texas Negro denied entry to the state's white law school on the grounds that the state would build an "equal" facility for Negroes, the Court considered the reality of such a facility immediately attaining equal status in faculty, library facilities, and general distinction, and rejected the Texas proposal as not affording the type of equality that the Fourteenth Amendment required. Still it failed to "reach petitioner's contention" that *Plessy* v. *Ferguson* should be reexamined in the light of contemporary knowledge respecting the purposes of the Fourteenth Amendment and the effects of racial segregation.[85] But the sensitivity of the ruling to other than the precise legal factors in the case suggested that the Court was not oblivious to such factors. Similarly, in ruling dining-car practices on the Southern Railway a violation of the Interstate Commerce Act, the justices considered the unfortunate impact of curtains, partitions, and signs, emphasizing the artificiality of a difference in treatment. The defendant railroad followed the practice of reserving ten tables for white passengers and one for Negroes, separated from the other by a curtain, and clearly marked "For Colored Only." Such action, Justice Burton maintained for a unanimous Court, came clearly under the Act's proscription of subjecting any particular person "to any undue or unreasonable prejudice or disadvantage."[86]

These cases, touching only the most obvious forms of discrimination, left many American Negroes frustrated at the cautiousness with which the Court was proceeding to guarantee them the rights that they felt were theirs as a result of American birth and citizen-

84. McLaurin *v.* Oklahoma State Regents, 339 U.S. 637 (1950).

85. Sweatt *v.* Painter, 339 U.S. 629 (1950). On this and the earlier cases see J. D. Hyman, "Segregation and the Fourteenth Amendment," *Vanderbilt Law Review,* IV (1951), 555–573; and Robert J. Harris, *The Quest for Equality: The Constitution, Congress and the Supreme Court* (Baton Rouge, 1960), pp. 130 ff.

86. Henderson *v.* U.S.. 339 U.S. 816 (1950).

ship. However, the rulings handed down on June 5, 1950, came with the early shots of the Korean war echoing across the nation. The resultant reassessment of national concerns now brought America's racial situation into clearer focus, and with the struggle for the minds of men now taking violent international forms, a new urgency developed for upgrading the poor American image created by the Communist-exploited second-class citizenship of the Negro. Negro leadership, especially in the N.A.A.C.P., was thereby encouraged to press even harder for legal relief from the discrimination that black people suffered in housing, jobs, voting, and particularly access to public schools and public facilities.

Still, many Americans found unsatisfactory the performance of the Vinson Court through the 1949–50 term. The Chief Justice, seemingly borrowing a page from the Court's Japanese relocation performance, went even further in steering the high bench away from explosive public controversies, confining its jurisdiction to narrowly limited legal points. Agreeing with Frankfurter that in such a period of national pressures, and particularly legislative activism, such a role was not only the right but the sensible path to preserving judicial prestige and power, he seemed at times to be courting favor with both Congress and the executive by shaping the law to acquiesce in the current desires of each. Public criticism, particularly informed legal criticism, was acute. The avoidance of constitutional issues drew broad-scale fire, and critics were particularly disturbed by the shrunken size of the Court's docket, which was the smallest since the early years of the 1930s. "If an efficiency expert took a look at the business of our highest tribunal," wrote two legal scholars in the *University of Pennsylvania Law Review*, "he might well come away with the notion that more time is devoted to deciding *not* to decide a case than to the disposition of those which get from one to four or five opinions from the Justices."[87] The article, entitled "What the Supreme Court Did Not Do in the 1950 Term," was the second such annual evaluation of the Court's inaction.[88] Burton C. Bernard took a similar tack in

87. Fowler V. Harper and Edwin D. Etherington, "What the Supreme Court Did Not Do in the 1950 Term," *University of Pennsylvania Law Review*, C (1951), 354–409.

88. The earlier article was Fowler V. Harper and Alan S. Rosenthal, "What the Supreme Court Did Not Do in the 1949 Term: An Appraisal of Certiorari," *University of Pennsylvania Law Review*, XCIX (1950), 293–325.

the *Michigan Law Review,* urging the Court to "modify its rules of avoidance" particularly in First Amendment cases, insisting that having disengaged itself from its heavy prior duties as adjudicator of economic rights, it should now have time for civil liberties and should use that time constructively.[89] James D. Barnett, writing in the *Oregon Law Review,* similarly deplored the Court's caution. "Escape from a decision today," he wrote, "simply postpones the performance of a duty until tomorrow."[90] A conservative critic in the *Florida Law Review,* assessing "What Is Wrong with the Current Supreme Court," began with the charge that "it puts law ahead of justice," and went on particularly to call for reassessment of its doctrine of delimiting its own jurisdiction, its doctrine of dodging constitutional issues, and its doctrine of not deciding the federal question if the case could be decided on a nonfederal issue.[91] Some of the strongest, and in some cases intemperate, comments came in the popular media. Irving Dilliard, writing in the *Atlantic* in December, 1949, viewed with alarm the path on which the Truman appointees seemed to have launched the Court. If its new appointees keep it on its present course, he predicted direfully, "it will be less concerned about the rights of individual citizens than it was when an economic conservative like Republican Justice George Sutherland wrote Bill of Rights decisions in the Scottsboro fair trial and the Huey Long press gag cases. What a bitter irony that will be."[92] Fred Rodell, a year and a half later, went further, charging in *Look*

89. Burton C. Bernard, "Avoidance of Constitution Issues in the United States Supreme Court," *Michigan Law Review,* L (1951), 267.

90. James D. Barnett, "Avoidance of Judicial Decision upon Constitutional Ground When Decision Can Be Based on Other Ground," *Oregon Law Review,* XXVIII (1949), 209.

91. Basil H. Pollitt, "What Is Wrong with the Supreme Court of the United States," *Florida Law Journal,* XXV (1951), 234. See also John P. Roche, "Judicial Self-Restraints," *American Political Science Review,* XLIX (1955), 762–772.

92. Irving Dilliard, "Truman Reshapes the Supreme Court," *Atlantic Monthly,* CLXXXIV (December, 1949), 34. At the other extreme, southern racists condemned the Court's left-wing tendencies, Mississippi Congressman Rankin typically maintaining that as a result of the Court's mild blow at restrictive covenants, "the Communists won their greatest victory." The Court's action, he charged, "destroyed the value of property owned by tens of thousands of loyal Americans in every state of the Union." *Congressional Record,* 80th Cong., 2d Sess., p. 5256.

that the Court's record in recent terms demonstrated that it was "incompetent, indolent and irresponsible."[93]

Such criticism, however, did not affect the justices to the degree that growing national pressures did. Indeed, the new military crisis seemed to convince the Court majority of the validity of its present course.

93. Fred Rodell, "Our Not So Supreme Court," *Look,* XV (July 31, 1951), 60.

CHAPTER 9

The Korean Crisis and the Cold War Constitution

ON February 9, 1950, Republican Senator Joseph McCarthy of Wisconsin made a speech in Wheeling, West Virginia, in which he claimed that he held in his hand the names of 205 Communists currently employed by the United States State Department. Shortly he read into the *Congressional Record* a version of that speech carefully reducing the number to 57, but proclaiming that "when a great democracy is destroyed, it will not be because of enemies from without, but rather because of enemies from within."[1] Four months later, on June 24, the administration found itself forced to deal with another open assault, this time, ironically, from the Communists themselves. On June 25, 1950, North Korean forces marched south across the thirty-eighth parallel to challenge the South Korean government, a government that the United States felt bound by

1. *Congressional Record,* 81st Cong., 2d Sess., pp. 1954–1957. Although McCarthy derived heavy Republican support, seven Republican senators moved in mid-1950 to divorce themselves from his accusations of treason and his methods. See the Declaration of Conscience in *Congressional Record,* 81st Cong., 2d Sess., pp. 7894–7895. The literature on McCarthy is voluminous and, while largely nonconstitutional, cannot avoid dealing with the Senator's callous flouting of procedural guarantees. See especially Jack Anderson and Ronald W. May, *McCarthy, the Man, the Senator, and the "Ism"* (Boston, 1952); William F. Buckley, and Brent Bozell, *McCarthy and His Enemies* (Chicago, 1954); and Richard H. Rovere, *Senator Joe McCarthy* (New York, 1959). See also the useful compilation by Earl Latham (ed.), *The Meaning of McCarthyism* (Boston, 1965).

international commitment to defend. The executive branch was quickly subjected to sharp fire from legislative leaders and from large segments of the general public in confronting both challenges. And as frustration over the seemingly unresolvable Korean conflict mounted, along with the unpopularity of the draft, uneven wage and price controls, and mounting inflation, McCarthy and others of his ilk exploited such discontent further by broadening and intensifying their disloyalty charges. In the ensuing atmosphere it was virtually impossible to consider constitutional questions with objectivity.[2] As a result, far-reaching decisions on vital points of law, particularly in the civil liberties area, bore the scar of overzealous security concerns, and precedents were established as restrictive on individual liberties as at any time in recent constitutional history.

Although foreign policy had been the major concern of the Truman administration in the years since 1945, and was the area in which it made its most significant accomplishments, the many constitutional questions that America's dramatic new world posture had created had not been carefully resolved prior to Korea. The new international crisis initially brought the spotlight to bear most fully upon them.

Full-scale participation in the United Nations, as in other formal postwar alliances, particularly the North Atlantic Treaty Organization, had committed the United States to the maintenance of world peace through collective security. It had also committed the nation to military arrangements raising fundamental constitutional questions of effective international security actions and congressional control of the war-making power. Section 6 of the United Nations Participation Act, which had been passed by Congress in 1945, authorized the President to negotiate military agreements with the Security Council to earmark American military contingents for the Council subject to congressional approval of the agreements negotiated.[3] The Act went further, however, to indicate that the Presi-

2. See H. W. Ehrmann, "Zeitgeist and the Supreme Court," *Antioch Review,* XI (December, 1951), 424–436.

3. 59 Stat. 619 (1945). See Jacob Robinson, *Human Rights and Fundamental Freedoms in the Charter of the United Nations* (New York, 1946); Edwin Borchard, "The Charter and the Constitution," *American Journal of International Law,* XXXIX (1945), 767–777; Jacob D. Hyman, "Constitutional Aspects of the Covenant," *Law and Contemporary Problems,* XIV (1949), 451–478; and *House Report* No. 137, 82nd Cong., 1st Sess. (1951).

dent did not need further authorization to make such forces available in any specific challenge to international collective security. Congress thus acknowledged the President's power to commit the United States to military actions under the United Nations Charter without congressional consent. The same constitutional issues in a slightly different form were raised by N.A.T.O.[4] Article 5 of the treaty pledged the United States to automatic intervention in case any member suffered armed attack. The provision sought to avoid any specific obligation on the part of the United States to a war without formal consent of Congress. But it obviously left in the hands of the President the authority to deploy American armed forces in such a fashion that should the challenge be great, they would find themselves in a war situation in implementing the treaty's provisions. The action thus further vitiated congressional check upon Presidential discretion in the use of troops, enabling him to commit the United States to war under such a treaty without the need for congressional approval in the form of a formal declaration.

The Korean war served as dramatic confirmation of this development. President Truman, in accordance with a request from the U.N. Security Council, based upon U.S. treaty commitments to the body, ordered American military forces into the fighting in Korea.[5] This action was taken even though prior to this time the United States had never assigned American forces to the Council for peacekeeping operations. The resultant massive Korean "police action" was not war in a formal constitutional sense, for it was never declared so by Congress.

Although unsuccessful in the long run, sharp congressional opposition arose to the constitutionality of such action. Senator Robert A. Taft of Ohio, the "Mr. Republican" of the day, was, like his father, a champion of congressional power and Republicanism in its purest form. Taft, a prewar isolationist, felt strongly that the growing centralization of the power of the President to commit the nation to international ventures, with virtually no effective con-

4. Executive Document 1, 81st Cong. 1st Sess. (1949). See Richard H. Heindel, Thorstein V. Kalijarvi, and Francis O. Wilcox, "The North Atlantic Treaty in the United States Senate," *American Journal of International Law,* XLIII (1949), 633–655.

5. Senate Foreign Relations and Armed Services Committees, Hearings, *Military Situation in the Far East,* 82nd Cong., 1st Sess., p. 3369.

gressional check, was a usurpation of the congressional war power, and violative both of the Constitution and the laws of the United States. Taft was joined by a number of conservative congressmen and senators, equally determined to bring about a revival of congressional prerogative in the foreign policy area in the same way that Congress had reasserted its domestic authority.[6] President Truman stood firm, however, insisting that the President possessed the constitutional power to move troops anywhere abroad at his own discretion.[7] In the final analysis, Congress in April, 1951, adopted a lengthy resolution acceding to Presidential prerogative but urging that "in the interests of sound constitutional process, and of national unity and understanding, Congressional approval should be obtained on any policy requiring the assignment of American troops abroad."[8] The resolution constituted a form of congressional surrender, however, leaving Congress with the devices of denying congressional appropriations and ultimately impeachment as the only specific tools with which to check Presidential prerogative in this area.[9]

6. Taft initially supported the Truman action, *Congressional Record,* 81st Cong., 2d Sess., pp. 9319–9323, only later charging that the President, in sending troops abroad, had "usurped power and violated the Constitution and laws of the United States." *Congressional Record,* 82nd Cong., 1st Sess., p. 57. By 1951, he was antagonistic both to further executive commitment of troops abroad unilaterally, and to the growing military influence in foreign policy decisions. *Congressional Record,* 82nd Cong., 1st Sess., p. 2046. For an explicit statement of his position see Robert A. Taft, *A Foreign Policy for Americans* (Garden City, N.Y., 1951) pp. 21–36. For a rebuttal contending that the President had unquestioned authority to move troops outside the United States without congressional authority see Henry Steele Commager, "Does the President Have Too Much Power?," *The New York Times Magazine,* Apr. 1, 1951, pp. 15 ff.

7. Harry S. Truman, *Memoirs,* (2 vols., Garden City, N.Y., 1955), II, 355 ff.

8. 82nd Cong. 1st Sess., S. Res. 99, reprinted in Senate Report No. 175, *Assignment of Ground Forces of the United States to Duty in the European Area,* pp. 2-3. The issue of whether the Korean action was technically a war, in the legal sense, was raised in a number of court cases, all of which the Supreme Court refused to hear. See A. Kenneth Pye, "The Legal Status of the Korean Hostilities," *Georgetown Law Journal,* XLV (Fall, 1956), which contains a discussion of the pertinent cases, pp. 45–47.

9. On the issue of the President's precise source of constitutional authority for his Korean action, there was confusion at the outset, even on the part of some of his most loyal supporters. Some of the latter contended initially that the President's move was based on a cease-fire order of the Security Council and hence stemmed from our treaty commitments to the United Nations. Others contended that the President had such authority as commander-in-chief. Some

On subjects less strategic, and less related to the President's massive foreign policy authority, calls for limitation of the blanket use of the treaty power were more effective. Article 55 of the U.N. Charter committed the signatories to promote ". . . universal respect for, and observance of human rights and fundamental freedoms for all without distinction as to race, sex, language or religion." In a case in 1948, challenging the California Alien Land Law, four of the members of the Supreme Court made clear their general conviction that that law was unconstitutional as a "barrier to the fulfillment of the Charter" to which the United States was committed by treaty.[10] Two years later, a California district court read the justices' earlier contention into law, holding the Alien Land Law invalid on these grounds.[11] Reaction, particularly from conservatives and states' rights advocates, was hostile in the extreme. Critics not only maintained that this action set a dangerous precedent for the setting aside of numerous restrictive state and federal statutes, particularly in the area of civil rights and property rights, they adopted the *argumentum ad horrendum* that this and other treaties, if interpreted this broadly, could well become the occasion for the exercise of federal authority otherwise restricted by explicit constitutional limitations.[12]

---

critics argued that the action was illegal in the absence of a congressional declaration of war. In time the second position came to prevail through the support of strong constitutional authorities such as Senator Wayne Morse—see *Congressional Record,* 81st Cong., 2d Sess., pp. 9228–9243—although in final analysis it seems dubious whether the issue was centrally constitutional and whether even with a congressional declaration, Truman would have escaped the bitter criticism to which he was subjected. See Charles A. Lofgren, "Mr. Truman's War: A Debate and Its Aftermath," *Review of Politics,* XXXI (April, 1969), pp. 223–241.

10. Oyama *v.* California, 332 U.S. 633 (1948).

11. Fujii *v.* State, 217 F. 2d 481 (1950). The ruling was affirmed, 242 P. 2d 617 (1952), but on Fourteenth Amendment grounds. See Manley O. Hudson, "Charter Provisions on Human Rights in American Law," *American Journal of International Law,* XLIV (1950), 543–548; and Charles Fairman, "Finis to Fujii," *American Journal of International Law,* XLVI (1952), 687–690. The Court also modified California legislation against alien fishermen, ruling unconstitutional a state law that in practice had prevented a resident Japanese alien from earning his living as a commercial fisherman in the state's waters. Takahashi *v.* Fish & Game Comm's., 334 U.S. 410 (1948).

12. For Senator Bricker's opposition see *Congressional Record,* 81st Cong., 1st Sess., p. 8261.

Similar apprehensions were voiced in other regards. Eleanor Roosevelt had been one of a number of liberal Americans interested in the framing of a Universal Declaration of Human Rights to "set a common standard of achievement for all peoples and all nations." Its sponsors hoped eventually to afford beleaguered individuals throughout the world access to international machinery as a remedy for the destruction or deprivation of their rights and the destruction of their individualism. The Declaration was agreed upon by the U.N. General Assembly in 1948 in highly watered-down form.[13] It did not, however, provide for direct access to international procedures by the individual, but was to be implemented only on the initiative of governments. In the same year the General Assembly unanimously adopted a Genocide Convention which President Truman transmitted to the Senate in early 1949, asking for ratification. This was essential to give it the effect of a binding treaty. Conservative congressional leaders promptly leaped on both suggestions as another attempt to undermine American nationalism and self-determination through the treaty power. Particularly concerned that the Universal Declaration embodied economic, social, and cultural rights, as well, the senators first insisted upon two separate conventions to separate the latter, which they branded as "socialistic if not communistic," from the narrower commitment to civil and political rights.[14] Even these they worried about, for fear that the Declaration, even though it lacked any enforcement provision, might someway evolve into a self-executing treaty and hence become the basis for action against local American political and civil rights patterns.[15]

The Genocide Convention fared even less well. A subcommittee of the Senate Foreign Relations Committee held public hearings early in 1950 in which representatives from the State Department

13. U.N. General Assembly, 2d Sess., Doc. A/811 (1948). See Egon Schewlb, *Human Rights and the International Community* (Chicago, 1964); and Moses Moskowitz, *Human Rights and World Order* (New York, 1958).

14. Milton R. Konvitz, *Expanding Liberties: Freedom's Gains in Postwar America* (New York, 1966), pp. 355–356.

15. See Zechariah Chafee, Jr., "Federal and State Powers under the UN Covenant on Human Rights," *Wisconsin Law Review* (1951), 389–473, 623–656; Oscar Schachter, "Charter and Constitution: The Human Rights Provisions in American Law," *Vanderbilt Law Review,* IV (1951), 399–659; and Lawrence Preuss, "Some Aspects of the Human Rights Provisions of the Charter and Their Execution in the United States," *American Journal of International Law,* XLVI (1952), 289–296.

and from groups as far ranging as the C.I.O., the Federal Council of Churches, the American Legion, and the Loyal Order of Moose had urged approval.[16] In May, it reported the convention favorably to the full committee, but with various crippling qualifications and reservations, a number strongly supported by the American Bar Association. These greatly undermined its thrust. By this time, however, Senator McCarthy was fueling his engines of assault upon the State Department and even the weakened convention now came under fire as a Communist plot concocted by subversives in that agency, against the Constitution and the government. Hence the full committee never got around to acting on the convention, although by the mid-1960s it had been ratified by sixty-seven other nations.

By early 1952, the new nativists moved to the offensive. Senator John Bricker of Ohio, with the support of a number of state legislatures and the American Bar Association, introduced a comprehensive constitutional amendment to limit the treaty power. Designed to prevent destruction of American federalism and the American social order through treaties that would have the effect of internal law, the amendment contained a provision that would have made any treaty that conflicted with the Constitution of no force and effect, and put in the hands of both houses of Congress and even the state legislatures further checks on treaty negotiation. Congress would also have been given the power to regulate all executive and other agreements with any foreign power or international organization.[17] The amendment, stated one senator at the time, "would restrain some future Roosevelt who might be tempted to indulge in another spree at Yalta."[18]

Opposition to the Bricker amendment was strong from the outset, however. Insisting that it would handicap the President in his ability to negotiate effectively with foreign nations, critics also

16. 81st Cong., 2d Sess., Hearings Before a Subcommittee of the Committee on Foreign Relations, United States Senate, *The Genocide Convention* (1950).

17. Senate Report No. 412, 82nd Congress, 2d Sess. For contemporary support of the amendment see F. E. Holman. "Treaty Law Making: A Blank Check for Writing a New Constitution," *American Bar Journal,* XXXVI (1950), 707 ff.; and E. P. Deutsch, "Peril in the Treaty-making Clause," *American Bar Association Journal,* XXXVII (1951), 659 ff.

18. Quoted in Alfred H. Kelly and Winfred A. Harbison, *The American Constitution: Its Origins and Development* (New York, 1963), p. 863. See also *Congressional Record,* 82nd Cong., 2d Sess., pp. 912–913.

argued the dangers of the provision that treaties were only to become effective as internal law through legislation that would be valid in the absence of a treaty. It would give the states, they contended, the sort of veto power in the treaty area that had been instrumental in making the federal government's power utterly ineffective under the Articles of Confederation.[19] Curiously, although the amendment would, its opponents charged, curtail the power of the President in conducting foreign policy, its provisions in no way limited his military power as commander-in-chief, and thus did not reach the one area of international policy under which he was freest to utilize the nation's power in foreign activities.

The amendment, which was constantly hung over Harry Truman's head while President, was not pushed to Senate vote until early 1954, when his successor Dwight D. Eisenhower was in the White House. Eisenhower, and his Secretary of State, John Foster Dulles, both opposed the measure, and when the vote came in February, it was one short of the required constitutional two-thirds majority necessary to start the amendment through the state legislatures.[20]

It thus fell to the Supreme Court in the 1950s to draw tighter lines and definitions around the treaty power. The context in which this was done involved other important aspects of America's new international role. As new treaties of alliance grew in the late 1940s and early 1950s, American military and civilian personnel assigned to carry out America's overseas commitments spanned the globe. Questions grew regarding the legal status of American citizens stationed within the boundaries of an allied, but foreign nation.[21]

19. See especially Zechariah Chafee, Jr., "Amending the Constitution to Cripple Treaties," *Louisiona Law Review,* XII (1952), 345–382; Arthur E. Sutherland, "Restricting the Treaty Power," *Harvard Law Review,* LXV (1952), 1305–1338; and Henry Steele Commager, "The Perilous Folly of Senator Bricker," *The Reporter,* IX (Oct. 13, 1953), 12–17.

20. Eisenhower had expressed opposition in a letter sent to the majority leader of the Senate on Jan. 25, 1954, an action influential in the rejection of the measure. A second try, with a watered-down version, failed as well and when the Democrats gained control of Congress in 1954, and McCarthy's influence waned, the possibility for revival largely vanished. See Glendon A. Schubert, "Politics and the Constitution: The Bricker Amendment during 1953," *Journal of Politics,* XVI (1957), 257–298; and Konvitz, *Expanding Liberties,* pp. 357–58.

21. 64 Stat. 109 (1950). On the subject see Sedgwick N. Green, "Applicability of American Laws to Overseas Areas Controlled by the United States," *Harvard*

The ordinary rule of international law would have given the foreign ally complete sovereignty over all persons within its boundaries. The United States insisted upon retaining jurisdiction over such personnel, however, and so-called Status of Forces Agreements were negotiated with a number of nations defining respective jurisdiction. Then in 1950, in another reflection of its unconcern for civil liberties, Congress set up a Uniform Code of Military Justice, making not only service personnel but their civilian dependents subject to court martial for crimes committed abroad. Thus again, treaty arrangements indirectly had important impacts upon traditional constitutional provisions and practices.

Court evaluation of this stricture awaited the termination of Korean hostilities. Then the justices accepted a case involving a former Korean serviceman, now discharged, but returned to Korea after arrest in Pittsburgh by Air Force police and convicted by a court-martial for murder of a Korean citizen. Robert Toth, who had been honorably discharged, was tried under Article 3(a) of the Universal Code of Military Justice Act. Justice Black, for the Court, held the article unconstitutional. Clearly reflecting his own lack of confidence in the commitment of the military to civil liberties, and his clear hostility toward the unwarranted assumption of unauthorized power by military authorities, Black maintained that such military action could not be sustained on any power of Congress, or upon the President's power as commander-in-chief, or on any theory of martial law.[22] Two years later, Black gave a "plurality" opinion for four members of a highly divided Court in a controversial case of the wife of a member of the armed forces stationed overseas charged with the murder of her husband.[23] Grounds for

---

Law Review, LXVIII (1955), 781–812; Gordon D. Henderson, "Courts-Martial and the Constitution: the Original Understanding," *Harvard Law Review,* LXXI (1957), 293–324; William G. McLaren, "Military Trials of Civilians," *American Bar Association Journal,* XLV (1959), 255 ff.; Arthur E. Sutherland, "The Flag, the Constitution and International Argeement," *Harvard Law Review,* LXVIII (1955), 1374–1381; and Frederick B. Wiener, "Courts-Martial and the Bill of Rights; the Original Practice," *Harvard Law Review,* LXXII (1958), 1–49; 266–304.

22. Toth *v.* Quarles, 350 U.S. 11, 13–14 (1955).

23. Reid *v.* Covert, 354 U.S. 1 (1957). The decision represented reversal of a 1956 ruling, reached in the same case, 351 U.S. 487 (1956), and a companion case, Kinsella *v.* Krueger, 351 U.S. 470 (1956).

the military trial were found in the Status of Forces agreement negotiated by the government under which both nations involved had granted exclusive jurisdiction over all offenses committed by Americans to military courts.

The case again raised the old question of whether the "Constitution follows the flag." But it also led the justice to examine the broader issue of whether the treaty power could validate, by its own force, practices that conflict with other portions of the Constitution. Here Black eased the mind of at least some of the early advocates of the Bricker amendment. Treaties are subject to the limits of constitutional supremacy just as are acts of Congress, he ruled. Quoting Article VI of the Constitution, he stated: "There is nothing in this language which intimates that treaties and laws enacted pursuant to them do not have to comply with the provisions of the Constitution. . . . It would be manifestly contrary to the objectives of those who created the Constitution, as well as those who were responsible for the Bill of Rights—let alone alien to our entire constitutional history and tradition—to construe Article VI as permitting the United States to exercise power under an international agreement without observing constitutional prohibitions."[24] He thus reiterated his general feeling that "we should not break faith with this nation's tradition of keeping military power subservient to civilian authority."

Black had been equally adamant earlier, in opposing the uninhibited use of Presidential power in the domestic area. In December, 1951, in the midst of the Korean war, the nation's steelworkers gave notice of intent to strike. When federal mediation failed, a nationwide steel strike was called for April 4, 1952. Truman, on the grounds that this would imperil American defense and jeopardize national security, directed his Secretary of Commerce to seize and operate the steel mills to assure production of vital defense material. Truman's authority to take such action was not

24. Reid *v.* Covert, 354 U.S. 1, 16–17 (1957). In the subsequent case of Wilson *v.* Girard, 354 U.S. 524 (1957), the Court found "no constitutional barrier" to a soldier being tried in a Japanese court, under a "status of forces" treaty agreement with Japan, for the murder of a Japanese woman. In 1960, however, the Court held that Congress lacked the power to authorize military trials of any civilian for any offense, thus throwing back to that body the necessity for establishing civilian courts in which the constitutional rights of such persons would be guaranteed. Kinsella *v.* U.S. *ex rel* Singleton, 361 U.S. 234 (1960).

specifically granted by statute. Yet Truman felt, in issuing the executive order, that the national crisis was grounds for claiming "inherent power" in the office of the President to act for the national welfare, even without specific statutory authority.[25]

Truman also felt that constitutional history was on his side. Presidents had intervened in major industrial disputes on numerous occasions before 1952 without specific legal authorization and even to the derogation of law in some instances.[26] The full powers of the Presidency, in emergency crises, had been underwritten and extended through World War II and in the postwar period. Further, since the 1930s, the Court had been highly reluctant to intervene in matters of economic policy, and had maintained the general position that measures of the elected branches of the federal government were entitled always to a strong presumption of constitutionality.

The Supreme Court of 1952, however, with the liberals in the majority and Vinson, Reed, and Minton in dissent, nullified the government's action in a sharply worded majority opinion. The President had no authority to act as he did, Justice Black maintained, because the subject was within the sphere of congressional authority. When the President entered that sphere without congressional authority, he violated the principle of separation of powers.[27] Others of the concurring justices went so far as to contend that the inherent executive power, even if it existed, did not provide the President with a license to violate statutes.[28] Vinson, in his dissent, was prepared to accede to this type of federal power, just as he was prepared to rationalize its use in most other areas. He stressed the emergency nature of the times, and insisted that judicial, legislative, and executive precedents throughout our history demonstrated that in this case the President acted in full con-

25. Executive Order 10340, *Federal Register,* XVI, p. 3503; see Alan F. Westin, *The Anatomy of a Constitutional Law Case* (New York, 1958), pp. 14–18; and Bernard Schwartz, *Commentary on the Constitution: The Powers of Government* (2 vols., New York, 1963), II, 65–73.

26. Edward S. Corwin, *The President: Office and Powers,* (New York, 1957), p. 154; B. M. Rich, *The Presidents and Civil Disorder* (Washington, 1941); and John L. Blackman, Jr., *Presidential Seizure in Labor Disputes* (Cambridge, Mass., 1967).

27. Youngstown Sheet & Tube Co. *v.* Sawyer, 343 U.S. 579 (1952).

28. *Ibid.,* pp. 604 ff., 632, 637.

formity with his duties under the Constitution.[29] Writing a few years later, Truman expressed similar views. "The President must always act in a national emergency," he insisted. "A wise President will always work with Congress, but when Congress fails to act or is unable to act in a crisis, the President, under the Constitution, must use his power to safeguard the nation."[30] In the immediate case, however, judicial activism reasserted itself so resoundingly and popularly that Justice Black's name was even talked of in some quarters as a Democratic Presidential candidate in the elections of the following fall.

By 1952, many Americans were convinced that Truman was neither competent to exercise properly the powers of his office nor adequately concerned with safeguarding the security of the nation. Such a view stemmed from the growing national hysteria about "Communists in government" and the continual insinuation, if not direct allegation by those fanning the flames of such hysteria, that an administration that had been guilty of "coddling Communists" was hardly prepared to act fully in the national interest. And it was in the security area that the most bitter executive-legislative struggle occurred in the early years of the 1950s. Here the Korean Conflict played particularly into the hands of anti-administration leaders in Congress, creating an atmosphere that encouraged leaders such as McCarthy, and conservative Democratic Senator Patrick McCarran of Nevada, the House Committee on Un-American Activities (H.U.A.C.), and other congressional committees to push for the kind of restrictive security legislation that the administration had successfully sidetracked in earlier, less hysterical times.

The Internal Security Act, or McCarran Act, of 1950 was a massive and hopelessly complex conglomeration of a variety of previous security suggestions plus many of the features of the Mundt-Nixon Bill. It was clearly designed to go beyond the Truman loyalty program, widen security investigations to all areas of American life, and shift the authority for security matters over to the hands of congressional leadership. Specifically the measure, the most

29. *Ibid.*, p. 667. For discussion of the case see Paul G. Kauper, "The Steel Seizure Case: Congress, the President and the Supreme Court," *Michigan Law Review*, LI (1952), 144–182; and Edward S. Corwin, "The Steel Seizure Case—A Judicial Brick Without Straw," *Columbia Law Review*, LIII (1953), 53–66.
30. Truman, *Memoirs*, II, 478.

severe since the Sedition Act of 1918, was composed of two parts, Title I, known as the Subversive Activities Control Act, and Title II, entitled the Emergency Detention Act.[31] Under the former, Communist organizations were required to register with the Attorney General and furnish complete membership lists and financial statements. Although membership and office holding in a Communist organization was not, by the Act, a crime, the measure did make it illegal knowingly to conspire to perform any act that would "substantially contribute" to the establishment of a totalitarian dictatorship in the United States. It also forbade employment of Communists in defense plants and the granting of passports to Communists and established a bipartisan Subversive Activities Control Board to assist the Attorney General in exposing subversive organizations.

Title II provided that when the President declared an internal security emergency, the Attorney General was to apprehend persons who were likely to engage in, or conspire with others to engage in, acts of espionage or sabotage and intern them "in such places of detention as may be prescribed by the Attorney General." Congress subsequently authorized funds for special camps for such purposes.[32] Other provisions of the measure denied entrance to the country to aliens who belonged to Communist organizations or "who advocate the economic, international, and governmental doctrines of any other form of totalitarianism." Naturalized citizens who joined Communist organizations within five years of acquiring citizenship were eligible to have their papers revoked.

Truman vetoed the measure, branding it "the greatest danger to freedom of speech, press and assembly, since the Alien and Sedition Laws of 1798."[33] "Our position in the vanguard of freedom," he contended, "rests largely on our demonstration that the free expression of opinion, coupled with government by popular consent, leads to national strength and human advancement. Let us not, in cowering and foolish fear, throw away the ideals which are the fundamental basis of our free society." Congress passed the measure

31. 64 Stat. 987 (1950).

32. Konvitz, *Expanding Liberties,* p. 401. By 1957, the camps were discontinued and no further funds were appropriated for this purpose. See William Hedgepath, "America's Concentration Camps: The Rumor and the Realities," *Look,* XXXII (May 28, 1969), 85–91.

33. House Document No. 708, 81st Congress, 2d Sess.

over his veto by voice vote, after Congressman Rankin had charged that the veto was written by one of the President's subversive accomplices, probably Justice Frankfurter, and was "Communist propaganda."[34]

But Congress was not through. Two years later it passed, again over the President's veto, the Walter-McCarran Immigration and Nationality Bill.[35] Although rectifying 160 years of racial discrimination by providing that the right of a person to become a naturalized citizen of the United States shall not be denied or abridged because of race, it included new provisions to prevent the admission of possible subversives and to permit the expulsion of dangerous aliens. Thus political and ideological discrimination was substituted for racial and religious bias.

Congressional superpatriots were vigorous on other loyalty fronts as well. In February, 1951, Truman created a special commission on internal security and individual rights, headed by Fleet Admiral Chester Nimitz, to intensify the administration's security program, insisting, however, that proper attention be paid to civil liberties. Such action smacked of whitewash to critics, and Nimitz was branded "an innocent dupe behind which the treasonous [Truman] Administration hoped to sulk." Senator McCarran then effectively killed the commission by parliamentary maneuver.[36]

But if such commissions were to have no power, congressional committees with far less honorable concerns gained authority unprecedented in American history. By the late 1940s, the House Committee on Un-American Activities fell victim to its own success in hitting the headlines and developed sharp competitors.[37] In

34. Congressional Record, 81st Cong., 2d Sess., p. 15632. See John P. Sullivan and David N. Webster, "Some Constitutional and Practical Problems of the Subversive Activities Control Act," *Georgetown Law Journal,* XLVI (Winter, 1957–58), 299–314; and John D. Crawford, "Free Speech and the Internal Security Act of 1950," *Georgetown Law Journal,* XXXIX (1951), 440–465.

35. 66 Stat. 143 (1952). For the Truman Veto Message see House Document No. 520, 82nd Congress, 2d Sess. See also Erwin A. Jaffe, "Passage of the McCarran-Walter Act: The Reiteration of American Immigration Policy" (unpublished Ph.D. dissertation, Rutgers University, 1962).

36. Harold M. Hyman, *To Try Men's Souls: Loyalty Tests in American History* (Berkeley, 1959), p. 335.

37. Telford Taylor, *Grand Inquest: The Story of Congressional Investigations* (New York, 1955), pp. 78–79; Robert K. Carr, *The House Committee on Un-American Activities, 1945–1950* (Ithaca, 1952), pp. 459–461. See also Edward J. Heubel, "Reorganization and Reform of Congressional Investigations, 1945–1955" (unpublished Ph.D. dissertation, University of Minnesota, 1955).

1946, the Senate established a permanent Senate Investigating Subcommittee, which promptly staked its claim in the field of subversion exposure. In 1950, Senator Patrick McCarran, Chairman of the Senate Judiciary Committee, established a subcommittee on internal security with himself as chairman. Its subsequent investigations overshadowed H.U.A.C., both in the range of subjects with which the members concerned themselves and in the passion for publicity surrounding its activities. By the early 1950s although H.U.A.C. had been embarrassed by the jailing of its former chairman for padding his office payroll,[38] the committee passed to the new leadership of Congressman Harold Velde of Illinois, who gave quick indication that he would take the line of Dies and Rankin, together with a leaf or two from the junior senator from Wisconsin. McCarthy had himself gained a committee chairmanship with Republican recapture of Congress in 1950, and his Committee on Governmental Operations, with a large, aggressive, and ruthless staff, now had a license to pry into any facet of federal activity. Such bodies, however, did not limit themselves to government, probing into subversion in the movie and entertainment industries, examining various private organizations, and eventually zeroing in on the academic community and the churches.[39]

Committee actions, however, alarmed civil libertarians, by their growing disregard for the type of procedural guarantees and safeguards of individual liberty normally afforded any citizen in any court of law.[40] Witnesses were browbeaten and given no right to counsel. No opportunity was afforded to examine charges, often irresponsible and from dubious sources. Opportunity to cross-

38. Walter Goodman, *The Committee: The Extraordinary Career of the House Committee on Un-American Activities* (New York, 1968), pp. 269–270; Carr, *House Committee on Un-American Activities,* p. 218.

39. The literature on the subject, mostly deploring loyalty excesses, is voluminous. See especially Alan Barth, *Government by Investigation* (New York, 1955) and *The Loyalty of Free Men* (New York, 1951); John W. Caughey, *In Clear and Present Danger: The Crucial State of Our Freedoms* (Chicago, 1958); John Cogley, *Report on Blacklisting* (2 vols., New York, 1956); Henry Steele Commager, *Freedom, Loyalty and Dissent* (New York, 1954); Walter Gellhorn, *Security, Loyalty, and Science* (Ithaca, 1950), and *Individual Freedom and Governmental Restraints* (Baton Rouge, 1956); Carey McWilliams, *Witch Hunt: The Revival of Heresy* (Boston, 1950); Merle Miller, *The Judges and the Judged* (New York, 1952); Clair Wilcon (ed.), *Civil Liberties Under Attack* (Philadelphia, 1951).

40. For a good summary of popular liberal hostility see Herbert Block, *The Herblock Book* (Boston, 1952), Chaps. 5, 12, 13.

examine witnesses was denied. Past affiliations and activities of individuals were thrown at them as evidence of their guilt, and they were expected to prove themselves innocent in front of a congressional "jury" obviously biased at the outset. The result was to induce many witnesses to "take the Fifth Amendment," refusing to testify on the grounds that any statement made might tend to incriminate them.[41] McCarthy, Velde, and Senator William Jenner, McCarran's successor as head of the Senate Internal Security Committee, promptly leaped upon such action as clear proof of a witness's guilt, and the term "Fifth Amendment Communist" became another device for character assassination by such committee leaders. The device was but one further example of the unfortunate nature of committee absolutism and extremism. Undoubtedly numerous witnesses abused the privilege and hid behind the constitutional guarantee that it afforded. Yet by branding anyone who so behaved a Communist, the committees were precluded from developing more practical, sensitive, and effective devices for drawing lines that might have been useful and at least partially justified their operation in the sensitive security area.[42]

The Vinson Court was highly aware of the loyalty-security pressures of the times. In fact, one bitter critic of the day charged that "the McCarthy-McCarran era could scarcely roll the repression along fast enough to keep pace with the Vinson Court's approval of it."[43] Early in its fall term of 1950, the court took several freedom of speech cases, and promptly tipped its hand as to its current attitude.

41. Edwin N. Griswold, *The Fifth Amendment Today* (Cambridge, Mass., 1955); Lewis Mayers, *Shall We Amend the Fifth Amendment* (New York, 1959); Oetje J. Rogge, *The First and the Fifth* (New York, 1960); Sidney Hook, *Common Sense and the Fifth Amendment* (New York, 1957); "Congressional Investigations: A Symposium," *University of Chicago Law Review*, XVIII (1951), 421–661; L. B. Frantz and Norman Redlich, "Does Silence Mean Guilt?," *Nation*, CLXXVI (June 6, 1953); and Bernard Meltzer and Harry Kalven, "Invoking the Fifth Amendment," *Bulletin of the Atomic Scientists*, IX (1953), 176–186.

42. The H.U.A.C. was particularly active in handing out contempt citations for various forms of refusal to cooperate with it. See Carl Beck, *Contempt of Congress: A Study of the Prosecutions Initiated by the Committee on Un-American Activities, 1945–1957* (New Orleans, 1959). Numerous state antisubversive bodies grew in the period. Many operated with an equal unconcern for the rights of the individuals. See Walter Gellhorn (ed.), *The States and Subversion* (Ithaca, 1952).

43. John P. Frank, *Marble Palace: The Supreme Court in American Life* (New York, 1961), p. 252.

The cases, and further ones in the 1951 and 1952 terms, involved a variety of city ordinances and state laws restricting freedom of expression in one form or another. In three cases decided the same day, January 15, 1951, the justices upheld the right of two religious enthusiasts to speak in public parks[44] and on street corners,[45] even, in the latter case, where the individual involved was preaching a gospel of hate against certain religious groups. Vinson, speaking for the Court, urged that the proper remedy for such action lay in subsequent punishment if appellants' speech should result in disorder or violence. The third case involved a pro-Communist college student whose exhortations to a largely hostile street-corner crowd differed little except in political slant from those of the right-wing rabble-rousing Terminiello, whose case had come up in the previous term. Yet the Court, speaking through Vinson, reached an opposite conclusion, although not without bitter protest from Black and Douglas, Black deploring the fact that the ruling "made it a dark day for civil liberties in our Nation."[46] Black was equally upset by a Court ruling of five months later which upheld a "Green River" ordinance against magazine salesmen. Justice Reed for the Court dwelt upon the need for "balancing of the conveniences between some householders' desire for privacy and the publisher's right to distribute publications."[47] This decision, wrote Black, "marks a revitalization of the judicial view which prevailed before this Court embraced the philosophy that the First Amendment gives a preferred status to the liberties it protects. I adhere to that preferred position philosophy."[48] Douglas expressed similar sentiments in a 1953 case, in which the court upheld a city ordinance providing for a "uniform" licensing system for meetings in public streets and parks.[49]

44. Niemotko *v.* Maryland, 340 U.S. 268 (1951).

45. Kunz *v.* New York, 340 U.S. 290 (1951).

46. Feiner *v.* New York, 340 U.S. 315, 323 (1951).

47. Breard *v.* Alexandria, 341 U.S. 622 (1951).

48. *Ibid.,* p. 650.

49. Poulos *v.* New Hampshire, 345 U.S. 395 (1953). The two justices found themselves on opposite sides of another 1952 case involving captive audiences on public buses, forced to listen to radio programs while in transit. Black concurred with the majority that the predominantly musical programs did not violate the First Amendment, but Douglas in dissent contended that protesting listeners were having their "freedom of attention" violated by the practice. Public Utilities Commission *v.* Pollak, 343 U.S. 451 (1952).

Greater acrimony arose over an Illinois group libel statute making it unlawful for persons or corporations to publish or exhibit any material "exposing the citizens of any race, color, creed or religion to contempt, derision, or obloquy. . . ." Frankfurter, for the pragmatic majority, declared such legislation eminently reasonable, and even if not, he contended, it was the Court's duty to accept "the trial-and-error inherent in legislative efforts to deal with obstinate social issues."[50] Black, dissenting with Douglas, Reed, and Jackson, maintained that the decision manifested the shocking results of "the reasonable man test" in the civil liberties field. "No legislature is charged with the duty or vested with the power to decide what public issues Americans can discuss," he wrote. "State experimentation in curbing of freedom of expression is a startling and frightening doctrine in a country dedicated to self-government by its people."[51]

Balancing won, however, and was even extended to new areas. Movie censorship in the United States had consistently been upheld prior to this period as legitimate restriction upon a predominantly economic activity.[52] In a case in May, 1952, Justice Clark brought movies within the protection of the First Amendment by way of the Fourteenth, indicating that they were a "significant medium for the communication of ideas."[53] The decision, however, and a similar one rendered a week later,[54] were limited to immediate and explicit forms of censorship, and the Court, having intruded into the area, left it promptly with no clear-cut guidelines as to how far censorship might extend without coming in conflict with First Amendment pro-

50. Beauharnais *v.* Illinois, 343 U.S. 250, 262 (1952).

51. *Ibid.*, p. 270. On the case see Loren P. Beth, "Group Libel and Free Speech," *Minnesota Law Review*, XXXIX (1955), 167–184; and David Riesman, "Democracy and Defamation: Control of Group Libel," *Columbia Law Review*, XLII (1942), 727–780, for background on the broader issue.

52. Such a ruling had been set down by the Court in 1915 in Mutual Film Corp. *v.* Ohio Industrial Commission, 236 U.S. 230 (1915), and had not been fully overruled, even though in a 1948 antitrust case (U.S. *v.* Paramount Pictures, 334 U.S. 131 [1948]) Justice Douglas for the Court had stated: "We have no doubt that moving pictures, like newspapers and radio, are included in the press whose freedom is guaranteed by the First Amendment," at 166.

53. Burstyn *v.* Wilson, 343 U.S. 495 (1952).

54. Gelling *v.* Texas, 343 U.S. 960 (1952). See Melville Nimmer, "The Constitutionality of Official Censorship of Motion Pictures," *University of Chicago Law Review*, XXV (1958), 625–657.

tections. The ruling did leave the Court as the immediate "umpire" of censorship actions, however, with its position to be determined on the basis of its own concept of "reasonableness."

The free speech issue came most clearly into focus in connection with the government's prosecution of the Communist party leaders under the Smith Act. The turbulent nine-month trial had finally resulted in the Communists' conviction.[55] The conviction was upheld in a federal court of appeals, with Chief Judge Learned Hand writing the opinion.[56] The Supreme Court, in taking appeal, limited its consideration to questions of the constitutionality of the Smith Act, "inherently or as construed and applied in the instant case." It went on, with Vinson writing the opinion, to confirm the convictions.[57]

Such a verdict necessitated an exploration of the relationship of free speech to action, and a definition of the point at which free speech became punishable. The Communist leaders were not charged with a conspiracy to overthrow the government but with a conspiracy to form a party to teach and advocate the overthrow of the government. And Vinson in his opinion admitted that any such attempt was doomed to failure at the outset because of the inadequate numbers and lack of power of the party. Further, he admitted that the Communists under trial had made no attempt, in the period

55. John Somerville, *The Communist Trials and the American Tradition* (New York, 1956); Milton R. Konvitz, *Fundamental Liberties of a Free People* (Ithaca, 1957), pp. 307–333; John A. Gorfinkel and Julian W. Mack, II, "Dennis v. United States and the Clear and Present Danger Rule," *California Law Review, XXXIX* (1951), 475–501; Edward S. Corwin, "Bowing Out—'Clear and Present Danger,'" *Notre Dame Lawyer,* XXVII (1952), 325–359; and Wallace Mendelson, "Clear and Present Danger: From Schenck to Dennis," *Columbia Law Review,* LII (1952), 313–333.

56. Dennis *v.* United States, 183 F. (2d) 201, 212 (1950). See also Hand's own enunciation of his views, Learned Hand, *The Bill of Rights* (Cambridge, Mass., 1958) pp. 29 ff., in which he contends that judicial review of legislation should be confined to those critical situations involving the allocation of power between the federal government and the states and, perhaps, between departments of the federal government itself. The Court can determine whether other officials of the government have acted within the general authority vouchsafed to them by the Constitution, but should not review the substantive validity of such action. The limitations of the Bill of Rights thus are, to Hand, admonitions to legislative bodies, state and federal, that, even if unheeded, should not be enforced judicially at the risk of the judiciary becoming a "third legislative chamber."

57. Dennis *v.* U.S., 341 U.S. 494 (1951).

1945 to 1948, to turn theory into practice. Examining a formula proposed by Hand—"whether the gravity of the evil, discounted by its improbability, justifies such invasion of free speech as is necessity to avoid the danger"—he contended that the clear-and-present danger test "cannot mean that before the Government may act, it must wait until the *putsch* is about to be executed, the plans have been laid and the signal awaited. . . ." "We must . . . reject the contention," he contended, "that success or probability of success is the criterion."[58] Black and Douglas resented what they considered a prostitution of the old Holmes rule to reach an unjustified conclusion. The Court's decision, they maintained, repudiated the rule directly. The decision, Black wrote, "waters down the First Amendment so that it amounts to little more than an admonition to Congress." However, the two justices found themselves alone and forced to express the hope that "in calmer times, when present pressures, passions and fears subside, this or some later Court will restore the First Amendment liberties to the high preferred place where they belong in a free society."[59]

The decision extended the Douds ruling of thirteen months earlier one frustrating step further. In so doing, it demonstrated the limited practicality of either total activism or total judicial hands-off in free speech cases. By embodying the ultimate in Frankfurterian self-restraint, the Court came close to abandoning altogether the concept of judicial limitation, and demonstrated its total ineffectiveness as an agency for defending the liberty of the individual against any government program publicly justified as a response to internal subversion. But the case also made clear the inadequacy of the preferred freedom position. Due to its absolute nature, its logical thrust called for the Court to negate any legislation that in any way infringed First Amendment freedoms, and offered no other alternative. Once rejecting such a course, there was no middle ground for the judiciary by which brakes might in any way be applied to modify, soften, or otherwise make more equitable programs that

58. *Ibid.*, pp. 509–510.

59. *Ibid.*, p. 581. Following the ruling, the Justice Department obtained the conviction and imprisonment of some forty regional, state, and Hawaiian Communist leaders for violating the Smith Act. See Robert Mollan, "Smith Act Prosecutions: The Effect of the Dennis and Yates Decisions," *University of Pittsburgh Law Review,* XXVI (1965), 710.

the executive and Congress were clearly determined to carry out. Clearly, if the Court was to exercise a constructive function in the area of individual freedom and governmental restraints, it had to adopt a more realistic and practical approach than one of "all or nothing at all."

The Court was also called on in the period to evaluate aspects of national and state loyalty-security programs, and to rule on the behavior of congressional committees. In both cases it chose to take the narrowest possible view of the issues presented to it and to keep its rulings as protected as possible from the embarrassment of hostile attack and even defiance. In early April, 1951, the Court upheld a Maryland statute requiring candidates for public office in the state to file with their nomination certificates, affidavits that they were not "subversive persons."[60] Fortunately for the oath's champions, the Maryland courts had given a precise meaning to the terms, designating a subversive person as one engaged in attempts to overthrow the government by force and violence. The oath requirement was thus upheld unanimously.

Two weeks later, the Court heard challenges to the federal loyalty-security program. In two divergent and somewhat confused opinions, it applied certain restrictions while simultaneously upholding its major thrust. In *Joint Anti-Fascist Refugee Committee* v. *McGrath,*[61] it had been confronted with a sharp protest to the Attorney General's practice of listing and specifically classifying an organization as "Communist." Three organizations sought declaratory judgments to have their names removed from the list on the grounds that they were not subversive and that their inclusion on the list was an arbitrary act. Five of the justices upheld the complaining organizations, although no majority opinion emerged. Justice Burton, announcing the "judgment" of the Court, maintained that the Attorney General's actions were "patently arbitrary." He specifically objected to the practice of listing organizations as subversive without prior notice and hearing, maintaining that such a practice violated due process of law as guaranteed by the Fifth Amendment. Controversy surrounded the ruling and demands rose that suitable hearings should be granted to organizations be-

60. Gerende *v.* Board of Supervisors of Elections, 341 U.S. 56 (1951).
61. 341 U.S. 123 (1951).

fore their inclusion.[62] However, in practice, the list continued to be used during the Truman administration, and no procedural reforms were instituted in that period.

The same day, the Court sustained a loyalty board barring Miss Dorothy Bailey, the training officer in the Federal Security Agency, from government employment on the basis of accusations against her made by persons whose identity was never revealed to her or to the board.[63] To Justice Douglas, one of four dissenters, this was unacceptable procedure. Miss Bailey, he reminded the Court, was on trial for her reputation, her job, and her professional standing. A disloyalty trial, he maintained, "is the most crucial event in the life of a civil servant. If condemned, he is branded for life as a person unworthy of trust or confidence. To make that condemnation without meticulous regard for the decencies of a fair trial is abhorrent to fundamental justice."[64]

The times were against Douglas, however. Although no further direct challenges to the federal loyalty program ensued, charges against the various and even more restrictive city and state loyalty ordinances and laws were consistently turned aside. Particularly revealing in this regard was the Court's sustaining of New York's Feinberg Law, providing for removal of public school teachers on disloyalty grounds for membership in subversive organizations.[65] The law, which *The New York Times* attacked as a "blunderbuss" bill "erecting into law the untenable and illiberal theory of 'guilt by association,' "[66] nonetheless did provide for full notice and hearing before organizations were branded as subversive. The teachers, it was thus felt, had a fair warning regarding the type of affiliations

62. Eleanor Bontecou, *The Federal Loyalty-Security Program* (Ithaca, 1953), pp. 202–204; Barth, *Loyalty of Free Men,* pp. 106–107; and Seth Richardson, "The Federal Employee Loyalty Program," *Columbia Law Review,* LVII (1951), 546.

63. Bailey *v.* Richardson, 341 U.S. 918 (1951). See Harold W. Chase, *Security and Liberty; the Problem of Native Communists, 1947–1955* (New York, 1955); and Thomas I. Cook, *Democratic Rights v. Communist Activity* (New York, 1954).

64. See Douglas' concurring opinion in Joint Anti-Fascist Refugee Committee *v.* McGrath, 341 U.S. 123, 180–181 (1951).

65. Adler *v.* Board of Education, 342 U.S. 485 (1952). For background see Lawrence H. Chamberlain, *Loyalty and Legislative Action* (Ithaca, 1951), p. 199; and Morris Arval, "Academic Freedom and Loyalty Oaths," *Law and Contemporary Problems,* XXVIII (1963), 487 ff.

66. *The New York Times,* Mar. 5, 1952, p. 28.

they might make. This position was sustained by the Supreme Court. The majority chose not to probe the question of earlier membership, before the organizations were proscribed, however, despite Douglas and Black's contention that "youthful indiscretions, mistaken causes, misguided enthusiasm, all long forgotten, can now become the ghosts of a harrowing present" and a device for "raising havoc with academic freedom."[67]

Only with the return of the Republicans to the executive branch with the election of Eisenhower in November, 1952, did the Court throw out a state loyalty statute—in this case, an Oklahoma statute so patently tied to the principle of "guilt by association" that even Justice Clark saw it as a device for "stifling the flow of democratic expression and controversy at one of its chief sources."[68]

The Court was equally pusillanimous in challenging the procedures of various congressional committees. In the months before Korea, it had twice sustained the activities of H.U.A.C. in a situation growing out of refusal by a witness to produce subpoenaed records.[69] In December, 1950, it relented momentarily, permitting a witness before a grand jury to take the Fifth Amendment and refuse to testify concerning Communist party activity, Black convincing the Court that such revelation made the individual promptly subject to prosecution under the Smith Act, and thus the potential victim of unwarranted, coerced self-incrimination.[70] Such a privilege had to be invoked at the right time, however. Early the following year, the Court ruled that a witness who began by admitting her Communist party activities, could not then invoke the privilege when asked about the disposition of party records.[71]

Two cases directly challenging committee authority also brought

67. Adler *v.* Board of Education, p. 509.

68. Wieman *v.* Updegraff, 344 U.S. 183 (1952). One authority, in assessing the implications of the case, felt that it "flatly rejected the old, bad idea that 'there is no constitutionally protected right to public employment.' The government may not exclude a public servant from employment on arbitrary or discriminatory grounds." Robert G. McCloskey, *The American Supreme Court* (Chicago, 1940), p. 204.

69. U.S. *v.* Bryan, 339 U.S. 323 (1950); U.S. *v.* Fleishman, 339 U.S. 349 (1950). See Carr, *House Committee on Un-American Activities,* pp. 406 ff; and William H. Brown, "Judicial Review of Congressional Investigative Powers with Special Reference to the Period 1945–1957" (unpublished Ph.D. dissertation, American University, 1959).

70. Blau *v.* United States, 340 U.S. 332 (1951).

71. Rogers *v.* United States, 340 U.S. 367 (1951).

interesting results. When a right-wing superpatriot witness before the House Select Committee on Lobbying Activities refused to disclose names of his financial supporters and purchasers of his propaganda literature, the Court unanimously reversed his contempt of Congress conviction on the grounds that the committee had not been granted authority by the House to broaden its investigation beyond narrow lines of inquiry.[72] The Court, however, carefully limited this consideration to the immediate committee under consideration, and its ruling clearly and carefully was cast so as not to be a precedent against H.U.A.C. or other of the congressional committees with broad hunting licenses.[73]

Probably the most revealing Court split in the security area emerged from a case involving a state antisubversive body, the flamboyant Tenny Committee in California.[74] A witness cited for contempt instituted a suit of his own against members of the committee, alleging that he had not been summoned before the committee for a proper legislative purpose, but for the purposes of intimidation to force him to stop using his constitutional rights of free speech. In taking the case, the Supreme Court was confronted with defining such committee's proper role.[75] Frankfurter spoke for the Court in this regard, and following his general rule of acceding to legislative authority, maintained that the principle of legislative immunity protected the committee from this kind of liability. As long as the committee was following the intent of its legislative creation, Frankfurter maintained it was not for the courts to determine its proper limits.

Douglas and Black were irate in protest. To leave erring legislators

to self-discipline and the voters, and to step aside when a legislative committee, they contended, "departs so far from its domain" as to

72. U.S. *v.* Rumely, 345 U.S. 41 (1953). On Rumely's background see Richard Polenberg, *Reorganizing Roosevelt's Government: The Controversy over Executive Reorganization, 1936–1939* (Cambridge, Mass., 1966), pp. 57 ff.

73. While the ruling demonstrated that it was possible, at the risk of a contempt citation, to force a test of the jurisdiction of a congressional committee, contemporary observers doubted whether the precedent would be applied against H.U.A.C. See "Limits on Congressional Inquiry: Rumely v. United States," *University of Chicago Law Review,* XX (1953), 594.

74. Edward L. Barrett, Jr., *The Tenney Committee: Legislative Investigation of Subversive Activities in California* (Ithaca, 1951).

75. Tenney *v.* Brandhove, 341 U.S. 367 (1951).

deprive a citizen of a right protected by the Constitution, carried judicial self-restraint to a ridiculous extreme. "It is one thing," wrote Douglas, "to give great leeway to the legislative right of speech, debate and investigation, but when a committee perverts its power, brings down on an individual the whole weight of government for an illegal or corrupt purpose, the reason for the immunity ends."[76] This again represented a minority, civil libertarian position, and viewing this case, along with others in the loyalty-security area during 1950–53, it is easy to agree with C. Herman Pritchett that in attempting to limit legislative irresponsibility, "the Vinson Court contributed almost nothing."[77]

In the area of procedural rights not tied to security questions, the Vinson Court was equally prepared to sacrifice the individual's rights to its concept of reasonable social needs. Seemingly disregarding its 1943 McNabb rule, seven of the justices upheld confessions secured between arrest and arraignment in cases in 1951 and 1952.[78] In the following year, it sustained a proceeding in which a preliminary hearing was not given until eighteen days after arrest.[79] In another 1953 case, the justices sharply modified the prior standards regarding the limits of psychological coercion. Justice Jackson for the Court sustained confessions on the grounds that they were extracted from "mature and experienced men, sufficiently self-possessed to bargain as to the terms on which they would confess."[80] Frankfurter here joined Douglas and Black in condemning practices that he maintained would be permitted in few other English-speaking countries at the time. The Court also softened its previously firm rulings assailing discrimination against Negroes in the selection of jurors, taking the general position that state autonomy in local law enforcement should be respected to the utmost and should not be "eroded through indefinite charges of unconstitutional actions."[81]

76. *Ibid.*, p. 383.

77. C. Herman Pritchett, *Civil Liberties and the Vinson Court* (Chicago, 1954), p. 89.

78. Gallegos *v.* Nebraska, 342 U.S. 55 (1951); Stroble *v.* California, 343 U.S. 181 (1952).

79. Brown *v.* Allen, 344 U.S. 443 (1953).

80. Stein *v.* New York, 346 U.S. 156 (1953).

81. Cassell *v.* Texas, 339 U.S. 282 (1950), especially Jackson's dissent. See also Brown *v.* Allen, 344 U.S. 443 (1953), in which the Court blinked both at the practice of selecting jurors only from the county tax rolls, and of placing dots

Comic-strip fans were intrigued with a 1952 case involving search and seizure in which the Court sustained the use of a concealed "Dick Tracy"–type radio transmitter, which an undercover agent had used to implicate a Chinese laundry owner suspected of peddling opium. Despite minority protest against the use of such an ambulatory wiretap, the majority held that the electronic eavesdropping did not violate the Fourth Amendment.[82] The judges did balk at search based upon use by the police of a stomach pump to recover evidence from a victim suspected of swallowing morphine rather than be arrested on a narcotics charge. "Proceedings by which the conviction was obtained," wrote a horrified Justice Frankfurter, "do more than offend some fastidious squeamishness or private sentimentalism about combatting crime too energetically. It is conduct that shocks the conscience. . . . This course of proceedings by agents of government to obtain evidence is bound to offend even hardened sensibilities. They are methods too close to the rack and the screw to permit of constitutional differentiation." While the states have much leeway in their conduct of prosecutions, he added, holding the police action to be a violation of due process of law, "still they must respect certain decencies of civilized conduct."[83]

If the rights of American citizens seemed to be guaranteed only against flagrant violation, in the McCarthy era, the rights of aliens suffered even more. In fact, in the words of Leo Pfeffer, "one of the cruelest aspects of the cold war was the treatment accorded by the

---

on all the scrolls in the jury box bearing the names of Negroes. Although the practices had resulted in no Negro ever serving on a jury in the county in question, the Court felt that the fact that some names of Negroes were in the jury box, and the fact that the venire was drawn by a five-year-old child, could not have resulted in discrimination. In Shepherd *v.* Florida, 341 U.S. 50 (1951), and Avery *v.* Georgia, 345 U.S. 559 (1953), however, the Court struck down the use of white and yellow tickets to identify prospective white and Negro jurors. See David Fellman, *The Defendant's Rights* (New York, 1958), p. 103.

82. On Lee *v.* U.S., 343 U.S. 747 (1952). In a contemporary case, Schwartz *v.* Texas, 344 U.S. 199 (1952), the Court also upheld the use of wiretap evidence to obtain convictions in an amusing case in which one thief was prevailed upon to induce his former partner to talk over a wiretapped telephone with the latter, then convicted on evidence recorded from the conversation. See Jacob W. Landynski, *Search and Seizure and the Supreme Court* (Baltimore, 1966), pp. 212–213.

83. Rochin *v.* California, 342 U.S. 165 (1952). See Paul G. Kauper, *Frontiers of Constitutional Liberty* (Ann Arbor, 1956), p. 173. Frankfurter was by far the Court's most consistent champion of Fourth Amendment rights. See Glendon A. Schubert, *Constitutional Politics* (New York, 1960), pp. 610–611.

government to non-citizens suspected of possible disloyalty or subversive affiliation."[84] In January, 1950, the Supreme Court rejected the plea of the German-born wife of an American citizen for entry to the country.[85] The Attorney General had ordered exclusion, without a hearing, on the ground that her admission would be prejudicial to the national interest. He justified such procedure on the basis of a 1941 statute that gave the President authority to issue "reasonable Rules, regulations and orders" governing the entrance of aliens during a period of national emergency. But although the Supreme Court found the Fifth Amendment did not apply to Mrs. Knauff, public opinion forced a hearing, and the House of Representatives passed a bill permitting her to stay in the country. Eventually the Immigration Service reversed its decision, and after nearly three years on Ellis Island the war bride was admitted.[86]

In two cases in March, 1952, no such legislative intervention was forthcoming. Here the Court considered provisions of the Alien Registration Act of 1940 and the Internal Security Act of 1950, which directed the deportation of any alien who during his stay in the United States was, for no matter how short a period, a member of the Communist party or any other organization that advocated the violent overthrow of the government. In rejecting challenges to these provisions, the Court upheld the deportation of an Italian who had come to the United States in 1920, joined the Communist party in 1923, and resigned in 1929.[87] Similarly it sustained the deportation of a mother of three American-born children, who between 1919 and 1936 had been a dues-paying member of the party, although she had taken no active part in its activities.[88] It was immaterial, the Court held, that both these aliens had resigned from the party long before the Alien Registration Act was adopted and at a time when the Communist party was still a legal party entitled

84. Leo Pfeffer, *This Honorable Court* (Boston, 1965), p. 370. On the general subject see Milton R. Konvitz, *The Alien and the Asiatic in American Law* (Ithaca, 1946); and Robert J. Frye, "Deportation of Aliens; A Study in Civil Liberties" (unpublished Ph.D. dissertation, University of Florida, 1959).

85. U.S. *ex rel* Knauff *v.* Shaughnessy, 338 U.S. 537 (1950).

86. Mrs. Knauff's version of the episode is in Ellen R. Knauff, *The Ellen Knauff Story* (New York, 1952). See Jackson's later comment regarding the case in Shaughnessy *v.* U.S. *ex rel* Mezei, 345 U.S. 206, 225 (1953).

87. Harisiades *v.* Shaughnessy, 342 U.S. 580 (1952).

88. Carlson *v.* Landon, 342 U.S. 524 (1952).

to be on the ballot and elect its members to public office. In the case of the mother, it ruled that alien Communists could be held indefinitely without bail while the Attorney General's office determined proper deportation action.

A month later, the Court refused to consider a challenge to the constitutionality of a section of the Immigration Act of 1917 which made it a felony for an alien, against whom a specified order of deportation had been issued, to willfully fail or refuse to make application for travel and secure the documents necessary for his departure. Spector, an alien who came to the United States from Russia in 1913, was protesting a deportation order entered against him in 1930. Yet the thrust of the Court's rule gave him only the choice of signing the application and accepting deportation, or remaining in the United States in a federal penitentiary.[89]

In *Shaughnessy* v. *U.S. ex rel Mezei,* decided in March, 1953, the Court knuckled in further to the hysteria of the moment, upholding discretionary executive imprisonment of an alien confined without accusation of crime, or trial, with no other reason than an anonymous allegation that he was a danger to national security.[90] Justice Black protested vigorously against putting an alien's liberty completely at the mercy of the unreviewable discretion of the Attorney General, arguing that such liberty "is too highly prized in this country to allow executive officials to imprison and hold people on the basis of information kept secret from courts." Again demonstrating his faith in the judiciary as the protector of personal rights, he argued that Mezei should not be deprived of his liberty indefinitely except as the result of a fair open-court hearing in which evidence is appraised by the court, not by the prosecutor. Justice Jackson agreed, noting that simple justice could hardly menace the security of the country. "No one can make me believe," he wrote, "that we are that far gone."[91]

The Court's conservatism shone through in two other areas not ostensibly related to national security problems. One was religion. Criticism of the earlier McCollum rule striking down a released-time program, to say nothing of Black's "neutrality" contention regarding the proper relation of government to religion, had intensified in the

89. U.S. *v.* Spector, 343 U.S. 169 (1952).
90. Shaughnessy *v.* U.S. *ex rel* Mezei, 345 U.S. 206 (1953).
91. *Ibid.,* p. 228.

late 1940s and early 1950s. The Court was seemingly prepared in this area, as in others, to accede to hostile pressures. In March, 1952, it refused to hear a challenge to a New Jersey Bible-reading statute, dodging the question on the narrow grounds that the cause was moot as far as it related to the child in question, since she had graduated from the public schools before the appeal was taken to court.[92] A month later, speaking through Justice Douglas, the Court gave ground sharply on released time. Upholding a New York City program providing for religious instruction during school hours, but off school property, Douglas argued that any rigid system of religious separation between church and state would be absurd and impossible. Agreeing that government could not finance religious groups or undertake religious instruction, or blend secular and sectarian education, he made clear that such practices were different from noncoercive public ceremonies, prayers in legislative halls, and fire protection for religious groups and similar public services. "We cannot read into the Bill of Rights," he wrote, "a philosophy of hostility to religion."[93]

Douglas failed to convince three of his brethren that the New York program was not coercive. To his contention that the public schools did no more than accommodate their schedules to a program of outside religious instruction, Jackson replied that on the contrary the state was making religious sects beneficiaries of its power to compel children to attend secular schools. "The school serves as a temporary jail for a pupil who will not go to church," he argued. "It takes more subtlety of mind than I possess to deny that this is governmental constraint in support of religion."[94]

Probably the most fascinating case regarding religion in the period came in late 1952. Traditionally, courts had refused to endorse state legislation that regulated, in hierarchical churches, internal church administration, or the appointment of the clergy, or effected the transfer of church property from one faction to another. Similarly, when property rights were involved in decisions of church custom or law on ecclesiastical issues, civil courts had always accepted church

92. Doremus *v.* Board of Education, 342 U.S. 429 (1952). See Donald E. Boles, *The Bible, Religion and the Public Schools* (Ames, Iowa, 1965).

93. Zorach *v.* Clauson, 343 U.S. 306 (1952).

94. *Ibid.*, p. 324. On the case see Frank J. Sorauf, "Zorach v. Clauson: The Impact of a Supreme Court Decision," *American Political Science Review,* LIII (1959), 777–791.

rules. The Religious Corporations Law of New York had transferred the administrative control of Russian Orthodox Churches in North America from the Supreme Church Authority in Moscow to authorities selected by a convention of the North American Churches. Ties had promptly been severed with the previous authorities at all levels. Such legislation was clearly intended to protect the American churches from the infiltration of atheistic and subversive influence of the Russian hierarchy now under the dominion of the Soviet Union. But the Court stuck to its traditional position, holding that the new statute interfered with the free exercise of religion contrary to the First Amendment, made applicable to the states by the Fourteenth.[95] Regarding the security question involved, Justice Reed took the position that if continued control by traditional authorities presented the danger of subversive activities on the part of clergymen, the federal government and the state were competent to deal with such subversion through their own instrumentalities.

The Korean war period again focused attention upon the American Negro, particularly the Negro serviceman serving in the first war to be fought by an integrated military establishment. The success of this Truman program was watched with a critical eye, especially by southern whites, although the country generally approved of it. Such a development encouraged Negro leaders at home to argue that the time was at hand for further integration on the home front, and a cautious Supreme Court, in October, 1952, agreed to take cases challenging racial segregation in the public schools, postponing argument, however, pending further exploration of the facts.[96] The following June, the Court called for reargument, presenting opposing counsel with a series of questions, which in their briefs and oral arguments they were requested to discuss.[97] The postponement was disappointing to the litigants and their lawyers, but was looked upon by Thurgood Marshall and other antisegregation attorneys as a

95. Kedroff *v.* St. Nicholas Cathedral, 344 U.S. 94 (1952).

96. Brown *v.* Board of Education, 344 U.S. 1 (1952). On the preliminary stages of the case see Daniel M. Berman, *It Is So Ordered: The Supreme Court Rules on School Segregation* (New York, 1966), pp. 1–86; Leon Friedman (ed.), *Argument* (New York, 1969); and Alfred H. Kelly, "The School Desegregation Cases," in John A. Garraty (ed.), *Quarrels That Have Shaped the Constitution* (New York, 1964), pp. 243–268.

97. 345 U.S. 972 (1953). This material is contained in Friedman (ed.), *Argument.* For a pre-Brown consideration of the legal status of school segregation see Robert A. Leflar and Wylie H. Davis, "Segregation in the Public Schools—1953," *Harvard Law Review,* LXVII (1954), 377–435.

hopeful sign and an opportunity to broaden their appeals. It seemed a clear indication that the justices were prepared to examine the entire history of the Fourteenth Amendment, particularly the intent of its framers, and thus not be bound by the nearly sixty years of restrictive gloss placed upon its equal protection clause by narrow Supreme Court rulings.[98]

Chief Justice Vinson, however, was not prepared to move rapidly. Having failed to convince his colleagues that the government should be discouraged from taking too prominent a part in the cases, he held fast to the position that the judiciary should not be an aggressive instrument for invalidating school segregation. Thus prior to his death, on September 8, 1953, the Court under his leadership, although striking at discriminatory employment practices,[99] and further subtle schemes of Negro disfranchisement,[100] was not prepared to hear reargument. It thus fell to a new Chief Justice to lead the Court through consideration of the school segregation issue and to accept responsibility for the most explosive and controversial judicial ruling in one hundred years.

98. Thurgood Marshall of the N.A.A.C.P. enlisted a team of distinguished historians and constitutional lawyers to research the background of the Fourteenth Amendment in hopes of demonstrating that the framers of it intended to prohibit public school segregation. Included were Horace Bond, Robert K. Carr, Robert Cushman, Jr., John P. Frank, John Hope Franklin, Walter Gellhorn, Howard Jay Graham, Alfred H. Kelly, Milton R. Konvitz, and C. Vann Woodward. Results were inconclusive, however, and sufficiently disappointing that the Court ultimately relied on other types of "social science" data. See Alfred H. Kelly "The Fourteenth Amendment Reconsidered: The Segregation Question," *Michigan Law Review,* LIV (1955), 1049–1086; and Alexander M. Bickel, "The Original Understanding and the Segregation Decision," *Harvard Law Review,* LXIX (1955), 1–65. A later study, Robert Kaczorowski, "Civil Rights Legislation During Reconstruction: The Intent of the Framers" (unpublished Ph.D. dissertation, University of Minnesota, 1971), contends, persuasively, that such intent was clear, and contemplated full civil rights.

99. Brotherhood of Railroad Trainmen *v.* Howard, 343 U.S. 768 (1952). The case involved the attempt by the Jim Crow Brotherhood to use its influence to try to eliminate Negro trainmen and get their jobs for members of the brotherhood. Black, over the dissent of Minton, Vinson, and Reed, struck down the practice, indicating that bargaining agents who enjoyed the advantages of the Railway Labor Act's provision must execute their trust without lawless invasions of the rights of other workers.

100. Terry *v.* Adams, 345 U.S. 461 (1953). The case involved a preprimary process of the selection of candidates by all-white "Jaybird" groups with the deliberate purpose of preventing Negroes from having a vote in the selection of candidates for the primary, the party convention, and the general election. On the case see Clay P. Malick, "Terry v. Adams: Governmental Responsibility for the Protection of Civil Rights," *Western Political Quarterly,* VII (1954), 51–64.

CHAPTER 10

Eisenhower Quiescence and the Warren Court

EARL WARREN became Chief Justice of the United States through an interim appointment by President Dwight D. Eisenhower on October 5, 1953.[1] His appointment was purely political, representing a concession to the liberal wing of the Republican party at a time when the President was being criticized for giving too much ground to the conservative Taft element. Warren's own background gave few hints as to either his judicial philosophy or his concept of the proper role of courts. A long-time public servant in California, and one time district attorney of urban Alameda County, he had a long record of concern with effective law enforcement, having served on various public bodies dealing with police training, criminal identification, and similar aspects of police activities. As district attorney he had set out to disassociate politics from graft and particularly organized crime in Oakland, and had also been an outspoken and aggressive advocate of streamlining California court procedures in order to insure more rapid and effective justice. As Governor of the state he had established an enviable record for honest government and social progress, demonstrating particular concern with education and public services, setting up a

1. The appointment was not confirmed by the Senate until March 1, 1954, and then over the opposition of three southern members of the Senate Judiciary Committee. Eisenhower, however, moved rapidly, insisting that the Court must be at full membership during the reargument of the school segregation cases. Daniel M. Berman, *It Is So Ordered: The Supreme Court Rules on School Segregation* (New York, 1966), pp. 88–90.

state crime commission and developing ways to accommodate the large popular migration to the region in the postwar years. Although he had acquiesced in the confinement of the Japanese,[2] he was a known supporter of civil rights, a factor which had emerged from his preconvention campaign for the Presidency in 1948.[3]

Having demonstrated the constructive power that could be wielded by state government, Warren, in his California years, had been an enthusiastic supporter of state sovereignty. He had testified adversely against turning over the tidelands oil lands of the coastal states to the federal government in a controversy that had roused national attention.[4] He was in turn pleased to endorse Congress's passage in May, 1953, of the Submerged Lands Act, vesting in the states ownership of such lands.[5] In a statement that later came back to haunt him, he had spoken out strongly against any interference with state voting and districting procedures, particularly defending the sanctity of state bicameralism in its traditional form.[6] His general career thus suggested more clearly his philosophy of government and approach to social problems than any attitudes toward the proper judicial role, although there is little to indicate that he did not hold in 1953 the position that he articulated two years later, that "judges [are] not monks or scientists, but participants in the living stream of our national life."[7]

In confronting the complex and supercharged question of public

2. Bradford Smith, "The Education of Earl Warren: Treatment of Nisei in California During World War II," *Nation,* CLXXXVII (Oct. 11, 1958), 206–208.

3. John D. Weaver, *Warren: The Man, the Court, the Era* (Boston, 1967), p. 150; Leo Katcher, *Earl Warren: A Political Biography* (New York, 1967), p. 219: and Henry M. Christman (ed.), *The Public Papers of Chief Justice Earl Warren* (New York, 1966), pp. 14–18.

4. For a careful analysis of the Warren testimony on the subject see Ernest R. Bartley, *The Tidelands Oil Controversy: A Legal and Historical Analysis* (Austin, 1953), pp. 72, 106, 116–119.

5. The Supreme Court in 1947 had ruled (U.S. *v.* California, 332 U.S. 19) that the United States had domination over the resources of the soil under the marginal sea adjoining California. The 1953 Act, 67 Stat. 29, reversed this ruling. In 1965, however, the Court once again entered the area, limiting state jurisdiction to areas within three geographical miles of the coastline, and excluding further areas being claimed by California as within "historic state boundaries." U.S. *v.* California, 381 U.S. 139 (1965).

6. The speech, on October 29, 1948, was made while Warren was campaigning for the Vice-Presidency. It is reprinted in Wallace Mendelson, *The Constitution and the Supreme Court* (New York, 1965), pp. 638–639. See also Katcher, *Earl Warren,* p. 436.

7. Earl Warren, "Law and the Future," *Fortune,* LII (November, 1955), 106.

school segregation, Warren revealed much regarding his approach to the law. The landmark case of *Brown* v. *Board of Education* told a great deal about his ability as Chief Justice, his judicial technique, and particularly his unabashed and primary commitment to justice and his willingness to shape the law to achieve it. One of his first actions as Chief Justice was to preside while the Court heard reargument on the school segregation cases. The process took an unprecedented ten hours over a three-day period with counsel for both sides, plus the government, exploring every aspect of the situation from the historical background of the Fourteenth Amendment to the actual social and psychological impact upon Negro children of segregated education.[8] When the decision was announced for a unanimous Court on May 17, 1954, it was indubitably clear that Warren had succeeded in doing what Vinson had had neither the ability nor the desire to accomplish previously. He had rallied a divergent membership behind a unanimous legal position that wiped nearly sixty years of judicial gloss off the Equal Protection Clause. In so doing, he had made very clear his intention to have the Court stride forth on an issue of national concern, where the other two branches of Congress were cautiously equivocating. The style of his opinion was direct, simple, and forthright with a candor which was disarming, and to many friends of the Court, disturbingly frank and dangerously careless regarding form. The fact that its references to precedent seemed to be less important than social and psychological data, included to show the social reasons for the Court's action, virtually guaranteed that it would draw highly critical fire.

The decision, holding basically that in the field of education the doctrine of "separate but equal" had no place, was clear demonstration of Warren's own conviction of the importance of public education in a democratic society.[9] His willingness to interpret the Fourteenth Amendment in line, not with precedent, but with what experts had convinced the Court was the historic intention of its framers, seemed to demonstrate his willingness to bring modern institutions into line with traditional and professed American values.

8. Alfred H. Kelly, "The School Desegregation Cases," in John A. Garraty (ed.), *Quarrels That Have Shaped the Constitution* (New York, 1964), pp. 243–268; Leon Friedman (ed.), *Argument* (New York, 1969); and Berman, *It Is So Ordered,* pp. 92 ff.

9. Brown *v.* Board of Education, 347 U.S. 483 (1954).

On the other hand, the care which he took to reassure the nation that implementation processes would have to be worked out calmly and carefully did much to ease rational minds that he was no irresponsible revolutionary. Advocates of immediatism and gradualism were invited to present briefs and arguments before the Court in the following term. After consideration of these, the Chief Justice indicated, careful guidelines would be set forth.

The same provision was applied to a similar federal case involving the schools of the District of Columbia, decided the same day. Although the Fifth Amendment did not contain an equal protection clause, Warren maintained that the concepts of due process of law and equal protection of the law both stemmed from "our American ideal of fairness," and while they were not interchangeable, it was true that "discrimination may be so unjustifiable as to be a violation of due process."[10] He thus ruled against segregation in the District, again returning the case to docket for further consideration of the proper remedies and decrees.

Immediate reaction to the rulings was strong but mixed. Northerners hailed them as a long-overdue step toward squaring fact and fiction in the area of the country's professed commitment to equality. The Voice of America promptly beamed their terms around the world as an indication of the nation's new credentials as leader of the free world. Southerners were as hostile as proponents were vigorous.[11] Cries were raised that the Court had been brainwashed by "foreign sociologists" (a reference to the famous footnote eleven, which cited a number of works exploring the impact of segregated education on Negro children), and as the decade advanced, numerous southern spokesmen, although denouncing the Court's use of "scientific evidence" regarding racial equality as irrelevant to the law, rallied behind a new wave of scientific racism, demonstrating the Negro's innate inferiority.[12]

When the second Brown decision came down the following May, the Court retreated. Technically it had granted Negro schoolchildren

10. Bolling *v.* Sharpe, 347 U.S. 497–499 (1954).

11. The southern urban press, however, was surprisingly calm and conciliatory. Benjamin Muse, *Ten Years of Prelude: The Story of Integration Since the Supreme Court's 1954 Decision* (New York, 1964), pp. 16 ff.; Harry M. Ashmore, *The Negro and the Schools* (Chapel Hill, N.C., 1954), pp. 132 ff.; and *The New York Times,* May 18, 1954, p. 19.

12. I. A. Newby, *The Challenge to the Court: Social Scientists and the Defense of Segregation, 1954–1966* (Baton Rouge, 1967), pp. 5, 171–172.

the constitutional right under the Fourteenth Amendment to attend racially nonsegregated schools. Now Chief Justice Warren, resorting awkwardly to the principles of equity law, denied immediate remedy, remanding the cases to the lower courts and ordering them to work out equitable ways of admitting the parties of the cases "to the public schools on a racially non-discriminatory basis with all deliberate speed."[13] The ruling, a masterpiece of legal contradiction, stood nonetheless as judicial acknowledgment of the cold fact that the cases called for a social revolution in the South and unless implemented carefully would produce massive retaliation against the very Negroes they were designed to benefit. The South interpreted the move as an invitation to intransigence. The states of the old Confederacy promptly set out on programs of massive resistance to the new judicially pronounced policy, seeking to utilize every legal and political weapon at their disposal to forestall implementation. Thus initially compliance with the rulings was orderly and meaningful only in the border states and in northern and western states with permissive segregation statutes.

The Brown decision promptly identified the Warren Court in the public mind as generally liberal and as the aggressive protector of Negro rights. At the outset, however, such an image was misleading. During his first two terms as Chief Justice, Warren rendered few other liberal opinions, generally voting with the former Vinson majority over the dissents of Black and Douglas. His record in these two terms again saw the Court avoiding other controversial issues and looking carefully to the new President, Dwight D. Eisenhower, for some signs of guidance as to its proper ideological path.[14]

13. Brown *v.* Board of Education, 349 U.S. 294, 301 (1955). For a discussion of the response of the various lower federal court judges to the assignment see Jack Peltason, *Fifty-Eight Lonely Men: Southern Federal Judges and School Desegregation* (New York, 1961).

14. For a discussion of those years see Clyde E. Jacobs, "The Warren Court—After Three Terms," *Western Political Quarterly,* IX (1956), 937–954; and C. Herman Pritchett, *The Political Offender and the Warren Court* (Boston, 1958), pp. 9–11, 62. In the three most explosive issues of the term Warren voted with the conservatives. The cases found Jackson affirming a state conviction based on evidence obtained through illegal searches and seizures (Irvine *v.* California, 347 U.S. 128 [1954]); Burton upholding New York's suspension of a physician's license for refusal to cooperate with a congressional committee (Barsky *v.* Board, 347 U.S. 442 [1954]); and Frankfurter sustaining the deportation of an alien due to past Communist party membership (Galvan *v.* Press, 347 U.S. 522 [1954]). In the latter case the Court also ruled that under the Internal Security Act of 1950, an alien's joining of the Communist party, whether the act was deliberate or innocent, was sufficient to justify deportation.

Eisenhower had come to the White House in early 1953, a popular military hero from World War II, beloved and respected by his countrymen, but with no very clear vision of the road ahead, other than that the Republican party should be as close to its middle as possible. Generally a passive and easygoing individual, he had no desire either to undo the major programs of the New and Fair Deals or to strike out on bold new paths and develop new approaches to government. His concept of the Presidency, unlike that of either of his two predecessors, was essentially that of a mediating agency, harmonizing the functioning of the team, and ratifying decisions and policies carefully prepared by responsible subordinates or by congressional leadership.[15] The result was that during his eight years in office, the leadership for the formulation of new policies was clearly shunted to Congress or to executive underlings. Significant executive actions, particularly the setting forth of new programs with important constitutional implications, were highly minimal. Thus when the Supreme Court in the 1950s looked to the White House it found few clues that would help it in reaching proper policy decisions, even on questions of national significance.

Congressional leadership at the outset of the Eisenhower administration was largely handled by Senator Robert A. Taft. Taft was quietly enthusiastic about the prospect of the reemergence of congressional leadership, and hoped that the actions of errant Republican congressmen, particularly the more flamboyant "Red" hunters, might now be curtailed in order to expand the image of congressional responsibility.[16] Senator McCarthy, however, had other ideas. Following the Eisenhower election, McCarthy had indicated that the job of "Red" hunting could now be taken over by the new administration.[17] When Eisenhower gave no immediate signs of leaping into the fray, the impatient senator continued and even expanded his efforts along these lines, leading highly irresponsible, but headline-making probes of the Voice of America, the State De-

15. See Richard E. Neustadt, *Presidential Power: The Politics of Leadership* (New York, 1960); Robert J. Donovan, *Eisenhower: The Inside Story* (New York, 1956), pp. 67–72; and Emmet John Hughes, *The Ordeal of Power: A Political Memoir of the Eisenhower Years* (New York, 1963), pp. 346 ff.

16. Arthur S. Link and William B. Catton, *American Epoch* (New York, 1963), pp. 742–743.

17. Richard Rovere, *Senator Joe McCarthy* (New York, 1959), p. 187.

partment's overseas information program,[18] the Protestant clergy (which he charged was riddled with subversion), and finally the army. His sensational disclosures and his general condescension toward the weakness of the executive branch in the "Red" hunting area annoyed and antagonized the President, who was reluctant to apply the brakes due to the compromised position in which he found himself.[19]

The Republican campaign for the Presidency in 1952 had placed major stress on the "Communists in government" issue, and the administration had both a political and moral obligation, once in office, to at least go through the motions of dealing with what was, by this time, largely a nonexistent evil. The Eisenhower response was thus one of a cautious attempt at preemption in the security area. The President on April 27, 1953, promulgated an executive order setting up a new executive loyalty program, expanding the criteria of the earlier Truman program.[20] Discharge from federal service was now to be based on a simple finding that the individual's employment "may not be clearly consistent with the interests of national security." Seven categories of security criteria were set up, and while a number clearly were tied with sabotage, treason, and sedition, a person could now also be dismissed as a "security risk" if he were a sexual pervert, a drug addict, or even a heavy drinker or a garrulous gossip.

The President shortly announced the dismissal of several thousand employees "for security reasons," but his criteria were promptly challenged, particularly by indignant Democrats infuriated by what they charged was a clear attempt to impugn the loyalty of officials

18. Such actions led directly to the removal of many books from the shelves of overseas libraries and to the charge that the government was engaging in "book burning." See Donovan, *Eisenhower,* pp. 90–92; and Herbert Block, *Herblock's Here and Now* (New York, 1955), pp. 103–131, 146.

19. For Eisenhower's attitude toward McCarthy see Donovan, *Eisenhower,* pp. 243 ff.; Hughes, *The Ordeal of Power,* pp. 92–93; and Richard Rovere, *Affairs of State: The Eisenhower Years* (New York, 1956), pp. 367 ff.

20. *Federal Register,* XVIII (1954), p. 2489. On the order and its impact see Report of the Special Committee of the Association of the Bar of the City of New York, *The Federal Loyalty-Security Program* (New York, 1956); Ralph S. Brown, *Loyalty and Security: Employment Tests in the United States* (New Haven, 1958), pp. 23–30; and "Symposium—Federal Loyalty-Security Programs," *Ohio State Law Journal,* XVIII (1957), 283–383. See also Sandra Weinstein, *Personnel Security Programs of the Federal Government* (New York, 1954).

of the previous administration.[21] They were particularly irate when a gratuitously helpful H.U.A.C. attempted to subpoena former President Truman to explain his security inadequacies and softness on "Reds."[22] The bite of the program was most vividly seen when J. Robert Oppenheimer, former director of the Los Alamos Laboratory and head of the Institute for Advanced Study at Princeton, was denied access to classified material on the ground that he was a poor security risk. A special board had affirmed Oppenheimer's loyalty, but agreed that security regulations required that he continue to be denied such access.[23] Clearly hysteria about "alleged Communists" had not fully subsided.

Critics of the program were also antagonized by it since, like congressional committee hearings, loyalty board proceedings frequently involved gross violation of procedural due process, with the term "disloyalty to the United States" seldom defined accurately or consistently, with evidence often nothing more than guilt by association, and with "faceless informers" utilized as sources of damaging accusation, not to be questioned.

21. The Eisenhower program proceeded on different grounds from the Truman Program, which it superseded and abolished. The new President made clear at the outset that he intended to use the "summary dismissal" power left over from World War II (*Congressional Record,* 83rd Cong. 1st Sess., pp. 748 ff.) and needed no additional legislation. His program also did little to clarify the difference between security and loyalty although liberal critics hoped initially it might. Underlying it was the assumption that every federal employee worked in a sensitive position. This enabled its champions to speak as if anyone dismissed under it was dismissed as a "subversive." See *Congressional Quarterly Almanac,* X, 378–383, 712; XI, 16, 27, 40. See also John H. Schaar, *Loyalty in America* (Berkeley, 1957), pp. 123 ff.; Michael C. Slotnick, "The Anathema of the Security Risk: Arbitrary Dismissals of Federal Government Employees," *University of Miami Law Review,* XVII (1962), 10–50; and Brown, *Loyalty and Security,* pp. 40–41.

22. Mr. Truman replied with a polite letter that was at the same time a lecture to the committee on separation of powers and the independence of the executive. *The New York Times,* Nov. 13, 1953, p. 14.

23. See Cushing Strout (ed.), *Conscience, Science and Security: The Case of Dr. J. Robert Oppenheimer* (Chicago, 1963); Michael Wharton (ed.), *A Nation's Security: the Case of Dr. J. Robert Oppenheimer* (London, 1955); Charles P. Curtis, *The Oppenheimer Case: The Trial of a Security System* (New York, 1955); Harry Kalven, "The Case of J. Robert Oppenheimer before the Atomic Energy Committee," *Bulletin of Atomic Scientists,* X (September, 1954), 259–269; and Joseph and Stewart Alsop, "We Accuse!," *Harper's Magazine,* CCIX (October, 1954), 25–45. On the broader problem of security and science see Walter Gellhorn, *Security, Loyalty and Science* (Ithaca, 1950).

The response of congressional leadership was highly mixed. In August, 1954, Congress enacted an Immunity Act, largely as a result of growing complaints from aggressive committee leaders regarding the tendency of witnesses to take the Fifth Amendment.[24] The measure provided that in questions involving security matters, a committee, holding hearings, could obtain from a federal judge an order forcing a witness to testify, granting him immunity, however, from immediate prosecution on the basis of the evidence thus legally coerced.

Three weeks later, under the leadership of Senator Hubert Humphrey, liberal Democrats, tired of being smeared as "soft on Communism," pushed through Congress the Communist Control Act of 1954.[25] The measure, which was clearly tied to the imminent fall elections, outlawed the Communist party and initially sought to make party membership a crime. Responding to administration criticism that this would make it difficult to register Communists under the McCarran Act, because such action would thus be compulsory self-incrimination, the sponsors removed the membership provision. Congressional critics who had attacked the measure as a clear violation of First Amendment guarantees of free speech and association, now pointed to its incongruity. Its enactment, while possibly serving immediate partisan political purposes, led to practically no attempts at enforcement on the part of Justice Department officials.[26]

By the time such actions came, however, McCarthy's Communist-

24. 68 Stat. 745 (1954). On the measure see Samuel H. Hofstadter, *The Fifth Amendment and the Immunity Act of 1954* (New York, 1956). The previous March, the Court had ruled in Adams *v.* Maryland, 347 U.S. 179 (1954), that information secured from a witness before a congressional committee could not be used against him in a state court. The 1954 Immunity Act incorporated the same principle regarding "coerced" information. See Oetje J. Rogge, "The New Federal Immunity Act and the Judicial Function," *California Law Review,* XLV (1957), 110.

25. 68 Stat. 775 (1954). On the measure see Donald G. Morgan, *Congress and the Constitution: A Study of Responsibility* (Cambridge, Mass., 1966), pp. 246–268; and Carl A. Auerbach, "The Communist Control Act of 1954: A Proposed Legal-Political Theory of Free Speech," *University of Chicago Law Review,* XXIII (1956), 173–220.

26. Morgan, *Congress and the Constitution,* pp. 258–259. The measure added a new category of groups required to register—"communist-infiltrated" organizations. These, like Communists and "front" organizations, although outlawed, were expected to register with the Subversive Activities Control Board.

hysteria balloon had been sharply punctured. The exposure given the senator over national television in his showdown with the army had made millions of previously oblivious Americans aghast at his bullying techniques, his callous disregard for established rules of law, his total unconcern for the rights of others, and his appalling lack of human decency. Republican members of his committee, under such pressure, finally gained the courage to disassociate themselves from his techniques,[27] and Congress was eventually prodded to take long overdue action in blowing the whistle on further abuse of the investigative power, recommending and securing censure by a Senate Resolution, December 2, 1954.[28] Early the following year, the public learned that government witnesses, used frequently before committees and loyalty review boards to establish disloyalty, had perjured themselves. Particularly flagrant was the case of Harvey Matusow, who admitted that as a paid government witness he had given false testimony under oath at two important federal trials and had done so in one case under the persuasion of Assistant U.S. Attorney Roy Cohn.[29] Such developments threw the whole process of anti-Communist investigation into confusion and disrepute. By mid-1955, although the Justice Department continued to proceed against local Communist leaders under the Smith Act, the security issue slipped into the back pages as national sanity returned and national interest quickly focused on the opportunities for enjoying the materialism of the new age of normalcy.

Along with Eisenhower's loyalty order, the Immunity Act and the Communist Control Act constituted two of the few examples in the decade of law making carrying significant constitutional overtones. This general quiescence, coupled with the restoration of national calm, seemed clear indication that Congress, like the President, was not prepared to set off on new courses of action and adopt positive legislation. As a sharp departure from the situation under Truman, it confronted the Supreme Court, by 1955, with the

27. See Charles E. Potter, *Days of Shame* (New York, 1965); and Michael Straight, *Trial by Television* (Boston, 1954).

28. 83rd Cong., 2d Sess., Senate Resolution 301, in *Hearings Before a Select Committee to Study Censure Charges* (1954), pp. 1–2.

29. For admission of his guilt, which led to a prison sentence, see Harvey Matusow, *False Witness* (New York, 1955). On the general problem see Herbert L. Packer, *Ex-Communist Witnesses* (Stanford, 1962); and Richard H. Rovere, "The Kept Witnesses," *Harper's Magazine*, CCX (May, 1955), 25–34.

task of assessing what its proper role and proper course should be.

There was little question, given the personality of the Chief Justice, a man who had spent his life deciding, not brooding, that Warren would want the body to stride out on an active course in the pursuit of social justice. The problem was one of means.

Here the very passivity of the other two branches suggested an approach. Clearly the type of Black-Douglas activism that called for throwing out executive and legislative programs that violated individual liberties was not realistic. Neither, however, was it realistic to expect Warren to acquiesce in the type of Vinson-Frankfurter self-restraint and confine the Court to legal hair-splitting and the avoidance of difficult policy questions. Rather, the obvious course that beckoned was to follow and extend the techniques that Warren had used in *Brown* v. *Board of Education*—vigorous statutory interpretation, with an eye to bringing the operation of American legal institutions into harmony with professed American ideals. Such a position had much to recommend it to the membership of the 1955 Court. By steering a middle course between the preferred freedoms activism of Black and Douglas and the self-restraint of Frankfurter, it accomplished many of the goals of the former through the techniques of the latter. The Court was thus enabled to exert positive authority in a fairly traditional fashion at a time when obviously neither of the other two branches intended to stride forward rapidly in the social justice field. Without challenging executive and legislative programs directly it could make them work more equitably and could refocus much of their excessive stress on security so as to revive earlier concerns with civil liberties and individual freedom. Further, such an approach invited Congress, if it was unhappy with judicial interpretations, to reassert its intentions, either by amending the statute in question or adopting a new one. Thus no matter whether the Court's interpretation was accepted, it would have made, by its actions, a useful contribution to the legislative process by keeping squarely before Congress some of the major values of the American constitutional system. By late in the 1954–55 term, the results of this new philosophy began to be seen.

The Court by this period had a second Eisenhower appointee. John Marshall Harlan, III, was the grandson of the distinguished late-nineteenth-century antisegregationist whose 1896 dissenting contention that "the Constitution is colorblind" the Court had finally made majority position in *Brown* v. *Board of Education*. The junior Harlan was a Republican New York lawyer, moderate in his views, and highly skilled in the law, if possessing but brief judicial experience.[30] He contrasted sharply with the third Eisenhower appointee, Democrat and Catholic William J. Brennan, Jr., who took his seat on the bench at the beginning of the 1956 term after a career as a moderate liberal and defender of civil liberties on the New Jersey Supreme Court.[31] Harlan expressed himself strongly in two of four late-May–early-June cases examining aspects of the functioning of federal security bodies, identifying himself clearly with the conservative wing. Three of these cases raised questions regarding the methods of the House Un-American Activities Committee and congressional committees in general.[32]

Warren, speaking for the Court in each, recognized the right of Congress to hold investigations in connection with contemplated legislation and did not question committee authority to compel testimony in order to carry out its duties effectively. He pointed out, however, that even this power had limitations and "must not be used to inquire into private affairs unrelated to a valid legislative purpose." "It should not be extended to an area in which Congress is forbidden to legislate," he contended, "and should not be confused with any of the powers of law enforcement."[33] Harlan won-

30. Eisenhower had appointed Harlan to the United States Court of Appeals for the Second Circuit in January, 1954. At the time he was acting as chief counsel for the duPont Corporation in its famed antitrust suit. He had previously served as a chief counsel for the New York State Crime Commission from 1951 to 1953. On Harlan see Arthur A. Ballantine, "John Marshall Harlan for the Supreme Court," *Iowa Law Review*, XL (1955), 391–399; Loren P. Beth, "Justice Harlan and the Uses of Dissent," *American Political Science Review*, XLIX (1955), 1085–1104; and Edward L. Friedman, Jr., "Mr. Justice Harlan," *Notre Dame Lawyer*, XXX (1955), 349–359.

31. Brennan, during his judicial tenure in New Jersey, had been an outspoken advocate of court reforms to lessen delays in the administration of justice. He also was a foe of legal narrowness, and an advocate of the increased use of social science evidence by judges in reaching realistic decisions. See Francis P. McQuade and Alexander T. Kardos, "Mr. Justice Brennan and His Legal Philosophy," *Notre Dame Lawyer*, XXXIII (1958), 321–349; Daniel M. Berman, "Mr. Justice Brennan: A Preliminary Appraisal," *Catholic University of America Law Review*, VII (1958), 1–15; and William J. Brennan, *An Affair with Freedom* (New York, 1967).

32. Quinn *v.* U.S., 349 U.S. 155 (1955); Emspak *v.* U.S., 349 U.S. 190 (1955); Bart *v.* U.S, 349 U.S. 219 (1955).

33. Quinn *v.* U.S., p. 161.

dered in dissent about the legitimacy of known Communists callously taking the Fifth Amendment to avoid answering legitimate committee queries, even though acknowledging that there were times when such a provision, if sincerely invoked, could be justified.

The June 6 case of *Peters* v. *Hobby* was far more equivocal. Dr. John P. Peters of Yale had directly attacked the constitutionality of the secret witness procedure in the Truman Loyalty Program. The Court, while seemingly ruling for Peters in maintaining that the board had exceeded its authority, based such abuse strictly on the grounds of its lack of jurisdiction.[34] Thus the charge of civil liberties violation by the board was carefully skirted.

Ascertaining no immediate hostility to its rulings, the Court in the 1955–56 term became progressively bolder. Early gesturing toward Congress in late March, by upholding the provisions of the recent 1954 Immunity Act,[35] it unleashed a bombshell in early April by taking a sharp swing at state un-American activity bodies and programs, maintaining, in a case involving a Pennsylvania Communist, Steve Nelson, that with the passage of the Smith Act, Congress had superseded state legislation punishing sedition against the United States and had generally preempted the field.[36] The effect of the decision was to invalidate in part sedition statutes in forty-two states, Alaska, and Hawaii. The scheme of federal subversive regulation, Warren argued in his majority opinion, included the Smith Act, the Internal Security Act of 1950, and the Communist Control Act of 1954. These were so pervasive as to imply that Congress had left no room for supplementary state action. In addition, enforcement of state legislation inevitably presented a "serious danger of conflict with the administration of the federal program." The task of guard-

34. Peters *v.* Hobby, 349 U.S. 331 (1955). See Brown, *Loyalty and Security,* pp. 46–47, 408–410.

35. Ullman *v.* U.S., 350 U.S. 422 (1956). In the ruling the question was raised whether the Act granted true immunity by simply protecting the coerced witness from court prosecution. Frankfurter felt that it did. Douglas and Black, in dissent, protested bitterly that this was not true immunity since it opened the witness to many kinds of economic, social, and political penalties, often worse than legal prosecution.

36. Pennsylvania *v.* Nelson, 350 U.S. 497 (1956). For an inside view see Steve Nelson, *The 13th Juror: The Inside Story of My Trial* (New York, 1955). On the broader constitutional issue see Alan R. Hunt, "Federal Supremacy and State Legislation," *Michigan Law Review,* (1955), 407–438; and Roger C. Cramton, "The Supreme Court and State Power to Deal with Subversion and Loyalty," *Minnesota Law Review,* XLIII (1959), 1025–1082.

ing the United States against subversive action, Warren maintained, was one for the federal government. In the Hanson case later in the term, the Court used the same preemption concept to invalidate state "right-to-work" laws.[37]

A week later, on April 9, Justices Clark and Frankfurter joined the liberal wing to condemn the dismissal of a Brooklyn College professor, Harry Slochower, solely because he had invoked the Fifth Amendment before a congressional committee. Such summary dismissal violates due process of law, Clark concluded, insisting that it was improper to infer a sinister meaning from the utilizing of a constitutional right designed to protect the innocent who might otherwise be ensnared by ambiguous circumstances.[38] Later the same month Black wrote an opinion destined to arouse states' rights champions throughout the nation. In a case cited as *Griffin* v. *Illinois,* he ruled that in criminal trials, states can be required to furnish transcripts for indigent defendants, making clear in the process his conviction that "there can be no equal justice where the kind of trial a man gets depends on the amount of money he has."[39] The decision, while innocuous in itself, seemed to presage federal interference with state administration of criminal justice, a threat strongly resented, especially by local judicial leaders.

But the Court was not through. Directly focusing on the nationally odorous perjured witness issue, it sent back to the Subversive Activities Control Board findings regarding Communism that had been based upon such testimony, including that by Harvey Matusow. Its opinion urged further and fairer proceedings. "The untainted administration of justice is certainly one of the most cherished aspects of our institution," wrote Justice Frankfurter for a Court split six to three. "This Court is charged with supervisory functions in relation to proceedings in the federal courts. Therefore, fastidious regard for the honor of the administration of justice requires the Court to make certain that the doing of justice be made so manifest that only irrational or perverse claims of its disregard can be asserted."[40]

37. Railway Employees *v.* Hanson, 351 U.S. 225 (1956).
38. Slochower *v.* Board, 350 U.S. 513 (1956).
39. Griffin *v.* Illinois, 351 U.S. 12 (1956).
40. Communist Party *v.* Subversive Activities Control Board, 351 U.S. 115, 124 (1956). Clark, dissenting with Reed and Minton, chided the majority for avoiding the issue of the constitutionality of the Internal Security Act. See p. 130.

The Court closed its session on another security note. In the case of *Cole* v. *Young* it explored the question of the application of the Internal Security Act of 1950 to government employees who had no contact with restricted information.[41] Confining its ruling primarily to statutory interpretation, Harlan's careful majority opinion nonetheless raised pointed questions regarding the validity of dismissing employees in nonsensitive positions, thus forcing modification of the program to limit its application to "sensitive agencies" only. Cole's situation as a food and drug inspector for the New York District of the Food and Drug Administration was hardly sensitive, even if evidence seemed to indicate that he had had close association with individuals reliably reported to be Communists, had contributed funds to groups on the Attorney General's list, and had attended social gatherings of an allegedly subversive organization.

The response of Congress to the Court's performance during the term, while not openly hostile, was less than enthusiastic in a number of areas. Southerners highly antagonistic toward the desegregation rulings saw in the Nelson and Hanson cases further clear challenge to state sovereignty and threat of federal negation of state programs and policies. They were joined by Senator McCarthy, now rapidly declining in vigor, who charged that the Court's rulings had "handed another solid victory to the Communist Party."[42] Action was begun in Congress to override the *Cole* v. *Young* decision, with a "Cole Repealer Bill" introduced designed to authorize executive discretion in the extension of sensitive programs.[43] On the other hand, one hundred lawyers from all parts of the country issued a manifesto defending the Court against attacks "reckless in their abuse, . . . heedless of the value of judicial review . . . and dangerous in fomenting disrespect for our highest law . . . ," contending that the appeal for resistance "to decisions of the Court, by

41. Cole *v.* Young, 351 U.S. 536 (1956). Charles Fairman, "The Supreme Court," *Harvard Law Review,* LXX (1956), 165.

42. *Congressional Record,* 84th Cong., 2d Sess., pp. 6063–6064. See Leon I. Salomon (ed.), *The Supreme Court* (New York, 1961), pp. 112 ff.

43. The sponsor of the measure, Senator Karl Mundt, called on Congress to reject judicial decisions "which stultify the power of the Government of the United States to defend itself." *Congressional Record,* 84th Cong., 2d Sess., p. 10173.

any lawful means, is to utter a self-contradiction, whose ambiguity can only be calculated to promote disrespect for our fundamental law."[44]

But if the Court needed defenders in October, 1956, it needed a storm cellar a year later. For despite its continued adherence to statutory construction, the net effect of its broad range of rulings in major areas of public policy was to lead its critics to accuse it of a type of judicial legislation totally beyond its authority and outside its proper function.

The 1956 term began quietly enough with cases in November validating policy action in the taking of a blood sample from a suspected alcoholic driver to determine his sobriety,[45] and with a little-noticed but significant opinion by Justice Frankfurter, throwing out a Michigan obscenity statute as a violation of the freedom of the press, guaranteed by the First Amendment. The case, *Butler* v. *Michigan,* involved a state statute that banned books containing obscene, immoral, or lewd language for their potentially harmful influence upon youths. "Surely," wrote the justice, "this is to burn the house to roast the pig." "The incidence of this enactment is to reduce the adult population of Michigan to reading what is fit for children."[46] The case was a quiet landmark in the gradually evolving judicial concern with modernizing the law of obscenity, and although substituting no judicial standard, made clear that state standards clearly based upon unrealistic and generally Victorian values, could not in all practicality be sustained.[47]

By May, 1957, the Court's new-type activism had reemerged in

44. *The New York Times,* Oct. 28, 1956, p. 63.

45. Breithaupt *v.* Abram, 352 U.S. 432 (1957).

46. Butler *v.* Michigan, 352 U.S. 380, 383 (1957).

47. The Supreme Court to this date had not officially rejected the obscenity rule set forth by an English court in 1868 in the case of Regina *v.* Hicklin, L.R. 3 Q.B. 360 (1868), which had been adopted by a U.S. federal court in 1879 in U.S. *v.* Bennett, 16 Blatchf. 338 (1879), F. Cas. No. 14,571. The rule indicated that the test of obscenity was whether the tendency of the matter charged as obscene was "to deprave and corrupt those whose minds are open to such immoral influence, and into whose hands a publication of this sort might fall." Terrence J. Murphy, *Censorship: Government and Obscenity* (Baltimore, 1963), pp. 41–51; James J. Kilpatrick, *The Smut Peddlers* (London, 1960), pp. 109–129; and William B. Lockhard and Robert C. McClure, "Literature, the Law of Obscenity, and the Constitution," *Minnesota Law Review,* XXXVIII (1954), 324 ff.

the security field. In two cases involving the refusal of state bar associations to admit to their membership candidates otherwise qualified with real or alleged Communist backgrounds, a divided Court found such actions a denial of due process of law. It thus put constitutional limits on the legal profession's hitherto almost absolute power of regulating admission to its ranks.[48] Harlan and Clark expressed in dissent the view of many of the immediate critics of the rulings, maintaining that the decisions presented an unacceptable intrusion into a matter of state concern.

The same day the Supreme Court justices suceeded in thoroughly alienating large segments of big business. The Justice Department had, for a number of years, been prosecuting a massive antitrust suit against the duPont Corporation, charging it with violation of Section 7 of the Clayton Act.[49] Justice Brennan now ruled that its ownership of 23 per cent of General Motors stock had clearly given it illegal preference over competitors in the sale of automotive finishes and fabrics to that industrial giant, and that duPont's commanding position as a General Motors customer was promoted by its stock interest and was not gained solely on competitive merit. The effect of this ruling, the *Wall Street Journal* complained, was to throw "suspicion on any corporation that does business with any other company any of whose stock it might own."[50] Call was promptly made for Congress to revise the Clayton Act to wipe out the suggestion in the Court's decision that bigness is in itself illegal and contrary to the best interests of the country.

The Court climaxed its June 3 decision day with a poorly drafted but nonetheless sweeping decision by Justice Brennan exploring in

48. Schware *v.* Board of Bar Examiners, 353 U.S. 232 (1957); Konigsberg *v.* State Bar, 353 U.S. 252 (1957). See the bar's reaction in William H. Rehnquist, "The Bar Admission Cases: A Strange Judicial Aberration," *American Bar Association Journal,* XLIV (1958), 229 ff.

49. U.S. *v.* duPont & Co., 353 U.S. 586 (1957). Harlan, who had been counsel for the company prior to his judicial appointment, disqualified himself, as did Clark and Whittaker. With Frankfurter and Burton dissenting, the ruling was thus four to two. See George W. Stocking, "The duPont-General Motors Case and the Sherman Act," *Virginia Law Review,* XLIV (1958), 1–40; and Joel B. Dirlam and Irwin M. Stelzer, "The duPont-General Motors Decision: In the Anti-Trust Grain," *Columbia Law Review,* LVIII (1958), 24–43.

50. *Wall Street Journal,* June 5, 1957, p. 9. See Bruce Bromley, "Business's Views of the duPont-General Motors Decision," *Georgetown Law Journal,* XLVI (1958), 646–654; and William G. McGovern, "The Power and the Glory: The duPont-GM Decision," *Georgetown Law Journal,* XLVI (1958), 655–671.

detail the problem of witnesses confronted with serious charges against them based upon "classified" information in F.B.I. files, and their inability to have access to the charges against which they were expected to defend themselves.[51] The case involved a labor union official, Clinton E. Jencks, who had filed a non-Communist affidavit with the National Labor Relations Board in 1950. The government, in seeking to prove that the affidavit was false, had used the testimony of paid F.B.I. informers, including the admitted perjured Harvey Matusow, who had made oral and written reports that were alleged to show Jencks's Communist activities. Counsel requested that the reports be produced by the government for the inspection of the trial judge. It was in turn requested that he examine them for materiality and relevancy and turn over to the defense such materials as met these tests. Such request was refused.

Brennan's opinion not only threw out the conviction on the grounds of this refusal, but, in a broad and impressive fashion, he stated that future witnesses should clearly be afforded such a privilege. He neglected to make clear, however, the extent to which this afforded such a witness access to classified information, and whether, in future cases, the trial judge would have any role in such a process.

The Jencks case, which had the effect of forcing new trials for several Communists indicted under the Smith Act, was jumped upon by critics as dangerous to national security. Many agreed with Justice Clark in his outspoken and near-inflammatory dissent that "unless the Congress changes the rule announced by the Court today, those intelligence agencies of our Government engaged in law enforcement may as well close up shop for the Court has opened their files to the criminal and thus afforded him a Roman holiday for rummaging through confidential information as well as vital national secrets."[52] Congress subsequently did enact a Jencks Act in late August, 1957, although the measure tightened up and made

51. Jencks *v.* U.S., 353 U.S. 657 (1957). Brennan at no point in his majority opinion made clear whether the decision was based on constitutional or statutory grounds. In addition, he quoted John Marshall out of context in an attempt to show that in the Burr trial Marshall had laid the basis for the principle he was here setting forth. See Walter F. Murphy, *Congress and the Court: A Case Study in the American Political Process* (Chicago, 1962), p. 121. Court critics were quick to pick up Brennan's error. See L. Brent Bozell, "Blueprint for Judicial Chaos," *National Review,* IV (July 20, 1957), 80–85.

52. *Ibid.,* pp. 681–682.

more precise the ambiguous terms of Brennan's ruling rather than openly and categorically rejecting it.[53]

Two decision days later, on what critics came to refer to as "Red Monday," June 17, 1957, the Court took further steps to upgrade the rights of the individual in dealing with the security power of governmental officials. In a decision so carefully written and fastidious in its drawing of legal distinctions as to be virtually undecipherable by the average layman,[54] Harlan brought an abrupt halt to further prosecutions under the Smith Act's organizing proscriptions.[55] He also drew a sharp distinction between advocating, advising, and teaching a course of action designed to facilitate overthrow of the government, which he maintained was punishable, and advocating, advising, and teaching such a course of action as "abstract doctrine," which he ruled was not. Since the immediate parties fell in the second category, the case had the effect of reversing the convictions of the top leaders of the Communist party in California, and by implication the leaders of other state parties throughout the country. Black, joined by Douglas, in a concurring opinion, while obviously pleased that the "calmer times" for which he had yearned in his Dennis dissent were returning, still decried the process of resuscitating the First Amendment by statutory construction, and maintained that the entire Smith Act should have been ruled unconstitutional.[56] Harlan next took on the State Department's loyalty dismissal of a high-level employee, John Stewart Service. He insisted that the Department, which had not been able to find formal grounds for dismissal after seven loyalty hearings, could not arbitrarily dismiss simply because its leaders desired such action.[57] The

53. 71 Stat. 595 (1957). See Robert G. McCloskey, "Useful Toil or Paths of Glory?," *Virginia Law Review,* XLIII (1957), 803; David Fellman, "Constitutional Law in 1956–57," *American Political Science Review,* LII (1958), 159; and "The Jencks Legislation: Problems in Prospect," *Yale Law Journal,* LXVII (1958), 674–699.

54. Walter Murphy refers to the opinion as a "model of technical correctness and dullness," containing no vivid phrase which might have been a rallying cry for its champions. Murphy, *Congress and the Court,* p. 122.

55. Yates *v.* U.S., 354 U.S. 298 (1957). See Robert Mollan, "Smith Act Prosecutions: The Effect of the Dennis and Yates Decisions," *University of Pittsburgh Law Review,* XXVI (1965), 725 ff.

56. *Ibid.,* p. 339. See Daniel M. Berman, "Constitutional Issues and the Warren Court," *American Political Science Review,* LIII (1959), 500–502.

57. Service *v.* Dulles, 354 U.S. 363 (1957).

case marked the first participation in a major security decision by recently appointed Justice Charles Evans Whittaker, who, observers noted carefully, sided with the liberal majority.[58]

Warren, who earlier had raised the Court's collective eyebrows regarding H.U.A.C.'s procedures, now dealt a crippling blow to that body's investigatory activities, and for good measure, struck at what he considered to be similar abuse of power on the part of the "Red" hunting Attorney General of New Hampshire, Louis Wyman. Warren's opinions clearly reflected his own strong sense of the unwarranted injustice visited upon witnesses by committee arbitrariness. In the federal Watkins case,[59] he traced the history of H.U.A.C., condemning its broad-scale intrusion into the lives and affairs of private citizens, and scolded Congress, in granting it its "hunting license," for affording it the authority to investigate things "un-American" without the guidelines of a practical definition of that term. Investigations in the future, Warren made clear, would, in the eyes of his Court, have to be related clearly and explicitly to a legitimate legislative purpose. "There is no Congressional power to expose for the sake of exposure." In the New Hampshire case,[60] the Chief Justice, assisted by strong, academic-freedom-oriented, concurring opinions by Harlan and Frankfurter, struck out at the badgering of a left-wing college professor, Paul M. Sweezy, who had been invited to speak at the state university. The decision again cut away sharply at state activities in the loyalty-security area and, as in the Watkins case, curtailed sharply the investigatory power of public officials, particularly when such power came from ambiguous and sweeping types of legislative authorization.

A week later, the Court closed the term on a note of further activism. In a Washington, D.C., case involving a Negro, Andrew

58. Whittaker, a lifelong Republican, had had a brief career as an Eisenhower-appointed federal district judge and a member, since 1956, of the United States Court of Appeals. His judicial philosophy seemed to be closer to the Frankfurter wing, and his general position of self-restraint was predicted at the time. See Daniel M. Berman, "Mr. Justice Whittaker; A Preliminary Appraisal," *Missouri Law Review,* XXIV (1959), 1–15; and Marlin M. Volz, "Mr. Justice Whittaker," *Notre Dame Lawyer,* XXXIII (1958), 159–179.

59. Watkins *v.* U.S., 354 U.S. 178 (1957). On the case see Allan L. Bioff, "Watkins *v.* United States as a Limitation on Power of Congressional Investigating Committees," *Michigan Law Review,* LVI (1957), 272–284.

60. Sweezy *v.* New Hampshire, 354 U.S. 234 (1956).

Mallory, who had confessed to raping a white woman, a unanimous Court, speaking through Justice Frankfurter, dismissed the conviction on the grounds that law-enforcement officers had not arraigned the Negro until seven and a half hours after his arrest, and during that delay had obtained a full confession through use of a lie detector and other intimidating devices that the mentally retarded youth had not understood.[61] The majority, however, was far less concerned about the unreliable character of the confession than they were in making sure that law-enforcement officers be deprived of the fruits of their violation of the federal criminal code, which required that any arraignment must take place "without unnecessary delay." The ruling, imposing sharp restriction on law-enforcement officials in the District that Congress administered, touched off bitter criticism from the District's press and the District's chief of police. The latter charged that the Court's position had endangered law enforcement in an area in which racial relations were particularly explosive.[62]

Congressional reaction, guarded before, was now openly critical. Although liberals, such as Senator Thomas Hennings of Missouri, publicly applauded the Court for its wisdom and courage,[63] hostile

61. Mallory *v.* U.S., 354 U.S. 449 (1957). On the question of coerced confessions, the Court had generally ruled for the appellant. In a complex but explosive case involving use of a psychiatrist trained in hypnosis, the Court had set aside a murder conviction on the grounds that it had been extracted involuntarily by methods violative of due process. Leyra *v.* Denno, 347 U.S. 556 (1954). A similar ruling freed an Alabama Negro who had been interrogated intermittently over a period of eleven days, denied a preliminary hearing required under Alabama law, and denied counsel. Fikes *v.* Alabama, 352 U.S. 191 (1957). Likewise, a conviction for murder was not permitted to stand, when, despite other adequate supporting evidence, it rested in part upon a confession extracted from a mentally ill, nineteen-year-old boy who was arrested without a warrant, never taken before a magistrate and advised of his right to counsel and to remain silent, held incommunicado for three days, given only one meal and two sandwiches in forty hours, and told by the sheriff that only through a confession could he be protected from a mob of thirty or forty people assembled outside the jail. Payne *v.* Arkansas, 356 U.S. 560 (1958).

62. See Donald J. Kemper, *Decade of Fear: Senator Hennings and Civil Liberties* (Columbia, Mo., 1965), pp. 147–148; and Special Subcommittee to Study Decisions of the Supreme Court, House Committee on the Judiciary, *Hearings on Mallory v. United States* (1957). For scholarly comment see James E. Hogan and Joseph M. Snee, "The McNabb-Mallory Rule: Its Rise, Rationale and Rescue," *Georgetown Law Journal,* XLVII (1958), 1–44; and C. C. Abeles, "The McNabb Rule: Upshaw through Mallory," *Virginia Law Review,* XLIII (1958), 915–932.

63. Kemper, *Decade of Fear,* pp. 164, 173–176; Murphy, *Congress and the Court,* pp. 180–181.

A TREE GROWS AND GROWS IN WASHINGTON

Critics of growing judicial activism in the 1950's urged Congressional curtailment, a call aimed particularly at Senate leader Everett Dirksen. (L. D. Warren, Cincinnati *Enquirer*)

voices were more numerous and much more shrill. During the latter stages of the debate on the 1957 Civil Rights Act, Senator William Jenner of Indiana introduced an omnibus anti-Court bill "to limit the appellate jurisdiction of the Supreme Court in certain cases," charging that "by a process of attrition and accession, the extreme liberal wing of the Court has become a majority; and we witness today the spectacle of a Court constantly changing the law, and even changing the meaning of the Constitution, in an apparent determination to make the law of the land what the Court thinks it should be."[64] Jenner's measure would have stripped the Court of appellate jurisdiction in cases involving the validity of the functions of Congressional committees, the security programs administered by the executive branch, state laws and regulations dealing with subversion, the acts and policies of boards of education designed to deal with subversion, and the acts of state courts and boards of bar examiners concerning admissions to the practice of law in their states.

Subsequently, Congressman Howard Smith of Virginia, a conservative banker, segregationist, and author of the Smith Act, introduced legislation to limit the discretion of the Court in construing statutes of Congress as preempting fields of legislation for the government and withdrawing them from state control.[65] Pressure also grew from angry law-enforcement officials for overriding the effect of the Mallory decision by amending the Federal Code of Criminal Procedure to provide that no confession could be inadmissible solely because of delay in taking an arrested person before an arraigning officer.[66]

Such legislative proposals were a conspicuous feature of the entire session of the Eighty-fifth Congress, going from committee to subcommittee to floor and in several instances reaching the voting stage in one house or the other. Generally the bills were reported on favorably by the Senate Judiciary Committee, a somewhat ironic

64. *Congressional Record,* 85th Cong., 1st Sess., p. 12806. On the background of the measure see Morgan, *Congress and the Constitution,* pp. 269 ff. Senator Hennings, during the course of the proceedings, wrote Judge Learned Hand for an opinion on the Jenner bill. Hand's strongly negative assessment was highly persuasive in the Senate in encouraging opponents of the measure. Katcher, *Earl Warren,* p. 392.

65. Murphy, *Congress and the Court,* pp. 91–92.

66. Kemper, *Decade of Fear,* pp. 103–104; Murphy, *Congress and the Court,* pp. 177–181, 206–207, 221–223.

twist in light of that body's earlier vigorous denunciation of Roosevelt's 1937 "Court-packing" plan on the grounds that an "independent judiciary was the only certain shield for individual rights." Jenner's measure, which its proponents quickly perceived as too ambitious, was later rewritten as the Jenner-Butler Bill, with a number of specific statutes substituted as more direct devices for counteracting disliked Court rulings.[67]

Eventually, and as the result, primarily, of parliamentary maneuvering, none of the strongly anti-Court measures was enacted. Thus a Congress that had granted the President virtually unlimited constitutional authority in the use of American military and economic resources for the conduct of foreign policy,[68] but conversely had set out to emasculate judicial authority, was turned away from taking formal action in the latter regard. Even so, the fact that the Court was clearly under a kind of indirect fire throughout its entire 1957–58 term, had a pronounced effect upon its rulings. Thus, although Anthony Lewis was probably correct a few years later in suggesting that its critics were really more interested in changing its orientation than its jurisdiction or technical authority,[69] their formal suggestions did have the effect of calling public attention to specific judicial action, a development to which the Court reacted with a new note of care and caution.[70]

67. Morgan, *Congress and the Constitution,* 287–291. Republican John M. Butler, the Senate leader for limiting the appellate jurisdiction of the Supreme Court, had, somewhat ironically, been so impressed with the Court's Steel Seizure ruling in 1952, that shortly after it was handed down, he had introduced an American Bar Association–sponsored joint resolution to amend the Constitution by removing from Congress its power to limit appellate jurisdiction of the Supreme Court. Murphy, *Congress and the Court,* p. 78.

68. In the Middle East Resolution, enacted in March, 1957, the Congress had responded to a request by President Eisenhower in passing a resolution authorizing him to give military and economic assistance to Middle East nations, adding that "if the President determines the necessity thereof, the United States is prepared to use armed forces to assist any nation or group of nations requesting assistance against armed aggression from any country controlled by international communism." *Congressional Record,* 85th Cong., 1st Sess., p. 2232. On the legislative history of the measure see Morgan, *Congress and the Constitution,* pp. 204–225.

69. Anthony Lewis, "The Supreme Court and Its Critics," *Minnesota Law Review,* XLV (1961), 305–322. See also Harold W. Chase, "The Warren Court and Congress," *Minnesota Law Review,* XLIV (1960), 595–639.

70. One of the most interesting countermoves to the Eighty-fifth Congress's sustained assault on the Court came by Senator Jacob Javits of New York, who in early 1959 introduced a proposal to place the appellate jurisdiction of the

Defenders of the Warren Court in the late 1950's saw it as a major obstacle to the abuse of citizens' rights. (From *Herblock's Special for Today,* Simon & Schuster, 1964)

The most obvious and direct effect of the congressional pressure was to create new tensions within the body itself. Up to the fall of 1957, Frankfurter had been consistently voting with the Chief Justice and the liberal-activist wing of the Court on a number of key issues.[71] Sensitive to the growing charge that the Court, even though

Court over constitutional issues beyond legislative interference. The Judiciary Committee subcommittee held a one-day hearing on the proposal which was promptly buried in committee. See *Congressional Record,* 86th Cong., 1st Sess., pp. 2996–2997. See also *The New York Times,* May 29, 1959, p. 8.

71. Despite this fact, Warren assigned him few majority opinions to write, in the 1957 term, for example, assigning him none of the opinions in any of the fourteen civil liberties cases in which they voted together. See S. Sidney Ulmer, "Supreme Court Behavior and Civil Rights," *Western Political Quarterly,* XIII (1960), 293.

resorting primarily to statutory construction, had assumed for itself the role of judging policy rather than law, he now eased back toward his earlier self-restraint posture. In March, 1958, in *Trop* v. *Dulles,* he split openly with the Chief Justice in a case that afforded him a good platform to express his views. Warren had ruled a section of the Nationality Act of 1940, which prescribed loss of citizenship for desertion from the armed services, unconstitutional as "cruel and unusual punishment" forbidden by the Eighth Amendment. To him such punishment did violence to civilized standards by taking away the "right to have rights." "It is not easy to stand aloof and allow want of wisdom to prevail," Frankfurter wrote, "but it is not the business of this Court to pronounce policy." "Self-restraint is the essence of the judicial oath," he went on, "for the Constitution has not authorized the judges to sit in judgment on the wisdom of what Congress and the Executive Branch do."[72]

Warren replied in equally forceful and revealing language. "We are oathbound to defend the Constitution. This obligation requires that Congressional enactments be judged by the standards of the Constitution. . . . We cannot push back the limits of the Constitution merely to accommodate challenged legislation. We do well to approach this task cautiously, as all our predecessors have counseled. But the ordeal of judgment cannot be shirked."[73] Observers now watched closely to see who would prevail.

The effect of these pressures in various areas of judicial concern during the term was clear. Concessions to conservatism came in a number of judicial retreats in the session. On the same day as the Trop ruling, the Court, speaking through Justice Frankfurter, held that under a section of the same Nationality Act of 1940, Congress could deprive a person of citizenship for voting in a foreign election on the grounds that this was a reasonable exercise of the power to regulate foreign affairs.[74] Two months later, the same justice blew the bugle of retreat on the preemption issue. Over dissents by War-

72. Trop *v.* Dulles, 356 U.S. 86, 127–28 (1958).

73. *Ibid.*, pp. 103–104.

74. Perez *v.* Brownell, 356 U.S. 44 (1958). See John P. Roche, "The Loss of American Nationality: The Development of Statutory Expatriation," *University of Pennsylvania Law Review,* XCIX (1950), 25–71; Leonard B. Boudin, "Involuntary Loss of American Nationality," *Harvard Law Review,* LXXIII (1960), 1510–1531; and Eleanor M. Kraft, "Constitutional Law: Citizenship: Statutory Expatriation," *Cornell Law Review,* XLIV (1959), 593–600.

ren and Douglas, he held that the Wagner and Taft-Hartley Acts did not preempt the field of labor relations. State courts were free, he maintained, to entertain damage suits against a union, by union members who had been expelled from the organization.[75]

Conservatives also saw as conciliatory two rulings on June 30, 1958, granting concessions to local security actions. *Beilan* v. *Board of Education* concerned a Philadelphia schoolteacher discharged for "incompetence" after refusing to answer questions from the superintendent as to possible Communist party affiliations. The teacher had also resorted to the Fifth Amendment before the House Un-American Activities Committee.[76] Conservative claim that the decision was a rejection of the earlier Slochower position, however, was exaggerated since Justice Burton, speaking for the majority, carefully distinguished between the dismissal in this case, which unlike the earlier was not for a specific charge of disloyalty. In *Lerner* v. *Casey,* the Court upheld the dismissal of a New York subway employee who invoked the Fifth Amendment.[77] But again, such invocation was not made the key point to the dismissal—rather other aspects of the employee's doubtful trust and reliability were stressed.

On the other hand, a number of actions by the high bench during the term suggested that while retreat might take place in certain areas, resoluteness would prevail in others. In December, 1957, it clearly precluded the use of wiretap data, achieved through a state-issued warrant in federal court proceedings,[78] and in January it threw out a city ordinance clearly being used to prevent recruitment of union members as an unwarranted prior restraint on freedom of speech.[79] Frankfurter, in dissent, protested that such action was an unwarranted judicial infringement upon state and local discretion. In June, it ruled sharply against denial of a passport to prominent left-wing figures Rockwell Kent and Weldon B. Dayton, even though Justice Douglas, for the Court, carefully avoided reaching the constitutional question of the right to travel and turned his majority

75. International Association of Machinists *v.* Gonzales, 356 U.S. 617 (1958).

76. Beilan *v.* Board, 357 U.S. 399 (1958).

77. Lerner *v.* Casey, 357 U.S. 468 (1958).

78. Benanti *v.* U.S., 355 U.S. 96 (1957). See Edwin J. Bradley and James E. Hogan, "Wiretapping: From Nardone to Benanti and Rathbun," *Georgetown Law Journal,* XLVI (1958), 418–442.

79. Staub *v.* Baxley, 355 U.S. 313 (1958).

opinion on the fact that the Secretary of State had relied upon erroneous statutory interpretation in his passport denial.[80] Further, on the same day that Burton and Harlan were sustaining the dismissal of the teacher and the public employee, Justices Brennan and Douglas were ruling that California constitutional and statutory provisions that made tax immunity for religious and charitable institutions dependent upon loyalty oaths did not meet basic requirements of procedural due process.[81] And Justice Harlan spoke for a unanimous Court in denouncing Alabama's efforts to drive the N.A.A.C.P. out of the state by demanding the names and addresses of all the members of the organization.[82]

The term thus ended with the Court more sharply divided than it had been since Warren's appointment. But although Congress again moved to chop away at its rulings, and even the President expressed annoyance regarding its passport decisions, such critical positions drew less support than had the inflammatory proposals of the Eighty-fifth Congress.[83]

Thus despite further sharp critiques from the Conference of Chief Justices of the States, and a Special Committee on Communist Tactics, Strategy, and Objectives of the American Bar Association,[84]

80. Kent *v.* Dulles, 357 U.S. 116 (1958).

81. Speiser *v.* Randall, 357 U.S. 513 (1958); First Unitarian Church *v.* Los Angeles, 357 U.S. 545 (1958).

82. N.A.A.C.P. *v.* Alabama *ex rel* Patterson, 357 U.S. 449 (1958). On the background of such legislation generally see Walter F. Murphy, "The South Counterattacks: The Anti-NAACP Laws," *Western Political Quarterly,* XII (1959), 371–390. See also Joseph B. Robison, "Protection of Associations from Compulsory Disclosure," *Columbia Law Review,* LVIII (1958), 614–649; and Leon R. Yankwich, "The Right of Privacy," *Notre Dame Lawyer,* XXVII (1952), 499–528.

83. Eisenhower had asked Congress for emergency legislation to allow the State Department to continue its policies concerning issuance of passports, but bills were already pending in Congress on the subject and both got lost in the last days of the Congress as other items got higher priority. See C. Herman Pritchett, *Congress Versus the Supreme Court* (Minneapolis, 1961), pp. 89–95.

84. Both statements are reprinted in Pritchett, *Congress Versus the Supreme Court,* pp. 137–159. Basic to the report of the Conference of Chief Justices were such articles as Philip B. Kurland, "The Supreme Court, The Due Process Clause, and the *in personam* Jurisdiction of State Courts," *University of Chicago Law Review,* XXV (1958), 569–624; Roger C. Cramton, "Pennsylvania v. Nelson: A Case Study in Federal Pre-Emption," *University of Chicago Law* Review, XXVI (1958), 85–108; Francis A. Allen, "The Supreme Court, Federalism and State Systems of Criminal Justice," *University of Chicago Law School Record,*

the drama of Congress versus the Supreme Court was declining. At the same time, however, a drama with equally important constitutional implications was reaching a legal showdown in Little Rock, Arkansas. Once again the Court was to be plunged into the center of national controversy, this time in defense of executive, and to a certain extent congressional, policy.

The four years since the initial Brown decision had seen interesting patterns emerge in the area of race relations. In line with the Court's new interpretation of the equal protection clause, dozens of suits were filed, largely in federal district courts, attacking explicit aspects of the legal structure of racial segregation. The legal division of the N.A.A.C.P., particularly its counsel Thurgood Marshall, rendered valuable support in many. The result was to see the courts strike down a wide range of segregation patterns in municipal facilities including public parks,[85] bathing beaches[86] and swimming pools,[87] public housing facilities,[88] golf courses,[89] and, in a case growing out of the celebrated Montgomery, Alabama, bus boycott, segregation in local and state transportation systems.[90]

VIII (1958), spec. suppl., 3 ff.; and Bernard D. Meltzer, "The Supreme Court, Congress and State Jurisdiction over Labor Relations," *Columbia Law Review*, LIX (1959), 6–60, 269–302. See also William B. Lockhart, "A Response to the Conference of State Chief Justices," *University of Pennsylvania Law Review*, CVII (1959), 802–810; William O. Douglas, "The Supreme Court Will Not 'Take a Back Seat,'" *The New York Times*, Nov. 9, 1958, p. 1; John Marshall Harlan, "Address Before the New York County Lawyers Association," *The New York Times*, Nov. 26, 1958, p. 31; and Robert J. Steamer, "Statesmanship or Craftsmanship: Current Conflict Over the Supreme Court," *Western Political Quarterly*, XI (1958), 265–277. Liberal forces within the American Bar Association sought to counter the A.B.A. critique with a position that, analyzing the same opinions, arrived at largely opposite results. The maneuver was fought bitterly by conservatives within the body but, although not approved, tempered somewhat the sting of the initial condemnation. See Murphy, *Congress and the Court*, pp. 226–227.

85. Holcombe, Mayor of Houston *v.* Beal, 193 F. (2d) 384 (1951), cert. den., 347 U.S. 974 (1954).

86. Mayor & City Council of Baltimore *v.* Dawson, 350 U.S. 877 (1955).

87. City of St. Petersburg *v.* Alsup, 238 F. (2d) 830 (1956), cert. den., 353 U.S. 922 (1957).

88. Housing Authority of San Francisco *v.* Banks, 120 Cal. App. (2d) 1 (1953), cert. den., 347 U.S. 974 (1954).

89. New Orleans Park Assn. *v.* Detiege, 358 U.S. 54 (1955).

90. Gayle *v.* Browder, 352 U.S. 903 (1956). See also Wolfe *v.* North Carolina, 364 U.S. 177 (1960). For background see Martin Luther King, Jr., *Stride Toward Freedom: The Montgomery Story* (New York, 1958).

But while Southerners seldom fought the courts vigorously at this level, their commitment to massive resistance in their opposition to school desegregation intensified. From a constitutional standpoint, such opposition took interesting forms. Senator Eastland of Mississippi publicly proclaimed open defiance. "The South," he stated, "will not abide by nor obey this legislative decision by a political court."[91] Senator Richard Russell of Georgia suggested that the Court was a "pliant tool" and a "political arm of the executive branch of the government," and called for its power to be curbed.[92] On the positive side, southern state legislatures immediately went into action passing a wide range of statutes to afford legal "interposition" to prevent the federal policy that the Supreme Court had announced from being put into effect.[93] Such legislation included pupil-assignment or placement laws intended to permit local school boards to shuffle students among districts so as to maintain segregation; "freedom-of-choice" laws designed to prevent or reduce the possibility of children of one race being forced to attend school with children of another; tuition-grant plans, providing children who wished to attend other than public schools with state financial support for such action; and even measures closing the public schools or providing for the withholding of public funds from any school that was desegregated.[94] Teachers, in turn, were assailed, with a number of southern legislatures prescribing discipline of teachers for violation of state policies on the school

91. Quoted in Lucius J. and Twiley W. Barker, *Freedoms, Courts, Politics, Studies in Civil Liberties* (Englewood Cliffs, N.J., 1965), p. 177. See also Muse, *Ten Years of Prelude,* p. 20, and "The South vs. the Supreme Court," *Look,* XX (Apr. 3, 1956), 23–47.

92. Barker and Barker, *Freedoms, Courts, Politics,* p. 177.

93. For an analysis of patterns of compliance and defiance see Robert R. McKay, "With All Deliberate Speed: A Study of School Segregation," *New York University Law Review,* XXXI (1956), 991–1090. See also Albert Blaustein and Clarence Ferguson, *Desegregation and the Law* (New Brunswick, N.J., 1962), pp. 210 ff.; Hubert H. Humphrey (ed.), *Integration* v. *Segregation* (New York, 1964), pp. 91–150; Peter A. Carmichael, *The South and Segregation* (Washington, 1965); and Reed Sarratt, *The Ordeal of Desegregation: The First Decade* (New York, 1966).

94. See, for example, Daniel Meader, "The Constitution and the Assignment of Pupils to Public Schools," *Virginia Law Review,* XLV (1959), 517–571; Southern Education Reporting Service, *Southern School News* (May, 1964), 5B–6B; Muse, *Ten Years of Prelude,* pp. 73 ff.; and Milton R. Konvitz, *Expanding Liberties: Freedom's Gains in Postwar America* (New York, 1966), Chap. 6.

segregation question. And in the face of mounting legal actions, ten of the eleven southern states enacted new laws or tightened old ones concerning barratry—the illegal solicitation of lawsuits.[95] Such actions were directed primarily at the N.A.A.C.P., whose lawyers were representing complainants in most school desegregation cases.

By early 1956, two significant actions had taken place. When a Negro, Autherine Lucy, was granted admission to the University of Alabama by a federal court order, "interposition" in the form of direct violence resulted. Alabama students, and large numbers of outside agitators, assumed the responsibility of driving Miss Lucy from the campus. Such violence succeeded temporarily, but shortly a U.S. district court judge ordered that she be readmitted, and was subsequently upheld by the Supreme Court.[96] At this point however, university officials expelled her permanently, claiming the action was necessary to avoid further violence. Significantly, no federal action was forthcoming in support of the federal judiciary.

In March, 1956, ninety-six members of the South's congressional delegation issued a Southern Manifesto, attacking the Supreme Court's desegregation decisions on constitutional grounds and commending those states "which have declared the intention to resist enforced integration by any lawful means."[97] Leadership for such action had come from Senator Harry F. Byrd of Virginia, whose own state had been a leader in creating programs of massive resistance. Coming in a Presidential election year, the action threw the gauntlet to Presidential candidates Dwight D. Eisenhower and Adlai Stevenson, both of whom deplored it. Each, however, took as the wise political tack, the course of stressing that the Southerners had committed themselves to support their efforts against integration only by "lawful means."

Once reelected, Eisenhower took cautious steps to go farther. With his Attorney General, Herbert Brownell, he pushed for federal

95. "The South's Amended Barratry Laws: An Attempt to End Group Pressures through the Courts," *Yale Law Journal,* LXXII (1963), 1613–1645.

96. Muse, *Ten Years of Prelude,* pp. 53–55; Anthony Lewis, *Portrait of a Decade: The Second American Revolution* (New York, 1964), pp. 107–108. For the case see Lucy *v.* Adams, 134 F. Supp. 235 (1955); for Supreme Court action, Lucy *v.* Adams, 350 U.S. 1 (1955).

97. *The New York Times,* Mar. 12, 1956, pp. 1, 19. See Robert McKay, "With All Deliberate Speed: Legislative Reaction and Judicial Development, 1956–1957," *Virginia Law Review,* XLIII (195), 1205–1245.

legislation to bring the federal government more directly into the civil rights area.[98] His requested Civil Rights Act would have created a bipartisan Civil Rights Commission to investigate violations, particularly of the right to vote, and would have increased the power of the Civil Rights Division in the Department of Justice, authorizing the Attorney General to initiate proceedings in civil rights cases. Incorporating a number of Harry Truman's previously unsuccessful civil rights proposals, the measure went to Congress in a new atmosphere of northern demands for positive action in the area of the attainment of greater racial equality.

The measure promptly met other forms of "massive resistance" as Southerners heading key congressional committees promptly set out to destory the bill through parliamentary maneuvering.[99] The measure that eventually emerged from the same Eighty-fifth Congress that had been so intent on limiting the Supreme Court's power, did little more than set up federal fact-finding agencies in areas where voting irregularities were charged.[100] Even these were defied in many parts of the South once the Commission sought to carry out its charge. Its one important contribution established for the first time uniform qualifications for federal jurors to insure more equitable racial composition of such bodies.[101]

Eisenhower, although expressing open disappointment at the weakness of the measure, reluctantly signed it into law on September 9, 1957. At just that time, however, he could have used a much stronger bill. For one week earlier, Governor Orval Faubus of Arkansas, an acknowledged segregationist, had ordered state troops into the city of Little Rock to prevent implementation of a federal

98. On the Eisenhower action see J. W. Anderson, *Eisenhower, Brownell, and the Congress: The Tangled Origins of the Civil Rights Bill of 1956–1957* (University, Ala., 1964).

99. Lewis, *Portrait of a Decade*, pp. 111–112.

100. 71 Stat. 634 (1957). For a digest of law and its legislative history, see Congressional Quarterly Service, *Revolution in Civil Rights* (Washington, 1965). For the work of the commission see Foster Rhea Dulles, *The Civil Rights Commission: 1957–1965* (East Lansing, Mich., 1968); and Wallace Mendelson, *Discrimination* (Englewood Cliffs, N.J., 1962).

101. In the following year, in Eubanks *v.* Louisiana, 356 U.S. 584 (1958), the Court underwrote the thrust of the provision condemning the state exclusion of Negroes from grand juries, insisting that "local tradition and the general thinking of the community cannot justify [noncompliance] with the constitutional mandate."

court order approving the admission of a handful of Negro students to that city's Central High School.[102]

Eisenhower's dilemma, however, was also partially self-induced. Walter Lippmann had observed correctly only a month earlier that in the field of achieving integration, "there is no policy." Further, Lippmann went on, "there is not only no policy, there is no program, no guidance, no rules on how to proceed. For the federal government, which has the duty of realizing the principle, has abstained from working out ways and means for realizing it."[103] Eisenhower was thus pushed to take positive executive action in support of integration for the first time, and his actions were thus landmarks and guidelines for the confrontation of further segregationist challenges.

Confronted with military defiance of federal authority, he reluctantly dispatched several companies of the United States Army to Little Rock under Section 333, Title 10, of the United States Code, which authorized the suppression of insurrection and unlawful combinations that hindered the execution of either state or federal law. He also nationalized, and thus neutralized, the Arkansas National Guard. The Black children thus attended school for a year under military protection and Arkansas's massive resistance was held at bay by bayonets.

The Little Rock School Board then turned back to the courts and obtained from a district court judge a two-and-a-half-year suspension of the integration program on the grounds that "conditions of chaos, bedlam, and turmoil" made this necessary. The United States Court of Appeals promptly reversed the stay[104] and the question was now squarely in the lap of the Supreme Court for resolution. The justices thus met in extraordinary session in August, 1958, to consider the cases.

For the Chief Justice, the situation was a significant one. Having

102. The literature on Little Rock is voluminous. See especially Brooks Hays, *A Southern Moderate Speaks* (Chapel Hill, N.C., 1959); Daisy Bates, *The Long Shadow of Little Rock* (New York, 1962); Loren Miller, *The Petitioners* (Cleveland, 1966), pp. 356–359; Dale Alford and L'Moore Alford, *The Case of the Sleeping People* (Little Rock, 1959); Muse, *Ten Years of Prelude*, pp. 122–45; and Lewis, *Portrait of a Decade*, pp. 46–69.

103. Walter Lippmann, "Integration Lacks Rules of Procedure," *Minneapolis Tribune*, Aug. 28, 1958, p. 6.

104. Aaron *v.* Cooper, 257 F. 2d 33 (1958).

just gone through a year in which congressmen and senators had called for a variety of proposals for undermining the Court's considered judicial policy, he was particularly sensitive to actions by state legislators or executive officials directly defying the orders of federal district courts. Upholding the circuit court, Warren, in an unprecedented decision signed independently by all nine of the justices, left no doubt as to the broad issue involved. "This case," he wrote, "involves a claim by the Governor and Legislature of a state that there is no duty on state officials to obey Federal court orders resting on this Court's considered interpretation of the United States Constitution. This claim we reject categorically."[105] "It is the legal and moral duty of every state official to follow the Court's interpretation of the Constitution." "No state official can war on the Constitution without violating his oath to support it," he went on, "or else the Constitution becomes a solemn mockery."[106] The ruling was thus a resounding endorsement of the President's cautious action, and, in the spirit of the supporters of the Civil Rights Act of the previous year, sought to achieve new levels of legal equality for Negro citizens.[107]

The case had nonlegal impacts as well, however, and particularly on the southern mind. During the arguments before the bench, the

105. In the argument before the Court, the attorney for the Little Rock School Board, Richard C. Butler, had aroused the Chief Justice, as well as other members of the bench, with his line of reasoning that the people of Arkansas were confused by statements from Governor Faubus and others that Supreme Court decisions were not the law of the land, and that a two-and-one-half-year delay of the integration program would provide time in which "a national policy could be established." Frankfurter's response was to demand to know "why the two decisions of this Court were not a national policy?" To this Butler replied that he felt they were until Governor Faubus had said he would call out the troops. This action, he insisted, gave the people of Arkansas "a right to have a doubt" about obeying Court orders. To this Warren replied, heatedly, "I have never heard such a statement made in a court of justice before. . . . I have never heard a lawyer say that the statement of a governor as to what was legal or illegal should control the action of any court." *The New York Times*, Aug. 31, 1958, Sec. 4, p. 1.

106. Cooper *v.* Aaron, 358 U.S. 1, 18 (1958). This did not close the issue, as Governor Faubus now moved to withhold funds from integrated schools. A three-judge federal district court struck down his action, however, and the Supreme Court sustained the court. Faubus *v.* Aaron, 361 U.S. 197 (1959).

107. Its constitutional implications were strong for federal-state relations as well. See Robert S. Rankin, *The Impact of Civil Rights upon Twentieth-Century Federalism* (Urbana, Ill., 1963).

United States Solicitor General, J. Lee Rankin, had deplored the example set by Little Rock officials. "I am not worried about the Negro children in Little Rock," he contended. "I worry about the white children who are told, as young people, that the way to get your rights is to violate the law and defy the lawful authorities."[108] The Court was now making clear that it would no longer tolerate such examples, and segregationists in the South found themselves forced to reassess their position in light of the obvious reality that all the power of the federal government would now be thrown behind the rulings of federal courts, and henceforth they could not count on a politically cautious executive to look away when defiance came. The point was also made by Congress, when Title I of the 1960 Civil Rights Act made it a federal crime for a person to obstruct or interfere with a federal court order, or to attempt to do so by threats of force.[109]

The Eisenhower administration during its last two years in office did not move strongly in the segregation area. Ordinarily it was content to confront direct challenges rather than to develop aggressive new approaches to the securing, particularly, of integrated school facilities. When it did move, as in Louisiana, in the fall of 1960, the Supreme Court was quick to support it. In the immediate situation it upheld the sharp decision by a federal district judge assailing the state's take-over of the New Orleans public schools to prevent court-ordered integration. The judge, Skelly Wright, had assailed the doctrine of interposition as an "amorphous concept," "a preposterous version of the Constitution," and "not a constitutional doctrine," and the Court in a per curiam opinion gave no indication of disagreeing.[110]

In other areas, where it was not called upon to implement administration acts, the justices moved cautiously. In June, 1959,

108. *The New York Times,* Sept. 14, 1958, Sec. 4, pp. 1–2.

109. 74 Stat. 86 (1960). On the measure see Daniel M. Berman, *A Bill Becomes a Law: The Civil Rights Act of 1960* (New York, 1962).

110. Bush *v.* Orleans School Board, 118 F. Supp. 916, 922, 926 (1960); and 364 U.S. 500 (1960). The occasion for the opinion stemmed from Louisiana's passage, in extraordinary legislative session, of twenty-five measures to prevent five first-grade Negro girls from being installed in all-white schools by the Orleans Parish School Board. The Court, on the other hand, refused to strike down an Alabama pupil placement law, even though its supporters had flaunted it as a scheme to defy integration.

they refused, speaking through Justice Douglas, to throw out a state literacy test, ruling that when impartially administered, it was allowable and not a violation of the Fifteenth Amendment. Douglas hastened to admit, however, that such a test, although fair on its face, might "be employed to perpetuate that discrimination which the Amendment was designed to uproot."[111] In early 1960, it blocked an attempt by Little Rock officials to force Daisy Bates, a local N.A.A.C.P. leader, to turn over that organization's records and membership lists, thus again cutting away at actions clearly designed to intimidate and harass civil rights advocates.[112] A week later, it reversed unanimously a Georgia Federal District Court ruling that had declared unconstitutional a portion of the 1957 Civil Rights Act. That section had permitted the Attorney General to institute civil suits and injunctive relief in voter registration cases.[113] On May 16, ten days after the passage of a second and stronger Civil Rights Act, it sustained action for declaratory and injunctive relief under the 1957 measure brought by Negro citizens. The state of Alabama had claimed that the Act did not authorize such relief even though charges were clear that voting rights had been denied by racially discriminatory practices. The Court ruled otherwise.[114] The general public was thus given notice that just as the justices were prepared to support executive action in advancing civil rights, it would support implementation of congressional action. And in light of the expanded 1960 Act, such a posture was encouraging to blacks and their white champions.

Public focus on the civil rights question, and judicial participation in it, tended to subordinate various actions of the Court in other areas to a minor position in the public eye. Here, Court actions also showed marked tendencies to acquiesce in executive and congressional leadership. This was particularly clear during the 1958–

111. Lassiter *v.* Northampton Election Board, 360 U.S. 45, 53 (1960).

112. Bates *v.* Little Rock, 361 U.S. 516 (1960). A month later, in a famous ruling, the "Shufflin' Sam" case, Thompson *v.* Louisville, 362 U.S. 199 (1960), the Court struck at another form of local harassment, the overzealous use of loitering and vagrancy statutes against unpopular individuals. Konvitz, *Expanding Liberties,* pp. 269–273.

113. U.S. *v.* Raines, 362 U.S. 17 (1960).

114. U.S. *v.* Alabama, 362 U.S. 602 (1960) The measure had been amended since its initial passage to afford such protection, a fact that Alabama had chosen to ignore.

59 term. The justices early in the session had again avoided ruling on key provisions of the Smith Act, ducking a challenge by an indicted Communist to its membership clause.[115] In three procedural cases in the spring of 1959, it showed caution in further nationalizing the procedural guarantees of the Bill of Rights against the states. In two cases involving double jeopardy, it sustained the conviction of two individuals, tried under state jurisdiction, who were subsequently tried under federal, even though the record was clear that state authorities, after failing to secure convictions, had turned material over to the federal government, requesting it to make a similar attempt.[116] In the search and seizure area, it gave a green light to health inspectors to search, without a warrant, premises suspected of harboring health hazards, making clear that here the Fourth Amendment right had to be balanced against the general welfare.[117]

June brought clear signs of further retreat. By this time membership had again changed, with Ohioan Potter Stewart having replaced Harold Burton at the beginning of the term, solidifying the conservative majority.[118] On June 8, 1959, Justice Clark, over the sharp dissent of Brennan, Warren, Douglas, and Black, virtually erased the earlier Sweezy ruling, and cut sharply at Warren's ruling in the Nelson case. The case again involved New Hampshire's one man antisedition committee, state Attorney General Louis Wyman, who had now transferred his attentions to a left-wing summer camp in the New Hampshire mountains. Although Brennan protested sharply that Wyman's investigations were conducted purely for the sake of exposure, and had no relevance to protecting the state from serious subversion, Clark disagreed. He denied that First Amendment rights of the defendant, Willard Uphaus, had been violated, and insisted that public interests overbalanced private ones in the security area. Addressing himself also to the question of

115. Scales *v.* U.S. 358 U.S. 917 (1958).

116. Bartkus *v.* Illinois, 359 U.S. 121 (1959); Abbate *v.* U.S., 359 U.S. 121 (1959).

117. Frank *v.* Maryland, 359 U.S. 360 (1959).

118. Stewart, following the pattern of Eisenhower appointees, was a Republican, and appointed by the President to a lower court judgeship. As a member of that Court of Appeals for the Sixth Circuit, Stewart had quickly gained a reputation for clear, concise opinions. See J. Francis Paschal, "Mr. Justice Stewart on the Court of Appeals," *Duke Law Journal,* (1959), 340–350. The youngest appointee, at forty-three, since Douglas, his views were clearly conservative, and self-restraint oriented. See Daniel M. Berman, "Mr. Justice Stewart, a Preliminary Appraisal," *University of Cincinnati Law Review,* XXIX (1959), 401–421.

federal preemption, Clark made clear that the majority for which he spoke did not feel that the battery of federal security laws precluded state action in the field. All the Nelson opinion proscribed, he maintained, was "a race between federal and state prosecutors to the courthouse door," and he contended that the state clearly had power to "proceed with prosecutions for sedition against the state itself."[119]

Harlan similarly renewed the broad "hunting license" of H.U.A.C., which Warren had curtailed so sharply in his Watkins rulings. Upholding the contempt conviction of a Vassar psychologist, Lloyd Barenblatt, for refusing to answer questions posed by the committee, he made clear that the power to investigate Communism "rests on the right of self-preservation," contending that the vagueness of the committee's charge from the House was not relevant as a factor in determining the sweep of its power. Such a sweep, his opinion made clear, should also not be limited too strictly by adherence to narrow legislative purpose.[120] The same spirit was clearly present in a case in the 1959 term, in which the Court upheld dismissal of public employees for invoking the Fifth Amendment before a subcommittee of that body.[121]

On the other hand, Warren was able to muster a liberal majority to apply new and more precise standards to the federal government's loyalty security program, now under attack by organizations as diverse as the New York City Bar Association and the League of Women Voters.[122] Although Harlan, in ordering reinstatement of an employee working in the Pacific Trust Islands who had been dismissed for security reasons, confined his opinion to condemnation of improper procedures on the part of the Secretary of the Interior in taking such action,[123] Warren, in a case involving security clearance for the vice president of a firm working on a Navy con-

119. Uphaus *v.* Wyman, 360 U.S. 72, 76 (1960). On the background of the case see Willard Uphaus, *Commitment* (New York, 1963).

120. Barenblatt *v.* U.S., 360 U.S. 109 (1959). See Michael Slotnick, "The Congressional Investigatory Power: Ramifications of the Watkins-Barenblatt Enigma," *University of Miami Law Review*, XIV (1960), 381–411; Alexander Meiklejohn, "The Barenblatt Opinion," *University of Chicago Law Review*, XXVII (1960), 328–340; and Harry Kalven, Jr., "Mr. Alexander Meiklejohn and the Barenblatt Opinion," *University of Chicago Law Review*, XXVII (1960), 315–328.

121. Nelson *v.* Los Angeles County, 362 U.S. 1 (1960).

122. See N.Y. City Bar Assn., *Fed. Loyalty-Security Program*.

123. Vitarelli *v.* Seaton, 359 U.S. 535 (1959).

tract, dealt a sharp blow to accepted methods of operating the whole security program.[124] Zeroing in particularly upon the government's use of anonymous information to deny clearance to classified information, he expressed irate hostility at such resort to "faceless informers," and made clear that the Court was unwilling to accept a security program that "is in conflict with our long accepted notions of fair procedures."[125] Although conservatives complained, and counteraction was proposed in Congress, the decision resulted, for once, in constructive remedy by the other branches. In early 1960, President Eisenhower issued an executive order[126] setting up a new industrial security program with vastly improved procedural safeguards, including fair hearings, and the right of confrontation and examination of all charges, under all ordinary circumstances, and the same spirit quickly came to prevail in the operation of other security programs.

The Court closed its term with a June 29 decision in an area into which it had been moving warily, but significantly, even though, as yet, public awareness of its position was slight.[127] Toward the end of the 1956–57 term, it had sought to clarify the law of obscenity so as to make it more realistic and practical in a modern context. Its majority was particularly concerned with what had become a national problem, the commercial exploitation of pornographic materials. It equally deplored the lack of national guidelines that the nation's many and varied local censors had in confronting the situation. Knowledgeable national leaders were clearly calling for such a move. Shortly after Frankfurter's February, 1957, Butler decision, the American Law Institute, a group of judges, scholars, and lawyers, proposed as part of its Model Penal Code a new standard for obscenity. The Institute argued that "society may legitimately seek to deter the deliberate stimulation and exploitation of emo-

124. Greene *v.* McElroy, 360 U.S. 474 (1959). See Joseph L. Rauh, Jr., "Nonconfrontation in Security Cases: The Greene Decision," *Virginia Law Review,* XLV (1959), 1175–1190.

125. *Ibid.,* pp. 506–507.

126. Executive Order 10865, *Federal Register,* XXV (1960), p. 1583. See *The New York Times,* Feb. 21, 1960, E7, pp. 4–8.

127. Barker and Barker, *Freedoms, Courts, Politics,* pp. 85–87. The fact that the Roth and Alberts cases came one week after the "Red Monday" cases, and that there was no indication at the time of how the Roth rule would be put into practice, undoubtedly accounts for much of the ignoring of the ruling.

tional tensions arising from the conflict between social convention and the individual's sex drive."[128]

In the Roth and Alberts cases of June, 1957, Justice Brennan examined the question in detail.[129] Arguing that from the outset of American history, the states had placed permissible legal restrictions on libel, slander, blasphemy, and profanity, he maintained that obscenity, as "material utterly without redeeming social importance," was not subject to First Amendment protection. "All ideas having even the slightest redeeming social importance—unorthodox ideas, controversial ideas, even ideas hateful to the prevailing climate of opinion—have the full protection of the guaranties," Brennan argued. "But obscenity is not within the area of constitutionally protected speech or press." The question remained, however, what was obscene, Brennan hastening to add that sex and obscenity were not synonymous. Obscene material, Brennan maintained, rejecting older and more rigid tests, is material which deals with sex in a manner appealing to prurient interest. The test of obscenity was to be a modern application of Judge Woolsey's landmark ruling in the 1933 Ulysses case.[130] It was whether or not "to the average person, applying contemporary community standards, the dominant theme of the material taken as a whole appeals to prurient interest." In setting forth such a definition, Brennan further made clear that the Court was concerned that in its application, standards "for judging obscenity safeguard the protection of freedom of speech and press for material which does not treat sex in a manner appealing to prurient interest."[131]

128. See James C. N. Paul and Murray L. Schwartz, *Federal Censorship: Obscenity in the Mail* (New York, 1961), pp. 141–142.

129. The Alberts *v.* California case was decided together with Roth *v.* U.S., 354 U.S. 476 (1957). On the Roth case see especially C. Peter Magrath, "The Obscenity Cases: Grapes of Roth," in Philip B. Kurland (ed.), *Supreme Court Review* (1966), 7–77; and William B. Lockhart and Robert C. McClure, "Censorship of Obscenity: The Developing Constitutional Standards," *Minnesota Law Review*, XLV (1960), 18–121.

130. U.S. *v.* One Book Called "Ulysses," 5 Fed. Supp. 182 (1933). The case had had limited importance as a precedent since it involved a federal customs regulation, and hence was a special situation not highly pertinent to local censorship problems.

131. Roth *v.* U.S., 354 U.S. 476, 487–488. Black and Douglas both dissented sharply, objecting strongly to the taking of any form of expression outside the First Amendment, and maintaining that that amendment was meant to be a block to censorship in any form.

The test, given the five clear variables within it, hardly added up to anything definite and precise, and clearly, since it would now apply both to printed material and to movies, it would have to take on legal preciseness as individual situations arose. This was made clear by the fact that on the same day it was set forth, the Court, in a case differing factually from Roth and Alberts, sustained action in New York State by public officials to prevent sale of material violative of a New York obscenity measure.[132]

In December, 1959, the Court added another dimension. Exploring the selling practices of obscenity distributors, it voted unanimously to invalidate a California law that made punishable mere possession by a bookseller of obscene literature, contending that unless the seller was clearly aware of what he was purveying, he could not justly be accused of "pandering."[133] The decision was indirect but positive endorsement of the A.L.I.'s position, and one stressed strongly by Warren in his concurring opinion in Roth, placing strong focus on the personal motives of the merchandiser of the product.

The June 29, 1959, case involved movie censorship, which the Court in 1952 had brought within First Amendment protection, but which was clearly to be subject to the Roth test as far as obscenity was concerned. Yet in the case, involving a movie version of D. H. Lawrence's celebrated novel *Lady Chatterley's Lover,* the Court unanimously threw out a ban on the film by the Regents of the University of the State of New York, who had deplored its setting forth of wrong ideas (in this case adultery) as "desirable, accepted, and proper forms of behavior."[134] The ruling left confused and unresolved the question of whether, if the justices could have agreed that the movie was obscene, they would have moved it out from under the umbrella of First Amendment protection. Thus the justices wound up the decade in the uncomfortable position of having tried to provide a workable standard for others to apply in the obscenity area, but with no takers, being forced to clarify it them-

132. Kingsley Books, Inc. *v.* Brown, 354 U.S. 436 (1957).

133. Smith *v.* California, 361 U.S. 147 (1959).

134. Kingsley Pictures Corp. *v.* Regents, 360 U.S. 684 (1959). See Ira H. Carmen, *Movies, Censorship and the Law* (Ann Arbor, 1966), pp. 96–100; and Richard S. Randall, *Censorship of the Movies: The Social and Political Control of a Mass Medium* (Madison, Wis., 1968), pp. 52–54.

selves by the trying process of applying it in different media, different situations, and to meet different challenges.[135]

As the Eisenhower years drew to a close, the success of the Court's carefully chosen role was measurable by a variety of yardsticks. The Court had indubitably reasserted its authority and no longer could be viewed as the mincing, acquiescent, issue-dodging body it had been under Vinson. But its very activism produced new waves of criticism, both from within and without. The fact that a Republican, sitting under a Republican President who had appointed him, was Chief Justice, clearly precluded partisan criticism. This was particularly true since the chief champions of the Court were liberal Democrats. The most vigorous congressional attacks had been carried on largely by a coalition of conservative Republicans and segregationist southern Democrats, resentful both of the Court's power and its policy directions. Undoubtedly the fact that the body and its leaders were identified in the public mind from the outset with the popular Brown ruling gave it a kind of general acceptance that made certain of its more controversial rulings less unpalatable. The same was true of its general willingness to accede to clear directions from Congress and the President on the few occasions when those were set forth. It had fully acquiesced in the 1954 Immunity Act, the Civil Rights Act of 1957, and the Jencks Act,[136] passed to clarify one of its own rulings. And when Eisenhower and the Justice Department took positive executive action in the civil rights area, the Court was a willing supporter.[137]

In evaluating the Court's course, it should be borne in mind that in the years between 1953 and 1960 it was given few clear and explicit prior guidelines to follow from either of the other two

135. The Court was split internally on a case-to-case approach, favored at this time by Frankfurter, Whittaker, and Harlan (who felt that in each instance there should be a careful judicial examination of both the film or book in question and the statute involved) and opposed by Black, who felt it turned the body into a "Supreme Board of Censors" when the application of standards of obscenity should be carried out by the local community, if anyone. See P. D. McNary, "Motion Picture Censorship and Constitutional Freedom," *Kentucky Law Journal* L (Summer, 1962), 440.

136. In the first cases under the Jencks Act, the Court sought carefully to conform to its provisions. See Rosenberg *v.* U.S., 360 U.S. 367 (1959); Palermo *v.* U.S., 360 U.S. 343 (1959).

137. See Robert A. Horn, "The Warren Court and the Discretionary Power of the Executive," *Minnesota Law Review,* XLIV (1960), 639–672.

branches. It thus had to appraise the climate of the period largely from the reactions that poured forth when its rulings became too aggressive. Thus its members labored under a felt need to accommodate its leader's aggressive desire for social justice, with the caution displayed by the other two branches of the government. To ignore those branches' general attitude regarding the need for stability in public law, and the danger of altering standards of social control too rapidly and radically, it was constantly aware, was to court a vocal hostility that clearly endangered its own credibility and authority.

The decade ended with the Court prepared to continue carrying on in the same fashion. Alert to the election returns in 1960 as a weathervane for what it might expect from a new executive and Congress, it hoped for clearer guidelines in the policy area. At the same time, there was little question that the majority of its members, and certainly its leader, expected it to continue to pull its weight no matter what the outcome.

CHAPTER 11

The New Frontier and the Constitution as an Instrument for Social Change

---

IN his campaign for the Presidency in 1960, John F. Kennedy sounded his commitment to the position that "we need to get America moving again." Playing constantly upon the turgidity and circumspection of the Eisenhower administration, his "New Frontier," he made clear, would be a dynamic one, calling the American people to face up to the dramatic challenges of a new and different world. "Ask not what America will do for you," Kennedy stated in his inaugural address, "but what together we can do for the freedom of man."[1] And that address, like the Democratic platform on which he ran, placed major focus upon the achievement of civil rights and civil liberties for all, "all too often disregarded by the previous Republican administration." Specifically the platform had attacked such "abuses" as "sullying the name and honor of loyal and faithful American citizens in and out of government, jeopardizing American rights by unfair loyalty and security proceedings; infringement upon the rights of American citizens to travel and pursue lawful trades and engage in other lawful activities," while proclaiming at the same time the need to create an "affirmative new atmosphere in which to deal with racial divisions and inequalities which threaten

1. Department of State *Bulletin,* Feb. 6, 1961, p. 3. On the "New Frontier" emphasis see Arthur M. Schlesinger, Jr., *A Thousand Days: John F. Kennedy in the White House* (Boston, 1965), p. 4.

both the integrity of our democratic faith and the proposition, on which our Nation was founded, that all men are created equal."[2]

That the new administration would pursue this announced policy, along with the others to which it was committed, was quickly evidenced as its new personnel assumed the reins of government. Drawing young and vigorous men and women to Washington, many from the liberal, intellectual community, the activism of the new administration quickly became its public trademark, tarnished though that image would become when a strong coalition of Republicans and conservative Democrats dug in their heels to oppose many of its new policies. Clearly the most dramatic question of the day, and the one that drew the most vigorous response from both advocates and critics, was the extension of civil rights.

The Civil Rights Acts of 1957 and 1960, for which the Republicans claimed full credit in their 1960 platform,[3] had been significant, if cautious, beginnings. The history of the enforcement of the 1957 measure had been one of constant frustration, and open defiance,[4] and in many respects the 1960 Act had been far more remedial than innovative, affording more rigid and explicit machinery for enforcing voting rights through court-appointed and voter referees to monitor situations in which disfranchisement was a threat, and requiring particularly the preserving of voting records and registration papers that had been deliberately destroyed earlier, before they could be examined by the Civil Rights Commission.[5] The Supreme Court, in turn, had complemented the measure. Only a week after Kennedy's election, it had struck down as unconstitutional an Alabama gerrymandering law that had been successfully used to disqualify Negro voters in Tuskegee from taking part in that predominantly Negro city's elections, thereby striking directly at an-

2. Kirk H. Porter and Donald B. Johnson, *National Party Platforms, 1840–1964* (Urbana, Ill., 1966), pp. 597–599.

3. Porter and Johnson, *National Party Platforms,* p. 618. The platform, clearly the product of the liberal, Rockefeller wing of the party, also stated: "We supported the position of the Negro school children before the Supreme Court. We believe the Supreme Court school decision should be carried out in accordance with the mandate of the Court."

4. See Foster Rhea Dulles, *The Civil Rights Commission: 1957–1965* (East Lansing, Mich., 1968); and Wallace Mendelson, *Discrimination* (Englewood Cliffs, N.J., 1962).

5. On the pasage of the measure see Daniel M. Berman, *A Bill Becomes a Law: The Civil Rights Act of 1960* (New York, 1962).

other southern attempt to invalidate the Negro franchise.[6] Negro leadership was also demanding Kennedy administration activism in the civil rights area. Roy Wilkins, N.A.A.C.P. chairman, called for immediate action to promote equal voting, education, employment, and other opportunities. Martin Luther King presented the President with a nearly one-hundred-page memorandum, indicating the sort of programs that Negro Americans considered minimal in light of the times.[7]

Initially the President was cautious. Fully cognizant of the difficulties engendered in pushing through the Civil Rights measures and the watering down that they had suffered, he was reluctant to go initially to Congress to call for new civil rights legislation. Rather he chose to resort to executive action as an initial device for advancing equality in various areas. On March 6, 1961, he created, by executive order, a new President's Committee on Equal Employment Opportunity.[8] The committee began its work a month later, quickly exhibiting the kind of energy and élan that civil rights advocates had sought in vain from the prior administration. By the end of its first year of operations it could boast that it had successfully adjusted more complaints in twelve months than had a previous Eisenhower committee in over seven years. It had begun the task of obtaining properly qualified personnel to implement the committee's program in the field; enlisted the active cooperation of the nation's leading manufacturers through its Plans for Progress campaign; and instituted a comprehensive compliance reporting system that required the employers of approximately 15 million workers to supply the committee with information that would greatly facilitate the promotion of equal employment opportunity.[9]

The same new tone was evident in other executive actions. Catching the public eye by informal challenging of segregation on a

6. Gomillion *v.* Lightfoot, 364 U.S. 339 (1960). On the case see Bernard Taper, *Gomillion v. Lightfoot, the Tuskegee Gerrymander Case* (New York, 1962).

7. Theodore C. Sorensen, *Kennedy* (New York, 1965), p. 476; Schlesinger, *Thousand Days,* p. 951.

8. Executive Order 10925, Mar. 7, 1961. See Harry Golden, *Mr. Kennedy and the Negroes* (Cleveland, 1964), pp. 82 ff.

9. Michael I. Sovern, *Legal Restraints on Racial Discrimination in Employment* (New York, 1966), pp. 105–106. See also Theodore W. Khell, *Report on the Structure and Operations of the President's Committee on Equal Employment Opportunity* (Englewood Cliffs, N.J., 1962).

variety of private fronts,[10] high administration officials left no doubt of their intention to carry through the Democratic platform's promise of "using the full powers of the government—legal and moral—to insure the beginning of good-faith compliance with the Constitutional requirement that racial discrimination be ended in public education."[11] All U.S. judges were put on notice that the government was determined to carry out the Constitution and court orders, regardless of political consequences. The Justice Department was encouraged to push both school segregation cases, and cases in other areas that would facilitate the end to discrimination, not only in public facilities, but also in voting rights. The task was accepted warmly by Burke Marshall, Kennedy's choice to head the Civil Rights Division, who early made clear that the law would not validate social change but induce it.[12] The Interstate Commerce Commission was prodded into issuing desegregation orders to southern interstate transportation companies and terminals and began entering cases, as amicus curiae, in suits brought by Negroes charging racial bias where segregation had been invalidated by law. When in early 1961 "freedom riders" chartered integrated bus trips into Dixie to test the desegregation of interstate travel facilities,[13] Attorney General Robert F. Kennedy sent several hundred federal marshals to Montgomery, Alabama, to confront the violence that such action had induced, placing the city under martial law and employing state national guardsmen and police to restore order. The practice of "sit-in" demonstrations, a technique begun by Negro students in early 1960 in southern lunch counters ostensibly serving

10. Kennedy administration officials deliberately tested a variety of Washington, D.C., color lines, refusing to speak before segregated audiences, boycotting segregated private clubs, and pressuring federal employee unions and recreation associations to relinquish segregation practices. See Sorensen, *Kennedy,* p. 477.

11. Porter and Johnson, *Party Platforms,* p. 599.

12. Golden, *Mr. Kennedy and the Negroes,* pp. 85, 141–142. For his own version of his activities see Burke Marshall, *Federalism and Civil Rights* (New York, 1964).

13. Donald B. King and Charles W. Quick (eds.), *Legal Aspects of the Civil Rights Movement* (Detroit, 1965), pp. 111–126. See also Anthony Lewis, *Portrait of a Decade: The Second American Revolution* (New York, 1964), pp. 87–93; and James Peck, *Freedom Ride* (New York, 1962). Robert S. Rankin and Winfried R. Dallmayr, *Freedom and Emergency Powers in the Cold War* (New York, 1964), pp. 228 ff., has a useful discussion.

the general public,[14] did not initially bring similar direct support. When cases began making their way through the courts involving the legality of such challenges to ancient segregation practices, however, Civil Rights Division attorneys were assigned to extend assistance to the rebuffed litigants.[15]

In November, 1962, Kennedy took a long-awaited step, prohibiting racial and religious discrimination in all housing built or purchased with federal aid.[16] The President had made much of Eisenhower's refusal to implement "with the stroke of the pen" a Civil Rights Commission recommendation that such an order be issued, but had dragged his feet on it, to the annoyance of Negro leaders. Nonetheless, when finally issued, it was widely hailed as an important step in breaking down the enforced residential segregation under which most Negroes lived.

The order came only two months after a civil rights showdown unprecedented since Civil War days. Growing southern hostility to the speed with which integration was being demanded and gained had led the governor of Mississippi to openly defy a federal court order ordering the admission of one Negro student, James Meredith, to that state's public university.[17] In light of continued defiance, which eventually resulted in a circuit court contempt citation for Governor Barnett,[18] Kennedy was forced to order federal troops to the scene, stating: "Our nation is founded on the principle that

14. King and Quick, *Legal Aspects of the Civil Rights Movement,* pp. 87–101. See also Earl L. Carl, "Reflections on the 'Sit-Ins,'" *Cornell Law Quarterly,* XLVI (1961), 444–457; and Frank E. Schwelb, "The Sit-In Demonstration: Criminal Trespass or Constitutional Right," *New York University Law Review,* XXXVI (1961), 779-809.

15. Sorensen, *Kennedy,* p. 480. Federal prerogatives at the time were limited, given the status of the law, which in this situation clearly favored racial discrimination. As yet there was no precedent for treating nongovernmental discrimination as the action of a state for the purposes of the Fourteenth Amendment. The Solicitor General of the time discussed the issue in Archibald Cox, *The Warren Court: Constitutional Decision as an Instrument of Reform* (Cambridge, Mass., 1968), pp. 31–41.

16. Executive Order 11063, *Federal Register,* XXVII (1962), 11527. For the literature on the subject see King and Quick, *Legal Aspects of the Civil Rights Movement,* pp. 441–443.

17. On the Meredith affair see Walter Lord, *The Past That Would Not Die* (New York, 1965); James Silver, *Mississippi: The Closed Society* (New York, 1966); and James Meredith, *Three Years in Mississippi* (Bloomington, Ind., 1966).

18. See Sheldon Tefft, "United States *v.* Barnett: ''Twas a Famous Victory,'" *Supreme Court Review* (1964), pp. 123–136.

observance of the law is the eternal safeguard of liberty and defiance of the law is the surest road to tyranny."[19] And although such resoluteness did not forestall further states' rights flouting of federal power—the governor of Alabama, George Wallace, shortly taking similar action[20]—the new administration's strong and unswerving determination to push ahead, in spite of all defiance, blocked out a policy that set clear guidelines for all within the federal government to follow.

The administration's civil rights attitude was certainly not lost upon the Supreme Court. Its membership fell clearly in line even though the sort of challenge presented to it demanded a different type of action. In early December, 1960, the justices had anticipated the I.C.C.'s future role, sustaining the use of the commerce clause of the Constitution to strike at segregation in a privately owned restaurant in an interstate bus terminal.[21] Four months later it had extended the principle to a private restaurant located within an off-street automobile parking building, owned and operated by an agency of the state of Delaware.[22] Although it turned the latter case on the equal protection clause of the Fourteenth Amendment, its thrust was clear. In the future the kind of "state action" that the amendment controlled would be interpreted so as to cover discriminatory action by parties even remotely connected with the state.

The Court also had continued to block established patterns of harassing proponents of civil rights, patterns fashioned by their enemies. In a widely reported case on December 12, 1960, it had struck down an Arkansas statute requiring public school teachers to file annual affidavits listing every organization to which they had belonged or regularly contributed during the preceding five years. These measures, clearly aimed to intimidate those with ties to

19. "President's Address on Mississippi Situation," *Congressional Quarterly Almanac,* XVIII (1962), 895.

20. Wallace, although threatening to "stand in the door way" of any schoolhouse under court order and defy the federal government to remove him, caved in quickly under federal confrontation at the University of Alabama. Lewis, *Portrait of a Decade,* pp. 189–191; Sorensen, *Kennedy,* p. 492; Schlesinger, *Thousand Days,* p. 964.

21. Boynton *v.* Virginia, 364 U.S. 454 (1960).

22. Burton *v.* Wilmington Parking Authority, 365 U.S. 715 (1961). On the case see Thomas P. Lewis, "Burton *v.* Wilmington Parking Authority—a Case Without Precedent," *Columbia Law Review,* LXI (1961), 1458–1467.

civil rights bodies, the Court denounced as a "comprehensive interference with associational freedom."[23] Later the same term, it continued on the same path, striking down a Louisiana attempt to drive the N.A.A.C.P. from the state on the grounds that it would not file an annual list of its membership and officers. It further denied that that body was under obligation to prove that its out-of-state members and officers were non-Communists.[24]

The clear, new, activist guidelines now afforded by the Kennedy administration reassured the justices in the civil rights area. The results again saw civil rights advances made judicially paralleling those being pushed by the executive department. The issues that the Court chose to adjudicate were in some cases new and in some cases merely refinements of earlier challenges. In *Garner* v. *Louisiana,* in December, 1961, the Court threw out the convictions of sit-in demonstrators for violating a "disturbing of the peace" statute. Chief Justice Warren, for a unanimous Court bench, could not see how Negroes remaining quietly in their seats at a lunch counter until served were engaging in "violent, boisterous, or disruptive acts," or behaving in "such a manner as to unreasonably disturb or alarm the public." He thus maintained that the convictions were so totally devoid of evidentiary support as to violate the due process clause of the Fourteenth Amendment.[25] Two months later, in a per curiam ruling, the Court sustained an appeal by Negroes seeking temporary and permanent injunctions to enforce their constitutional rights to nonsegregated service in interstate and intrastate transportation.[26] In May, 1962, it ordered integration of a Memphis airport restaurant clearly serving interstate passengers.[27]

Other cases were illustrative of the Court's continuing hostility to the use of legal devices for the intimidation of Negro civil rights supplicants. In January, 1963, the justices threw out Virginia's recently amended barratry statute. While not quarreling with the state's traditional right to regulate the conduct of lawyers, Justice Brennan made clear that such a right could not be used to deny

23. Shelton *v.* Tucker, 364 U.S. 479 (1960).

24. Louisiana *v.* N.A.A.C.P., 366 U.S. 293 (1961). See Harry Kalven, Jr., *The Negro & the First Amendment* (Chicago, 1965), pp. 74 ff.

25. Garner *v.* Louisiana, 368 U.S. 157 (1961); Kalven, *Negro & First Amendment,* pp. 125 ff.

26. Bailey *v.* Patterson, 369 U.S. 31 (1962).

27. Turner *v.* Memphis, 369 U.S. 350 (1962).

civil rights attorneys, in this case specifically N.A.A.C.P. attorneys, their freedom of speech to contact Negroes who might need legal counsel in civil rights cases.[28] *Edwards* v. *South Carolina* the following month raised the question of the permissible limits of freedom of speech involved in peaceful civil rights demonstrations, and the power of local authorities to break them up. In the immediate instance student civil rights marchers had disregarded police order to disperse, and had stayed on the State House grounds, singing patriotic and religious songs and listening to a "religious harangue" by one of their leaders. No violence or threat of violence was present. Returning to the 1949 Terminiello case, Justice Stewart for the Court fully sustained the Negroes and gave a shot in the arm to peaceful civil rights demonstrators. The courts of South Carolina have defined a criminal offense so as to permit conviction of the petitioners if their speech "stirred people to anger, invited public dispute, or brought about a condition of unrest," he wrote. "A conviction resting on any of those grounds may not stand."[29]

In March, the Court again returned to the freedom of association question. When Florida sought to drive the N.A.A.C.P. from that state on the grounds of its "subversive nature," the Court declared that a "substantial connection" must be shown to exist between an organization and illegal activities or objectives. In the case of the N.A.A.C.P., a five-man majority maintained, this "nexus" test was not met with regard to that body and Communist activities.[30]

28. N.A.A.C.P. *v.* Button, 371 U.S. 415 (1963). See "The South's Amended Barratry Laws: An Attempt to End Group Pressures through the Courts," *Yale Law Journal,* LXXII (1963), 1330–1341; and Milton Konvitz, *Expanding Liberties: Freedoms Gains in Postwar America* (New York, 1966), pp. 67–69.

29. Edwards *v.* South Carolina, 372 U.S. 229, 237–238 (1963). On this and pertinent subsequent cases see Harry Kalven, Jr., "The Concept of the Public Forum: Cox v. Louisiana," *Supreme Court Review* (1965), pp. 1–32.

30. Gibson *v.* Florida Legislative Investigating Committee, 372 U.S. 539 (1963). Southern opponents continued unsuccessfully to harass the organization, however. See N.A.A.C.P. *v.* Alabama, 377 U.S. 288 (1964). The Court's own civil rights advocacy was seen in an interesting Colorado case. When Colorado courts dismissed the complaint of a Negro applicant for a job as an airline pilot on grounds that this was a federal question, and the state Anti-Discrimination Law was superseded by federal law, the Court reversed the state and upheld the appellant's right under its law. Black for the Court maintained that "we are not convinced that commerce will be unduly burdened if Continental [Airlines] is required by Colorado to refrain from racial discrimination in its hiring of pilots in that State." Colorado Anti-Discrimination Commission *v.* Continental Air Lines, 372 U.S. 714 (1963).

The Court's most significant and dramatic constitutional move in this period, however, took place in May of 1963. In landmark rulings the Court raised in more explicit terms the whole question of "state action" in the area of segregated facilities. For years, southern merchants and professional men, supposedly serving the general public, had hidden behind a great, complex network of local segregation ordinances requiring segregation in a great range of privately owned facilities. Maintaining that as a result of these laws their "hands were tied," they had been able for years to strike the pose of being willing to integrate their facilities, but being unable to do so since such action would force them to break the law. In the five May cases,[31] the Court, for all practical purposes, "untied the hands" of such private parties, insisting not only that such laws could not be enforced, but maintaining that other kinds of local statutes—trespass ordinances, disorderly conduct laws, disturbing-of-the-peace statutes—could not be utilized to prevent integration of facilities serving the general public. Such "state action," it maintained, constituted clear violation of the equal protection clause of the Fourteenth Amendment.

The sit-in rulings, while not forcing integration of private facilities, clearly put strong moral pressure upon their owners to make them available, voluntarily, to all would-be patrons. The question remained whether such moral pressure would be acceded to. Douglas had maintained, in a concurring opinion, that "when the doors of a business are open to the public, they must be open to all regardless of race."[32] The Chief Justice, who wrote the majority opinion, was not prepared, however, to have the Court move to such a position or compel such action.[33]

But the Kennedy administration was already moving along those

31. Peterson *v.* City of Greenville, 373 U.S. 244 (1963); Shuttlesworth *v.* City of Birmingham, 373 U.S. 262 (1963); Lombard *v.* Louisiana, 373 U.S. 257 (1963); Gober *v.* City of Birmingham, 373 U.S. 374 (1963); Avent *v.* North Carolina, 373 U.S. 375 (1963). See also Wright *v.* Georgia, 373 U.S. 284 (1963), decided the same day, in which the Court sustained the right of Negro youths to play basketball in a public park in Savannah, Georgia. For a general discussion see Thomas P. Lewis, "The Sit-In Cases: Great Expectations," *Supreme Court Review* (1963), pp. 101–151.

32. Lombard *v.* Louisiana, 373 U.S. 267, 281 (1963).

33. In the weeks before the term ended, the Court had struck at segregation in public parks in Memphis, Watson *v.* Memphis, 373 U.S. 526 (1963); and at a pupil placement scheme in the Knoxville, Tennessee, public schools designed to preserve segregation. Goss *v.* Board of Education, 373 U.S. 683 (1963).

very lines. A day after the announcement of the sit-in rulings, Kennedy told a news conference that "as a result of the Supreme Court decision, yesterday, we are considering whether any additional proposals will be made to the Congress." Stressing that there were already proposals there dealing with voting, and extension of the Civil Rights Commission and the Conciliation Service, the President went on: "I think there may be other things that we could do which would provide a legal outlet for a desire for a remedy other than having to engage in demonstrations which bring them into conflict with the forces of law and order in the community."[34] The statement was a preview of the comprehensive measure that he shortly was to unveil.

The proposed Civil Rights Act could draw upon precedents of the Truman administration and even back a century in American history. Federally guaranteed access to all public facilities and accommodations had been an objective of the Radical Republicans of the post–Civil War period, only to be legally hamstrung by the famous Civil Rights Cases of 1883.[35] The failure of the Truman fight for a permanent F.E.P.C. plus open accessibility to housing and education had induced a number of states to pass legislation in the field. And even though patterns of compliance varied greatly, progress was evident in a number of northern areas.[36] The South was a different matter, however. Negro pressure for fair treatment and equal opportunity, especially in the form of open demonstrations, had resulted, in a number of areas, in official retaliation through the use of tear gas, clubs, fire hoses, police dogs, electric cattle prods, and indiscriminant jailing of Negro participants, even women and children. The behavior of Birmingham, Alabama, Police Commissioner Eugene "Bull" Connor especially, given wide publicity on television and in the press, caused, in millions of Americans, revulsion, shame,

34. Harold W. Chase and Allen H. Lerman, *Kennedy and the Press: The News Conferences* (New York, 1965), pp. 449–450.

35. The Civil Rights Cases, 109 U.S. 3 (1883).

36. Bureau of National Affairs, *State Fair Employment Practice Laws and Their Administration* (Washington, 1964); Milton R. Konvitz and Theodore Leskes, *A Century of Civil Rights* (New York, 1961), pp. 155–251; and Arnold H. Sutin, "The Experience of State Fair Employment Commissions: A Comparative Study," *Vanderbilt Law Review*, XVIII (1965), 965–1046.

and outrage, producing a clamor for uniform national standards to be enforced against local police brutality.[37]

On June 11, 1963, the President announced that he was sending to Congress a legislative proposal to provide "the kind of equality of treatment which we would want ourselves."[38] The Kennedy bill involved two broad and general principles. The first was a ban on discrimination in places of public accommodation. This kind of discrimination, more than any other, had been the object of Negro sit-ins, pickets, and demonstrations. Southerners promptly objected that the proposal was a violation of property rights, to which the President replied that property had its duties as well as its rights. The second gave authority to the Attorney General to seek desegregation of public education on his own initiative, particularly when lack of means or fear of reprisal prevented aggrieved students or their parents from doing so. The implementation of the Supreme Court's decision, the President made clear, could no longer be left solely to those who lacked the resources to bring suits or withstand intimidation.[39]

Promptly a bipartisan coalition of Northerners and Westerners, conscious of the elections of the following year, backed the bill with effective lobbying and set out to push it through the complex legislative channels. Southern reaction was strong and hostile, as was that of property-conscious conservatives, particularly members of the recently formed John Birch Society. A few hours after Negro leaders hailed Kennedy's speech as a Second Emancipation Proclamation, Medgar Evers, a prominent N.A.A.C.P. official in Mississippi, was shot in the back by an irate white racist, and on Capitol Hill a special caucus of southern senators vowed to block any civil rights legislation. Senator Barry Goldwater, shortly to become the Republican party's 1964 Presidential candidate, openly condemned the equal accommodations section and vowed to fight against it. On the

37. President Kennedy was fond of "paying tribute" to Connor whose brutality toward civil rights advocates had aroused the nation. See Leslie W. Dunbar, *A Republic of Equals* (Ann Arbor, 1966), p. 80.

38. Ianniello, *Milestones Along the March,* p. 98.

39. On the background of the measure see Donald G. Morgan, *Congress and the Constitution: A Study of Responsibility* (Cambridge, Mass., 1966), pp. 292–330; King and Quick, *Legal Aspects of the Civil Rights Movement,* pp. 303–327; and Bickel, *Politics and the Warren Court,* pp. 92–108.

other hand, civil rights leaders, sensing they had the support of many, called for a massive march on Washington in late August, and on the twenty-eighth of that month nearly 200,000 Negroes and whites joined in the greatest civil rights demonstration to date, meeting at the foot of the Lincoln Memorial to call for "jobs and freedom."[40]

John F. Kennedy was not to live to see the measure enacted. Felled by an assassin's bullet on November 22, 1963—an action that eventually produced a broad-scale and controversial investigation by a commission headed reluctantly by Chief Justice Warren[41]—the duty of shepherding the measure through to law fell to his successor, Lyndon B. Johnson.

Skeptics from the outset were dubious about the enthusiasm that the former Texas senator would throw into such a campaign. They were surprised and pleased when Johnson, as a national leader cut free from his southern constituency and obligations, proved a more effective champion than Kennedy had been. The new President, meeting promptly with Negro leaders, assured them of his determination to see the bill through without compromise; and on July 2, 1964, after an effective bipartisan campaign in Congress led by Senators Dirksen and Humphrey, the bill was signed into law as the Civil Rights Act of 1964.[42] The measure brought the legislative branch up even with the executive and judicial in the crusade for civil rights for all Americans.

The 1964 Civil Rights Act contained eleven titles covering a vast number of subjects from education and accommodations to the creation of new techniques for the achievement of the integration principle. It particularly gave the Attorney General the green light to proceed with positive federal moves to attain the ends that private citizens had previously had to seek through the courts. Appropriate action was immediately forthcoming and a number of suits were

40. Benjamin Muse, *Ten Years of Prelude* (New York, 1964), pp. 272–274; King and Quick, *Legal Aspects of the Civil Rights Movement*, pp. 272–274; and Lewis, *Portrait of a Decade*, pp. 253–257.

41. On Warren's attitude toward accepting the assignment see Leo Katcher, *Earl Warren: A Political Biography* (New York, 1967), pp. 456–457; and John D. Weaver, *Warren: The Man, the Court, the Era* (Boston, 1967), pp. 302–303.

42. 78 Stat. 241 (1964). On Johnson's role see Rowland Evans and Robert Novak, *Lyndon B. Johnson: The Exercise of Power* (New York, 1966), pp. 376–380; and Jack Bell, *The Johnson Treatment* (New York, 1965), pp. 165–175.

begun to break down defiance previously unchallengeable due to the inability of the federal government to bring pressure. This was especially true of the application of the controversial new Title II—the equal accommodations section—but was also true in the education area. Here other agencies helped, with the Office of Education, authorized by Title VI to withhold federal support from programs where discrimination was present. The agency lost little time, issuing regulations in April, 1965, requiring a "good faith, substantial start" toward segregation by school districts receiving federal funds.[43]

The Supreme Court made clear early its intention of supporting the new measure, both by following its broad principles and by sustaining its enforcement. During the final stages of legislative maneuvering, it had moved strongly to strike down Virginia's "massive resistance" to public school integration, ordering the public schools of Prince Edward County, which had been closed to Negro children for five years, to reopen. Justice Black, speaking for a unanimous Court, stated clearly that the Constitution did not permit the abolition of public schools in one county of a state while they remained open in others.[44] He then went one step farther, vigorously denouncing further challenges to the Court's integration policy. Maintaining that the pace of desegregation generally would have to pick up, he contended that the requirement of desegregation "with all deliberate speed" was not a license to deliberate forever. Ten years was a long enough period of grace, he stated, making clear that further delays would not be countenanced.[45] Two weeks before the bill was signed, the Court had made equally clear that an amusement park that advertised for the patronage of the general public could neither deny entry to Negroes nor utilize its employees as "public officials" to eject Negroes who entered its grounds.[46] The same day

43. "Federal Aid Cutoff Prompted Limited School Desegregation," *Congressional Quarterly Almanac,* XXI (1965), 568–569.

44. Griffin *v.* Prince Edward County, 377 U.S. 218 (1964). On the background of the situation see Robbins L. Gates, *The Making of Massive Resistance: Virginia's Politics of Public School Desegregation* (Chapel Hill, N.C., 1964); Robert C. Smith, *They Closed Their Schools: Prince Edward County, Virginia* (Chapel Hill, N.C., 1965); and Benjamin Muse, *Virginia's Massive Resistance* (Bloomington, Ind., 1961). The most comprehensive statement of the southern position on integrated education came in 1962 in James J. Kilpatrick, *The Southern Case for School Segregation* (New York, 1962).

45. Griffin *v.* Prince Edward County, 377 U.S. 218, 234 (1964).

46. Griffin *v.* Maryland, 378 U.S. 130 (1964).

it had sustained sit-in demonstrators where evidence failed to show that their actions were in any way a "breach of the peace," with Justice Goldberg contending that the Civil Rights Act of 1866 had been broadly conceived to wipe out all racial discrimination in public places, both as to state law and as between private parties.[47]

Such rulings were the result of prior actions, however. Now the Court, which had followed closely the passage of the Civil Rights Act—Black as early as August, 1964, paying tribute to "one of the most thorough debates in the history of Congress"[48]—unanimously turned away challenges to it in early December. In each instance, owners of private facilities, one an Atlanta motel, the other a Birmingham restaurant, had sought injunctions to prevent enforcement of the public accommodations provision of Title II. Justice Clark, speaking for the Court, held the title a valid exercise of congressional power under the commerce clause, maintaining that Congress had a rational basis for finding that racial discrimination in such facilities had a direct and adverse effect on the free flow of interstate commerce.[49] On the same day, Clark, in a ruling that drew hostile dissents from four members of the bench, threw out trespass convictions of peaceful lunch-counter sit-in demonstrators by the dubious device of making the Civil Rights Act retroactive to cover cases begun before the measure's passage.[50] The Court applied the same principle in a case the following February.[51] Then moving outside the new law, it threw out at the same time a Florida statute prohibiting biracial cohabitation of persons of different races,[52] and the conviction of peaceful picketers. Observers were quick to pick up the

47. Barr *v.* City of Columbia, 378 U.S. 146 (1964); Bell *v.* Maryland, 378 U.S. 226 (1964). See also Robinson *v.* Florida, 378 U.S. 153 (1964); and Bouie *v.* City of Columbia, 378 U.S. 347 (1964). For a general discussion of the cases see Monrad G. Paulsen, "The Sit-In Cases of 1964: 'But Answer Came There None,'" *Supreme Court Review,* 1964, 137–170. For an assessment of Goldberg's "history" see Alfred H. Kelly, "Clio and the Court: An Illicit Love Affair," *Supreme Court Review* (1965), pp. 145–149.

48. Morgan, *Congress and the Constitution,* p. 296.

49. Heart of Atlanta Motel *v.* U.S., 379 U,S. 184 (1964); Katzenbach *v.* McClung, 379 U.S. 294 (1964).

50. Hamm *v.* Rock Hill, 379 U.S. 306 (1964). Black in an outraged dissent maintained that "the idea that Congress has power to accomplish such a result has no precedent, so far as I know, in the nearly 200 years that Congress has been in existence" (at 318).

51. Blow *v.* North Carolina, 379 U.S. 684 (1965).

52. McLaughlin *v.* Florida, 379 U.S. 184 (1964).

fact that in the latter case, *Cox* v. *Louisiana,*[53] which twice reached the Court, the body modified its 1963 Edwards rule to make clear that there were limits that could legitimately be placed on civil rights demonstrations. "We emphatically reject," said the Court, "the notion . . . that the First and Fourteenth Amendments afford the same kind of freedom of those who would communicate ideas by conduct such as patrolling, marching, and picketing on streets and highways, as these amendments afford to those who communicate ideas by pure speech."[54]

In its next block of civil rights cases, the Court moved back to the explosive question of voting rights, examining explicitly southern procedures, from registration to the actual casting of the ballot. On March 8, 1965, it roundly condemned the practices of Mississippi registrars in violating the rights of voters through the enforcement of clearly discriminatory state literacy tests and attendant laws.[55] The right to vote without racial distinction is guaranteed by federal statute, Black made clear for the majority, in the process validating the Attorney General's power to sue state officials to protect that right. Similarly in a Louisiana case, he ruled that evidence amply supported a district court's finding that the state's "interpretation" clause, giving registrars the unbridled discretion over whether a Negro could qualify to vote, was part of a plan to deprive Negroes of voting rights.[56] Evidence in the two cases again demonstrated the clear need for direct monitoring of the election process.

Nonetheless, the degree of cooperative action between the executive, legislative, and judicial branches that existed in the civil rights area in the years between 1960 and 1965 was paralleled in no other field. After all, as Earl Warren himself pointed out, these were the civil rights years and "the very atmosphere in which we live is charged with the subject."[57] The other numerous constitutional issues that arose in these explosive years normally produced sharp tugging and pulling and seldom full public acquiescence in the resolution eventually made. Certain significant areas of executive-

53. Cox *v.* Louisiana, 379 U.S. 536 (1965); Cox *v.* Louisiana, 379 U.S. 559 (1965). See Kalven, "Concept of the Public Forum," pp. 5 ff.

54. Cox *v.* Louisiana, 379 U.S. (1965).

55. U.S. *v.* Mississippi, 380 U.S. 128 (1965).

56. Louisiana *v.* U.S., 380 U.S. 145 (1965).

57. Katcher, *Earl Warren,* pp. 452–453.

"BY TH' WAY, WHAT'S THAT BIG WORD?"

Northern liberal hostility to the alleged hypocrisy of Southern voting practices elicited the above. (Mauldin, St. Louis *Post-Dispatch*)

judicial cooperation did exist, however. One such example involved public regulation of business.

The nation's antitrust structure had not produced major issues of constitutional adjudication through the years of the 1940s and 1950s even though certain actions indicated the government had not been idle in the period. In 1950, Congress had opened the door to more rigid enforcement of the Clayton Act's vital Section 7 through a significant amendment, the Celler-Kefauver Act.[58] The measure extended proscriptions against mergers far beyond the simple acquisition of controlling stock in a competitive corporation. It made clear that both stock and asset acquisitions were covered, and the Supreme Court, in its 1957 duPont case, had proceeded on this ground against that industrial giant.[59] The Kennedy administration, seemingly loath to leave any major area of public policy tranquil, promptly set out on a new antitrust movement, indicating its desire to use the antitrust structure, particularly Section 7, as a device for striking at corporate bigness and encouraging freer and more healthy economic competition.

The Warren Court again took its cue from the administration, and in the words of one analyst engaged in a pattern of activity in the broad economic area that was generally "prounion, antibusiness, procompetition, proemployee in personal-injury suits against employers, and pro-small business in a conflict between a large and small business not involving antitrust action."[60] In the antitrust area it was particularly quick to sustain antimerger moves and to uphold the principal arm of antimerger enforcement, the Federal Trade Commission. During the years between 1962 and 1965 the Court

58. 64 Stat. 1125 (1950). On the background of the measure see Betty Bock, *Mergers and Markets*, 5th ed. (New York, 1966); David M. Martin, *Mergers and the Clayton Act* (Berkeley, 1959); Joel B. Dirlam, "The Celler-Kefauver Act: A Review of Enforcement Policy," in *Administered Prices: A Compendium on Public Policy* (Washington, 1963), pp. 97–133; and Jesse W. Markham, "Merger Policy Under the New Section 7: A Six-Year Appraisal," *Virginia Law Review*, XLIII (1957), 489–528.

59. U.S. *v.* duPont, 353 U.S. 586 (1957). In the case the Court maintained that the statute had always covered both. See *The New York Times*, Oct. 25, 1964, Sec. III, pp. 1, 11.

60. Harold J. Spaeth, "Warren Court Attitudes Toward Business," in Glendon Schubert (ed.), *Judicial Decision-Making* (New York, 1963), pp. 79–108; and Spaeth, "An Analysis of Judicial Attitudes in the Labor Relations Decisions of the Warren Court," *Journal of Politics*, XXV (May, 1963), 290–311.

handed down eight major antitrust rulings. In the Brown Shoe case of 1962,[61] in the first major test of the Celler-Kefauver Amendment, the Court fully sustained that provision, ruling against the acquisition by Brown Shoe of a small competitive company on the grounds that the merger would increase concentration in manufacturing in the shoe industry and substantially reduce competition in the retailing of shoes in a number of cities. In a sequel case in 1964, it further demonstrated its opposition to the growth of big business by mergers, no matter how small the merged company, ordering Alcoa to divest itself of a small competitor whose share of the market was less than one-twentieth of that of the acquiring firm.[62]

Two other cases in the 1963–64 term were revealing of the majority's attitude. On April 6, 1964, the Court applied in stringent terms to a Lexington, Kentucky, bank merger the prohibition in Section 1 of the Sherman Act against combinations in restraint of trade. Any horizontal merger of companies that were "major competitive factors" in a market violated the Sherman Act, Justice Douglas contended. A monopoly need not result. Factors justifying the merger, if any, were deemed irrelevant.[63] The same day the body ruled that one natural gas company's acquisition of the stock and assets of another with which it was not a direct competitor "had a sufficient tendency to lessen competition" to violate the antimerger provision of the Clayton Act and ordered divestiture "without delay." The fact that no competition between the two companies existed, the Court maintained, was irrelevant as long as the operations of one proved to be a "substantial factor" in the market of the other.[64] Thus the Court seemed to take a broad view of the antimerger effects of both antitrust statutes.

Although by this time the Kennedy administration's tenure was over and its early aggressiveness in the antitrust area had become

61. Brown Shoe Co. *v.* U.S., 370 U.S. 274 (1962).

62. U.S. *v.* Aluminum Company of America, 377 U.S. 271 (1964).

63. U.S. *v.* First National Bank & Trust of Lexington, 376 U.S. 665 (1964). The previous year the Court had brought certain of the activities of the stock exchange under the reach of the antitrust laws, condemning as a violation the denial of direct-wire connections by the exchange to out-of-town, over-the-counter broker dealers. Silver *v.* New York Stock Exchange, 373 U.S. 341 (1963).

64. U.S. *v.* El Paso Natural Gas Co., 376 U.S. 651 (1964). See also U.S. *v.* Continental Can Co., 378 U.S. 441 (1964); U.S. *v.* Penn-Olin Chemical Co., 378 U.S. 158 (1964); and G. E. and Rosemary D. Hale, "Potential Competition under Section 7: The Supreme Court's Crystal Ball," *Supreme Court Review* (1964), pp. 171–189.

history, the Warren Court was prepared to follow through. Typically focusing upon the social effects of corporate action, and employing standards of proof that tended to eliminate the mountains of economic data that formerly accompanied antitrust trials, Warren tended to subordinate the requirement of actual proof of injury to that of a demonstration that such a tendency existed. Further, in a case in 1965, the Court took the position that post-acquisition evidence of a merger's deleterious effect was admissible as grounds for undoing it, arguing, however, that such evidence should not be totally determinative in such a finding.[65] The rulings continued to disturb business leaders. The old maxim that bigness was badness seemed to have been reinvigorated. A number of business leaders protested vehemently that such a policy tended to freeze institutional rigidities into the whole business structure.[66]

The other areas of major constitutional adjudication in the first half of the 1960s found the justices breathing heavily of the heady activist air that the Kennedy administration had generated and cinching up its belt to complete a wide range of unfinished business that it had cautiously avoided pending clear administration guidelines. Clearly such a view was not acceptable to Frankfurter and those of like view and once again the inevitable jockeying between self-restraint advocates and those anxious to reinvigorate earlier activism took place. But such tensions, clearly evident in 1961 and 1962, were eased by the appointment by President Kennedy of two "new frontiersmen"–type justices—Byron R. "Whizzer" White to replace the ailing Whittaker in April, 1962, and Arthur J. Goldberg, former C.I.O. counsel and Secretary of Labor, to the chair vacated by Frankfurter's retirement at the beginning of the 1962–63 term.[67] With their accession, activism expanded, even though it did not go

65. F.T.C. *v.* Consolidated Foods, 380 U.S. 592 (1965).

66. The Court, on the other hand, took a different position with regard to state "fair trade" laws. It had struck at such legislation in 1951 (Schwegman Brothers *v.* Calvert, 341 U.S. 484), only to be "overruled" by Congress by the 1952 McGuire Act, 66 Stat. 631 (1952), exempting state-approved fair trading from the antitrust structure. When challenge to the measure came in 1964, the Court maintained a posture of self-restraint stating "whether it is good policy to permit such laws is a matter for Congress to decide." Hudson Distributors *v.* Lilly, 377 U.S. 386 (1964).

67. White soon proved a disappointment to champions of judicial activism, tending as frequently to join the Harlan-Stewart wing as to vote with the Chief Justice, Black, Douglas, and Brennan. See Weaver, *Warren,* p. 245; Clifford M. Lytle, *The Warren Court and Its Critics* (Tucson, 1968), p. 109.

so far as Black and Douglas would have preferred, that is, in returning to the preferred freedoms concept and throwing out in toto legislation violative of First Amendment rights. Rather, the Court chose to continue its pattern of statutory interpretation, adding two new techniques. On one level it placed heavy emphasis upon the obligation of bodies carrying out policies which it found questionable, to adhere to proper procedures, and on a number of occasions voided otherwise defensible convictions for this reason. But it also displayed a clear willingness, in certain limited areas, to rule portions of laws unconstitutional when clearly their application had produced violations of personal freedom. Thus, for example, five members of the bench found no difficulty in throwing out a section of the 1959 Landrum-Griffin Act making it criminal for a member of the Communist party to serve as an officer or employee of a labor union, maintaining that it was unconstitutional as a bill of attainder.[68] A similar trend was present in the loyalty-security area.

The Court had for a number of years found ways to avoid confronting certain of the more controversial sections of the Smith Act and particularly of the McCarran Act of 1950. Now it came to terms directly with various aspects and provisions of both, and in the process did not hesitate to examine other security legislation whose application it felt was producing unwarranted results. Here again it took its cue from Kennedy administration attitudes. Robert F. Kennedy, as Attorney General, had created an unfortunate image early in his tenure by calling for a broad expansion of the permissible use of wiretapping. Public hostility erupted quickly, forcing early retreat.[69] Such action tended to overshadow the new Attorney Gen-

68. U.S. *v.* Brown, 381 U.S. 436 (1965). In the labor area generally, although rendering no significant constitutional decisions, the Warren Court tended to be unsympathetic to unfair labor practices, to rule for the individual in workmen's compensation cases, and generally to side with federal statutes when a case of preemption arose. See Spaeth, "Analysis of Judicial Attitudes in the Labor Relations Decisions of the Warren Court," p. 296; Alfred Kamin, "The Union as Litigant: Personality, Pre-Emption, and Propaganda," *Supreme Court Review* (1966), pp. 253–291; Thomas P. Lewis, "Fair Representation in Grievance Administration: Vaca *v.* Sipes," *Supreme Court Review* (1967), pp. 81–126; and Ralph K. Winter, Jr., "Judicial Review of Agency Decisions: The Labor Board and the Court," *Supreme Court Review* (1968), pp. 53–75.

69. Jacob W. Landynski, *Search and Seizure and the Supreme Court* (Baltimore, 1966), pp. 229–230. For a general study see Edward V. Long, *The Intruders: The Invasion of Privacy by Government and Industry* (New York, 1966). The Court

eral's very real concern for liquidating the McCarthyite heritage, which still dominated much of the government's attitude toward both its employees and American Communists and their sympathizers. Kennedy made clear early that he felt the Communist party as a political organization was no danger to the United States, and argued for the dismissal of unsupported security charges, expressing also his dislike for informers and the use of coerced information. He was also outspoken in his conviction that visa and travel restrictions should be softened, here agreeing with his brother in the White House that it was time to correct the impression held by many foreigners that the United States was a sort of police state obsessed with security.[70]

The activist wing of the Court needed little more in the way of encouragement. When Frankfurter, in June, 1961, sustained the registration provision of the 1950 McCarran Act, insisting that the Communist party, per se, must register with the Subversive Activities Control Board, as the Act demanded,[71] Chief Justice Warren, and Justices Black, Douglas, and Brennan, wrote lengthy separate dissents. The Chief Justice was concerned that the board had depended upon dubious testimony, and was clearly of the opinion that a "communist-action" group must be construed under the statute as one engaged in direct advocacy of overthrow of the government by violence. Black, on the other hand, maintained that the entire law

---

took a number of cases dealing with wiretap and "bugging" actions in these years. In Pugach *v.* Dollinger, 365 U.S. 458 (1961), it denied that wiretap evidence could be enjoined by a federal court from use in a state criminal trial, even though its use was prohibited in federal courts. In Silverman *v.* U.S., 365 U.S. 505 (1961), it reversed for the first time a conviction obtained with the assistance of electronic eavesdropping, in this instance a "spike mike" shoved into the wall of a gamblers' headquarters in such a way that it touched the heating duct and converted the heating system into a sound conductor which the police then monitored. In Lanza *v.* New York, 370 U.S. 139 (1962), a badly divided bench rejected a protest against the use of wiretap evidence secured in a jail by monitoring the conversation between an inmate and his visiting brother. And in Lopez *v.* U.S., 373 U.S. 427 (1963), it sustained a conviction based on evidence obtained by an I.R.S. agent on a concealed tape recorder of attempted bribery of the agent. Harlan, for the Court, drew a distinction between the use of electronic devices to eavesdrop on conversations that would otherwise be beyond the range of the government's ears and the mere recording of a conversation to whose contents the government was already privy by right.

70. Schlesinger, *Thousand Days,* pp. 699–700.

71. Communist Party *v.* S.A.C.B., 367 U.S. 1 (1961).

"embarks this country . . . on the dangerous venture of outlawing groups that preach doctrines nearly all Americans detest."[72] This, he contended, was a gross violation of the First Amendment. He also condemned the Act for forcing self-incrimination, allowing the legislature to identify the guilty and inflict the punishment rather than the courts, and for violating due process of law by short-cutting the Bill of Rights. The idea of group guilt clearly was, to the justice, an un-American concept.

The same day the Court rendered decisions in two cases involving the Smith Act's membership clause. Drawing a clear line between knowing and mere passive membership in a subversive group, it sustained a conviction for the former,[73] but reversed one for the latter.[74] Thus, although the membership clause was saved, it was read so narrowly that the likelihood of further arrests under it became highly remote. And shortly after the decisions, the government quietly dropped the prosecution of a number of Communist party members who had been indicted under it.

Two weeks later the Court examined the government's security program for its own employees, insisting, once again, in a case involving dismissal of a short-order cook in a privately owned cafeteria in a navy ordinance installation, that in all such proceedings the party involved was fully entitled to a meaningful, fair, decent, and dignified hearing.[75] It still, however, upheld dismissal, but over the sharp protest of the same four-man dissenting minority.

With the appointment of the two Kennedy judges, particularly the replacement of Frankfurter by Goldberg, that minority became a majority. Such impact quickly became evident when, in February, 1963, with Goldberg writing the opinion, the Court ruled unconstitutional sections of the 1940 and 1952 Nationality Acts.[76] Those sections had automatically (without judicial trial) stripped an American of his citizenship, in this case for remaining outside the

72. *Ibid.*, at 139.

73. Scales *v.* U.S., 367 U.S. 203 (1961). For reaction to the case see Lucius J. and Twiley W. Barker, *Freedoms, Courts, Politics: Studies in Civil Liberties* (Englewood Cliffs, N.J., 1965), pp. 122–125.

74. Noto *v.* U.S., 367 U.S. 290 (1961).

75. Cafeteria & Restaurant Workers Union *v.* McElroy, 367 U.S. 886 (1961).

76. Kennedy *v.* Mendoza-Martinez, 372 U.S. 144 (1963). On Goldberg's background see Daniel P. Moynihan (ed.), *The Defenses of Freedom: The Public Papers of Arthur J. Goldberg* (New York, 1964).

jurisdiction of the United States in time of war for the purpose of evading or avoiding training and service in the nation's armed forces.[77] A year later it struck at further provisions of the same measures, insisting that a citizen could live abroad without fear of loss of citizenship.[78] One month later, speaking again through Goldberg, the Court struck down Section 6 of the 1950 McCarran Act, maintaining that domestic Communists might travel abroad for a "wholly innocent purpose" without losing their passports. Such denial, it contended, was invalid under the Fifth Amendment.[79] Similarly when the Subversive Activities Control Board attempted to force organizations to register with it as "communist-fronts," based upon testimony collected from dubious sources in the early 1950s, the Court reversed their action on the basis that the evidence was "stale" and hence inadmissible.[80]

The Court did not deviate from such a pattern under the Johnson administration. In May, 1965, it ruled unconstitutional that portion of the Postal Service and Federal Employees Salary Act of 1962 that required persons to whom "Communist political propaganda" was addressed to request in writing the delivery of such materials.[81] Further, Black derived a degree of pleasure from the move since it constituted the first time in American history that the First Amendment had been used to void an Act of Congress.

A similar spirit pervaded the Court's ongoing struggle with the House Un-American Activities Committee and with various state loyalty programs. Prior to the retirement of Whittaker and Frankfurter, the old majority had followed the Barenblatt and Uphaus

77. In other cases relating to the armed forces, the Court sustained the right to claim conscientious objector status for other than religious reasons, U.S. *v.* Seegar, 380 U.S. 163 (1965), and ruled that the right of a member of the armed services to vote could not be violated by a state, Carrington *v.* Rash, 380 U.S. 89 (1965).

78. Schneider *v.* Rusk, 377 U.S. 163 (1964).

79. Aptheker *v.* Secretary of State, 378 U.S. 500 (1964). The Court balked at reversing State Department denial of a passport to a citizen seeking to visit Castro's Cuba, however, Zemel *v.* Rusk, 381 U.S. 1 (1965), even though Attorney General Robert Kennedy was on record as supporting the removal of restrictions on American travel to any foreign country. Schlesinger, *Thousand Days,* p. 700.

80. American Committee for Protection of the Foreign Born *v.* S.A.C.B., 380 U.S. 503 (1965); Veterans of the Abraham Lincoln Brigade *v.* S.A.C.B., 380 U.S. 513 (1965).

81. Lamont *v.* Basic Pamphlets, 381 U.S. 70 (1965).

rules, sustaining the committee in cases when witnesses had refused to answer questions concerning their membership in the Communist party during an investigation of Communist propaganda in the South.[82] Three months later, however, Justice Stewart moved to join the liberal wing on the question, voting for acquittal in a case in which the committee had sought to force a witness to answer questions that were neither pertinent to the purposes of its immediate hearing nor to his own activities directly. The witness, Deutch, although answering questions about himself, refused to answer those pertaining to others, and the Court took a long stride back toward the Watkins precedent in confining the committee's investigatory powers to subjects relevant to the immediate legislative purpose.[83]

The Stewart switch was significant in the area of state loyalty programs as well. In December, 1961, the conservative Ohioan wrote an eloquent opinion voiding for vagueness a Florida statute requiring state and local public employees to swear that they had never lent their "aid, support, advice, counsel, or influence to the Communist Party," and subjecting them to discharge for refusal. "It would be blinking reality," Stewart wrote, "not to acknowledge that there are some among us always ready to affix a Communist label upon those whose ideas they violently oppose." And he went on to question the fighting of Communists by "a statute which either forbids or requires the doing of an act in terms so vague that men of common intelligence must necessarily guess at its meaning and differ as to its application."[84] The ruling was an invitation to state and local employees in other parts of the country to launch legal action against humiliating loyalty statutes of similar vagueness, a process encouraged and aided by such organizations as the American Civil Liberties Union. In cases in 1964 and 1966, the Court acted similarly regarding such statutes in Washington[85] and Arizona.[86] It also

82. Wilkinson *v.* U.S., 365 U.S. 399 (1961). Braden *v.* U.S., 365 U.S. 431 (1961).

83. Deutch *v.* U.S. 367 U.S. 456 (1961); and see Russell *v.* U.S., 369 U.S. 749 (1962). In a later case, involving a charge of illegal search and seizure against the Senate Judiciary Committee, the Court fell back on congressional immunity to void the charge. Dombrowski *v.* Eastland, 387 U.S. 82 (1967).

84. Cramp *v.* Board of Public Instruction, 368 U.S. 278, 286–877 (1961).

85. Baggett *v.* Bullitt, 377 U.S. 360 (1964).

86. Elfbrandt *v.* Russell, 384 U.S. 11 (1966). On the case see Jerold H. Israel, "Elfbrandt v. Russell: The Demise of the Oath?," *Supreme Court Review* (1966), pp. 193–252.

struck hard at state antisubversive committees, declaring unconstitutional portions of two Louisiana antisubversive laws, thus making it possible for federal courts to enjoin the unwarranted activities of that state's local un-American activities committee.[87] Finally, returning to New Hampshire, it once more placed the brakes on that state's perennially hypertonic, Red-hunting attorney general.[88]

Although its critics continually charged that such activities were an indication of the body's softness on Communism, the charge missed much of the subtlety of the Court's operations. By its Yellin decision in 1963, the Court had insisted that if H.U.A.C. did not strictly follow its own rules for the protection of witnesses it could not ask the Courts to punish a witness for contempt, but it still left the body elbow room to operate within legitimate areas as long as it followed legitimate procedures.[89] Similarly, in its Gojack ruling, late in the 1965 term, although it struck at unauthorized subcommittee hearings, it focused its ruling upon their illegitimate nature and unwarranted excesses.[90] Thus, although by mid-1966 even Senator Everett Dirksen was condemning the "unseemly spectacles" which H.U.A.C.'s sensational activities seemed chronically to elicit,[91] that body's continued existence seemed little threatened either by judicial interpretation or by public or congressional hostility.[92]

But if the Court's demand for fair procedure on the part of loyalty bodies had its scattered critics, its aggressive new commitment to broadening and nationalizing the whole area of fair trial produced wrath from an even wider range of opponents. The Court had begun as early as 1940 gingerly to attempt to spell out the essential ingredients to a "fair trial," but at best its efforts had been piecemeal and had generally been oriented toward insistence upon rigid ad-

87. Dombrowski *v.* Pfister, 380 U.S. 479 (1965).

88. DeGregory *v.* Atty. Gen. of New Hampshire, 383 U.S. 825 (1966).

89. Yellin *v.* U.S., 374 U.S. 109 (1963).

90. Gojack *v.* U.S., 384 U.S. 702 (1966).

91. *The New York Times,* Aug. 22, 1966.

92. The civil rights revolution produced growing criticism of the Committee's racist bias. See American Civil Liberties Union, *The Case Against the House Un-American Activities Committee* (New York, 1964), pp. 31–36; and Anne Braden, *House Un-American Activities Committee: Bulwark of Segregation* (New York, 1964). The Committee eventually moved to undercut its critics with a flamboyant investigation of the Ku Klux Klan in the fall of 1965. See Walter Goodman, "H.U.A.C. Meets the K.K.K.," *The New York Times Magazine,* Dec. 5, 1965, pp. 48 f.

herence by the federal courts and federal officials to various of the guarantees of Amendments Four through Eight. It seemed to hope thereby that such an example might be followed by state and local authorities. By the 1960s, especially in light of the Kennedy administration's strong call for upgrading and standardizing criminal justice throughout the nation, it again moved to the position that the time for deliberate speed was past, and the time for judicially induced action to raise the level of state procedures was at hand. Its ruling in *Mapp* v. *Ohio,* on June 19, 1961,[93] proved its first dramatic announcement.

The Mapp case, like the federal Mallory case of 1957,[94] fell into the area of pretrial procedures, demanding a new degree of literalness in adherence to traditional guarantees. The Mallory ruling, after several years of application, had virtually eliminated prearraignment interrogation. Judge Holtzoff, of the Circuit Court of Appeals of Washington, D.C., observed in 1963, "the only delay recognized under the Mallory rule is the delay necessary for the clerical procedures involving the arraignment."[95] Mapp struck at arrest procedures and did so at the state level. Police in Cleveland had entered the home of a Negro woman, without warrant, hunting policy slips and a bombing suspect. Neither was found. But after violently suppressing the protesting householder, they did discover, after thorough and destructive search, a quantity of obscene material, and Dollree Mapp was tried and found guilty of possessing such matter. Justice Clark, for a six-to-three Court, threw out the conviction, ruling that the state courts must enforce the Fourth Amendment guarantee against unreasonable search and seizure by excluding illegal evidence. He thus specifically overruled the 1949 *Wolf* v. *Colorado* decision on the exclusionary point. The ruling forced state and local police to use judge-approved warrants for the first time in U.S. history.

The impact of the decision was immediately disturbing to many U.S. police departments.[96] Police procedures such as roundups and

93. Mapp *v.* Ohio, 367 U.S. 643 (1961). For the Kennedy views see Schlesinger, *Thousand Days,* pp. 697–698.

94. Mallory *v.* U.S., 354 U.S. 449 (1957).

95. U.S. Congress, Senate, *Hearings on the Mallory and Durham Rule,* Committee on the District of Columbia, 88th Cong., 1st Sess., Oct. 3, 1963, p. 321.

96. A typical response was that of Los Angeles Chief of Police W. H. Parker. See *U.S. News and World Report,* Apr. 20, 1964, pp. 70–71. Well before Mapp a number of states had already ruled as a matter of local law that evidence illegally

"rousts" (running strangers out of town); the use of nebulous vagrancy and disorderly conduct ordinances and the police dragnet were promptly threatened. But more significant from a constitutional standpoint was the ruling's clear intimation that the Court was returning to the position of the dissenters in the 1948 Adamson case, and starting on a program of systematic nationalization of the entire Bill of Rights. Opponents of such a move became more convinced when the following year the Court ruled that the Fourteenth Amendment made applicable to the states the Eighth Amendment's prohibition against cruel and unusual punishment;[97] and the Sixth Amendment's guarantee of right to counsel.[98]

The Sixth Amendment ruling, however, proved immensely popular and threw a large segment of American public opinion behind the Court's new course. The case, *Gideon* v. *Wainwright,* involved a white Florida indigent convicted on an improper charge, without adequate counsel, who personally fought his way to the Supreme Court from inside a Florida prison with an appeal so eloquent that the Court appointed prominent Washington D.C. attorney Abe Fortas to argue his cause. The ruling, which established the right to counsel in state courts of all indigents accused of felonies, ap-

---

seized by federal officers should be barred from state proceedings; see J. A. C. Grant, "The Tarnished Silver Platter: Federalism and Admissibility of Illegally Seized Evidence," *University of California at Los Angeles Law Review,* VIII (1961), 1, 28; and in Elkins *v.* U.S., 364 U.S. 206 (1960), the Supreme Court had rejected the "silver platter" doctrine, which had previously allowed illegal evidence seized by state officers to be handed over—on a silver platter—to federal officers to be admitted in a federal trial, so long as there was no federal participation in the illegal activities of the state police. See Yale Kamisar, "Wolf and Lustig Ten Years Later: Illegal State Evidence in State and Federal Courts," *Minnesota Law Review,* XLIII (1959), 1083–1198; and Claude R. Sowle, *Police Power and Individual Freedom: The Quest for Balance* (Chicago, 1962), pp. 77–103.

97. Robinson *v.* California, 370 U.S. 660 (1962).

98. Gideon *v.* Wainwright, 372 U.S. 335 (1963). The following year the Court moved the right to counsel back to the pretrial stage of indictment in a complex case in which Massiah's codefendant, having decided to help the federal authorities, had persuaded him to make incriminating statements that were recorded by a federal agent. The Court ruled that the Sixth Amendment forbade the use against him of incriminating statements that had been elicited from him by federal officials "after he had been indicted and in the absence of counsel." Massiah *v.* U.S., 377 U.S. 201 (1964). Regarding federal action in the area, Congress, in enacting the Criminal Justice Act of 1964, 78 Stat. 552 (1964), sought to insure counsel to the indigent as well as other rights.

pealed to the nation's instinct for fair play and equality before the law for rich and poor and the case was dramatized both in a best-selling book[99] and an hour-long TV documentary over a nationwide network. Although the police feared that should the Gideon rule be retroactive it would be the basis for "opening the jailhouse doors to hundreds of prisoners,"[100] such action was not forthcoming. More rational heads among police leaders were also eased by a 1963 ruling upholding the right of Los Angeles police to make arrest and seizure after entering a narcotics-peddling couple's apartment without a warrant, the Court finding that the police had "probable cause" to suspect what they would find.[101]

But the Court was just beginning. In June, 1964, it extended the Fifth Amendment's prohibition against compulsory self-incrimination to the states, insisting that the citizen had the same right in state courts as in federal to remain silent unless he chose to speak, assuring that there should be no penalty for such silence.[102] On the same day, it made clear that neither a state nor the federal government could coerce a witness to testify and have the evidence, so coerced, usable by a different jurisdiction.[103] Self-incrimination now protected a state witness against incriminating himself under federal law as well as state law and vice versa.

One week later the Court again returned to the pretrial area. Danny Escabedo, alleged to have been involved in the murder of his brother-in-law, was eventually convicted and sentenced to prison on evidence extracted by police during the pretrial period. Even though his lawyer had been in the police station at the time, Escabedo had been denied the opportunity to talk with him, and had not been informed as to rights he might have in such circumstances. Justice Goldberg for the Court condemned the action sharply and now moved the Constitution and lawyers into the police station. "The fact that many confessions are obtained during this period," wrote the justice, for a five-man majority, "points up its critical nature as a

99. Anthony Lewis, *Gideon's Trumpet* (New York, 1964).

100. "The Revolution in Criminal Justice," *Time,* LXXXVI (July 16, 1965), p. 23.

101. Ker *v.* California, 374 U.S. 23 (1963). Cf. Wong Sun *v.* U.S., 371 U.S. 471 (1963).

102. Malloy *v.* Hogan, 378 U.S. 1 (1964). The case overruled Adamson *v.* California, 332 U.S. 46 (1947).

103. Murphy *v.* New York Waterfront Commission, 378 U.S. 52 (1954).

stage when legal aid and advice are surely needed. Our Constitution, unlike some, strikes the balance in favor of the right of the accused to be advised by his lawyers of his privilege against self-incrimination. A system of law enforcement which comes to depend on the confession, will, in the long run," he contended, "be less reliable than a system which depends on extrinsic evidence independently secured through skillful investigation. If the exercise of constitutional rights will thwart the effectiveness of a system of law enforcement, then there is something very wrong with that system."[104]

The response to the Escabedo ruling was explosive. Police officials moaned that their most effective tool for extracting confessions had now been taken from them. Former New York Police Commissioner Michael Murphy, in a symposium on the ruling, charged Chief Justice Warren and Justice Brennan to their face with "unduly hampering the administration of criminal justice, while 'vicious beasts' were loose on the street."[105] Other critics charged the Court with "coddling criminals," and in right-wing communities from southern California and Texas to Columbus, Ohio, IMPEACH EARL WARREN bumper stickers now gained a complementary SUPPORT YOUR LOCAL POLICE. Republican Presidential candidate Barry Goldwater sought to turn the Court's rulings into a major campaign issue in the 1964 election, continually charging it with contributing to the breakdown of law and order in the cities, alleging that its rulings inferred "that a criminal defendant must be given a sporting chance to go free, even though nobody doubts in the slightest he is guilty." "No wonder," Goldwater contended, "that our law enforcement officers have been demoralized and rendered ineffective in their jobs."[106]

But the Warren Court had its defenders as well. Critics well aware of the types of psychological devices used by the modern police interrogator as a way of tricking confessions out of witnesses hailed this rule, which now gave the witness constitutional protection when

104. Escabedo *v.* Illinois, 378 U.S. 478, 488–489 (1964). On the background of the Court's entry into this area see Arnold N. Enker and Sheldon H. Elsen, "Counsel for the Suspect: Massiah v. United States and Escabedo v. Illinois," *Minnesota Law Review,* XLIX (1964), 47–91.

105. *Time,* LXXXVI (Sept. 17, 1965), 74.

106. Alexander M. Bickel, "Barry Fights the Court," *New Republic,* CLI (Oct. 10, 1964), 9–11; Katcher, *Earl Warren,* pp. 454–455.

"What This Country Needs Is More Law and Order!"

The Supreme Court became a major scapegoat for national problems during the 1964 Presidential campaign. (Scott Long, Minneapolis *Tribune*)

investigations shifted to accusations.[107] A leading legal scholar, University of Michigan Law Professor Yale Kamisar, answered Police Commissioner Murphy's assault by calling his position "simplistic, narrow-minded, and politically expedient," and a "police effort to make the Court a scapegoat for society's inability to cope with crime."[108]

The Escabedo ruling thus raised both tempers and questions and clearly needed further clarification. Especially essential was a statement of the precise pretrial and prearraignment standards to which the Warren Court expected states and local authorities to adhere. Ideally such a task was one for the legislative branch. Indeed, *Time* magazine editorialized in July, 1965, "rule making by constitutional interpretation has limits; such rules tend to be confined to the happenstances in particular cases and are often more confusing than clarifying. The burden is now on Congress and state legislatures, which are ideally equipped for the fact finding required in so vast and varied a country as the U.S."[109]

Such legislative action was only sporadically forthcoming, however, and the Court was eventually moved to clarify its own ruling. But before that process took place, it returned once again to the process of nationalizing others of the procedural rights in the Bill of Rights. In *Stanford* v. *Texas,* in early 1965, it struck at state issuance of general warrants, which Justice Stewart contended were historically anathema to the American people from the time of the British issuance of writs of assistance in the pre-Revolutionary era.[110] In April, it insisted that the Sixth Amendment right of a witness to confront and cross-examine his accusers was guaranteed in state courts.[111] Three weeks later, it ruled that comment to the jury by

107. Yale Kamisar, "Equal Justice in the Gatehouses and Mansions of American Criminal Procedure," in A. E. Dick Howard (ed.), *Criminal Justice in Our Time* (Charlottesville, Va., 1965), pp. 1–95; David L. Sterling, "Police Interrogation and the Psychology of Confession," *Journal of Public Law,* XLV (1965), 25–65; Ed Cray, *The Big Blue Line: Police Power vs. Human Rights* (New York, 1967): Paul Chevigny, *Police Power: Police Abuses in New York* (New York, 1969); and see Chief Justice Warren's references in Miranda *v.* Arizona, 384 U.S. 436, 440 (1966).

108. *Time,* LXXXVI (Sept. 17, 1965), 74.

109. "The Revolution in Criminal Justice," *Time,* LXXXVI (July 16, 1965), 23.

110. Stanford *v.* Texas, 379 U.S. 476 (1965).

111. Pointer *v.* Texas, 380 U.S. 400 (1965).

a prosecutor in a state criminal trial on a defendant's silence as proof of his guilt clearly violated the self-incrimination clause of the Fifth Amendment made applicable to the states by the Fourteenth.[112]

The two cases produced sharp intra-Court sparring, however. Justice Harlan in the former made clear that he had not departed from his view that the "incorporation doctrines, whether full blown or selective, are both historically and constitutionally unsound and incompatible with the maintenance of our federal system."[113] In the latter he even more directly deplored "the creeping paralysis with which this Court's recent adoption of the 'incorporation' doctrine is infecting the operation of the federal system."[114] He was answered by newly appointed Justice Goldberg, who made clear that while it was good that the states should be able to try social and economic experiments, "I do not believe that this includes the power to experiment with the fundamental liberties of citizens safeguarded by the Bill of Rights."[115]

While strong opposition arose to the Court's new prescription for equal justice, direct action to countermand it was not forthcoming from legislative sources. The Court's strong emphasis upon the historic nature of the rights it was insisting must be protected, was impressive, as was its clear desire to protect people from police brutality. Further, to countermand the Court's position meant legislatively altering some of the most basic guarantees of the Bill of Rights, a step which even the most critical congressman hesitated to take. But the Court's action in assaulting another form of deviant local patterns in implementing the public law did produce strong congressional counteraction. This involved its major restructuring of apportionment practices and its unprecedented entry into an area that it had historically left to the states from the beginning of American history.

The Founding Fathers had been ambiguous with regard to the

112. Griffin *v.* California, 380 U.S. 609 (1965).

113. Pointer *v.* Texas, 380 U.S. 400, 409 (1965).

114. Griffin *v.* California, 380 U.S. 609 (1965).

115. Pointer *v.* Texas, 380 U.S. 400, 413 (1965). See the follow-up case of Chapman *v.* California, 386 U.S. 18 (1967), in which Harlan, in dissent, alludes to the important study by Harry Kalven, Jr., and Hans Zeisel, *The American Jury* (Boston, 1966).

way representatives should be apportioned among the several states. They had made clear, however, that this should be done according to their respective numbers. But they had left the states to set up explicit guidelines. Senators were thus to represent the states, but it seemed clear that the House of Representatives was to represent the people. The inference, from leaders like James Madison, was that this meant a reasonable equality, with one man's vote having the same general weight as that of his neighbor, both in state legislative bodies and in the national House.[116] The Court's early designation of this question as "political" prevented adjudication, even though by 1946 the dissenters in the *Colegrove* v. *Green*[117] case had suggested that there were clearly due process and equal protection questions involved. Nonetheless, despite Douglas' protest in *South* v. *Peters* in 1950,[118] the Court, as late as November, 1960, was still cautious in claiming the power to make adjustments in the area. Its *Gomillion* v. *Lightfoot* opinion of that year had important overtones, however. Throwing out a state gerrymandering law clearly inferred that a majority of the justices felt that state legislative districting action did not lie wholly outside judicial control. And Justice Whittaker, in a brief concurring opinion, expressed his view that clearly this question, and by implication, other comparable issues, were equal protection questions coming under the Fourteenth Amendment.[119]

Circumstances, by 1960, seemed to invite calls for judicial relief in this area. Rural domination of state legislatures, so obvious in many states, was clearly growing, as rural voters diminished in numbers. Yet those in power had no intention of modernizing those legislatures to give equal votes to urban and suburban dwellers and thereby destroy their own power. The same was true in a number of states where unequal congressional districts existed. Further, the increased emphasis upon making the Negro's vote count fully was an added incentive. A citizen whose vote was diluted because he hap-

116. Alexander Hamilton, and others of his view, preferred a system that would insure a "weighted" vote, but, somewhat ironically, weighted in favor of men of wealth and station in urban areas so as to downgrade the potential political influence of radical and divisive backcountry agrarians. Andrew Hacker, *Congressional Districting* (Washington, 1964), p. 9.

117. Colegrove *v.* Green, 328 U.S. 549 (1946).

118. South *v.* Peters, 339 U.S. 276 (1950).

119. Gomillion *v.* Lightfoot, 364 U.S. 339, 349 (1960).

pened to live in one section of the state should, proponents claimed, have the same ability to remove such strictures on his political power as a person denied the vote because of his color. And by March, 1962, the Warren Court accepted the appeal of urban Tennessee voters, in a state that had not been redistricted since 1901 (even though the state constitution required reapportionment every ten years), and took the plunge into the "political thicket" of reapportionment.

The *Baker* v. *Carr* decision[120] was revolutionary in altering the traditional federal hands-off policy over districting and apportionment. It also brought shifts in traditional separation of powers by setting up the federal district courts, much as in the desegregation area, as instruments for affording relief in the voting area. The latter were assigned the task of determining the time and speed with which actions should be taken to wipe out former "rotten boroughs" and attain a degree of equality for state voters. Bitter protest came from the Court's leading advocates of self-restraint, Harlan and particularly Frankfurter. The latter expressed fear that the Court was taking action that would destroy its own prestige and power; questioned whether the district courts should be the agents to devise "what should constitute the proper composition of the legislatures of the fifty states"; and made clear that the problem should not be assaulted by the judiciary, but "appeal must be to an informed, civically militant electorate." "In a democratic society like ours," Frankfurter argued, "relief must come through an aroused popular conscience that sears the conscience of the people's representative."[121] But the justice did not prevail, and the Court, itself an unrepresentative minority, thus set out to erase the power of rural minorities to curb majority rule, seeking thereby to make the political process more representative and equitable.[122]

The result of the decision was ponderous. Although Brennan for the Court had left unclear the precise criteria for representation that that body would hold as not incompatible with the equal protection clause of the Fourteenth Amendment, the citizens of a num-

120. Baker *v.* Carr, 369 U.S. 186 (1962).

121. *Ibid.*, pp. 267–270.

122. The contradiction is explored revealingly in Carl A. Auerbach, "The Reapportionment Cases: One Person, One Vote—One Vote, One Value," *Supreme Court Review* (1964), pp. 1–87.

ber of malapportioned states still set out to gain relief under it. In a short time legal action was begun in thirty-nine of the fifty states to challenge a variety of local patterns and practices.[123] Complications and complexities inevitably arose. The district courts thus found themselves obliged to return, in short order, to the justices for more explicit guidance.

This the Court was not reluctant to give. In March, 1963, in a case in which Attorney General Robert F. Kennedy argued the cause for the United States, as amicus curiae, the Court heard new challenge to the formerly "political" Georgia County-Unit system.[124] Justice Douglas somewhat triumphantly ruled that its use, as applied to primary elections for U.S. senator and statewide officers, denied underrepresented voters within a single constituency equal protection. Then, turning somewhat shakily to history, Douglas contended that "the conception of political equality from the Declaration of Independence, to Lincoln's Gettysburg Address, to the Fifteenth, Seventeenth, and Nineteenth Amendments can mean only one thing, one person, one vote."[125] The decision, although it applied the principle only within a given constituency, opened the door to its potential extension, and the Court was sympathetic to appeals to do so. Early the following year, it was applied to the federal House of Representatives, with the Court ruling that Article I, Section 2, of the federal Constitution, which provides that repesentatives in Congress be chosen "by the People of the several States," meant choice as nearly as practicable by weighing each citizen's vote equally.[126] Explicitly this was to mean that a state's congressional districts should be equal in population, the Court using Article I to preclude Congress from using its legislative authority to stave off reapportionment.[127]

123. On the general subject see Robert G. Dixon, Jr., *Democratic Representation: Reapportionment in Law and Politics* (New York, 1968); Royce Hanson, *The Political Thicket, Reapportionment and Constitutional Democracy* (Englewood Cliffs, N.J., 1966); Robert B. McKay, *Reapportionment: The Law and Politics of Equal Representation* (New York, 1965); Glendon A. Schubert, *Reapportionment* (New York, 1965); and Hacker, *Congressional Districting.*

124. Gray *v.* Sanders, 372 U.S. 386 (1963).

125. *Ibid.*, p. 381.

126. Wesberry *v.* Sanders, 376 U.S. 1 (1964).

127. The deliberate turning of the case so as to preclude congressional retaliation is explored in Harold J. Spaeth, *The Warren Court* (San Francisco, 1966), p. 87.

But many congressmen and senators were already aroused, and the Court's next round of decisions, in June, 1964, produced loud demands for direct congressional counteraction. The cases involved challenges to a number of state reapportionment plans, which voters in various states found unacceptable. Chief Justice Warren, in the central case of *Reynolds* v. *Sims,*[128] met them by the insistence that the "one man, one vote" rule would now be the rule of thumb for all representative bodies, including the upper houses of the state legislatures. And in the companion case of *Lucas* v. *General Assembly of Colorado,*[129] he made equally clear that the Court stood ready to strike down plans that did not conform to the rule. The case involved voter protest that a Colorado Senate reapportionment plan, based on other than equitable population factors, denied them equal protection, even though the voters of Colorado had approved the plan through popular referendum by a nearly two-to-one majority. The state in the case had made much of the voters' willingness to dilute their own legislative voice and give disproportionate power to rural minorities. The Court, however, insisted it was not concerned with the rights of minorities. It was concerned with the rights of individuals, and Warren made clear "it was a precept of American constitutional law that certain rights exist which a citizen cannot trade, barter, or even give away." "A citizen's constitutional rights," he further contended, "can hardly be infringed simply because a majority of the people choose that it be."[130]

Justice Harlan, who steadfastly continued to oppose the Court's whole reapportionment involvement, again protested the single rule, population basis for voting, suggesting that this waved aside at least ten other relevant considerations for establishing legislative districts, and ignored the fact that "legislators can represent their electors only by speaking for their interests—economic, social, political. . . ."[131] Congressional action sought explicitly to counter-

128. Reynolds *v.* Sims, 377 U.S. 533 (1964). See also W.M.C.A. *v.* Lomenzo, 377 U.S. 633 (1964), and on it Calvin B. T. Lee, *One Man One Vote: W.M.C.A. and the Struggle for Equal Representation* (New York, 1967); Maryland *v.* Towes, 377 U.S. 656 (1964); Davis *v.* Mann, 377 U.S. 678 (1964); Roman *v.* Sincock, 377 U.S. 695 (1964).

129. Lucas *v.* General Assembly of Colorado, 377 U.S. 713 (1964).

130. *Ibid.*, pp. 736–737.

131. To Harlan, properly relevant considerations were: history; economics; or other sorts of group interests; area; geographical considerations; a desire to insure effective representation for sparsely settled areas; availability of access

mand the two rulings. Various proposals were introduced for delaying the carrying out of the rulings, or leaving it up to the current state legislatures to work out both timetables and individual methods of implementation. A bill was introduced into the House to remove state legislative apportionment from the jurisdiction of the federal courts, and Senator Everett Dirksen of Illinois went further, proposing a constitutional amendment to override the Sims and Lucas rulings, making it possible for the people of a state, through a referendum, to use "factors other than population" in apportioning one house of a bicameral legislature.[132]

Pro-reapportionment forces were strong, however, with a variety of responsible national bodies, including the League of Women Voters, generally endorsing the Court's position. Contending that the vagueness of "other factors" would allow discrimination against Negroes and other minorities, they found convincing logic in Warren's contention that "neither history alone, nor economic or other sorts of group interests, are permissible factors in attempting to justify disparities from population-based representation." "Citizens not history or economic interests cast votes," Warren had contended. "People, not land or trees or pastures vote. As long as ours is a representative form of government, and our legislatures are those instruments of government elected directly by and directly representative of the people, the right to elect legislators in a free and unimpaired fashion is a bedrock of our political system."[133] Similarly, such citizens were apprehensive of delaying tactics since they saw in them the creation of the ironical situation, as one senator put it, of having "the rotten boroughs decide whether they should continue to be rotten."[134] Rather, they saw nothing unreasonable in the Reynolds timetable, which urged that action be taken as soon as reasonably possible to alter legally challenged systems, and that unless strong reasons were present, that no further state elections be conducted under invalid plans. Similarly, the fact that the Court

---

of citizens to their representatives; theories of bicameralism (except those approved by the Court); occupation; an attempt to balance urban and rural power; and the preference of a majority of voters in the state. Reynolds *v.* Sims, 377 U.S. 533, 622–623 (1964).

132. Dixon, *Democratic Representation,* p. 400.

133. Reynolds *v.* Sims, 377 U.S. 533, 562, 580 (1964).

134. Andrew Hacker, "One Man, One Vote—Yes or No?," *The York Times Magazine,* Nov. 8, 1964, p. 32.

"But there must be some way around him."

Rather than compliance, the Court's reapportionment rulings produced vigorous reaction, especially on the part of local politicians. (Brooks, in the Birmingham *News*)

had made clear that it did not demand "mathematical exactness" in establishing equitable districts, a point reiterated in the 1965 term,[135] seemed a responsible understanding of the type of problems involved. Thus, although opponents continued to devise constitutional obstructions, the general, if not always enthusiastic, acquiescence of practically all of the states to the Court's policy gave indication that the Court-imposed "one man, one vote" rule would henceforth be the voting test, with the Court standing by permanently to see that it was adhered to.

The other area of significant constitutional interpretation by the Warren Court in the Kennedy and early Johnson years involved problems growing out of various First Amendment freedoms. Here, as in its other concerns, the Court was activist, placing its major emphasis upon the rights of the individual when those rights seemed unjustifiedly curtailed by the authority of the state. Probably the most controversial and in many ways unpopular of its postures in this regard involved the ever touchy question of church-state relations. The Court had generally avoided further controversy in the field through the Eisenhower years. Yet its activism in other areas following 1960 invited reopening of smoldering questions, especially in the "establishment" area.

The Warren Court's first significant religious cases did not occur until 1961. Then, in a series of Sunday Closing Law decisions, it held by varying majorities that state "blue laws" violated neither the establishment of religion nor the free exercise thereof.[136] In the third of the cases, *Braunfeld* v. *Brown,* it especially appeared to take lightly the contention that such laws infringed upon free exercise of religion.[137] On the other hand, the Court was quick to defend the right to individual conscience in the religious field. When a Maryland citizen, appointed to the office of notary public by the governor, was refused a commission to serve because he would not declare his belief in God, the Court ruled that such a test for public

135. Burns *v.* Richardson, 383 U.S. 73 (1966).

136. McGowan *v.* Maryland, 366 U.S. 420 (1961); Two Guys from Harrison-Allentown, Inc., *v.* McGinley, 366 U.S. 582 (1961); Braunfeld *v.* Brown, 366 U.S. 599 (1961); Gallagher *v.* Crown Kosher, 366 U.S. 617 (1961).

137. On the cases generally see Candida Lund, "Religion and Commerce—The Sunday Closing Cases," in C. Herman Pritchett and Alan F. Westin (eds.), *The Third Branch of Government* (New York, 1963), pp. 275–308.

office could not be enforced. It constitutionally invaded the appellant's freedom of belief and religion, guaranteed by the First Amendment, and protected by the Fourteenth from infringement by the states.[138] Further, the case was symbolic of things to come; in June, 1962, speaking through Justice Black, in an opinion relying on poorly researched historical foundations,[139] it granted relief to New York parents whose children had been compelled against their beliefs to recite a compulsory state-composed prayer at the opening of the day in the public school classroom. Such a program, which utilized public, tax-supported facilities for a type of religious observance, was unconstitutional, the Court delared, as a violation of the principle of separation of church and state.[140]

The ruling was both widely misunderstood and assaulted. Conservative religious leaders, especially, attacked the Court for promoting atheistic and agnostic beliefs and encouraging secularization in the United States. As in the area of criminal procedure, the Court seemed to have struck at traditional practices that kept society on an even keel, even though some members of it might be penalized as a result. Sentiments of apprehension were thus also stirred. Southern representatives, particularly, sought to draw such hostility behind their assault on the Court's integration policies. "They put the Negroes in the schools," Representative George W. Andrews of Alabama asserted. "Now they have driven God out." And Representative L. Mendel Rivers of South Carolina maintained that the Court "had now officially declared its disbelief in God."[141]

Rationality prevailed at other levels, however. Liberal churchmen saw the decision as a significant move to upgrade religion by disassociating it from a meaningless ritualistic ceremony, and saw the Court drawing defensible lines that vigorously underwrote freedom of conscience in religious matters. President Kennedy, the victim in the 1960 campaign of various forms of religious bigotry frequently from the same sources as those attacking the Court, gave the ruling

138. Torcaso *v.* Watkins, 367 U.S. 488 (1961).

139. Paul L. Murphy, "Time to Reclaim: The Current Challenge of American Constitutional History," *American Historical Review,* LXIX (Oct., 1963), 64–65; Leonard W. Levy, "School Prayer and the Founding Fathers," *Commentary,* XXXIV (Sept., 1962), 225–230.

140. Engle *v.* Vitale, 370 U.S. 421 (1962).

141. Quoted in Leo Pfeffer, *This Honorable Court* (Boston, 1965), pp. 421–422. See also Katcher, *Earl Warren,* pp. 423 ff.

"Nice Kitty Can't Come In?"

Defenders of the Court's prayer and Bible reading rulings saw them as essential to the avoidance of open hostility over the church-state issue. (From *Straight Herblock* [Simon & Schuster, 1964])

a type of indirect approval. Asked at a news conference to comment on the Court's action, he responded, "I think that it is important for us, if we are going to maintain our constitutional principle, that we support the Supreme Court decisions, even though we may not agree with them. In addition, we have, in this case, a very easy remedy. And that is, to pray ourselves. And I would think that it would be a welcome reminder to every American family that we can pray a good deal more at home, we can attend our churches with a good deal more fidelity, and we can make the true meaning of prayer much more important in the lives of all of our children."[142]

The Supreme Court thus weathered another storm, and gradual public understanding of its posture was sufficient in the months that followed so that when a year later the Court ruled that it was unconstitutional for the public schools to conduct Bible reading and recitation of the Lord's Prayer, as part of the school program,[143] actions far more universal than that struck down in New York, public response was remarkably subdued. This did not prevent attempts to countermand the decisions. A New York congressman, Frank Becker, introduced a constitutional amendment to this effect.[144] But although individuals as diverse as Fulton J. Sheen and Governor George Wallace of Alabama testified in its support, the proposal, opposed strongly by the nation's leading constitutional lawyers, resulted in no concrete action.[145] The effort did not close the church-state question, however. Especially as Congress moved to extend various forms of public aid to both public and private parochial schools, with various states following suit, and as legal suits were instituted against tax exemption on church property, it was clear that complicated and sticky problems would continue to arise and be a source of friction and intense feeling for years to come.

142. Chase and Lerman, *Kennedy and the Press,* p. 274.

143. School District of Abbington Township *v.* Schempp; Murray *v.* Curlett, 374 U.S. 203 (1963).

144. Pfeffer, *This Honorable Court,* p. 423. See Robert S. Gallagher, "God's Little Helpers," *The Reporter,* XXX (June 4, 1964), 24–26.

145. "Senate Fails to Amend School Prayer Ruling," *Congressional Quarterly Almanac,* XXII (1966), 512–516. On the same day as the Schempp and Murray cases, the Court in a "free exercise" case ruled that a Seventh Day Adventist could not be denied unemployment compensation after she had refused to accept Saturday work, a precept condemned by her religion, Sherbert *v.* Verner, 374 U.S. 398 (1963). The decision seemed to conflict with the earlier Braunfeld *v.* Brown ruling, a point stressed strongly by four dissenters.

Questions of freedom of expression produced similar results. In the censorship area the ambiguities of the judicial rulings of the late Eisenhower years came home to roost in the period. In the area of printed materials, books, magazines, and pamphlets, the Court extended the Roth rule in various ways. Caught between millions of Americans disturbed by the rebellion of youth and the revolution in sexual mores, to say nothing of growing violence and crime, and others equally hostile to unintelligent and overzealous censorship policies and the adverse effect they had upon creativity and cultural expression, the Court found itself obliged to try to ease the minds of the former and make peace with the latter—a difficult task in light of the impreciseness of the rule it had to apply. Certain actions were relatively simple. On the same day it struck at union coerciveness in sustaining the freedom of members to protest union policies with which they disagreed,[146] Brennan, for the Court, struck at the coercive tactics of public officials, ruling that a state, in seizing allegedly obscene materials, must show respect for basic and elementary procedural safeguards.[147] A year later, in a substantive ruling, in which the Court was unable to agree on an opinion, Harlan, in considering magazines designed to appeal to homosexuals, maintained that these could not be banned from the mails.[148] Such magazines, he maintained, were not obscene because it was not shown that they were "patently offensive." He thus added a further test to Roth, maintaining that such "patent offensiveness" in addition to "prurient interest appeal" must be demonstrated in order to declare a work obscene.

In February, 1963, with only Harlan dissenting, the Court ruled that a system of informal sanctions employed by the legislatively established Rhode Island Commission to Encourage Morality in Youth, abridged First Amendment freedoms.[149] The commission had followed the practice of notifying book and magazine distributors that certain designated publications were objectionable for sale, distribution, or display to persons under eighteen, and such notices had been followed up by police visitations and threats of legal action if compliance did not occur. A similar local pattern of censorship in Kansas, in this case seizure of books by a local judge at

146. International Association of Machinists *v.* Street, 367 U.S. 740 (1961).
147. Marcus *v.* Search Warrant, 367 U.S. 717 (1961).
148. Manual Enterprises *v.* Day, 370 U.S. 478 (1962).
149. Bantam Books, Inc. *v.* Sullivan, 372 U.S. 58 (1963).

the request of the state attorney general, was also thrown out.[150] On the same day, in a movie censorship case, *Jacobellis* v. *Ohio,* the Court again stressed the need for demonstrating that obscene material was "without redeeming social importance" and in the process made clear that the "contemporary community standards" test of the Roth case had to be determined on the basis of the "national community," thereby adopting a principle first enunciated by Judge Learned Hand in 1913.[151] Said Brennan for the Court: "It is after all a national Constitution we are expounding."[152]

The decision drew comment from Justice Stewart, revealing in its candor, regarding the status of judicial standards on the obscenity question. "I shall not today attempt further to define the kinds of material I understand to be embraced within [hard-core pornography];" wrote Stewart, "and perhaps I could never succeed in intelligibly doing so. But I know it when I see it, and the motion picture involved in this case is not that."[153] Warren, dissenting in the case, went further. "I believe that there is no provable 'national standard' and perhaps that there should be none. At all events, this Court has not been able to enunciate one, and it would be unreasonable to expect local courts to divine one."[154]

The censorship of printed material issue came to its somewhat confused climax late in the 1965 term. In three decisions, involving a variety of types of alleged obscenity, the Court moved to the American Law Institute position, and struck hard at the way such material was presented and merchandised. Attacking especially the flamboyant techniques of Ralph Ginzburg, publisher of a variety of erotic materials, the Court clearly made their advertising a central concern, because, as Justice Brennan wrote, such advertising made the reader "look for titillation not for saving intellectual content."[155] Attacking "the sordid business of pandering," and material that had

150. A Quantity of Books *v.* Kansas, 378 U.S. 205 (1964).

151. U.S. *v.* Kennerley, 209 F. 119, 121 (D.C.S.C.N.Y., 1913).

152. Jacobellis *v.* Ohio, 378 U.S. 184, 195 (1964).

153. *Ibid.,* p. 197.

154. *Ibid.,* p. 200. On the cases and their implications see C. Peter Magrath, "The Obscenity Cases: Grapes of Roth," *Supreme Court Review* (1966), 7–77.

155. Ginzburg *v.* U.S., 383 U.S. 463, 475 (1966). See also Memoirs *v.* Massachusetts, 383 U.S. 413 (1966); and Mishkin *v.* New York, 383 U.S. 502 (1966). The ruling, which resulted in Ginzburg's conviction, was a departure from the Court's pattern from 1957 to 1966, of consistently overturning obscenity convictions. Alexander N. Bickel, "Obscenity Cases," *New Republic,* CLVI (May 27, 1967), 15–17.

the "leer of the sensualist about it," the Court added yet another standard to the confusion that it had created in the obscenity field, and drew sharp criticism as a result.[156]

No one was sharper than Justice Douglas in his dissent. Douglas, who with Black had more and more moved to the position that the First Amendment should be read with literal exactness as preventing any restriction on free speech and expression of any kind,[157] continued to maintain his cynicism about the Court's obscenity course. Wrote the justice:

> The use of sex symbols to sell literature, today condemned by the Court, engulfs another exception on First Amendment rights that is as unwarranted as the judge-made exception concerning obscenity. This new exception condemns an advertising technique as old as history. The advertisements of our best magazines are chock-full of thighs, ankles, calves, bosoms, eyes, and hair, to draw the potential buyers' attention to lotions, tires, food, liquor, clothing, authors, and even insurance policies. The sexy advertisement neither adds to nor detracts from the quality of the merchandise being offered for sale. And I do not see how it adds to or detracts one whit from the legality of the book being distributed. A book should stand on its own, irrespective of the reasons why it was written or the wiles used in selling it. I cannot imagine any promotional effort that would make chapters 7 and 8 of the Song of Solomon any the less or any more worthy of First Amendment protection than does its unostentatious inclusion in the average edition of the Bible. . . .[158]

Movie censorship, in the meantime, had been ushered down a parallel but somewhat different aisle. In *Times Film Corporation* v. *Chicago* in early 1961, the Court ruled that movies could be

156. See John E. Semonche, "Definitional and Contextual Obscenity: The Supreme Court's New and Disturbing Accommodation," *U.C.L.A. Law Review,* XIII (August, 1966), 1173–1213; Leon Friedman, "The Ginzburg Decision and the Law," *American Scholar,* XXXVI (Winter, 1966–67), 71–91; and "Dissent to the High Court's Harsh Verdict," *Life,* LX (Apr. 22, 1966), 26. See also Richard H. Kuh, *Foolish Figleaves: Pornography in and Out of Court* (New York, 1967); and Charles Rembar, *The End of Obscenity: The Trials of Lady Chatterley, Tropic of Cancer and Fanny Hill* (New York, 1968).

157. On Black see Irving Dilliard (ed.), *One Man's Stand for Freedom: Mr. Justice Black and the Bill of Rights* (New York, 1963), pp. 31–48, 467–483. On Douglas, William O. Douglas, "The Bill of Rights Is Not Enough," *New York University Law Review,* XXXVIII (April, 1963), 207–242.

158. Ginzburg *v.* United States, 383 U.S. 463, 482–483 (1966).

licensed for exhibit, even though by doing so it placed them in a second-class relationship with other means of communication and threatened them with prior restraint.[159] In the Jacobellis case, the Court went on to suggest standards that licensing must observe, making clear that movies, when obscene, clearly came out from under the protection of the First Amendment with such obscenity to be determined by the Roth test on the expanded terms of the "whole national community" consideration.[160] The ruling, however, still left in the hands of local movie censors the initiative and control of applying such a standard. Such an ambiguous situation the Court moved to correct. In *Freedman* v. *Maryland,* in March, 1965,[161] it held unanimously that the burden of proving that a film should not be shown rested with the censor; that a censor's ban was subject to judicial review, and that the courts must grant the exhibitor prompt review of any such ban. The effect of the ruling was to destroy the discretionary and often frivolously used power of dozens of local censorship boards and individuals by subjecting their actions to nationally monitored and judicially determined standards.

Although the First Amendment absolutists, Black and Douglas, did not prevail in the censorship area, their position came very close to prevailing in another revolutionary legal departure of the 1960s. The law of libel in the United States had come from English common law, and had, along with such crimes as slander and defamation of character, traditionally been considered an area of speech outside of First Amendment protection. As late as 1952, in the Illinois group libel case,[162] the Court has reaffirmed this principle by sustaining a conviction under the law over sharp free speech violation protests. The case had been one of the few in which the Court had had opportunity to consider constitutional aspects of state libel laws even though such laws were numerous and were applicable to speech and press in a number of ways. By the early 1960s, with the civil rights movement intensifying, a number

159. Times Film *v.* Chicago, 365 U.S. 43 (1961).

160. Jacobellis *v.* Ohio, 378 U.S. 184 (1964).

161. Freedman *v.* Maryland, 380 U.S. 51 (1965). See Ira H. Carmen, *Movies, Censorship and the Law* (Ann Arbor, 1966); and Richard S. Randall, *Censorship of the Movies* (Madison, Wis., 1968).

162. Beauharnais *v.* Illinois, 343 U.S. 250 (1952).

of southern officials turned to such laws as devices to harass outspoken civil rights advocates. A Mississippi N.A.A.C.P. official, for example, had been sued for $40,000 when he stated that a local police chief and prosecutor had manufactured a charge against him of indecent assault on a hitchhiker.[163] And when *The New York Times* ran a full-page advertisement paid for by the Committee to Defend Martin Luther King and the Struggle for Freedom in the South, critical generally of the vicious treatment by Alabama officials of civil rights demonstrators, an elected commissioner of Montgomery brought a libel suit against the newspaper for a half-million dollars, charging it with printing erroneous and defamatory statements of "fact," an action punishable under an Alabama libel statute. The Alabama Supreme Court affirmed the judgment, but the Supreme Court reversed,[164] and for the first time in American history ruled that libelous utterance, with certain important qualifications, was protected under the First Amendment.

Under the free speech section of that amendment, Justice Brennan ruled, one must be free to criticize public officials. Since some error of fact is inevitable in vigorous debate of public issues, the right to criticize is not to be forfeited or penalized when the statements complained of are made in good faith. The only thing that would defeat the privilege was "actual malice," which Brennan defined to mean knowledge that a statement was false, or a reckless disregard of whether it was false or not. Further, Brennan made clear that impersonal criticism of government was absolutely privileged, even though such criticism necessarily implies indirect criticism of individuals associated with it. Such criticism, he maintained, is to be encouraged, not merely in the interests of free speech, but in the interests of checking governmental power over the people, and of maintaining a democratic society. There can be no libel on

163. Spaeth, *Warren Court,* p. 151.

164. New York Times *v.* Sullivan, 376 U.S. 254 (1964). On the case see Harry Kalven, Jr., "The New York Times Case: A Note on 'The Central Meaning of the First Amendment,'" *Supreme Court Review* (1964), pp. 191–221; James M. Shoemaker, Jr., "New York Times Co. v. Sullivan—The Scope of Privilege," *Virginia Law Review,* LI (January, 1965), 106–120; and William J. Brennan, "The Supreme Court and the Meiklejohn Interpretation of the First Amendment," *Harvard Law Review,* LXXIX (1965), 1–20.

government, he maintained, and no punishment for "seditious libel."[165]

Eight months later the Court extended *The New York Times* doctrine to apply to criminal libel cases, reversing unanimously the conviction of a local district attorney in Louisiana who had publicly criticized local judges as lazy and inefficient, and charged that they had hampered his enforcement of the vice laws by refusing to authorize the money necessary to conduct investigations. Even when utterance is false, Brennan maintained for the Court, "the great principles of the Constitution which secure freedom of expression in this area preclude attaching adverse consequences to any except the knowing or reckless falsehood." Otherwise, he maintained, "it becomes a hazardous matter to speak out against a popular politician, with the result that the dishonest and incompetent will be shielded."[166]

The public's right to criticize officials did not include the freedom of the press to interfere with justice, however. Returning to the question of the conflict between free press and fair trial, which in the 1940s it had resolved in favor of the former, the Court moved sharply to shift the balance back toward favoring the individual. The case, which made national headlines, involved Texas promoter and financier and alleged swindler Billy Sol Estes. The Court, following the rule of a 1963 case that had assailed the use of motion-picture films of an "interview" between a sheriff and an accused bank robber,[167] ruled for Estes. Over his protest television had been used extensively both in trial and pretrial activities. Such televising over the petitioner's objections, the Court ruled, was inherently invalid as infringing the fundamental right to a fair trial guaranteed by the due process clause of the Fourteenth Amendment. The pub-

165. New York Times *v.* Sullivan, 376 U.S. 254, 292 (1964). In the *Times* case, attorneys for Sullivan had been able to show errors in the advertisement which *The Times* carried. The question then became one of permissible and nonpermissible error, and again the factor of "malice" became the criterion. For reaction from the world of letters see "The New York Times' Vital Victory," *Saturday Review,* XLVII (Apr. 11, 1964), 69–70. See also R. H. Smith, "Important Victory for a Free Press," *Publishers' Weekly,* CLXXXV (Mar. 16. 1964), 33.

166. Garrison *v.* Louisiana, 379 U.S. 64 (1964). The rule was applied later in the same term to reverse the conviction of an appellant arrested for disturbing the peace who had maintained that his arrest was "the result of a diabolical plot" by local officials and had been charged with libel for so stating. Henry *v.* Collins, 380 U.S. 356 (1965).

167. Rideau *v.* Louisiana, 373 U.S. 723 (1963).

lic's right to be informed about court proceedings, Justice Clark stated for the majority, is satisfied if reporters are free to attend and to report on the proceedings through their respective media. Where the procedure employed by the state involves the probability that prejudice to the accused will result, that procedure is lacking in due process, whether or not isolatable prejudice can be demonstrated.[168] Similarly, in the equally famous Samuel Sheppard murder case involving a Cleveland osteopath who had been "convicted" by newspaper publicity and editorializing prior to his actual trial, the Court ultimately drew lines around the people's right to know. Justice Clark, for the Court, while insisting that freedom of discussion should be given the widest range compatible with the fair and orderly administration of justice, held that it must not be allowed to divert a trial from its purpose of adjudicating controversies according to legal procedures based on evidence received only in open court.[169]

The Court's willingness to create new areas of freedom encouraged parties feeling that their liberties were restricted by unwarranted types of coercion, to apply for judicial relief. Late in the 1964 term, the Court, in finding new legal ways to accommodate such an appeal, took a step that many observers felt was indicative of its future course. The law of privacy was poorly defined within the American constitutional structure, even though there were a number of guarantees for the individual, particularly within the Fourth Amendment, that suggested such a general area of protection.[170] Since 1890, civil libertarians had been attempting to read a right to privacy into the Constitution, but with highly limited success.[171] The Warren Court, however, was, if anything, creative and open to new ways to "modernize" traditional civil liberties, and took significant first steps in this regard in 1965. The situation involved a challenge to Connecticut's eighty-year-old birth-control law, forbidding the use of contraceptives, or the dispensation of information regarding their

168. Estes *v.* Texas, 381 U.S. 532 (1965).

169. Sheppard *v.* Maxwell, 384 U.S. 333 (1966). On the case see Paul A. Holmes, *The Sheppard Murder Case* (New York, 1961); and Samuel H. Sheppard, *Endure and Conquer* (Cleveland, 1966).

170. Works on the subject include Morris Ernst and Alan U. Schwartz, *Privacy: The Right To Be Let Alone* (New York, 1962); and Alan F. Westin, *Privacy and Freedom* (New York, 1967).

171. The initial suggestion had been in Samuel D. Warren, Jr., and Louis D. Brandeis, "The Right of Privacy," *Harvard Law Review,* IV (1890), 193–220.

use. The Court had taken a case challenging the law's latter provisions in the 1960 term, but although deploring the regulation, had found that it raised no constitutional point since the party involved could not legitimately claim that the law completely precluded him from getting birth-control information.[172] Now Douglas, for the Court, found a way to strike down the measure. Analyzing a number of modern rights not found specifically in the first ten amendments, he found that these were valid projections from that document. "Specific guarantees in the Bill of Rights have penumbras, formed by emanations from those guarantees that help give them life and substance," he argued. Then pointing out that First Amendment protection had been afforded to individuals acting in a variety of political and social ways, he went on to contend that that amendment has such a "penumbra where privacy is protected from government restriction."[173] And, he argued, such a right of privacy presses for recognition.

It was Justice Goldberg's concurring opinion that startled constitutional lawyers, however. Over the vigorous protest of Black and Stewart, the justice, with the concurrence of Chief Justice Warren and Justice Brennan, called for the creation of a whole body of extra-constitutional rights, arguing that this action was thoroughly within the spirit of the Ninth Amendment and the due process clause of the Fourteenth. With such tools, Goldberg argued, the Court was in a position to strike down all state legislation that violates "fundamental principles of liberty and justice" or that was contrary to the "traditions and [collective] conscience of our people."[174] Black was horrified. Contending that Connecticut's law was not forbidden by any provision of the federal Constitution as that Constitution was written, the justice, while continuing to call for full incorporation of the various explicit guarantees of the Bill of Rights against the states, deplored such a proposal, which he contended would turn the Court into a "bevy of Platonic guardians," a role that he contended he would find "most irksome."[175]

172. Poe *v.* Ullman, 367 U.S. 497 (1961).

173. Griswold *v.* Connecticut, 381 U.S. 478, 483 (1965).

174. Griswold *v.* Connecticut, 381 U.S. 478, 488–493 (1965).

175. *Ibid.*, pp. 526–527. As to the Court applying principles that represented the "collective conscience" of citizens, Black retorted that "the scientific miracles of this age have not yet produced a gadget which the Court can use to determine what traditions are rooted in the [collective] conscience of our people" (at 519).

With the close of the Court's 1964–65 term, the justices had finished a variety of judicial business left dangling from the Eisenhower years and had generally put a judicial seal of approval upon a variety of "New Frontier" programs and objectives, carried on and in some cases implemented further by President Johnson. In so doing, they were to create a vast amount of new business for years to come in the form of clarifying the reach of rulings on reapportionment, religion, libel, obscenity, and criminal procedure. The question remained whether Mr. Johnson, now his own man following the smashing defeat of Barry Goldwater and right-wing Republicanism in the November, 1964, election, would start off on new paths that might strongly influence the climate for the resolution of such questions.

CHAPTER 12

The Great Society, Vietnam, and the Warren Court's Concluding Activism

BY the early months of 1965, it was clear not only to the Eighty-ninth Congress, but to the nation that Lyndon B. Johnson had strong ideas of his own regarding the proper course for the United States both domestically and in the foreign area. As that Congress began to function, it was further clear that the resolute Texan would leave no stone unturned in his drive to achieve his "Great Society." Three weeks before his inauguration, Johnson began sending messages and bills to Congress, and by mid-April he had transmitted ninety-seven messages together with seventy-eight pieces of draft legislation. The Eighty-ninth Congress responded with one of the most remarkable records of legislative achievement in American history. Its first session in 1965 was compared with Franklin D. Roosevelt's "Hundred Days"[1] and numerous New Dealish actions were taken, many of which had been proposed and considered visionary years earlier.

Various of the measures had significant constitutional implications. All were important socially and economically. The Appalachian Regional Development Act, appropriating $1.1 billion for the economic development of that vast impoverished area, complemented broader programs functioning under the Economic Opportunity Act of 1964, generally aimed at achieving success in the "war

1. James M. Burns (ed.), *To Heal and to Build: The Programs of President Lyndon B. Johnson* (New York, 1968), pp. 4–5.

on poverty."[2] An enormous extension and a major revision of the Housing Act was passed, the Housing and Urban Development Act of 1965 approving grants for a four-year urban research program and authorizing federal aid for the construction of 240,000 units of low-rent public housing.[3] At first Congress denied an administration request for directly subsidized federal rent supplements to low-income families, but voted for it in the spring of 1966, in the meantime creating a new Cabinet-rank agency, the Department of Housing and Urban Development (HUD), which consolidated a number of federal agencies concerned with the cities.[4] Its first head, Robert C. Weaver, was also the first Negro Cabinet member in American history. Beating down the persistent opposition of the American Medical Association, Johnson proposed a health care plan for persons over sixty-five, fulfilling proposals Harry Truman had made twenty years earlier and Kennedy had supported.[5] Financed through social security, it provided for hospital and nursing home care. Other health legislation authorized mental health centers, aid to retarded children, and research into cancer, heart disease, and stroke. It also required cigarette manufacturers to imprint packages with the message that "cigarette smoking may be hazardous to your health," raising an issue that later aroused free speech advocates when federal action was urged to ban cigarette advertising.

Acting on a proposal originally submitted by President Kennedy in July, 1963, Congress revised and modernized the immigration laws in the first basic overhaul of these statutes since 1924.[6] The national-origins quota system, with its arbitrary ceilings for approved nationality groups, was scrapped, as was the policy of Asian exclusion. Numerical limits were imposed only on the total number of immigrants from each hemisphere. The new law brought to an end the dominant place assigned to Anglo-Saxon immigration by previous generations.

The two measures with the strongest constitutional overtones were the Elementary and Secondary Education Act of 1965[7] and the

2. 79 Stat. 5 (1965).
3. 79 Stat. 451 (1965).
4. 79 Stat. 667 (1965).
5. 79 Stat. 286 (1965).
6. 79 Stat. 911 (1965).
7. 79 Stat. 27 (1965). On the measure see Eugene Eidenberg and Roy D. Morey, *An Act of Congress: The Legislative Process and the Making of Education Policy* (New York, 1969).

Voting Rights Act of the same year.[8] In enacting the former, Congress resolved a long-standing church-state controversy over federal assistance to parochial schools by appropriating federal funds on a large scale for the first time for primary and secondary schools both public and private. Although separationists viewed the measure with a degree of alarm, there was precedent for tax support in the name of "public welfare."[9] Nonetheless, challenges to the measure, and to various state emulative moves, were launched in various courts shortly after it went into operation.

Continued southern intransigence in obstructing voting registration and the actual casting of the ballot led President Johnson to go to the people in calling for further federal remedial action. In a nationwide address, calling for new civil rights legislation, he pointed out that "every device of which human ingenuity is capable has been used to deny this right." "Experience has clearly shown," he went on, "that the existing process of law cannot overcome systematic and ingenious discrimination. No law that we now have on the books can insure the right to vote when local officials are determined to deny it."[10] The Voting Rights Act, which the President proposed as a solution, was subsequently passed by Congress and signed into law on August 6, 1965. The measure empowered the Attorney General to send federal registrars to any county he suspected of practicing discrimination. This included those with voting qualification tests that clearly impeded registration, and more explicitly those where 50 per cent or more of the voting-age population had failed to register and vote in 1964. The measure also instructed him to file suits to suspend unwarranted prerequisites to voting, such as literacy tests.

The measure, which for the first time assured any actual protec-

8. 79 Stat. 437 (1965). On the measure see Alexander M. Bickel, *Politics and the Warren Court* (New York, 1965), pp. 116–129.

9. For varying contemporary views on the subject see Carl N. Degler, "Aid for Parochial Schools: A Question of Education Not Religion," *The New York Times Magazine*, Jan. 31, 1965, pp. 11 ff.; "Big Federal Move into Education," *Time*, LXXXV (Apr. 30, 1965), 44–45; "School Aid Bill," *Science*, CXLVII (Feb. 12, 1965), 717–719; "Take Back Your Aid," *Newsweek*, LXVI (Nov. 29, 1965), 86; "Congress Shall Make No Law," *Saturday Review*, L (Feb. 18, 1967), 74; L (Mar. 18, 1967), 46.

10. See Lynne Ianniello (ed.), *Milestones Along the March* (New York, 1965), pp. 11–24.

tion of the voting process, was constitutionally a clear departure from the previous 1957 and 1960 Acts. It confronted recalcitrant southern officials directly with effective federal power, something the executive branch had at its disposal, and something clearly unavailable either to Congress or the judiciary. It seemed clearly to assure that in states like Mississippi, where fewer than 7 per cent of the potentially eligible Negroes were registered to vote in 1965, there would be new participation for the Negro in the political process in the future. Further, Attorney General Nicholas Katzenbach lost no time in making clear his intention of acting under the measure's provisions. The federal government early in the previous year had adopted the Twenty-fourth Amendment, abolishing the poll tax in federal elections,[11] and the Supreme Court had struck down a Virginia dodge in this area in April.[12] Katzenbach now filed suits to outlaw the poll tax in four more states, an action that brought subsequent Supreme Court approval in March of 1966.[13]

By the latter months of 1965, Johnson was ebullient over his domestic achievements. Saluting Congress as the "fabulous 89th," he stated: "From your committees and both your houses have come the greatest outpouring of creative legislation in the history of this nation. . . ."[14] And Congress's record was indeed remarkable. In fact, the pace of the session had been so breathless as to cause a major revision of the image, widely prevalent in preceding years, of Congress as structurally incapable of swift decision and prone to frustrate demands for progress.

But Johnson's foreign policy brought changed congressional behavior also, this time in contrast to the "rubber stamp" domestic image its Republican critics were assigning it. The unilateral executive handling of crises in the Dominican Republic and South Vietnam shattered the bipartisan foreign policy image of earlier years and produced highly vocal and mounting criticism from a determined band of senators. When the President sent more than thirty thou-

11. The Twenty-third Amendment, which had been adopted in March, 1961, had seen the long overdue right to vote in federal elections extended to residents of the District of Columbia.

12. Harmon *v.* Forssenius, 380 U.S. 528 (1965).

13. Harper *v.* Virginia, 383 U.S. 663 (1966).

14. "Congress, 1965—The Year in Review," *Congressional Quarterly Almanac* (1965), p. 65.

sand troops to the Dominican Republic to end a civil war, with unconvincing allegations of the danger of a Communist take-over, critics from both parties castigated the action and denounced the doubts it raised about whether the United States intended to impose a Pax Americana on the world.[15]

But it was Presidential actions in Vietnam that were to prove Johnson's fatal error. As the President, responding mainly to the military, involved the nation more and more in the internal affairs of that nation, with minimal positive results, popular hostility became so great as to snuff out hopes for further domestic reform. This involvement served to undo much of the work of the Eighty-ninth Congress, and eventually topple the Democrats from power and drive the President from the White House. The by-products of the move were the energizing of an amorphous peace movement, the loss of confidence in the President of a vast part of the intellectual and academic community, a mounting nationwide resistance to the draft, the embittering of Black leadership, who regarded Vietnam as a drain on America's obligation to help the poor, intensification of the alienation of youth and the generation gap, and the channeling of the forces of student insurgency on college campuses. Most of these developments produced constitutional problems.

The situation in Vietnam had become more and more a part of domestic American politics, especially with the 1964 Presidential campaign. Johnson's opponent, Barry Goldwater, did not miss an occasion to denounce the administration's "no win" policy, and the President rebutted, somewhat contradictorily assailing those who would enlarge the conflict, but also making promises that the United States would not "run out" and leave South Vietnam "for the Communists to take over."[16] Then in August, 1964, the President ordered retaliatory air raids against North Vietnam in response to an attack by North Vietnamese gunboats on American destroyers in the Gulf of Tonkin. He also promptly moved to take advantage of the crisis by extracting from Congress a resolution authorizing him, as Commander-in-Chief, to "take all necessary measures to repel any armed attack against the forces of the United States and to

15. *The New York Times,* Sept. 16, 1969, pp. 1, 4, 16.
16. Alfred Steinberg, *Sam Johnson's Boy* (New York, 1968), pp. 766–767.

prevent further aggression."[17] The resolution was so ambiguously worded that it seemed a rubber stamp of previous Presidential action and a blank-check authorization for conducting Asian actions as the President chose. Contemporary attempts, especially by Senators Daniel Brewster of Maryland and Gaylord Nelson of Wisconsin, to place qualifications on it were voted down.[18]

From a constitutional aspect this Tonkin Gulf resolution had controversial implications. In handing over to President Johnson one of the few foreign affairs powers reserved to Congress by the Constitution—the power to declare war—the overwhelming majority of Senate members gave little consideration to the propriety of delegating legislative authority on such a scale to the executive. Conspicuously missing in the resolution were qualifications on the activities or location of the armed forces when they were attacked and stipulations as to who might be the aggressed or the aggressor. Without such designations the Congress soon found it had licensed the President to escalate the war in Vietnam at will.

The one constitutional critic in the Senate debates on the resolution was Senator Wayne Morse of Oregon, a student of constitutional law and former law school dean. Morse challenged vigorously the constitutionality of the measure. "I do not intend to give to any President the power to make war by way of a predated declaration of war," he contended. "The power to make war is vested in Congress and not in the President. Congress has no constitutional authority to grant such authority to the President."[19]

Yet Morse found little positive Senate support for his challenge. And although he suggested that if the Supreme Court should consent to review the act—a prospect that he himself considered doubtful—it would declare the resolution unconstitutional, modern precedents were largely against him. On the subject the Court since the 1930s had found not only that the Congress was competent to make such sweeping delegations, but that the President alone might exer-

17. See Roger H. Hull and John C. Novogrod, *Law and Vietnam* (Dobbs Ferry, N.Y., 1968), pp. 176 ff.; and Richard A. Falk, *Legal Order in a Violent World* (Princeton, 1968), pp. 245 ff.

18. *Congressional Record,* 88th Cong., 2d Sess., pp. 18403–18410. See also Joseph C. Goulden, *Truth Is the First Casualty: The Gulf of Tonkin Affair—Illusion and Reality* (Chicago, 1969).

19. *Ibid.,* p. 18430.

cise extensive power in external affairs with or without congressional approval.[20]

Whether Senator Morse, or those who later moved to his position, were right or wrong was ultimately of little concern to Lyndon B. Johnson. Acting on the advice of generally "hawkish" consultants, civilian and military, he proceeded to escalate the war stage by stage until by the middle of 1968 the total of American forces had passed half a million. By the end of the year casualties exceeded 30,000 American dead and 100,000 wounded even though "victory" in the normal military sense was nowhere in sight. Through this development, despite a growing "credibility gap" regarding President Johnson's professed and actual intentions, Congress continued to vote the huge appropriations demanded for support of the venture even though at the same time supporting resolutions asserting that "the executive and legislative branches of the United States Government have joint responsibility and authority to formulate the foreign policy of the United States," and stating that in the future American armed forces should not be committed to hostilities on foreign territory without "affirmative action by Congress specifically intended to give rise to such commitment."[21]

20. The issue had been one wrestled with by the Founding Fathers. Alexander Hamilton, in defending George Washington's unilateral issuance in 1793 of a Proclamation of Neutrality, argued strongly that the President possessed an inherent body of executive prerogative above and beyond those rights and duties specifically mentioned in the Constitution. The enumeration of executive powers, he argued in his *Pacificus* essays, unlike that of congressional power, was not restrictive, and did not limit other prerogatives inherent in the office. This was especially true in the sensitive area of foreign policy, he argued, rebutting critics who had charged Washington with infringing upon the province of Congress to which the Constitution assigned the authority to declare war. The President, he contended, "must necessarily possess a right of judging what is the nature of the obligation which the treaties of the country impose on the government." Henry Cabot Lodge (ed.), *The Works of Alexander Hamilton* (12 vols., New York, 1904), IV, 159. At Jefferson's urging, Madison, writing as *Helvidius,* replied. Arguing vigorously that only Congress had the power to decide what treaty obligations were binding on the nation, he went on to blast "the extraordinary doctrine, that the powers of making war, and treaties, are in their nature executive." This vicious doctrine, he pointed out, emanated from British sources; for in Great Britain treaty and war powers "are *royal prerogatives,* hence executive functions. It would never do for a democracy; it smacked of monarchy—worse still, of British monarchy." Gaillard Hunt (ed.), *The Writings of James Madison* (9 vols., New York, 1900–10), VI, 139, 143, 150.

21. *The New York Times,* Nov. 17, 1967, pp. 1, 2. On November 30, the Senate unanimously adopted the Mansfield resolution calling on the President to seek United Nations help in ending the war in Vietnam. *Congressional Record,* 90th Cong., 1st Sess., p. 34348.

Eventually, in 1968, the Senate Foreign Relations Committee under Chairman J. William Fulbright held closed hearings on the original Tonkin Gulf crisis that had produced the war. Evidence seemed strong from a prolonged committee staff investigation of the attacks that the order for "retaliation" against the North had been prepared long before the Tonkin Gulf incident, and the hearings raised the question whether the whole "incident" had not been deliberately designed to provoke a military response that could be used as justification for bombing North Vietnam. Secretary of Defense Robert S. McNamara dismissed the charges as "monstrous" even though he was unprepared to declassify much of the information that might have thrown light on the events. "Every thing related to the Tonkin incidents is secret except that which the Pentagon deems should be made public," Fulbright complained, and after the hearings he told a television audience that "the decision to go to war and then to bring the [Tonkin Gulf] resolution to Congress was based on inadequate evidence and conflicting reports. . . . I would like to see a full-scale re-examination of the purposes, the objectives of our policy in Vietnam."[22]

But if the causes of the war and the constitutional issues surrounding the President's role in bringing it on were really not honestly confronted, the political, social, economic, and constitutional problems that the war produced on the domestic scene could not be so cavalierly avoided. America's racial dilemma, now fanned into new immediacy with growing black discontent, was a good case in point.

The year 1965 had seemed in many ways a high point for the civil rights movement with combined executive, legislative, and judicial support all extending previous goals. The executive branch had set out immediately to implement the new Voting Rights Act. When South Carolina challenged the constitutionality of the measure, the Supreme Court promptly took cases on the subject, ultimately sustaining the measure fully. Chief Justice Warren, for the Court, made clear that the measure's voluminous legislative history had disclosed unremitting and ingenious defiance in certain parts of the country of the Fifteenth Amendment, and that the forms of

22. *Congressional Quarterly Almanac* (1968), pp. 713–715.

relief that Congress had afforded were a valid effectuation of that constitutional provision.[23]

The opinion complemented a series of rulings during the 1965–66 term in the civil rights area. In these the Court continued its protection of civil rights demonstrators from unwarranted harassment;[24] struck further at southern schemes for noncompliance with school desegregation;[25] and opened facilities to equal access in a case involving land willed to a city for a public park for whites only.[26] Over a surprising dissent by Justice Black, it also struck at divergent treatment of white and Negro patrons of Louisiana public libraries.[27]

Similar cooperation had produced sharp and effective federal response to violent southern hostility to the civil rights movement generally. Brutal and violent suppression of a civil rights march from Selma, Alabama, to that state's capital in March, 1965, and the subsequent duplicity of Governor George Wallace, in promising President Johnson he would protect the marchers, then indicating he was unable to do so,[28] once again poured federal troops into the South and partisans of the movement into integrated lines of march. On the other hand, the summer of 1964 had seen unprotected college students working for civil rights in Mississippi brutally assaulted and murdered, and through all such action a refusal of southern courts to bring in indictments against such brutality, even when federal officials afforded them evidence of form and nature.[29] The

23. South Carolina *v.* Katzenbach, 383 U.S. 301 (1966). See also Katz *v.* Morgan, 384 U.S. 641 (1966). Later, in a case in 1969, the Court moved again to enforce the measure against Virginia and Mississippi "interposition," denying that changes in the state's voting law were enforceable in the absence of federal approval required by Sec. 5 of the 1965 Act. Allen *v.* State Board of Education, 393 U.S. 544 (1969).

24. Shuttlesworth *v.* Birmingham, 382 U.S. 86 (1965).

25. Bradley *v.* School Board, 382 U.S. 103 (1965); Rogers *v.* Paul, 382 U.S. 198 (1965).

26. Evans *v.* Newton, 382 U.S. 296 (1965).

27. Brown *v.* Louisiana, 383 U.S. 131 (1966).

28. Rowland Evans and Robert D. Novak, *Lyndon B. Johnson: The Exercise of Power* (New York, 1966), p. 495; Benjamin Muse, *The American Negro Revolution: From Nonviolence to Black Power, 1963–1967* (Bloomington, Ind., 1968), pp. 168–171.

29. On the Mississippi experience see Len Holt, *The Summer That Didn't End* (London, 1966); and Elizabeth Sutherland, *Letters from Mississippi* (New York, 1965). See also Leon Friedman (ed.), *Southern Justice* (New York, 1965),

constitutional question that arose from both situations was the extent of the ability of the federal government to intervene to enforce state law and demand the punishment of state crimes against United States citizens. The issue came to a dramatic head legally when civil rights worker Mrs. Viola Liuzzo was shot and killed while returning by automobile from the Selma march. Although a federal official had witnessed the shooting and clearly identified the assassin, Alabama courts had refused to convict him of murder.[30]

In late March, 1966, the Court addressed itself to the question. Long-standing precedents hamstrung the federal government, permitting it only to move against "state action" depriving citizens of their federal rights. Similar movement against private individuals was legally difficult. It now found that in the murder of three civil rights workers near Philadelphia, Mississippi, a conspiracy existed among police officers and private citizens, particularly Klansmen, that clearly constituted "state action."[31] Subsequent conviction of a number of the principals resulted—an unprecedented action on the part of a southern state court. Further, a case involving the ambush slaying of a prominent Washington, D.C., Negro traveling through Georgia was made federal by invoking a statute making it a crime for private individuals to interfere with the rights of citizens to travel from state to state.[32]

But the justices were not happy with their own rulings. Six of their number joined in two concurring opinions deploring the inability of the federal government to move against private citizens who deprived other Americans of their basic rights—including their lives. They also indicated clearly to Congress that they would feel bound to uphold any appropriate law aimed at punishing such

---

pp. 136–164, 187–280. The lack of uniformity in federal and state jury selection procedures was dramatized by a 1961 Justice Department survey that showed that the ninety-two federal district courts had ninety-two different systems of selecting jurors, and far greater variations existed among state and county courts. "White Man's Justice," *Civil Liberties* (March, 1967), p. 2.

30. *The New York Times,* Oct. 23, 1965, p. 1. For later conviction of the assassin and his accomplices under an 1870 federal law, see *The New York Times,* Dec. 4, 1965, p. 1.

31. U.S. *v.* Price, 383 U.S. 787 (1966).

32. U.S. *v.* Guest, 383 U.S. 745 (1966). There is a good discussion of the case in Archibald Cox, *The Warren Court: Constitutional Decision as an Instrument of Reform* (Cambridge, Mass., 1968), pp. 60 ff.

individuals who used violence to deny persons their Fourteenth Amendment rights. Although President Johnson announced the following day that the Justice Department was drafting such a law, its immediate enactment was not forthcoming.[33]

Already black disillusionment with the hollowness of securing further legal guarantees of their rights was producing violent response. The "black power" movement, growing slowly to this time, was greatly escalated as black leaders like Stokely Carmichael convinced their followers that de jure segregation and voting rights could not bring about an end to de facto discrimination, even if they were defined so broadly and liberally as to include voting protection and equal access to everything from schools to private housing, hotels, restaurants, and clubs.[34]

The Watts riots in Los Angeles in August, 1965, brought the level of this frustration home to white America. Promptly a commission was appointed to investigate the causes of the violent looting, burning, and destruction of property. But this McCone Commission's report, while investigating local economic and social conditions, tended to play down the broader implications of the activity and avoided confronting the role that black bitterness over Vietnam had played, particularly as the growing escalation had pulled what seemed to young blacks to be a disproportionate number of their race into the military.[35] It also ignored what Bayard Rustin, a modern black intellectual who was in Watts during the riots, felt were the clear broader implications: "The whole point of the outburst in Watts," wrote Rustin, "was that it marked the first major rebellion of Negroes against their masochism and was carried on with the express purpose of asserting that they would no longer quietly submit to the deprivation of slum life."[36] Martin Luther King

33. On June 20, 1966, the Court moved in the area, ruling that under the 1964 Civil Rights Act, sit-in cases could be removed from a local to a federal court for trial. Georgia *v.* Rachel, 384 U.S. 780 (1966); but see also City of Greenwood *v.* Peacock, 384 U.S. 808 (1966).

34. Stokely Carmichael and Charles V. Hamilton, *Black Power: The Politics of Liberation* (New York, 1967).

35. A Report by the Governor's Commission on the Los Angeles Riot, *Violence in the City—An End or a Beginning?* (Los Angeles, 1965).

36. Bayard Rustin, "The Watts 'Manifesto' and the McCone Report," *Commentary,* XLI (March, 1966), 30. For other criticism of the report see Robert M. Fogelson, "White on Black: A Critique of the McCone Commission Report on the Los Angeles Riots," *Political Science Quarterly,* LXXXII (September, 1967), 337–367; and Robert Blauner, "Whitewash over Watts: The Failure of the McCone Commission Report," *Transaction,* III (March–April, 1966), 3–9.

articulated well the coming together of the two sources of discontent when in a bitter denunciation of national policy he stated:

> To do too little to relieve the agony of Negro life is as inflammatory as inciting a riot. To put an Asian war of dubious national interest far above domestic needs in the order of priorities and to pit it against reforms that were delayed a century is worse than a blind policy; it is a provocative policy.[37]

Federal response was not forthcoming, and indeed, by 1966 the government was spending more for Vietnam than for the entire federal welfare program. Black discontent mounted. Riots in Chicago and Cleveland in the summer of 1965 produced at most a mild Bail Reform Act,[38] but no broad remedial legislation for the ghettoes or for more pressing urban problems such as unemployment, slum housing, and hostile police. The Detroit and Newark riots of the following summer finally spurred federal action. Mr. Johnson in July, 1967, established the National Advisory Commission on Civil Disorders with Governor Otto Kerner of Illinois as chairman to investigate. The commission report, released in March, 1968, was pessimistic in the extreme.[39] While submitting detailed recommendations for a comprehensive program to insure equality, social justice, and peace, and warning against resort to blind repression or capitulation to lawlessness, it also placed major responsibility for the nation's racial disorders on white racism and warned that "our nation is moving toward two societies, one black, one white—separate and unequal. . . . To continue our present course will involve the continuing polarization of the American Community, and will involve ultimately the destruction of basic democratic values."[40]

Distressed and sensitive Americans called for immediate implementation of the report's recommendation, many now coming to support Negro leader A. Philip Randolph's earlier submitted "Freedom Budget," which had called for the government to spend

37. *The New York Times,* Apr. 14, 1966, p. 1.

38. 80 Stat. 214 (1966). On the measure see Patricia Wald and Daniel J. Freed, "The Bail Reform Act of 1966," *American Bar Association Journal,* LII (1966), 940–945.

39. *Report of the National Advisory Commission on Civil Disorders* (New York, 1968).

40. *Ibid.,* p. 1.

over $100 billion in ten years to eradicate poverty,[41] but President Johnson clearly felt military priorities came first and little immediate action other than steps to suppress the manifestations of black discontent was forthcoming.

The assassination of Martin Luther King in April, 1968, finally pressured Congress into minor action. The rioting that had followed this outrage had resulted in the biggest military buildup to deal with a civil disorder in American history, and one day after King's funeral, the House of Representatives passed and sent to the President a "fair housing bill" designed to ban racial discrimination in the sale or rental of 80 per cent of housing in the United States. The measure ultimately passed Congress as the Civil Rights Act of 1968.[42] Its other provisions provided criminal penalties for injuring or interfering with persons exercising specified rights such as attending school or working, voting, serving on a jury, or enjoying public accommodations, with similar protection afforded civil rights workers urging or helping others to exercise their rights.[43] Riot-shy congressional leaders, led by Senator J. Strom Thurmond of South Carolina, insisted, however, upon provisions providing heavy criminal penalties for traveling in or using the facilities of interstate commerce, such as telephones, to incite or take part in a riot. Penalties were also provided for manufacturing or teaching the use of firearms or explosives for use in a civil disorder. The measure thus made "evil intent" punishable, with critics quick to charge that the antiriot provisions were so loosely worded as to abridge First Amendment guarantees of free speech and to restrict freedom of travel. Black reaction to the bill was mixed: N.A.A.C.P. types were pleased with the positive sections, but the more militant black nationalists designated it as merely a measure to create further legal rights that a great majority of black Americans had little opportunity or real ability to enjoy, and argued that its latter sections threatened the promised gains of the former.

The Supreme Court's actions in these years were revealing, es-

41. *The New York Times,* Oct. 27, 1967, pp. 1, 2.

42. Public Law 90–284 (1968).

43. The measure also contained an Indian rights section that prohibited tribal government from making or enforcing law that violated specified constitutional rights. It also prohibited states from assuming civil or criminal jurisdiction over Indian areas without the consent of the Indian tribes affected.

pecially of the Chief Justice's own impatience at the lower pace of fair actions being carried out by the other two branches of the government in the civil rights area. Members of the Court's liberal wing frequently joined him. In a series of cases involving the omission of Negroes from juries and grand juries, the Court struck consistently at discriminatory local practices.[44] In *Jones* v. *Alabama,*[45] it even examined the disparities between the percentage of Negroes on the tax rolls and on venires. Unless there was some reasonable relation, it maintained, fair trial had been denied. While insistent also that Negroes be assured every proper procedural guarantee, even the Chief Justice was unprepared to afford damages to a civil rights leader against a judge for his "illegal sentencing," even though the Civil Rights Act of 1871 seemed to allow action against "any person" who under "color of law" deprived another person of his civil rights.[46]

The Court was equally adamant in seeing that fairness was done in the desegregation area. In a series of school cases in May, 1968, it struck down "freedom of choice" plans in Virginia and Arkansas and a "free transfer" plan in Mississippi.[47] In the Virginia case, it looked closely at whether the state plan adopted actually broke down the pattern of racial segregation in that state's schools. "The burden on a school board today," wrote Justice Brennan in ruling to the contrary, "is to come forward with a plan which promises realistically to work, and promises realistically to work *now*."[48] Discrimination in other public facilities got similar judicial treatment. In *U.S.* v. *Johnson* in April, 1968, it held that the 1964 Civil Rights Act, although it limited the action of would-be users

44. Whitus *v.* Georgia, 385 U.S. 545 (1967); Coleman *v.* Alabama, 389 U.S. 22 (1967). In the jury area the Court did rule, however, that it was possible to exclude jurymen who had scruples against the death penalty from participating in a case in which, should the defendant have been found guilty, the death penalty could have been demanded. Witherspoon *v.* Illinois, 391 U.S. 510 (1968). The case sufficiently aroused Illinois Senator Everett Dirksen that he eventually used it as grounds for switching and opposing Associate Justice Abe Fortas' appointment as Chief Justice.

45. Jones *v.* Alabama, 389 U.S. 24 (1967).

46. Pierson *v.* Ray, 386 U.S. 547 (1967).

47. Green *v.* County School Board, 391 U.S. 430 (1968); Raney *v.* Board of Education, 391 U.S. 443 (1968); Monroe *v.* Board of Commissioners, 391 U.S. 450 (1968).

48. Green *v.* County School Board, p. 439.

to injunctive relief, still did not foreclose the possibility of action against outsiders who blocked the entry of Negroes to facilities that they were clearly entitled to use. It went on in June, 1969, to rule that private clubs with "memberships" open to whites only were still not private and must integrate.[49]

Judicial power, activism, and impatience showed most strongly in cases involving equal rights to housing. When California voters, by a margin of almost two to one, approved an amendment to the state constitution that nullified earlier legislation barring racial discrimination in the sale or rental of any private dwelling of more than four units, the Court upheld California's supreme court, which had nullified the action.[50] The question turned on the difficult definition of "state action," the issue being whether the voters in enacting Proposition 14 had involved the state in discrimination in violation of the equal protection clause of the Fourteenth Amendment. By adopting the proposition, the Court ruled, the state had become "at least a partner in the act of discrimination," adding that when "the electorate assumes to exercise the law making function," it is "as much a state agency as any of its elected officials."[51]

Such an unprecedented move to find unique legal ways to achieve a social purpose also characterized a Missouri case in 1968. Here the Court removed by judicial action the exemptions in the federal fair housing act of that year by holding them in conflict with an 1866 federal statute still on the books, which provided that all citizens had the same right to ". . . inherit, purchase, lease, sell,

49. U.S. *v.* Johnson, 390 U.S. 563 (1968). Daniel and Kyles *v.* Paul, 395 U.S. 298 (1969). In a widely reported decision in June, 1967, the Court shocked southern racists by ruling unanimously that Virginia's antimiscegenation law was unconstitutional. Holding that marriage is one of the "basic civil rights of man," Chief Justice Earl Warren wrote: "To deny this fundamental freedom on so unsupportable a basis as . . . racial classifications . . . so directly subversive of the principle of equality at the heart of the Fourteenth Amendment, is surely to deprive all the state's citizens of liberty without due process of law." Loving *v.* Virginia, 388 U.S. 1, 12 (1967). The opinion invalidated similar laws in fifteen other states.

50. Reitman *v.* Mulkey, 387 U.S. 369 (1967).

51. *Ibid.*, at 379. On the case see Charles L. Black, Jr., "'State Action,' Equal Protection, and California's Proposition 14," *Harvard Law Review,* LXXXI (1967), 69–109; and Kenneth L. Karst and Harold W. Horowitz, "Reitman *v.* Mulkey: A Telophase of Substantive Equal Protection," *Supreme Court Review* (1967), pp. 39–80.

hold, and convey real and personal property."[52] That measure, wrote Justice Stewart, precluded all racial discrimination in the sale and rental of property. That that act lay partially dormant for many years does not diminish its force today, he contended. "Clearly it was the intention of its framers to enact a comprehensive statute forbidding every form of racial discrimination affecting basic civil rights . . . , including the right to purchase or lease property." And the justice went on, over the bitter protest of Justices Harlan and White, to invoke the Thirteenth Amendment as ample constitutional justification for the 1866 measure and its breadth. The following year, the body used both the 1866 and 1968 Acts to sustain a local fair housing ordinance enacted by city council, even though the voters, in supporting a racist counter charter amendment, had moved for its revocation.[53]

The dramatic nature of such judicial action, however, was lost in the malaise of Vietnam that engulfed the country by 1966. Public concern for civil rights had waned sharply and other constitutional issues had displaced them. Foremost among these were the legitimacy of governmental actions taken in the name of the national emergency, particularly the stepped-up drafting of young men, the use of the draft to suppress dissent, and other attempts to contain mounting and at times violent protest against the most unpopular war in American history.

The central issues of the constitutionality of the war did not reach the Court directly, even though dissenters in various cases raised disturbing issues. Rather the debate tended to rage in nonjudicial circles, where, however, it was warmly pursued. It generally took two forms. One involved the legality of United States involvement in the war and the lawfulness of U.S. actions under international law and in the name of certain treaty commitments.[54] The second involved Senator Morse's concern for the President's authority, as chief executive, to act unilaterally, in spite of, or because of, the Tonkin Gulf resolution. Critics continued to hold such action a violation of separation of powers,

52. Jones *v.* Mayer, 392 U.S. 409 (1968). See Gerhard Casper, "Jones v. Mayer: Clio Bemused and Confused Muse," *Supreme Court Review* (1968), pp. 89–132.

53. Hunter *v.* Erickson, 393 U.S. 385 (1969).

54. See David W. Robertson, "The Debate Among American International Lawyers About the Vietnam War," *Texas Law Review,* XLVI (1968), 898–913.

insisting that the Congress was naïve in assuming that once having handed the President a blank check he could be depended upon, through self-discipline, to use that plenary power with restraint and in constitutional ways.[55]

The issues that did reach the Supreme Court were either denied certiorari or handled in a limited and gingerly fashion. Nonetheless they were still illustrative of the kinds of domestic problems that the war was producing. When a young Georgia Negro legislator-elect, Julian Bond, spoke out sharply against the war, seeming to support S.N.C.C. opposition to it and to the draft, he was twice denied his seat on the ground that his remarks showed that he could not take the oath of office in good faith.[56] Earl Warren, for the Supreme Court, held that Bond was entitled to his seat and that he could not be deprived of it on the basis of statements he made that were protected by the First Amendment. The Court reasoned that the freedom to make such statements about national policy were essential to the operation of a democratic government and that legislators especially "be given the widest latitude to express their views on issues of policy."[57] In May, 1967, however, the Court dismissed the appeal of seventeen antiwar demonstrators convicted of disorderly conduct in a 1964 rally in New York City, taking the position that the case was without sufficient merit to warrant review.[58] Justices Douglas and Fortas dissented, Douglas particularly suggesting that "where First Amendment rights are involved, as

55. Stanley Faulkner, "War in Vietnam: Is It Constitutional?," *Georgetown Law Journal,* LVI (1968), 1132–1143; and "Congress, the President, and the Power to Commit Forces to Combat," *Harvard Law Review,* LXXXI (1968), 1771–1805.

56. Bond *v.* Floyd, 385 U.S. 116 (1966). During the course of the oral argument the following exchange took place: Justice Fortas: ". . . Where did Mr. Bond ever say that he would not support the Constitution?" Georgia Attorney General Arthur K. Bolton: "He said that people should not participate and he said that he had no obligation to support the war." Justice White: "What does that mean?" Mr. Bolton: "I don't think my opinion matters, and I don't know what the Georgia Legislature thought it meant." Justice Fortas: "You will concede that there is an ambiguity." Justice Stewart: "Are you telling us that there is a requirement to support a war that Congress hasn't even declared? You're differentiating legislators from other people?" Mr. Bolton: "Yes." Justice Stewart: "There is no obligation on anyone to support Viet Nam, is there?" Mr. Bolton: "No."

57. Bond *v.* Floyd, at 136.

58. Turner *v.* New York, 386 U.S. 773 (1967).

they were here, we have been meticulous to insist upon clean-cut violations of ordinances protecting law and order lest broad or fuzzy applications be used to suffocate or impair their exercise of those constitutional rights. Issues of that character and gravity are tendered here and I would resolve them."[59]

Yet the Court clearly had no intention of doing so. In two subsequent cases involving the refusal of inductees to serve in the armed forces on the grounds that "the present United States military activity in Vietnam is illegal,"[60] and that "waging of a war of aggression" is a "crime against peace" imposing "individual responsibility,"[61] the Court denied certiorari. Both Douglas and Stewart protested, however, contending that it was dodging large and deeply troubling questions.[62]

Disturbed American young people, frustrated in their inability to reach the public conscience through this sort of noncompliance, turned to other forms of civil disobedience. In one celebrated case an army doctor, Captain Howard B. Levy, refused to instruct Special Forces ("Green Beret") medical aidmen in treating skin disease in Vietnam and was charged with promoting disloyalty and disaffection among the troops by making statements disloyal to the United States and prejudicial to good order and discipline.

59. *Ibid.,* at 775.

60. Mora *v.* McNamara, 389 U.S. 934 (1967).

61. Mitchell *v.* U.S., 386 U.S. 972 (1967).

62. The Mitchell case had raised the troublesome issue of the fact the dissenters did not so much oppose war in general as the Vietnam war in particular. This contention, raised more and more by potential draftees, came to be known as the Nuremberg defense. It took its name from the Treaty of London of August 6, 1945, which said that "waging a war of aggression" was a "crime against peace" and that it imposed individual responsibility. The theory behind the treaty was the same as that underlying Allied prosecutions of Nazi war criminals at the Nuremberg Trials following World War II: that individuals could be held accountable for heinous crimes that they were ordered to commit by a higher commander. Douglas in his dissent alluded to the defense, indicating there was a considerable body of opinion that our actions in Vietnam constituted the waging of an aggressive "war." The case, he said, presented questions of whether the Treaty of London was the supreme law of the land, whether the waging of an aggressive war was justiciable in this context, whether "the Viet Nam episode is a 'war' in the sense of the Treaty," whether the defendant had standing to raise the question, and whether the defense could be raised in amelioration of punishment. Admitting that these were sensitive and delicate questions, he still contended, "I think they should be answered." Mitchell *v.* U.S., 386 U.S. 972 (1967).

At pretrial proceedings the army law officer presiding permitted Levy's counsel to introduce evidence of Special Forces' brutality in Vietnam. The counsel, Charles Morgan Jr., the southern regional director of the American Civil Liberties Union and a veteran of southern civil rights skirmishes, called a number of witnesses to the stand to testify as to Special Forces' behavior in Vietnam, but the army law officer ruled that Morgan had failed to support the charge that Special Forces' personnel were guilty of atrocities.[63]

The burning of draft cards, as an act of "symbolic speech," did arouse the nation. In fact, it so aroused Congress that legislation was passed imposing extreme penalties on such action. The Supreme Court initially denied certiorari in one such case,[64] but did take a second, *U.S.* v. *O'Brien*.[65] In its ruling in May, 1968, Warren for the Court sustained the 1965 amendment to the Universal Military Training and Service Act of 1948 extending the draft and making it a federal crime knowingly to destroy a draft card. Even if such activity were constitutionally protected speech, Warren maintained, when speech and nonspeech elements are combined,

63. Prior to the opinion of the court-martial, the Supreme Court in Levy *v.* Corcoran, 387 U.S. 915 (1967), had refused to accept his case for review. Levy had attempted unsuccessfully to have a three-judge federal district court convened to rule on the constitutionality of sections of the Uniform Code of Military Justice, which he said were unconstitutional infringements on his free speech. In two subsequent cases the Court considered military justice. In O'Callahan *v.* Parker, 395 U.S. 258 (1969), it held that members of the armed forces could not be prosecuted by court-martial for offenses that are not "service-connected." Justice Douglas pointed to the serious deficiencies of trial by court-martial compared to trial by civilian court, including absence of indictment by grand jury, trial of enlisted men by officers, conviction by two-thirds vote, and the danger of command-influence, and noted that a court-martial's basic purpose was not to secure justice but to preserve military discipline. See Grant S. Nelson and James E. Westbrook, "Court-Martial Jurisdiction Over Servicemen for Civilian' Offenses: An Analysis of O'Callahan v. Parker," *Minnesota Law Review,* LIV (November, 1969), 1–65. In Noyd *v.* Bond, 395 U.S. 683 (1969), the claim was presented that members of the armed forces are entitled, both constitutionally and by statute, to be free of imprisonment pending review of their court-martial convictions by the military appellate court. Ducking the issue entirely, the Court held that before the federal courts could entertain the claim, the Court of Military Appeals first had to be given an opportunity to decide the question.

64. Miller *v.* U.S. 389 U.S. 930 (1967).

65. U.S. *v.* O'Brien, 391 U.S. 367 (1968). On the background of the law and the Miller and O'Brien cases see Dean Alfange, Jr., "Free Speech and Symbolic Conduct: The Draft-Card Burning Case," *Supreme Court Review* (1968), pp. 1–52.

and the latter are sufficiently important to warrant governmental interest, they can be suppressed. Douglas again dissented, raising in this and a further case in the same term[66] the question of the extent to which the government could call war powers into use in the absence of a declaration of war, a question on which, he argued, the litigants and the country were entitled to a ruling.

> . . . the question whether there can be conscription when there has not been a declaration of war, has never been decided by this Court. It is an important question. It is a recurring question. It is coming to us in various forms in many cases as a result of the conflict in Vietnam. I think we owe to those who are being marched off to jail for maintaining that a declaration of war is essential for conscription an answer to this important undecided constitutional question.[67]

The Court, however, was prepared to handle issues such as conscription on a narrow case-to-case basis. When a theological student classified IV-D returned his draft card in protest and was reclassified I-A without a hearing, the Supreme Court protested, insisting that preinduction judicial review was not precluded in the case, and that the student's activities could not justify his reclassification.[68] On the other hand, where a Negro conscientious objector was denied that status, and a district court held a section of the Military Selective Service Act of 1967 unconstitutional in denying preinduction judicial review, the Supreme Court reversed the ruling, maintaining that protests against misclassification could

66. Holmes *v.* U.S., 391 U.S. 936 (1968).

67. *Ibid.*, p. 949. Two rulings were revealing of the Court's tacit acknowledgment of "war" circumstances. In U.S. *v.* Acme Process Equipment Co., 385 U.S. 138 (1966), Black for a unanimous Court upheld the government's cancellation of a war contract because three of a rifle manufacturer's key employees had accepted compensation for awarding subcontracts in violation of the Anti-Kickback Act. In Becker *v.* Philco Corp., 389 U.S. 979 (1967), both Warren and Douglas expressed doubts in dissent about the "military-industrial complex" and its "war" intentions.

68. Oestereich *v.* Selective Service Board, 393 U.S. 233 (1969). Earlier in the famed Seegar case (U.S. *v.* Seegar, 380 U.S. 163 [1965]), the Court had broadened the conscientious objector provisions of the Selective Training and Service Act of 1940 to cover not merely orthodox religious pacifism, but those who had a sincere and meaningful belief that occupied a place in their lives "parallel to that filled by the orthodox belief in God." This still left Selective Service boards with the power to determine, in considering applications for C.O. status, whether the belief was "truly held." On the case see Clyde E. Jacobs and John F. Gallagher, *The Selective Service Act* (New York, 1967), pp. 147–189.

validly await induction.[69] Even in general dissent cases, the Court insisted on examining the circumstances. When a protestor at a Washington Monument antidraft rally, himself ineligible for service, maintained to a crowd that if inducted, "the first man I want to get in my sights is L.B.J.," the Court reversed his conviction, maintaining that his statement was crude political hyperbole, and, as such, protected speech.[70]

But if the courts were frequently lenient with antiwar protest, leaders in high administration, including the Justice Department, were not. General Lewis B. Hershey, disturbed by Stop-the-Draft demonstrations, recommended in October, 1967, that local draft boards invoke the delinquency provisions of the Selective Service regulations against antiwar demonstrators, suggesting to the boards that "misguided registrants" who participated in "illegal demonstrations" should be declared delinquent, reclassified I-A, and subjected to immediate induction. His letter promptly brought angry denunciations from many national leaders and bodies as divergent as the American Association of University Professors and the American Civil Liberties Union, who viewed with alarm the use of the draft as a bludgeon to silence opposition to the war. It drew support from conservative congressmen, however, Representative Edward Hebert of Louisiana urging, "Let's forget the First Amendment. When is the Justice Department going to get hep and do something to eliminate this rat-infested area? At least the effort can be made."[71] And the Justice Department responded shortly thereafter, indicting pediatrician Dr. Benjamin Spock

69. Clark *v.* Gabriel, 393 U.S. 256 (1968). Shortly afterward in McKart *v.* U.S., 395 U.S. 185 (1969), Marshall finally settled the question, much discussed among lawyers and lower federal courts, whether a man under prosecution for refusing to be inducted can raise his legal defenses if he had ignored the administrative appeals available with the Selective Service system. The Court answered the question affirmatively, at least where the defense involves only the interpretation of a congressional statute. In this case, the issue was whether the petitioner was a "sole surviving son" and therefore exempt from the draft. Since local draft boards and Selective Service appeal boards have no special competency in statutory interpretation, the petitioner could raise his defense in his criminal prosecution. More headline-making was the refusal of former heavyweight boxing champion Muhammad Ali (Cassius Clay) to submit to induction on the ground that he was a minister of the Black Muslim faith and as such entitled to deferment, and the refusal of the Supreme Court to hear his case, Ali, aka Clay *et al. v.* Gordon, 386 U.S. 1002, 1018, 1027 (1967).

70. Watts *v.* U.S., 394 U.S. 705 (1969).

71. *Congressional Record,* 90th Cong., 1st Sess., pp. 11929–11930.

and Yale Chaplain William Sloan Coffin, Jr., along with three other chronic antidraft spokesmen, for conspiracy to "counsel, aid, and abet" violations of the Selective Service law. Sentenced in a Boston federal court in the summer of 1968 by Judge Francis W. Ford, who contended, "Where law and order stops, obviously anarchy begins. . . . It would be preposterous to allow those who, as the jury found, conspired to incite Selective Service registrants to violate the law to escape under the guise of free speech,"[72] the case was appealed to a United States circuit court. The four defendants found guilty were then given liberty on their own recognizance pending the outcome of their appeal, and subsequently freed on reversal.

The action clearly seemed to be an effort to make an example of excessive protest and keep antiwar activities to a qualified level. It thus seemed to reflect Johnson's own somewhat ambiguous posture on dissent. The President had, on one hand, frequently presented arguments against dissent, contending that it would only prolong the war and aid the enemy, a posture endorsed by General William C. Westmoreland, commander of U.S. forces in Vietnam, in a stateside speech.[73] On the other hand, Johnson had also, in other appearances, defended the right of dissent, stating in May, 1967, that the nation needed the "free spirit of its youth," suggesting that the "debate will go on" and that "it will have its price."[74]

Public response to protest, both antiwar and antiestablishment, tended to be more hostile than sympathetic. This type of noncompliance with the law and civil disobedience was linked by many with the nation's broader defiance of law and order, from the black ghettoes to cynical criminals and irresponsible youthful nonconformists. For many, such divergent actions blurred into a national pattern of rising lawlessness and "crime in the streets." Many disturbed Americans in seeking a scapegoat heaped blame on Earl Warren and the Supreme Court. The "law-and-order" issue, both emotionally and actually, thus became the central one in domestic American politics and had to be confronted by all three branches

72. Jessica Mitford, "Guilty as Charged by the Judge," *Atlantic,* CCXXIV (August, 1969), 57.

73. *The New York Times,* Apr. 25, 1967, p. 14.

74. "On Viet Nam Dissent," *Congressional Quarterly Weekly Report* (June 2, 1967), p. 937.

of the government. The result produced a tangle of constitutional developments, many of grave significance.

The legal status of the issue had changed perceptibly in the early years of Vietnam escalation. Having followed the injunction of Kennedy leadership to upgrade the rights of the poor and the depressed in the area of criminal procedure, the Supreme Court had watched the outcome of its 1965 Escabedo ruling carefully. Leading members of that body had hoped that it would be an invitation to Congress to join the Court's venture and bring something close to uniform justice to the nation's federal and local courts. But the setting forth of national guidelines in the criminal procedure area was not part of the Eighty-ninth Congress's otherwise active program and record of legislation.[75]

Thus the Court felt called upon to act and did in the Miranda case at the end of the 1965 term.[76] The generalities with which the Court had disposed of the necessity for pretrial rights in the earlier Escabedo case had opened the way for confusion in both state and federal courts, both having arrived at varying and even contradictory conclusions about the decision in subsequent cases.[77] The Court was now prepared, wrote Chief Justice Warren, in the first of the major criminal law opinions in which he had written the majority, to "give concrete constitutional guidelines for law-enforcement agencies and courts to follow." Those guidelines, while simple and direct, again aroused controversy. In an ambitiously researched opinion, exploring both the long historical background of various procedural guarantees and modern techniques of police interrogation, Warren set forth three basic rules. A person must be informed in clear and unequivocal terms that he has the right to remain silent and that anything said can and will be used against him in court. He must be apprised of his right to have counsel,

75. The principal 1965 measure enacted by Congress had been the Law Enforcement Assistance Act, 79 Stat. 828 (1965), which had provided grants for the study of new police procedures and for demonstration projects using new police techniques. The federal government's role had been chiefly monetary and very indirectly advisory. The measure had complemented the Criminal Justice Act of 1964, 78 Stat. 552 (1964), on which see Robert U. Kutak, "The Criminal Justice Act of 1964," *Nebraska Law Review*, XLIV (1965), 703–750.

76. Miranda *v.* Arizona, 384 U.S. 486 (1966).

77. *Time*, June 24, 1966, pp. 53–54. See also Richard J. Medalie, *From Escabedo to Miranda* (Washington, 1966); and William J. Chambliss, *Crime and the Legal Process* (New York, 1969), p. 222.

with the state expected to foot the bill if he is indigent. If the interrogation continues without the presence of an attorney, "a heavy burden rests on the Government to demonstrate that the defendant knowingly and intelligently waives his privilege against self-incrimination and the right to counsel."

Four dissenters—Harlan, White, Stewart, and Clark—protested the ruling vigorously. Harlan accused the majority of peddling poor constitutional law by ignoring the carefully developed "totality of circumstances" doctrine and replacing it with hard and inflexible rules based on the Fifth Amendment. White contended that the Court was making "new law and new public policy," which could well have the undesirable social effect of "returning a killer, a rapist, or other criminal to the streets to repeat his crime whenever it pleases him."[78] On the other hand, many of the most progressive police departments in the country promptly indicated that they had been adhering to such practices for some years and that the Court certainly afforded them no new rules or difficult restrictions. As to the loud cry from others, and from alarmists generally that the ruling encouraged crime and criminals, two prominent law-enforcement officials had answers. Said Attorney General Ramsey Clark, "Court rules do not cause crime. People do not commit crimes because of decisions restricting police questions or because they think they might not be convicted."[79] David Acheson, then U.S. Attorney for Washington, D.C., added: "Changes in court decisions and prosecution practices have about the same effect on the crime rate as an aspirin would have on a tumor of the brain."[80] Whoever was right, there was no doubt that the ruling called for a higher level of police work on the part of many of the nation's departments, and police better educated and more knowledgeable in the Constitution and the Bill of Rights.[81]

78. Miranda *v.* Arizona, 384 U.S. 486, 517, 542 (1966).

79. Quoted in Leo Katcher, *Earl Warren: A Political Biography* (New York, 1967), p. 472. For one police chief's response see O. M. Wilson, "Crime, the Courts, and the Police," *Journal of Criminal Law, Criminology, and Police Science,* LVII (1966), 291–307.

80. Irving R. Kaufman, "Miranda and the Police: The Confession Debate Continues," *The New York Times Magazine,* Oct. 2, 1966, p. 47; James Vorenberg, "Is the Court Handcuffing the Cops?," *The New York Times Magazine,* May 11, 1969, p. 32.

81. In follow-up studies on the impact of Miranda conducted by students at Yale and Georgetown Universities, and by faculty members at the University of Michigan, observing directly police procedures and confessions, evidence was

The Supreme Court was not unmoved by the wide public criticism of its rulings. The addition of Justice Abe Fortas, at the beginning of the 1965 term, an attorney well known for his role in behalf of Clarence Gideon in that famous and popular right-to-counsel case, had insured the Miranda majority. But the body in the 1966–67 term, following, in some ways, an unpredictable shift to the conservative side by Hugo Black, generally upheld broader police powers. Congress at the time was strongly considering a new crime bill for the District of Columbia that called for overruling the earlier Mallory decision, permitting police interrogation of suspects, and authorizing investigative arrests.[82] Possibly in reaction, the Court majority, which in the previous June had hastened to make clear that the Escabedo and Miranda rulings were not retroactive,[83] now moved toward the restrictive side in a majority of its criminal procedure rulings.

---

strong that the ruling had had little impact on actual police practices. Either surprisingly few suspects were shown to have taken advantage of the new rules, or police found ways of getting around them. The Yale study showed that in New Haven the police advised less than one-fourth of suspects of their rights, and paradoxically got most of their confessions and incriminating statements from those who had been warned of those rights. "Interrogations in New Haven: The Impact of Miranda," *Yale Law Journal,* LXXVI (1967), 1519–1648. The Georgetown study showed that police were violating rules by questioning suspects on the street, in squad cars, or at the station before the lawyers arrived. Richard J. Medalie and Peter H. Wolf (eds.), *Crime: A Community Response,* Proceedings on the Conference on the Report of the President's Commission on Crime in the District of Columbia (Washington, 1967). The Michigan study questioned whether street interrogation was essential to effective crime control in demonstrating that such questioning was "remarkably unproductive of admissions of guilt." Albert J. Reiss and Donald J. Black, "Interrogation and the Criminal Process," *Annals of the American Academy,* CCCLXXIV (1967), 47–57.

82. President Johnson had vetoed the measure, contending that it raised serious constitutional questions, particularly in its provisions permitting police to detain citizens for questioning and authorizing suppression of allegedly obscene matter. The bill, he further pointed out, would not diminish crime in the District but would make an already confusing law-enforcement situation worse. Robert Kennedy and Wayne Morse agreed. Both had refused to sign a conference committee report on the measure on grounds that it posed a serious threat to civil liberties. *Congressional Quarterly Almanac* (1966), pp. 577–578.

83. Johnson *v.* New Jersey, 384 U.S. 719 (1966). John P. MacKenzie contends that the case was an "innovation," but not because of its lenity. Rather, "it was in fact an unprecedented limitation on the retroactive effect of a constitutional ruling, more severely restricting Miranda's application to past cases than even the fairly recent decisions limiting the retroactive impact of Mapp v. Ohio and Griffin v. California." John P. MacKenzie, "The Warren Court and the Press," in Richard H. Sayler, Barry B. Boyer, and Robert E. Gooding, Jr. (eds.), *The Warren Court: A Critical Analysis* (New York, 1969), p. 121.

"Now, boys, before you begin—please keep in mind the recent United States Supreme Court decision in the case of Ernesto Miranda v. Arizona on Writ of Certiorari from the Supreme Court of Arizona."

While skilled crooks quickly took advantage of the Court's new criminal procedure rulings, many minority citizens and poor people were oblivious of the rights they extended. (Leo Garel, *Wall Street Journal*)

Starting with an alleged double jeopardy situation in which a defendant had been put through two trials, the Court, speaking through Justice White, ruled that certiorari should not have been granted and declined an invitation to rule that the provision was binding on the states.[84] A month later it held that the use of "decoys and undercover agents" to acquire narcotics convictions was not illegal per se and that an agent invited to the home of a purchaser and offered marijuana for sale could arrest the seller without violating the Fourth Amendment.[85] In the nationally headlined Jimmy Hoffa case of the same day, the Court upheld the use by the government of an informer hired to ingratiate himself with the Teamster boss. The informer had then turned over evidence of admitted jury tampering. Such action, the Court ruled, was not a violation of the Fourth Amendment or of the Fifth Amendment's provision on self-incrimination since the statements made to the informer that implicated Hoffa were made voluntarily.[86] In a second case growing out of the same situation, the Court moved a long way toward sustaining the introduction of information secured by wiretap.[87] On the basis of a sworn statement that one of Hoffa's attorneys had endeavored to bribe a prospective juror, two federal judges in the district in which the trial was being conducted had authorized the use of a tape recorder for the specific and limited purpose of ascertaining the truth of the allegation. Such action the Court also validated.

Earl Warren was particularly upset by both rulings and especially the former. His chronic distaste for the use of informers permeated his somewhat angry dissent.[88] Police were not upset,

84. Cichos *v.* Indiana, 385 U.S. 76 (1966).
85. Lewis *v.* U.S., 385 U.S. 206 (1966).
86. Hoffa *v.* U.S., 385 U.S. 293 (1966)
87. Osborn *v.* U.S., 385 U.S. 323 (1966).
88. Hoffa *v.* U.S., 385 U.S. 293, 317–319. Partin, the informer, Warren pointed out, was a "jailbird languishing" in jail on charges which included embezzlement, kidnaping, manslaughter, perjury, and assault, "facing indictments far more serious than the one confronting the man against whom he offered to inform." His bail was then "suddenly reduced from $50,000 to $5,000." "Here the government reaches into the jailhouse" to employ an informer for infiltration to determine if crimes would be committed, he stated. Warren then went on to charge that "the affront to the quality and fairness of federal law enforcement which this case presents is sufficient to require an exercise of our supervisory powers." For the dubious evidence thus obtained, he contended, the government paid an enormous price. If Hoffa had had an informer infiltrate the government's camp, he would have been guilty of obstructing justice.

however, and were pleasantly surprised when in January, 1967, Douglas extended the self-incrimination provisions of the Fifth Amendment to protect police accused of traffic ticket fixing.[89] Prosecutors were equally pleased by a case involving Texas's recidivist or habitual criminal statute. That measure provided that a jury was to be informed before sentencing of a defendant's past convictions; and when it was challenged, the Court ruled that the practice did not offend the due process clause of the Fourteenth Amendment. The possibility of prejudice here, wrote Justice Harlan over dissents by Warren and Fortas, "is outweighed by the validity of the state's purpose in permitting introduction of the evidence."[90]

Other rulings again showed similar concern that the police not be unduly "handcuffed." In *McCray* v. *Illinois,*[91] the Court upheld a warrantless arrest on information by an informer in a narcotics case. There was no duty on the part of the state, wrote Justice Stewart, to reveal in Court the informer's identity at a pretrial hearing, if he was known to be reliable. The ruling was followed by a sustaining of the right of the police without warrant to enter a house "in hot pursuit" of a suspect, search the house for the felon, his weapons, and the fruits of the crime without violating the Fourth Amendment.[92] In fact, Brennan made clear in his majority opinion that the premise that property interests control the government's search and seizure rights is no longer controlling. The Fourth Amendment's principal object, he contended, was the protection of privacy, not property.[93] On the other hand, where public health inspectors had entered property without a warrant in order

89. Garrity *v.* New Jersey, 385 U.S. 493 (1967). The police officers had been given the choice of incriminating themselves or forfeiting their jobs and pension rights, and had chosen to make confessions. The confessions, the Court ruled, were not voluntary and could not be used in subsequent criminal prosecutions in state courts. In a companion case, Spevack *v.* Klein, 385 U.S. 511 (1967), the Court, in a case involving disbarment of an attorney for refusal to answer questions in a disciplinary proceeding, held that since the self-incrimination clause had been absorbed into the Fourteenth Amendment, its protection extended to lawyers as well as other persons, and that it should not be "watered down by imposing the dishonor of disbarment and the deprivation of a livelihood as a price for asserting it." On the cases see Robert B. McKay, "Self-Incrimination and the New Privacy," *Supreme Court Review* (1967), pp. 193–232.

90. Spencer *v.* Texas, 385 U.S. 554, 560 (1967).

91. McCray *v.* Illinois, 386 U.S. 300 (1967).

92. Warden *v.* Hayden, 387 U.S. 294 (1967).

93. *Ibid.,* p. 303.

to investigate possible violations of fire, health, and building regulations, the Court overruled its 1959 *Frank* v. *Maryland* decision, and insisted that search warrants still must be secured in such circumstances, emphasizing that normally there was adequate time to do so.[94]

The trend, however, did not indicate that the Court was deserting the citizen. In several cases procedural rights were extended, and in at least two, police practices were curtailed, to the anger of a number of police spokesmen. The Court continued to insist that the state had an obligation to furnish transcripts to indigent plaintiffs.[95] A bailiff was held to have prejudiced a trial by statements he made to a jury.[96] The Court continued to insist that confessions be truly voluntary.[97] An involuntary confession in one Texas case from a Negro first offender questioned intermittently for nine days without benefit of counsel was thrown out and his conviction overturned.[98] Further following the rule from the old Tom Mooney case, the Court maintained that the Fourteenth Amendment could not tolerate a state criminal conviction secured by the knowing use of false evidence.[99] In addition, the right to a speedy trial, set forth in the Sixth Amendment, was applied to the states in a case involving a university professor's 1964 trial for a sit-in trespass.[100] And Colorado's Sex Offender's Act could not, it was held, bypass a defendant's right to a full judicial hearing, including the right to counsel, summon witnesses in his own behalf, and to cross-examine.[101]

94. Camara *v.* Municipal Court, 387 U.S. 523 (1967); See *v.* City of Seattle, 387 U.S. 541 (1967). See Wayne R. LaFave, "Administrative Searches and the Fourth Amendment: The Camara and See Cases," *Supreme Court Review* (1967), pp. 1–38.

95. Long *v.* District Court of Iowa, 385 U.S. 192 (1966); Entsminger *v.* Iowa, 386 U.S. 748 (1967); Gardner *v.* California, 393 U.S. 367 (1969).

96. Parker *v.* Gladden, 385 U.S. 363 (1966).

97. Sims *v.* Georgia, 385 U.S. 538 (1967); 389 U.S. 404 (1967).

98. Clewis *v.* Texas, 387 U.S. 707 (1967). In Anders *v.* California, 387 U.S. 738 (1967), the Court looked into the role of counsel, holding that an indigent petitioner's right to counsel had been violated when an appointed counsel had taken the position that his appeal had "no merit" and had refused to aid him further.

99. Miller *v.* Pate, 386 U.S. 1 (1967). The case involved a murder conviction based in part on a pair of men's underwear shorts, stained not with blood, as the prosecution said, but with paint, as the prosecution knew.

100. Klopfer *v.* North Carolina, 386 U.S. 213 (1967).

101. Specht *v.* Patterson, 386 U.S. 605 (1967).

Later in the term, it made more explicit that the Sixth Amendment right to have the compulsory process for obtaining witnesses in state criminal trials was made applicable to the states by the Fourteenth Amendment.[102] But the imposition of new requirements on state procedures was more dramatic in the area of juvenile justice. Here Justice Fortas, in a widely publicized ruling, followed up his earlier Kent decision,[103] which had held that a waiver hearing for a juvenile must measure up to the essentials of due process and fair treatment. In juvenile courts, Fortas now maintained, there must be a notice of charges, notice of the right to be represented by counsel, and appointment of counsel if the parents are unable to afford it; the right to confront and cross-examine complainants and other witnesses and adequate warning of the privilege against self-incrimination and the right to remain silent.[104] Justice Stewart, the only dissenter, charged that "the decision converted juvenile proceedings into criminal prosecutions" and was inviting "a long step backwards into the Nineteenth Century."[105]

The Berger and Wade cases brought the bitterest criticism from "law-and-order" advocates. In the former,[106] the Court struck down New York's eavesdropping law as so broad in its sweep as to permit trespassory intrusion into a constitutionally protected area. Under it police could obtain permission to tap or bug without any requirement that the crime suspected and the conversations sought be specified, that a time limit be placed on the eavesdrop, that it be stopped when the specific information was sought, or that exigent circumstances be shown. Although the Court suggested that a more carefully drawn statute that would place police under more strict court supervision might withstand constitutional challenge, the immediate impact of the ruling was to wipe out a variety of

102. Washington *v.* Texas, 388 U.S. 14 (1967).

103. Kent *v.* U.S., 383 U.S. 541 (1966). See Monrad G. Paulsen, "Kent v. United States: The Constitutional Context of Juvenile Cases," *Supreme Court Review* (1966), pp. 167–192.

104. *In re* Gault, 387 U.S. 1 (1967). On the case and the issue see Norman Dorson, *Frontiers of Civil Liberty* (New York, 1968), pp. 213–232; and Monrad G. Paulsen, "The Constitutional Domestication of the Juvenile Court," *Supreme Court Review* (1967), pp. 233–266.

105. *In re* Gault, 387 U.S. 1, 79 (1967).

106. Berger *v.* New York, 388 U.S. 41 (1967).

other state wiretap statutes and place large obstacles to the passage of broadly permissive measures in states that did not have them. Coupled with the Court's insistence the same day in the Wade case[107] that although a police lineup was not compulsory self-incrimination, a defendant was entitled to counsel in such a lineup, the ruling brought wails of protest even though the Court had hastened to rule that the latter case was not retroactive and that it was permissible for the police to identify outside the station and use such information in court if the totality of the surrounding circumstances warranted.[108]

A month following the end of the Court's term in June, 1967, the Detroit and Newark riots broke out with the resultant death of dozens and property damage in the millions. The country was inflamed. Together with the mounting pace of antiwar protest, new cries were raised for antiriot legislation with numerous senators and representatives proposing measures that would prohibit crossing state lines to incite or take part in riots, one House bill also authorizing an additional $25 million for local law-enforcement agencies to prevent and control riots. President Johnson, in a special message to Congress on February 6, called for implementation of the report of the President's Commission on Law Enforcement and Administration of Justice.[109] Congress responded with the Safe Streets and Crime Control Act of 1967,[110] a $50 million program intended to stimulate state and local action and spending on crime prevention and control through updated personnel training, modern equipment, and innovative anticrime techniques. The measure passed in the House in August, 1968, only to run into liberal-conservative battling in the Senate, failing ultimately to be signed into law. Congress did enact, however, a crime law for the District of Columbia,[111] authorizing police to arrest persons for certain misdemeanors without a warrant, but on a probable cause, attacking the Mallory ruling by repealing the requirement that arrested persons be arraigned without delay; and authorizing police to question any arrested person for a period of up to three hours after advising him of his rights, provided that any statement

107. U.S. *v.* Wade, 388 U.S. 218 (1967).
108. Stovall *v.* Denno, 388 U.S. 293 (1967).
109. For the text of the message see *The New York Times,* Feb. 7, 1967, p. 24.
110. H.R. 5037.
111. 81 Stat. 734 (1967).

made by the arrested person during the three hours could not be excluded from evidence at trial solely because of delay in arraignment.

Again the Supreme Court was alert to executive and legislative attitudes. Its personnel had been changed over the summer with the resignation of Justice Tom Clark and his replacement by Thurgood Marshall, former counsel for the N.A.A.C.P. and the first Negro to ascend the high bench. Again its patterns were relatively conciliatory, although by no means totally concessionary. Early in the term it struck at forced confessions[112] and condemned the use of evidence obtained in violation of the Gideon rule.[113] In his first opinion for the Court, Justice Marshall extended the requirement of counsel to post-trial hearings, where revocation of probation would result in substantial confinement.[114] In *Katz* v. *U.S.*,[115] Justice Stewart extended further the Berger ruling of the previous term. Federal agents had secured evidence against a gambler by bugging a public telephone booth, which he used to place bets. The Court reversed his conviction, but outlined a procedure by which bugging could be constitutionally employed. Ruling that the old Olmstead rule—that the Fourth Amendment forbids only physical invasion of a constitutionally protected area —was no longer controlling, Stewart held that what the Fourth Amendment actually protected was people, not places. "The narrow view that property interests or technical notions of trespass control the right of the government to search and seize," he maintained, is no longer binding. And he suggested that if government agents had followed "the procedure of antecedent justification that is central to the Fourth Amendment" and had secured prior judicial approval for the eavesdropping, their actions could well have been justified.[116]

112. Beecher *v.* Alabama, 389 U.S. 35 (1967).

113. Burgett *v.* Texas, 389 U.S. 109 (1967).

114. Mempa *v.* Rhay, 389 U.S. 129 (1967). See also McConnell *v.* Rhay, 393 U.S. 2 (1968), in which the Court ruled that the Mempa rule should be applied retroactively.

115. Katz *v.* U.S., 389 U.S. 347 (1967). On the case see Edmund W. Kitch, "Katz v. United States: The Limits of the Fourth Amendment," *Supreme Court Review* (1968), pp. 133–152.

116. *Ibid.*, p. 354. Black in his dissent fell back on constitutional literalism. Finding no formal constitutional restraints on official wiretapping or eavesdropping in the Fourth Amendment, he deplored the departure from the Olmstead

The Court also interpreted the self-incrimination provisions of the Fifth Amendment in controversial ways. In cases involving conviction of gamblers for violation of federal wagering tax statutes, which required a gambler to register and pay an occupational tax, it held that such action made the gamblers subject to federal or state prosecution, and thereby violated the Fifth.[117] On the other hand, in another case it held that registration under the National Firearms Act was not compulsory self-incrimination.[118] In March,

---

rule, which he felt should stand. Protection for the individual in this area he felt came from the exclusionary rule to bar evidence obtained by means of such intrusions. As to the protection of privacy, Black found that the Fourth Amendment protected privacy only to the extent that it prohibited unreasonable searches and seizures of "persons, houses, papers and effects." "No general right is created by the Amendment so as to give this Court the unlimited power to hold unconstitutional everything which affects privacy," he argued. Later, in Lee *v.* Florida, 392 U.S. 378 (1968), the Court reversed its earlier ruling in Schwartz *v.* Texas, 344 U.S. 199 (1952), holding, over dissents by Black, White, and Harlan, that wiretap information was not admissible in state courts.

117. Marchetti *v.* U.S., 390 U.S. 39 (1968); Grosso *v.* U.S., 390 U.S. 62 (1968). Warren dissented in a highly revealing way. The case invited contrast with the earlier Albertson case (382 US. 70, [1965]), allowing Communist party members to avoid registration by invoking the privilege. The Chief Justice, however, found "a critical distinction" from that case. There the registration requirement "clashed head-on with protected First Amendment rights," while here gambling could "in no sense be called a protected activity." As one authority commented: "The suggested distinction is breathtaking in its ingenuity. If taken seriously, it would mean that anyone's Fifth Amendment freedom from self-incrimination would depend on whether he could also claim the protection of some other Constitutional provision. But of course the Fifth Amendment makes no distinction between the criminal charges one may face, giving speakers preferred status over gamblers; it extends the privilege to all. The Chief Justice, it must be concluded, was just reluctant to inhibit government control of gambling, no matter what he had agreed to in other cases." Anthony Lewis, "Earl Warren," in Sayler, *et al., The Warren Court,* p. 22.

118. Haynes *v.* U.S., 390 U.S. 85 (1968). In subsequent self-incrimination cases, the Court held that a group can claim the privilege, even when doing so threatens their job, Uniformed Sanitation Men *v.* Sanitation Commissioner, 392 U.S. 280 (1968); but a corporation cannot, in its corporate capacity, Campbell Painting Corp. *v.* Reid, 392 U.S. 286 (1968). In a highly controversial case in May, 1969, it reversed the federal marijuana conviction of Timothy Leary. Leary had been convicted under the federal marijuana tax act, which required that the names of all who pay the tax be turned over to state law-enforcement officers. The Court held that compliance with the tax act would compel Leary to incriminate himself. Leary had also been convicted of importing marijuana. As to that conviction, the Court said the statute's presumption that one who possessed marijuana will be said to know it was illegally imported, could not withstand the fact that a significant amount of marijuana is grown within the United States. Leary *v.* U.S., 395 U.S. 6 (1968).

1968, the question of pretrial identification by photographs came up. Here Harlan ruled that their use was not prejudicial and was an aid to F.B.I. agents making an investigation.[119] But despite mounting criticism, the Court did not back away from its Miranda rule, insisting in a case in May, 1968, that the same standards it set forth in criminal proceedings should apply in Internal Revenue Service investigations.[120]

Two bodies of rulings drew wide public comment. In three cases decided on May 20, 1968, Justice White for the Court held for the first time that the Sixth Amendment right to trial by jury applied to the states through the due process clause of the Fourteenth. The first involved a misdemeanor case,[121] the second a criminal contempt case.[122] And while considering the possibility in the third, the Court, while not ruling so in the immediate case, made clear that in the case of petty offenses this could be the case, depending on the size of the potential penalty involved.[123] Clearly the rulings most significant for law-enforcement officers involved "stop and frisk" legislation in Ohio and New York. The Court sustained both, holding that police could detain a citizen on the street on grounds of reasonable suspicion, but without probable cause for arrest. If police had reasonable suspicion that crime was about to be committed they did not need to believe that it was imminent in order to frisk the citizen or search him by patting down his outer clothing for dangerous weapons. If such weapons were found, the Court agreed, they would be admissible in evidence.[124] In *Wainwright* v. *New Orleans*[125] the Court considered the appeal of a law student who was stopped on the street by police looking for a murder suspect. The defendant identified himself but refused to remove his jacket to satisfy the police that he had no tattoo, as the subject

119. Simmons *v.* U.S., 390 U.S. 377 (1968).

120. Mathis *v.* U.S., 391 U.S. 1 (1968).

121. Duncan *v.* Louisiana, 391 U.S. 145 (1968).

122. Bloom *v.* Illinois, 391 U.S. 194 (1968).

123. Dyke *v.* Taylor Implement Co., 391 U.S. 216 (1968). In DeStefano *v.* Woods, 392 U.S. 631 (1968), the Court ruled that the Duncan and Bloom cases were not retroactive.

124. Terry *v.* Ohio, 392 U.S. 1 (1968); Peters *v.* New York, 392 U.S. 40 (1968). But see Sibron *v.* New York, 392 U.S. 40 (1968), where the Court saw a different issue when narcotics were "frisked" from a party. For a discussion of the cases see Walter R. LaFave, "Street Encounters and the Constitution; Terry, Sibron, Peters, and Beyond," *Michigan Law Review,* LXVII (1968), 39–64.

125. Wainwright *v.* New Orleans, 392 U.S. 598 (1968).

was believed to have. The police arrested the defendant and took him to a station house where his jacket was forcibly removed. He subsequently was convicted of assaulting a police officer. The Court dismissed his appeal over the strong dissents of Justices Warren and Douglas, the latter maintaining that "I fear with Terry and Wainwright that we have forsaken the Western tradition and taken a long step toward the oppressive police practices not only of Communist regimes but of modern Iran, 'democratic' Formosa, and Franco Spain, with whom we are now even more closely allied."[126]

But the Court by June of 1968 was clearly living on borrowed time. That Presidential election year saw the "law-and-order" issue embraced by both major party candidates and southern white racist George Wallace, with its members being charged with responsibility for the "law-and-order" problem by at least two of the three. In this climate it was not surprising that President Johnson's call for progressive and sensitive anticrime legislation should be turned by Congress into a "green light" for a massive, restrictive piece of legislation embodying a number of provisions clearly punitive of the judiciary. The Omnibus Crime Control and Safe Streets Act of 1968[127] was the most extensive anticrime legislation in the nation's history. It bore little resemblance to the legislation President Johnson had originally proposed in 1967 and had requested again in a 1968 crime message. Taken as a whole it was a defeat for the administration and congressional liberals, but despite the urging of civil libertarians and a number of members of Congress that he veto the measure, the President reluctantly signed it into law on June 19, expressing his opinion at the time that a number of its features were "unwise." Title II of the Act specifically overturned Supreme Court rulings in Mallory, Miranda, and the 1967 Wade case.[128] Confessions by defendants, it made clear, were admissible in evidence if they were "voluntary"

126. *Ibid.*, p. 615.

127. Public Law 90–351 (1968). On the general controversy over the law and order issue see V. A. Leonard, *The Police, The Judiciary and the Criminal* (Springfield, Ill., 1969), esp. Chap. 1.

128. The Title was based, at least partially, on an unfortunate misconception of the Miranda case, that despite the Court's explicit ruling that it was not retroactive (Johnson *v.* New Jersey, 384 U.S. 719 [1966]), it had the effect of forcing the police to release persons who had previously confessed to criminal activity. See Sayler *et al., The Warren Court,* p. 121.

even if the suspect had been warned of his constitutional rights. Police could hold a suspect up to six hours (or more in certain circumstances) before arraignment and still obtain an admissible confession. Further, the trial judge in a federal prosecution was to determine the issue of voluntariness out of the hearing of the jury, basing that determination on such criteria as time lapse between arrest and arraignment, whether the defendant knew the nature of the offense with which he was charged, when he was advised of or knew of his right to remain silent and to have counsel, and whether he was without the assistance of counsel when questioned and when giving the confession. Although the provisions had no effect on state courts and although liberals were able to force deletion of a provision forbidding the Supreme and other federal courts from reviewing a trial judge's decision that a confession was "voluntary" if the decision had been affirmed by the state's highest court, the Act nonetheless set a tone for "unshackling" the police, a development watched favorably by "law-and-order" advocates.

The measure had other controversial provisions that drew strong pro and con reactions. Its Wiretapping Title not only authorized judge-approved taps to monitor a wide range of activities, but authorized any law officer, or any other person obtaining information in conformity with such a process, to disclose or use it as appropriate.[129]

Sent to the President on June 6, with the nation further outraged over the shooting of Senator Robert F. Kennedy the pre-

129. Under the measure the Attorney General could apply to any federal judge for a warrant approving wire or oral intercepts relating to a wide range of specified federal offenses punishable by death or imprisonment for more than one year, namely, violations of the Atomic Energy Act; espionage; sabotage; treason; rioting; unlawful payments of loans to labor organizations; murder; kidnaping; robbery; extortion; bribing public officials or witnesses; sports bribes; wagering offenses; influencing or injuring an officer, juror, or witness; obstructing criminal investigations; Presidential assassination, kidnaping or assault; interference with commerce by threats or violence; racketeering offenses; unlawfully influencing an employee benefit plan; theft from interstate shipment; embezzlement from pension and welfare funds; interstate transportation of stolen property; counterfeiting; bankruptcy fraud; narcotics violations; extortionate credit transactions; or any conspiracy to commit such offenses. In addition the measure authorized the principal prosecuting attorney of any state or political subdivision to apply to a state judge for a warrant approving wire or oral intercepts relating to any crime dangerous to life, limb, or property and punishable by imprisonment for more than one year.

vious day, Congress hesitated to weaken further its already limited gun control section. Even so the section was still inadequate for many, but too strong for the National Rifle Association and firearms enthusiasts generally. Congressman Emanuel Celler expressed minority liberal opposition to the measure, arguing that it was a "cruel hoax on citizens for whom crime and the fear of crime are facts of life. . . . It is built on false premises. Its promises are illusory. It is destructive of the tenets of our liberty." The criminal law sections, he went on, were unconstitutional and "would turn the clock backward." The permissive wiretapping section did not contain "proper safeguards" and amounted to an "assault on our way of life." House Minority Leader Gerald Ford, however, expressed a more widely held view when he stated: "I refuse to concede that the elected representatives of the American people cannot be the winner in a confrontation with the Supreme Court." And Richard H. Poff, head of the G.O.P. task force on crime, hailed the measure, admitting that it contained many imperfections, but contending that these could "be readily cured by separate legislative enactment."[130] The ball was thus again thrown back to the high bench. But that body in its first session under Richard M. Nixon and last under Earl Warren was afforded no opportunity to rule on the constitutionality of its provisions.[131]

130. "Congress Passes Extensive Anti-Crime Legislation," *Congressional Quarterly Almanac* (1968), p. 237.

131. The Court in its 1968–69 term encouraged federal-state cooperation in the area of combating organized crime, ruling that the definition of "extortion" should be broad (U.S. *v.* Nardello, 393 U.S. 286 [1969]); ruled that informers' tips were not enough to provide "probable cause" that a crime was being committed (Spinelli *v.* U.S., 393 U.S. 410 [1969]); and held that prison inmates could use "jailhouse lawyers" (Johnson *v.* Avery, 393 U.S. 483 [1969]). It also held that electronically obtained evidence was only excludable against those from whom it was obtained, not against others implicated by it, going on to hold that if illegal surveillance had occurred, defendants with standing to object must be allowed to examine the entire record of such surveillance without any preliminary screening of that record by the judge (Alderman *v.* U.S., 393 U.S. 165 [1969]). In Davis *v.* Mississippi, 394 U.S. 721 (1969), it ruled that police could not, without a warrant, detain a suspect to obtain his fingerprints. Holding dogmatically to its Miranda rule, it reversed the murder conviction of a man questioned in his bedroom without being apprised of his constitutional rights. Justice Black, speaking for a six-to-two majority, ruled that the decision did not broaden Miranda but merely reaffirmed the principle that a suspect must be warned of his rights when in custody or otherwise deprived of his freedom

In areas outside the storm center of law-and-order, racial tension, and war, the Supreme Court, despite changing personnel, did not depart appreciably, in the Great Society years, from general patterns launched in its previous terms in the 1960s. Unique rulings were made as unique cases raised unexpected constitutional controversy, but a floating majority of five or six liberal activists were generally successful in applying Warrenesque interpretations in areas ranging from free speech, obscenity, and libel, to loyalty voting problems and antitrust.

In the First Amendment area, the Court generally took a permissive attitude toward political speech. Hugo Black surprised both his brethren and legal commentators alike in late 1966, however, upholding the conviction of over one hundred civil rights advocates arrested under a Florida trespass statute for demonstrating at a segregated jail where other students protesting segregation had been lodged. People who want to propagandize protests or views, Black held, do not have the right to do so whenever and however and wherever they please. The state, no less than a private owner of property, he ruled, has power to preserve the property under its control for the use to which it is lawfully dedicated.[132] Stewart held the following spring that civil rights marchers must not bypass orderly judicial processes when refusing to obey anti-parade injunctions.[133] Neither ruling became the precedent for a

---

of action in any way (Orozco v. Texas, 394 U.S. 324 [1969]). In Frazier *v.* Cupp, 394 U.S. 731 (1969), it also followed Miranda, but made clear that the Miranda rule, that after a defendant had indicated his wish to consult an attorney before speaking, questioning could not proceed until counsel was obtained, need not be applied to cases tried before that ruling in 1966.

132. Adderly *v.* Florida, 385 U.S. 39 (1966). Douglas split with the Alabaman for one of the few times in a First Amendment case, arguing in dissent that this could not be treated as an ordinary trespass case. The assembly and petition were peaceful, he contended. There was no threat to the safety of the jail or interference with its functioning. The protestors, he felt, were legitimately exercising the right to petition the government for the redress of grievances, using the only type of access to public officials open to them. He futher deplored with three dissenting brethren the invitation the ruling seemed to issue to use trespass and other comparable laws as a "blunderbuss to suppress civil rights."

133. Walker *v.* Birmingham, 388 U.S. 307 (1967). On the case see Sheldon Tefft, "Neither Above the Law Nor Below It: A Note on Walker v. Birmingham," *Supreme Court Review* (1968), pp. 181–192.

new restrictiveness.[134] Rather, to the contrary, the Court tended more often to throw out legal impediments to freedom of expression as long as its use was not an overt threat to public order.

State loyalty oaths continued to be questioned and struck down. In an important Maryland ruling, *Whitehill* v. *Elkins*,[135] Justice Douglas ruled that a teachers' loyalty oath was "in the First Amendment field," and that such laws as supported it were hostile to academic freedom. The Maryland scheme, he maintained, resulted in "an overbreadth that makes possible oppressive or capricious application as regimes change."[136] The ruling was thus a follow-up to the landmark Keyishian case of the previous January,[137] in which over the bitter dissents of Clark, Harlan, White, and Stewart, Brennan for the Court had struck at New York's previously validated Feinberg Law, "a highly efficient *in terrorum* mechanism,"[138] and in the process had given constitutional status to the concept of academic freedom. Academic freedom, he wrote, is a "special concern of the First Amendment, which does not tolerate laws that cast a pall of orthodoxy over the classroom."[139] While New York could protect its educational system from perversion, he maintained, it could not do so by vague and uncertain standards, but only by "sensitive tools" that clearly informed teachers of the sanctions being established.

Once in the area, the Court found itself with other business. Student leaders of the "Free Speech Movement" on the Berkeley campus of the University of California in 1964 asked it to reverse their conviction for refusal to leave a public building—the school's administration building—after closing hours. The Court refused, dismissing their appeal for want of jurisdiction.[140] In a modern-day Scopes situation, an Arkansas high school teacher, teaching

134. See Cameron *v.* Johnson, 381 U.S. 741 (1965); 390 U.S. 611 (1968); and Gregory *v.* City of Chicago, 394 U.S. 111 (1968). In the latter case the Court considered the role of onlookers threatening violence against peaceful civil rights marchers, upholding the marchers' right to conduct legitimate demonstrations. The Chicago police as a result of the onlookers' threats had attacked the marchers in an attempt to disperse them.

135. Whitehill *v.* Elkins, 389 U.S. 54 (1967).

136. *Ibid.,* p. 62.

137. Keyishian *v.* Board of Regents, 385 U.S. 589 (1967).

138. Adler *v.* Board of Education, 342 U.S. 485 (1952).

139. Keyishian *v.* Board of Regents, p. 603.

140. Savio *v.* California, 388 U.S. 460 (1967).

biology in a Darwinian fashion in defiance of substantially the same state antievolution law that had produced the famed 1920s case, had her conviction reversed. The law, the Court held, was a violation of the First Amendment through the Fourteenth, restricting an establishment of religion.[141] More controversial was the famed Tinker case of 1969. Here children had defied a school regulation and worn black armbands to protest American action in Vietnam. Speaking through Justice Fortas the Court sustained the children's actions as permissible symbolic speech, ruling that in the absence of evidence that such a rule was necessary to avoid substantial interference with school discipline or the rights of others, the rule was not permissible under the First and Fourteenth Amendments.[142] Justice Black, in a highly emotional dissent,[143] denounced the ruling caustically, suggesting that if it were allowed to stand the country would be entering a new era in which the Supreme Court and the pupils would ultimately run America's public schools.[144]

In other First Amendment areas the cases reaching the Court primarily called for clarification of prior rulings. In the obscenity area, the Court returned from considering the way material was

141. Epperson *v.* Arkansas, 393 U.S. 97 (1968).

142. Tinker *v.* Des Moines School District, 393 U.S. 503 (1969). On the issue of school board authority see Stephen R. Goldstein, "Scope and Sources of School Board Authority to Regulation of Student Conduct and Status: A Nonconstitutional Analysis," *University of Pennsylvania Law Review*, CXVII (1969), 373–430.

143. Tinker *v.* Des Moines School District, p. 515. The opinion was consistent with Black's generally changing attitude toward First Amendment freedoms, but was also a reflection of his alarm at the times. "If the time has come," he wrote, "when pupils of state-supported schools, kindergartens, grammar schools or high schools can deny and flaunt orders of school officials to keep their minds on their own school work, it is the beginning of a new revolutionary era of permissiveness in this country fostered by the judiciary."

144. In other education-related cases, the Court granted a taxpayer standing to sue to challenge the use of tax-purchased school books in private religious schools (Flast *v.* Cohen, 392 U.S. 83 [1968]), but then upheld the practice (Board of Education *v.* Allen, 392 U.S. 236 [1968]). It also reversed the dismissal of a teacher whose competence had been questioned and dismissal ordered for criticizing the allocation of school funds, and making false statements regarding the true need for tax increases. Such expressions, it held, were protected under the Times-Sullivan rule, Justice Marshall holding that they addressed themselves to matters of public concern and presented no questions of faculty discipline or harmony. Pickering *v.* Board of Education, 391 U.S. 563 (1968).

promoted and marketed to considering its content.[145] Making clear that its standards for the suppression of obscenity were still strict, it threw out a variety of obscenity convictions based on "pulp books," "girlie magazines,"[146] and in one instance for sending an allegedly obscene book through the mails, a case in which the defendant had previously received a ten-year sentence.[147] The justices, however, took a more favorable look at legislation aimed at protecting minors. In a widely read ruling in April, 1968,[148] it approved the constitutionality of the New York statute making it a crime to sell any material to children under seventeen years of age that presented a salacious view of nudity, sexual conduct, or sado-masochistic abuse. Justice Brennan for the Court maintained that the statute expressed a valid state interest in protecting the well-being of youth, a contention seriously challenged by Black, Douglas, and Fortas, who continued to maintain that the First Amendment was designed to keep the state and the hands of all state officials off the printing presses of America and off the distribution systems for all printed literature. Fortas particularly was concerned that the Court had adopted a theory of "variable obscenity" that left booksellers guessing as to what sales might violate the law. "Bookselling," he argued, "should not be a hazardous profession."[149]

But if sellers were to be monitored, consumers were not. When police attempted to move against a defendant with a private collection of films, proclaimed obscene by arresting police who projected them in the defendant's home with his projector (the opinion did not say whether the impromptu film festival was a form of entertainment or standard police practice), the Court blocked their

145. C. Herman Pritchett, *The American Constitution* (New York, 1968), p. 499, contends that "the Ginzburg decision is perhaps best understood as one of Mr. Dooley's 'illiction returns' decision, a reassurance by the Court to the country that the permissiveness of its standards on obscenity did have limits. In fact, the decision was widely interpreted in this manner, and it stimulated many proposals for the drafting of new obscenity legislation."

146. Redrup *v.* New York, 386 U.S. 767 (1967).

147. Aday *v.* U.S., 388 U.S. 447 (1967).

148. Ginsberg *v.* New York, 390 U.S. 629 (1968).

149. *Ibid.*, p. 674. On the case see Samuel Krislov, "From Ginzburg to Ginsberg: The Unhurried Children's Hour in Obscenity Litigation," *Supreme Court Review* (1968), pp. 153–198.

action.[150] The Constitution, wrote Justice Marshall, "protects the right to receive information and ideas regardless of their worth." A citizen he wrote, should expect "to be free from governmental intrusion into his privacy and the control of his thoughts. Our whole constitutional heritage rebels at the thought of giving the government the power to control men's minds."[151]

As to the libel area, following the Court's Times-Sullivan and Garrison rulings, the question remained how far the new "freedom to libel" doctrine would be extended. In February, 1966, the Court explored the question of who might be considered a "public official," and expanded the term to include a governmental employee having or appearing to the public to have substantial responsibility for control over the conduct of governmental affairs. The term, Justice Brennan maintained, should be interpreted in the light of the compelling interest in debate on public issues.[152] Thus the rule opened still another group of citizens to permissible criticism and left as the important legal criterion in future cases the question of proof as to whether the kind of charges launched against public figures were sufficiently irresponsible and inaccurate as to meet the "malicious" test.[153] Then, in companion

150. Stanley *v.* Georgia, 394 U.S. 557 (1969). The Court's same concern with private behavior was apparent in Recznik *v.* City of Lorain, 393 U.S. 166 (1968), in which it held a police raid of a crap game in a private home a violation of the Fourth Amendment.

151. In movie censorship cases the Court continued to see to it that the Freedman *v.* Maryland rule was followed, Teitel Film Corp. *v.* Cusack, 390 U.S. 139 (1968), and adequate and speedy legal action was followed when censorship arose. It also struck down a Dallas movie censorship ordinance whose standards it found too vague. Interstate Circuit *v.* Dallas, 390 U.S. 676 (1968).

152. Rosenblatt *v.* Baer, 383 U.S. 75 (1966). A lower federal court added a further dimension. When Dr. Linus Pauling, a Nobel prize–winning scientist and leader of the movement to ban nuclear testing, brought action against false editorial statements that he had "contemptuously refused to testify" before a Senate committee, and had been cited for contempt of Congress, the Eighth Circuit Court held that such statements were conditionally privileged, even though false, since by his statements and actions Pauling had projected himself into the arena of public controversy and in the very "vortex of the discussion of a question of pressing public concern," and thus came within the ambit of the "public official" doctrine. Pauling *v.* Globe-Democrat Publishing Co., 362 F. 2d 188 (1966).

153. For later application of the rule see U.S. *v.* Johnson, 383 U.S. 169 (1966); Ashton *v.* Kentucky, 384 U.S. 195 (1966); Mills *v.* Alabama, 384 U.S. 214 (1966). In the widely reported case of Time Inc., *v.* Hill, in which Richard Nixon appeared unsuccessfully for the appellee, (385 U.S. 374 [1966]), the Court ex-

cases, in 1967, the Court broadened its concept beyond "public officials" to "public figures"—either those who thrust themselves into the vortex of public disputes or who have a status in life that commands wide attention.[154]

The cases involved intriguing situations. In one, the well-known right-wing leader General Edwin A. Walker had filed suits totaling more than $20 million against the Associated Press and television companies for statements made about his activities on the University of Mississippi campus during the rioting surrounding the James Meredith episode in 1962. He was reported to have "assumed command of the crowd" and "led a charge of students against federal marshals." The second involved Georgia football coach Wally Butts, who had been charged, on the basis of information inadvertently heard over a bad telephone connection, with "fixing" a college football game by giving his team's secrets in advance to the opposing coach. When the *Saturday Evening Post* published an article inferring that the charges were true, Butts had instituted a libel suit against the magazine. The Court ruled against the General but for the coach. Walker's appearance on the campus during the rioting was "hot news," which had to be written quickly, and though there might have been errors in the dispatch

---

tended the rule to cover freedom of the press, even when a magazine story had deliberately invaded the privacy of a family for clearly commercial purposes. Brennan for the Court held that private individuals suing under such circumstances must prove "knowing or reckless falsity." Admitting that the ruling struck the concept of privacy a serious blow, he nonetheless contended that freedom of discussion takes priority. "We create grave risk of serious impairment of the indispensable service of a free press in a free society," he wrote, "if we saddle the press with the impossible burden of verifying to a certainty the facts associated in news articles with a person's name, picture or portrait, particularly as related to nondefamatory matter."

154. Curtis Publishing Co. *v.* Butts; Associated Press *v.* Walker, 388 U.S. 130 (1967). On the cases see Harry Kalven, Jr., "The Reasonable Man and the First Amendment: Hill, Butts, and Walker," *Supreme Court Review* (1967), pp. 267–309. The definition of "public figures" even extended to the past. When the daughter of Henry Clay Frick asked a Pennsylvania Court to enjoin publication of a book about her father, on the ground that it unfairly presented him as an exploiter of workingmen, under a state law permitting recovery of damages for statements "tending to blacken the memory" of the dead, a judge dismissed the suit, upholding the author's right to make an unflattering historical assessment of Frick. *The New York Times,* May 21, 1967, p. 1; Aug. 10, 1967, p. 39; Sept. 8, 1967, p. 21.

there was "not the slightest hint of severe departure from accepted publishing standards." The *Post* story, on the other hand, was not "hot news." The magazine, wrote Justice Harlan, had ignored "elementary precautions" and with adequate time for investigation had failed to exercise proper responsibility. The rulings seemed to leave the possibility of anyone entering the public area filing a successful libel action greatly in doubt. Critics, while welcoming protection for the uninhibited discussion of public issues, also wondered whether such freedom did not undermine the valid social values that underlay the law of defamation.[155]

In cases involving other areas of personal freedom, the Court inevitably wound up on the permissive side. In early 1967 it sustained travel to Communist Cuba, denying that such a right was violative of sections of the Immigration and Nationality Act as alleged by State Department officials.[156] The ruling thus left open to the State Department only the sanction of canceling the passports of persons who visited off-limits countries, an action taken with Yale professor Staughton Lynd following his 1966 peace mission to North Vietnam.[157] The State Department also moved to remove

155. In the following term the Times-Sullivan rule was applied to TV broadcasting. A deputy sheriff had been charged over the air with criminal conduct. Even though the charge was false and the defendant had made no effort to investigate it, the plaintiff, the Court ruled, failed to prove that the defendant entertained serious doubt as to the truth of the statement. The fact that he had not taken time to explore the charge was irrelevant, wrote Justice White. A failure to investigate does not in itself establish bad faith. St. Amant *v.* Thompson, 390 U.S. 727 (1968). The Court also refused to consider a libel suit brought by defense plant employees who had been reported to the government by the employer as security risks, even though Chief Justice Warren protested vigorously that this refusal endangered "the right to millions of workers to vindicate their reputations and to make a living in the military-private industrial complex." Becker *v.* Philco Corp., 389 U.S. 979 (1967). Arnold Rose, the well-known sociologist, also found that the rule precluded successful libel action against being called a Communist. Arnold Rose, *Libel and Academic Freedom: A Lawsuit Against Political Extremists* (Minneapolis, 1968).

156. U.S. *v.* Laub, 385 U.S. 475 (1967).

157. Subsequently the court of appeals for the District of Columbia held that the Passport Act of 1926 does not give the State Department the right to control a person's travel, but only to say where the individual can take his passport. Lynd *v.* Rusk, 389 F. 2d 940 (1967). The State Department issued regulations limiting the authority of the Secretary of State to impose travel bans, to periods when a country is at war with the United States, when armed hostilities are in progress in a country, or when travel would seriously impair the conduct of United States foreign affairs. *The New York Times,* Mar. 15, 1967.

citizenship from a naturalized citizen for voting in Israeli elections. Justice Black reversed the ruling, holding that the citizenship clause of the Fourteenth Amendment protected every citizen against forcible destruction of his citizenship, making clear that unless a citizen voluntarily relinquished that citizenship, it could not be removed.[158] The decision clearly invalidated all statues providing for expatriaton of citizens because of involvement in the affairs of a foreign state, although it did not affect the government's power to denaturalize where naturalization was obtained by fraud.[159]

The Court also continued its assault on the old loyalty program of the 1950s. In November, 1965, it ruled unanimously, to the gratification of Justices Black and Clark, that the Subversive Activities Control Board could not force individuals to register under the McCarran Act without engaging in unconstitutional violations of the Fifth Amendment right against self-incrimination.[160] Clark was quick to point out that as Attorney General in 1948 he had advised the Senate Judiciary Committee that such a registration requirement could be unconstitutional. The following term the Chief Justice delivered a final coup de grace to the S.A.C.B., declaring unconstitutional the provision of the McCarran Act making it a crime for any member of a Communist-action organization "to engage in any employment in any defense facility." The language of the statute, Warren contended, swept "indiscriminately across all types of associations with Communist-action groups, without regard to the quality or degree of membership. . . . The statute quite literally establishes guilt by association alone, without any need to establish that an individual's association poses the threat

158. Afroyim *v.* Rusk, 387 U.S. 253 (1967).

159. The Court took a number of deportation cases, moving generally to narrow the government's discretionary authority in that area. See Immigration Service *v.* Errico, 385 U.S. 214 (1966); Woodby *v.* Immigration Service, 385 U.S. 276 (1966); Benenyi *v.* Immigration Director, 385 U.S. 630 (1967); and Boutilier *v.* Immigration and Naturalization Service, 387 U.S. 118 (1967). The latter case was the one exception, the Court there upholding deportation of a homosexual over the bitter dissent of Justice Douglas who argued that to permit deportation of aliens "affected with a psychopathic personality," under which the action had been taken, was to operate with "much too vague a constitutional standard."

160. Albertson *v.* S.A.C.B., 382 U.S. 70 (1965). On the case see John H. Mansfield, "The Albertson Case: Conflict Between the Privilege Against Self-Incrimination and the Government's Need for Information," *Supreme Court Review* (1966), pp. 103–166.

feared by the Government in proscribing it."[161] The ruling rendered the Internal Security Act virtually useless. It was not until Congress in December, 1967, came to the rescue of S.A.C.B. by establishing a procedure by which the body could hold hearings on cases referred to it by the Attorney General and itself determine whether individuals were Communists, that it acquired a gainful function.[162]

Rulings in the reapportionment and voting areas were also primarily clarifying. In fact, by 1968, just four years after the explosive *Reynolds* v. *Sims* ruling, public outcry on the issue had virtually vanished. Despite some bitter tail-end attempts to amend the Constitution or even call a new constitutional convention to undo the Court's prior action, the mood even among most politicians was that the reapportionment decisions were acceptable and that the reforms they introduced were defensible. Liberal critics, on the other hand, had some doubts whether, in light of the results, the "modernization" of legislatures and other representative bodies that reapportionment had seemed to promise had not been more optimistic than realistic.[163]

The stormy 1968 election also raised difficult constitutional issues. Third parties sprouting on the right and left sought places on the ballot and ran into inhibiting state elections statutes. The serious

161. U.S. *v.* Robel, 389 U.S. 258 (1967).

162. "Subversive Activities," *Congressional Quarterly Almanac* (1967), p. 742.

163. Among the more significant cases were: Fortson *v.* Morris, 385 U.S. 231 (1966), in which the Court held valid Georgia's power to solve by legislative choice the problem of an indecisive gubernatorial election. No candidate in the 1966 election received a majority of the votes, and under the state constitution the general assembly was to select the governor from the top two contenders. The Court held the one-man-one-vote doctrine inapplicable, since nothing in the Constitution "either expressly or impliedly dictates the method a State must use to select its Governor"; Sailors *v.* Kent Board of Education, 387 U.S. 105 (1967), in which the Court held a school board was "not a legislature in the classical sense" and hence was not covered by the one-man-one-vote rule; Dusch *v.* Davis, 387 U.S. 112 (1967), in which the Court held valid a plan in which the eleven members of a city council were elected at large, but one councilman had to reside in each of the city's seven boroughs; Avery *v.* Midland County, 390 U.S. 474 (1968), in which it held the one-man-one-vote rule did apply to local governmental units such as counties, towns, and cities; Kirkpatrick *v.* Preisler, 394 U.S. 526 (1969), in which a Missouri reapportionment plan that contained a variance of 3.1 percent from perfect mathematical equality was ruled unconstitutional; and Wells *v.* Rockefeller, 394 U.S. 542 (1969), in which the Court struck down a New York redistricting statute on the grounds of gerrymandering.

possibility that George Wallace's American Independent party might poll enough votes to throw the election into the House of Representatives, raised with new immediacy the perennial debate over the modern relevancy of the electoral college. A month before the election the Court ruled there was no time to consider the merits of obtaining ballot status for candidates of a last-minute "Californians-for-an-Alternative-in-November" group,[164] but a week later it did strike at Ohio's restrictive election law, which gave such a decided advantage to the two old established parties as to virtually prevent a new party from running its candidates in the election. Cynics pointed to the fact that the Court found a place for Wallace's right-wing American Independent party on the ballot but not for the left-wing Socialist Workers. But the Court made what was to it a viable legal distinction between the claims of the two.[165] After the narrow election of Nixon, the Court took cases exploring Alabama's attempt to keep black National Democratic Party of Alabama candidates off the ballot in that state, finding that the use of the state's Corrupt Practices Act as an impediment violated the equal protection clause of the Fourteenth Amendment.[166] It also expressed a solicitude for the rights of all qualified citizens to vote, holding in April, 1969, that a ballot could not be denied to unsentenced jail inmates seeking to exercise the franchise.[167]

In the antitrust area, business leaders by 1965 had become so disturbed by the residual Kennedy administration's and the Supreme Court's activism, that Attorney General Nicholas Katzenbach felt compelled to reassure them by making clear that the Justice Department planned a breathing spell before pushing antitrust

164. Californians for an Alternative in November *v.* California, 393 U.S. 1 (1968).

165. Williams *v.* Rhodes, 393 U.S. 23 (1968).

166. Hadnott *v.* Amos, 394 U.S. 358 (1969); *In re* Herndon, 394 U.S. 399 (1969). The election also produced a strong move, in light of the very real possibility that George Wallace's candidacy might throw it into the House of Representatives, for abolition of the electoral college, and in September, 1969, the House passed a bill proposing an amendment to that effect. Strong arguments existed on both sides regarding the desirability of the move. See James A. Michener, *Presidential Lottery* (New York, 1969); and Alexander M. Bickel, *The New Age of Political Reform: The Electoral College, the Convention and the Party System* (New York, 1969).

167. McDonald *v.* Board of Elections, 394 U.S. 802 (1969).

strictures to their complete limits.[168] The Supreme Court, however, did not move to endorse the Attorney General on this score. In June of 1966, in three significant cases, it ruled that the F.T.C. might ask for, and the lower courts might grant, temporary injunction banning F.T.C.-challenged mergers even before the F.T.C. held an administrative hearing on the case.[169] It also ruled that a lower court was too lenient in merely ordering a large burglar-alarm company to sell three subsidiaries after it was found guilty under the Sherman Act of monopolizing a segment of the industry. The remedy, the Court felt, should be continuing government surveillance to police compliance with the decree.[170] Finally, it ruled that a 1958 merger between the Pabst and Blatz brewing companies violated the antitrust laws, even though the two firms accounted for only 4.49% of national beer sales.[171] Even Hugo Black expressed surprise that control of such a small share of the market tended to infringe the antitrust statutes.[172] Questions now arose as to whether the rulings did not virtually eliminate the possibility of future horizontal mergers while casting doubt on whether vertical combines might survive a court test.

Cases in the years between 1966 and 1969 showed no major policy change. Arrangement by a single producer with distributors, franchise dealers, consignees, and agents still drew judicial rebuke,[173] with the Court on the other hand acting far more leniently on the question of conglomerates, and Justice Fortas in 1968 approving the Penn-Central merger, the largest in the nation's history.[174] The

168. *The New York Times,* May 9, 1965, p. 36. On business apprehensions see Sylvester Petro, "The Growing Threat of Antitrust," *Fortune,* LXII (November, 1962), 128–131.

169. F.T.C. *v.* Dean Foods Co., 384 U.S. 597 (1966).

170. U.S. *v.* Grinnell Corp., 384 U.S. 563 (1966).

171. U.S. *v.* Pabst Brewing Co., 384 U.S. 546 (1966).

172. The Court was not content to apply the antitrust structure merely to business combinations. In June, 1965, it denied labor unions their exemption from the antitrust structure when, by agreeing with one set of employers to impose excessive wage scales on their competitors, they were clearly acting to assist in the elimination of competition. United Mine Workers *v.* Pennington, 381 U.S. 657 (1965).

173. U.S. *v.* Arnold, Schwinn Co., 388 U.S. 365 (1967). See also F.T.C. *v.* Procter & Gamble Co., 386 U.S. 568 (1967).

174. Penn-Central Merger and N. & W. Inclusion Cases, 389 U.S. 486 (1968). In an interesting dissent in B. & O. R.R. *v.* U.S., 386 U.S. 372 (1967), Fortas had earlier protested against judicial interference with an I.C.C. merger order, sug-

net result, as one authority pointed out in late 1968, was to make businessmen highly aware of the legal impediments to be surmounted in the achievement of a successful merger; to enhance the role of the Justice Department as an agency in determining whether to proceed in given cases and how; and to arouse an increasing cynicism about the Court as an effective policy maker in this area, the growing record seeming to show that the judiciary at both the appellate and top level tended to follow Justice Department guidelines in the rulings it rendered.[175]

By the latter years of the 1960s, it became clear to many observers that Earl Warren wished relief from the demanding tasks of the Chief Justiceship. It was also clear that he hoped to hand the reins to a legal activist of his general persuasion whom he hoped would continue the work in which he had engaged since 1953. The pending election of Richard M. Nixon, a long-time political enemy, to the Presidency led Warren in 1968 to tender his resignation. Lyndon Johnson then named to the Chief Justiceship Associate Justice Abe Fortas, an old crony but a judge with a distinguished record, very much in Warren's judicial mold. Critics, however, saw this move by an unpopular, vulnerable, lame-duck President as a golden opportunity to stir up public wrath against the Warren Court on everything from desegregation and reapportionment to its obscenity and criminal procedure rulings. By the time the dust had settled, Johnson had been forced to withdraw the nomination along with that of another Texas friend, Homer Thornberry, whom he had named to assume Fortas' associate justice seat, and Warren, true to the

---

gesting that this was a disturbing return to old-fashioned judicial laissez-faire-type interference with legitimate governmental regulation. Douglas retorted that Fortas was posing erroneous specters. Our position today, he wrote, shared by the Solicitor General and the Department of Justice, "is not one of judicial negation but of insistence that the I.C.C. fulfill Congress's directive to supervise in the public interest the destiny of this Nation's transportation system" (p. 438).

175. Sayler *et al.*, *The Warren Court,* pp. 144–146. In the Permian Basin Area Rate Cases, 390 U.S. 747 (1968), the Court had even moved to upgrade the policy-making authority of other agencies dealing with business, attempting, through judicial interpretation, to breathe new life and sanctions into the Federal Power Commission, an agency that through most of its history had been excessively litigious, preferring rather than to set forth policies and enforce them to move quickly to the courts for its sanctions.

spirit of public service that had marked his entire career, agreed to serve one more term as the nation's judicial head.

In the spring of 1969, the seventy-eight-year-old Californian, pledged to retire in late June, closed his career, either writing or seeing into ruling case law a series of typical opinions reflecting both his judicial and social philosophy. In late April, the Court, speaking through Justice Brennan, struck down, in a controversial ruling, state laws requiring one year of residence in the state for welfare recipients before welfare payments could be made. Such laws, Brennan maintained, were a denial of equal protection and a violation of the broad guarantee of freedom to travel.[176] The ruling was another strong blow at federalism and in the words of Nixon's new Secretary of Health, Education, and Welfare, Robert H. Finch, made the enactment of national welfare standards inevitable.[177] Warren, in dissenting, acknowledged the importance of the latter but saw federal action since the 1930s as authorizing state discretion in the area of creating viable local requirements and encouraging the states to adopt liberal programs, and could see no reasonable grounds for departure.[178] A week later Justice Douglas overruled the 1948 decision in *MacDougall* v. *Green*,[179] making clear that

176. Shapiro *v.* Thompson, 394 U.S. 618 (1969).

177. "Court Rules Out Welfare Residency Requirement," *Congressional Quarterly Weekly Report* (Apr. 25, 1969), p. 5944.

178. The Court since the 1966 term had shown a growing interest in cases involving the poor and depressed. In 1967, in Williams *v.* Shaffer, 385 U.S. 1037 (1967), Warren and Douglas protested the refusal of certiorari in a case involving eviction of a poor tenant, arguing that the defendant had had no real judicial recourse. "The problem of housing for the poor is one of the most acute facing the Nation," Douglas wrote. And while admitting that "this Court does not sit to cure social ills that beset the country," he still contended that "when we are faced with a statute that apparently violates the Equal Protection Clause by patently discriminating against the poor and thereby worsening their already sorry plight, we should address ourself to it." A few months later the Court did take such a case, insisting on fair procedure in eviction actions (Thorpe *v.* Housing Authority, 386 U.S. 670 [1967]; 393 U.S. 268 [1969]). In Damico *v.* California, 389 U.S. 416 (1967), it afforded a welfare client federal relief where local laws were not working, and in Levy *v.* Louisiana, 391 U.S. 68 (1968); and Glona *v.* American Guarantee, 391 U.S. 73 (1968), it turned to the equal protection clause to insure the legal rights of illegitimate children and their parents. In King *v.* Smith, 392 U.S. 309 (1968), it held that an A.F.D.C. mother could not be deprived of funds as the result of having a nonfather in the home; and in Powell *v.* Thompson, 392 U.S. 514 (1968), it held that alcoholism was a disease so that arrest of a chronic alcoholic under criminal statutes was not warranted.

179. MacDougall *v.* Green, 335 U.S. 281 (1948).

while states still had wide discretion over election matters, a scheme such as that in Illinois requiring two hundred signatures from each county before a minor party could get on the ballot, violated the "one man, one vote" principle guaranteed under the equal protection clause by discriminating against voters residing in populous counties.[180] In June the Court upheld the Voting Rights Act of 1965 against local attempts to reinstate literacy tests, Harland pointing out that especially since the local schools were not yet integrated and black students did not have opportunity for equal education, such reinstatement was not as yet warranted.[181] The old 1927 *Whitney* v. *California*[182] case was overruled when the Court threw out an Ohio criminal syndicalism law, charging it with unjustifiably punishing advocacy and assembly, areas that it maintained were guaranteed by the First Amendment.[183] Douglas and Black, in a concurring opinion, used the occasion to call for an end to the judicial use of the clear-and-present-danger doctrine, Douglas denouncing it especially in light of Vietnam protest. He also condemned all loyalty hearings conducted by the government since 1947 as an unconstitutional encroachment upon individual freedom.[184]

Warren's parting valediction came on June 16. For some time attempt had been made to draw the federal courts into the complex question of the refusal of the House of Representatives to seat controversial Negro Congressman Adam Clayton Powell. In fact Justice Warren Burger, appointed by President Nixon to succeed Warren to the Chief Justiceship, had ruled as a member of the Court of

180. Moore *v.* Ogilvie, 394 U.S. 814 (1969).
181. Gaston Co. *v.* U.S., 395 U.S. 285 (1969).
182. Whitney *v.* California, 274 U.S. 357 (1927).
183. Brandenburg *v.* Ohio, 395 U.S. 444 (1969).
184. *Ibid.*, p. 450. In the free expression area, the Court ruled in Red Lion Broadcasting Co. *v.* F.C.C., 395 U.S. 367 (1969), that radio and television broadcasters had a duty, under the F.C.C.'s fairness doctrine and personal attack rule, to present different points of view about controversial public issues. The radio and television industry had claimed the fairness doctrine violated its right to freedom of speech and press, and that broadcasters could not be prohibited from airing whatever they chose and excluding whomever they chose. The Court rejected those claims, holding that the public's First Amendment right to hear different sides of public issues was paramount to the broadcasters' right to be free of government regulation. "Because of the scarcity of radio frequencies," Justice White said, "the government is permitted to put restraints on licensees in favor of others whose views should be expressed on this unique medium."

Appeals for the District of Columbia, that Powell had no standing since the case involved a "political question" that if decided would constitute a violation of the separation of powers and produce an embarrassing confrontation between Congress and the courts.[185] Warren reversed the ruling on the grounds that the Court should act to declare the House's action beyond the limits of its constitutional power.[186] The House had improperly excluded Powell, he maintained, a duly elected representative who met all constitutional qualifications. Stating further that the Constitution in giving to the House the power to be the judge of the qualifications of its own members left the House without the authority to exclude any duly elected representative who met the requirements for membership expressly stated in the Constitution, Warren drew a line between exclusion and expulsion, upholding the House's constitutional authority to the latter but denying it to the former in this case. Typical of Warren was the strong tone running through the opinion expressing the need of the courts to guarantee open democratic processes and the ability of the voters to be represented by leaders of their own choosing. Reaction to the decision was strong, since, as Fred P. Graham wrote in *The New York Times,* "political it was not."[187] Four bills were promptly introduced into Congress in direct response to it, Senator Eastland proposing a joint resolution which would prohibit the Supreme Court or any inferior court from considering suits against either House of Congress, its members, any committee, or congressional employees acting "within the scope . . . of official duties."[188] None eventually passed.

On Warren's final day, June 23, 1969, the Court, activist and controversial under his leadership to the end, issued rulings bound to

185. Powell *v.* McCormack, 395 F. 2d. 577 (1968).

186. Powell *v.* McCormack, 395 U.S. 486 (1969). On the background of the case, both immediate and long range, see P. Allan Dionisopoulos, *Rebellion, Racism, and Representation: The Adam Clayton Powell Case and Its Antecedents* (DeKalb, Ill., 1970).

187. Fred P. Graham, "Ruling on Powell," *The New York Times,* June 22, 1969, p. 6E.

188. "The Powell Case: More Legislative Battles in Store?," *Congressional Quarterly Weekly Report* (June 27, 1969), p. 1125. The Court did not consider the issues of Powell's seniority, back pay, and $25,000 fine assessed by the Ninety-first Congress, but rather sent the case back to the court of appeals with instructions to conduct further proceedings on these points in light of its general ruling.

create further litigation. In nationalizing the double-jeopardy provisions of the Fifth Amendment and overruling the thirty-two-year-old ruling in *Palko* v. *Connecticut,* it held that the right not to be tried twice for the same crime was clearly fundamental to the entire American system of justice.[189] In the criminal procedure area, the Court, still insistent upon justice outside as well as inside the courtroom, held that the Fourth Amendment required a warrant for any search incident to arrest that went beyond the suspect's immediate surroundings. Again it overruled an earlier decision, the Rabinowitz case of 1950,[190] in so seeking to place judicial strictures on excessive police activities.[191]

Earlier in the day, President Nixon had made an unprecedented appearance before the body to introduce his new Chief Justice and to pay tribute to Earl Warren. Nixon, who had so strongly condemned the Court in his campaign for the Presidency and had pledged to reverse its activism with judges pledged to judicial restraint, extended best wishes to the Chief Justice for the years ahead. In a brief address he also praised Warren personally as an "example of humanity," symbolizing in his person and his office the "integrity, fairness and dignity of the Supreme Court." "His example," the President said, ". . . as the chief law official of this country, has helped to keep America on the path of continuity and change, which is so essential for our progress." Warren responded by thanking Nixon for his appreciation of the value of the Supreme Court in the life and government of the nation, and reminding the President that the Court had no constituency and served no majority or minority, but only "the public interest as we see it, guided only by the Constitution and our own consciences." Then possibly in retrospective comment, he expressed the hope that the Court would never agree on all matters, dealing as it did with "the most important and controversial things of life." Otherwise, he said, its vitality would be lost and it would no longer be a real force in national affairs.[192]

189. Benton *v.* Maryland, 395 U.S. 784 (1969). See also North Carolina *v.* Pearce, 395 U.S. 711 (1969).

190. U.S. *v.* Rabinowitz 339 U.S. 56 (1950).

191. Chimel *v.* California, 395 U.S. 752 (1969).

192. "New Chief Justice," *Congressional Quarterly Weekly Report* (June 27, 1969), p. 1126. For a summary of Burger's lower court record see *Congressional Quarterly Weekly Report* (May 30, 1969), pp. 841–844.

Other commentators saw Warren's contribution in a different light.[193] As a progressive politician, cognizant of the nation's need for reform and modernization of its institutions and particularly the urgency with which it was necessary to bring some degree of harmony between professed American commitments to liberty, justice, and equality, and actual American practices, he had utilized the judiciary as a constructive policy-making instrument in a wide range of areas. Intent more upon social ends than upon legal subtleties and refinements, and candidly prepared to say so, he had pushed the nation, through his Court's legal rulings, to take public actions that Congress was unprepared to recommend and the executive was incapable, unilaterally, of effectively securing. That such a policy role would invite controversy was a risk Warren had been prepared to take. That the result would be that an eighteenth-century document, the Constitution, would at the end of the seventh decade of the twentieth century play a greater role in the everyday life of the average American than ever before in his history was a result for which he could legitimately take no small amount of credit and much genuine satisfaction.

193. Anthony Lewis, "A Man Born to Act, Not to Muse," *The New York Times Magazine,* June 30, 1968, pp. 9 ff.

CHAPTER 13

The Historical Implications of the Revolution in Public Law

THE average American of the 1960s was highly conscious of the changed role of the Supreme Court in American life and the American body politic. Even though he might not appreciate how the Court had attained its position of prominence he could certainly recognize how the Court had changed. In the past, the Court had served as a brake on the social mechanism, but now it seemed to be pushing ahead of public opinion and assuming the lead in setting forth new standards of social control and public behavior. In short, the Supreme Court under Earl Warren had become the most innovative of the three branches of the American government.

Its attainment of its new position seemed in retrospect the inevitable result of the public law revolution of the 1930s and its impact on American life and institutions. The overwhelming popular endorsement, at the ballot box, of the New Deal had constituted a clear public acceptance of big government. It was the government's task, from here on, a majority agreed, to take actions in the public interest that in a complex and enormous industrial state an individual could not meaningfully take for himself. Thus the condition of the average individual, his protection against massive impersonal forces such as poverty, unemployment, the business cycle, and his general lack of economic security, which the depression had demonstrated a laissez-faire system could not insure, were now to be turned over to government, whose responsibility it was to afford remedies and solutions. New Deal leaders argued persuasively that only if such elemental economic guarantees were achieved could man be free to cope with the great range of social and political problems chronically confronting him.[1] By the 1950s, the permanence of such an approach to public policy became clear. Eight years of Eisenhower Republicanism demonstrated that even the nation's more conservative party was prepared to preserve and extend rather than reverse or alter the basic New Deal programs.

The popular endorsement of big government and the changed responsibilities it thrust upon both the legislative and executive branches could not help but have profound impact upon the judiciary. With the help of Roosevelt's 1937 "Court-packing" shock treatment, the justices came to acknowledge the government's prerogative in the economic management of the leviathan state—so much so that in the years following the late 1930s, the Court virtually erased from its constitutional agenda regulation-of-property cases. No constitutional act between 1937 and 1969 regulating property was declared unconstitutional and very few state laws regulating industry or providing welfare programs were invalidated as interferences with contract rights or private property. In so reassessing and readjusting its role, the Court found that, if it were to maintain a position of status and power within the governmental structure, it would have to find new areas for adjudication. The elections returns were clear here also.

The American people, responding both to the growth of big government at home and the threat of dictatorial tyranny abroad, were anxious by the late 1930s for reassurance that such government could be limited and their personal rights and individual freedoms guaranteed. The Court had started cautiously down this path in the early 1930s, and now welcomed the opportunity to expand and extend its activities. While abandoning its role as evaluator of the need for state and national economic legislation, it still felt

1. William E. Leuchtenburg, *Franklin D. Roosevelt and the New Deal, 1932–1940* (New York, 1963), pp. 338–340, stresses this theme, with added emphasis upon the New Deal assumption that government cannot reform man, but by altering institutions can create the conditions in which he can more effectively master his own destiny.

a clear obligation to allocate power between state and federal units and among the branches of the government in the economic area, and to oversee the proper execution of the law by administrative agencies.[2] This it continued to do. By the postwar years, it responded further to public clamor, and expanded its concern into areas where local authority, particularly the power of intolerant majorities, tended to limit the individual's ability to make free choices. It also assumed new obligations in the civil rights area, where national demands for modernization were growing.

By this period, time had demonstrated that such considerations demanded special attention. New Deal assumptions, that the solution to many pressing modern social and political problems would come as an automatic spin-off from the attainment of economic security, had proved overoptimistic. Clearly if the individual's social and political rights were to be raised to the same level as his economic rights, positive governmental action would have to be taken in their behalf as well. The accomplishment of such action seemed a particularly relevant task for the courts. Achievement of such rights necessitated the clearing out of a legal thicket of archaic interpretations, which Congress and the executive were either ill-fitted or slightly motivated to undertake.[3]

Meaningful racial integration of public schools and other public facilities could not be achieved until the "separate but equal" gloss on the equal protection clause of the Fourteenth Amendment was removed. This was a task for the courts. Neither was Congress the agency to strike at the use of local laws and regulations "interpreted" by local law-enforcement officials in such a way as to harass and intimidate local minorities and reform groups seeking a new level of individual rights. Similarly, the national legislature could not solve the problem of rural domination of state legislatures. And while it could act in the voting rights area, it was very clear

2. Martin Shapiro, *The Supreme Court and Administrative Agencies* (New York, 1968).

3. The report of President Truman's Civil Rights Committee, *To Secure These Rights* (Washington, 1947), called for a mutual assault by all branches of government, but in the late 1940s it quickly became clear that, especially with the seniority system, and southern domination of key congressional committees, little help would come from Congress. See James M. Burns, *Congress on Trial* (New York, 1949) and *Deadlock of Democracy* (New York, 1963); and David Truman, *The Congressional Party* (New York, 1959).

in the late 1940s and early 1950s, that it would not do so until pressure was so strong that it had no other choice. In like fashion, neither Congress nor the executive was the agent to reinterpret the meaning of the constitutional guarantees of the Bill of Rights and apply them to states and cities in such a way as to produce uniform national standards of criminal procedure, or to supervise the administration of criminal justice in federal and state courts. In the religious area, the First Amendment, on its face, prohibited congressional action in the form of protection for unpopular religious minorities or individuals, as it did reinterpretation of speech and press freedoms, leaving the judiciary the only practical agency for affording relief from the arbitrary power of local comstocks, and self-appointed censors of the reading and viewing tastes of the community.

Along with such political and jurisdictional considerations, the courts were peculiarly qualified to act in these areas for traditional reasons as well. What appellants sought who brought cases in these fields was application of a variety of traditional principles and values associated with the American tradition of democratic government to contemporary problems. The Court's historic role had been to construe established statutes and legal language in the context of both initial meaning and intent and current societal demands. The judicial tradition directed itself naturally, not merely to discovering the precise locus of the productive language of constitutional provisions and statutes, but to ascertaining their thrust and deep and enduring implications as well as their overall philosophical justification for a republican state. Unhampered by the same need for compromise and concern for constituency expedient for the other two branches, the judiciary was able to move quickly and directly toward the assuring of abstract public values, such as justice, fairness, natural rights, and morality in individual and public relationships, in a far less qualified way. It was thus in a unique position to act, as one commentator put it, as the "conscience of the nation."[4]

As its more revolutionary decisions drew sharp and mixed public

4. Philip B. Kurland, "The Court Should Decide Less and Explain More," *The New York Times Magazine,* June 9, 1968, p. 35. See also Kurland, "Earl Warren, The 'Warren Court,' and the Warren Myths," *Michigan Law Review,* LXVII (1968), 353.

comment, the Court quickly responded that this was its purpose. Particularly under Earl Warren, it was persistently literal minded. There was no reason, its majority felt, why historically professed American ideals and their practice could not be harmonized and why the hypocrisy and immorality that had pervaded the behavior of earlier generations of Americans—Americans who while professing deep belief in liberty and equality found innumerable ways to qualify and destroy each—could not be eliminated. Thus, while the Court was conscious of playing a new power role, and acting as a balance wheel in protecting the rights of the individual against the power of big business, big labor, and big government, it was also conscious of its obligation to make American traditions and values operative in the context of a modern industrial society even in face of the reluctance or obstructions of the other two branches.

Such a posture created serious problems, however. While it may have prodded Congress into taking action in the civil rights area that it had been reluctant previously to take, or encouraged the executive branch, particularly the Justice Department, to become more directly involved in the civil rights movement, it also opened the Court to charges of departing from its traditional role and becoming primarily a "legislative body" rewriting the laws of the nation and setting forth its own version of proper public policy. Further, in insisting that it was seeking to spur the practice of professed American ideals and to revitalize traditional and historical constitutional principles, the Court found itself on shaky grounds in at least two respects. The invoking of "history" for some of its moot departures smacked too often of pure rationalization and the creation of a usable past as protective coloration for its actions. The result was that its "historical" claims were frequently disputed even by its own members.[5] At the same time, it ran headlong into one of the central historical contradictions of the American experience; namely that millions of Americans clearly preferred to maintain the discrepancy that existed between theory and practices in many areas, on one hand to profess their belief in such

5. On the problem of using history in judicial decision-making see Alfred H. Kelly, "Clio and the Court: An Illicit Love Affair," *Supreme Court Review* (1965), pp. 119–158; Paul L. Murphy, "Time to Reclaim: The Current Challenge of American Constitutional History," *American Historical Review,* LXIX (1963), 64–79; and Charles A. Miller, *The Supreme Court and the Uses of History* (Cambridge, Mass., 1969).

abstract concepts as freedom, liberty, and equality; on the other, to abstain so far as possible from actions to implement such precepts.[6]

Finally, the results of the Court's new decisions frequently produced sharp social dislocations and hence bitter controversy. Unleashing dissident minorities from legal and social strictures and pressures that had repressed and held them in check for many years resulted, at times, in the immediate abuse of their new freedom and the inability or unwillingness on their part to accept the responsibility that such freedom entailed. The Court was thus subjected to charges of fostering irresponsible action, whether it be by militant civil rights advocates, Communist agitators, criminals flouting the law, unscrupulous purveyors of pornography, or devious labor, business, and political figures hiding behind the Fifth Amendment.

The patterns of approval and disapproval of this constitutional revolution took a variety of significant forms. Nowhere was this more evident than on the high bench itself. While a constantly changing majority of the Court supported judicial activism, with the activists by the mid-1960s jockeying with each other to devise new and legitimate ways to project the Court even further into the policy area,[7] a sharp and critical minority did not. The grounds for their dissent exposed the serious problems activism created. Central was the question whether the Court was not bypassing the other two branches of the government and, as an appointive body, insulated from direct control by the electorate, improperly taking over functions that the people should seek to have performed by their elected representatives. This position was a recurring theme of the advocates of judicial self-restraint. They argued that the behavior of the pre-1937 Court had afforded a clear lesson of the dangers of judicial supremacy; but more importantly, that such supremacy adversely affected the more democratic branches of the government, by playing down the importance of citizens engaging in the political process in such a way as healthily to manage their own affairs along republican lines.

Such a note had been sounded early by Chief Justice Stone. That

6. See Stuart Chase, *American Credos* (New York, 1962), pp. 152–167.

7. See Griswold *v.* Connecticut, 381 U.S. 479 (1965), especially Goldberg's concurring opinion and Black's dissent.

penetrating critic of pre-1937 judicial activism expressed fear in 1945 that the new Court was "in danger of becoming a legislative and Constitution-making body, enacting into law its own predilections."[8] Jackson shortly before his death had reiterated the theme, expressing doubt that the activists could find in a "4,000 word eighteenth-century document or its nineteenth-century amendments . . . some clear bulwark against all dangers and evils that today beset us internally." "This," he contended, "seems to me to be a doctrine wholly incompatible with faith in democracy."[9] In his aroused dissent in *Baker* v. *Carr,* Felix Frankfurter addressed himself to the point, condemning the Court's plunge into the reapportionment area. "To charge courts with the task of accommodating the incommensurable factors of policy . . . is to attribute, however flatteringly, omnicompetence to judges," the justice wrote. "The Framers of the Constitution persistently rejected a proposal that embodied this assumption and Thomas Jefferson never entertained it."[10] And the old Holmesian went on to insist that if the Court persisted in making itself the instrument for finding policy solutions to accommodate the wants of dissident citizens, it would undercut their willingness to make vital their proper avenues of relief, the state legislatures and the Congress. A vigorous lead from the Court, he maintained, inhibited and weakened popular responsibility in the areas of liberty, equality, and justice.

And the theme was continued through the 1960s. John Marshall Harlan, III, seldom lost an opportunity to express his disagreement with what he considered the Court's virtually inviting appeals on a great variety of public questions. Accusing the majority of "straying from the appropriate bounds of its authority," he contended that its actions presented "a jarring picture of Courts threatening to take action in an area which they have no business entering, inevitably on the basis of political judgments which they are incompetent to make." Referring to the later reapportionment rulings, the justice wrote that "these decisions give support to a current mistaken view of the Constitution and the constitutional function of this Court.

8. Alpheus T. Mason, *Harlan Fiske Stone: Pillar of the Law* (New York, 1956), p. 779.

9. Robert H. Jackson, *The Supreme Court in the American System of Government* (Cambridge, Mass., 1955), pp. 57–58.

10. Baker *v.* Carr, 369 U.S. 186, 268 (1962).

This view, in a nutshell, is that every major social ill in this country can find its cure in some constitutional 'principle,' and that this Court should 'take the lead' in promoting reform when other branches of government fail to act." "The Constitution," he contended, "is not a panacea for every blot upon the public welfare, nor should this Court, ordained as a judicial body, be thought of as a general haven for reform movements."[11]

Both Frankfurter and Harlan, as well as a number of the other justices, also fretted about the Court's ability to gain compliance for its policies and about the real threat to its status and power that defiance of them posed. "Disregard of inherent limits in the effective exercise of the Court's 'judicial power,'" wrote Frankfurter, "may well impair the Court's position as the ultimate organ of 'the supreme Law of the Land' in that vast range of legal problems, often strongly entangled in popular feeling, on which this Court must pronounce."[12] And the fact that the justices, on certain occasions, felt compelled to defend publicly certain of their "unpopular" pronouncements, indicated their sensitivity to this point.[13]

Defenders against such criticism inevitably denied that the Court was actively seeking to stamp its version of public policy on the nation. Earl Warren stated: "There are many people, and I fear some lawyers, who believe that whenever the Court disapproves of some facets of American life, it reaches out and decides the question in accordance with its desires. We can reach for no cases. They come to us in the normal course of events or we have no jurisdiction."[14] Nonetheless, the size of the Court's agenda by the 1960s and the divergent areas in which it took appeals, indicated that when they came, it was fully prepared to adjudicate cases from virtually all areas.

11. Reynolds *v.* Simms, 377 U.S. 533, 620, 624–625 (1964). Harlan had expressed himself similarly in an off-the-bench address to the American Bar Association in 1963. See *The New York Times,* Aug. 14, 1963, p. 18.

12. Baker *v.* Carr, 369 U.S. 186, 267 (1962).

13. Especially after the first of the prayer rulings, Engle *v.* Vitale, 370 U.S. 421 (1962), various of the justices addressed themselves publicly to responsible critiques of the Court's action. See Leo Katcher, *Earl Warren: A Political Biography* (New York, 1967), p. 424. See also John H. Laubach, *School Prayers: Congress, the Courts and the Public* (Washington, 1969).

14. The address was given to the California State Bar Association. See Katcher, *Earl Warren,* p. 452, and *The New York Times,* Sept. 26, 1963, p. 29.

Defenders made clear that the Court was not seeking to act independently of the other branches. When entering various areas, they pointed out, it had clearly cast its rulings in such a way as to invite congressional or legislative standards as guidelines for their subsequent implementation. This was true, it was claimed, in the segregation area, in the area of criminal procedure, in the area of censorship and obscenity, and in the area of reapportionment. Critics retorted, however, that the Court never seemed to have the patience to await such legislative standard-making. Rather, the justices insisted, often at an impatiently early date, in taking cases that enabled them to inject their own judicial standards as the guiding ones. To a justice such as Harlan, this questionable action was made more questionable by the fact that the judicial standards afforded were monolithic and inflexible, seldom taking into consideration the "totality of circumstances" involved in areas in which they were now ordered to be applied. Defenders, on the other hand, pointed out that cases came when need for adjudication of pressing issues arose, and insisted that only if the Court responded by insisting upon the early establishment of uniform national standards could any level of consistent practice in the area of civil liberties, civil rights, voting rights, and uniform procedural guarantees be assured throughout the nation.[15]

Similarly divergent patterns of response were forthcoming from students of the Court. That body, as it more and more expanded its policy-making role, became a new focus for scholarly concern. The results had a major impact in various fields of American education.

One of the clear by-products of the "revolution" of 1937 had been the public realization and acknowledgment, despite the image that earlier courts had so carefully projected to the contrary, that the judges constituted a policy-forming agency of government, with discretionary powers. Such realization permitted a type of academic analysis of the Court's procedure and behavior that an earlier generation could not and would not have countenanced. The process

15. A chronic bone of contention was the Court's frequent departure from stare decisis, the view, as Justice Brandeis once put it, that "in most matters it is more important that the applicable rule of law be settled than that it be settled right." Justices such as Black and Douglas, always ready to look beneath precedents for the policy they represented, had far fewer compunctions about departing from established precedents than did Frankfurter and those of his bent, the latter dissenting frequently from decisions overruling prior cases. See Anthony Lewis, *Gideon's Trumpet* (New York, 1964), pp. 84–96.

was begun, carefully and cautiously, by C. Herman Pritchett of the Political Science Department of the University of Chicago. Pritchett, influenced by Herman C. Beyle's study of attribute-cluster-blocs in state legislatures,[16] published an article in 1941 undertaking to identify and describe bloc voting in the nonunanimous decisions of the Supreme Court. The premise of this inquiry was that "the Supreme Court on decision day takes on the aspect of a small legislature in which votes are cast pro and con on significant issues of public policy," and that divisions of opinion among the justices grew out of their "conscious and unconscious preferences and prejudices" on these public policy issues.[17] The technique, which came to be referred to as "bloc analysis," was subsequently utilized to show persistent divisions on the Court with votes of subgroups or blocs of justices placed in alternative liberal or conservative categories. The technique, although it drew criticism from the outset for grossly oversimplifying the justices' stands for the purposes of counting and statistical analysis,[18] nonetheless made clear, even if in a somewhat insensitive way, the proclivity of the justices for following policy lines in their decision making.

Glendon Schubert, who subsequently became the recognized leader of a new school of behavioral research in public law, considered the technique seminal. It "conceptualized the Supreme Court as a small decision-making group, whose voting and opinion behavior could best be explained in terms of imputed differences in the attitudes of individual justices toward the recurrent issues of public policy that characterize cases that reach the Court for decision."[19] Later behavioralists developed more refined systems of attitudinal measurement, particularly Guttman cumulative scaling. This research technique, which social psychologists developed for the army in World War II, was applied to judicial decisions, and its use in analyzing nonunanimous cases showed, its advocates claimed, whether differences among the justices could be accounted for by a single dominant

16. Herman C. Beyle, *Identification and Analysis of Attribute-Cluster-Blocs* (Chicago, 1931).

17. C. Herman Pritchett, "Divisions of Opinion Among Justices of the U.S. Supreme Court, 1939–1941," *American Political Science Review,* XXXV (1941), 890–898.

18. Mark DeWolf Howe, "Justice in a Democracy," *Atlantic Monthly,* CLXXXIV (December, 1949), 34–36.

19. Glendon A. Schubert, *Judicial Decision-Making* (Glencoe, Ill., 1963), p. 2.

variable or by other complex factors. Scalogram analysis, which was subsequently added, provided a technique for arranging the respondent justices in rank orders according to their degree of attachment to the particular value or variable involved, and revealed the consistency and intensity of the underlying attitude of the justices.[20]

Other methods of judicial analysis grew, such as emphasis upon the Court as an interest group, group interaction, role playing by the judges and lawyers, and assessment of how judges were criticized and rewarded and how pressure was brought to bear upon the judiciary. Students of judicial strategy also emerged, and sought to describe the kind of factors that a policy-oriented judge would weigh and the strategic and tactical courses that would be open to a judge who wished to maximize his influence with his colleagues.[21]

Each new technique developed in the political science field had its impact upon the traditional teaching of public law in colleges and universities. Courses in the judicial process joined courses in the legislative and administrative process. Small group theory, role-playing, game theory, formal logic, vector analysis, systems theory, mathematical prediction were all applied to the work of the courts. Indeed, the area of "judicial behavior" became one of the most active fields of research in the precincts of public law.[22] Given the fact that it was posited upon the preliminary assumption that the courts were policy-making agencies, this could not help but add documentation to the general public's growing feelings along these lines.[23]

Many outstanding legal scholars were generally unimpressed with such a turn. Such "scientific" analysis, particularly when at times

20. See Glendon A. Schubert, *Quantitative Analysis of Judicial Behavior* (East Lansing, Mich., 1959), pp. 269 ff.

21. Walter F. Murphy, *Elements of Judicial Strategy* (Chicago, 1964).

22. Text material in the field was abundant. Examples were Theodore L. Becker, *Political Behavioralism and Modern Jurisprudence* (Chicago, 1965); Henry J. Abraham, *Judicial Process,* 2d ed. (New York, 1968); Samuel Krislov, *The Supreme Court in the Political Process* (New York, 1965); Walter F. Murphy and C. Herman Pritchett (eds.), *Courts, Judges, and Politics: An Introduction to the Judicial Process* (New York, 1961); Glendon A. Schubert, *Judicial Behavior: A Reader in Theory and Research* (Chicago, 1964), and *Judicial Policy-making* (Chicago, 1965); and Robert Scigliano, *The Courts: A Reader in the Judicial Process* (Boston, 1962).

23. One behavioralist study found that less than 20 per cent of the Warren Court's rulings were decided on strictly legal considerations, with public policy considerations the central motivation for judicial behavior. Harold J. Spaeth, "Judicial Power as a Variable Motivating Supreme Court Behavior," *Midwest Journal of Political Science,* VI (February, 1962), 54–82.

the evidence assessed and plugged into the computation system was poorly chosen and handled insensitively and heavy-handedly, led one lawyer to insist that the new study of "judicial behavior" was a field "in which counters never think and thinkers never count." Another critic deplored an approach that he felt seemed to prove primarily that the members of the Supreme Court are "guilty of hypocrisy, or foolishness."[24] And legal liberals generally deplored the fact that such scholarship, obsessed as it was with method and procedure, produced in its adherents an attitude of neutrality and detachment that prevented them from considering the social ends that modern jurisprudence sought. To constitutional lawyers like Charles L. Black, Jr., and Fred Rodell of the Yale Law School, and J. Lee Rankin, one-time Solicitor General of the United States, the significance of the Warren Court particularly was in the values it set out to achieve and extend through the courts as instruments.[25] By sublimating legal process to moral ends and to the goals of meaningful justice, while managing not to overlook the latest election returns, they felt the Court had achieved a new level of statesmanship.

Law school activists, however, were by no means the only law school voices. Conservative and traditional legal scholars were clearly apprehensive about many of the Court's revolutionary departures and particularly about the methods it was using in attaining its ends. Conceiving of the body as almost solely a legal institution, they were quick to challenge its questionable legal standards and techniques. This was true, somewhat ironically, even though the Warren Court acted, on most occasions, more like the political science model of a policy-forming institution, than the legal model of a judicial institution.

Learned Hand, in his famous lectures at the Harvard Law School in the late 1950s, was one of the more extreme and most influential of this school. Going even further than Frankfurter in insisting on the need for a new judicial respect for self-restraint, he called for

24. Wallace Mendelson, "The Neo-Behavioral Approach to the Judicial Process: A Critique," *American Political Science Review,* LVII (1963), 603.

25. Charles L. Black, Jr., *The People and the Court* (New York, 1960); Fred Rodell, "It Is the Earl Warren Court," *The New York Times Magazine,* Mar. 13, 1966, pp. 30 f; J. Skelly Wright, "The Role of the Courts: Conscience of a Sovereign People," *The Reporter,* XXIX (Sept. 26, 1963), 27–30; and Katcher, *Earl Warren,* p. 4.

a virtual judicial abdication of most of the power of judicial review, and acceptance of a far more passive role in the policy area.[26] In a reply, Herbert Wechsler saw the problem as far more complex. Wechsler was concerned less over the Court's policies and its use of power than he was over the way it reached its decisions. He particularly deplored the Court's carelessness in failing to reach "principled" decisions. A "principled decision," he explained, "is one that rests on reasons with respect to all the issues in the case, reasons that in their generality and their neutrality transcend any immediate result that is involved."[27] Unless, in his opinion, the Court quit acting like a "naked power group" and began searching for high and universal standards, through the process of collective legal reasoning, it would quickly lose its authority and its aura of respect, one of its traditional sources of power.

Wechsler's "neutral principles" analysis stirred up an ongoing controversy through the world of legal scholarship. Defenders insisted that he was right and that the Court should declare as law only such principles as would in the foreseeable future gain general assent. "The Court," wrote Alexander Bickel of the Yale Law School, echoing many of the views of his colleague Louis Pollak, "is a leader of opinion, not a mere register of it, but it must lead opinion, not merely impose its own; and—the short of it is—it labors under the obligation to succeed."[28] He thus called for an activism of high principles.

Critics, on the other hand, wondered if Wechsler's approach did

26. Learned Hand, *The Bill of Rights* (Cambridge, Mass., 1958). Hand's position was relied upon heavily by congressional critics of the Court in the late 1950s, with one of the Court's defenders, Senator Thomas Hennings of Missouri, so disturbed by it that he wrote the retired justice for clarification. See Katcher, *Earl Warren,* p. 392. Hand made clear that while he favored self-restraint, he did not endorse the proposed Jenner move to curtail the Court's jurisdiction.

27. Herbert Wechsler, *Principles, Politics and Fundamental Law* (Cambridge, Mass., 1961), p. 27.

28. Alexander M. Bickel, *The Least Dangerous Branch—the Supreme Court at the Bar of Politics* (Indianapolis, 1962), p. 239. Professor Robert H. Bork, also of Yale Law School, expressed similar views in a popular magazine article in 1968. Calling on the Court to assume a different role, one better suited to the political realities of American society, he urged it to use its rich and subtle repertory of judicial techniques available to educate, to frame and expose issues for other branches of government, to require them to face up to hard choices and their consequences. Robert H. Bork, "The Supreme Court Needs a New Philosophy," *Fortune,* LXXVIII (December, 1968), 138, 170, 177.

not in many ways parallel Hand's. If the Court could only act when it could formulate a standard that would yield defensible results in all future imaginable cases, they contended, it might be unable to act at all. If standards were placed so high that few or none could be found, Wechsler's approach was simply another road to judicial surrender. More pragmatically, the Court's defenders contended that recent cases reaching the Supreme Court did not lend themselves to traditional types of adjudication. The Court, with more and more ordinary decisions being made by administrators, was getting the "trouble" or "pathological" or "no-law" cases.[29] The reason was precisely because no readily ascertainable legal rule was available to satisfactorily dispose of the issues elsewhere in government. Since there thus was no law to be discovered, the Court was obligated to make its own, by balancing the interests of competing parties involved in difficult and frequently novel modern conflicts, but conflicts that still demanded constitutional solutions. Further, such defenders contended that under these circumstances, the Court's clear obligation was not to concern itself with abstract legal standards, but with the effects of given decisions and the attempt to make those effects an application, in broad principle, of the goals and values of American society.[30] In this regard, the Chief Justice's own position was revealing, even if shocking to traditionalists. "A legal system," Warren contended, "is simply a mature and sophisticated attempt, never perfected, to institutionalize a sense of justice and to free men from the terror and unpredictability of arbitrary force."[31]

Such controversy again revealed deep concern for the judiciary's new path and a renewed need for a variety of scholarly analyses, and an enlarged role for the historian. Politicial scientists focused

29. Martin Shapiro, *Law and Politics in the Supreme Court* (Glencoe, Ill., 1964), p. 20. See also Arthur S. Miller and Ronald F. Howell, "The Myth of Neutrality in Constitutional Adjudication," *University of Chicago Law Review,* XXVII (Summer, 1960), 661–695; and Louis H. Pollak, "Racial Discrimination and Judicial Integrity: A Reply to Professor Wechsler," *University of Pennsylvania Law Review,* CVIII (1959), 1–34.

30. The position was remarkably similar to that maintained a century earlier by Grant's one-time Secretary of the Treasury, George Boutwell. Writing to Hamilton Fish in 1873, Boutwell contended that "a court without political opinions is a myth . . . and as the Supreme Court must be political, let it be right politically rather than wrong." Sidney Ratner, "Was the Supreme Court Packed by President Grant?," *Political Science Quarterly,* L (Sept., 1935), 351.

31. Ernest Havemann, "Storm Center of Justice," *Life,* LVI (May 22, 1964), 118.

on the Court as a policy instrument, studied it internally, and plotted the interactions of its members, departing to a large extent from a larger view of issues of public law. Such scholars had little concern for the origins of problems that eventually came to command public law solutions; the way Court decisions, acts of Congress, and executive orders were promulgated so as to cope with such problems and attune to the intellectual climate of given periods, and the impact and results of this type of executive, legislative, and judicial solution. They seemed singularly uninterested in the Court's professed purpose of successfully readapting the broad, traditional values of American society to modern conditions and in assessing whether such action was one of judicial rationalization or concrete actuality. This sharp and limiting focus, combined with the lawyer's traditional emphasis upon the judiciary as primarily a disembodied legal institution, found a growing school of modern constitutional historians filling the gap.[32]

Less educated and frequently less sophisticated response to the Court's new role and to the new constitutionalism came from the general public. While reaction was more directed to individual decisions and policies, interest and concern were enormous. As the Court rendered decisions in more and more controversial and central areas, its activities became headline news, and its actions, as never before in American history, were portrayed and evaluated by the news media, from columnists, cartoonists, and editorial writers through books, magazines, and radio broadcasts. Following such striking rulings as the school-prayer case and the *Gideon* v. *Wainwright*, right-to-counsel ruling, hour-long, nationwide TV interpretations were produced, with surprisingly high viewer response.

The general public's reaction, while often glandular and visceral, was nonetheless significant. Unlike the 1920s, when the Court's bias toward special privilege and vested interest led many average citizens to despair of any judicial relief from pressing problems, many of the Court's modern decisions drew popular commendation. Wide favorable response emerged to the Hughes Court's blow at biased southern justice in the Scottsboro cases of the 1930s and its curtailing of the power of local dictators in the cases involving Mayor Hague

32. A cry for such action was launched by a University of Minnesota professor in 1963, with considerable salutary results. See Murphy, "Time to Reclaim," pp. 78–79.

"You Know What? Those Guys Act Like They Really Believe That"

Despite criticism, a majority of Americans supported the *Baker* v. *Carr* and *Gideon* rulings, seeing them as conforming with American values. (From *Straight Herblock* [Simon & Schuster, 1964])

and Huey Long. The defense of the rights of religious minorities, especially in the second of the flag-salute cases, was welcomed as an indication of a judicial concern for the welfare of those helpless in the face of majority tyranny. Equally popular with certain segments, were the Court's 1952 blow at excessive Presidential prerogative in the Steel Seizure case, and its call for equal justice for the Negro in *Brown* v. *Board of Education* and the Sit-In decisions. Its clear desire to extend equal justice to the indigent in a number of late 1950, and 1960 rulings and its curtailment of excessive search and seizure and invasion of privacy, to say nothing of its blow at the traditional tyranny of rural legislators in *Baker* v. *Carr,* also found strong adherents and champions.[33]

Such rulings had the significant by-product of projecting the Court, in the public eye, into the role of an agency for affording relief to and protecting the rights of minorities, especially when those rights tended to become neglected in the political processes of government. With the other branches susceptible to prevailing winds, and frequently reluctant, even when majority support seemed evident, to take on politically dangerous subjects, the judiciary seemed to gain a new attraction as an avenue to concerned justice. Private organizations from the American Civil Liberties Union and the N.A.A.C.P. to the left-wing National Lawyers Guild and various organizations with specific interests at stake such as the National Education Association and the legal wings of religious, labor, and ethnic organizations were willing and anxious to assist in bringing cases to test and challenge restrictions to individual freedoms and civil rights. So, also, was the Justice Department. Thus many average citizens, intimidated by the complexities and challenges of gaining relief through the legislative process, turned to the courts first.[34] This was especially true as judicial activism triumphed and the Court made clear its willingness to find ways to take appeals in

33. Harris pollsters found in 1966 that more than three-fourths of the people supported the reapportionment decisions, desegregation of schools and public accommodations were supported two to one, with even 44 per cent of Southerners approving the school-desegregation decision. See G. Theodore Mitau, *Decade of Decision: The Supreme Court and the Constitutional Revolution, 1954–1964* (New York, 1967), pp. 5–8.

34. The theme is explored in various ways in Hans J. Morgenthau, *The Decline of the Democratic Process* (Chicago, 1962); and Hans J. Morgenthau (ed.), *The Crossroads Papers* (New York, 1965).

cases involving pressing modern social impasses. Its guarantee of the right to counsel to all Americans was also significant in the process, both symbolically and practically.

On the other hand, many of the Court's more controversial decisions were highly unpopular and raised serious question whether it was carrying out its proper function. This was particularly true of its prayer rulings, various of its allegedly "pro-Communist" decisions, its obscenity rulings, and certain of its holdings in the area of criminal procedure, which, its critics claimed, with more passion than evidence, hamstrung the local police and coddled criminals.[35] Earl Warren summed up a large segment of this kind of public reaction well when he stated:

> Too often we find people who believe fervently in that portion of the rule of law that protects them . . . but who are intolerant of that portion which protects other people. Many a person who believes implicitly that the Constitution is designed to protect him in the enjoyment and use of his property has little patience with those who insist on freedom of expression, freedom to teach, freedom of association, from discrimination, and freedom to participate fully in government.[36]

Actions to alter the Court's function and the new constitutionalism formed an important part of public policy from Roosevelt's "Court-packing" maneuver to the assault on Abe Fortas in the late 1960s. The question became one of options. Americans were generally committed to the acceptance of the Court as the interpreter of the Constitution and the nation's law and what distressed them was the impact of its rulings rather than the way they were reached or the broader role of the Court. Thus it was normally far easier to rally support against certain rulings, or certain justices, than against the body's modern constitutional function.

Congress, despite the vociferous demands of its southern members following 1954 for countermanding the Court's desegregation rulings, failed, even under the pressure of the Jenner-Butler crusade, to alter the Court's jurisdiction. Rather, it legislated, somewhat piecemeal, to alter the impact of specific Court decisions, in measures such

35. On the latter issue see Robert F. Drinnan, *Democracy, Dissent and Disorder: The Issues and the Law* (New York, 1969).

36. Katcher, *Earl Warren,* p. 452. For a general summary of the nature of the opposition see Clifford M. Lytle, *The Warren Court and Its Critics* (Tucson, 1968).

as the Jencks Act, the District of Columbia Crime Bill, and the Omnibus Crime Control and Safe Streets Act of 1968. Attempts to amend the Constitution to alter the prayer rulings and reapportionment decisions were unsuccessful, even if, at times, warmly supported. Its members seemed to prefer pressuring the Court to change its own mind, by loud public assault, or more subtlely by flexing its approval-power muscles, especially when liberal justices such as Arthur Goldberg or Thurgood Marshall were put forward. Such action reached a climax when Lyndon Johnson appointed Abe Fortas Chief Justice to replace Earl Warren in 1968. Southern senators, especially Dixiecrat-states'-righter-turned-Republican Strom Thurmond, used this occasion to blast particularly the Court's law-and-order and obscenity rulings, at one point in the hearings of the Senate Judiciary Committee demanding unsuccesfully that Fortas justify over fifty cases, some such as Mallory, going back to eight years before the justice had ascended the bench.[37]

Similarly, Presidents prudently abstained from judicial affairs, possibly chastened by Franklin Roosevelt's finger-burning. Truman, whose appointments to the Court were among the weakest since the 1920s, could scarcely assail a body that was generally of his own point of view. Eisenhower, while allegedly expressing later concern over the appointment of Earl Warren,[38] confined his activities to an occasional negative comment on a specific ruling such as the Jencks decision or the passport rulings, and refused generally to endorse the proposed Jenner-Butler legislation.[39] John Kennedy and Lyndon Johnson steered assiduously away from comment on Court rulings, the former occasionally picking up a civil rights gauntlet laid down

37. *Congressional Quarterly Almanac,* XXIV (1968), 531. Thurmond, an acknowledged racist, sublimated those views to focus on more popularly inflammatory issues. To dramatize Fortas' immorality, he arranged to have movies and printed materials which the Court had ruled not to be legally obscene shown to a select audience of senators with viewers returning to the Senate floor to then condemn both the films and the justice. John Corry, "Strom's Dirty Movies," *Harper's,* CCXXXVII (December, 1968), 30–40. See also Andrew Kopkind, "The Significance of Abe Fortas," *New Statesman,* (Sept. 20, 1968), pp. 340–341.

38. Eisenhower is reported to have called Warren's appointment "the biggest damfool mistake I ever made." See Joseph W. Bishop, Jr., "The Warren Court Is Not Likely To Be Overruled," *The New York Times Magazine,* Sept. 7, 1969, p. 31.

39. Walter F. Murphy, *Congress and the Court* (Chicago, 1962), pp. 117, 140, 170–171.

by the justices and following the explosive school-prayer case, urging public acceptance of the Court and its honest intentions. Hubert Humphrey, campaigning for the Presidency in 1968, deplored assaults upon the justices, especially charges that the Court had exacerbated the nation's law and order problem. Only Richard Nixon made a concerted assault upon the Court's role, promising if elected President, to make appointments that would shift its judicial activism to judicial self-restraint, but still not proposing any alteration in its structure, function, or jurisdiction.[40]

Slightly different patterns emerged as state and local officials confronted the new constitutionalism. Strong resentment existed among many state officials over the Court's monitoring of state policies and state activities, particularly in areas involving local segregation patterns; apportionment and voting practices; education, censorship, and loyalty activities; welfare programs, especially following the *Shapiro* v. *Thompson* ruling;[41] and particularly the functioning of state courts in the area of criminal procedure. These were areas in which many state officials preferred to retain deviant local patterns and the Court's insistence upon uniform national standards in all was often highly galling to localist champions.[42]

In the late 1950s, with Southerners frequently serving as prime movers, the Conference of State Chief Justices counterattacked. At its 1958 meeting it issued a long critique of the Court's rulings, condemning particularly the body's activism, "policy-making," and departure from stare decisis. "We believe that strong state and local governments are essential to the effective function of the American system of federal government," the report read, "that they should not be sacrificed needlessly to leveling, and sometimes deadening, uniformity; and that in the interest of active, citizen participation in self-government—the foundation of our democracy—they should be sustained and strengthened."[43] The chief justice of Michigan was so intent upon making the assault personal that he turned a submeet-

40. "Nixon's Beliefs on the Court," *Congressional Quarterly Weekly,* May 23, 1969, p. 798.

41. Shapiro *v.* Thompson, 394 U.S. 618 (1969).

42. The General Assembly of Virginia, for example, set up in 1958, as an official agency, the Virginia Commission on Constitutional Government which issued periodic position papers and pamphlets on proper constitutionalism from the states' rights viewpoint.

43. The full text of the report is contained in C. Herman Pritchett, *Congress versus the Supreme Court, 1957–1960* (Minneapolis, 1961), pp. 141–159.

ing of the convention, ostensibly called to honor Chief Justice Warren, into a forum for an attack on the former governor's judicial leadership.[44] Warren, with admirable self-control, remained aloof from such ill-mannered assaults, but could not resist when addressing the entire body on administrative problems of the federal courts, to hit out at Court obstructionists. In what was clearly a reference to southern defiance of the Court's desegregation rulings, he stated, "I urge all of you to fight court congestion as you would the plague, and to eliminate stoppages and delays from whatever cause, regardless of the effort called for or the personal feelings involved."[45] And he made clear that in his opinion "improvement of the administration of justice is the greatest single cause of our profession," with all other causes clearly to be sublimated to it.[46]

Although nothing specifically came of the maneuver, local government champions were not discouraged. At a meeting in Chicago in 1962, the Council of State Governments developed a three-package proposal for "returning the Constitution to the states and the people."[47] The body, which sought from the outset to disassociate itself from racism and keep its ranks clear of members of far-right groups, set out through its Volunteer Committee on Dual Sovereignty to push its proposals quietly through state legislatures, and within a short time had succeeded in getting one or more of them enacted by at least seventeen, mostly in the South, Southwest, and Midwest. Its amendments, which developed as an immediate response to the *Baker* v. *Carr* ruling, would have cut sharply into the Court's power, and although pushed as a way for better assuring assertion of the popular will, would have enabled a minority of the citizens in a limited number of states to control national policy in a variety of key areas.

The first would have permitted the legislatures of two-thirds of the states to amend the Constitution without approval of Congress. Since reapportionment had not at the time taken place and thirty-

44. *The New York Times,* Feb. 21, 1959, p. 44.

45. Katcher, *Earl Warren,* p. 393.

46. Open southern hostility was by no means universal. In July, 1963, 104 deans and professors in southern law schools, eighteen of them professors of constitutional law, issued a statement condemning southern programs of interposition, and calling for acquiescence in and respect for the Supreme Court and its rulings. *Minneapolis Tribune,* July 20, 1963, p. 4.

47. The full text of the amendments is in *State Government,* XXXVI (Winter, 1963), 10–15.

eight states had legislatures controlled by legislators individually representing only 15 per cent of the nation's population, the measure would have made it possible for a small minority to alter the nation's basic constitutional structure. The second sought to keep legislatures "sacred" by requiring that states keep full and complete jurisdiction over their apportionment. The third proposed to create a "Court of the Union," comprising the fifty state chief justices, in all their multitude, to meet on extraordinary occasions to review, and if necessary, overrule, judgments of the Supreme Court.

Warren effectively blew the whistle on this action. Appalled by lack of opposition to such dangerous threats to the traditional structure of American government, he called, in an address at Duke University, for strong opposition to all the amendments and chided the legal profession generally for failing to fight a move that "would make profound changes in the judiciary, the relationship between the federal and state governments and even the stability of the United States Constitution."[48]

Local law-enforcement agencies were unable to mount such a systematic national campaign. Nonetheless, their constant cry that the Court's criminal procedure rulings were "handcuffing" the police and making local law enforcement impossible, drew sympathetic congressional ears, and played a role in the District of Columbia Crime Bill, the Omnibus Crime Bill of 1968, and in Richard Nixon's campaign for the Presidency.[49]

At the more informal level, various organizations and pressure

48. *The New York Times,* Apr. 28, 1963, p. 44. Charles L. Black, Jr., of the Yale Law School had been the only legal scholar to sound the alarm. See his "Proposed Amendment of Article V: A Threatened Disaster," *Yale Law Journal,* LXXII (April, 1963), 957–966.

49. Nixon had been particularly devious on the law-and-order issue, especially the Court's Miranda ruling. As a result of it, he had contended, no more than "one in eight major crimes committed now results in arrest, prosecution, conviction and punishment." The figure was from the President's Crime Commission, but carefully blurred the fact that the largest single factor in the total number of unpunished crimes was cases where no arrest was made. Rulings on the admission of evidence in court do not seriously affect the number of arrests made. Rather, the Crime Commission made clear that the rate of convictions in cases brought to court is high, the reverse of the picture Nixon conjured up of criminals walking blithely out of court after seeing the evidence against them disallowed on minor technicalities. Nixon, in blasting the Miranda ruling, since there the confession was disallowed as evidence, also neglected to point out that even so Miranda was convicted. See Lewis Chester, Godfrey Hodgson, and Bruce Page, *An American Melodrama: The Presidential Campaign of 1968* (New York, 1969), pp. 230–231.

groups found ways of expressing hostility to the nation's new constitutional arrangement. The American Bar Association, after its brief flirtation with civil rights and civil liberties causes in the late 1930s and early 1940s, returned to conservative foundations by the 1950s. Although passing a resolution in 1950 deploring suggestions for striking at the Court's jurisdiction,[50] the body, especially after the Warren Court's 1956–57 term, spearheaded an attack particularly upon its Communist rulings, which the head of its Committee on Communism claimed represented "overzealous protection of theoretical individual rights."[51] The entire body, which under Eisenhower had gained the prerogative of screening all appointments to the Court,[52] was subsequently pressured to endorse the Jenner Bill, an action that after first indicating its general distrust of the Warren Court, it reluctantly refused to do.[53] But when its Bill of Rights Committee then called for endorsement of Warren and the majority justices and "the sympathy of the Bar with, and their enthusiastic regard for the institution of a courageous and independent judiciary, . . ."[54] the House of Delegates voted to oppose acceptance of the report, indicating that such views represented those of the committee and not of the association.[55] Warren's response was quietly to resign from the organization, which, in reality, comprised only a minority of the nation's lawyers, indicating that while he no longer chose to belong, "he expected to continue to cooperate with the association as he had done for many years in the past."[56]

The Chief Justice earned a certain measure of reward in the 1960s. In calling the nation's attention to the Counsel of State Governments' crippling amendments, he rebuked the association for failing, particularly as an organization devoted to preserving the Constitu-

50. *Congressional Record,* 85th Cong., 2d Sess., p. 4410.

51. See John Nolan, "The Supreme Court versus the ABA," *Commonweal,* LXX (May 15, 1959), 179.

52. Joel B. Grossman, *Lawyers and Judges: The ABA and the Politics of Judicial Selection* (New York, 1965), p. 72.

53. *Congressional Record,* 85th Cong., 2d Sess., p. 4410.

54. Washington *Post & Times-Herald,* Mar. 2, 1959, p. 19. See also David Fellman, "Constitutional Law in 1958-1959," *American Political Science Review,* LIV (1960), 167, 171–172.

55. Dorothy C. Tompkins, *The Supreme Court of the United States* (Berkeley, 1959), pp. 195–196.

56. *The New York Times,* Feb. 21, 1959, p. 44.

tion, to stand up and fight against such serious threats to it.[57] The action forced the president of the body to admit that it had been derelict in its responsibilities,[58] even though a good many of its House of Delegates, then supporting Barry Goldwater for the Presidency, agreed with the amendments, if not in form, at least in spirit. Possibly in a further attempt to compensate, when the initial assault upon Abe Fortas became particularly raucous and irresponsible, the A.B.A. publicly went on record as feeling that Fortas was "highly qualified" to become Chief Justice.[59]

Finally there was a body of conservative and right-wing opinion whose opposition to the Court, to its opinions, and to its role affected the constitutional development of the nation. Initially hopeful of the success of congressional moves to limit the Court's power,[60] a variety of such groups, following the failure of such formal action, directed their energies into sponsoring "grass roots" movements for achieving the same ends popularly. Irony existed, in some regards, in these movements. Many of their leaders had been outspoken champions of the Court and its power when it was throwing out Roosevelt's New Deal in the 1930s. David Lawrence, editor of *U.S. News and World Report,* was a case in point. Lawrence, who had praised the "Nine Honest Men" of 1937 for resisting unwarranted majoritarian pressures and saving the nation and the Constitution,[61] now turned his journal into a sounding board for extreme criticism of the Court's excessive use of power, at one point calling for taking the appointment of its members out of the hands of the President and making seats on it elective for short terms.[62] Other bodies

57. Minneapolis *Tribune,* Apr. 28, 1963.

58. Katcher, *Earl Warren,* pp. 451–452. The Association at its annual meeting in 1963 did express its concern for the civil rights movement and the obligation of the legal profession within it. *The New York Times,* August 14, 1963.

59. *Congressional Quarterly Almanac* (1968), p. 532.

60. When Congress was considering the proposed Jenner-Butler Bill in 1957 and 1958, a number of groups testified as to the Court's communistic tendencies. Included were the States Rights Party of Louisiana, the Defenders of the American Constitution, Inc., and the Ladies of the Grand Army of the Republic. One ex-Communist warned of its excessive commitment to humanism and "Protagorean Paganism." Donald G. Morgan, *Congress and the Constitution: A Study in Responsibility* (Cambridge, Mass., 1966), p. 276.

61. David Lawrence, *Nine Honest Men* (New York, 1936). See also David Lawrence, *Supreme Court or Political Puppets?* (New York, 1937).

62. For citations to key *U.S. News* articles, critical of the Court, see Tompkins, *Supreme Court of the U.S.,* pp. 174 ff.

ranging from the National Association of Manufacturers, the Chamber of Commerce of the United States, the American Legion, the Daughters of the American Revolution, to the National Association of Chiefs of Police and the *National Review* magazine, offered a range of similarly oriented proposals.[63]

Most extreme, and in some ways most futile of such activities was a national campaign to impeach the Chief Justice. Such a campaign had been launched as early as 1958 by a collaboration of racists, superpatriots, and wealthy opponents of "race mixing" and the civil liberties and civil rights rulings of the Court generally. Signboards, particularly sponsored by the John Birch Society, blossomed across the nation carrying the IMPEACH EARL WARREN message, and the Birch Society prepared impeachment postcards and instruction kits, at one point launching a national contest with a cash award for the best essay on "Grounds for Impeachment of Earl Warren."[64] Although admittedly realizing the impossibility of such a move, its sponsors found it was more successful in attracting adherents, members, and money than any other of their stands,[65] although by the mid-1960s even this aspect of it was languishing and it was quietly terminated.

Certain wealthy sympathizers also made the Court a prime target; H. L. Hunt, a Texas oil millionaire who maintained that Calvin Coolidge was the last great American President, subsidized radio and television shows devoted to attacks on the Chief Justice and underwrote the Manion Forum, another source of "informed" vitriol, conducted by an ultraconservative Notre Dame Law School professor. Clarence Manion had earlier been one of the principal champions of the Bricker Amendment, and in the 1920s had condemned the original authors of the Bill of Rights for awarding American man an excessively dangerous amount of freedom.[66] Unfortunately such groups could not curtail the zeal of their adherents, and when Fulton Lewis Jr., before a Boston audience, and Mitchell Paige, a retired

63. For a strong *National Review* assault, typically throwing the Court against itself by indicting it through the dissents of its own members, see "Exit Warren," *National Review,* XX (July 16, 1968), 684–687.

64. For the Society's position on the Court see J. Allen Broyles, *The John Birch Society: Anatomy of a Protest* (Boston, 1964), pp. 114–117.

65. Katcher, *Earl Warren,* p. 417. See also John D. Weaver, *Warren: The Man, the Court, the Era* (Boston, 1967), pp. 284–286.

66. Clarence Manion, "The Shrinking Bill of Rights," *Notre Dame Lawyer,* I (1926), 156.

Marine colonel, before one in Los Angeles called for Warren to be hanged, many Americans were shocked.[67]

The very extremism and irresponsibility of such actions tended to produce reaction and counteraction, particularly when the motives of their advocates were exposed. By the mid-1960s, although frequently antagonized and shocked, most rational Americans waved aside the impeachment movement good-naturedly, chalking it up to another aspect of the peculiarly un-American value system of the nation's lunatic fringe, only to turn to talk of impeachment themselves when the magnitude of Abe Fortas' financial indiscretions were publicly revealed in May of 1969.[68]

Any summary of the impact of such divergent grounds of dissatisfaction with the new constitutionalism would be futile. Such studies as were made produced results more ambiguous than revealing. In a Gallup Poll in 1968 when the question was asked "What kind of rating would you give the Supreme Court?" 8 per cent responded *excellent;* 28 per cent, *good;* 32 per cent, *fair;* 21 per cent, *poor,* with 11 per cent expressing no opinion. Support for the body came from the better educated and the younger, with the South the region most strongly in opposition.[69] Similar Gallup polls earlier had produced only slightly higher endorsement, but by contrast had never recorded any substantial support for moves to limit the Court and alter the nation's constitutional structure such as the "Court of the Union" proposal. The conclusion seemed to indicate that it was the current Court's performance that citizens rated low, not the body nor even its functioning or operation. Similarly, although the point was frequently raised by right-wingers that the Court was undemocratic and elitist, that charge was picked up by few. Thus, as a Yale law professor wrote in *The New York Times* in late 1969:

> . . . no sugar coating could have been thick enough to make some of the Court's major decisions—notably in the sensitive areas of electoral equality, race relations and criminal procedure—palatable to large segments of the population, including a great many highly vocal politicians. . . . But in

67. Katcher, *Earl Warren,* p. 3. A more reasoned right-wing assault was Rosalie M. Gordon, *Nine Men Against America: The Supreme Court and Its Attack on American Liberties* (New York, 1958). On the Gordon book see Glendon A. Schubert, *Constitutional Politics: The Political Behavior of Supreme Court Justices and the Constitutional Policies That They Make* (New York, 1960), pp. 16–18.

68. *Congressional Quarterly Weekly Report,* May 16, 1969, p. 705.

69. *The New York Times,* July 10, 1968, p. 19.

these areas it is my judgment . . . that (1) the Court was right and (2) most people knew it was right.[70]

Thus a quarter century after the constitutional revolution of the late 1930s—a period during much of which it played a major role in the governmental process—the Supreme Court, as an institution, still seemed to enjoy a position of prestige and respect. Even the Warren Court's excessive activism, which at times disturbed legal commentators, scholars, politicians, business leaders, and average Americans alike, brought little successful concrete counteraction. The American people, although at times disturbed by its tendency to sacrifice the general will to the rights of unpopular individuals, still conceded the Court an important role as a balance wheel and check upon the tyranny of the majority. Under big government it was still vital to have a body that would assume the duty of assuring fairness in the enforcement of great bodies of new laws and preserve the best aspects of the federal system. Even "new left" assailants of the "establishment" did not bypass the body, but turned to it as one institution still capable of rendering justice. For many the Court was also an effective national conscience. Even those who assailed specific rulings frequently expressed approval of its articulation in broad principles of the goals of American society and for its clear quest for seeking their attainment through the Constitution in the markedly changed circumstances which the post-1937 world combined.

That the Court was itself nonelective and insulated from the direct reins of popular control or even that its decision-making was at times legally assailable worried most Americans less than whether its decisions had the proper effect upon their society. Used to the world of modern administrative government and bureaucratic management, they took for granted that control by nonelective agencies was a proper modus vivendi for the conduct of life in a complex modern industrial republic.[71] For many the Court had unique qualifications for determining and enforcing the basic operating principles of a democratic system. Recognizing that not all representative institu-

70. Bishop, "Warren Court Is Not Likely To Be Overruled," p. 33.

71. For interesting assessments of acquiescence to nonelective bureaucracies and their role in a democratic society see Henry S. Kariel, *The Decline of American Pluralism* (Stanford, 1961); and Grant McConnell, *Private Power and American Democracy* (New York, 1966).

tions are elective, and not all elective institutions are representative, most Americans trusted the Court to do its best to maintain a balance between majority power and private rights, and were confident that as a responsible judicial-political agency upon which they had come to rely, it could continue to deepen and reenforce the assurances that their representative institutions might someday achieve the full democratic purposes of the Constitution.

Selected Bibliography

Bibliographical Aids

While no single guide to all cases exists, Norman U. Small (ed.), *The Constitution of the United States of America: Analysis and Interpretation* (Washington, 1964), is a valuable guide to leading decisions. Supreme Court cases themselves are available in three editions, the official *United States Reports*, the *Supreme Court Reporter*, and the *Lawyers' Edition*. Federal district and circuit court cases are reported in the *Federal Reporter* to 1932 after which district court cases are printed in the *Federal Supplement* and circuit court cases in the *Federal Reporter*. These volumes are selective, however. For the complete listing of district and circuit court cases consult the federal records office of the appropriate district. Briefs are not included in the reports. *Supreme Court Briefs* are held by most major law libraries and are available on microcard. State court records are compiled both by the states and by the West Publishing Co., St. Paul, Minnesota, in its regional reporters. Many law reviews include regular case notes on the leading state cases handed down by the pertinent state court during its regular session.

Papers of the Justice Department are contained in its library. In addition, the activities of the Attorney General's office are reported in the *Annual Reports of the Attorney General* and the Attorney General's interpretation of the law is contained in the *Opinions of the Attorney General*. Executive and administrative order, proclamations, and rulings are contained in the *Code of Federal Regulations* and orders and statements of federal commissions in the *Federal Register*. The *Uniform Crime Reports for the United States and Its Possessions* has been published annually since 1930 by the Federal Bureau of Investigation.

Federal laws are listed by the Congress by which they were passed in *United States Statutes at Large,* while the *United States Code* is a topical compilation of statutes that are currently in effect. The most useful reference for the study of history is the *United States Code Annotated,* which not only lists the laws but provides a cross reference, historical notes, and the laws' interpretations by the courts. For actions in Congress see the *Journals* of the United States Senate and House of Representatives and the *Congressional Record.* For Senate committee hearings prior to March 4, 1935, see the *Index of Congressional Committee Hearings* and from 1935 to 1959 use the *Cumulative Index of Congressional Committee Hearings, 1935-1959.* Committee hearings of the House of Representatives to 1951 are in the *Index to Congressional Committee Hearings* and after 1951 the *Supplemental Index to Congressional Committee Hearings.*

References to works in constitutional history can be found in the annual volumes of *Writings on American History* (Washington, 1902–1958). Dorothy C. Tompkins, *The Supreme Court of the United States: A Bibliography* (Berkeley, 1959), is a selective, annotated bibliography of materials concerning the Court's organization, method of operation, and personnel. Alexander D. Brooks, *A Bibliography of Civil Rights and Civil Liberties* (New York, 1962), is annotated and includes audio-visual materials. Alan F. Westin (ed.), *An Autobiography of the Supreme Court* (New York, 1963), contains a bibliography of articles and speeches of the justices. A list of the writings of Edward S. Corwin is included in Alpheus T. Mason and Gerald Garvey (eds.), *American Constitutional History: Essays by Edward S. Corwin* (New York, 1964), while Richard S. Kirkendall (ed.), *The Truman Period as a Research Field* (Columbia, Mo., 1967), surveys the research and publications on the Truman period and opportunities for research.

Articles appearing in law reviews are listed in the *Index to Legal Periodicals* and selective articles are summarized in the *C.C.H. Legal Periodical Digest* for the years 1949 to 1964. Association of American Law Schools, *Selected Essays in Constitutional Law* (4 vols., Chicago, 1938), is a collection of notable articles on constitutional law and history selected from law reviews. Besides the major law journals, periodicals of particular use to the historian are *The Supreme Court Review,* published annually since 1961; *The Journal of Law and Economics,* published semiannually since 1958; *The Law and Society Review;* the *American Journal of Legal History;* Donald A. Giannella (ed.), *Religion and the Public Order,* an annual review of chuch-state relations since 1965, which includes a review of books on the subject; and the *Harvard Civil Rights and Civil Liberties Law Review,* a publication devoted to the civil rights revolution and the modern manifestations of the relations between the citizen and the state. *The Southern School News,* begun in 1956 by a group of southern newspaper editors and educators, is a monthly publication that attempts to report what has happened in southern schools since the 1954 school desegregation decision. *The Race Relations Law Reporter* aims to give a "complete, impartial presentation of basic materials including court cases, litigation, orders, regulations . . ." in the race relations area.

Papers and Manuscripts

Included in this listing are only those persons whose papers have been deposited in a collection under their name. Some of the papers of justices and other leading legal figures not included may be found in the collections of others. For these see *The National Union Catalogue of Manuscript Collections* (Washington, 1959–1966).

Justices of the Supreme Court

Louis D. Brandeis collection, School of Law, University of Louisville; Pierce Butler MSS., Minnesota Historical Society; Harold H. Burton MSS., Truman Library (TL); Benjamin N. Cardozo MSS., Columbia University and American Jewish Archives (many are reported to have been destroyed); John H. Clarke MSS., Western Reserve University; Felix Frankfurter MSS. (TL); Oliver Wendell Holmes MSS., Library of Congress (LC) and the Harvard Law School; Charles Evans Hughes MSS. (LC); James C. McReynolds MSS., University of Virginia; Sherman Minton MSS. (TL); Frank Murphy MSS., University of Michigan; Edward T. Sanford MSS., University of Tennessee; Harlan Fiske Stone MSS. (LC); George Sutherland MSS. (LC); William Howard Taft MSS., (LC) and Yale University.

Attorneys General

J. Howard McGrath MSS. (TL); William D. Mitchell MSS. (LC) and Minnesota Historical Society; A. Mitchell Palmer MSS. (LC).

Others

Truman Arnold MSS., University of Wyoming; Zechariah Chafee MSS., Harvard Law School; John W. Davis, Columbia Oral History Collection (COHC); Charles Foly (COHC); Learned Hand MSS. (LC); James Landis MSS. (LC) and (TL); Judson King MSS. (LC); Pat McCarran MSS., Nevada State Museum; Roscoe Pound MSS., Nebraska State Historical Society; Thomas Reed Powell, Harvard Law School; Donald Richberg MSS.

(LC); Jouett Shouse MSS., University of Kentucky; Robert Wagner MSS., Georgetown University.

Of value to the constitutionalist also are the papers of the American Civil Liberties Union, Princeton University, Columbia University, and the New York Public Library; the National Association for the Advancement of Colored People (LC); the National Lawyers Guild, University of California at Berkeley. The papers of the American Bar Association and the Liberty League are in several depositories; see the *National Union Catalogue*. In addition the Justice Department Library contains papers, statements, and speeches of various legal figures.

Various published compilations of various justices' opinions are available. These include John P. Frank (ed.), *Mr. Justice Black: The Man and His Opinions* (New York, 1949); Irving Dilliard (ed.), *One Man's Stand for Freedom: Mr. Justice Black and the Bill of Rights* (New York, 1963); Alexander M. Bickel, *The Unpublished Opinions of Mr. Justice Brandeis* (Cambridge, Mass., 1957); Alfred Lief (ed.), *The Social and Economic Views of Mr. Justice Brandeis* (New York, 1930); Stephen J. Friedman (ed.), *Justice William J. Brennan, Jr., An Affair with Freedom* (New York, 1967); Beryl H. Levy (ed.), *Cardozo and the Frontiers of Legal Thinking, with Selected Opinions* (Cleveland, 1969); A. L. Sainer (ed.), *Law as Justice: Notable Opinions of Mr. Justice Cardozo* (New York, 1938); Vern Countryman (ed.), *Douglas of the Supreme Court: A Selection of His Opinions* (Garden City, N.Y., 1959); Samuel J. Konefsky (ed.), *The Constitutional World of Mr. Justice Frankfurter: Some Representative Opinions* (New York, 1949); Felix Frankfurter, *Of Law and Men* (New York, 1956). The latter volume contains Frankfurter's nondecisional comments. Useful in this regard also is Max Freedman (ed.), *Roosevelt and Frankfurter: Their Correspondence, 1928–1945* (Boston, 1967). Others include: Barbara Frank Kristein (ed.), *A Man's Reach: The Selected Writings of Judge Jerome Frank* (New York, 1965); Daniel P. Moynihan (ed.), *The Defenses of Freedom: The Public Papers of Arthur J. Goldberg* (New York, 1966); Hershel Shanks (ed.), *The Art and Craft of Judging: The Decisions of Judge Learned Hand* (New York, 1968); David L. Shapiro (ed.), *The Evolution of a Judicial Philosophy: Selected Opinions and Papers of Justice John M. Harlan* (Cambridge, Mass., 1969); Max Lerner (ed.), *The Mind and Faith of Justice Holmes* (New York, 1943); Alfred Lief (ed.), *Representative Opinions of Mr. Justice Holmes* (New York, 1931); Harold Norris (ed.), *Mr. Justice Murphy and the Bill of Rights* (Dobbs Ferry, N.Y., 1965); Henry M. Christman (ed.), *The Papers of Chief Justice Warren* (New York, 1966); and Edward D. White, *Legal Traditions and Other Papers* (St. Louis, 1927). See also Carl B. Swisher (ed.), *Selected Papers of Homer Cummings* (New York, 1939).

The justices's nonjudicial writing ranges widely in style and content, from Justice Douglas' works, which range from volumes on mountain climbing to comparisons between the American and Indian Constitutions (here see William O. Douglas, *We The Judges* [Garden City, N.Y., 1956]), to revealing lectures on the judicial process. In the latter category see especially Hugo Black, *A Constitutional Faith* (New York, 1968), a strong statement of the justice's activist philosophy; Learned Hand, *The Bill of Rights* (Cambridge, Mass., 1958), an equally eloquent statement of the need for judicial self-restraint; Robert H. Jackson, *The Supreme Court in the American System of Government* (Cambridge, Mass., 1955); Wiley B. Rutledge, *A Declaration of Legal Faith* (Lawrence, Kans., 1947) and Owen J. Roberts, *The Court and the Constitution* (Cambridge, Mass., 1951). Alan F. Westin (ed.), *An Autobiography of the Supreme Court* (New York, 1963), is a collection of articles and speeches of the Supreme Court justices from John Jay to Earl Warren that provides a picture of how they saw the Court; and his *The Supreme Court: Views from Inside* (New York, 1961), using the same kind of materials from 1948 to 1960, attempts to show how the modern justices arrive at their decisions.

Among the more useful compilations of source material relevant to the constitutional historian are: Donald O. Dewey, *Union and Liberty: A Documentary History of American Constitutionalism* (New York, 1969); Stanley I. Kutler, *The Supreme Court and the Constitution: Readings in American Constitutional History* (Boston, 1969); Thomas I. Emerson, David Haber, and Norman Dorson (eds.), *Political and Civil Rights in the United States: A Collection of Legal and Related Materials,* 3d ed. (2 vols., Boston, 1967); and James M. Smith and Paul L. Murphy, *Liberty and Justice: A Historical Record of American Constitutional Development,* 2d ed. (2 vols., New York, 1968).

Biographies

Fred L. Israel and Leon Friedman (eds.), *The Justices of the United States Supreme Court, 1789–1966: Their Lives and Major Opinions* (New York, 1969), contains articles on individual justices written by specialists on the individual and the times. Allison Dunham and Philip B. Kurland (eds.) *Mr. Justice,* 2d ed. (Chicago, 1964), includes sketches on Holmes, Hughes, Brandeis, Sutherland, Stone, Cardozo, Murphy, and Rutledge. John P. Frank and Yousuf Karch, *The Warren Court* (New York, 1964), contains biographical sketches of the members of the Warren Court.

Specific judicial biographies vary greatly in quality and legal sophistication with some of the most valuable work on the justices buried in the law reviews. The following works are of particular interest to the historian. Wallace Mendelson, *Justices Black and Frankfurter: Conflict in the Court,* 2d ed. (Chicago, 1966), contrasts the ideas and judicial theories of the Court's leading activist and advocate of judicial self-restraint. Stephen P. Strickland (ed.), *Hugo Black and the Supreme Court*: *A Symposium* (Indianapolis, 1967), contains an analysis of the justice's opinion by nine lawyers, teachers, and constitutional scholars, and explores their impact. "Mr. Justice Black: Thirty Years in Retrospect," *U.C.L.A. Law Review,* XIV (January, 1967), is a valuable symposium that includes a biographical essay and Black's opinion in such areas as First Amendment freedoms, demonstrations, the judicial function, antitrust, labor law, and due process. Useful also are Daniel M. Berman, "The Political Philosophy of Hugo L. Black" (unpublished Ph.D. dissertation, Rutgers University, 1957); and "Mr. Justice Black," *Yale Law Journal,* LVI (February, 1956).

The works on Brandeis are voluminous. See Yale University Law School, *Louis Dembitz Brandeis, 1856–1941: A Bibliography* (New Haven, 1958). Among the more important are Alpheus T. Mason, *Brandeis and the Modern State* (Washington, 1936) and *Brandeis: A Free Man's Life* (New York, 1956); Felix Frankfurter, *Mr. Justice Brandeis* (New Haven, 1932), a collection of essays by Charles Evans Hughes, Max Lerner, Frankfurter, and others; Frankfurter *et al.,* "Mr. Justice Brandeis," *Harvard Law Review,* LIV (December, 1941); Max Lerner, "The Social Thought of Mr. Justice Brandeis," *Yale Law Journal,* XL (November, 1931); and Paul A. Freund, "Mr. Justice Brandeis: A Centennial Memoir," *Harvard Law Review,* LXX (March, 1957).

On Brennan see Francis P. McQuade and Alexander T. Kardos, "Mr. Justice Brennan and His Legal Philosophy," *Notre Dame Lawyer,* XXXIII (May, 1958). On Butler see the informative work by David J. Danelski, *A Supreme Court Justice Is Appointed* (New York, 1964), which also affords valuable insights into what went into choosing a Supreme Court justice in the 1920s. See also Francis J. Brown, *The Social and Economic Philosophy of Pierce Butler* (Washington, 1945). There is no satisfactory biography of Cardozo. See, however, Beryl H. Levy, *Cardozo and Frontiers of Legal Thinking* (Cleveland, 1969); George S. Hellman, *Benjamin N. Cardozo, American Judge* (New York, 1940); Walter Gouch, "The Legal Theory of Justice Benjamin Cardozo" (unpublished Ph.D. dissertation, Johns Hopkins University, 1954); Dean Acheson, "Mr. Justice Cardozo and Problems of Government," *Michigan Law Review,* XXXVII (February, 1939); and Learned Hand, "Mr. Justice Cardozo," *Columbia Law Review,* XXXIX (1939). The most useful insights into the man and his philosophical approach to the law are revealed in his four short volumes: *The Nature of the Judicial Process* (New Haven, 1921), *The Growth of the Law* (New

Haven, 1924), *The Paradoxes of Legal Science* (New York, 1928), and *Law and Literature and Other Essays* (New York, 1931). H. Landon Warner, *The Life of Mr. Justice Clarke: A Testament to the Power of Liberal Dissent in America* (Cleveland, 1959), is a sympathetic work on the anti-war justice. In this regard see his own *America and World Peace* (New York, 1925). Joseph E. McLean, *William Rufus Day, Supreme Court Justice from Ohio* (Baltimore, 1956), should be supplemented by Vernon William Roelofs' "William R. Day: A Study in Constitutional History" (unpublished Ph.D. dissertation, University of Michigan, 1942) and "Justice William R. Day and Federal Regulation," *Mississippi Valley Historical Review,* XXXVII (June, 1950). Douglas also is revealed through his own writing, but see Leon D. Epstein, "Justice Douglas: A Case Study in Judicial Review" (unpublished Ph.D. dissertation, University of Chicago, 1949); and Fred Rodell, "Justice Douglas," *University of Chicago Law Review,* XXV (Autumn, 1958).

The literature on Felix Frankfurter is also voluminous, and much of it is panegyrical. See, however, Helen S. Thomas' excellent study *Felix Frankfurter, Scholar on the Bench* (Baltimore, 1960); Samuel J. Konefsky, *The Constitutional World of Mr. Justice Frankfurter* (New York, 1939); Clyde Jacobs, *Justice Frankfurter and Civil Liberties* (Berkeley, 1961); Paul A. Freund and Albert M. Sacks, "Mr. Justice Frankfurter," *University of Chicago Law Review,* XXVI (Winter, 1959); Louis L. Jaffe, "The Judicial Universe of Mr. Justice Frankfurter," *Harvard Law Review,* LXII (January, 1949); and "Mr. Justice Frankfurter" (Symposium), *Yale Law Journal,* LXVI (December, 1957). On the legal realists generally see Wilfred E. Rumble, Jr., *American Legal Realism: Skepticism, Reform, and the Judicial Process* (Ithaca, 1968). On Jerome Frank, see Julius Paul, *The Legal Realism of Jerome N. Frank: A Study of Fact-Skepticism and the Judicial Process* (The Hague, 1959). Valuable also is David E. Ingersoll, "Karl Llewellyn, American Legal Realism, and Contemporary Legal Behavioralism," *Ethics,* LXXV (1966). The Holmes bibliography is equally extensive as those of Frankfurter and Brandeis combined. Mark DeWolfe Howe, Holmes's literary executor, produced two volumes of a projected six-volume biography before his death, and edited two valuable collections of Holmes's letters, *The Holmes-Pollock Letters* (2 vols., Cambridge, Mass., 1941) and *The Holmes-Laski Letters* (2 vols., Cambridge, Mass., 1953). Max Lerner, *The Mind and Faith of Justice Holmes* (New York, 1943), includes a bibliography of writing of the justice to that date. Among the more perceptive studies are Felix Frankfurter, *Mr. Justice Holmes and the Supreme Court* (Cambridge, Mass., 1938); and Samuel J. Konefsky, *The Legacy of Holmes and Brandeis* (New York, 1956), a work assessing the influence of the ideas of the two dissenters. See also Francis

Biddle, *Justice Holmes, Natural Law and the Supreme Court* (New York, 1961); and J. Willard Hurst, *Justice Holmes and Legal History* (New York, 1964), both lectures sponsored by the Holmes Devise, a bequest to the nation by the justice, which is also being used to sponsor a multivolume history of the Supreme Court, no volumes of which have as yet appeared in well over ten years. As to Holmes's later influence, law review material is abundant. See especially Samuel Krislov, "Oliver Wendell Holmes: The Ebb and Flow of Judicial Legendry," *Northwestern University Law Review,* LII (September-October, 1957); and "Mr. Justice Holmes: Some Modern Views," *University of Chicago Law Review,* XXXI (Winter, 1964). A useful explicit study is Walter P. Kremm, "Justice Holmes on Constitutionality and Evidence of His Influence on the Vinson Court" (unpublished Ph.D. dissertation, University of North Carolina, 1961).

Charles Evans Hughes has had one uncritical biographer, Merlo J. Pusey, *Charles Evans Hughes* (2 vols., New York, 1952), a study which is popular and weak on constitutional materials and diverse other analysis. Samuel Hendel, *Charles Evans Hughes and the Supreme Court* (New York, 1951), is a careful and competent study. Valuable also are Felix Frankfurter and Edwin McElwain, "The 'Administrative Side' of Chief Justice Hughes: The Business of the Supreme Court as Conducted by Chief Justice Hughes," *Harvard Law Review,* LXIII (November, 1949); Robert H. Jackson, "The Judicial Career of Chief Justice Hughes," *American Bar Association Journal,* XXVII (July, 1941); and Alpheus T. Mason, "Charles Evans Hughes: An Appeal to the Bar of History," *Vanderbilt Law Review,* VI (December, 1952). Eugene H. Gerhart, *America's Advocate: Robert H. Jackson* (Indianapolis, 1958), is general and slights the judicial career of the one-time Attorney General. Works stronger on judicial materials include Robert J. Steamer, "The Constitutional Doctrines of Mr. Justice Robert H. Jackson" (unpublished Ph.D. dissertation, Cornell University, 1954); Glendon Schubert, *Dispassionate Justice: A Synthesis of the Judicial Opinions of Robert H. Jackson* (Indianapolis, 1969); Walter F. Murphy, "Mr. Justice Jackson, Free Speech, and the Judicial Function," *Vanderbilt Law Review,* XII (October, 1959); "Symposium: Robert H. Jackson, 1892–1954," *Columbia Law Review,* LV (April, 1955); and "Mr. Justice Jackson—a Symposium," *Stanford Law Review,* VIII (December, 1955).

Although only a fraction of his judicial career spans the period, Matthew McDevitt, *Joseph McKenna* (Washington, 1946), is useful for that segment. McReynolds' career has been assessed in three dissertations: Doris S. Blaisdell, "The Constitutional Law of Mr. Justice McReynolds" (unpublished Ph.D. dissertation, University of Wisconsin, 1953); Stephen

T. Early, "James Clark McReynolds and the Judicial Process" (unpublished Ph.D. dissertation, University of Virginia, 1954); and John B. McGraw, "Justice McReynolds and the Supreme Court, 1914–1941" (unpublished Law dissertation, University of Texas, 1949). See also Stirling P. Gilbert, *James Clark McReynolds* (privately printed, 1946). J. Woodford Howard, Jr., *Mr. Justice Murphy: A Political Biography* (Princeton, 1968), is particularly valuable for the accounts of labor struggle in the 1930s and the growth of civil liberties and the judiciary in the 1940s. Useful specific studies include Archibald Cox, "The Influence of Justice Murphy on Labor Law," *Michigan Law Review,* LXVIII (April, 1950); Thurgood Marshall, "Mr. Justice Murphy and Civil Rights," *Michigan Law Review,* XLVIII (April, 1950); and John P. Roche, "The Utopian Pilgrimage of Mr. Justice Murphy," *Vanderbilt Law Review,* X (February, 1957). F. William O'Brien, *Justice Reed and the First Amendment: The Religion Clauses* (Washington, 1958), explores an area of major concern to that New Deal justice. Mark J. Fitzgerald, "Justice Reed: A Study of a Center Judge" (unpublished Ph.D. dissertation, University of Chicago, 1950), is more general. An early work on Roberts was William O. Trapp, "The Constitutional Doctrines of Justice Owen J. Roberts" (unpublished Ph.D. dissertation, Cornell University, 1943). More insightful and revealing are Felix Frankfurter, "Mr. Justice Roberts," *University of Pennsylvania Law Review,* CIV (December, 1955); and Erwin N. Griswold, "Owen J. Roberts as a Judge," *University of Pennsylvania Law Review,* CIV (December, 1955). Wiley Rutledge has fared well biographically. Fowler B. Harper, *Justice Rutledge and the Bright Constellation* (Indianapolis, 1965), is a penetrating analysis of the justice's philosophy and work on the bench and a defense of the liberal wing of the Court during the later New Deal period. Wallace Mendelson, "Mr. Justice Rutledge's Mark upon the Bill of Rights," *Columbia Law Review,* L (January, 1950); and "A Symposium to the Memory of Wiley B. Rutledge," *Iowa Law Review,* XXXV (Summer, 1950), are alternately critical and sympathetic. Also useful are Robert H. Birkby, "Justice Wiley B. Rutledge and Individual Liberties" (unpublished Ph.D. dissertation, Princeton University, 1963); and Alfred O. Canon, "The Constitutional Thought of Wiley Rutledge" (unpublished Ph.D. dissertation, Duke University, 1953). Helaine M. Barnett and Kenneth Levine, "Mr. Justice Potter Stewart," *New York University Law Review,* XL (May, 1965), is a preliminary evaluation of the Ohio justice's attitudes in the free expression, procedure, and federalism areas.

Alpheus T. Mason, *Harlan Fiske Stone: Pillar of the Law* (New York, 1956), was a controversial landmark in judicial biography. Drawing heavily from Stone's private correspondence and papers, Mason not only offered a detailed analysis of Stone's judicial career, but revealed information about the inner working of the body unprecedented in its candor and sufficiently disturbing to at least one justice that he threatened to destroy his papers rather than let them fall into the hands of scholars unprepared to respect the privileged nature of much judicial communication. Samuel J. Konefsky, *Chief Justice Stone and the Supreme Court* (New York, 1945), is more general, less internal, and less valuable. Useful insights are afforded in Learned Hand, "Chief Justice Stone's Conception of the Judicial Function," *Columbia Law Review,* XLVI (September, 1946); Alpheus T. Mason, "The Core of Free Government, 1938-40: Mr. Justice Stone and 'Preferred Freedoms,'" *Yale Law Journal,* LXV (April, 1956); and Herbert Wechsler, "Stone and the Constitution," *Columbia Law Review,* XLVI (September, 1946). Joel F. Paschal, *Mr. Justice Sutherland: A Man Against the State* (Princeton, 1951), perhaps overstates Sutherland's stature. Less uncritical is Jay B. Saks, "Mr. Justice Sutherland: A Study in the Nature of the Judicial Process" (unpublished Ph.D. dissertation, Johns Hopkins, 1940). Allen E. Ragan, *Chief Justice Taft* (Columbus, Ohio, 1938) has been largely superseded by Alpheus T. Mason, *William Howard Taft: Chief Justice* (New York, 1965), although the latter by focusing on Taft's success in marshaling the Court, erects a structure which precludes thorough treatment of that body's record under the former President. Walter F. Murphy, *Elements of Judicial Strategy* (Chicago, 1964), has valuable Taft material, as does Murphy's "In His Own Image: Mr. Chief Justice Taft and Supreme Court Appointments," *Supreme Court Review* (1961), pp. 159–193. Fred Vinson awaits a careful and sympathetic biographer. Work to date includes John P. Frank, "Fred Vinson and the Chief Justiceship," *University of Chicago Law Review,* XXI (Winter, 1954); "In Memoriam: Fred M. Vinson," *Northwestern University Law Review,* XLIX (March-April, 1954); and James J. Bolner, "Mr. Chief Justice Vinson" (unpublished Ph.D. dissertation, University of Virginia, 1962). The same is even more true of Earl Warren, given his lengthier and more significant career in the Chief Justiceship. Work to date on the Californian is journalistic and sympathetic. See Leo Katcher, *Earl Warren: A Political Biography* (New York 1967); John D. Weaver, *Warren: The Man, the Court, the Era* (Boston, 1967); and especially Anthony Lewis, "Earl Warren," in Richard H. Saylor, Barry B. Boyer, and Robert E. Gooding, Jr., *The Warren Court: A Critical Analysis* (New York, 1969), pp. 1–31. The first of the Chief Justices relevant to this study, Edward D. White, received valuable early treatment by Sister Marie Carolyn Klinkhamer, *Edward Douglas White* (Washington, 1943); and less penetrating attention in Harold F. Hartman, *Constitutional Doctrines of Edward D. White*

(Ithaca, 1936); and Robert B. Highsaw, "Mr. Justice White: A Judicial Biography" (unpublished Ph.D. dissertation, Harvard University, 1945). A promising start toward a new biography is W. E. Joyce, "Edward D. White: The Louisiana Years," *Tulane Law Review,* XLI (July, 1967). Francis Biddle, *In Brief Authority* (New York, 1962) is a valuable autobiographical statement by F.D.R.'s wartime Attorney General.

General Works

Standard constitutional history textbooks that include extensive material on the post–World War I period include Alfred H. Kelly and Winfred A. Harbison, *The American Constitution: Its Origins and Development,* 4th ed. (New York, 1970); Carl B. Swisher, *American Constitutional Development,* 2d ed. (Boston, 1954); and Arthur E. Sutherland, *Constitutionalism in America: Origin and Evolution of Its Fundamental Ideas* (New York, 1965). Leo Pfeffer, *This Honorable Court* (Boston, 1965), is a popular treatment from a liberal view by the counsel for the American Jewish Congress. Encyclopedic and factual and generally noninterpretive, Bernard Schwartz, *A Commentary on the Constitution of the United States* (5 vols., New York, 1963–68), summarizes constitutional development in the twentieth century and complements his earlier work, *The Supreme Court: Constitutional Revolution in Retrospect* (New York, 1957), an evaluation of the impact of the constitutional revolution of 1937 in the area of personal freedom, and federalism. The former is individually titled *The Powers of Government* (2 vols., New York, 1963); *The Rights of Property* (New York, 1965); and *The Rights of the Individual* (2 vols., New York, 1968).

Several able constitutional scholars have produced valuable analytical works covering phases of this period. Alpheus T. Mason has augmented his biographies of Brandeis, Taft, and Stone with a more general overview, *The Supreme Court from Taft to Warren,* 2d ed. (Baton Rouge, 1969), and with two period studies, *Security Through Freedom* (Ithaca, 1955), and *The Supreme Court: Vehicle of Revealed Truth or Power Group, 1930–1937* (Boston, 1953). His students have also filled various interstices through Gottfried Dietze (ed.), *Essays on the American Constitution* (Englewood Cliffs, N.J., 1964). C. Herman Pritchett's works also span the latter portion of the period and put together with his text, *The American Constitution,* 2d ed. (New York, 1969), bring together much useful information for the historian. Relevant here are *The Roosevelt Court: A Study in Judicial Politics and Values, 1937–1947* (New York, 1948); *Civil Liberties and the Vinson Court* (Chicago, 1954); *The Political Offender and the Warren Court* (Boston, 1958); and *Congress Versus the Supreme Court, 1957–1960* (Minneapolis, 1961). A Pritchett student, Walter F. Murphy, in *Congress and the Court* (Chicago, 1962), expands constructively on the theme of the latter volume.

Other works that cut through sizable portions of the period include Wesley McCune, *The Nine Young Men* (New York, 1947), a journalistic discussion of the Court from 1937 to 1947, which stresses personalities and their role in the adjudication of various key cases; Carl B. Swisher's two sets of lectures, *The Growth of Constitutional Power in the United States* (Chicago, 1946) and *The Supreme Court in Modern Role,* rev. ed. (New York, 1965); Frank R. Strong, "Trends in Supreme Court Interpretation of Constitution and Statute," *Wayne Law Review,* VI (Summer, 1960), an ambitious though concise attempt to trace major constitutional theories and their application from the New Deal to 1960; Paul A. Freund, *The Supreme Court of the United States: Its Business, Purposes, and Performance* (Cleveland, 1961), and *On Law and Justice* (Cambridge, Mass., 1968); and Charles S. Hyneman, *The Supreme Court on Trial* (New York, 1963), a comparative analysis of the judicial and political process as alternative instruments for making public policy. The latter work is particularly useful in exploring the Court's role as an initiator of desegregation reforms. Through essays by leading constitutional scholars, Alfred H. Kelly (ed.), *Foundations of Freedom in the American Constitution* (New York, 1954), sets forth in historical perspective the idea of constitutional liberty, its background, major premises, strengths, weaknesses, and points of stress. Alexander M. Bickel, *The Least Dangerous Branch: The Supreme Court at the Bar of Politics* (New York, 1962), deals effectively with subjects of recent adjudication from film censorship and anti–birth control legislation to congressional investigations, loyalty and security dismissals, legislative apportionment, and segregation, and is augmented effectively by the same scholar's *Politics and the Warren Court* (New York, 1965), a compilation of *New Republic* articles and law review pieces. Harold J. Spaeth, *The Warren Court: Cases and Commentary* (San Francisco, 1966), is a combination of textbook and casebook with attitudinal analysis of the justices, and a critique of certain legalistic factors considered to be significant motivators of the behavior of the Supreme Court.

Works on the 1950s and 1960s of particular value to the historian include G. Theodore Mitau, *Decade of Decision: The Supreme Court and the Constitutional Revolution, 1954–1964* (New York, 1967); Martin Shapiro, *Law and Politics in the Supreme Court* (New York, 1964), a study that examines various of the Court's policy-making functions from political economist, labor lawyer, and tax policy maker to champion of the Bill of Rights; Donald G. Morgan, *Congress and the Constitution: A Study of Responsibility* (Cambridge, Mass., 1966), which contains valuable information on subjects from the Bituminous Coal Conservation Act of 1935 to the 1964 Civil Rights Act; James E. Clayton, *The Making of Justice: The Supreme Court in Action* (New York, 1964), which, using the Court's 1962 term as a reference point, analyzes the Court's role in American government and the types of problems it faces in maintaining its legitimacy. Robert L. Cord, "Judicial Theories of Limited Government and Procedural Guarantees under the Fourteenth Amendment, as Expressed in Supreme Court Decision, 1942–1966" (unpublished Ph.D. dissertation, Syracuse University, 1967), relates the theory of limited government to the judicial philosophies advanced to justify the growth of procedural rights under the due process clause of the Fourteenth Amendment. Max Freedman, William M. Beaney, and Eugene V. Rostow, *Perspectives on the Court* (Evanston, 1967), interprets the recent reformulation of fundamental law from the perspectives of journalism, political science, and the legal profession. Finally, Archibald Cox, *The Warren Court: Constitutional Decision as an Instrument of Reform* (Cambridge, Mass., 1968), offers valuable evaluations by President Kennedy's Solicitor General.

The nature of the Court as a political institution and its relation to other branches of the government has been a popular theme for investigation. Walton H. Hamilton and George D. Braden, "The Special Competence of the Supreme Court," *Yale Law Journal* (June, 1941), early pointed out that in the days of the post-1937 Court the constitutional issues the body was getting had increasing nonlegal overtones that set it off from most ordinary litigation. This fact, they contended, afforded its members more discretionary policy-making opportunities. The limits to which the justices should go in exercising this new judicial review promptly became a divisive factor, Arthur M. Schlesinger, Jr., "The Supreme Court, 1947," *Fortune,* XXXV (January, 1947), alerting the public to the configurations of the activist–self-restraint controversy in a popular if somewhat oversimplified way. As Black and Frankfurter emerged as polar opposites on this issue in the late 1940s, each developed scholarly champions. Wallace Mendelson, *Justices Black and Frankfurter: Conflict in the Court,* 2d ed. (Chicago, 1966), and *The Supreme Court: Law and Discretion* (Indianapolis, 1967) trace the continuing patterns of this division with a Frankfurterian bias showing at many points. Walter F. Berns, *Freedom, Virtue and the First Amendment* (Chicago, 1957), assaults Black's "preferred freedoms" approach and asserts that freedom is not as central a value to modern society as virtue and order. C. B. Blackmar, "The Supreme Court as a Governmental Institution," *St. Louis University Law Journal,* XII (Winter, 1967), argues that judicial power is inherently opposed to popular government. Charles L. Black,

Jr., *The People and the Court: Judicial Review in a Democracy* (New York, 1960), defends the Court's activist role, especially in civil liberties, as does Martin Shapiro, *Freedom of Speech: The Supreme Court and Judicial Review* (Englewood Cliffs, N.J., 1966). A balanced assessment is Victor G. Rosenblum, *Law as a Political Instrument* (Garden City, N.Y., 1955). On the historic background of the controversy see Howard E. Dean, *Judicial Review and Democracy* (New York, 1966). The Supreme Court's relation with the executive branch, particularly its check upon Presidential power, is explored in Glendon A. Schubert, *The Presidency in the Courts* (Minneapolis, 1957).

Business, Labor, and Property in the 1920s

The expansion of federal functions in this period is recounted in Carroll H. Wooddy, *The Growth of the Federal Government, 1915–1932* (New York, 1934). Carl McFarland, *Judicial Control of the Federal Trade Commission and the Interstate Commerce Commission, 1920–1930* (Cambridge, Mass., 1932), is a comparative study of the relations between the courts and these commissions that describes the evolution of administrative justice in related fields. Myron W. Watkins, "An Appraisal of the Work of the Federal Trade Commission," *Columbia Law Review,* XXXII (February, 1932); and G. Cullom Davis, "The Transformation of the Federal Trade Commission, 1914–1929," *Mississippi Valley Historical Review,* XLIX (December, 1962), evaluate critically the F.T.C. as a regulatory agency.

More specific studies include Bernard C. Gavit, *The Commerce Clause of the United States Constitution* (Bloomington, Ind., 1932), the standard early legal treatise on the clause and its varied interpretations and use prior to the New Deal; Thomas Reed Powell, "The Supreme Court and State Police Power, 1922–1930," *Virginia Law Review,* XVII, XVIII (April, May, June, November, and December, 1931, and January, 1932); and Robert E. Rodes, Jr., "Due Process and Social Legislation in the Supreme Court, 1873–1937—A Post Mortem," *Notre Dame Lawyer,* XXXIII (December, 1957). An earlier and still valuable treatment of the latter subject is Virginia Wood, *Due Process of Law* (Baton Rouge, 1951). Maurice Finklestein, "From Munn v. Illinois to Tyson v. Banton: A Study in the Judicial Process," *Columbia Law Review,* XXVI (November, 1927), is a useful historical trace, while the history of the spending power is analyzed in Edward S. Corwin, "The Spending Power of Congress Apropos the Maternity Act," *Harvard Law Review,* XXXVI (March, 1923).

Much has been written on the subject of labor in this period. General discussions include Edward Berman, *Labor and the Sherman Act*

(New York, 1930); Charles O. Gregory, *Labor and the Law,* 2d ed. (New York, 1961); and Wayne L. McNaughton, *Development of Labor Relations Law* (Washington, 1941). Elias Lieberman, *Unions Before the Bar: Historic Trials Showing the Evolution of Labor Rights in the United States* (New York, 1960), has useful chapters on the 1920s. Felix Frankfurter and Nathan Greene, *The Labor Injunction* (New York, 1930); and Edwin E. Witte, *The Government in Labor Disputes* (New York, 1932), are standard treatments. Edward Berman, "Supreme Court Interpretation of the Railway Labor Act," *American Economic Review,* XX (December, 1930), analyzes the Supreme Court's interpretation of the Railway Act of 1926 prohibiting railroads from pressuring employees into revoking their membership in unions. Joel I. Seidman, *Yellow Dog Contracts* (Baltimore, 1932); and R. G. Fuller, *Child Labor and the Constitution* (New York, 1929), are useful contemporary studies.

Civil Liberties, Liberalism, and Legal Reform to 1937

The classic civil liberties study on World War I and the 1920s is Zechariah Chafee, Jr., *Free Speech in the United States* (Cambridge, Mass., 1941). More specific studies on the problems of the war period include William Preston, *Aliens and Dissenters: Federal Suppression of Radicals, 1903–1933* (Cambridge, Mass., 1963); Gilbert C. Fite and Horace C. Peterson, *Opponents of War, 1917–1918* (Madison, 1957); Donald O. Johnson, *The Challenge to American Freedoms: World War I and the Rise of the American Civil Liberties Union* (Lexington, Ky., 1963); Harry N. Scheiber, *The Wilson Administration and Civil Liberties, 1917–1919* (Ithaca, 1960); and Joan M. Jensen, *The Price of Vigilance* (Chicago, 1968). The standard work on the "Red Scare" is Robert K. Murray, *Red Scare: A Study in National Hysteria, 1919–1920* (Minneapolis, 1955); but Louis F. Post, *The Deportations Delirium of Nineteen-Twenty: A Personal Narrative of an Historical Official Experience* (Chicago, 1923), captures the immediacy of a beleaguered participant. Stanley Coben, *A. Mitchell Palmer: Politician* (New York, 1963), is an admirable analysis of the "fighting Quaker" Attorney General, portraying him as a victim of the times and his own ambition.

There is no satisfactory general study of civil liberties in the post–"Red Scare" years of the decade. Topical works cover a number of key issues, however. The Sacco-Vanzetti case and the Tom Mooney case, although raising greater public passion than constitutional questions, nonetheless were vehicles stimulating strong cries for legal and judicial reform. The most thorough work on the former is Louis Joughin and Edmund M. Morgan, *The Legacy of Sacco and Vanzetti* (New York, 1948), and the most recent Herbert B. Ehrmann, *The Case That Will Not Die: Commonwealth vs. Sacco and Vanzetti* (Boston, 1969). Richard H. Frost, *The Mooney Case* (Stanford, 1968) explores the case's social and political impact cogently and revealingly. Benjamin Gitlow, *I Confess: The Truth About American Communism* (New York, 1940), is an autobiographical exorcism by the principal in the significant 1925 case. Eldridge F. Dowell, *History of Criminal Syndicalism Legislation in the United States* (Baltimore, 1939), explores the roots of the state legislation used to arrest Gitlow and many others, and traces its application through the decade. Lawrence H. Chamberlain, *Loyalty and Legislative Action: A Survey of Activity by the New York Legislature, 1919–1949* (Ithaca, 1951), is a case study at the state level and is augmented by Thomas E. Vadney, "The Politics of Repression, a Case Study of the Red Scare in New York," *New York History,* XLIX (January, 1968). Davis B. Tyack, "The Perils of Pluralism: The Background of the Pierce Case," *American Historical Review,* LXXIV (October, 1968); and Kenneth B. O'Brien, Jr., "Education, Americanization and the Supreme Court in the 1920's," *American Quarterly,* XIII (Summer, 1961), are valuable explorations of the cultural and social factors underlying judicial behavior. The best works on censorship include Paul S. Boyer, *Purity in Print: The Vice Movement and Book Censorship in America* (New York, 1968), a useful chronicle of the history of censorship with special emphasis on the 1920s; Morris L. Ernst and William Seagle, *To the Pure: A Study of Obscenity and the Censor* (New York, 1928); William L. Curry, "Comstockery: A Study in the Rise and Decline of a Watchdog Censorship, 1875–1950" (unpublished Ph.D. dissertation, Columbia University, 1957), which surveys a wide range of materials to assess the motivations behind such censorship; James C. N. Paul and Murray L. Schwartz, *Federal Censorship: Obscenity in the Mail* (New York, 1961); Robert W. Haney, *Comstockery in America: Patterns of Censorship and Control* (Boston, 1960); and Mary Ware Dennett, *Who's Obscene?* (New York, 1930), a contemporary account by one who felt its sting. Harry Shulman, "The Supreme Court's Attitude on Liberty of Contract and Freedom of Speech," *Yale Law Journal,* XLI (December, 1931), was a prescient contemporary analysis of the beginnings of the shift from economic due process to civil liberties due process, a development turning on an interpretation of the Fourteenth Amendment that Charles Warren had deplored as constitutionally indefensible in a famous article, "The New 'Liberty' Under the Fourteenth Amendment," *Harvard Law Review,* XXXIX (February, 1926), published shortly after the landmark Gitlow decision.

The Negro in this period is discussed by Charles S. Mangum, Jr., *The Legal Status of the Negro* (Chapel Hill, N.C., 1940), in the context of his moral and social conditions. Bernard H. Nelson, *The Fourteenth Amendment and the Negro Since 1920,* 2d ed. (New York, 1967), includes selected cases to 1943. Robert L. Zangrando, "The Efforts of the National Association for the Advancement of Colored People to Secure Passage of a Federal Anti-Lynching Law, 1920–1940" (unpublished Ph.D. dissertation, University of Pennsylvania, 1963), evaluates this campaign in terms of public and political reaction, Negro esprit, and N.A.A.C.P. organizational growth. Dan T. Carter, *Scottsboro: A Tragedy of the American South* (Baton Rouge, 1969), is the most definitive account of the famed right to counsel and impartial jury cases that became a landmark in southern justice. The problems of other minority groups are treated in Milton R. Konvitz, The *Alien and the Asiatic in American Law* (Ithaca, 1946); and William M. Gibson, *Aliens and the Law* (Chapel Hill, N.C., 1940).

The New Deal and the Old Court, 1934–1937

Robert L. Stern, a contemporary legal observer, provides an excellent general treatment of the New Deal's program in the courts in "The Commerce Clause and the National Economy, 1933–1946," *Harvard Law Review,* LIX (May, July, 1946); while Erik M. Eriksson, *The Supreme Court and the New Deal* (Los Angeles, 1941), is a detailed evaluation of the pre-1937 rulings on New Deal legislation. Edward S. Corwin, *The Commerce Power Versus States Rights* (Princeton, 1936), analyzes the conflicting interpretations of the commerce power that lay in the background of the New Deal constitutional crisis, his earlier *Twilight of the Supreme Court* (New Haven, 1934) being a New Deal–oriented questioning of the use of judicial power. His third work from this period, *Court over Constitution* (Princeton, 1938), focuses on the governmental crisis produced by judicial rejection of New Deal legislation. F. D. G. Ribble, *State and National Power over Commerce* (New York, 1937), argues for a modern Marshallian expansiveness of the commerce clause.

The functioning of early New Deal agricultural legislation is explored in Edwin G. Nourse, *Marketing Agreements under the A.A.A.* (Washington, 1935); Edwin G. Nourse, Joseph S. Davis, and John D. Black, *Three Years of the Agricultural Adjustment Administration* (Washington, 1937), which also points out the reforms it clearly needed; and Paul L. Murphy, "The New Deal Agricultural Program and the Constitution," *Agricultural History,* XXIX (October, 1955). Russell L. Post, "Constitutionality of Government Spending for General Welfare," *Virginia Law Review,* XXII (November, 1935), is a general examination of the constitutional issues involved in the AAA case, while Charles S. Collier, "Judicial Bootstraps and the General Welfare Clause; The A.A.A. Opinion," *George Washing-*

ton Law Review, IV (January, 1936), also evaluates the controversial Butler ruling.

Early New Deal efforts at governmental regulation in the labor-management area are described by Lewis P. Lorwin and Arthur Wubnig, *Labor Relations Boards* (Washington, 1935). Labor policy generally and the constitutional factors involved in the struggle to create a national labor policy are treated in Irving Bernstein, *The New Deal Collective Bargaining Policy* (Berkeley, 1950). Ralph H. Baker, *The National Bituminous Coal Commission* (Baltimore, 1941), explores the background of New Deal mine legislation, while Eugene V. Rostow, "Bituminous Coal and the Public Interest," *Yale Law Journal,* L (February, 1941), analyzes the effects of government regulation on this industry. The best studies of the case that ruled the NIRA unconstitutional are Edward S. Corwin, "The Schechter Case—Landmark or What?," *New York University Law Quarterly Review,* XIII (January, 1936); Thomas Reed Powell, "Commerce, Pensions, and Codes," *Harvard Law Review,* XLIX (November, December, 1935); and J. A. C. Grant, "Commerce, Production, and the Fiscal Power of Congress," *Yale Law Journal,* LXV (March, April, 1936). Other useful works are Jane P. Clark, "Emergencies and the Law," *Political Science Quarterly,* XLIX (June, 1934), an analysis of the constitutional issues involved in the Minnesota Moratorium Case; John P. Dawson, "The Gold-Clause Decisions," *Michigan Law Review,* XXXIII (March, 1935), which discusses monetary policy; and Helen Martell, "Legal Aspects of the Tennessee Valley Authority," *George Washington University Law Review,* VII (June, 1939), a good constitutional study of the federal power program.

The Crisis of 1937

Florence S. Hellman has compiled bibliographies of contemporary materials on the Court-packing crisis, U.S. Library of Congress, Division of Bibliography, *List of References on the Supreme Court with Particular Reference to the Doctrine of Judicial Review* (Washington, 1935); *List of Speeches on the United States Supreme Court Issue as Printed in the Congressional Record,* compiled by Anne L. Baden under the direction of Florence S. Hellman (Washington, 1937); and *The Supreme Court Issue: A Selected List of References* (Washington, 1938).

The background forces that ultimately exploded into the 1937 crisis are traced by Dean Alfange in *The Supreme Court and the National Will* (Garden City, N.Y., 1937) and Robert K. Carr, *The Supreme Court and Judicial Review* (New York, 1942). Joseph Alsop and Turner Catledge, *The 168 Days* (Garden City, N.Y., 1938), is a contemporary, journalistic, blow-by-blow account of the Court-packing fight. Leonard Baker, *Back to*

Back: The Duel Between F.D.R. and the Supreme Court (New York, 1967), covers much the same ground from the vantage point of thirty years of perspective. Richard C. Cortner, *The Wagner Act Cases* (Knoxville, 1964), analyzes the role of a governmental agency in constitutional adjudication and the maneuvering of the interest groups involved in the cases that reversed laissez-faire constitutionalism. William E. Leuchtenburg has published three articles preparatory to a full-length monograph: "The Case of the Contentious Commissioner: Humphrey's Executor v. U.S.," in Harold M. Hyman and Leonard W. Levy (eds.), *Freedom and Reform: Essays in Honor of Henry Steele Commager* (New York, 1967); "The Origins of Franklin D. Roosevelt's 'Court-Packing' Plan," *Supreme Court Review* (1966); and "Franklin D. Roosevelt's Supreme Court "Packing" Plan," in Wilmon H. Droze *et al., Essays on the New Deal* (Austin, 1969). E. Kimbark MacCall, "The Supreme Court and Public Opinion—a Study of the Court Fight of 1937" (unpublished Ph.D. dissertation, University of California, 1953), is a useful assessment of popular reactions. Edward S. Corwin, *Constitutional Revolution, Ltd.* (Claremont, Calif., 1941), explores the immediate impact of the "switch in time which saved nine," as does Bernard Schwartz, *The Supreme Court: Constitutional Revolution in Retrospect* (New York, 1957). Robert H. Jackson, *The Struggle for Judicial Supremacy* (New York, 1941), is an apology for F.D.R.'s tactics and a sanguine evaluation of their constitutional results, whereas Merlo J. Pusey, *The Supreme Court Crisis* (New York, 1937), is a contemporary assault on those tactics. William O. Douglas, "Stare Decisis," Eighth Annual Cardozo Lecture before the Association, April 12, 1949, *The Record of the Association of the Bar of the City of New York,* IV (May, 1949), is a classic "old left" defense of the new post-1937 judicialism, especially its departure from prior precedents; while Charles P. Curtis, Jr., *Lions Under the Throne* (Boston, 1947), defends responsibly exercised judicial power while deploring aspects of the Court's excesses during the 1930s.

Constitutional Revolution: Economic Implications, 1937–41

C. Herman Pritchett, *The Roosevelt Court: A Study in Judicial Politics and Values, 1937–1947* (New York, 1948), is a valuable general overview, profitably augmented by Kenneth Culp Davis, "Revolution in the Supreme Court," *Atlantic Monthly,* CLXVI (July, 1940); Charles Fahy, "Notes on Developments in Constitutional Law, 1936–1949," *Georgetown Law Journal,* XXXVIII (November, 1949); and Vincent M. Barnett, Jr., "The Supreme Court and the Capacity to Govern," *Political Science Quarterly,* LXIII (September, 1948).

The major constitutional problems of the 1930s are insightfully discussed in a retrospective piece by Robert L. Stern, "The Problems of Yesteryear—Commerce and Due Process," *Vanderbilt Law Review,* IV (April, 1951); and by Robert G. McCloskey, "Economic Due Process and the Supreme Court: An Exhumation and Reburial," *Supreme Court Review* (1962). The problem of state interference with interstate commerce is treated in detail in a series of articles published under "Governmental Market Barriers: A Symposium," *Law and Contemporary Problems,* VIII (April, 1941), and in Joseph E. Kallenbach, *Federal Cooperation with the States under the Commerce Clause* (Ann Arbor, 1942). Edward L. Barrett, Jr., summarizes the problems created in the commerce area by the revolution in federalism in "State Taxation of Interstate Commerce: 'Direct Burdens,' 'Multiple Burdens' or What Have You?," *Vanderbilt Law Review,* IV (April, 1951); and Thomas Reed Powell, "Insurance as Commerce," *Harvard Law Review,* LVII (September, 1944), discusses the Polish Alliance and Southeastern Underwriters cases.

The early interpretation of the Wagner Act, particularly as the courts expanded its coverage, is discussed in Herbert O. Eby, *The Labor Relations Act in the Courts* (New York, 1943); and Ervin K. Zingler, "The N.L.R.B. and the Federal Courts," *Southern Economic Journal,* VII (April, 1941). Charles O. Gregory questions Frankfurter's claim to be an advocate of judicial self-restraint in light of his actions in the Hutcheson and Apex rulings in "The New Sherman-Clayton-Morris-LaGuardia Act," *University of Chicago Law Review,* VIII (April, 1941); and Mozart G. Ratner and Norton J. Come, "The Norris-LaGuardia Act in the Constitution," *George Washington Law Review* XI (June, 1943), assesses the judicial treatment of the measure. The legislative and judicial aspects of the Fair Labor Standards Act are detailed in Orme W. Phelps, *The Legislative Background of the Fair Labor Standards Act: A Study of the Growth of National Sentiment in Favor of Government Regulation of Wages, Hours and Child Labor* (Chicago, 1939); John S. Forsythe, "Legislative History of the Fair Labor Standards Act," *Law and Contemporary Problems,* VI (Summer, 1939); Herman A. Wecht, *Wage-Hour Coverage* (Philadelphia, 1951), a detailed exploration of the judicial treatment of the law; and E. Merrick Dodd, "The Supreme Court and Organized Labor, 1941–1945," *Harvard Law Review,* LVIII (September, 1945), and "The Supreme Court and Fair Labor Standards, 1941–1945," *Harvard Law Review* LIX (February, 1946).

In the area of agriculture see Donald C. Blaisdell, *Government and Agriculture: The Growth of Federal Farm Aid* (New York, 1940); Andrew F. Oehman, "The Agricultural Adjustment Act of 1938," *Georgetown Law Review,* XXVI (March, 1938), a contemporary article on the legislative history of the measure, especially its constitutional aspects; and Ashley

Sellers and Jesse E. Baskette, Jr., "Agricultural Marketing Agreement and Order Programs, 1933–1943," *Georgetown Law Journal,* XXXIII (January, 1945), a good description of changing governmental actions in the agricultural area.

Constitutional Revolution: Civil Liberties, 1937–46

Edward S. Corwin, *Liberty Against Government: The Rise, Flowering and Decline of a Famous Judicial Concept* (Baton Rouge, 1948), is a historical and theoretical analysis of the idea of civil liberty. "Civil Liberties—a Symposium," *University of Chicago Law Review,* XX (Spring, 1953), contains a number of useful articles on a variety of problems. Virginia Wood, *Due Process of Law, 1932–1949: The Supreme Court's Use of a Constitutional Tool* (Baton Rouge, 1951), is a general study of due process in relation to free speech, social and economic legislation, and criminal procedure. Charles Fairman attacks the validity of Justice Black's thesis, especially his Adamson dissent, in "Does the Fourteenth Amendment Incorporate the Bill of Rights? The Original Understanding," *Stanford Law Review,* II (December, 1949); is rebutted by William Crosskey, "Legislative History and the Constitutional Limitations on State Authority," *University of Chicago Law Review,* XXII (Autumn, 1954); and returns the challenge in "A Reply to Professor Crosskey," *University of Chicago Law Review,* XXII (Autumn, 1954).

Robert B. McKay, "The Preference for Freedom," *New York University Law Review,* XXXIV (November, 1959), is an analytical defense of Cardozo's "preferred freedoms" concept that focuses on freedom of speech in the context of the clear and present danger rule and probable danger test. Zechariah Chafee, Jr., *Free Speech in the United States* (Cambridge, Mass., 1948), is an expanded and updated revision of the Harvard Law School professor's earlier influential *Freedom of Speech* (New York, 1920). Joseph Tanenhaus, "Picketing as Free Speech: The Growth of the New Law of Picketing from 1940 to 1952," *Cornell Law Quarterly,* XXXVIII (Fall, 1952), and "Picketing as Free Speech: Early Stages in the Growth of the New Law of Picketing," *University of Pittsburgh Law Review,* XIV (Spring, 1953), discuss the early debate over picketing as a form of free speech, especially the rise of the conservative approach to picketing law; and Jerold S. Auerbach, *Labor and Liberty: The La Follette Committee and the New Deal* (Indianapolis, 1966), describes the committee's successful casting of labor's problems in civil liberties terms. Donald R. Manwaring stresses the vital role of the Jehovah's Witnesses in securing a favorable rendering of the "free exercise" clause in *Render unto Caesar: The Flag Salute Controversy* (Chicago, 1962). For the problem of loyalty and security conceived by conservative congressmen see August R. Ogden, *The Dies Committee: A Study of the Special House Committee for the Investigation of Un-American Activities* (Washington, 1945). Lester E. Mosher discusses the clean politics movement, the history of the Hatch Act, its political activity provisions, and the constitutional problems it raised in "Government Employees Under the Hatch Act," *New York University Law Quarterly Review,* XXII (April, 1947).

In the area of civil rights see Alison Reppy, *Civil Rights in the United States* (New York, 1951); Morroe Berger, *Equality by Statute: The Revolution in Civil Rights,* 2d ed. (Garden City, N.Y., 1967), a general study that emphasizes the New York experience with civil rights legislation; Robert K. Carr, *Federal Protection of Civil Rights: Quest for a Sword* (Ithaca, 1947), which deals with the early work of the Civil Rights Division of the Justice Department in its attempts to use Sections 18 U.S.C. and 241 and 242 of the federal antilynching law; and Abraham Wilson, "The Proposed Legislative Death Knell of Private Discriminatory Employment Practices," *Virginia Law Review,* XXXI (September, 1945), which describes the congressional debate concerning the question of whether the F.E.P.C. should be continued, expanded and made a permanent peacetime agency of the federal government. In the voting rights area, Sidney A. Jones, Jr., "The White Primary and the Supreme Court," *National Bar Journal,* III (March, 1945), analyzes *Smith* v. *Allwright* and traces the historical roots of the struggle to secure Negro voting rights in the South.

Total War and the Constitution

Clinton Rossiter analyzes constitutional government in modern war and concludes that no form of government can survive that excludes dictatorship when the life of the nation is at stake. Clinton Rossiter, *Constitutional Dictatorship: Crisis Government in the Modern Democracies* (Princeton, 1948). His *The Supreme Court and the Commander-in-Chief* (Ithaca, 1951) interprets the Court's handling of war problems. Edward S. Corwin, *Total War and the Constitution* (New York, 1947), emphasizes the extent to which President Roosevelt broke through normal constitutional processes in the war crisis; while Nathan Grundstein, "Presidential Subdelegation of Administrative Authority in War-time," *George Washington Law Review,* XVI (April, 1948), demonstrates the extent to which the Court accepted the constitutionality of the wartime executive mechanism. Arthur T. Vanderbilt has done an exhaustive analysis of the wartime administrative machinery in "War Powers and Their Administration," *Annual Survey of American Law, 1942* (1945).

Quincy Wright, "Congress and the Treaty-making Power," *Proceedings of the American Society of International Law* (1952), is a valuable piece illustrating the problems which the Bricker Amendment sought to deal with and the dangers in the solution it proposed; these dangers are elaborated in Henry Steele Commager, "The Perilous Folly of Senator Bricker," *The Reporter,* IX (Oct. 13, 1953). Zechariah Chafee, Jr., "Amending the Constitution to Cripple Treaties," *Louisiana Law Review,* XII (May, 1952), presents cogent arguments against the amendment, while Glendon Schubert, "Politics and the Constitution: The Bricker Amendment During 1953," *Journal of Politics,* XVI (May, 1954), discusses Bricker Amendment "politics."

Harold Stein (ed.), *American Civil-Military Decisions: A Book of Case Studies* (University, Ala., 1963), is a series of explorations from 1931 to the 1950s summarizing emerging trends in civil-military politics; Louis Smith details World War II military rule in *American Democracy and Military Power: A Study of Civil Control of the Military Power in the United States* (Chicago, 1951); and the issue of military jurisdiction over civilians is discussed by Gordon D. Henderson, "Courts-Martial and the Constitution: The Original Understanding," *Harvard Law Review,* LXXI (December, 1957); and by Frederick B. Wiener, "Courts-Martial and the Bill of Rights: The Original Practice," *Harvard Law Review,* LXXII (November, December, 1958). Military government in Hawaii is analyzed in excellent studies by J. Garner Anthony, "Hawaiian Martial Law in the Supreme Court," *Yale Law Journal,* LVII (November, 1947), and Charles Fairman, "The Supreme Court on Military Jurisdiction: Martial Rule in Hawaii and the Yamashita Case," *Harvard Law Review,* LIX (July, 1946); while Adolf R. Reel, *The Case of General Yamashita* (Chicago, 1949), argues that there were serious constitutional inequities in his trial. The constitutional aspects of postwar military trials of German and Japanese war criminals is carefully analyzed in Charles Fairman, "Some New Problems of the Constitution Following the Flag," *Stanford Law Review,* I (June, 1949).

The W.R.A., especially the economic, social, and political pressures that affected its establishment, its policies, and its administration of the relocation process, is examined in Albert B. Turner, "The Origins and Development of the War Relocation Authority" (unpublished Ph.D. dissertation, Duke University, 1967). Dorothy S. Thomas *et al., Japanese American Evacuation and Resettlement* (3 vols., Berkeley, 1946–54), is a comprehensive treatment of the Japanese experience in the United States during the war, with the third focusing on constitutional implications. Morton Grodzins, *Americans Betrayed: Politics and the Japanese Evacuation* (Chicago, 1949), emphasizes the dubious legal and constitutional aspects of the wartime Japanese-American detention program, while Eugene V. Rostow, "The Japanese-American Cases—a Disaster," *Yale Law Journal,* LIV (June, 1945), is a vigorous indictment of both government policy and the critical court decisions. Sidney Fine, "Mr. Justice Murphy and the Hirabayashi Case," *Pacific Historical Review,* XXXIII (May, 1964), is a tribute to the most courageous of the justices on this issue.

J. Willard Hurst, "Treason in the United States," *Harvard Law Review,* LVIII (December, 1944, and July, 1945), is an excellent survey of treason law from Aaron Burr to World War II; and Cyrus Bernstein, "The Saboteur Trial: A Case History," *George Washington Law Review,* XI (February, 1943), is a detailed treatment of the Nazi invaders. Mulford Q. Sibley and Phillip E. Jacob, *Conscription of Conscience: Conscientious Objectors, 1940-1947* (Ithaca, 1952), presents the legal complexities of the status of the conscientious objector, especially in a "popular" war; and Christopher H. Clancy and Jonathan A. Weiss, "The Conscientious Objector: Problems in Conceptional Clarity and Constitutional Considerations," *Maine Law Review,* XVII (1965), discusses the clash between loyalty to the state and respect for an individual's basic beliefs through an analysis of the Court's treatment of problems arising under existing statutory exemption provisions. The impact of the human rights provisions of the United Nations Charter on constitutional rights and federal law is evaluated in a lengthy, cogent analysis by Zechariah Chafee, Jr., "Federal and State Powers under the U.N. Covenant on Human Rights," *Wisconsin Law Review,* 1951 (May, July, 1951).

Economic Issues after 1945

Grant McConnell assesses the impact upon formal legal and governmental institutions of corporate and other wielders of private power in *Private Power and American Democracy* (New York, 1966). John A. Hetherington, "State Economic Regulation and Substantive Due Process of Law," *Northwestern University Law Review,* LIII (March-April, 1953), traces areas of state economic regulation of business, trade, and professional activities and the Court's abandonment of substantive due process. Jo D. Lucas, "Constitutional Law and Economic Liberty," *Journal of Law and Economics,* XI (April, 1968), in examining economic due process, concludes that the Court is likely to continue its inaction toward legislative decisions in this area, although it could move into it with its concern for equality shown in the civil rights area.

"Symposium on Anti-Trust," *Kentucky Law Journal,* LI (Spring, 1963), consists of a series of articles on various aspects of antitrust law including its historical development and recent trends in the actions of the Court,

Congress, commissions, and states in this area. Richard B. Wilson, "Antitrust Policy and Constitutional Theory," *Cornell Law Quarterly,* XLVI (Summer, 1961), is an analytical discussion of recent antitrust policy and theory in which the author concludes that the Court has veered away from the idea of imperfect or even workable competition. "The Fiftieth Anniversary of the Federal Trade Commission," *Columbia Law Review,* LXIV (March, 1964), is a symposium that traces the historical and contemporary problems of the F.T.C., including procedural impartiality, false advertising, mergers, and competition; and Charles J. Steele, "A Decade of the Celler-Kefauver Anti-Merger Act," *Vanderbilt Law Review,* XIV (October, 1961), traces the reasons for the ineffectiveness of the F.T.C. in combating mergers and the reasons why delays in litigation are so pronounced. Irston R. Barnes, "The Primacy of Competition and the Brown Shoe Decision," *Georgetown Law Journal,* LI (Summer, 1963), analyzes the Court's decision and the proper use of economic evidence in antimerger proceedings under the Clayton Act; and Derek C. Bok, "The Tampa Electric Case and the Problem of Exclusive Arrangements Under the Clayton Act," *Supreme Court Review* (1961), analyzes this aspect of the act in terms of the reforms of the 1940s and 1950s and in the context of the intellectual and institutional influences upon its development. Carl Kaysen, *United States v. United Shoe Machinery Corporation: An Economic Analysis of an Anti-Trust Case* (Cambridge, Mass., 1956), is a study by a law clerk to a justice of the United States District Court of Massachusetts.

Seymour M. Lipset, "The Law and Trade Union Democracy," *Virginia Law Review,* XLVII (January, 1961), is a general discussion of the conditions accounting for the dominant pattern of union government, various past efforts to change union practices by legislation, particularly the Labor-Management Reporting and Disclosure Act of 1959. Stephen K. Bailey, *Congress Makes a Law: The Story Behind the Employment Act of 1946* (New York, 1964), analyzes legislative policy-making as the interaction of ideas, institutions, interests, and individuals, using psychological and sociological tools of analysis. Harry A. Millis and Emily C. Brown, *From Wagner Act to Taft-Hartley* (Chicago, 1950), is an anti–Taft-Hartley piece deploring the retreat from the Wagner Act arrangements in light of its successful functioning. Useful on their subjects are: Archibald Cox, "The Influence of Mr. Justice Murphy on Labor Law," *Michigan Law Review,* XLVIII (April, 1950); Dexter L. Hanley, "Union Organization on Company Property," *Georgetown Law Review,* XLVII (Winter, 1958); Robert F. Koretz, "Employer Interference with Union Organization Versus Employer Free Speech," *George Washington Law Review,* XXIX (December, 1960); and R. Alton Lee, *Truman and Taft-Hartley: A Question of Mandate* (Lexington, Ky., 1966). Richard A. Givens, "Federal

Protection of Employees Rights Within Trade Unions," *Fordham Law Review,* XXIX (December, 1960), discusses the historical problems out of which emerged *Steele* v. *Louisville and Nashville Railroad* and the problem of the relation of concentrated power to the obligations of trade unions toward the employees they represent. Harry H. Wellington, "The Constitution, the Labor Union, and 'Governmental Action,'" *Yale Law Journal,* LXX (January, 1961), is a case study of Negro exclusion from a labor union, exploring the question of whether a labor union comes under state action, and, if so, the Court's responsibility for federal labor policy. His "Machinists v. Street: Statutory Interpretation and the Avoidance of Constitutional Issues," *Supreme Court Review* (1961), analyzes the avoidance doctrine as practiced in this case.

Alan F. Westin, *The Anatomy of a Constitutional Law Case: Youngstown Sheet and Tube Co. v. Sawyer: the Steel Seizure Decision* (New York, 1961), is a documentary portrait of this case that goes into the full sweep of the American constitutional process, from the way social and political issues are shaped into legal controversies to the criteria and techniques by which the Court resolves the issues. Robert J. Banks, "Steel, Sawyer and the Executive Power," *University of Pittsburgh Law Review,* XIV (Summer, 1953), is an argument and presentation on the Presidential abuse of power; also see Edward S. Corwin, "The Steel Seizure Case—a Judicial Brick Without Straw," *Columbia Law Review,* LIII (January, 1953); and Paul G. Kauper, "The Steel Seizure Case: Congress, the President and the Supreme Court," *Michigan Law Review,* L (December, 1952).

General Works on Civil Liberties Since World War II

Lucius J. Barker and Twiley W. Barker, Jr., *Freedoms, Courts, Politics: Studies in Civil Liberties* (Englewood Cliffs, N.J., 1965), attempts to place civil liberties problems in the practical political context in which they must be solved, by emphasizing the interdependence of judges, legislators, and administrators in formulating civil liberties policies and the role of organized interest groups, community attitudes, and public opinion in the process. Bar Association of St. Louis, *Constitutional Freedom and the Law* (St. Louis, 1965), is a useful topical survey of the recent development of key civil liberties issues. Milton R. Konvitz, *Expanding Liberties: Freedom's Gains in Postwar America* (New York, 1966), traces the expansion of old liberties and the evolution of new ones since World War II. Other valuable studies include: Paul G. Kauper, *Civil Liberties and the Constitution* (Ann Arbor, 1966); Milton R. Konvitz and Clinton Rossiter (eds.), *Aspects of Liberty: Essays Presented to Robert E. Cushman* (Ithaca, 1958), which contains several good articles on civil liberties questions; Alan Reitman (ed.), *The Price of Liberty* (New York, 1968), a series of pieces from the A.C.L.U. viewpoint on privacy, loyalty-security questions, church-state relations, freedom of expression, and civil rights; Norman Dorson, *Frontiers of Civil Liberties* (New York, 1968), a collection with a similar orientation; and Rocco J. Tresolini, *Justice and the Supreme Court* (Philadelphia, 1963), a nontechnical account of eight civil liberties decisions and the judges who rendered them.

Among the more general law review articles in this area are: "Symposium on Civil Liberties," *Western Reserve Law Review,* XIII (December, 1961), which includes works on privacy, search and seizure, and antidiscrimination in housing and travel; Clifford M. Lytle, "Congressional Response to Supreme Court Decisions in the Aftermath of the School Segregation Cases," *Journal of Public Law,* XII (1963), reviews Congressional attacks on the Court by conservative and southern members for its rulings in civil liberties and civil rights questions, and legislation proposed to rectify them; while J. Patrick White, "The Warren Court Under Attack: The Role of the Judiciary in a Democratic Society," *Maryland Law Review,* XIX (Summer, 1959), compares this attack to other attacks on the Court in earlier periods. Anthony Lewis, "The Supreme Court and Its Critics," *Minnesota Law Review,* XLV (January, 1961), in a well-reasoned defense which classifies critics into those motivated by the results of particular decisions, those critical of its exercise of judicial review, and academic criticism directed at the Court's reasoning. Robert J. Cushman, "Incorporation: Due Process and the Bill of Rights," *Cornell Law Quarterly,* LI (Spring, 1966), is an excellent history of the incorporation process; Louis Henkin, " 'Selective Incorporation' in the Fourteenth Amendment," *Yale Law Journal,* LXXIII (November, 1963), analyzes the major judicial arguments on how many of the Bill of Rights should be incorporated. C. Herman Pritchett, "The Supreme Court Today: Constitutional Interpretation and Judicial Self-Restraint," *South Dakota Law Review,* III (Spring, 1958), is a review of trends to 1958 in Court interpretations that emphasizes preferred freedoms and judicial restraint and should be read with "The Judicial Revolution and American Democracy," in Thomas R. Ford (ed.), *The Revolutionary Theme in Contemporary America* (Lexington, Ky., 1965). Norman Redlich, "Are There 'Certain Rights Retained by the People?,' " *New York University Law Review,* XXXVII (November, 1962), ably traces the Black-Frankfurter split over the Bill of Rights since the Adamson case and relates it to decisions applying the First Amendment against the states; and Samuel Krislov, "Mr. Justice Black Reopens the Free Speech Debate," *U.C.L.A. Law Review,* II (January, 1964), analyzes Black's "emergency absolutism," Frankfurter's "balancing role" for the Court, and the constitutional theory of Alexander

Meiklejohn and its contribution to Black's approach. On the latter point see Alexander Meiklejohn, "The First Amendment Is an Absolute," *Supreme Court Review* (1961).

The Church-State Question

Perhaps the most exhaustive single volume on the church-state question is by a legal authority of the Jewish community, Leo Pfeffer, *Church, State and Freedom,* rev. ed. (Boston, 1967). Other useful works include Loren P. Beth, *The American Theory of Church and State* (Gainesville, Fla., 1958); Wilber G. Katz, *Religion and American Constitutions* (Evanston, 1964); Philip B. Kurland, *Religion and the Law of Church and State and the Supreme Court* (Chicago, 1962); Mark DeWolfe Howe, *The Garden and the Wilderness: Religion and Government in American Constitutional History* (Chicago, 1965), a denunciation of the Court's "history" in interpreting separation; and Robert F. Drinan, *Religion, the Courts, and Public Policy* (New York, 1963), a valuable insight by a liberal Catholic scholar. Alvin W. Johnson and Frank H. Yost, *Separation of Church and State in the United States* (Minneapolis, 1948), is a revised and enlarged edition of Johnson's *The Legal Status of Church-State Relationships in the United States,* published in 1934. Conrad H. Moehlman, *The Wall of Separation Between Church and State: An Historical Study of Recent Criticism of the Religious Clause of the First Amendment* (Boston, 1951), is a defense of the Jeffersonian neutrality position. Dallin H. Oaks (ed.), *The Wall Between Church and State* (Chicago, 1963), explores the same theme in the light of a dozen years of development. On the historical role of the neutrality position see Paul L. Murphy's "Introduction" to the reprint edition of Sanford H. Cobb, *The Rise of Religious Liberty in America: A History* (New York, 1970).

Law review material abounds. David Fellman, "Religion in American Public Law," *Boston University Law Review,* XLIV (Summer, 1964), is a useful survey from the early national period that emphasizes recent developments. "Symposium on Religion and the Constitution," *Journal of Public Law,* XIII (1964); "Symposium: Expanding Concepts of Religious Freedom," *Wisconsin Law Review,* 1966 (Spring, 1966); and "Symposium: Constitutional Problems in Church-State Relations," *Northwestern University Law Review,* LXI (November-December, 1966), all contain valuable articles. Donald A. Giannella, "Religious Liberty, Nonestablishment, and Doctrinal Development: Part I. The Religious Liberty Guarantee; and Part II. The Nonestablishment Principle," *Harvard Law Review,* LXXX (May, 1967, and January, 1968), examine the relation and conflict between free exercise and establishment and are a critique of the "balancing test" used to assess religious liberty claims; while Alan Schwarz, "The Nonestablishment Principle: A Reply to Professor Giannella," *Harvard Law Review,* LXXXI (May, 1968), is a rebuttal to Giannella's emphasis on the principles of voluntarism and political neutrality in interpreting the nonestablishment clause which urges the use of the no-imposition-of-religion principle.

More specific works include Vashti C. McCollum, *One Woman's Fight,* rev. ed. (Boston, 1961), which throws a personal light on the first released-time case; and Frank J. Sorauf, "Zorach v. Clauson: The Impact of a Supreme Court Decision," *American Political Science Review,* LIII (September, 1959), which explores the reception, impact, and pattern of compliance of the second. Theodore Sky, "The Establishment Clause, the Congress and the Schools: An Historical Perspective," *Virginia Law Review,* LII (December, 1966), traces the history of this clause from the original intent through major judicial interpretations, but focuses on recent cases and the implications of the Elementary and Secondary Education Act of 1965. Virgil C. Blum, "Religious Liberty and Bus Transportation," *Notre Dame Lawyer,* XXX (May, 1955), argues that denial of public funds for this purpose is a deprivation of the equal protection clause of the Fourteenth Amendment, thus taking a typically Catholic position on a subject explored carefully in Theodore Powell, *The School Bus Law: A Case Study in Education, Religion and Politics* (Middletown, Conn., 1960). Paul A. Freund, "Public Aid to Parochial Schools," *Harvard Law Review,* LXXXII (June, 1969), concludes that the Court should restrict its ruling in *Board of Education* v. *Allen* to general welfare services and shared-time instruction in the public schools; while Arthur E. Sutherland, "Establishment of Religion—1968," *Case Western Reserve Law Review,* XIX (April, 1968), argues that the establishment clause merely prohibits the establishment of a state church and in no way prohibits aid to education that may incidentally benefit religious institutions. Fred A. Hurvich, "Religion and the Taxing Power," *University of Cincinnati Law Review,* XXXV (Fall, 1966), examines the background and present status of tax exemptions for religious bodies and concludes that such exemptions should be reconsidered.

Donald E. Boles, *The Bible, Religion and the Public Schools,* 3d ed. (Ames, Iowa, 1965), is a standard work. William K. Muir, *Prayer in the Public Schools: Law and Attitude Change* (Chicago, 1967), examines the question in the context of the role of the law in affecting attitudinal changes; while John H. Laubach, *School Prayers: Congress, the Courts and the Public* (Washington, 1969), explores the issue politically. Philip B. Kurland, "The Regents' Prayer Case: 'Full of Sound and Fury, Signifying . . . ,'" *Supreme Court Review* (1962); and Paul G. Kauper, "Prayer,

Public Schools and the Supreme Court," *Michigan Law Review,* LXI (April, 1963), discuss the issue and judicial history of *Engel* v. *Vitale* and evaluate the decision. Louis H. Pollak, "The Supreme Court, 1962 Term, Forward: Public Prayers in Public Schools," *Harvard Law Review,* LXXVII (November, 1963), extends Kauper in an examination of the Schempp and Murray cases. Suggestive in this regard also is Ernest J. Brown, "Quis Custodiet Ipsos Custodes?—The School Prayer Cases," *Supreme Court Review* (1963). Edmond Cahn, "The Establishment of Religion Puzzle," *New York University Law Review,* XXXVI (November, 1961), treats the Sunday blue-law cases; Francis J. Conklin, "Conscientious Objector Provisions: A View in the Light of Torasco v. Watkins," *Georgetown Law Journal,* LI (Winter, 1963), is critical of that ruling. R. L. Rabin, "When Is a Religious Belief Religious: United States v. Seeger and the Scope of Free Exercise," *Cornell Law Quarterly,* LI (Winter, 1966), studies the theological and constitutional implications of the Seeger ruling; and "Black Muslims in Prison: Of Muslim Rites and Constitutional Rights," *Columbia Law Review,* LXII (December, 1962), contains valuable information on cases in which Muslim religious doctrine and practices have collided with local and state statutes. Milton R. Konvitz, *Religious Liberty and Conscience: A Constitutional Inquiry* (New York, 1968), is a useful statement of the state of the constitutional problem in the late 1960s.

Loyalty-Security and Procedural Rights

The best general works that deal with various constitutional aspects of security issues and Communism include Osmond K. Fraenkel, *The Supreme Court and Civil Liberties,* 2d ed. (Dobbs Ferry, N.Y., 1963); Walter Gellhorn, *Individual Freedom and Governmental Restraints* (New York, 1956), and *American Rights: The Constitution in Action* (New York, 1960); and Morton Grodzins, *The Loyal and the Disloyal* (Chicago, 1956). Clyde E. Jacobs, *Justice Frankfurter and Civil Liberties* (Berkeley, 1961), and C. Herman Pritchett, *Civil Liberties and the Vinson Court* (Chicago, 1954), while general, have useful sections on loyalty-related rulings.

Alistair Cooke, *Generation on Trial: U.S.A. v. Alger Hiss* (New York, 1950), is among the better works on the Hiss-Chambers trial. See also William A. J. Jowett, *The Strange Case of Alger Hiss* (London, 1953), for the view of a prominent English legal expert. Francis Biddle, *The Fear of Freedom* (Garden City, N.Y., 1951), is a liberal study of civil liberties and national security by F.D.R.'s World War II Attorney General. Harold D. Lasswell, *National Security and Individual Freedom* (New York, 1950); Walter Gellhorn, *Security, Loyalty and Science* (Ithaca, 1950);

Alan Barth, *The Loyalty of Free Men* (New York, 1951), and *Government by Investigation* (New York, 1955), are popular, anti-McCarthy, anti-loyalty hysteria works. Clair Wilcox (ed.), *Civil Liberties Under Attack* (Philadelphia, 1951), contains essays reflective of liberal fears in the McCarthy era, as does Henry S. Commager, *Freedom, Loyalty, Dissent* (New York, 1954); and Thomas I. Cook, *Democratic Rights versus Communist Activity* (Garden City, N.Y., 1954). Harold W. Chase, *Security and Liberty: The Problem of Native Communists, 1947–1955* (Garden City, N.Y., 1955), should be read with the same author's "The Libertarian Case for Making It a Crime to Be a Communist," *Temple Law Quarterly,* XXIX (Winter, 1956). An interesting latter-day reassessment is Kathleen L. Barber, "The Legal Status of the Communist Party: 1965," *Journal of Public Law,* XV (1966).

Eleanor Bontecou, *The Federal Loyalty-Security Program* (Ithaca, 1953), is a careful study of the loyalty program, which, while dated, is still useful for reference purposes. Thomas I. Emerson and David M. Helfeld, "Loyalty Among Government Employees," *Yale Law Journal,* LVIII (December, 1948), traces the growth of the loyalty program, 1938–48. For an interesting and continuing dialogue on this article see J. Edgar Hoover, "A Comment on the Article, 'Loyalty Among Government Employees,'" Emerson and Helfeld, "Reply by the Authors," and Hoover, "Rejoinder by Mr. Hoover," *Yale Law Journal,* LVIII (February, 1949). Seth W. Richardson, "The Federal Employee Loyalty Program," *Columbia Law Review,* LI (May, 1951), is a reasoned defense of the Truman program by the former chairman of the Loyalty Review Board. See also Murray Seasongood, "The Loyalty Review Board," *University of Cincinnati Law Review,* XXV (Winter, 1956); and Dudley B. Bonsal, *The Federal Loyalty-Security Program: Report of the Special Committee of the Association of the Bar of the City of New York* (New York, 1956), the most complete and generally critical treatment of the Eisenhower loyalty program. Valuable special studies are Ralph S. Brown, *Loyalty and Security: Employment Tests in the United States* (New Haven, 1958); and Donald L. King, "The Legal Status of the Attorney General's List," *California Law Review,* XLIV (October, 1956).

Detailed treatment of Smith Act prosecutions has been made in Edward S. Corwin, "Bowing Out 'Clear and Present Danger,'" *Notre Dame Lawyer,* XXVII (Spring, 1952); Wallace Mendelson, "Clear and Present Danger: From Schenck to Dennis," *Columbia Law Review,* LII (March, 1952), and "The Degradation of the Clear and Present Danger Rule," *Journal of Politics,* XV (August, 1953); John A. Gorfinkel and Julian W. Mack, II, "Dennis v. United States, and the Clear and Present Danger Rule," *California Law Review,* XXXIX (December, 1951); and Robert

Mollan, "Smith Act Prosecutions: The Effect of the Dennis and Yates Decisions," *University of Pittsburgh Law Review,* XXVI (June, 1965), which examines the history of prosecutions of Communist party leaders under the "advocacy," "organizational," and "membership" clauses of the Smith Act. Arthur E. Sutherland, "Freedom and National Security," *Harvard Law Review,* LXIV (January, 1951), focuses on the role of Congress and security legislation in a discussion of the Truman loyalty program, the Internal Security Act of 1950, and the S.A.C.B. A valuable study of the McCarran Act has been done by John P. Sullivan and David N. Webster, "Some Constitutional and Practical Problems of the Subversive Activities Control Act," *Georgetown Law Journal,* XLV (Winter, 1957). Carl A. Auerbach, "The Communist Control Act of 1954: A Proposed Legal-Political Theory of Free Speech," *University of Chicago Law Review,* XXIII (Winter, 1956), evolves a constitutional defense of the measure. Relevant here also is "Constitutional Law—Federal Anti-Subversive Legislation—the Communist Control Act of 1954," *Michigan Law Review,* LIII (June, 1955). Donald J. Kemper, *Decade of Fear: Senator Hennings and Civil Liberties* (Columbia, Mo., 1965) is especially useful for its treatment of the Jenner-Butler bill and the late 1950 assault on the Court. Leonard B. Boundin traces the problem of government interference with the right to travel from the British common law through *Edwards* v. *California* in "The Constitutional Right to Travel," *Columbia Law Review,* LVI (January, 1956); while William B. Gould, "The Right to Travel and National Security," *Washington University Law Quarterly,* 1961 (December, 1961), analyzes the impact of the Cold War and national security on this right. E. R. Knauff, "Passport Refusals for Political Reasons: Constitutional Issues," *Yale Law Journal,* LXI (February, 1952); and Louis L. Jaffe, "The Right to Travel: The Passport Problem," *Foreign Affairs,* XXXV (October, 1956), are valuable studies.

M. Nelson McGeary, *The Development of Congressional Investigative Power* (New York, 1940), is an early work on an important topic. "Congressional Investigations: A Symposium," *University of Chicago Law Review,* XVIII (Spring, 1951), shows the increasing concern for constitutional problems. Telford Taylor, *Grand Inquest: The Story of Congressional Investigations* (New York, 1955), is a highly critical, but journalistic account of the excesses of congressional investigations. O. John Rogge, "Inquisitions by Officials: A Study of Due Process Requirements in Administrative Investigations," *Minnesota Law Review,* XLVII (May, 1963), XLVIII (January, May, 1964), is a three-part study that explores investigative practices of governmental agencies and the constitutional rights of persons subpoenaed to appear before them. Robert B. McKay, "Congressional Investigations and the Supreme Court, *California Law Review,* LI

(May, 1963), discusses the trends of the Supreme Court in dealing with the congressional investigative power since 1953. Nanette Dembitz, "Congressional Investigation of Newspapermen, Authors, and Others in the Opinion Field—It's Legality under the First Amendment," *Minnesota Law Review,* XL (April, 1956), is a useful special study.

Works on the F.B.I. vary from extreme criticism to uncritical praise. Max Lowenthal, *The Federal Bureau of Investigation* (New York, 1950), assaults the agency and its leadership with a meat-ax, as does Fred J. Cook, *The F.B.I. Nobody Knows* (New York, 1964). Don Whitehead, *The F.B.I. Story: A Report to the People* (New York, 1956), presents the pro side, as does Harry and Bonaro Overstreet, *The F.B.I. in Our Open Society* (New York, 1969), the latter also assailing the Lowenthal and Cook works. The House Un-American Activities Committee has met similar divergent treatment. Robert K. Carr, *The House Committee on Un-American Activities, 1945–1950* (Ithaca, 1952); and Walter Goodman, *The Committee: The Extraordinary Career of the House Committee on Un-American Activities* (New York, 1968), are both critical, but scholarly. William F. Buckley, Jr. (ed.), *The Committee and Its Critics* (Chicago, 1962), is sympathetic and defensive. Carl Beck, *Contempt of Congress: A Study of the Prosecutions Initiated by the Committee on Un-American Activities, 1945–1957* (New Orleans, 1959), explores the body's procedural insensitivity. Samuel H. Hofstadter, *The Fifth Amendment and the Immunity Act of 1954* (New York, 1955), is a valuable special study of the rationale, functioning, and dangers of the measures; and O. John Rogge, "Compelling the Testimony of Political Deviants," *Michigan Law Review,* LV (December, 1956), considers the background, history, and terms of the Immunity Act, the validity of the Court's decision in *U.S.* v. *Ullman.* Erwin Griswold, *The Fifth Amendment Today* (Cambridge, Mass., 1955), is challenged in Sidney Hook, *Common Sense and the Fifth Amendment* (New York, 1957); and Lewis Mayers, *Shall We Amend the Fifth Amendment?* (New York, 1959). Leonard G. Ratner, "Consequences of Exercising the Privilege Against Self-Incrimination," *University of Chicago Law Review,* XXIV (Spring, 1957), surveys developments to that time. The Watkins and Barenblatt cases are analyzed in the following articles: Allan L. Bioff, "Watkins v. United States as a Limitation on Power of Congressional Investigating Committees," *Michigan Law Review,* LVI (December, 1957); Avrum M. Cross, "Congressional Investigation of Political Activity—Watkins v. United States Re-examined," *Michigan Law Review,* LVIII (January, 1960); and Michael Slatnick, "The Congressional Investigatory Power: Ramifications of the Watkins-Barenblatt Enigma," *University of Miami Law Review,* XIV (Spring, 1960). Useful also is Harry Kalven, Jr., "Mr. Alexander Meiklejohn and the Barenblatt Opinion," *University of*

Chicago Law Review, XXVII (1960). Other useful loyalty-security studies include Joseph L. Rauh, "Non-Confrontation in Security Cases—the Greene Decision," *Virginia Law Review,* XLV (November, 1959); Robert B. McKay, "The Right of Confrontation," *Washington University Law Quarterly,* 1959 (April, 1959); Daniel H. Pollitt, "The Right of Confrontation: Its History and Modern Dress," *Journal of Public Law,* VIII (Fall, 1959); Norman Redlich, "Rights of Witnesses Before Congressional Committees: Effects of Recent Supreme Court Decisions," *New York University Law Review,* XXXVI (June, 1961); and Frank C. Newman, "Federal Agency Investigations: Procedural Rights of the Subpoenaed Witness," *Michigan Law Review,* LX (December, 1961). Ronald L. Goldfarb, *The Contempt Power* (New York, 1963), is a broad treatise exploring all aspects of the legal issue. Williard E. Uphaus, *Commitment* (New York, 1963), is an autobiographical treatment of the *Uphaus* v. *Wyman* case by the "victim."

Other aspects of the loyalty era constitutionally are explored in Harold W. Chase, "The Warren Court and Congress," *Minnesota Law Review,* XLIV (March, 1960), a critical analysis of the relationship of court decisions and congressional power; Samuel B. Groner, "State Control of Subversive Activities in the United States," *Federal Bar Journal,* IX (October, 1947), is an interesting discussion of the background and status of state control of subversive activities before the Steve Nelson ruling, and is a useful complement to Walter Gellhorn (ed.), *The States and Subversion* (Ithaca, 1952). Alan R. Hunt, "Federal Supremacy and State Legislation," *Michigan Law Review,* LIII (January, 1955), examines constitutional objections to state antisubversive laws based on the idea that federal power in this area is exclusive or that Congress has preempted this field. Roger C. Cramton, "The Supreme Court and State Power to Deal with Subversion and Loyalty," *Minnesota Law Review,* XLIII (May, 1959), analyzes the Nelson case and the federal preemption doctrine. The best book on the subject of the famed California oath is David P. Gardner, *The California Oath Controversy* (Berkeley, 1967); but see also John W. Caughey, *In Clear and Present Danger: The Crucial State of Our Freedoms* (Chicago, 1958), by a professor in the center of the conflict; and the more general study by Harold M. Hyman, *To Try Men's Souls: Loyalty Tests in American History* (Berkeley, 1959).

Milton R. Konvitz, *Civil Rights in Immigration* (Ithaca, 1953), is a scholarly study of the restrictiveness of American immigration law; Ellen R. Knauff, *The Ellen Knauff Story* (New York, 1952), is a valuable study on the laws of naturalization and their punitive impacts on a war bride. John P. Roche, "The Loss of American Nationality: The Development of Statutory Expatriation," *University of Pennsylvania Law Review,* XCIX

(October, 1950), analyzes the constitutional basis of congressional expatriation legislation before the McCarthy era, while his "The Expatriation Cases: 'Breathes There the Man, With Soul So Dead . . . ?,'" *Supreme Court Review* (1963), brings developments up to *Kennedy* v. *Mendoza-Martinez* and the Joseph Henry Cort cases.

Freedom of Expression

Alexander Meiklejohn, *Political Freedom: The Constitutional Powers of the People* (New York, 1965), is an expansion of his classic work *Free Speech and Its Relation to Self-Government,* which analyzes the meaning of the First Amendment in light of the author's sanguine view of human nature and its relations to rational self-government. A more pessimistic view leads Walter F. Berns, in *Freedom, Virtue and the First Amendment* (Chicago, 1965), to place considerably less importance on freedom as a positive value. Hugo L. Black, "The Bill of Rights," *New York University Law Review,* XXXV (April, 1960), leans far toward Meiklejohn. Elliot L. Richardson, "Freedom of Expression and the Functions of the Courts," *Harvard Law Review,* XXV (November, 1951), analyzes the issues involved in the clash between First Amendment guarantees and legislative restriction on those guarantees. Martin Shapiro, *Freedom of Speech: The Supreme Court and Judicial Review* (Englewood Cliffs, N.J., 1966), discusses the role of the Supreme Court within the American political system and urges it to protect this right through its power of judicial review. Laurent B. Frantz and Wallace Mendelson debate the use of "balancing of interests" in free speech cases in which Frantz attacks this principle while Mendelson strongly supports it as the essence of the judicial process. Laurent B. Frantz, "The First Amendment in the Balance," *Yale Law Journal,* LXXI (July, 1962); answered by Wallace Mendelson in "On the Meaning of the First Amendment: Absolutes in the Balance," *California Law Review,* L (December, 1962); to which Frantz replies in "Is the First Amendment Law? A Reply to Professor Mendelson," *California Law Review,* LI (October, 1963); to which Mendelson responds in "The First Amendment and the Judicial Process: A Reply to Mr. Frantz," *Vanderbilt Law Review,* XVII (March, 1964). A portion of this exchange is anthologized in Martin Shapiro (ed.), *The Supreme Court and Constitutional Rights* (Chicago, 1967). Louis B. Lusky surveys the history of the "clear and present danger" rule in "The Present Status of the 'Clear and Present Danger Test'—a Brief History and Some Observations," *Kentucky Law Journal,* XLV (Summer, 1957); as does Wallace Mendelson in "Clear and Present Danger: From Schenck to Dennis," *Columbia Law Review,* LII (March, 1952), and "Clear and Present Danger—Another Decade," *Texas*

Law Review, XXXIX (April, 1961). Robert S. Lancaster, "Judge Hand's Views on the Free Speech Problem," *Vanderbilt Law Review,* X (February, 1957), complements Hand's Harvard lectures: Learned Hand, *The Bill of Rights* (Cambridge, Mass., 1958).

O. John Rogge, *The First and the Fifth, with Some Incursions into Others* (New York, 1960), is especially concerned with the right of free speech and the right of silence in the late 1950s in light of the McCarthy investigations. William W. Van Alstyne has written two articles on the problem of free speech on the campus: "Political Speeches at State Universities: Some Constitutional Considerations," *University of Pennsylvania Law Review,* CXI (January, 1963), discusses arbitrary screening of speakers in relation to standards of equal protection and free speech; and "Procedural Due Process and State University Students," *U.C.L.A. Law Review,* X (January, 1963), focuses on the implications of increasing student activism. Loren P. Beth, "Group Libel and Free Speech," *Minnesota Law Review,* XXXIX (January, 1955), explores a controversial concept. C. J. Black, "He Cannot Choose But Hear: The Plight of the Captive Auditor," *Columbia Law Review,* LIII (November, 1953), empathizes with the victim. Harry Kalven, Jr., "The Concept of the Public Forum: Cox v. Louisiana," *Supreme Court Review,* (1965), examines the problems of free speech in public places raised by civil rights sit-in protestors.

On problems of press freedom, Frank Thayer, *Legal Control of the Press* (Brooklyn, 1962), is a standard work. See also William A. Hachten, *The Supreme Court on Freedom of the Press: Decisions and Dissents* (Ames, Iowa, 1968), an anthology that explores major decisions in the areas of newspapers and broadcasting as well as motion pictures. Harry Kalven, Jr., "The New York Times Case: A Note on 'The Central Meaning of the First Amendment,'" *Supreme Court Review* (1964), asserts that this decision is the best and most important the Court has produced in this area. William H. Pedrick, "Freedom of the Press and the Law of Libel: The Modern Revised Translation," *Cornell Law Quarterly,* XLIX (Summer, 1964), reviews concepts of libel and defamatory statements and emphasizes the impact of *The New York Times* case on them. Alfred Friendly and Ronald L. Goldfarb analyze the problems of free press and fair trial, its definition, dimensions, and remedies, in *Crime and Publicity: The Impact of News on the Administration of Justice* (New York, 1967). Harvey Gelb, "Fair Trials and Free Speech," *George Washington Law Review,* XXXI (March, 1963), goes into the problems of jury selection, change of venue, continuance, prior restraint, and contempt; while "Symposium on a Free Press and a Fair Trial," *Villanova Law Review,* XI (Summer, 1966), presents the viewpoint of a newspaperman, radio and TV newsman, prosecutor, defense attorney, bar association, judges, and academician. Other valuable works in the area include Donald M. Gillmor, *Free Press and Fair Trial* (Washington, 1966); John Lofton, *Justice and the Press* (Boston, 1965); Conference on Prejudicial News Reporting in Criminal Cases: Northwestern School of Law and Medill School of Journalism, *Papers and Proceedings: Free Press, Fair Trial* (Evanston, 1964); Harold R. Medina, *Freedom of the Press and Fair Trial* (New York, 1967); American Bar Association, *Fair Trial and Free Press* (Chicago, 1966); American Newspaper Publishers Association, *Free Press and Fair Trial* (New York, 1967); Special Committee on Radio and Television of the Association of the Bar of the City of New York, *Radio, Television, and the Administration of Justice: A Documented Survey of Materials* (New York, 1965), and *Freedom of the Press and Fair Trial: Final Report with Recommendations* (New York, 1967).

Richard H. Kuh discusses every kind of pornography and the law in a broad context that presents a reasoned valuation of the pros and cons of censorship in *Foolish Figleaves? Pornography in—and Out of—Court* (New York, 1967). Robert W. Haney, *Comstockery in America: Patterns of Censorship and Control* (Boston, 1960), affords a valuable trace on the problem. Harry M. Clor, *Obscenity and Public Morality: Censorship in a Liberal Society* (Chicago, 1969), is an evaluative analysis. Terrence J. Murphy, *Censorship: Government and Obscenity* (Baltimore, 1963), makes the case for reasoned suppression. M. C. Slough and P. D. McAnany, "Obscenity and Constitutional Freedom—Parts I and II," *St. Louis University Law Journal,* VIII (Spring, Summer, 1964), is an historically oriented analytical study of the development of constitutional standards of interpreting obscenity in both literature and motion pictures that relates them to the legal and social problems they create. William R. Lockhart and Robert McClure's influential articles: "Literature and the Law of Obscenity, and the Constitution," *Minnesota Law Review,* XXXVIII (March, 1954), and "Censorship of Obscenity: The Developing Constitutional Standards," *Minnesota Law Review,* XLV (November, 1960), are anthologized in part in John Chandos (ed.), *To Deprave and Corrupt* (New York, 1962). Morris L. Ernst, an early student of the subject, has joined with Alan U. Schwartz in surveying recent developments in *Censorship: The Search for the Obscene* (New York, 1964). The cases of the 1960s have produced extensive evaluations. John E. Semonche, "Definitional and Contextual Obscenity: The Supreme Court's New and Disturbing Accommodation," *U.C.L.A. Law Review,* XIII (August, 1966), is a critical analysis of the development of standards, especially since the Ginzburg and Mishkin cases. C. Peter Magrath, "The Obscenity Cases: Grapes of Roth," *Supreme Court Review* (1966), criticizes the failure to develop viable definitions to guide judicial behavior. Here see also Henry

P. Monoghan, "Obscenity, 1966: The Marriage of Obscenity Per Se and Obscenity Per Quod," *Yale Law Journal,* LXXVI (November, 1966), and "Obscene Literature," *Vanderbilt Law Review,* XVIII (October, 1965). Charles Rembar, *The End of Obscenity: The Trials of "Lady Chatterley," "Tropic of Cancer," and "Fanny Hill"* (New York, 1968) is a humorous discussion of the tactics and strategy of the publishers and the would-be censors by the attorney who argued the cases. Samuel Krislov, "From Ginzburg to Ginzburg: The Unhurried Children's Hour in Obscenity Legislation," *Supreme Court Review* (1968), relates the general problems of obscenity in the Court and concludes that juvenile control promises to be the best application of "variable obscenity" restrictions. The nature and problems of movie censorship is analyzed by Richard S. Randall, *Censorship of the Movies: The Social and Political Control of a Mass Medium* (Madison, Wis., 1968), which also gives a history of official censorship and its various legal approaches, and examines the implications of the tension between the right of free expression and the requirements of mass democratic society; and Ira H. Carmen, *Movies, Censorship, and the Law* (Ann Arbor, 1966) a more analytical study of the impact of censorship rulings on local patterns. Suggestive here also is Thomas I. Emerson, "The Doctrine of Prior Restraint," *Law and Contemporary Problems,* XX (Autumn, 1955).

Criminal Procedure

Useful general studies include Arnold S. Trebach, *The Rationing of Justice: Constitutional Rights and the Criminal Process* (New Brunswick, N.J., 1964); Fred E. Inbau and John E. Reid, *Criminal Interrogation and Confessions* (Baltimore, 1962); Wayne R. LaFave, *Arrest: The Decision to Take a Suspect into Custody* (Boston, 1965); Jerome H. Skolnick, *Justice Without Trial: Law Enforcement in Democratic Society* (New York, 1966); and Edward Barrett, "Police Practices and the Law—from Arrest to Release or Charge," *California Law Review,* L (March, 1962). Claude R. Sowle (ed.), *Police Power and Individual Freedom: The Quest for Balance* (Chicago, 1962), is a collection of papers prepared by the International Conference on Criminal Law Administration in 1960 and explores criminal law administration in the areas of arrest and detention, search and seizure, police interrogation, and self-incrimination. William J. Chambliss, *Crime and the Legal Process* (New York, 1969), is a useful anthology. Yale Kamisar, Thurman Arnold, and Fred E. Inbau's *Criminal Justice in Our Time* (Charlottesville, Va., 1965); and Kamisar's *Criminals, Cops and the Constitution* (New York, 1964), are general treatments. Walter V. Schaefer, *The Suspect and Society: Criminal Procedure and*

Converging Constitutional Doctrines (Evanston, 1967), deals with the constitutional implications of procedure from the time of arrest to arraignment, especially search and seizure, self-incrimination, and right to counsel. Lawrence Hermen, "The Supreme Court and Restrictions on Police Interrogation," *Ohio State Law Journal,* XXV (Fall, 1964), surveys procedural rights as they are affected by police interrogation. One unique study, with procedural interests, "A Symposium on the Warren Commission Report," *New York University Law Review,* XL (May, 1965), contains articles on various aspects of the commission's report, including studies of the commission from a procedural standpoint, the fundamentals of fact-finding, Oswald's role, and trial by newspaper.

David Fellman, *The Defendant's Rights* (New York, 1958), is a discussion of the rights of the accused and the general tendencies of state law. Henry B. Rothblatt and Emma A. Rothblatt, "Police Interrogation: The Right to Counsel and to Prompt Arraignment," *Brooklyn Law Review,* XXVII (December, 1960), treats these rights on the national and state levels and is an especially good analysis of the McNabb and Mallory cases. C. C. Abeles, "The McNabb Rule: Upshaw Through Mallory," *Virginia Law Review,* XLIII (October, 1957), traces the admissibility of "coerced" confessions, 1943–57. Stanley Milledge, "Escobedo—Toward Eliminating Coerced Confessions," *University of Miami Law Review,* XIX (Spring, 1965), is a discussion of the case that emphasizes the more immediate precedents for the decision. Arnold N. Enker and Sheldon H. Elsen, "Counsel for the Suspect: Massiah v. United States and Escobedo v. Illinois," *Minnesota Law Review,* XLIX (November, 1964), is an analysis of the direction of these cases that criticizes the Court for creating "unnecessary and undesirable impediments to police investigation." The subject is brought up to Miranda by Richard J. Medalie in *From Escobedo to Miranda: The Anatomy of a Supreme Court Decision* (Washington, 1966). Karl P. Warden, "Miranda—Some History, Some Observations, and Some Questions," *Vanderbilt Law Review,* XX (December, 1966); Yale Kamisar, "A Dissent from the Miranda Dissents: Some Comments on the 'New' Fifth Amendment and the Old 'Voluntariness' Test," *Michigan Law Review,* LXV (November, 1966); and Sheldon H. Elsen and Arthur Rosett, "Protections for the Suspects Under Miranda v. Arizona," *Columbia Law Review,* LXVII (April, 1967), show the centrality of that ruling.

Jacob W. Landynski, *Search & Seizure and the Supreme Court* (Baltimore, 1966), is a valuable overall analysis with good attention to historic developments. Francis A. Allen, "Federalism and the Fourth Amendment: A Requiem for Wolf," *Supreme Court Review* (1961), analyzes the right of privacy in the context of the obligations and restraints imposed by a federal system upon the Court in its efforts to nationalize individual rights. Richard A. Watson, "Federalism v. Individual Rights: The Legal Squeeze on Self-Incrimination," *American Political Science Review,* LIV (December, 1960), evaluates the effect of judicial concepts of federalism upon the right against self-incrimination. Nathan R. Sobel, "The Privilege Against Self-Incrimination 'Federalized,'" *Brooklyn Law Review,* XXXI (December, 1964), reviews, historically, the major interpretations of self-incrimination and the effect the Mallory case had in nationalizing this right. Robert B. McKay, "Self-Incrimination and the New Privacy," *Supreme Court Review* (1967), outlines some of the present difficulties of interpreting the self-incrimination privilege and examines the "true" policies of the privilege. Peter H. Wolf, "A Survey of the Expanded Exclusionary Rule," *George Washington Law Review,* XXXII (October, 1963), examines the consequences of the application of the exclusionary rule in terms of its broader significance since *Mapp* v. *Ohio.* Paul Bender, "The Retroactive Effect of an Overruling Constitutional Decision," *University of Pennsylvania Law Review,* CX (March, 1962), analyzes the Mapp case and the problem of retroactivity it raised. Telford Taylor, *Two Studies in Constitutional Interpretation* (Columbus, Ohio, 1968), traces the history of search and seizure law and practice from the colonial period to the present. Wayne R. LeFave, "'Street Encounters' and the Constitution: Terry, Sibran, Peters and Beyond," *Michigan Law Review,* LXVII (November, 1968), examines police-citizen contacts in relation to stop and frisk, the Fourth Amendment, field interrogation and identification, and protective search. B. J. George, Jr., "Scientific Investigation and Defendants' Rights," *Michigan Law Review,* LVII (November, 1958), comments on the problems raised by scientific methods of crime detection for the areas of search and seizure, self-incrimination, and due process. Herman Schwartz, "The Legitimation of Electronic Eavesdropping: The Politics of 'Law and Order,'" *Michigan Law Review,* LXVII (January, 1969), examines constitutional considerations raised by wiretapping and eavesdropping in the light of recent Supreme Court decisions, the probable extent of such activity, the limitations imposed upon it by Title III of the Omnibus Crime Control and Safe Streets Act of 1968, and the A.B.A.'s standards relating to electronic surveillance; while Edmund W. Kitch, "Katz v. United States: The Limits of the Fourth Amendment," *Supreme Court Review* (1968), concludes that while the Court has apparently abandoned the limiting principle set down in *Olmstead* v. *United States* in applying the Fourth Amendment to a person's conversations, it has failed to enunciate a new principle.

William M. Beaney, *The Right to Counsel in American Courts* (Ann Arbor, 1955), shows that this right is not enjoyed as consistently and widely as necessity requires and traces its history as a chronic problem in the affording of "fair trial." "The Right to Counsel: A Symposium," *Minnesota Law Review,* XLV (April, 1961), updates the study, while Tom C. Clarke, "The Sixth Amendment and the Law of the Land," *St. Louis University Law Journal,* VIII (Fall, 1963), traces the historical basis of the right, its development in major cases, and the future outlook since the "1963 Revolution" of the Gideon and Douglas cases. In relating the story of *Gideon* v. *Wainwright,* Anthony Lewis presents insights into the history of the Court, constitutional and criminal law, the philosophies of various justices, and the modus operandi of the Court in *Gideon's Trumpet* (New York, 1964). Jerold H. Israel, "Gideon v. Wainwright: The 'Art' of Overruling," *Supreme Court Review* (1963), discusses some basic questions raised by overruling prior decisions; while William W. Van Alstyne, "In Gideon's Wake: Harsher Penalties and the 'Successful' Criminal Appellant," *Yale Law Journal,* LXXIV (March, 1965), goes into other problems stemming from Gideon such as unreasonable conditions and the right of fair trial, the unconstitutionally convicted, double jeopardy, and equal protection. Philip Fahringer, "Equal Protection and the Indigent Defendant: Griffin and Its Progeny," *Stanford Law Review,* XVI (March, 1964), attempts to determine the ultimate impact of the equal protection rationale of the Griffin case through an analysis of prior and subsequent cases. Arval A. Morris, "Poverty and Criminal Justice," *Washington Law Review,* XXXVIII (Winter, 1963), reviews the problem of poverty and due process in relation to transcripts, the rights to counsel and appeal, and federal habeas corpus. Dallin H. Oaks and Warren Lehman, *A Criminal Justice System and the Indigent: A Study of Chicago and Cook County* (Chicago, 1968), is a case study that also surveys the law and practice regarding assistance for indigent criminal defendants.

Other aspects of criminal procedure are discussed by Sheldon Tefft, "United States v. Barnett: ' 'Twas a Famous Victory,' " *Supreme Court Review* (1964), an analysis of the case as limiting the punishment that can be inflicted by the courts in contempt cases tried without juries; Harry Kalven, Jr., and Hans Zeisel, *The American Jury* (Boston, 1966), the principal report of the jury study of the University of Chicago Law School, which answers the question of how differently a judge and a jury would decide the same case and offers a general theory of jury decision-making; Ronald Goldfarb, *Ransom: A Critique of the American Bail System* (New York, 1965), which describes the inequities of the bail system, its danger to society, and its abuses in recent civil rights demonstrations. Lawrence Newman, "Double Jeopardy and the Problem of Successive Prosecutions: A Suggested Solution," *Southern California Law Review,* XXXIV (Spring, 1961), explores the Abbate and Bartkus rulings of 1959 and the solution of a joint trial conducted by both state and federal officials; as does George C. Pontikes, "Dual Sovereignty and Double Jeopardy: A Critique of Bartkus v. Illinois and Abbate v. U.S.," *Western Reserve Law Review,* XIV (September, 1963), which is also critical of the decisions. "Symposium on Juvenile Criminal Procedure," *Wayne Law Review,* XI (Spring, 1965), is a series of articles on a variety of areas such as juvenile courts, delinquency prevention, offenses, procedural rights; while Chester J. Antieau, "Constitutional Rights in Juvenile Courts," *Cornell Law Quarterly,* XLVI (Spring, 1961), examines the process by which juveniles have been denied traditional constitutional rights. Norman Dorson and Daniel A. Rezneck, "In re Gault, and the Future of Juvenile Law," *Family Law Quarterly,* I (December, 1967), is augmented by Monrad G. Paulsen, "The Constitutional Domestication of the Juvenile Court," *Supreme Court Review* (1967).

The right of privacy has been treated by Alan F. Westin, *Privacy and Freedom* (New York, 1967), in relation to the nature and use of privacy-invasion devices by government, industry, and private individuals, and the response of legislatures, the press, and other institutions. Other general studies include Edward V. Long, *The Intruders: The Invasion of Privacy by Government and Industry* (New York, 1967); Samuel Dash, *The Eavesdroppers* (New Brunswick, N.J., 1959); and Jerry M. Rosenberg, *The Death of Privacy* (New York, 1969). Evan Y. Semerjian, "Proposals on Wiretapping in Light of Recent Senate Hearings," *Boston University Law Review,* XLV (Spring, 1965), discusses legislative and judicial positions regarding this device; while Leon Yankwich, "The Right of Privacy: Its Development, Scope and Limitations," *Notre Dame Lawyer,* XXVII (Summer, 1952), discusses privacy in relation to news media and news reporting.

Ernest Katin, "Griswold v. Connecticut: The Justices and Connecticut's 'Uncommonly Silly Law,'" *Notre Dame Lawyer,* XLII (July, 1967), evaluates the opinion and notes its significance regarding legislation affecting public morals. "Symposium: Comments on the Griswold Case," *Michigan Law Review* LXIV (December, 1965), explores the background, concepts, and implications of the case with special emphasis upon the suggestions of new "Ninth Amendment Freedoms." Peter Smith, "Comment: The History and Future of the Legal Battle over Birth Control," *Cornell Law Quarterly,* XLIX (Winter, 1964), traces the legislative and judicial history of this controversy up to the Poe case.

Voting Rights

Andrew Hacker traces the development of congressional representation, examines the relationship of the judiciary to the problem of legislative redistricting, and shows inequities in the franchise in *Congressional Districting: The Issue of Equal Representation,* rev. ed. (Washington, 1964). Robert B. McKay, *Reapportionment: The Law and Politics of Equal Representation* (New York, 1965), assesses *Baker* v. *Carr* and the significance it holds for the nation's political process. Glendon A. Schubert, *Reapportionment* (New York, 1965), is a useful anthology. Royce Hanson, *The Political Thicket: Reapportionment and Constitutional Democracy* (Englewood Cliffs, N.J., 1966), treats the historical, legal, and political aspects of this issue through to the defeat of the Dirksen Amendment in 1965. Robert G. Dixon, Jr., *Democratic Representation: Reapportionment in Law and Politics* (New York, 1968), is a comprehensive and complete account of the recent and continuing reapportionment revolution. For a useful, in-depth study, see Calvin B. T. Lee, *One Man, One Vote: WMCA and the Struggle for Equal Representation* (New York, 1967). "Reapportionment Symposium," *Michigan Law Review,* LXIII (December, 1964), includes analyses of cases and congressional response. Robert G. McCloskey, "The Supreme Court, 1961 Term, Forward: The Reapportionment Case," *Harvard Law Review,* LXXVI (November 1962), discusses the historical and legal problems underlying *Baker* v. *Carr.* "Symposium on Baker v. Carr," *Yale Law Journal,* LXXII (November, 1962), includes studies on urbanization and reapportionment, the Colgrove case, malapportionment and judicial power, and a statistical study of malapportionment. Stanley H. Friedelbaum, "Baker v. Carr: The New Doctrine of Judicial Intervention and Its Implications for American Federalism," *University of Chicago Law Review,* XXIX (Summer, 1962), argues that a new epoch in American federalism began with the case. Phil C. Neal, "Baker v. Carr: Politics in Search of Law," *Supreme Court Review* (1962), analyzes the reapportionment problem and the Court's response to it in terms of adapting the distribution of political power to new circumstances. Carl A. Auerbach, "The Reapportionment Cases: One Person, One Vote—One Vote, One Value," *Supreme Court Review* (1964), examines the constitutionality and desirability of the above principle. James B. Atleson, "The Aftermath of Baker v. Carr—an Adventure in Judicial Experimentation," *California Law Review,* LI (August, 1963), outlines the various standards used in the post-Baker cases and analyzes the interests and justifications for malapportionment as advanced by the state courts. William P. Irwin, "Representation and Election: The Reapportionment Cases in Retrospect," *Michigan Law Review,* LXVII (February, 1969), is an analysis by a political scientist of the reapportionment cases in terms of their merits and their implications for democratic theory and practice.

The problem of Negro voting rights is discussed by Donald S. Strong, *Negroes, Ballots, and Judges* (University, Ala., 1968), in a highly critical account of southern judicial and legislative resistance to the Civil Rights

Acts of 1957, 1960, and 1964, which analyzes court cases, the conflict between regional values and the responsibilities of a judge, and legislative acts in Louisiana, Mississippi, and Alabama. Foster R. Dulles, *The Civil Rights Commission, 1957–1965* (East Lansing, Mich., 1968); and Ira M. Heyman, "Federal Remedies for Voteless Negroes," *California Law Review,* XLVIII (May, 1960), discuss the workings of the 1957 law. Bernard Taper, *Gomillion v. Lightfoot: The Tuskegee Gerrymander* Case (New York, 1963), is an interesting depth study of the first break in the justiciability of voting arrangements. Jo Desha Lucas, "Dragon in the Thicket: A Perusal of Gomillion v. Lightfoot," *Supreme Court Review* (1961), analyzes this case in terms of the Fourteenth and Fifteenth Amendments, concluding that its usefulness is limited to racial discrimination cases and not to cases involving the right to vote. Alexander M. Bickel, "The Voting Rights Cases," *Supreme Court Review* (1966), examines the cases evolving from the 1965 Voting Rights Act; and L. Thorne McCarty and Russell B. Stevenson, "The Voting Rights Act of 1965: An Evaluation," *Harvard Civil Rights and Civil Liberties Review,* III (Spring, 1968), evaluates the successes and failures of the Act in its first two years with emphasis upon its effect on Mississippi elections.

Civil Rights

Wallace Mendelson, *Discrimination* (Englewood Clifs, N.J., 1962) is a résumé of the five-volume report of the United States Commission on Civil Rights that presents the facts of discrimination and a picture of the Negro's position in American life. See also the commission's *Freedom to the Free* (Washington, 1963), which summarizes historical developments in the civil rights area. The best works on the general subject include Milton R. Konvitz, *Expanding Liberties* (New York, 1966); Donald B. King and Charles W. Quick (eds.), *Legal Aspects of the Civil Rights Movement* (Detroit, 1965), a series of essays discussing the legal struggle toward the goal of equality; Loren Miller, *The Petitioners: The Story of the Supreme Court of the United States and the Negro* (Cleveland, 1966), a chronicle of what the Court has said and done concerning the rights of Negroes from 1789 to 1965 by a Negro judge; Morroe Berger, *Equality By Statute,* rev. ed. (New York, 1968); Jack Greenberg, *Race Relations and American Law* (New York, 1959); Milton R. Konvitz, *A Century of Civil Rights* (New York, 1961) and *The Constitution and Civil Rights* (New York, 1962); J. A. Lapence, *Protection of Minorities* (Berkeley, 1960); and Robert J. Harris, *The Quest for Equality: The Constitution, Congress and the Supreme Court* (Baton Rouge, 1960). There is a useful symposium on various civil rights matters in the *Wayne Law Review,*

IX (Spring, 1963). Laurent B. Frantz, "Congressional Power to Enforce the Fourteenth Amendment Against Private Acts," *Yale Law Journal,* LXXIII (July, 1964), discusses the constitutionality of this alternative; while Glenn Abernathy, "Expansion of the State Action Concept under the Fourteenth Amendment," *Cornell Law Quarterly,* XLIII (Spring, 1958), discusses the idea that a state has positive responsibilities to protect the individual against constitutionally unreasonable discrimination on the part of other private persons. Arnold J. Lien, *Concurring Opinion: The Privileges and Immunities Clause of the Fourteenth Amendment* (St. Louis, 1957), has valuable historical material. Federal legislation is discussed by Howard Schneider, "The Civil Rights Act of 1957 and Contempt of Court," *Cornell Law Quarterly,* XLIII (Summer, 1958); while Leon Freidman (ed.), *Southern Justice* (Cleveland, 1967), contains essays by nineteen lawyers handling civil rights cases in the South that show how all levels of public authority have turned the law against Negroes. Harry A. Shapiro, "Limitations in Prosecuting Civil Rights Violations," *Cornell Law Quarterly,* XLVI (Summer, 1961), discusses the difficulties of the federal government in enforcing the 1948 criminal civil rights statute presented by the Screws case and the efforts of the Civil Rights Division of the Justice Department to secure convictions. "Civil Rights and the South: A Symposium," *North Carolina Law Review,* XLII (December, 1963), includes articles on federal civil rights legislation, civil rights in North Carolina, desegregation, housing discrimination, property rights, and employment, that present a southern, and generally states' rights, view. Howard M. Feuerstein, "Civil Rights Crimes and the Federal Power to Punish Private Individuals for Interference with Federally Secured Rights," *Vanderbilt Law Review,* XIX (June, 1966), examines relevant cases and legislation and proposed remedies for private interference with civil rights. Duane Lockard, *Toward Equal Opportunity: A Study of State and Local Anti-Discrimination Laws* (New York, 1968), discusses the proponents and opponents, legislative dynamics, and background of state and local legislation. Lloyd H. Riley, "Miscegenation Statutes, a Re-evaluation of Their Constitutionality in Light of Changing Social and Political Conditions," *Southern California Law Review,* XXXII (Fall, 1958), is a review of the history of statutes and litigation in state courts; while Harvey M. Applebau, "Miscegenation Statutes: A Constitutional and Social Problem," *Georgetown Law Review,* LIII (Fall, 1964), surveys their background, consequences of violation, judicial interpretation, and the three leading grounds upon which they have been attacked. Jay A. Higbee, *Development and Administration of the New York State Law Against Discrimination* (University, Ala., 1968), is a case-by-case survey of public hearings, litigation, and conciliation activities of the state's Commission for Human Rights. Frederick D. Ogden, *The Poll Tax in the South* (University, Ala., 1968), is an in-depth study of that institution and its relation to contemporary American politics.

Clement E. Vose, *Caucasians Only: The Supreme Court, the N.A.A.C.P. and the Restrictive Covenant Cases* (Berkeley, 1959), in emphasizing the role of interest groups in the judicial process and the interplay of historic forces in recent constitutional development, shows the importance of sociopsychological, economic, and political factors in understanding the substance of the Court's decisions and the process by which they are determined. Donald M. Cahen, "The Impact of Shelly v. Kraemer on the State Action Concept," *California Law Review,* XLIV (October, 1956), is fruitfully augmented by William R. Ming, "Racial Restrictions and the Fourteenth Amendment: The Restrictive Covenant Case," *University of Chicago Law Review,* XVI (Winter, 1949), which contains suggestive material on the legal and social background by a counsel for the N.A.A.C.P. Gerhard Casper, "Jones v. Mayer: Clio, Bemused and Confused Muse," *Supreme Court Review* (1968), is a historical survey of fair housing from the civil rights act of 1866 to that of 1968, exploring particularly the problems raised by the latter. Commission on Race and Housing, *Where Shall We Live?* (Berkeley, 1958), and *Privately Developed Interracial Housing: An Analysis of Experience* (Berkeley, 1960), are research reports of the commission. See also Chester Rapkin and William G. Grigsby, *Demand for Housing in Racially Mixed Areas: A Study of Neighborhood Change* (Berkeley, 1960).

The problem of discrimination in employment is discussed by Michael I. Sovern, *Legal Restraints on Racial Discrimination in Employment* (New York, 1966), a comprehensive work that not only treats the abuses and remedies of such discrimination but the various equal employment opportunity programs and agencies as well. Sanford J. Rosen, "The Law and Racial Discrimination in Employment," *California Law Review,* LIII (August, 1965), is an excellent analysis of the major modes of employment discrimination by employers and unions, the constitutional bases for legal responses thereto, and judicial enforcement of the orders of the F.E.P.C. Herbert R. Northrup and Richard L. Rowan, *The Negro and Employment Opportunity* (Ann Arbor, 1965); Paul H. Norgren and Samuel E. Hill, *Toward Fair Employment* (New York, 1964); Daniel H. Pollitt, "Racial Discrimination in Employment: Proposals for Corrective Action," *Buffalo Law Review,* XIII (Fall, 1963), all examine the state of racial discrimination in private and public employment; while Vern Countryman, "The Constitution and Job Discrimination," *Washington Law Review,* XXXIX (Spring, 1964), looks at what has been done and what can be done at the federal level. Useful in this regard also is

Samuel Krislov, *The Negro in Federal Employment: The Quest for Equal Opportunity* (Minneapolis, 1967). Louis Ruchames, *Race, Jobs, and Politics* (New York, 1953), focuses on the F.E.P.C. and other related programs; and Theodore W. Kheel, *Report on the Structure and Operations of the President's Committee on Equal Employment Opportunity* (Englewood Cliffs, N.J., 1962), is more recent. Ray Marshall, *The Negro and Organized Labor* (New York, 1965), explores that subject. A valuable special study is Michael I. Sovern, "The National Labor Relations Act and Racial Discrimination," *Columbia Law Review,* LXII (April, 1962), which probes the success of the measure in preventing unions from engaging in racially discriminatory practices; as is William B. Gould, "The Negro Revolution and the Law of Collective Bargaining," *Fordham Law Review,* XXXIV (December, 1965). State fair employment policies are treated in Bureau of National Affairs, *State Fair Employment Practice Laws and Their Administration* (Washington, 1964); and Arnold H. Sutin, "The Experience of State Fair Employment Commissions: A Comparative Study," *Vanderbilt Law Review,* XVIII (June, 1965), which surveys techniques and procedures, and substantive principles developed by them in enforcing the law.

Segregation in the schools is treated generally by Henry A. Bullock, *A History of Negro Education in the South: From 1619 to the Present* (Cambridge, Mass., 1967) with a useful section on the aftermath of the 1954 Brown ruling. Ira DeA. Reid (ed.), "Racial Desegregation and Integration," *Annals of the American Academy of Political and Social Science,* CCCIV (March, 1956), relates the struggle for human rights to both stateways and folkways. Albert P. Blaustein and Clarence C. Ferguson, Jr., *Desegregation and the Law: The Meaning and Effect of the School Segregation Cases,* 2d ed. (New York, 1964), is augmented by Daniel M. Berman, *It Is So Ordered: The Supreme Court Rules on School Segregation* (New York, 1966), a useful detailed analysis of the Brown Case. Paul G. Kauper, "Segregation in Public Education: The Decline of Plessy v. Ferguson," *Michigan Law Review,* LII (June, 1954), has good historical data. Charles Fairman reviews criticism of the Court, particularly from the South, in "Attack on Segregation Cases," *Harvard Law Review,* LXX (November, 1956); while the Court's action is further defended in Charles L. Black, Jr., "The Lawfulness of the Segregation Decisions," *Yale Law Journal,* LXIX (January, 1960); and Ira M. Heman, "The Chief Justice, Racial Segregation and Friendly Critics," *California Law Review,* XLIX (March, 1961), which is a more broadly based review of legal response to the Court. The southern response to school desegregation is presented in James J. Kilpatrick, *The Southern Case for School Segregation* (New York, 1962); and analyzed in Robbins L. Gates, *The Making of Massive Re-*

sistance: Virginia's Politics of Public School Desegregation, 1954–1956 (Chapel Hill, N.C., 1964). Useful in this regard also is Robert C. Smith, *They Closed Their Schools: Prince Edward County, Virginia, 1951–1964* (Chapel Hill, N.C., 1965), and the more general study, Numan V. Bartley, *The Rise of Massive Resistance: Race and Politics in the South During the 1950's* (Baton Rouge, 1969). Robert B. McKay, "The Repression of Civil Rights as an Aftermath of the School Desegregation Cases," *Howard Law Journal,* IV (January, 1958), is a discussion of the legislative, judicial, and economic harassment by southern state and local institutions seeking to destroy the N.A.A.C.P. The subject is also explored in Walter F. Murphy, "The South Counterattacks: The Anti-N.A.A.C.P. Laws," *Western Political Quarterly,* XII (June, 1959); and Thomas I. Emerson, "Freedom of Association and Freedom of Expression," *Yale Law Journal,* CXXIV (November, 1964). More general is David Fellman, *The Constitutional Right of Association* (Chicago, 1963); and Joseph B. Robinson, "Protection of Association from Compulsory Disclosure," *Columbia Law Review,* LVIII (May, 1958), the latter of which explores the Communism issue as well. Private education and race are discussed by Arthur S. Miller, *Racial Discrimination and Private Education: A Legal Analysis* (Chapel Hill, N.C., 1957); and "Note: The Wall of Racial Separation: The Role of Private and Parochial Schools in Racial Integration," *New York University Law Review,* XLIII (May, 1968), calls for the courts to apply the public function theory of state action to nonpublic schools to end any racially discriminatory practices therein. De facto segregation and the major cases and concepts that it involves are reviewed by Owen M. Fiss, "Racial Imbalance in the Public Schools: The Constitutional Concepts," *Harvard Law Review,* LXXVIII (January, 1965); and "Symposium: De Facto School Segregation," *Western Reserve Law Review,* XVI (May, 1965), which includes legal remedies, constitutional problems, Fourteenth Amendment guarantees against it, educational implications, and a historian's perspective on the problem. Useful also are a series of articles by John Kaplan, "Segregation Litigation and the Schools—Part I: The New Rochelle Experience," *Northwestern Law Review,* LVIII (March-April, 1963), "Segregation Litigation and the Schools—Part II: The General Northern Problem," LVIII (May-June, 1963), and "Segregation Litigation and the Schools—Part III: The Gary Litigation," LIX (May-June, 1964), all of which analyze the actions taken by northern communities after the Brown decision.

In the area of race and marriage, Walter Wadlington, "The Loving Case: Virginia's Anti-Miscegenation Statute in Historical Perspective," *Virginia Law Review,* LII (November, 1966), traces the legislative and judicial history of the statute and presents a valuable analysis of the arguments for and against the constitutionality of this kind of law, agreeing that it is unconstitutional. Robert F. Drinan, "The Loving Decision and the Freedom to Marry," *Ohio State Law Journal,* XXIX (Spring, 1968), relates this decision to the broader question of statutory prohibitions regulating the formation of the marriage contract.

The direct action technique and the change in the nature of the civil rights movement of the late 1950s and 1960s is discussed in Arnold M. Rose (ed.), "The Negro Protest," *Annals of the American Academy of Political and Social Science,* CCCLVII (January, 1965). "The Negro American," *Daedalus,* XCIV (Fall, 1965, Winter, 1966), includes a wide range of articles by prominent scholars. Ira M. Heyman, "Civil Rights 1964: Responses to Direct Action," *Supreme Court Review* (1965), is a direct action protest. Martin Luther King, *Stride Toward Freedom: The Montgomery Story* (New York, 1958), tells the story of the beginning of the direct action story by a leader. Alfred Kamin, "Residential Picketing and the First Amendment," *Northwestern University Law Review,* LXI (May-June, 1966), analyzes the use of labor tactics—i.e., picketing, boycotting—by civil rights groups. Robert G. Dixon, Jr., "Civil Rights in Transportation and the I.C.C.," *George Washington Law Review,* XXXI (October, 1962), examines the involvement of the I.C.C. with racial discrimination in transportation and includes a good discussion of the legal implications of the 1961 Freedom Rides.

Daniel H. Pollitt, "Dime Store Demonstrations: Events and Legal Problems of the First Sixty Days," *Duke Law Journal,* 1960 (Summer, 1960), is an excellent discussion of the immediate events and legal problems of the early stage of the 1960 sit-ins. Frank E. Schwelb, "The Sit-In Demonstration: Criminal Trespass or Constitutional Right?," *New York University Law Review,* XXXVI (April, 1961), treats the constitutional aspects of the sit-ins. Monrad G. Paulsen, "The Sit-In Cases of 1964: 'But Answer Came There None,'" *Supreme Court Review* (1964), discusses the question as to what extent the Fourteenth Amendment forbids states to support private choice when that choice could not be made by the states themselves; and Thomas P. Lewis, "The Sit-In Cases: Great Expectations," *Supreme Court Review* (1963), concludes that Congress is in a much better position to deal with discrimination in places of public accommodations. Harry T. Quick, "Public Accommodations: A Justification of Title II of the Civil Rights Act of 1964," *Western Reserve Law Review,* XVI (May, 1965), is an in-depth analysis that considers not only the act, the legislative history leading up to it, and the court decisions respecting Title II, but the nature of private property and the Title's relation to state law as well. Hugh D. Graham, *Crisis in Print: Desegregation and the Press* (Nashville, 1967), is a Tennessee case study.

"Symposium, 1965," *Notre Dame Lawyer,* XL (1965), analyzes the social and legal implications of urban racial violence and goes into the role of the police in riots, the social and psychological factors of violence, and the changing patterns of violence. William M. Kephart, *Racial Factors and Urban Law Enforcement* (Philadelphia, 1957), is a sociological study of the integration of Negroes into the Philadelphia police department and the relationship between black policemen and black offenders. David W. Abbott, Louis H. Gold, and Edward T. Rogowsky, *Police, Politics, and Race: The New York City Referendum on Civilian Review* (Cambridge, Mass., 1969), surveys the reasons behind the defeat of the referendum by surveying the attitudes of white Brooklyn voters immediately after the election.

Civil Rights and Civil Liberties in a Changing World

The Center for the Study of Democratic Institutions has issued position papers and other publications dealing with many of the constitutional issues of the 1960s. On the announcement of the retirement of Chief Justice Warren, a symposium was conducted to offer a series of perspectives on the degree to which the Court was successful in adapting fundamental law to the social upheavals and economic developments of the years of his Chief Justiceship: *Michigan Law Review,* LXVII (December, 1968), subsequently published in book form as Richard H. Sayler, Barry B. Boyer, and Robert E. Gooding, Jr. (eds.), *The Warren Court: A Critical Analysis* (New York, 1969).

On specific issues, "Symposium: Law of the Poor," *California Law Review,* LIV (May, 1966), contains articles that discuss the welfare system, administrative patterns and problems, discrimination in welfare, the constitutionality of the residency requirements, and poverty and cultural patterns. Albert M. Bendich, "Privacy, Poverty and the Constitution," *California Law Review,* LIV (May, 1966), is especially useful in exploring the constitutional problems of privacy, poverty, and the rights of welfare recipients. "Constitutionality of Residence Requirements for State Welfare Recipients," *Northwestern Law Review,* LXIII (July-August, 1968), argues that neither the violation of the right to interstate travel nor the equal protection clause provides a strong enough basis for striking down those requirements; while "Social Welfare—Paupers—Residency Requirements," *Case Western Reserve Law Review,* XIX (April, 1968), in discussing the Court's reasoning in *Thompson* v. *Shapiro,* concludes that it is arbitrary to find a violation of the Fourteenth Amendment in a state's attempt to protect itself from welfare seekers by durational residency requirements. James J. Graham, "Public Assistance: The Right to Receive; the Obligation to Repay," and "Civil Liberties Problems in Welfare Administration," *New York University Law Review,* XLIII (May, November, 1968), combines a history of welfare from medieval England to the present with an empirical study of welfare administration in New York to demonstrate how it abridges the statutory and constitutional rights of recipients and to urge more litigation to protect those rights.

The National Advisory Commission on Civil Disorders commissioned by President Johnson in the wake of the 1967 riots to determine the roots of rising militancy and the widening gap between white and black America reveals its finding in *Report of the National Advisory Commission on Civil Disorders* (Washington, 1968). *Supplemental Studies for the National Advisory Commission on Civil Disorders* (Washington, 1968) is a preliminary report of the perceptions and attitudes of black and white America. "Anatomy of a Riot: An Analytical Symposium of the Causes and Effects of Riots," *Journal of Urban Law,* XLV (Spring-Summer, 1968), includes articles ranging from discussions of First Amendment freedoms and the politics of mass participation, responses of police and courts to riots, and the use of military force, to analyses of ghetto life and the Detroit riots. Daniel Walker, *Rights in Conflict: Convention Week in Chicago, August 25–29, 1968: A Report* (New York, 1969), is a report to the city of Chicago of a study made of the confrontation between protestors and police during the 1968 Democratic National Convention that concludes that a police riot occurred there. Jack Greenberg, "Supreme Court, Civil Rights and Civil Dissonance," *Yale Law Journal,* LXXVII (July, 1968), demonstrates an interrelationship among the school desegregation decisions, early reversals of sit-in convictions, the spreading civil "dissonance," and the Court's recent tendency to let protest convictions stand. Abe Fortas, *Concerning Dissent and Civil Disobedience* (New York, 1968), is a brief tract explaining the view of the justice on the distinction between dissent and civil disobedience. It is answered by "new left" scholar Howard Zinn in *Disobedience and Democracy* (New York, 1968).

Protest in the schools is the subject of "Symposium: Student Rights and Campus Rules," *California Law Review,* LIV (March, 1966), which includes studies of the general background of growing student activism, the rules, rights, and responsibilities of school administrations, conflicting rights of free speech and property, and the Berkeley demonstrations. Ted Finman and Stewart Macaulay, "Freedom to Dissent: The Vietnam Protests and the Words of Public Officials," *Wisconsin Law Review,* 1966 (Summer, 1966), is a detailed study of American protest to the Vietnam war, the official response this protest caused, and the constitutional implications of both dissent and irresponsible accusations by government officials. William W. Van Alstyne has written two articles that review the treatment of student academic freedom in the courts and suggest it should be considered in relation to the due process and equal protection clauses of the Fourteenth Amendment: "Study Academic Freedom and the Rule-Making Powers of Public Universities; Some Constitutional Considerations," *Law in Transition Quarterly,* II (Winter, 1965), and "Judicial Trend Toward Student Academic Freedom," *University of Florida Law Review,* XX (Winter, 1968). Arval A. Morris, "Academic Freedom and Loyalty Oaths," *Law and Contemporary Problems,* XXVIII (Summer 1963), studies the restrictions on academic freedom and litigation stemming from refusals to take loyalty oaths. J. E. Leahy, "Loyalty and the First Amendment—a Concept Emerges," *North Dakota Law Review,* XLIII (Fall, 1966), examines the cases that formed the background for the freedom of association approach to loyalty cases and shows its culmination in the Elfbrandt decision. On the latter see Jerold H. Israel, "Elfbrandt v. Russell: The Demise of the Oath?," *Supreme Court Review* (1966); and "Comment, Loyalty Requirements vs. Academic Freedom," *Marquette Law Review,* LII (Fall, 1968), which sees the Keyishian decision as carrying the Court's new policy to its logical conclusion. See also "Loyalty Oaths," *Yale Law Journal,* LXXVII (March, 1968), which analyzes the Elfbrandt, Keyishian, and Whitehill cases and concludes that while defeating loyalty oaths as self-executing devices they fail to bring a new analysis to bear in this area.

Graham Hughes, "Civil Disobedience and the Political Question Doctrine," *New York University Law Review,* XLIII (March, 1968), examines the nature and effect of this doctrine in both its "discretionary" and "constitutional" formulations in relation to the Vietnam war protests. "Symposium: The Draft, the War and Public Protest," *George Washington Law Review,* XXXVII (March, 1969), considers civil disobedience, First Amendment protections of protest, and problems of Selective Service. Clyde E. Jacobs and John F. Gallagher, *The Selective Service Act: A Case Study of the Governmental Process* (New York, 1967), is a historical study of Selective Service with emphasis upon the administration of the modern Acts. Nicholas W. Puner, "Civil Disobedience: An Analysis and Rationale," *New York University Law Review,* XLIII (October, 1968), analyzes the nature of civil disobedience and the circumstances under which it may be permitted and practiced. L. R. Velvel, "Freedom of Speech and the Draft Card Burning Cases," *University of Kansas Law Review,* XVI (January, 1968), explores such questions as symbolic speech, and the constitutionality of the draft-card burning law. Dean Alfange, Jr., "Free Speech and Symbolic Conduct; the Draft-Card Burning Cases," *Supreme Court Review*

(1968), discusses *U.S.* v. *O'Brien* and indicts the Court for uncritically accepting the University Military Training and Service Act and avoiding the constitutional questions involved in the case. Norman Dorsen, *Frontiers of Civil Liberties* (New York, 1969), includes an essay on military service and conscientious objection to a particular war that considers the pertinence and meaning of the Nuremberg judgments to this subject. Theodore Hochstadt, "The Right to Exemption from Military Service of a Conscientious Objector to a Particular War," *Harvard Civil Rights and Civil Liberties Review,* III (Fall, 1967), is also useful.

The issue of Julian Bond's exclusion from the Georgia legislature is discussed in "Notes, the Julian Bond Case," *Virginia Law Review,* LII (November, 1966). C. P. Kindregan, "The Cases of Adam Clayton Powell, Jr., and Julian Bond: The Right of Legislative Bodies to Exclude Members-Elect," *Suffolk University Law Review,* II (Winter, 1968), explores the exclusion issue in depth. The proper judicial role in such controversies is assessed in "Note, Legislative Exclusion: Julian Bond and Adam Clayton Powell," *University of Chicago Law Review,* XXXV (Autumn, 1968); while two congressmen debate the issue in *Texas Law Review,* XLV (July, 1967), arriving at opposite conclusions.

The war in Vietnam has produced a debate over two legal questions. The first concerns the legality of the United States involvement in the war. The official position is argued in Leonard C. Meeker of the Office of the Legal Adviser, U.S. Department of State, "The Legality of United States Participation in the Defense of Vietnam," *The Department of State Bulletin,* LIV (March 28, 1966), reprinted in the *Yale Law Journal,* LXXV (June, 1966). F. B. Schick, "Some Reflection on the Legal Controversies Concerning America's Involvement in Vietnam," *International and Comparative Law Quarterly,* XVII (October, 1968), replies to the State Department by evaluating its position against principles and norms of international law and finds U.S. involvement indefensible on legal grounds. The Lawyers Committee on American Policy Towards Vietnam attacks U.S. involvement as a violation of international, constitutional, and treaty law. David W. Robertson, "The Debate Among American International Lawyers About the Vietnam War," *Texas Law Review,* XLVI (July, 1968), reviews the debate, which is extensively reproduced in the *Yale Law Journal* and the *American Journal of International Law* for 1966 and 1967. Roger H. Hull and John C. Novograd have made a good compilation of materials on the subject in *Law and Vietnam* (New York, 1968). See also Richard A. Falk, *Legal Order in a Violent World* (Princeton, 1968).

The second legal question of the U.S. involvement in Vietnam concerns its constitutionality under domestic law. "Note: Congress, the President, and the Power to Commit Forces to Combat," *Harvard Law Review,*

LXXXI (June, 1968), finds that power legitimately extended in the second section of the Gulf of Tonkin Resolution; Stanley Faulkner, "War in Vietnam: Is It Constitutional?," *Georgetown Law Journal,* LVI (June, 1968), concludes that power was used unconstitutionally in light of the broader principle of separation of powers, the SEATO treaty being an improper base, and condemns the judiciary for its unwillingness to examine the issue. Merlo J. Pusey, *The Way We Go to War* (Boston, 1969), continues that author's denunciation of Franklin D. Roosevelt in condemning Lyndon Johnson's preemptive actions.

The violence of the Vietnam war and the growing violence at home has been used by some to define American society as a violent one. This prompted President Johnson to appoint a National Commission on the Causes and Prevention of Violence whose report was published in 1970, *To Establish Justice, To Insure Domestic Tranquility: Final Report of the National Commission on the Causes and Prevention of Violence.* Chairman, Milton Eisenhower (Washington, 1970). Of the fourteen staff reports which accompanied the statement of general findings, Volumes I, and II (Hugh D. Graham and Ted R. Gurr, *Violence in America: Historical and Comparative Perspectives* (Washington, 1969) is of particular interest to the historian. Others deal with such subjects as violent aspects of protest and confrontation; assassination and political violence, and firearms and violence in American life. The rising concern over violence and three political assassinations gave rise to the demand for federal gun controls. Nicholas V. Olds, "Second Amendment and the Right to Keep and Bear Arms," *Michigan State Bar Journal,* XLVI (October, 1967), argues that this amendment prohibits unreasonable congressional infringements on the right, and that such controls should be aimed at correcting identified evils. "Note: Firearms; Problems of Control," *Harvard Law Review,* LXXX (April, 1967), suggests that legislation should identify the types of weapons that do not have a proper use in private hands, and the classes of people who should be denied access to firearms. M. K. Benenson, "Controlled Look at Gun Controls," *New York Law Forum,* XIV (Winter, 1968), doubts the efficacy and usefulness of gun laws, which, he feels, there is inadequate empirical information to support, particularly as an impediment to crime. Stanley Mosk, "Gun Control Legislation: Valid and Necessary," *New York Law Forum,* XIV (Winter, 1968), assuming that gun controls would reduce the amount of violence, rebuts opposition to such legislation based on the Second Amendment; while Frank Zimring, "Is Gun Control Likely to Reduce Violent Killings?," *University of Chicago Law Review,* XXXV (Summer, 1968), analyzes data obtained from the Chicago Police Department on reported homicides and serious, but not fatal, criminal assaults for the period 1965–66 and concludes that the evidence shows that the absence of firearms would reduce the number of violent killings. Carl Bakal, *The Right to Bear Arms* (New York, 1966), is a heavily documented antigun polemic that includes informative statistics and digests of existing local and federal firearms laws.

The growing concern over crime in America was recognized by President Johnson when he appointed a President's Commission on Law Enforcement and Administration of Justice to study those who commit crime, those who are its victims, and what can be done to prevent crime. Its report was published under the title *The Challenge of Crime in a Free Society: A Report* (Washington, 1967). Isidore Silver, "The President's Crime Commission Revisited," *New York University Law Review,* XLIII (October, 1968), is a chapter-by-chapter critique of the report by one of its participants, who suggests several areas in which the commission failed to deal adequately with the issues. "Challenge of Crime in a Free Society: A Symposium," *Notre Dame Lawyer,* XLIII (Symposium, 1968), includes articles on such subjects as the effect of social change on crime and law enforcement, riots, crime commission and state and local government crime control. Finally, a valuable aspect of recent research into criminal law has been follow-up studies exploring the relation of Supreme Court rulings to police practice and behavior. Two such studies conducted by scholars at Yale and Georgetown Universities are anthologized in Theodore L. Becker (ed.), *The Impact of Supreme Court Decisions* (New York, 1969), which also suggests useful avenues of research in other areas for the constitutional historian.

Index

71 72 73 10 9 8 7 6 5 4 3 2 1